The Invention of Terrorism in Europe, Russia and the United States

The Invention of Terrorism in Europe, Russia and the United States

Carola Dietze

Translated by David Antal, James Bell
and Zachary Murphy King

VERSO

London • New York

First published in English, revised and expanded from
the German edition, by Verso 2021
Translation © David Antal, James Bell and Zachary Murphy King 2021
Originally published as *Die Erfindung des Terrorismus in Europa,
Russland, und den USA 1858–1866* © Hamburger Edition, 2016

This translation was supported by funds made available by the 'Cultural
Foundations of Social Integration' Centre of Excellence at the University of
Konstanz, established in the framework of the German Federal and State Initiative
for Excellence, and the Collaborative Research Centre / Transregio 138 'Dynamics
of Security. Types of Securitization from a Historical Perspective', funded by the
DFG Deutsche Forschungsgemeinschaft / German Research Foundation.

1 3 5 7 9 10 8 6 4 2

Verso
UK: 6 Meard Street, London W1F 0EG
US: 20 Jay Street, Suite 1010, Brooklyn, NY 11201
versobooks.com

Verso is the imprint of New Left Books

ISBN-13: 978-1-78663-719-2
ISBN-13: 978-1-78663-720-8 (UK EBK)
ISBN-13: 978-1-78663-721-5 (US EBK)

British Library Cataloguing in Publication Data
A catalogue record for this book is available from the British Library

Library of Congress Cataloging-in-Publication Data
Library of Congress Control Number: 2020948730

Typeset in Minion Pro by Hewer Text UK Ltd, Edinburgh
Printed and bound by CPI Group (UK) Ltd, Croydon CR0 4YY

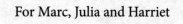

For Marc, Julia and Harriet

Contents

Introduction

For one brief moment in history after 1989, it appeared as if terrorist violence would become a thing of the past in the established democracies of the West. As the Algerian War reminds us, terrorist tactics had been used frequently in the bloody wars of decolonization. When these wars ended in the 1960s, largely with the independence of the colonies, terrorism as a means of action to achieve political ends then moved directly to Europe, Japan and the United States. In Germany, the Red Army Faction (Rote-Armee-Fraktion, RAF) and the 2 June Movement (Bewegung 2. Juni) held the public increasingly in suspense starting in the second half of the 1970s. In France, the Action Directe were active; in Italy, the Brigate Rosse; in Japan, the Nihon Sekigun; and in the United States, the Weather Underground group. In addition, the ever-recurring use of terrorist attacks was evident in seemingly perpetual conflicts, such as between Israel and the Palestinians, and in the civil wars raging from Sri Lanka to South America.[1] Moreover, even national governments occasionally resorted to terrorist tactics.

---

1 For a transnational and/or comparative perspective on this, see Linda Amiri, 'Western Europe, Second Front in the War for Algerian Independence (1954–1962)', in Carola Dietze and Claudia Verhoeven (eds.), *The Oxford Handbook of the History of Terrorism* (Oxford: Oxford University Press, 2014, published online: oxfordhandbooks.com); Petra Terhoeven, *Deutscher Herbst in Europa: Der Linksterrorismus der siebziger Jahre als transnationales Phänomen* (Munich: Oldenbourg, 2014); Terhoeven, 'Terrorism as Third Front: The New Left in Italy and West Germany during the 1960s and 1970s', in

Yet the demise of the Soviet Union and the Warsaw Pact in 1991 appeared to seal the fate of terrorism at least in Germany and Europe. Societal models propagated by left-wing terrorist groups lost a good measure of their persuasive power with the collapse of 'real socialism'. In view of this, the news in 1993 that Wolfgang Grams, a member of the RAF's 'third generation', had been killed in a shoot-out with special police forces at the train station of the town of Bad Kleinen seemed almost like a relic from the past. At the same time, the RAF announcement of its own dissolution in 1998 was thought by many to be the logical consequence of historical developments occurring worldwide, especially when groups that had fought primarily for ethnic-nationalist aims also began to lay down their arms. The Provisional Irish Republican Army (IRA) declared a ceasefire and its political organization, Sinn Féin, began negotiations that led in 1998 to the Good Friday Agreement. Likewise, the Euskadi Ta Askatasuna (ETA) entered talks that culminated in 2011 in the cessation of hostilities in Spain. Consequently, a prominent interpretation in the final years of the twentieth century was that terrorism had outlived its purpose as a means of political confrontation, at least in the Western democracies.

Careful observers at the time were already quite aware, however, that this impression was misleading. The very year in which Wolfgang Grams was shot in June, a bomb exploded in a transport van in February that had been left in the public parking garage under the World Trade Center in New York. The bomb tore a hole through the concrete seven storeys upward in the North Tower; six people died and over a thousand were wounded. The crime investigation revealed that this had been the work of Sunni extremists. In the same year that both the Good Friday Agreement was signed and the RAF in Germany announced its disbandment in April, bomb attacks were carried out against the US embassies

---

Dietze and Verhoeven, *The Oxford Handbook of the History of Terrorism*; Jeremy Varon, *Bringing the War Home: The Weather Underground, the Red Army Faction, and Revolutionary Violence in the Sixties and Seventies* (Berkeley: University of California Press, 2004); Varon, 'Refusing to Be "Good Germans": New Left Violence as a Global Phenomenon', *GHI Bulletin* 43/2 (2008), 21–43; see further Bruce Kapferer, *Legends of People, Myths of State: Violence, Intolerance and Political Culture in Sri Lanka and Australia* (Washington, DC: Smithsonian Institution Press, 2002); and Carlota McAllister, '"Terrorism" as an Artifact of Transition: Reckoning with Revolutionary Violence in Post-Cold War Latin America', in Dietze and Verhoeven, *The Oxford Handbook of the History of Terrorism*.

in Nairobi and Dar es Salaam in August by Osama bin Laden's network.[2] Meanwhile, current investigative findings in Germany indicate that, only a year after the RAF had laid down its arms, the right-wing extremist group National Socialist Underground (NSU) launched its first terrorist attack: a bomb explosion in a Nuremberg pub and, most likely, another against the so-called German Wehrmacht Exhibition then on display in Saarbrücken. More bomb attacks, murders and a nail-bomb explosion would follow, in which the victims were first- and second-generation immigrants and one police officer. Despite their murderous impact, these violent acts at first attracted little public attention, not least because, for many years, security authorities on both the national and state levels did not perceive them as a series of terrorist acts.[3]

The attacks on the World Trade Center in New York and the Pentagon in Arlington, Virginia, on 11 September 2001 (9/11) put terrorism on the political agenda in bold letters – worldwide. On the island of Bali, coordinated bombings of Paddy's Bar and the Sari Club nightclubs, both popular particularly among tourists from Australia and Europe, killed over 200 people in October 2002. Another 200 were wounded, many seriously. The Islamist organization Jemaah Islamiyah claimed responsibility for the attacks, as did Osama bin Laden, who is thought to have aided the group in carrying them out. Since most of the victims were Australian nationals, the attack became known in the Pacific region as the 'Southeast Asian' or 'Australian' 9/11. That same month, Chechen separatists burst into the Dubrovka Theatre in Moscow during a performance of the musical *Nord-Ost* and took 900 hostages. When special security forces stormed the building a couple of days later, at least 130 people died – many of them from inhaling an anaesthetic gas pumped into the building just prior to the raid. In September 2004, over a thousand hostages were taken in a school in Beslan, a town in the Republic of North Ossetia–Alania, part of the

---

2 See National Commission on Terrorist Attacks upon the United States, *The 9/11 Commission Report* (New York: W. W. Norton, 2004), 67–9, 71.

3 On recent acts of right-wing terrorism in Germany, see Barbara Manthe, 'Racism and Violence in Germany since 1980', in: *Global Humanities. Studies in Histories, Cultures, and Societies* 4 (2016), S. 35–53. For the NSU see Stefan Aust and Dirk Laabs, *Heimatschutz. Der Staat und die Mordserie des NSU* (Munich: Pantheon, 2014); and Matthias Quent, *Rassismus, Radikalisierung, Rechtsterrorismus. Wie der NSU entstand und was er über die Gesellschaft verrät*, 2., revised und complemented ed. (Weinheim und Basel: Beltz Juventa, 2016).

Russian Federation. According to official reports, more than 300 of the hostages were murdered when security forces took the building. A Chechen rebel leader claimed responsibility for the attack. On 11 March (11-M) of that same year, nearly 200 people died as a result of ten bomb explosions in fully occupied commuter trains in Madrid; officials also reported that more than 2,000 people were injured, many seriously. The following year, on 7 July 2005 (7/7), similar attacks occurred in the London Underground. Trains were also bombed a year later in Mumbai, and more than 170 people died in attacks there in November 2008. In January and November 2015, Europe and the world were shaken by the attacks in Paris on the editorial offices of the French satirical magazine *Charlie Hebdo*, a supermarket for kosher goods, the Stade de France, the audience of a rock concert at the Bataclan Theatre, and the guests of various cafés and restaurants in the 10th and 11th arrondissements. Official statistics listed nearly 150 fatalities; over 350 people were injured, 100 of those seriously.[4] These were followed by the bombings at the airport and a Metro station in Brussels in March 2016. In addition to these highly publicized attacks, many others could also be listed.

Today we experience a perpetual stream of images and news about attacks, hostage taking and kidnapping in China, Thailand, Bangladesh, India, Pakistan, Afghanistan, Iraq, Kuwait, Yemen, Israel, Lebanon, Egypt, Libya, Tunisia, Algeria, Morocco, Mali, Nigeria, Cameroon and Kenya. Since the militias serving the so-called ad-Dawlah-al-Islāmiyah (Islamic State, IS or ISIS) launched their campaigns for territorial conquest, both Syria and Turkey have increasingly become the targets of terrorism. In addition, further terrorist acts have been carried out in the United States, Australia, Great Britain, France, Belgium, the Netherlands, Norway, Sweden, Denmark and Russia. Within only a few years, terrorist violence has become endemic, leaving only a dwindling number of regions in the world untouched.

---

4 See, for example, Bruce Hoffman and Fernando Reinares, *The Evolution of the Global Terrorist Threat: From 9/11 to Osama bin Laden's Death* (New York: Columbia University Press, 2014); Mark Juergensmeyer, *Terror in the Mind of God: The Global Rise of Religious Violence* (Berkeley: University of California Press, 2000); Juergensmeyer, 'Religious Terrorism at the Turn of the 21st Century', in Dietze and Verhoeven, *The Oxford Handbook of the History of Terrorism*; and Pinar Kemerli, 'The Islamist Terrorist as the New Universal Enemy: Discourses on Terror at the United Nations', in ibid.

This intensification of terrorist violence within a few decades was immediately placed in historical perspective, particularly in regard to the 9/11 attacks in the United States. In order to gauge the scope and meaning of the events, commentators and politicians alike emphasized the new, unprecedented aspect of this violence: 'this newly disclosed threat of large-scale, sophisticated terrorism' was said to represent 'a wholly new set of threats', 'a new kind of war', indeed 'a new kind of evil'.[5] Such views went hand in hand with the conviction that these attacks were of historical significance worldwide. Commentators spoke of a 'turning point' in history, a fundamental 'break in the development of humanity' and the beginning of a new 'age of terrorism'.[6] The American journalist Fareed Zakaria also assumed that these attacks were an important caesura when he declared them to mark 'the end of the end of history'.[7] Major historical categories were also evoked in connection to the perpetrators or to interpret the significance of their targets. The perpetrators were characterized as 'barbarians' in a war against America, against the 'civilized world community' and Western modernity, or were said to represent a nexus of both worlds: 'the conjunction of 21st-century Internet speed and 12th-century fanaticism has turned our world into a tinderbox,' wrote Tina Brown in the *Washington Post*.[8] From this and

5 Anthony Lewis, 'A Different World', *New York Times*, 12 September 2001, A27; former Senator Pat Moynihan, quoted in Maureen Dowd, 'The Modernity of Evil', *New York Times*, 16 September 2001, WK11; Donald H. Rumsfeld, 'Interview with Tony Snow', *Fox News Sunday*, 16 September 2001, 9:05 a.m. EDT, archive.defense.gov; and George W. Bush, 'Remarks by the President upon Arrival. The South Lawn', 16 September 2001, 3:23 p.m. EDT, georgewbush-whitehouse.archives.gov. For Germany, see the documentary report by Jürgen Dörmann and Ulrich Pätzold, *Der 11. September: Wie die Tageszeitungen berichteten*, Hagen: Journalisten-Zentrum Haus Busch, 2002.

6 For example, Reed Johnson, 'Will War on Terrorism Define a Generation? Historians Ponder to What Extent the Attacks Will Be a True Turning Point for Society', *Los Angeles Times*, 23 September 2001, E1; Ralf Beste, Jürgen Hogrefe, Horand Knaup, Fabian Leber, Jürgen Leinemann, Holger Stark and Alexander Szandar, 'Wir sind eine Welt', *Spiegel Online*, 15 September 2001, spiegel.de; Martin Klingst and Gunter Hofmann, 'Ich will nicht nur Sicherheit: Bundesinnenminister Otto Schily über die Schwierigkeiten, eine Strategie gegen den neuen Terror zu finden', *Die Zeit*, 17 September 2001, 4.

7 Fareed Zakaria, 'The End of the End of History', *Newsweek* 138/13 (24 September 2001), 70, alluding to the argument put forth by Francis Fukuyama first in 'The End of History?', *National Interest* 16 (Summer 1989), 3–18.

8 George W. Bush, 'President Urges Readiness and Patience: Remarks by the President, Secretary of State Colin Powell, and Attorney General John Ashcroft', Camp David Thurmont, MD, 15 September 2001, 9:19 A.M. EDT, georgewbush-whitehouse.

other similar observations, historical images emerged that depicted the terroristic attacks since the turn of the millennium as, on the one hand, a new form of violence, and, on the other, a basically premodern, hence medieval, and religious (especially Islamist) one. Terrorism was being directed particularly against the secular, modern, highly industrialized societies and their institutions and representatives. These widely popular interpretations of history remained readily available – not the least because their historical content was not seriously challenged.

Such historical evaluations focusing on the new and unprecedented dimension of terroristic acts of violence soon helped legitimize new measures and strategies of security policy. 'The danger now, as he sees it, is to fall back into traditional responses to terrorism, which clearly haven't worked,' wrote David Remnick on 24 September 2001 in the *New Yorker* about Dennis Ross, the former Middle East envoy and chief negotiator for the Israeli–Palestinian peace process. 'He said, "We can't just do the usual thing – bomb a few targets, if it turns out to be Osama bin Laden. If we respond the same old way, nothing will change." '[9] When Deputy Secretary of Defense Paul D. Wolfowitz was asked about a possible Iraqi connection to the attacks, he answered,

I think the president made it very clear today that this is about more than just one organization, it's about more than just one event . . . And I think everyone has got to look at this problem with completely new eyes in a completely new light after what happened last Tuesday.[10]

The columnist William Safire suggested what exactly this might mean by posing the question several days later in the *New York Times*:

archives.gov; Gerhard Schröder, 'Abgabe einer Erklärung der Bundesregierung zu den Anschlägen in den Vereinigten Staaten von Amerika', *Deutscher Bundestag, Stenographischer Bericht*, 186, Sitzung, Berlin, 12 September 2001, dipbt.bundestag.de; and Tina Brown, 'Death by Error', *Washington Post*, 19 May 2005, washingtonpost.com. The statements by Tony Blair are in a similar vein, 'September 11 Attacks: Prime Minister's Statement', 11 September 2001, webarchive.nationalarchives.gov.uk; and by Vladimir V. Putin, 'Prezidentu Soedinennych Shtatov Ameriki Dzhordzhu Bushu', 11 September 2001, 00:00, kremlin.ru.

9 David Remnick, 'September 11, 2001', *New Yorker*, 24 September 2001, 54–75.

10 Paul D. Wolfowitz, 'Deputy Secretary Wolfowitz with the German Foreign Minister', 19 September 2001, archive.defense.gov.

Do we respond to our initial, catastrophic defeat in a wholly multilat-
eral way? ... [This] would fight yesterday's terrorist war. Or do we
recognize now the greater danger of germ warfare or nuclear attack
from a proven terrorist nation, and couple expected retribution for
this month's attack with a strategy of pre-emptive retaliation?[11]

New responses had to be found to counter the monstrousness and the
unprecedented nature of the attack.[12] As depicted here, the history of
terrorism figured as an argument used in politics; consequently, it was
also interpreted in a way that best served political aims. Thus, in a rather
circular process, the history of terrorism became both the determinant
and the product of political discourse.

All this underscores the political relevance of the history of terrorism.
As understandable as the recourse to norm-laden dualisms – such as
barbarism and civilization or the Middle Ages and modernity – may be to
express the dimension of events, such an approach offers no suitable
explanatory means with which to comprehend both recent and earlier
developments in the use of political violence. Therefore historiography
must apply its own methods and means to scrutinize the current narratives on the history of terrorism and, if necessary, to correct them and
reveal new contexts that help us better understand this phenomenon of
violence, past and present. The aim here is to show that the origins of
terrorism are in the nineteenth century, not recent contemporary history,
and to place them in the context of what is referred to both in general and
in an analytical sense as the emergence of Western modernity.[13] This
history provides the key for understanding current forms of terrorism
and its development within the context of the globalization of such
modernity in the late twentieth and early twenty-first centuries.

---

11 William Safire, 'The Ultimate Enemy', *New York Times*, 24 September 2001, A31.

12 On this, see Adrian Guelke, *Terrorism and Global Disorder: Political Violence in
the Contemporary World* (London: I. B. Tauris, 2006).

13 For a condensed version of this argument from the perspective of historiography
and history, see my 'Introduction: Writing the History of Terrorism' and 'The Invention
of Terrorism in Nineteenth Century Europe, Russia, and the United States', both in
Dietze and Verhoeven, *The Oxford Handbook of the History of Terrorism*. For my
fundamental critique of the term 'modernity', see 'Toward a History on Equal Terms: A
Discussion of Provincializing Europe', *History and Theory* 47 (2008), 69–84. In
accordance with this critique, the term is used in this book only as a source term or in
reference to relevant intellectual concepts; otherwise, it is applied as little as possible.

When, where and how did terrorism originate? These are the questions at the heart of this book. More concretely, the first step is to ask how this specific form of political violence was invented. How and by whom was this tactic then adopted, propagated and further developed? The reference to the 'invention' of terrorism – as opposed to the far more common reference to the origins or the emergence of terrorism – is deliberate and incorporates concepts from both sociology and philosophy that maintain the existence not merely of technological inventions but also of social, cultural and psychological ones.[14] The emergence of terrorism is the result of such inventions, whereby this term refers concretely to the thinking and actions of specific actors. These actors embraced the idea (as did the members of the NSU years later) of 'deeds over words'. Moreover, they experimented with older and newer forms of insurgent violence and used the ensuing media coverage for their purposes with varying degrees of success. By way of this media coverage, they also learned about and from one another. In the context of this learning process, they developed patterns of violent action that must be called terrorism, even though the perpetrators themselves and the societies in which they lived would not have used this term, with one exception to be mentioned later. This learning process, in which terrorism was subsequently invented, occurred in a relatively short span of time, namely in the eight years from 1858 to 1866, but stretched over a rather expansive geographical area: Europe, the United States and Russia – countries and continents that, by the mid-nineteenth century, were already connected to each other through a dense network of medial communications.[15]

---

14 On the concept of 'social invention', so key to the work of Talcott Parsons and for various advocates of a sociology inspired by philosophical anthropology, see Joachim Fischer, 'Von archaischen Menschengruppen zur Moderne: Philosophisch-anthropologische Konzepte zur Menschheitsgeschichte (Gehlen, Claessens, Dux, Popitz)', in Volker Steenblock and Hans-Ulrich Lessing (eds.), *Vom Ursprung der Kultur* (Munich: Verlag Karl Alber, 2014), 289–335, especially 327–31.

15 Therefore the invention of terrorism can be understood as an early example for the developing internationalism of the nineteenth century. On internationalism and its subsequent consequences for research, see Martin H. Geyer and Johannes Paulmann, 'Introduction: The Mechanics of Internationalism', in Geyer and Paulmann (eds.), *The Mechanics of Internationalism: Culture, Society, and Politics from the 1840s to the First World War* (Oxford: Oxford University Press, 2001), 1–25. On the spread of anarchism and anarchist terrorism as an aspect of the globalized economy and culture that developed at the end of the nineteenth century, see Richard Bach Jensen, *The Battle against Anarchist Terrorism, 1878–1934: An International History* (Cambridge: Cambridge University Press, 2013), 58.

Who were these inventors of terrorism? Initially two people perpetrated acts of violence that (1) conform to the criteria for terrorism, (2) resulted from independent and idiosyncratic processes of thought and action (and not primarily the imitation of some prior action by others), and (3) can be proven to have served as models for the actions of terrorists to come. These two men were Felice Orsini, who attempted to assassinate Napoleon III in 1858, and John Brown, who attacked the US Army arsenal in Harpers Ferry, Virginia, in 1859. The first individuals who verifiably adopted, copied and thereby further developed the terrorist acts of Orsini and Brown were Oskar Wilhelm Becker, who failed in his attempt to assassinate the Prussian king Wilhelm I in 1861; John Wilkes Booth, who shot US president Abraham Lincoln in 1865; and Dmitry Vladimirovich Karakozov, who tried to kill Tsar Alexander II in 1866. Therefore these five men were the fathers of modern terrorism, for it was they who invented and established terrorism in the three political contexts that would remain significant at least throughout the nineteenth and twentieth centuries, namely the social-revolutionary, ethnic-nationalist and radically right-wing contexts.[16]

In this book, the five perpetrators and their deeds will be studied in detail. Particular emphasis will be given to the historical contexts and political dynamics of the time and to the role models, views of the world, ideas, networks and other factors contributing to the decisions of these men to resort to terrorist violence. Likewise, it is important to examine the reactions, interpretations and effects that enabled their violent acts to succeed or caused them to fail.

The analysis of the origins of these terrorist acts is particularly fruitful in revealing extensive similarities among them. First, all five men were inspired by the legacy of the French and American revolutions. Each one attempted to implement rigorously the ideas of these revolutions (as they understood them) in places where these ideas had not fully materialized or to defend them against perceived threats. Two revolutionary ideas stood in the forefront, those of nationhood and of liberty. The idea of nationhood focused on political freedom and state

16 For more detail on this, p. 18 and Chapter 1, p. 52. On the assassination carried out by Charlotte Corday and Karl Ludwig Sand, which can be seen as an even earlier case of terrorism, see the discussion in the concluding chapter, pp. 610–15.

sovereignty, specifically on nation building and state building, 'a major issue in the period between the 1848–9 Revolution and the 1870s', emphasizes Friedrich Lenger. Lenger's observation refers to the German states but can also be applied to other regions in Europe, such as the Italian states.[17] With regard to the idea of liberty, the specific issue was the abolition of institutions of bondage, in particular the emancipation from slavery and indentured service, as well as the bestowal of social and political rights – or, as in John Wilkes Booth's case, the denial of these – to people previously enslaved.[18]

The second shared impetus pushing these men to violence was the impact of political blockades in their respective societies. Although each situation was shaped by its own specific historical factors, they all involved either the idea of liberty or nationhood or (again in the case of Booth) both. Terrorism, as a specific form of individual, political violence, originated in precisely those places – Italy, France and the United States – where the promises of the American and French revolutions, coupled with a revolutionary tradition, resonated particularly strongly but were only partially fulfilled. The conflicts that thereby ensued between social movements advocating the fulfilment of these promises and other societal forces seeking to prevent such implementation could not be resolved by way of either established political institutions or collective violence.[19] However, this way of using violence, this invention of terrorism, was immediately perceived as a universally deployable tactic and adopted also by counterrevolutionary actors and by political groups in other parts of the world, as is shown by Booth's assassination of US president Abraham Lincoln and the terrorist acts perpetrated by various people and groups in places like India and China. The revolutionary demands for personal, political and national liberty and equality or the struggle against the realization of precisely such demands remained the major impulses driving terrorist actions both then and in the future.

---

17 Friedrich Lenger, *Gebhardt: Handbuch der deutschen Geschichte*, vol. 15: *Industrielle Revolution* (Stuttgart: Klett-Cotta, 2003), §1, 26. For more, see also in Chapter 1, pp. 73–81.

18 On the origins of the idea of liberty, see Hans Joas, *The Sacredness of the Person: A New Genealogy of Human Rights* (Washington, DC: Georgetown University Press, 2013); see also Chapter 1, pp. 81–95.

19 On the concept of the blocked society, see below, p. 60–1; and on the concrete causes and types of blockades, Chapter 2, pp. 97–100; Chapter 4, pp. 185–92; Chapter 5, pp. 395–402; and Chapter 6, pp. 464–83.

A third and highly important aspect for all five cases is the well-documented finding that terrorism is dependent on the amplification of a symbolic act of violence by the media in order to be politically successful: 'Terrorism, it must be remembered, is primarily a communication strategy,' writes Peter Waldmann.[20] Therefore terrorism – at least as a transregional phenomenon – can only be understood in the context of mass media and a new mass public. That is, in the context of the revolution in transport and communication that took place before the mid-nineteenth century with the emergence of the popular press, telegraphy, steamship travel and railways on a global scale; furthermore, the most rapid development in such transregional communication occurred between Europe and the United States.[21] In other words, terrorism was invented and successfully developed as a tactic in those parts of the world where transport and communication technologies and the media landscape were especially advanced and where a politically interested public had become particularly pronounced, namely in Europe, Russia and the United States.[22]

---

20 Peter Waldmann, *Terrorismus: Provokation der Macht* (Munich: Gerling-Akademischer-Verlag, 1998), 15.

21 See more on this point in reference to the numerous nineteenth-century German states but with general implications in Lenger, *Gebhardt*, vol. 15, §1, especially 27–8; and also in a global reference in Christopher Alan Bayly, *The Birth of the Modern World: Global Connections and Comparisons* (Malden: Blackwell, 2004), 35–6, 261–2, 388; Jürgen Osterhammel, *The Transformation of the World: A Global History of the Nineteenth Century* (Princeton: Princeton University Press, 2015), deals above all with developments starting in the mid-nineteenth century and therefore maintains that the decisive turning point occurred later. A similar argument is put forth by, for example, Frank Bösch, *Mediengeschichte: Vom asiatischen Buchdruck zum Fernsehen* (Frankfurt am Main: Campus, 2011), Chapter 4, who, however, emphasizes at the same time the close connection between media and revolution for the period from the end of the eighteenth to the middle of the nineteenth century. That it was all but self-evident that Europe, the United States and Russia took a leading role in the area of media and communication is emphasized especially by Bayly in *The Birth of the Modern World*, 35–6. For example, he notes that more printed material was produced in Calcutta around 1800 than in Vienna or St Petersburg. Not until the following decades did Europe, Russia and the United States experience a take-off that resulted in an advantageous lead. On the developments relative to the invention of terrorism, see the depiction in greater detail below in Chapter 1, p. 85; Chapter 3, pp. 178–82; and Chapter 5, pp. 375–6 and pp. 403–6.

22 On this fundamental idea regarding the connection between the development of mass media and terrorism, see my project presentation 'Terror in the Nineteenth Century: Political Assassinations and Public Discourse in Europe and the United States, 1878–1901', *Bulletin of the German Historical Institute* 40 (Spring 2007), 91–7. I discussed this idea in December 2008 as a participant at the conference organized by Klaus Weinhauer and Jörg

However, this point does not level the differences existing between and within these geographical entities. Felice Orsini and John Brown – who were decisive for the invention of terrorism, successfully carried out acts of violence and became role models for the three emulators – respectively had the French and American environments of transport, communication and media at their disposal, which were quite advanced compared even with other countries in Europe and with Russia. Their emulators would develop terrorism further, but they would not achieve any immediate success using this tactic. No comparable media and communication environment existed where they operated, neither in the German countries, in the by-then civil-war ridden United States, nor in Russia. Yet this does not substantiate the existence of a form of media determinism; that is, transport, communication and media infrastructures alone could not determine the success or failure of violent acts. As the historical analysis shows, there were other pivotal factors.

This book represents a form of historiography best described as the 'transnational history of society'.[23] By way of the phenomenon of terrorism, this historical study analyses societal structures, technological and media developments and constellations, political dynamics, social movements, groups and networks, individual actors, sociopolitical ideas, and societal and media events, and it compares national and transnational processes of reception for Europe, Russia and the United States. In order to determine the interconnectedness and mutual

---

Requate entitled 'Mit Terroristen reden? Vom Umgang mit politischer Gewalt im Europa des 19. und 20. Jahrhunderts', and on 20 January 2009 in the colloquium of Jürgen Osterhammel and Sven Reichardt. See also the publication by Jörg Requate, 'Die Faszination anarchistischer Attentate im Frankreich des ausgehenden 19. Jahrhunderts', in Klaus Weinhauer and Jörg Requate (eds.), Gewalt ohne Ausweg? Terrorismus als Kommunikationsprozess in Europa seit dem 19. Jahrhundert (Frankfurt am Main: Campus, 2012), 99–120, in which the author also considers the impact of media developments but does not date their appearance until the last third of the nineteenth century (ibid., 108); in a similar vein, see Sven Reichardt, 'Die verdorbenen Burschen wollen von sich reden machen und finden auch noch ein Echo', Frankfurter Allgemeine Zeitung, 7 September 2011, N3. Both texts appeared after my publication and presentations.

23 On this, see the relevant discussion forum in Geschichte und Gesellschaft 27/3 (2001). The contributions by Jürgen Osterhammel, 'Transnationale Gesellschaftsgeschichte: Erweiterung oder Alternative?' (ibid., 464–79), and Albert Wirz, 'Für eine transnationale Gesellschaftsgeschichte' (ibid., 489–98), were very helpful in providing directional guidance for this book.

contingency of these decisive structures, processes, events, actors and ideas for the origins of terrorism, a wide range of historiographic approaches is necessary.[24]

For this purpose, a comparative approach to political history, social history and a history of ideas is combined here with biographical case studies and with the transnational history of communication, media and ideas. The structural starting points, societal premises, political developments and ideas, and the social movements to which the perpetrators felt they belonged will be compared by using approaches from social history, political history and the history of ideas.[25] What have now become well-developed methods of biographical research will be used to study both the actors as the inventors of terrorism and the planning and carrying out of their violent deeds. With the help of these methods, the course of the perpetrators' lives, their networks, world views, cognitive horizons, motivations, interpretations,

---

24 Such a transnational comparative history of terrorism had been called for by Robert Gerwarth and Heinz-Gerhard Haupt in 'Internationalising Historical Research', *European Review of History – Revue européenne d'Histoire* 14 (2007), 275–81; and by Sylvia Schraut in 'Terrorismus und Geschichtswissenschaft', in Alexander Spencer, Alexander Kocks and Kai Harbrich (eds.), *Terrorismusforschung in Deutschland* (Wiesbaden: VS Verlag für Sozialwissenschaften, 2011), 99–122. On the relation of the category of (media) events to the other named categories, see – together with further reference literature – Carola Dietze, 'Von Kornblumen, Heringen und Drohbriefen: Ereignis und Medienereignis am Beispiel der Attentate auf Wilhelm I.', in Friedrich Lenger and Ansgar Nünning (eds.), *Medienereignisse der Moderne* (Darmstadt: Wissenschaftliche Buchgesellschaft, 2008), 40–60. The decisive stimuli came from Reinhart Koselleck, 'Ereignis und Struktur', in Reinhart Koselleck and Wolf-Dieter Stempel (eds.), *Geschichte: Ereignis und Erzählung* (Munich: Fink, 1973), 560–70; Pierre Nora, 'Le retour de l'événement', in Jacques Le Goff and Pierre Nora (eds.), *Faire de l'histoire*, première partie: *Nouveaux problèmes* (Paris: Gallimard, 1974), 210–27; Manfred Hettling and Andreas Suter, *Struktur und Ereignis* (Göttingen: Vandenhoeck & Ruprecht, 2001); Egon Flaig, 'Ein semantisches Ereignis inszenieren, um ein politisches zu verhindern: Die entblößten Narben vor der Volksversammlung 167 v. Chr.', in Thomas Rathmann (ed.), *Ereignis: Konzeptionen eines Begriffs in Geschichte, Kunst und Literatur* (Cologne: Böhlau, 2003), 183–98; and Jacques Derrida, 'A Certain Impossible Possibility of Saying the Event', *Critical Inquiry* 33/2 (2007), 441–61.

25 Particularly helpful in this regard were Hartmut Kaelble's *Der historische Vergleich: Eine Einführung zum 19. und 20. Jahrhundert* (Frankfurt am Main: Campus, 1999); and Heinz-Gerhard Haupt and Jürgen Kocka's *Geschichte und Vergleich: Ansätze und Ergebnisse international vergleichender Geschichtsschreibung* (Frankfurt am Main: Campus, 1996).

intentions and expectations will be placed in a historical context.[26] Since the terrorist act relies on response and reaction to determine its success or failure, these become highly significant for the invention of terrorism. The theoretical and methodological reflections by Jürgen Osterhammel and Albert Wirz on the research of transfer have been particularly inspiring for this analysis of the national and transnational processes of reception.[27] In addition to the analysis of nationally transcending transfer processes, the studies on the history of reception also need to anchor reactions in a specific setting of time and place; that is, to track down the local and spatial circumstances and the concrete means of transport and communication.[28] It is only through the interplay of these various analytic levels and factors and the different perspectives resulting from them that a fruitful history of the invention of terrorism can be written.[29]

Genuinely historical research on the origins and development of terrorism is rare.[30] The most influential work on past terrorist activity

---

26 On this, see what continue to be, including for this study, the seminal discussions found in Andreas Gestrich's 'Einleitung: Sozialhistorische Biographieforschung', in Andreas Gestrich, Peter Knoch and Helga Merkel (eds.), *Biographie – sozialgeschichtlich: Sieben Beiträge* (Göttingen: Vandenhoeck & Ruprecht, 1988), 5–28; Jacques Le Goff, 'Writing Historical Biography Today', *Current Sociology* 43/2 (1995), 11–17; and Friedrich Lenger's *Werner Sombart, 1863–1941* (Munich: C. H. Beck, 1995), 13–16.

27 See Osterhammel, 'Transnationale Gesellschaftsgeschichte'; as well as Wirz, 'Für eine transnationale Gesellschaftsgeschichte'. Furthermore, crucial suggestions were put forth by Michael Werner and Bénédicte Zimmermann, 'Beyond Comparison: Histoire Croisée and the Challenge of Reflexivity', *History and Theory* 45 (2006), 30–50.

28 In this regard, the author has greatly profited from conferences on media and communication history organized by the Arbeitskreis Geschichte + Theorie in the years 2000 to 2003. Crucial for this book proved to be the conference in Mülheim an der Ruhr in 2003. On this, see Alexander C. T. Geppert, Uffa Jensen and Jörn Weinhold (eds.), *Ortsgespräche· Raum und Kommunikation im 19. und 20. Jahrhundert* (Bielefeld: Transcript, 2005), especially the contribution by Christian Holtorf, 'Die Modernisierung des nordatlantischen Raumes: Cyrus Field, Taliaferro Shaffner und das submarine Telegraphennetz von 1858', ibid., 157–78.

29 The following works served as models for such a multi-perspective approach at the start of the research for this study in 2005: Sidney Wilfred Mintz, *Sweetness and Power: The Place of Sugar in Modern History* (New York: Penguin Books, 1986); Bayly, *The Birth of the Modern World*; and Benedict Anderson, *Under Three Flags: Anarchism and the Anti-colonial Imagination* (London: Verso, 2006).

30 Dirk Blasius made this point as early as 1983 in his book *Geschichte der politischen Kriminalität in Deutschland* (Frankfurt am Main: Suhrkamp, 1983, 7), and it is still a valid one. See also, for example, Gerwarth and Haupt, 'Internationalising

and groups with a global perspective is by the political scientist David C. Rapoport. Taken together, his essay 'Fear and Trembling: Terrorism in Three Religious Traditions' and his 'four-wave theory' add up to a cross-cutting theoretical approach to the history of terrorism.[31] Rapoport argues that a religiously inspired premodern terrorism existed and – borrowing from Walther Laqueur – cites the Jewish Sicarii in their fight against the Roman Empire, the Assassins in medieval Persia and the Indian Thugs as examples. For him, modern terrorism begins in 1879 in Russia and can be divided into four ideological waves: anarchist, anti-colonial, New Left, and religious. He defines a wave as a 'cycle of activity in a given time period' exhibiting an international character, in which 'similar activities occur in many countries driven by a common predominant energy shaping participating groups and their mutual relationships'. As the names of these waves suggest, each is driven by a different energy. Rapoport maintains that a wave lasts for a generation; this prognostic capability is one reason why his theory is valued in the study of terrorism.[32] He explains the emergence of the first wave with advances in transport and communication technology (the invention of the telegraph, the expansion of railways and the founding of daily mass newspapers) and with the

Historical Research', 275; Martin Schulze Wessel, 'Terrorismusstudien', *Geschichte und Gesellschaft* 35/3 (2009), 363; Schraut, 'Terrorismus und Geschichtswissenschaft', 100, 104; Klaus Weinhauer and Jörg Requate, 'Terrorismus als Kommunikationsprozess: Eskalation und Deeskalation politischer Gewalt in Europa seit dem 19. Jahrhundert', in Weinhauer and Requate (eds.), *Gewalt ohne Ausweg?*, 11–12; and Karl Härter, Tina Hannappel, Conrad Tyrichter and Thomas Walter, 'Terrorismus für die Rechtsgeschichte? Neuerscheinungen zur Geschichte politischer Gewalt im 19. und 20. Jahrhundert', *Rechtsgeschichte: Zeitschrift des Max-Planck-Instituts für europäische Rechtsgeschichte* 22 (2014), 374.

31 See David Rapoport, 'Fear and Trembling: Terrorism in Three Religious Traditions', *American Political Science Review* 78/3 (1984), 658–77; as well as, for example, his work 'Terrorism', in Mary E. Hawkesworth and Maurice Kogan (eds.), *Encyclopedia of Government and Politics*, vol. 2 (London: Routledge, 2004), 1049–77; and 'The Four Waves of Modern Terrorism', in Audrey Kurth Cronin and James M. Ludes (eds.), *Attacking Terrorism* (Washington, DC: Georgetown University Press, 2004), 46–73.

32 David Rapoport, 'Generations and Waves: The Keys to Understanding Rebel Terror Movements', international.ucla.edu. On the reaction to his theory, see, for example, Berto Jongman, 'Research Desiderata in the Field of Terrorism', in Magnus Ranstorp (ed.), *Mapping Terrorism Research: State of the Art, Gaps and Future Direction* (New York: Routledge, 2006), 255–91.

dissemination of democratic ideas and the discovery of a strategy of terror by Russian revolutionaries.[33]

Rapoport's theory on the development of terrorism does an excellent job of capturing the international character of the major cycles of terrorism as they have been observed from the late nineteenth century to the beginning of the twenty-first century. And yet it does not include the groups of terrorists who failed to inspire emulators elsewhere in the world or whose demands did not correspond with the globally predominant topics at the time.[34] This essentially leads to an exclusion of nationalist groups in the history of terrorism.[35] In addition, this theoretical explanation is problematic from the viewpoint of historiography because the *explanans*, the explanation, of the four-wave theory (the discovery of the strategy of terrorism by Russian revolutionaries or the 'energy' driving the 'waves') is for historical research the *explanandum*, the phenomenon to be explained. Moreover, this theory deals with the history of major, known structures which are interpreted as a history of terrorism, but it lacks any analysis of specific historical situations or events. For this reason, the four-wave theory remains hypothetical and can claim to possess plausibility but not validity.

The exact opposite is true for the literature on political assassination: it focuses on political murder as an event.[36] The books that belong to this

---

33 See, for example, Rapoport, 'Terrorism', 1051–2, 1067.

34 Rapoport, 'Terrorism', 1051, himself cites the Assassins, the Thugs, the Sons of the American Revolution, and the Ku Klux Klan as examples. Additional groups that are not included in his history of terrorism are, for example, abortion opponents or nationalist associations like the Organisation Consul.

35 This also concurs with the criticism levelled by Klaus Weinhauer and Jörg Requate, who therefore extended Rapoport's waves to include a 'right-wing/rightist nationalist' phase, which stretches from World War I until the 1930s (Weinhauer and Requate, 'Terrorismus als Kommunikationsprozess', 17).

36 For examples of scholarly or popular books spanning time or geographic areas, see Alphons Nobel, *Mord in der Politik* (Hamburg: Hanseatische Verlagsanstalt, 1931); Wolfgang Plat, *Attentate: Eine Sozialgeschichte des politischen Mordes* (Düsseldorf: Econ, 1982); Franklin L. Ford, *Political Murder: From Tyrannicide to Terrorism* (Cambridge, MA: Harvard University Press, 1985); Lucian O. Meysels, *Morde machen Geschichte: Politische Gewaltakte im 20. Jahrhundert* (Vienna: Herold, 1985); Alexander Demandt (ed.), *Das Attentat in der Geschichte* (Cologne: Böhlau, 1996); Werner Raith and Thomas Schmid, *Politische Morde: 17 Fälle des 20. Jahrhunderts* (Göttingen: Verlag Die Werkstatt, 1996); George Fetherling, *The Book of Assassins* (New York: Wiley, 2001); Jörg von Uthmann, *Attentat: Mord mit gutem Gewissen* (Berlin: Siedler, 1996); Sven Felix Kellerhoff, *Attentäter: Mit einer Kugel die Welt verändern* (Cologne: Böhlau, 2003);

extensive genre usually present a select number of assassinations throughout world history, listed in chronological order or alphabetically by the names of the perpetrators. Some of these works provide a good introduction to the backgrounds, the course of events and the after-shock and impact of individual assassinations. Two such examples are the volume of collected essays published by Alexander Demandt, *Das Attentat in der Geschichte*, and Franklin L. Ford's monograph *Political Murder*. Ford, who explicitly refers to his method as 'episodic' and describes his approach as *l'histoire événementielle*,[37] aspires to present political murder throughout the expanse of world history from biblical times to the beginning of the 1980s and is particularly interested in the political consequences of assassination. In his analytical recapitulations, he offers cogent observations on the relationship between political systems and the murderous episodes and on the function of political assassination. He also succeeds in identifying worldwide trends and reception processes. In this respect, this genre makes valuable contributions to the history of political violence.

Nevertheless, the depictions of political murders tend to remain merely a point of departure and a resource for the history of the origins and development of terrorism. Since a perpetrator's political motivation for murder is the sole criterion that books belonging to this genre use to determine whether to include a killing or not, these books cover not only terrorist attacks but also assassinations that cannot be classified as terrorism. Furthermore, the treatment of individual cases – often by various authors – rarely leads to a consideration of the structures common to political murders and the factors linking them.[38] This then

Michael Sommer (ed.), *Politische Morde: Vom Altertum bis zur Gegenwart* (Darmstadt: Wissenschaftliche Buchgesellschaft, 2005); Greg Woolf, *Et Tu, Brute? The Murder of Caesar and Political Assassination* (Cambridge, MA: Harvard University Press, 2007). On specific countries and time periods, examples are James McKinley, *Assassination in America* (New York: Harper & Row, 1977); or Marcus Mühlnikel, *'Fürst, sind Sie unverletzt?' Attentate im Kaiserreich 1871–1914* (Paderborn: Ferdinand Schönigh, 2014).

37 Ford, *Political Murder*, 3.

38 Exceptions to this rule are found especially in French historiography on the early modern period. See George Minois, *Le couteau et le poison: L'assassinat politique en Europe (1400–1800)* (Paris: Fayard, 1997), whose study ends with the period in which terrorism emerged; and Renaud Villard, *Du bien commun au mal nécessaire: Tyrannies, assassinats politiques et souveraineté en Italie vers 1470 vers 1600* (Rome: Ecole Française de Rome, 2008).

precludes the formation of a coherent history on the development of terrorism.

The standard narrative for the global history of terrorism was greatly influenced by the historian Walther Laqueur in his study, published in 1977, on terrorism as a phenomenon of political violence.[39] As indicated above, Laqueur mentions the Sicarii, the Assassins and the Thugs as early forms of terrorism. He sees the turning point towards modern terrorism as being the French Revolution, when the word 'terror' (terreur) became laden with political–secular meaning. In Laqueur's opinion, the origins of the emergence of modern terrorism lie in the Enlightenment and the rise of the revolutionary principles of democracy and nationalism, especially the idea of nationhood. However, he argues that the most important organization was the Russian group Narodnaia Volia, founded in 1879, and describes the first high point of terrorist violence to be the anarchist 'propaganda of deeds' of the 1890s.[40] He furthermore examines separatist terrorism as exemplified by the Irish, Armenians and Macedonians and also addresses right-wing groups like the Romanian Iron Guard, the German Freikorps and the Zionist Irgun and LEHI, as well as the Muslim Brotherhood.[41]

This narrative, from the antique forerunners in religious violence and tyrannicide, the origins of revolutionary terrorism in the terror of the French Revolution, and its evolution by way of the Narodnaia Volia in tsarist Russia and anarchist individuals in Western Europe and the United States, is still considered valid today. There is also consensus on classifying terrorism according to the categories of social-revolutionary, ethnic-nationalistic and radically right-wing, even though these three types are not equally integrated into the history of terrorism.[42]

---

39 Walter Laqueur, Terrorism (Boston, MA: Little, 1977), republished as A History of Terrorism (New Brunswick, NJ: Transaction Publishers, 2002). In addition, see the sourcebook by Laqueur, The Terrorism Reader: A Historical Anthology (New York: New American Library, 1978), in which tyrannicide is considered rather important as the precursor to terrorism.

40 Laqueur, A History of Terrorism, 7–12.

41 Ibid., 12–14, 16.

42 Grant Wardlaw, Political Terrorism: Theory, Facts and Counter-measures (Cambridge: Cambridge University Press, 1982), Chapter 1, parts 2–3, or Waldmann, Terrorismus, Chapter 3. On the neglect of right-wing terrorism in historiography, especially in Germany, see Carola Dietze, 'Ein blinder Fleck? Zur relativen Vernachlässigung des Rechtsterrorismus in den Geschichtswissenschaften', in Tim

Since 1977, this standard narrative has only undergone one significant change and broadened its scope on a single score. The singular
change is that more recent literature attributes equal importance to the
actions of nineteenth-century Irish groups in originating modern
terrorism, alongside the violence perpetrated by Russian and anarchist
movements.[43] The scope of the narrative has been broadened since the
late 1990s to include religious terrorism as a new category to describe
developments since the 1970s, and more emphasis has been placed on
the danger of new weapons, particularly weapons of mass destruction.
In the eyes of several terrorism experts, these developments, taken
together, have created a 'new terrorism', one that is qualitatively distinct
from the terrorism experienced until the 1970s.[44]

Within the framework of this standard narrative on the emergence
and development of terrorism in the nineteenth century – with or without the above-mentioned change and topical expansion – many scholars

---

Schanetzky, Tobias Freimüller, Kristina Meyer, Sybille Steinbacher, Dietmar Süß und
Annette Weinke (eds.), *Demokratisierung der Deutschen. Errungenschaften eines Projekts*
(Göttingen: Wallstein, 2020), 189–205.

43 Important in this regard was Lindsay Clutterbuck, 'The Progenitors of Terrorism:
Russian Revolutionaries or Extreme Irish Republicans?', *Terrorism and Political Violence*
16/1 (2004), 154–81.

44 See Walter Laqueur, *The New Terrorism: Fanaticism and the Arms of Mass
Destruction* (New York: Oxford University Press, 1999); the sourcebook by Laqueur
(ed.), *Voices of Terror: Manifestos, Writings, and Manuals of Al Qaeda, Hamas, and
Other Terrorists* (New York: Reed Press, 2004), which combines an earlier compilation
of sources with sources on guerrilla war and extends it into the twenty-first century;
Laqueur, *No End to War: Terrorism in the Twenty-First Century* (New York: Continuum
International Publishing Group, 2003); Bruce Hoffman, *Holy Terror: The Implications
of Terrorism Motivated by a Religious Imperative* (Santa Monica: Rand, 1993);
Juergensmeyer, *Terror in the Mind of God*; David C. Rapoport (ed.), *Terrorism: Critical
Concepts in Political Science*, vol. 4: *The Fourth or Religious Wave* (London and New
York: Routledge, 2006); Peter R. Neumann, *Old and New Terrorism* (Malden: Polity
Press, 2009). For the inclusion of Irish and/or religious, specifically new terrorism in
the standard narrative, see also Gerard Chaliand and Arnaud Blin (eds.), *The History
of Terrorism: From Antiquity to Al Qaeda* (Berkeley: University of California Press,
2007); Leonard Weinberg, *Global Terrorism: A Beginner's Guide* (New York: Rosen,
2005), Chapter 2; Bruce Hoffman, *Inside Terrorism* (New York: Columbia University
Press, 2006) Chapter 1 and 139–41; Clifford Simonsen and Jeremy Spindlove (eds.),
Terrorism Today: The Past, the Players, the Future (Upper Saddle River: Pearson
Prentice Hall, 2007), Chapter 2; Alexander Straßner, *Sozialrevolutionärer Terrorismus*
(Wiesbaden: Verlag für Sozialwissenschaften, 2008); Michael Burleigh, *Blood & Rage:
A Cultural History of Terrorism* (London: Harper Press, 2008); and Randall D. Law,
Terrorism: A History (Cambridge: Polity Press, 2009).

have enriched research since the 1970s with important contributions. Next to Laqueur, a number of authors have also contributed to a history of ideas linked to nineteenth-century terrorism. Using strategy papers and statements made by terrorists themselves, they have analysed the conceptual origins of 'terrorist revolution' and the development of the professional revolutionary as a specific type. Furthermore, they have described the response to Jacobin terror and the idea of the 'propaganda of deeds' and examined the confrontations between Marx and Engels and the anarchists. In doing so, most of these scholars stress the importance of the failed revolutions of 1848–9 and the experience of the brutal repression of the Paris Commune of 1871, which appeared to make it necessary to change strategy and seek new tactics for the revolutionary struggle.[45] Popular treatments of the history of terrorism are fascinated by terrorist organizations like secret societies, an aspect of the history of terrorism that has been subject to little systematic research to date.[46] In addition, Matthew Carr has started to study cultural reactions, responses

45 See the following for various emphases on and in different combinations with the aspects mentioned: Albert Parry, *Terrorism: From Robespierre to Arafat* (New York: The Vanguard Press, 1976), Chapters 5–9; Laqueur, *Terrorism*, 48–9; Gerard Chaliand, *Terrorism: From Popular Struggle to Media Spectacle* (London: University of California Press, 1987); Noel O'Sullivan, 'Terrorism, Ideology and Democracy', in his *Terrorism, Ideology and Revolution* (Brighton: Wheatsheaf Books, 1986); Richard E. Rubenstein, *Alchemists of Revolution: Terrorism in the Modern World* (New York: Basic Books, 1987); Zeev Ivianski, 'The Terrorist Revolution: Roots of Modern Terrorism' (1989), in Rapoport, *Terrorism: Critical Concepts in Political Science*, vol. 4, 73–94; Rudolf Walther, 'Terror, Terrorismus', in Otto Brunner, Werner Conze and Reinhart Koselleck (eds.), *Geschichtliche Grundbegriffe Historisches Lexikon zur politisch-sozialen Sprache in Deutschland*, 8 vols. (Stuttgart: Klett-Cotta, 1972–97), vol. 6, 385; Martin A. Miller, 'The Intellectual Origins of Modern Terrorism in Europe', in Martha Crenshaw (ed.), *Terrorism in Context* (University Park: Pennsylvania State University Press, 1995), 27–62; Miller, *The Foundations of Modern Terrorism: State, Society and the Dynamics of Political Violence* (Cambridge: Cambridge University Press, 2013); and Jensen, *The Battle against Anarchist Terrorism*, 15–17. On the emergence of the professional revolutionary as a stock character type, see the male variations as presented in Claudia Verhoeven, *The Odd Man Karakozov: Imperial Russia, Modernity and the Birth of Terrorism* (Ithaca: Cornell University Press, 2009), 6; and the female forms in Ana Siljak, *Angel of Vengeance: The 'Girl Assassin', the Governor of St. Petersburg, and Russia's Revolutionary World* (New York: St Martin's Press, 2008).

46 For example, see Paul Elliott, *Brotherhoods of Fear: A History of Violent Organizations* (London: Blandford, 1998); and Andrew Sinclair, *An Anatomy of Terror: A History of Terrorism* (London: Macmillan, 2003).

and representations regarding terrorists and their violent deeds, particularly in the field of literature, and to integrate them into the history of terrorism. Christine Hikel and Sylvia Schraut have undertaken similar efforts in the field of terrorism, gender and memory, and the three historians Dirk Blasius, Martin A. Miller and Richard Bach Jensen have depicted the history of terrorism as the interaction between governmental use of force and insurgent violence.[47]

In mainstream historiography, the general consensus seems to be that terrorism was a product of European modernity, in both dimensions: a product of Europe and of modernity. Thus the assumption made by Noel O'Sullivan that 'terrorism in its modern form originated as a specifically European phenomenon' is one found explicitly or implicitly in most work on the history of terrorism.[48]

---

47 Matthew Carr, *The Infernal Machine: A History of Terrorism from the Assassination of Tsar Alexander II to Al-Qaeda* (New York: The New Press, 2006); Christine Hikel and Sylvia Schraut, *Terrorismus und Geschlecht: Politische Gewalt in Europa seit dem 19. Jahrhundert* (Frankfurt am Main: Campus, 2012); Blasius, *Geschichte der politischen Kriminalität in Deutschland*; Miller, *The Foundations of Modern Terrorism*; and Jensen, *The Battle against Anarchist Terrorism*.

48 O'Sullivan, *Terrorism, Ideology, and Revolution*, ix. See also Miller, 'The Intellectual Origins of Modern Terrorism in Europe'. For other authors, the assumption is implied by the fact that they deal solely with Europe or European examples for the nineteenth century, e.g. Parry, *Terrorism*, Chapter 4; Laqueur, *Terrorism*, 15–16; Ze'ev Iviansky, 'Individual Terror: Theory and Typology', *Journal of Contemporary History* 12/1 (1977), 45; Robert A. Friedlander, 'The Origins of International Terrorism', in Yonah Alexander and Seymour Maxwell Finger (eds.), *Terrorism: Interdisciplinary Perspectives* (New York: The John Jay Press, 1977), 34; Franklin L. Ford, 'Reflections on Political Murder: Europe in the Nineteenth and Twentieth Centuries', in Wolfgang J. Mommsen and Gerhard Hirschfeld (eds.), *Social Protest, Violence and Terror* (New York: St Martin's Press, 1982), 1–12; Wolfgang J. Mommsen, 'Non-legal Violence and Terrorism in Western Industrial Societies: An Historical Analysis', in ibid., 383–404; Chaliand, *Terrorism*, 78; Rubenstein, *Alchemists of Revolution*, 79; Wardlaw, *Political Terrorism*, 18; Dominique Venner, *Histoire du terrorisme* (Paris: Pygmalion/Gérard Watelet 2002); Carr, *The Infernal Machine*, 6; and Gérard Desmaretz, *Des guerres révolutionnaires au terrorisme: Les stratégies de la subversion* (Paris: Chiron, 2006). Russia is explicitly called the country of origin for terrorism by Verhoeven, *The Odd Man Karakozov* (for example, 4–6); Verhoeven, 'The Making of Russian Revolutionary Terrorism', in Isaac Land (ed.), *Enemies of Humanity: The Nineteenth-Century War on Terrorism* (New York: Palgrave Macmillan, 2008), 100; Weinhauer and Requate, 'Terrorismus als Kommunikationsprozess', 20; Lutz Häfner, ' "Russland als Geburtsland des modernen Terrorismus"? oder: "Das classische Land des politischen Attentats" ', in Weinhauer and Requate (eds.), *Gewalt ohne Ausweg?*, 67; and Miller, *The Foundations of Modern Terrorism*, 57.

As a consequence, the United States is relegated to the periphery in the standard narrative. According to this general depiction, terrorism arrived in America due to the immigration of the traditionally violence-prone Irish, as well as German and Russian socialists and anarchists like Karl Heinzen, Johannes Most and Emma Goldman, who were forced to flee Europe because of their radical political views.[49] This view corresponds perfectly with the perception in the United States at the time. Following his attempt to assassinate the industrialist Clay Frick in 1892, the Russian immigrant Alexander Berkman claimed to have carried out 'the first terrorist act in America'. Likewise, politicians and the general public thought stricter immigration laws would be a decisive contribution to combating terrorism.[50] In his analysis, Laqueur does admit that the conflicts between employees and employers in the United States were more violent from the start than they had been in Europe, and Albert Parry cites numerous violent confrontations that occurred in North America, starting with the wars between settlers and the indigenous population. Still, Parry does not consider them terrorism, since they were not 'acts of deliberate political terror of Socialist or anarchist category'. Neither does he view the assassinations of Abraham Lincoln in 1865 and of James Garfield in 1881 as terrorism because, in his opinion, these were not acts of revolutionary violence.[51] In so arguing, he adheres exactly to the definition of terrorism as violence in the service of socialist and anarchist aims, a definition that was widely accepted in the late 1960s and early 1970s in the social sciences. Laqueur even takes the stand that neither the Haymarket riot in Chicago nor the bombing of the *Los Angeles Times* building, typically considered examples of American terrorism,[52] were comparable with European terrorism, because the aim of such action in the United States had not been to topple the government or to force a system change; the aims were far more modest.[53] In contrast, Rapoport wrote as early as 1971 that the first successful terrorist

---

49 For example, see Laqueur, *Terrorism*, 19; or Miller, 'The Intellectual Origins of Modern Terrorism in Europe', 48.

50 Alexander Berkman, *Prison Memoirs of an Anarchist* (New York: Schocken Books, 1970), 59.

51 Parry, *Terrorism*, 94.

52 See, for example, Miller, 'The Intellectual Origins of Modern Terrorism in Europe', 48–50.

53 Laqueur, *Terrorism*, 19.

movements in the United States were the Sons of Liberty during the period of the American Revolution and the Ku Klux Klan. However, even Rapoport thought that the origins of modern terrorism lay in Europe, since these American movements – unlike the European ones – did not draw up a theoretical tract justifying their actions.[54]

Due in no small measure to this European orientation in the standard narrative of the history of terrorism, terrorism was long seen in the United States as a foreign phenomenon. In 2014, the publicist Michael Kronenwetter expressed this idea with a good measure of self-criticism:

> Before September 11, 2001, most Americans thought of terrorism as something foreign to the American experience. Terrorism was a terrible thing, we told ourselves, but it was something that happened in the Middle East. Or in Latin America. Or in Northern Ireland. Or on the mainland of Europe. It didn't happen here. Even when it undeniably did happen here – as when the Alfred P. Murrah building [in Oklahoma City] was destroyed by a truck bomb in 1995 – we dismissed it as an aberration.[55]

In the American mindset prior to the 9/11 attacks, terrorism only happened elsewhere. According to Kronenwetter, such an idea could only take hold because the terrorist attacks that occurred in the United States were not labelled as such. Instead they were called acts of resistance against the politics of Reconstruction following the Civil War or labour unrest or mass shootings perpetrated by lone gunmen. After the attacks on the World Trade Center and the Pentagon, notes Kronenwetter, this perception reversed completely: 'Americans have stopped thinking of terrorist attacks as rare, isolated, and almost anarchic events, and come to regard them as incidents in an ongoing war.'[56]

---

54 David Rapoport, *Assassination & Terrorism* (Toronto: Canadian Broadcasting Corporation, 1971), 46. Usually it is the popular books that depict the treatment of people who remained loyal supporters of the British Crown during the American Revolution and the Ku Klux Klan as terrorism. See Elliott, *Brotherhoods of Fear*, Chapters 2–3; Sinclair, *An Anatomy of Terror*, Chapter 19. The Ku Klux Klan is now also included in Miller, *The Foundations of Modern Terrorism*.

55 Michael Kronenwetter, *Terrorism: A Guide to Events and Documents* (Westport: Greenwood, 2004), vii.

56 Ibid., vii–viii.

But they see it still as an external threat, not a homegrown one. The historian Michael Fellman concurred with Kronenwetter's observation in 2010 when he wrote, 'Americans prefer to see terrorism as external to the "American way," as exceptional.'[57] Such an understanding does little to encourage more in-depth research of this phenomenon of political violence.

Perhaps this is the reason why the history of terrorism in the United States has not played much of a role in America's national historiography. Although a series of studies on class conflict in the United States, on American anarchism and on the Ku Klux Klan has been produced by historians since the beginning of the twentieth century and particularly since the 1970s,[58] the primary focus in these studies has not been on the violence involved. Especially in the historiography on left-wing radicalism, scholars have carefully avoided using the term 'terrorism' in order to circumvent common stereotyping. In her 2011 review of American research on terrorism, Beverly Gage thus concluded, 'When the 9/11 attacks occurred, then, Americans already had *histories* of terrorism . . . What did not exist was a coherent historiography of terrorism, a definable way to think about the role such violence has (or has not) played in the American past.'[59] As Gage also notes, little has changed in this regard since the attacks of 11 September 2001, although it now appears as if the term 'terrorism' is considered quite marketable. It is being applied to a broad spectrum of people and groups from the outlaw Jesse James and Confederate guerrillas during the Civil War to the bombings of Chicago's Haymarket Square and the buildings of the *Los Angeles Times* and Wall

---

57 Michael Fellman, *In the Name of God and Country: Reconsidering Terrorism in American History* (New Haven: Yale University Press, 2010), 1.

58 On violence in the US in connection with class conflict, see still Robert Hunter, *Violence and the Labour Movement* (London: Routledge & Sons, 1916); Louis Adamic, *Dynamite: The Story of Class Violence in America* (New York: Viking Press, 1931); and especially Melvyn Dubofsky, *We Shall Be All: A History of the Industrial Workers of the World* (Chicago: Quadrangle Books, 1969); Paul Avrich, *The Haymarket Tragedy* (Princeton: Princeton University Press, 1984); Avrich, *Sacco and Vanzetti: The Anarchist Background* (Princeton: Princeton University Press, 1991); and Kevin Kenny, *Making Sense of the Molly Maguires* (New York: Oxford University Press, 1998). On the Ku Klux Klan, see David Mark Chalmers, *Hooded Americanism: The First Century of the Ku Klux Klan, 1865–1965* (Garden City: Doubleday, 1965); Allen W. Trelease, *White Terror: The Ku Klux Klan Conspiracy and Southern Reconstruction* (London: Secker & Warburg, 1971); and in this book, pp. 588–9.

59 Beverly Gage, 'Terrorism and the American Experience: A State of the Field', *Journal of American History* 98/1 (2011), 81.

Street.[60] Yet the aspect of terrorism remains peripheral in the majority of these studies. The studies that do delve deeper into the subject of this type of violence limit their focus to individual events without seeking long-term lines of development or broader contexts. 'While both the word and concept of terrorism now appear more frequently and in a wide variety of books, few of those works are speaking to each other, and fewer still gesture toward any comprehensive understanding of terrorism's role in the American past', concludes Gage.[61]

Meanwhile, initial efforts have been undertaken to demonstrate the importance of assassinations and terrorist violence for American history, thanks to the work by the journalist James McKinley, the political scientists James M. Lutz and Brenda J. Lutz, and the historians Michael Fellman and Martin A. Miller. Following the assassination of John F. Kennedy, McKinley began his search for assassinations and their consequences in American history. On the basis of the available literature, he presented a number of prominent political murders without conducting his own research of these assassinations or embedding them in contexts and structures. Lutz and Lutz, Fellman, and also Miller define terrorism so broadly – roughly as a 'mutual exchange of intimidating violence' – that they are convinced the overwhelming number of violent phenomena in American history can be called terrorism.[62] However, such a definition blurs any analysis of terrorism.

Apart from their consensus with regard to the geographical location of Europe as the origins of terrorism, the authors who follow the standard narrative also assert that terrorism is a phenomenon of modernity. Although there were forerunners of this type of political violence in the centuries prior to the French Revolution,[63] terrorism in the modern

---

60 Particularly interesting among the work done on these events is the book by Beverly Gage, *The Day Wall Street Exploded: A Story of America in Its First Age of Terror* (New York: Oxford University Press, 2009).

61 Gage, 'Terrorism and the American Experience', 83.

62 See the definition and use of the term in Brenda J. Lutz and James M. Lutz, *Terrorism in America* (New York: Palgrave Macmillan, 2007), especially Chapters 1–3; and Miller, *The Foundations of Modern Terrorism*, in which state terror and terrorism are both subsumed under the term 'terrorism' (1–2). The quote is taken from Fellman, *In the Name of God and Country*, 2.

63 As a rule, precursors are considered to be political murder (especially tyrannicide); the violence perpetrated by the Sicarii, Assassins and Thugs; and sometimes guerrilla war. Besides the previously mentioned authors Rapoport and Laqueur, see also

sense is said to have emerged in the late eighteenth century and over the course of the nineteenth century in Europe. Usually, the dates of origin are cited as being 1876, when the strategy of the 'propaganda of deeds' was first proposed at a meeting of the Anarchist International, or 1879, the year Narodnaia Volia was founded.[64] Claudia Verhoeven has proposed the reaction of the Russian government to the assassination by Karkozov in 1866 to be the birth of modern terrorism, while Richard Bach Jensen has argued the Fenian campaign targeting London and two other British cities between 1881 and 1885 constitutes 'the first modern terrorist campaign'.[65]

But what exactly is modern about modern terrorism according to this historiography? How does this form of violence differ from its premodern forerunners? If the accusation of a tautological argument is to be avoided, then it must become clear what this difference is. For Rapoport, the difference between premodern and modern terrorism lies more in the *meaning* of the respective action than in the act itself: while the murderer of a tyrant kills a person who has corrupted a system, the terrorist seeks to bring down the system itself, which is thought to corrupt everyone who comes into contact with it.[66] Ze'ev Iviansky also emphasizes that terrorists did not attack political and public authorities as people but as embodiments of the social and economic orders they represented. Referring explicitly to work done by Uwe Backes, Sylvia Schraut generalizes this observation by arguing that terrorists radically questioned the legitimacy of the existing order and therefore sought to delegitimize both state rule and the state's monopoly on the use of force, which is why there could not have been terrorism without the necessity

---

Friedlander, 'The Origins of International Terrorism', 31; O'Sullivan, 'Terrorism, Ideology and Democracy', 10–11; Rubenstein, *Alchemists of Revolution*, 126; and Miller, *The Foundations of Modern Terrorism*, Chapter 2.

64 See Rapoport, *Assassination & Terrorism*, 45; and Rapoport, 'Terrorism', 1051; also Parry, *Terrorism*, xi–xii; Laqueur, *A History of Terrorism*, viii; Laqueur, *Terrorism*, 11–18; Iviansky, 'Individual Terror', 44; Friedlander, 'The Origins of International Terrorism', 31–4; Ford, 'Reflections on Political Murder'; Mommsen, 'Non-legal Violence and Terrorism', 397; O'Sullivan, *Terrorism*, ix–x; O'Sullivan, 'Terrorism, Ideology and Democracy', 4–6; Chaliand, *Terrorism*, 13, 77–8; Rubenstein, *Alchemists of Revolution*, xx, 79; Wardlaw, *Political Terrorism*, 18; Sinclair, *An Anatomy of Terror*, 132; and Carr, *The Infernal Machine*, 4–6.

65 Verhoeven, *The Odd Man Karakozov*, 6; and Jensen, *The Battle against Anarchist Terrorism*, 71.

66 Rapoport, *Assassination & Terrorism*, 37.

to legitimize state rule and without the state's claim to a monopoly on the use of force.[67] According to Franklin Ford, the new features of political murder in the nineteenth century were the revolutionary ideals (nationalism, egalitarianism, anarchism, and nihilism), the availability of new weapons (that increased the attacker's chances of success), the possibility of greater publicity through mass journalism, and decisive changes in the legal culture: whereas up to the eighteenth century, trials had taken place behind closed doors and executions had been public events, in the nineteenth century the trials became public and most of the executions occurred in closed chambers. Ford argues that terrorists learned quickly how to take advantage of the public trials to publicize their deeds and aims.[68] Rudolf Walther notes a shift in the means–ends relationship: the impact of deeds on third parties became more important than the deed itself.[69] In the eyes of Wolfgang Mommsen, the main difference between the premodern violence of underprivileged classes and terrorist violence was rooted in the nature of their demands. Groups like the Luddites or the underclasses prior to the revolutions of 1848–9 were backward-looking in their demands for the reinstatement of the old and just order, while terrorists' orientation towards the future, in contrast, came with an unleashing of the potential to violence. Whereas groups from the underclass doled out their violence in precise dosages, terrorists were prepared for a 'constant acceleration in the use of violence' until they achieved their goal: the destruction of the existing order for the sake of the better future promised by their ideology. O'Sullivan, Chaliand and Miller also see the abstract, ideological and utopian nature of the political aims of terrorists as a major difference to the political use

---

67 Iviansky, 'Individual Terror', 50; Schraut, 'Terrorismus – Geschlecht – Erinnerung', 13; Schraut, 'Terrorismus und Geschichtswissenschaft', 110; and specifically Carola Dietze, 'Legitimacy and Security from a Historical Perspective: A Case Study in the History of Terrorism', in Regina Kreide and Andreas Langenohl (eds.), *Conceptualizing Power in Dynamics of Securitization. Beyond State and International System* (Baden-Baden: Nomos, 2019), 135–73.

68 Ford, *Political Murder*, 106, 208; and Ford, 'Reflections on Political Murder', 4, 8. Like Ford, Richard Bach Jensen also stresses the roles of ideology (although the major anarchist thinkers, while embracing revolutionary violence, were initially ambiguous about and ultimately rejected terrorism), new weapons (especially dynamite), and the mass media as important factors (see Jensen, *The Battle against Anarchist Terrorism*, Chapters 1 and 2).

69 Walther, 'Terror, Terrorismus', 385.

of violence in earlier eras, while Jensen regards the first modern terrorist campaign as one that eschewed attempts at assassinating political leaders and instead turned to blowing up sites frequented by the public, in order to cause general terror.[70] Walther and Verhoeven identify the emergence of the modern, politically sovereign subject who seeks to intervene in the historical process as being a decisive criterion for modern terrorism. In addition, Verhoeven has argued not only that terrorism is a modern phenomenon, but also that terrorists – at least in nineteenth-century Europe and Russia – even had a modern image of themselves and that terrorism should therefore be ascribed to political modernism.[71]

All of these authors maintain that the subversive violence or violence from below experienced by societies before the French Revolution was typically restorative in aim, limited in scope, and targeted against single individuals or objects. By comparison, the modernism of terrorism lies in its struggle against a societal order, a struggle that is oriented towards the future, abstract, and driven by a philosophical, or rather an ideological, interpretation of history. Moreover, it is a struggle being fought out both in the streets and in courtrooms with the help of new weapons technology and mass media.[72]

Two contrary counternarratives have established themselves since the late 1990s, and even more prominently since 2001, to challenge

---

70 See Mommsen, 'Non-legal Violence and Terrorism', 388–9 (quote at 389); O'Sullivan, 'Terrorism, Ideology and Democracy', 5–6; Chaliand, *Terrorism*; Miller, *The Foundations of Modern Terrorism*, 95–6; and Jensen, *The Battle against Anarchist Terrorism*, 71–2. On the characteristics of violent acts by premodern underclass groups in relation to terrorist violence, see also Eric John Hobsbawm, ' "Political Violence" and "Political Murder": Comments on Franklin Ford's Essay', in Mommsen, *Social Protest, Violence, Terror*, 13–19.

71 Walther, 'Terror, Terrorismus', 385; Verhoeven, *The Odd Man Karakozov*, 4, 6; and Claudia Verhoeven, 'Time Bombs: Terrorism, Modernism, and Temporality in Europe and Russia during the Long Nineteenth Century', in Dietze and Verhoeven (eds.), *The Oxford Handbook of the History of Terrorism*.

72 In his book *Das Attentat*, Manfred Schneider has presented his argument that the emergence of 'paranoid reasoning' has produced terrorist assassinations and other forms of modern political violence. Even if his treatment of assassinations contains many interesting observations, Schneider's argument is not convincing because it does not become clear why and to what degree 'paranoid reasoning' is new or even a modern phenomenon. For example, a fruitful area of research for 'paranoid reasoning' would also be the Roman Empire.

this standard narration. According to the first counternarrative, modern terrorism begins with the attack against the Israeli Olympic team in Munich in 1972,[73] an assumption that results implicitly or explicitly from an emphasis on the role of technology in these violent acts. The hostage taking in Munich was the first act of terrorism to be broadcast on television in real time to a worldwide audience. While technical innovations may indeed justify the marking of a turning point within the history of terrorism, they do not indicate the beginning of (modern) terrorism, because the social logic prompting the exploitation of this technology had long been developed and tested often over time.

The second counternarrative posits that terrorism is a universal phenomenon spanning the entirety of time. Terrorist violence, argue the authors, has existed since the beginning of history and has been experienced all over the world.[74] The distinction between this interpretation and the standard narrative can be explained by the differences in the definitions of terrorism that are used. Those propagating the standard narrative define terrorism narrowly, as is also done in this book. Those authors who view terrorism as an anthropological phenomenon have a broader conception of this form of political violence. For them it is the use of violence by organized groups 'directed toward target audiences beyond the immediate victims in order to achieve political objectives',[75] or 'warfare deliberately waged against civilians with the purpose of destroying their will to support either leaders or policies that the agents of such violence

---

73 An example for this view is found in John Deutch, 'Terrorism', *Foreign Policy* 108 (1997), 10–22.

74 Among others, see Caleb Carr, *Lessons of Terror: A History of Warfare against Civilians: Why It Has Always Failed, and Why It Will Fail Again* (London: Little, Brown, 2002); Kronenwetter, *Terrorism*; Brenda J. Lutz and James M. Lutz, *Global Terrorism*, London: Routledge, 2004; Lutz and Lutz, *Terrorism: Origins and Evolution*, New York: Palgrave Macmillan, 2005; Brett Bowden and Michael T. Davis (eds.), *Terror: From Tyrannicide to Terrorism* (St Lucia: University of Queensland Press, 2008); and the relevant chapters in a series of general survey books, e.g. Gus Martin, *Understanding Terrorism: Challenges, Perspectives, and Issues* (Los Angeles: Sage, 2010). Miller, *The Foundations of Modern Terrorism*, has combined both narratives. In his definition of terrorism, which includes state terror, he refers to the 'emergence of several characteristics of terrorism' in the premodern period, and then assumes the (secularizing) turning point to have occurred in the French Revolution. See especially ibid., 2, 30–1, 57, and Chapter 3, quote at 10.

75 Lutz and Lutz, *Terrorism*, 19.

find objectionable',[76] or a form of violence encompassing both insurgent terrorism and state terror.[77] Such definitions broaden the history of terrorism into a history of murder, terror and psychological warfare that covers a multitude of different violent phenomena from Greek tactics for intimidating opponents, to tyrannicide, the Spanish Inquisition, the struggles in the Italian city states during the Renaissance, National Socialist and Stalinist state terror and finally the dropping of the atomic bombs on Hiroshima and Nagasaki. These are undoubtedly very important subjects, but the history of terrorism should not be lumped together with them. Otherwise it risks losing analytical incisiveness regarding its actual topic.[78] As a result, neither of these counternarratives represents a persuasive alternative as a framework for a systematic history of terrorism.

There are a number of studies on the prehistory of terrorism that attempt to correct details of the standard narrative or to fundamentally question its validity. For example, in a thorough study of the so-called Thugs, Kim A. Wagner recently proved that the interpretation of their use of violence as religiously motivated terrorism is part of a colonial conspiracy theory justifying the British mission to civilize India. In actuality, their activity was simply organized banditry, a criminality that was neither religiously nor politically motivated.[79] Johannes Dillinger has put forth the idea that terrorism has accompanied 'the modern states since their formation' in late medieval Europe. As an example of early modern terrorism, he cites the fear of mass poisoning, of arson and of regicide.[80] But just because the fear of these crimes and their concomitant conspiracy

---

76 Carr, *Lessons of Terror*, 6.

77 Miller, *The Foundations of Modern Terrorism*, 2.

78 The importance of analytically precise distinctions is emphasized, for example, by Ariel Merari, 'Du terrorisme comme stratégie d'insurrection', in Chaliand and Blin (eds.), *Histoire du terrorisme*, 23–55; and Schraut, 'Terrorismus und Geschichtswissenschaft', 106.

79 See Kim A. Wagner, *Thuggee: Banditry and the British in Early Nineteenth-Century India* (Basingstoke: Palgrave Macmillan, 2007); Wagner, *Stranglers and Bandits: A Historical Anthology of Thuggee* (New Delhi: Oxford University Press, 2009); and Wagner, 'Thugs and Assassins', in Dietze and Verhoeven (eds.), *The Oxford Handbook of the History of Terrorism*.

80 Johannes Dillinger, *Terrorismus: Wissen, was stimmt* (Freiburg: Herder, 2008), 21–6, quote at 26. See also Dillinger, 'Terrorists and Witches: Popular Ideas of Evil in the Early Modern Period', *History of European Ideas* 30 (2004), 167–82; and Dillinger, 'Organized Arson as a Political Crime: The Construction of a "Terrorist" Menace in the Early Modern Period', *Crime, histoire & sociétés* 10/2 (2006), 101–21.

theories reveal interesting parallels to the fear of terrorism, we cannot conclude that such fears and the reactions they evoke stem from similar types of violence. In the early modern period, regicide, arson and poisoning (insofar as the latter actually occurred) were usually implemented as very practical instruments for pursuing a specific aim, that aim being to eliminate or harm certain people and not to communicate a message in a symbolic way. Therefore such forms of violence do not constitute terrorism in the sense of the definitions commonly found in social-science research on the subject.

We are now seeing the publication of the first studies on the efforts to combat terrorism in the nineteenth century. Robert A. Friedlander has focused on the legal handling of political acts of violence and thus pointed out that the category *hostis humani generis* ('enemy of humanity') found in the legal discourse on piracy was adopted to prosecute terrorists. Mikkel Thorup has analysed the historical discourse of such ascriptions in a study spanning the entire modern era, and Richard Bach Jensen has researched national and international measures to combat terrorism in Europe and the Americas in the late nineteenth century. Both Joachim Wagner and Marcus Mühlnickel have described the security measures taken to prevent and protect against assassinations in the German Empire.[81] With regard to the political dimension of the fight against terrorism, the work on current developments by George Kassimeris and his co-authors has turned out to be fruitful to historical research.[82]

For the first time, this book presents the history of the origins of terrorism, its early reception and further development as a transnational history of terrorism and analyses it using methods of historical research in the context of societal and social history, political history,

---

81 See Friedlander, 'The Origins of International Terrorism'; Mikkel Thorup, *An Intellectual History of Terror: War, Violence and the State* (London: Routledge, 2010); Jensen, *The Battle against Anarchist Terrorism*; Joachim Wagner, *Politischer Terrorismus und Strafrecht im Deutschen Kaiserreich von 1871* (Heidelberg: Decker's Verlag, 1981); and Mühlnikel, 'Fürst, sind Sie unverletzt?'. In addition, see also Land, *Enemies of Humanity*; and Isabelle Duyvesteyn and Beatrice de Graaf (eds.), *Terroristen en hun bestrijders, vroeger en nu* (Amsterdam: Boom, 2007).

82 Kassimeris's introduction was particularly inspiring for this book, as were the contributions by Martin A. Miller, Jo-Marie Burt, Peter Oborne, Jonathan Stevenson, Leonard Weinberg and William Eubank, Richard Jackson, Christopher Michaelsen and Paul Wilkinson, in George Kassimeris (ed.), *Playing Politics with Terrorism: A User's Guide* (New York: Columbia University Press, 2008).

media history and the history of ideas in nineteenth-century Europe, Russia and the United States. For this study, the phenomenon of terrorist violence alone is decisive; in contrast, the terms used by the perpetrators themselves or by their contemporaries in connection with such acts are irrelevant.[83] It is important to keep in mind that the term 'terrorism' has its own history, one that is not congruent for long periods of time with the history of the phenomenon itself, as we understand it today.[84]

Two other aspects about this historical study are novel. For one, the yardstick of a uniform, social-scientific definition was applied before-hand to size up the many violent acts that have been called terrorism in one context or another. The five cases that were selected as a result of this process are closely scrutinized here and empirically proven to meet the defining criteria for terrorism. For another, the approach used here not only identifies those violent acts that constitute terror-ism but also examines their relations to and interactions with one another, instead of studying them as isolated episodes. The contexts shared by these acts are demonstrated by comparing the conditions, situations and dynamics involved and by observing how the transfer of ideas set processes of reception in motion among the perpetrators themselves. Such a uniform and scientifically grounded approach, coupled with evidence that demonstrates the interdependence of violent acts, makes it possible to comprehend and analyse the transna-tional process of inventing terrorism in the context of societal, social and media history and the history of ideas. This approach places terrorism in contemporary contexts and thereby offers a historical and empirical explanation of it, instead of asserting, in a relatively

---

83 This approach is consistent with the findings and claims presented by Schraut, 'Terrorismus und Geschichtswissenschaft', 104, 109.

84 On this point, see the older yet still relevant work by Iviansky, 'Individual Terror', and Walther, 'Terror, Terrorismus', as well as the more recent publications by Andreas Musolff, *Krieg gegen die Öffentlichkeit: Terrorismus und politischer Sprachgebrauch* (Opladen: Westdeutscher Verlag, 1996), Chapters 1, 2; Musolff, 'Verwendung von Kriegsterminologie in der Terrorismus-Debatte', in Frank Liedtke (ed.), *Begriffe besetzen: Strategien des Sprachgebrauchs in der Politik* (Opladen: Westdeutscher Verlag, 1991), 186–204; and Musolff, 'Die Terrorismus-Diskussion in Deutschland vom Ende der sechziger bis Anfang der neunziger Jahre', in Georg Stötzel and Martin Wengeler (eds.), *Kontroverse Begriffe: Geschichte des öffentlichen Sprachgebrauchs in der Bundesrepublik Deutschland* (Berlin: De Gruyter, 1995), 405–45.

arbitrary and occasionally sensationalist manner, that some single violent deed represents the first example of terrorism.

This study draws on a broad spectrum of sources and a selection of specialized historical literature, the compilation of which varies somewhat between the five cases studied here. Basically, sources of three major types were used. The first category consists of the personal testimonies of terrorists and people close to them as found in letters, memoirs, other texts of an autobiographical nature and material used by the perpetrators in connection with the terrorist act. The second is made up of government documents, such as police investigation files, court and prison records, government files, dispatches and correspondence between government institutions, letters from the populace addressed to public officials, official announcements and public statements, and reports filed by parliamentary inquiries establishing the circumstances of the crime, diagrams of the site, interrogations of the perpetrators, and protocols from witness examinations. Examples of the third source type are the media reports on the violence, particularly dispatches, newspaper articles and editorials, illustrations, contemporary magazine stories, speeches, lectures, sermons, book publications, and poems by pastors, intellectuals and writers. In addition to this, it is possible to consider some of the secondary literature on the history of terrorism in general and on the perpetrators studied here and their deeds in particular as a fourth type of source material because – depending on the perspective – such literature also frequently can be used as source material.

With regard to personal testimonies, the important sources on Felice Orsini and his attempted assassination of Napoleon III are his autobiographies, his letters and his testimony in court. These are all available in print. There are two versions of Orsini's autobiography: the translation of the original Italian manuscript under the title *Memoirs and Adventure of Felice Orsini, Written by Himself*, which was published in 1857 in Edinburgh, and *Memorie politiche scritte da lui medesimo e dedicate alla gioventù italiana*, a revised edition published in early 1858 in Turin in which Orsini deleted some biographical passages and added political arguments and appeals.[85] Orsini's letters were edited by Alberto Maria Ghisalberti and published as *Lettere di Felice Orsini* in 1936. The court

---

85 A second edition of this 1858 version appeared in March of that same year augmented by an appendix by the publisher Ausonio Franchi. Hereafter, references to the *Memorie politiche* will be citing the Trieste 2008 reprint, unless indicated otherwise.

transcripts were also published.[86] In addition, government records and various other documents are found in the Archives nationales in Paris. Unfortunately, these collections of sources were not available due to the archive's relocation to a new building.

No recent scholarly biography of Felice Orsini exists. The only study authored by a historian is Alessandro Luzio's *Felice Orsini: Saggio biografico* from 1914.[87] On the attack on Napolean III itself, there is a helpful depiction by Pierre François Gustave de la Gorce in the second volume of his *Histoire du Second Empire* (Book 13) from 1895 and an excellent study by Adrien Dansette, *L'attentat d'Orsini*, written in 1964. Besides these works, the book by Michael St John Packes, *Orsini: The Story of a Conspirator*, from 1958, proved helpful. Packes used print sources and historical literature to write a depiction that is often adorned to a degree far exceeding what can be historically reconstructed but embeds the subject in contexts well and is essentially reliable. Finally, the adventurous life of Felice Orsini has become the subject of numerous literary and popular books that lack in scholarly ambitions but do possess a source value of their own in questions concerning the culture of memory.[88]

The situation for source material on John Brown and the raid on Harpers Ferry is complex in several regards because the archival sources, such as letters by and to John Brown and other documents and artefacts, are scattered across various archives and libraries throughout the United States. Important collections whose archives were used for this study are located in the Abraham Lincoln Presidential Library, Springfield, Illinois; the Boston Public Library, Boston, Massachusetts; the Kansas

---

86 Constantin-Achille Dandraut (ed.), *Textuel: Procès Orsini contenant par entier les débats judiciaires devant la Cour d'assises de la Seine et la Cour de cassation* (Turin: Imprimerie nationale de G. Biancardi, 1858).

87 Alessandro Luzio, *Felice Orsini Saggio biografico* (Milan: Casa Editrice L. F. Cogliati, 1914). In addition, a short but good overview is found in Jesse Fryniwyd Tennyson, 'The Murder from Conviction, Orsini', in Tennyson, *Murder & Its Motives* (London: William Heinemann, 1924), 224–56.

88 See Edmond Lepelletier, *Le serment d'Orsini*, vol. 1: *Un caprice de Napoléon III* (Paris: Montgredien, 1900); Claude Gevel, *Deux Carbonari: Orsini et Napoléon III* (Paris: Éditions Emile-Paul Frères, 1934); Giorgio Manzini, *Avventure e morte di Felice Orsini* (Milan: Camunia, 1991); Alfredo Venturi, *L'uomo delle bombe: La vita e i tempi di Felice Orsini, terrorista e gentiluomo* (Bresso and Milan: Hobby & Work, 2009); Giancarlo De Cataldo, *Il Maestro, Il Terrorista, Il Terrone* (Rome: Laterza, 2011). On the bombing specifically, see Marcel Boulenger, *L'attentat d'Orsini* (Paris: Librairie Hachette, 1927); and Rinaldo Caddeo, *L'attentato di Orsini* [1858] (Milan: A. Mondadori, 1932).

State Historical Society in Topeka; the Ohio Historical Society in Columbus; and the Boyd B. Stutler Collection in the West Virginia State Archives in Charleston. Government documents on the attack on Harpers Ferry are kept chiefly at the US National Archives and Records Administration in Washington, DC, and at the Library of Virginia in Richmond. By now, these archives have digitalized a significant part of their inventories (including the majority of sources used here) and made them available on the Internet. Whenever the sources cited here were used in digitalized form, the corresponding website is given. However, it should be noted that the sources available in this manner change from time to time. Many of the sources used here are also found in print, which has also been noted. In addition, there are a number of older biographies that cite sources by and on John Brown (including material that was later lost) and several more recent publications.[89] Since none of these can be considered scientific works in a strict sense and since the reproduction of documents in these editions often deviates from one printed version to the next, the original source material has been used whenever possible.

The body of literature on John Brown is quite extensive. The first scholarly biography of Brown was written by Oswald Garrison Villard and published in 1910 with the title *John Brown, 1800–1859: A Biography Fifty Years After*. Unfortunately, in his attempt to curb the mythicization of John Brown, Villard often throws out the baby with the bathwater and is too imprecise. The best historical biography remains Stephen B. Oates's book *To Purge This Land with Blood: A Biography of John Brown* (1970). Although certain details in Oates's work have been corrected by recent research, the book stands out for its extensive use of source material, reliability and good judgement. This also holds true for *Allies for*

---

89 See especially James Redpath, *The Public Life of Captain John Brown* (Boston: Thayer and Eldridge, 1860); Franklin B. Sanborn, *The Life and Letters of John Brown, Liberator of Kansas, and Martyr of Virginia* (Boston: Houghton, Mifflin, 1906); Richard J. Hinton, *John Brown and His Men* (New York: Funk & Wagnalls Company, 1894); Louis Ruchames (ed.), *John Brown: The Making of a Revolutionary: The Story of John Brown in His Own Words and in the Words of Those Who Knew Him* (New York: Grosset & Dunlap, 1969); Benjamin Quarles (ed.), *Blacks on John Brown* (1972) (Cambridge: Da Capo Press, 2001); Zoe Trodd and John Stauffer (eds.), *Meteor of War: The John Brown Story* (Maplecrest: Brandywine Press, 2004); and Trodd and Stauffer (eds.), *The Tribunal: Responses to John Brown and the Harpers Ferry Raid* (Cambridge, MA: Belknap Press of Harvard University Press, 2012).

Freedom by Benjamin Quarles, which was first published in 1974 and focuses particularly on Brown's relations and cooperation with Afro-Americans; the same can be said for much of the book *Man on Fire: John Brown and the Cause of Liberty* by Jules Abel (1971), although Abel fails to document his sources precisely. Richard Owen Boyer's book *The Legend of John Brown: A Biography and a History* (1973) focuses solely on the years up to 1855 but achieves the best historical contextualization of John Brown for this period. Church historian Louis A. DeCaro Jr illustrates in *'Fire from the Midst of You': A Religious Life of John Brown* (2002) the role faith played in his protagonist's life on the basis of in part newly evaluated source material. In *John Brown's War against Slavery* (2009), the historian Robert McGlone discusses major questions of contention in the research on John Brown on the basis of his thorough rereading of the sources. In addition, two books deserve mention for incorporating cultural contexts very well. The first is a 'cultural biography' entitled *John Brown, Abolitionist: The Man Who Killed Slavery, Sparked the Civil War, and Seeded Civil Rights* (2005) by David S. Reynolds, a scholar of American literature; the second is the particularly good psychological study by Evan Carton, also an American literary scholar, with the title *Patriotic Treason: John Brown and the Soul of America* (2006). Likewise, the journalist and writer Tony Horwitz published a book in 2011 entitled *Midnight Rising: John Brown and the Raid That Sparked the Civil War* that offers a fresh approach to the telling of Brown's story partly thanks to sources rarely cited before. Another work to be noted is the double biography of John Brown and Frederick Douglass, published in 2013 by the independent scholar William S. King with the title *To Raise Up a Nation*. Last of all, in *Weird John Brown* (2015) the theologian Ted A. Smith revisits the religious thinking of John Brown and uses this as the starting point for his own political theology. Since these more recent depictions rely on earlier literature, they will only be mentioned later in relation to aspects or interpretations that are not found in earlier work.

Unlike John Brown's raid on Harpers Ferry, the attack by Oskar Wilhelm Becker on the Prussian king Wilhelm I has received little attention in historiography to date. For this reason, the depiction offered here is based on archival material on Becker and his deed – none of which has been published – found in the Stadtarchiv

Baden-Baden, the Generallandesarchiv Karlsruhe, and the Geheimes Staatsarchiv Preußischer Kulturbesitz (Secret State Archives, Prussian Cultural Heritage) in Berlin-Dahlem. Only short depictions of Becker's attack on King Wilhelm I exist to date in the literature, specifically in biographies of Wilhelm I and in a helpful article by the judge Reiner Haehling von Lanzenauer, 'Das Baden-Badener Attentat', published in 1995.[90]

Also unlike the case of John Brown, the source material on John Wilkes Booth and his assassination of Abraham Lincoln is relatively well organized and very well edited. Nearly all of the ego-documents by Booth that exist (and there are not many) are found with useful commentaries in a reliable volume entitled 'Right or Wrong, God Judge me': The Writings of John Wilkes Booth, edited by John Rhodehamel and Louise Taper. The recollections of his sister Asia Booth Clarke were published as a book entitled The Unlocked Book: A Memoir of John Wilkes Booth, which has recently been edited and republished by Terry Alford under the title John Wilkes Booth: A Sister's Memoir. In addition, innumerable eyewitness accounts of Lincoln's assassination and of the events occurring in the final days and hours prior to his murder have been recorded from different perspectives. These accounts were written at various points in time, and some of them are already partially influenced by other contemporary depictions (such as newspaper stories or trial records). A helpful compilation and comparative analysis of several of the more significant sources of this type have been undertaken by W. Emerson Reck in A. Lincoln: His Last 24 Hours (1987) and by Timothy S. Good in the volume he edited, entitled We Saw Lincoln Shot: One Hundred Eyewitness Accounts (1995).[91]

There exists an abundance of depictions of Booth's assassination of Lincoln – both of the event itself and of its background – the majority of which have not been written by professional historians.[92] Therefore we

90 Erich Marcks, Kaiser Wilhelm I. (Leipzig: Duncker, 1897), 152; Franz Herre, Kaiser Wilhelm I.: Der letzte Preuße (Cologne: Kiepenheuer & Witsch, 1980), 285–6.

91 The 1955 depiction by Jim Bishop, The Day Lincoln Was Shot (New York: Greenwich House, 1955), is accurately described by the author himself as 'pretty much a journalistic job' (ibid., 2). Unfortunately, it is not always reliable.

92 The catalogue of the Library of Congress registers around 400 separate publications (as of 2015); Blaine V. Houmes's Abraham Lincoln Assassination Bibliography (Clinton: Surrat Society, 1997), lists 3,000 contributions.

find events presented in many variations, some of which diverge signifi-cantly from others, with no shortage of conspiracy theories.[93] Yet histo-rians have also written reliable investigations of the assassination, its background, reactions to it, and the escape of and hunt for Booth.[94] Likewise, Booth specialists have produced other useful depictions that are based on the in part meticulous analysis of sources, including new material.[95] Contrary to what could be expected from this myriad of books dealing with the assassination, only two biographical works exist on John Wilkes Booth: *American Brutus: John Wilkes Booth and the Lincoln Conspiracies* (2004) by Booth expert Michael W. Kauffman, a work that has proven helpful in many regards for this book, and the biography *Fortune's Fool: The Life of John Wilkes Booth* (2015) by the historian Terry Alford.[96]

The source material and literature on Dmitry Vladimirovich Karakozov and his attempt to assassinate Alexander II is also broadly accessible, especially since important sources are available in printed form. For example, Aleksei Alekseevich Shilov published a scholarly edition with an informative commentary, first of Karakozov's proclama-tion and later of various interrogations of both Karakozov and people

---

93 The first critical and well-balanced accounts of the events are Lloyd Lewis's *Myths after Lincoln* (New York: Harcourt, 1929, republished under the title *The Assassination of Lincoln: History and Myth*, Lincoln: University of Nebraska Press, 1994); and a study that was first published in 1940 by George S. Bryan, *The Great American Myth* (Chicago: Americana House, 1990).

94 See especially Thomas Reed Turner, *Beware the People Weeping: Public Opinion and the Assassination of Abraham Lincoln* (Baton Rouge: Louisiana State University Press, 1982); William Hanchett, *The Lincoln Murder Conspiracies* (Urbana: University of Illinois Press, 1983); Thomas Reed Turner, *The Assassination of Abraham Lincoln* (Malabar: Krieger, 1999); Harold Holzer (ed.), *The Lincoln Assassination* (New York: Fordham University Press, 2010); and Martha Hodes, *Mourning Lincoln* (New Haven: Yale University Press, 2015).

95 See Edward Steers, *Blood on the Moon: The Assassination of Abraham Lincoln* (Lexington: University Press of Kentucky, 2001); Thomas Goodrich and Debra Goodrich, *The Darkest Dawn: Lincoln, Booth, and the Great American Tragedy* (Bloomington: Indiana University Press, 2005); and Anthony S. Pitch, *'They Have Killed Papa Dead!' The Road to Ford's Theatre, Abraham Lincoln's Murder, and the Rage for Vengeance* (Hanover: Steerforth Press, 2008).

96 Bill O'Reilly and Martin Dugard, *Killing Lincoln: The Shocking Assassination That Changed America Forever* (New York: Henry Holt and Co., 2011), is a well-written account of the events but is not a scholarly work.

close to him.[97] In addition, Mitrofan Mikhailovich Klevenskii and K. G. Kotel'nikov have published an authoritative edition of the stenographic transcripts of court proceedings and other sources linked to the case and have included an extremely helpful introduction and commentary.[98] Several memoirs by members of Karakozov's circle of friends have been published.[99] Further unpublished sources are found in Russian archives – especially in the State Archive of the Russian Federation (Gosudarstvennyi arkhiv Rossiiskoi Federatsii, GARF) in Moscow – some of which were examined by the author; however, this material proved of little value for the issue ultimately addressed here.

A large body of literature also exists on Dmitry Vladimirovich Karakozov and his attempt on the life of the tsar. As the first such attempt to emerge out of the revolutionary movement, it is mentioned in all biographies of Tsar Alexander II and in all books on the Russian revolutionary movement. The incident is rarely examined closely in either of the genres, and the depictions are sometimes very inconsistent with one another on the details.[100] There are books and essays that specifically depict Karakozov and his deed. As early as 1931, Boris Yakovlevich Bukhshtab examined the reaction of the Russian public to the attack in his essay 'Posle vystrela Karakozova'. Later, in 1968, E. G. Zil'berman and V. K. Kholyavin wrote a source-based and documented account

---

97 Aleksei Alekseevich Shilov, 'Iz istorii revoliutsionnogo dvizheniia 1860-kh godov', *Golos minuvshego* 10–12 (1918), 159–68; Shilov, 'Pokushenie Karakozova 4 aprelia 1866 g', *Krasnyi Arkhiv* 17/7 (1926), 91–137.

98 Mitrofan Mikhailovich Klevenskii and K. G. Kotel'nikov (eds.), *Pokushenie Karakozova: Stenograficheskii otchet po delu D. Karakozova, Kh. Khudiakova, N. Ishutina i dr.* 2 vols. (Moscow: Izdatel'stvo Tsentrarkhiva R.S.F.S.R., 1928–30).

99 For example, see the recollections noted in a letter by Pëtr Fëdorovich Nikolaev to Ch. Vetrinskiy (= V. E. Cheshikhiy), reprinted under the title 'N. G. Chernyshevskii i karakozovtsy', *Russkaia mysl'* 34/2 (1913), 102–7.

100 The most detailed and/or reliable depictions are those in the classic biography of Alexander II by Sergei Spiridonovich Tatishchev, *Imperator Aleksandr II, ego zhizn' i tsarstvovanie* (1903) (Moscow: AST, 2006), 423–33; and in Leonid Mikhailovich Liashenko, *Aleksandr II, ili Istoriia trekh odinochestv* (Moscow: Molodaia gvardiia, 2002); Franco Venturi, *Roots of Revolution: A History of the Populist and Socialist Movements in Nineteenth-Century Russia* (London: Weidenfeld & Nicolson, 1960), Chapter 14; Adam Ulam, *Prophets and Conspirators in Prerevolutionary Russia* (New Brunswick: Transaction Publishers, 1998), 1–8; Oleg Vital'evich Budnitskii, *Terrorizm v rossiiskom osvoboditel'nom dvizhenii* (Moscow: ROSSPEN, 2000), 34–9; Sydney Ronald Seth, *The Russian Terrorists: The Story of the Narodniki* (London: Barrie, 1967), 29–30; Walter G. Moss, *Russia in the Age of Alexander II, Tolstoy and Dostoevsky* (London: Anthem Press, 2002), 89–91.

entitled 'Vystrel: Ocherk zhizni i revolyutsionnoǐ bor'by D. Karakozova', which, however, goes beyond what can be historically reconstructed to a degree much like Michael St John Packe's book *Orsini*. In addition, the historian N. P. Eroshkin published a short but vivid and clearly written essay on Karakozova's deed in the journal *Voprosy istorii*. The most recent study on this topic is Claudia Verhoeven's book *The Odd Man Karakozov: Imperial Russia, Modernity, and the Birth of Terrorism*, published in 2009.

In order to extrapolate the reaction to acts of violence, an extensive array of newspapers was also examined. Since research for this book began before any database for digitalized newspapers existed, for several years this work depended on microfilm and even the original bound volumes of newspapers at various libraries in Europe and the United States. Except for those newspapers that have still not been digitalized to date, newspaper databases were reviewed later as they became available. The database used for researching American newspapers were, above all, 19th Century U.S. Newspapers, the New York Times Article Archive, Google News (in which a number of historical newspapers are found), Historical Newspapers Online (made available by Viewshare, a service of the Library of Congress in Washington, DC) and the digital collection Chronicling America: Historic American Newspapers, also by the Library of Congress.[101] For British newspapers, the database 19th Century British Library Newspapers and the Times Digital Archive were used; for German newspapers, primarily the Zeitungsinformationssytem (ZEFYS) of the Staatsbibliothek zu Berlin Preußischer Kulturbesitz; for French newspapers, the Gallica, the digital library of the Bibliothèque nationale de France; for Austria-Hungarian newspapers, ANNO – AustriaN Newspapers Online, the portal of the Österreichische Nationalbibliothek in Vienna for historical newspapers and periodicals.[102]

---

101 See Gale Cengage Learning, Nineteenth Century U.S. Newspapers, infotrac. galegroup.com; New York Times Article Archive 1851–Present, nytimes.com; Google News, All Newspapers, news.google.com; Viewshare: Interfaces to our Heritage, a Service Provided by Library of Congress, Historical Newspapers Online, viewshare.org; Library of Congress, Chronicling America: Historic American Newspapers, chroniclingamerica.loc.gov.

102 See Gale Cengage Learning, 19th Century British Library Newspapers infotrac. galegroup.com; Gale Cengage Learning, The Times Digital Archive, infotrac.galegroup. com; Zeitungsinformationssystem der Staatsbibliothek zu Berlin Preußischer

The violent acts and actors dealt with here, with the exception of Oskar Wilhelm Becker, have been the subject of historical inquiry and even intense controversy for about 150 years, a fact that represents both an advantage and a challenge for this study. The advantage lies in the availability of a multitude of edited volumes and depictions to be drawn upon for this study. This occurs here over long stretches precisely where the central theme – the invention of terrorism – recedes into the middle ground while biographical narration takes centre stage. The challenge lies in the necessity to drill through the layers of repeatedly adopted views and strongly solidified narratives and interpretations and to apply one's own critical inspection of the sources and literature, in order to provide a concrete and vivid depiction and analysis that reflects historical reality as accurately as possible. To document this protracted process of assessment throughout would have caused the notes to swell to a size greatly inhibiting readability. Therefore accounts and interpretations deviating from those presented here will be pointed out only in cases where it seems necessary for any number of reasons. However, the sources and literature crucial for this study or those also dealing with the matter at hand have been included in the notes, even if these differ in depiction and interpretation.[103]

In light of the long-standing interest in four of the five perpetrators, it should come as no surprise that in some cases the deeds carried out by Felice Orsini and John Brown and later emulated by Oskar Wilhelm Becker, John Wilkes Booth and Dmitry Vladimirovich Karakozov have already been labelled as terrorism. This is particularly true in the cases of Orsini, Brown and Karakozov. The reasons differ why various authors have called these deeds terrorist acts,[104] and many other cases of violence

Kulturbesitz, zefys.staatsbibliothek-berlin.de; Bibliothèque nationale de France, Gallica – la bibliothèque numérique de la BnF, gallica.bnf.fr, Österreichische Nationalbibliothek, ANNO – AustriaN Newspapers Online. Historische österreichische Zeitungen und Zeitschriften online, anno.onb.ac.at.

103 Because this study was completed in the summer of 2013, literature published up to this point has been worked into it as systematically as possible. While books and essays appearing after that date were still included, they could no longer be afforded the same degree and depth of consideration.

104 On Orsini, see especially Miller, 'The Intellectual Origins of Modern Terrorism in Europe', 36–9; Waldmann, *Terrorismus*, 56; and Marco Pinfari, 'Exploring the Terrorist Nature of Political Assassinations: A Reinterpretation of the Orsini Attentat', *Terrorism and Political Violence* 21/4 (2009), 580–94. On Karakozov, see p. 456–7, and on Brown,

in history have also been said – sometimes rather arbitrarily – to be terrorism. The cases are rare in which the term 'terrorism' has been used in an analytical sense.

A good example is the question whether John Brown was a terrorist or not – a very politically and normatively laden one in the American discussion of the politics of memory. In the past 150 years, the answer given to this question marked how one stood on the issue of equality and civil rights for Afro-Americans. Typically, John Brown was labelled a terrorist by those people who were rankled by the idea of equality for African Americans, while people who firmly supported and support the tradition of the abolitionist movement and the civil rights movement usually try to stress the difference between the means and the ends and thus to acquit John Brown of the charge of terrorism. Even in 2009 – on the occasion of the 150th anniversary of the raid on Harpers Ferry and the execution of John Brown – this issue exceeded the realm of scholarly debate and was discussed prominently in newspapers, on television and on Internet blogs.

The political–normative explosiveness of the question whether John Brown was a terrorist or not is precisely why the characterization of him has fluctuated greatly. Over the decades, African Americans continually nurtured a positive image of the man and defended him: 'Today at least we know: John Brown was right,' wrote W. E. B. Du Bois in 1909.[105] However, following the end of Reconstruction in the South in the late 1870s and the re-establishment of a racist regime featuring segregation and the political, economic and social exclusion of African Americans, various books and later also movies appeared in which John Brown was portrayed as a criminal, murderer and terrorist. In doing so, the term 'terrorism' was applied to him with strictly polemic–denunciatory intent.[106] In the course of the civil rights movement that started in the late 1950s, an increasing number of studies appeared which attempted to do John Brown justice in a critically objective sense. Just as in the debate in Brown's time after 1859, the terms 'uprising', 'insurrection', 'rebellion', 'guerrilla army', '(black) revolution' and 'invasion' dominate

---

see the following paragraphs. Miller is the only author who has already called Becker a terrorist (Miller, 'The Intellectual Origins of Modern Terrorism in Europe', 39).

105 W. E. B. Du Bois, *John Brown* (New York: Modern Library, 2001), 202.

106 For an overview, see Stephen B. Oates, 'John Brown and His Judges: A Critique of the Historical Literature', *Civil War History* 17/1 (1971), 11–19.

these studies.[107] Following the attacks of 11 September 2001, a new series of works appeared devoted to the question of whether and to what degree John Brown was a terrorist, a crucial question because – as David Reynolds asked – 'How can America, which regards terrorism as its greatest threat, admit to the fact that it was shaped by a terrorist of its own?'[108] Here Reynolds pinpoints the central predicament involved in America's renewed interest in the controversy over John Brown and the violence he committed.

The question of whether or not to remember John Brown as a terrorist and what political and normative import to give his memory does not pose itself in this way, however, if terrorism is examined at once analytically and historically.[109] John Brown plays a particularly important role in the history of terrorism. Following Felice Orsini and in cooperation with others, Brown both discovered and invented terrorism in the United States as a new strategy of political violence with which to achieve the aims of the American Revolution in a non-revolutionary situation. He sought to complete this revolution. Therefore John Brown is no longer solely relevant for the question about the role terrorism has played in American history but also for the question about the importance of the United States in the history of terrorism. Once we recognize, first, that terrorism was invented as a last resort to fulfil Enlightenment-inspired, revolutionary demands for political participation and national sovereignty as well as personal liberty, equality and

107 See, for example, Stephen B. Oates, *To Purge This Land with Blood: A Biography of John Brown* (Amherst: University of Massachusetts Press, 1979), Chapters 16–20; or the title of Robert McGlone's book, *John Brown's War against Slavery* (Cambridge: Cambridge University Press, 2009).

108 David S. Reynolds, *John Brown, Abolitionist: The Man Who Killed Slavery, Sparked the Civil War, and Seeded Civil Rights* (New York: Vintage Books, 2005), 500. See also ibid., 11, 165, 502–4; and Louis A. DeCaro Jr, 'Connections with the Past: Reflections on John Brown', afrolumensproject, WaybackMachine, Internet Archive, web.archive. org, afrolumens.org; McGlone, *John Brown's War*, Chapter 6, IV, here 136; and James Gilbert, 'A Behavioral Analysis of John Brown', in Peggy A. Russo and Paul Finkelman (eds.), *Terrible Swift Sword: The Legacy of John Brown* (Athens: Ohio University Press, 2005), 115. On the other hand, John Brown is labelled a terrorist by Lutz and Lutz, *Terrorism in America*, 140, 53; Fellman, *In the Name of God and Country*, 18, 29, 30; and Michael Stoneham, *John Brown and the Era of Literary Confrontation* (New York: Routledge, 2009), 7, 163.

109 Härter, Hannappel, Tyrichter and Walter make a similar argument for the history of terrorism in general in 'Terrorismus für die Rechtsgeschichte?', 376.

human dignity; second, that this tactic was initially a continuation of the American and French revolutions; and, third, that terrorists viewed themselves as continuing this tradition and were also interpreted as doing so by their contemporaries, then the stigma of labelling John Brown a terrorist falls away.[110]

---

110 All Russian dates are listed according to the Julian calendar, which was the civil calendar in that country throughout the nineteenth century; the orthography common before the revolution was adjusted to modern usage; however, the emphasis found in quotes is always taken from the original. Unless noted otherwise, all translations have been provided by the translators. If not explicitly stated to the contrary, Bible citations are taken from the King James Version.

1
Theoretical and historical premises

Components of a theory of terrorism: concept, logic of action, causes and effects

What is terrorism? Only a precise concept of terrorism, its causes, and the ways in which it operates can help identify this specific kind of violence and differentiate it from other forms of violence in history. In terms of scientific disciplines, the questions of what terrorism is, how it arises, and how it functions fall under the purview of the social sciences, in particular sociology and political science. A careful review of the literature on terrorism, however, has made it clear that the social sciences have no single comprehensive approach that explains all the questions that are important in a historical analysis of terrorism's origins. The aspects crucial to a historical inquiry into this topic are therefore discussed below.

The general purpose of the social sciences is to arrive at universally valid statements that hold true independently of time and space. This chapter's synthesis of approaches from political science and social science is thus itself a theory on the origins and functioning of terrorist violence. It is a theory with a claim to systematic universal validity even though it is embedded in a historical investigation based on specific times, spaces and actors, and hence on the uniqueness of each of them. As it turns out, however, the theory that emerges from the following synthesis is equally applicable to the analysis of all five incidents at the heart of this book, their perpetrators and the societies in which they lived. It thereby proves valid for understanding the rise of terrorism, at least in the nineteenth century. The degree to which it can explain terrorism's history since the mid-nineteenth century is discussed in the concluding chapter.

Concept

As repeatedly emphasized in the relevant literature, the notion of *terrorism* is problematic for various reasons. First, the word as used in today's political discourse does not refer to an analytical concept designating a particular kind of violence. It is instead a battle cry to defame a political opponent.[1] The argument is that political positions ultimately determine what terrorism is. Gerald Seymour sums it up in an aphorism: 'One man's terrorist is another man's freedom fighter.'[2] Second, Martha Crenshaw and Charles Tilly correctly warned against the term's objectifying effect. Terror and terrorism appeared to be virtually independent actors when former US president George W. Bush declared war on terrorism and his secretary of defense Colin L. Powell stated, 'Terrorism doesn't only kill people. It also threatens democratic institutions, undermines economies, and destabilizes regions.'[3] By contrast, Crenshaw and Tilly conceive of terrorism as a strategy used by different political actors with different goals and effects, depending on the situation.[4] Third, research on terrorism stresses again and again how difficult it is to define the term. In the early 1980s the Dutch terrorism researcher Alex Schmid found more than a hundred different definitions by different scientific and political institutions, and their number has only grown

---

1 See Martha Crenshaw, 'Thoughts on Relating Terrorism to Historical Contexts', in Crenshaw, *Terrorism in Context*, 7–12; and Louise Richardson, *What Terrorists Want: Understanding the Enemy, Containing the Threat*, 1st ed. (New York: Random House, 2006), 3–4.

2 Harold Seymour, *Harry's Game: A Novel* (New York: Random House, 1975), 61.

3 Secretary Colin L. Powell, 'Release of the 2001 Report "Patterns of Global Terrorism"', Statement upon the Release of "Patterns of Global Terrorism"', Washington, DC, 21 May 2002, US State Department archive, para. 8, 2001-2009.state.gov.

4 Charles Tilly, 'Terror, Terrorism, Terrorists', *Sociological Theory* 22/1 (2004), 5–13; Martha Crenshaw, 'Questions to Be Answered, Research to Be Done, Knowledge to Be Applied', in Walter Reich (ed.), *Origins of Terrorism: Psychologies, Ideologies, Theologies, States of Mind* (Cambridge: Cambridge University Press, 1990), especially 248.

since then.[5] This multiplicity explains the frequent assumption that the term does not lend itself to scientific study.[6]

A closer look shows that these objections to the term 'terrorism' are of only limited value. The sheer abundance of definitions for terrorism is undeniable, but well-conceived scientific ones converge in the essential points.[7] German sociologist Peter Waldmann, on whose terminology the study in this book rests, defines terrorism as 'violence against a political order from below which is planned and prepared [*planmäßig vorbereitet*] and meant to be shocking. Such acts of violence are supposed to spread feelings of insecurity and intense fear, but they are also meant to generate sympathy and support.'[8] The term 'political order' in German can include the social and economic order of a society, so that Waldmann's definition also covers these aspects of societal order as objects of violence (for example, aimed at by right-wing or social-revolutionary terrorists, such as the anarchists). Waldmann underlines the political dimension expressed in the political intentions and objectives of the violence committed by the terrorists.[9] Terrorism is thus a politically motivated strategy of resorting to spectacular violence with the goal of producing a powerful psychological effect in a society – fear on the one hand, sympathy on the other – in order to compel political change. This view limits the concept of terrorism to underground acts of violence against an inherently more powerful opponent (bottom-up),

5 See Alex P. Schmid, *Political Terrorism: A Research Guide to Concepts, Theories, Databases and Literature* (Amsterdam: North-Holland, 1984), 74, 119–58.

6 See Donatella Della Porta, *Clandestine Political Violence* (Cambridge: Cambridge University Press, 2013), 7–9. The very title of the book is her proposal for a different formulation.

7 Schmid even finds that 'in the field of terrorism there is no agreement about any single definition. But there is, in our view, considerable agreement about the main elements which definitions should contain.' Schmid, *Political Terrorism*, 110. On these elements and his definition see Schmid, *Political Terrorism*, 76–7, 111. For this reason, Christopher Daase has suggested using Ludwig Wittgenstein's concept of 'family resemblance' to capture the meaning of the term 'terrorism'. Christopher Daase, 'Terrorismus – Begriffe, Theorien und Gegenstrategien: Ergebnisse und Probleme sozialwissenschaftlicher Forschung', *Die Friedens-Warte: Journal of International Peace and Organization* 76/1 (2001), 55–79.

8 Waldmann, *Terrorismus*, 12, with minor changes, as translated in Carola Dietze and Claudia Verhoeven, 'Introduction', paper presented at the conference on 'Terrorism and Modernity: Global Perspectives on Nineteenth Century Political Violence', Tulane University, New Orleans, Louisiana, 23–6 October 2008.

9 Waldmann, *Terrorismus*, Chapters 1–2, here 12.

whereas acts of violence by the state against the population (top-down) are called 'terror'. More recent research literature reflects broad international agreement on the elements identified in this definition.[10] The repeatedly evoked problem of defining terrorism is thus not so much a terminological issue as it is a battle over political ascriptions.[11]

By contrast, the widely cited alternative distinction between terrorist and freedom fighter stems from a logical fallacy. As the Israeli terrorism researcher Boaz Ganor convincingly argues, terrorism and the fight for freedom describe two different aspects of political action. The former term refers to tactics; the latter, to the political objective. Individuals who practise insurgent violence can therefore be terrorists and freedom fighters, the one or the other, or neither.[12]

For these reasons, it is possible to use the word 'terrorism' as an analytical term without becoming mired in polemics or lapsing into anthropomorphization, as long as one strictly observes the criteria, for example, in the definition by Waldmann.[13] This definition serves in the

10 For Germany see also Friedhelm Neidhardt, 'Zur Soziologie des Terrorismus', *Berliner Journal für Soziologie* 1/2 (2004), 263–72; from the perspective of security policy, Kai Hirschmann, *Terrorismus* (Hamburg: Europäische Verlagsanstalt, 2003), 7–9; and from the criminological viewpoint, Anne Wildfang, *Terrorismus: Definition, Struktur, Dynamik* (Berlin: Duncker & Humblot, 2010). For the Netherlands, see Erwin Roelof Muller, Ramón F. J. Spaaij and A. G. W. Ruitenberg, *Trends in terrorisme* (Alphen aan den Rijn: Kluwer, 2003), 2–3. For the United Kingdom and Ireland, see Charles Townshend, *Terrorism: A Very Short Introduction* (Oxford: Oxford University Press, 2002), Chapter 1; and Richardson, *What Terrorists Want*, Chapter 1. For the United States, see Laqueur, *A History of Terrorism*, 79; Crenshaw, 'Thoughts on Relating Terrorism'; and Hoffman, *Inside Terrorism*, Chapter 1, 40–1. For Israel, see Boaz Ganor, *Defining Terrorism: Is One Man's Terrorist Another Man's Freedom Fighter?* (Herzliya: International Policy Institute for Counter-Terrorism, the Interdisciplinary Center, 1998); and Ariel Merari, 'Terrorism as a Strategy of Insurgency', in Chaliand and Blin, *The History of Terrorism*, 12–54. For Russia, see Murat Islamovich Dzliev, El'zad Seifullaevich Izzatdust and Mikhail Pavlovich Kireev, *Sovremennyi terrorizm: sotsial'no-politicheskii oblik protivnika* (Moscow: Akademiia, 2007), Chapter 1.1, 28–35. For Australia, see Grant Wardlaw, *Political Terrorism*, Chapter 1.1. Della Porta, *Clandestine Political Violence*, 9–10, likewise singles out these elements to define her term 'clandestine political violence'.

11 This position is also taken by Wildfang, *Terrorismus*, 9; and by Uwe Backes, 'Auf der Suche nach einer international konsensfähigen Terrorismusdefinition', *Jahrbuch Öffentliche Sicherheit* (2003), 153–65.

12 See Ganor, *Defining Terrorism*; and Merari, 'Terrorism as a Strategy of Insurgency', 27. See also Richardson, *What Terrorists Want*, 6–10.

13 See also Martha Crenshaw, 'Introduction: Reflections on the Effects of Terrorism', in Martha Crenshaw and Irving Louis Horowitz (eds.), *Terrorism, Legitimacy, and Power* (Middletown: Wesleyan University Press, 1983), 1–37.

following chapters to assess the violent acts committed by Felice Orsini and John Brown and by their imitators Oskar Wilhelm Becker, John Wilkes Booth and Dmitry Vladimirovich Karakozov. This approach will show that, or to what degree, the different acts of violence constitute terrorism.

Waldmann's definition, however, is complemented by additional criteria and observations relating to the causes of terrorist violence and to the conditions on which its success hinges. These criteria and observations come from several sources: first, Rainer Paris's analyses based on action theory; second, research by James C. Davies and Samuel Huntington in political science and sociology on the social causes of political violence; third, the work by historical sociologists and researchers of movements and protests like Donatella della Porta, Dieter Rucht, Sidney G. Tarrow and Charles Tilly; fourth, the results of terrorism research by Martha Crenshaw, Bruce Hoffman and Peter Waldmann, as well as by Luigi Bonanate, Janny de Graaf, Ze'ev Iviansky, Louise Richardson, Alex P. Schmid, Gabriel Weimann, Paul Wilkinson and Conrad Winn; and fifth, Reinhart Koselleck's study on the history of philosophy. This approach makes it possible not only to examine the deed itself but also to study its origin and effect for criteria and patterns typical of terrorist violence. It will then be possible to contextualize what exactly happened and further corroborate the definition-based finding that the acts of violence presented in the following pages were indeed terrorism.

Logic of action

How does terrorism work? Rainer Paris, a phenomenological sociologist who has analysed particular kinds of social action for their inherent ends and logics independent of their positive or negative moral value, has shown that terrorism serves the exercise of power and must be classified as a special case of provocation. He sees power 'not as possession . . . of resources and means of power but rather as a dynamic reciprocal process that plays out between at least two actors within a social relationship in which one presses his will upon the other and is able to prevail even against resistance'.[14] Building on this notion of the

---

14 Rainer Paris, Foreword (*Vorwort*), in *Stachel und Speer* (Frankfurt am Main: Suhrkamp, 1998), 7–8, 7.

sociology of power, Paris defines provocation 'as a deliberate, surprising norm violation intended to draw the other into an open conflict and prompt a reaction that morally discredits and exposes that party in the eyes of third parties'.[15] Paris's definition of provocation encompasses a number of elements that also appear in Waldmann's definition and that are crucial constituents of terrorist strategy – intentionality, norm violation, surprise, conflict orientation and dependence on a reaction. Paris includes the additional aspect of exposure that discredits.

The structural elements of provocation that Paris identifies entail specific social conditions, action logics and consequences. According to him, provocations are especially frequent where a power imbalance exists. They usually occur from the bottom up and are thus 'the preferred weapon of the weaker parties. The provocation positions the powerful as having power and simultaneously impugns their legitimacy.' Of course, provocations can sometimes appear opportune to the powerful person, too, 'if it is a matter of seeking occasion to impose sanctions or eliminate barriers to legitimacy that block you from activating your own power resources'.[16] A provocation, he continues, is aimed and direct, yet also calculated and dosed. The purpose is to insult, wound, expose and show up the powerful person and to disavow their legitimacy. The agitator proceeds indirectly. The idea is to make the other feel attacked so that he attacks in turn, for the agitator wants to discredit the other – but, if at all possible, in a way that gets the person to discredit himself.[17] Terrorism is an extreme manifestation of such action. Whether in history or in contemporary society, this social logic is decisive for identifying violence as terrorism.

By contrast, other factors extraneous to this logic of action, but nonetheless frequently mentioned as criteria in the literature, are irrelevant for defining an act of violence as terrorism. For example, it is immaterial whether an individual, a group, or a network is behind an attack and how many attacks are carried out.[18]

15 Rainer Paris, 'Der kurze Atem der Provokation', in *Stachel und Speer*, 58. See also Waldmann, *Terrorismus*, 34–9.
16 Paris, 'Der kurze Atem der Provokation', 68–9, and note 7.
17 Ibid., 61–4.
18 On the 'group' criterion, see also Paul R. Pillar, 'The Dimensions of Terrorism and Counterterrorism' (2001), in Russell Howard and Major Reid Sawyer (eds.), *Terrorism and Counterterrorism* (Dubuque: McGraw-Hill, 2006), 25.

The analysis must also account for the fact that terrorists adapt their tactics to the circumstances in order to exploit the potential of the method optimally as conditions change. What starts as a strategy of provocation can expand to a kind of war when a conflict has reached a certain degree of polarization.[19] That is why terrorism often accompanies other kinds of political violence, from vigilantism, civil wars and guerrilla war to Leninist-style revolutions, ethnic clashes and *coups d'état*. Identifying terrorist violence within such larger altercations becomes problematic at times, even with a clear analytical concept of terrorism.[20]

Authors vary in their answers to the question whether the political motives and objectives of the persons perpetrating terrorist acts are important for identifying terrorism. In the social-science research of the 1970s and 1980s, terrorism was generally seen as violence motivated by anarchist or socialist ideologies. Today, this kind of violence is often associated with Islamism. Objecting to such tendencies, Lawrence Freedman, for example, has pointed out that terrorism is politically and religiously open as a tactic: 'The methods of terrorism are not the monopoly of any cause or political philosophy.'[21] Nonetheless, researchers agree that ideologies shape the actual forms and manifestations of terrorist action. In that capacity, ideology serves as a kind of prism through which terrorists interpret their environment and the world. It prescribes their motives and political objectives as well as the weapons and targets that are deemed legitimate. Terrorists target the victim whose symbolic value is high in relation to their convictions and goals.[22]

---

19 See Waldmann, *Terrorismus*, 214.

20 See Crenshaw, 'Thoughts on Relating Terrorism', 12.

21 Lawrence Freedman, 'Terrorism and Strategy', in Lawrence Freedman, Christopher Hill, Adam Roberts, R. J. Vincent, Paul Wilkinson and Philip Winsor (eds.), *Terrorism and International Order* (London: Routledge, 1986), 56. See also Ganor, *Defining Terrorism*, 5; Richardson, *What Terrorists Want*, 10–14; and Pillar, 'Dimensions', 28.

22 See C. J. M. Drake, 'The Role of Ideology in Terrorists' Target Selection', *Terrorism and Political Violence* 10/2 (1998), 53–85; Magnus Ranstorp, 'Terrorism in the Name of Religion', *Journal of International Affairs* 50/1 (1996), 41–62; Hoffman, *Inside Terrorism*, 229–40; and Waldmann, *Terrorismus*, Chapters 6–7. On Al-Qaida and the Jihadi ideology specifically, see Quintan Wiktorowicz, 'A Genealogy of Radical Islam', in Howard and Sawyer, *Terrorism and Counterterrorism*, 207–29.

Apart from the generalization that terrorism can serve as a tactic for different motives and objectives, three political directions of terrorism stand out empirically in the nineteenth and twentieth centuries. Waldmann characterizes them as social-revolutionary, ethno-nationalist, and radical right-wing terrorism. Since the late twentieth century, this scope has come to encompass religiously motivated terrorism as well. Waldmann underlines how important it is to distinguish clearly between these 'basic ideas . . . that subscribe to and determine terrorist action', while the possibility of 'fluid transitions and overlaps' between the three secular political motivations. Substantively, Waldmann defines the three types of revolutions as

> the striving for a revolutionary change in social and political struc-
> tures according to Marx's ideas; the will of ethnic minorities or
> repressed peoples to gain state independence, or at least increased
> political autonomy; a third type encompasses law-and-order move-
> ments that purport to protect the existing social order while circum-
> venting the state and violating the law – one could describe them as
> right-wing radical or vigilante terrorism.[23]

Right-wing extremist terrorism is a special case in that it often combines elements of top-down state terror with bottom-up terrorism against the political order. Right-wing radical groups fight to defend the status quo and, depending on the situation, direct their violence less against the state than against certain social groups. In that sense, the phenomena of both right-wing terrorism and state-sponsored terrorism illustrate that powerful actors, too, sometimes resort to indirect means if it appears opportune to them.[24]

One conclusion for the historical analysis of the logic behind violent terrorist action is that terrorism serves the exercise of power and that

---

23 Waldmann, *Terrorismus*, Chapters 6–7, quotation at 99. See also Della Porta, *Clandestine Political Violence*, 10.

24 See p. 50, above, and Paris, 'Der kurze Atem der Provokation', 68, note 7. On right-wing terrorism, see Waldmann, *Terrorismus*, 15–121; and Friedhelm Neidhardt, 'Left-Wing and Right-Wing Terrorist Groups: A Comparison for the German Case', in Donatella Della Porta (ed.), *Social Movements and Violence: Participation in Underground Organizations* (Cambridge: Cambridge University Press, 1995), 263–72. On state-sponsored terrorism, see Hoffman, *Inside Terrorism*, 261.

the element of provocation aimed at delegitimizing and exposing powerful opponents can be added to Waldmann's definitional criteria as a key
constituent of terrorist tactics. Another conclusion is that terrorism,
although its goals can be indeterminate in principle, has been effective
empirically (at least in the nineteenth and twentieth centuries) in three
political manifestations: as social-revolutionary, ethno-nationalist and
right-wing radical terrorism.

Causes

What can be gathered from the social-science literature regarding the
causes of terrorism? The preceding description of the phenomenon
suggests that terrorism is a tactic of political action that follows rational
logics. It is misleading to keep dismissing terrorists simply as irrational
fanatics whose behaviour is psychopathologically conditioned.[25] There
is no such thing as a psychologically abnormal 'terrorist personality'.

If psychopathological approaches to explaining terrorism are
excluded, the question about its causes becomes even more pressing.
The use of terrorist violence is not a tactic of first choice. Lawrence
Freedman stresses that terrorism, as an indirect course of action that
depends on responses, is difficult to control and thus always at a disadvantage up against direct methods of military coercion. Accordingly,
terrorist attacks would be mounted primarily where excessively unequal
power relations would rule out modes of direct military control as a
sensible option. Martha Crenshaw agrees, noting that terrorism is
usually the result of a learning process and is not used until other means
have proven ineffective.[26] To understand how terrorism arose as a tactic
and why political actors use terrorist violence, it is necessary to analyse

---

25 For a study on the psychological dimensions of terrorism, see Reich, *Origins of
Terrorism*, especially the chapter by Crenshaw, 'The Logic of Terrorism: Terrorist
Behavior as a Product of Strategic Choice', in ibid., 7–24), whose view has prevailed in
the literature, though it does not preclude consideration of sociopsychological processes.
See also Walter Reich, 'Understanding Terrorist Behavior: The Limits and Opportunities
of Psychological Inquiry', in ibid., 261–79; Waldmann, *Terrorismus*, Chapter 9; and
Richardson, *What Terrorists Want*, 14–15. For an example of historical literature in
which psychological deviance is declared to be the cause of terrorism, see Albert Parry,
Terrorism, Chapter 3.

26 See Freedman, 'Terrorism and Strategy', 60–1; Crenshaw, 'The Logic of Terrorism',
10–11; and Muller, Spaaij and Ruitenberg, *Trends in terrorisme*, 73.

such patterns of interaction and learning as well as the specific circum-stances, models and processes of socialization and legitimation.[27]

The inquiry into terrorism's causes has a long tradition in a history of ideas, one which attempts to understand the genesis and recurring adoption of this form of political violence. Seeking to understand how violence is manifested in different guises (for instance as war, civil war, rebellion or political murder), how it can be prevented, and how peace can be maintained or restored within society, has occupied rulers, authors and philosophers of all cultures since time immemorial.[28] After the great revolutions of the eighteenth and nineteenth centuries, which were perceived by contemporaries as a new phenomenon, social philosophers and scholars in the young discipline of sociology at the time – such as John Stuart Mill, Karl Marx, Emile Durkheim and Max Weber – developed approaches for explaining the origin and success or failure of these new forms of political violence. Building on the ideas of those thinkers, sociologists, social psychologists and psychol-ogists conceived of several models that address the causes of political violence and are regarded as fundamental in research on terrorism as well.[29] This work, however, has not yielded a comprehensive social-scientific theory explaining the use of terrorist violence.[30]

Nonetheless, the various social-scientific models and factors have been helpfully compiled, evaluated and categorized into three levels of analysis in recent years: (1) society and the state, both national and international; (2) terrorist groups and organizations; and (3) the individual.[31] In practice, factors and constellations at all

27 A similar call is heard from the School of Critical Terrorism Studies at the Centre for the Study of Radicalisation and Contemporary Political Violence in Aberystwyth, Wales. See Richard Jackson, Marie Breen Smyth and Jeroen Gunning (eds.), *Critical Terrorism Studies: A New Research Agenda* (London: Routledge, 2009).

28 See John Gittings, *The Glorious Art of Peace: From the Iliad to Iraq* (Oxford: Oxford University Press, 2012).

29 See Charles Tilly, *From Mobilization to Revolution* (Reading: Addison-Wesley, 1978), Chapter 2.

30 See also Verhoeven, *The Odd Man Karakozov*, 4.

31 This breakdown synthesizes the categorizations of social-science literature. See Martha Crenshaw, 'The Causes of Terrorism', *Comparative Politics* 13/4 (1981), 379–99; Jeroen Gunning, 'Social Movement Theory and the Study of Terrorism', in Jackson, Smyth and Gunning (eds.), *Critical Terrorism Studies*, 156–77. Brynjar Lia and Katja Skjølberg, 'Causes of Terrorism: An Expanded and Updated Review of the Literature', FFI/Rapport – 2004/04307, Forsvarets forskningsinstitutt, Norwegian Defence Research Establishment,

these levels interact, jointly contributing to the genesis of terrorism.

At the first level, that of society at large, several consequences of modernization serve as conditioning and facilitating factors of insurgent violence in general and of terrorist violence in particular. These factors lie in the advanced complexity of modern society, which heightens its vulnerability. They are the mass media and improved communications and transport that enable the general population to engage in public discourse and mobility. They are also the enhanced accessibility of the public, fellow (or potential fellow) combatants and targets, a characteristic that followed upon urbanization and growing population density.[32]

Two key dynamics in the nineteenth century were democratization and economic modernization. Neither has lost relevance in the twentieth and early twenty-first centuries. How these dynamics affect forms of violence and whether they lower or raise a society's degree of violence is a matter of debate. Liberal theoreticians typically assume that modernization and democratization reduce the potential for violent conflicts in a society.[33] By contrast, sociologists and political scientists who tend to be associated with either the left or conservative camps have raised objections that have become important for research on terrorism. Starting from structural functionalism in the tradition of Durkheim,

---

Kjeller, 2004; Richardson, *What Terrorists Want*, Chapter 3; and Christopher Daase and Alexander Spencer, 'Stand und Perspektiven der politikwissenschaftlichen Terrorismusforschung', in Alexander Spencer, Alexander Kocks and Kai Harbrich (eds.), *Terrorismusforschung in Deutschland* (Wiesbaden: VS Verlag für Sozialwissenschaften, 2011), 25–47. Earlier research of continuing value is Paul Wilkinson, 'Social Scientific Theory and Civil Violence', in Yonah Alexander, David Carlton and Paul Wilkinson (eds.), *Terrorism: Theory and Practice* (Boulder, CO: Westview Press, 1979), 45–72; and Charles W. Kegley, 'The Causes of Terrorism', in Kegley (ed.), *International Terrorism: Characteristics, Causes, Controls* (New York: St Martin's, 1990), 97–112. For an analysis of the causes usually named in the field of politics and still used as a basis for political initiatives and military interventions, see Karin von Hippel, 'Responding to the Roots of Terror', in Magnus Ranstorp (ed.), *Mapping Terrorism Research: State of the Art, Gaps and Future Direction* (New York: Routledge, 2006), 94–105.

32 See Crenshaw, 'The Causes of Terrorism', 381. On urbanization see also Friedrich Lenger, *Metropolen der Moderne: Eine europäische Stadtgeschichte seit 1850* (Munich: C. H. Beck, 2013), Chapter 7.

33 See Lia and Skjølberg, 'Causes of Terrorism', 22–3. They trace this argumentation back to Immanuel Kant's essay *Zum ewigen Frieden* (1795). See Immanuel Kant, *Perpetual Peace: A Philosophical Essay* (London: George Allen and Unwin, 1917).

Samuel Huntington had the so-called Third World countries of the late 1960s in mind when he argued that rapid political and economic modernization leads to social instability and, hence, to an increase in violent conflicts.[34] Proponents of the 'theory of relative deprivation', whose basic ideas hark back to Alexis de Tocqueville and to the theory of revolution of Karl Marx and Friedrich Engels, confirm and specify this observation. According to James C. Davies, the likelihood of violent conflicts is especially high when expectations initially raised by economic or political improvements are dashed by sudden deterioration in the material or political situation. Ted Robert Gurr showed that violence is fostered particularly when there is political and economic discrimination against certain population groups, as well as when one group descends while other segments of the population rise, or when it ascends more slowly than other groups.[35] In this sense, processes of political, social and economic modernization must be seen as important facilitating factors of terrorist violence, especially when they involve profound changes over a short time.

Huntington and Davies claim universality for their answers to the question about the relations between modernization and violence. By contrast, social historians and historical sociologists have empirically studied the history of change in the forms of collective, sometimes also violent, political conflicts in Europe and the United States from the eighteenth century to the twenty-first as distinctive responses to the emergence of nation states, industrialization and parliamentary processes.[36] Charles Tilly's richly documented first work on this subject

34 Samuel P. Huntington, *Political Order in Changing Societies* (New Haven: Yale University Press, 1968), 39–59. See also Richardson, *What Terrorists Want*, 55.

35 See James C. Davies, 'Toward a Theory of Revolution', *American Sociological Review* 27/1 (February 1962), 5–19; Ted Robert Gurr, *Why Men Rebel* (Princeton: Princeton University Press, 1970); Gurr, 'The Calculus of Conflict', *Journal of Social Issues* 28/1 (1972), 27–47; and also Richardson, *What Terrorists Want*, 56.

36 See Tilly, *From Mobilization to Revolution*, Chapter 2; and Doug McAdam, Sidney G. Tarrow and Charles Tilly, *Dynamics of Contention* (Cambridge: Cambridge University Press, 2001); Charles Tilly, *The Politics of Collective Violence* (Cambridge: Cambridge University Press, 2003); Tilly, *Social Movements, 1768–2004* (Boulder, CO: Paradigm, 2004); Tilly, *Contentious Performances* (Cambridge: Cambridge University Press, 2008); Sidney G. Tarrow, *Power in Movement: Social Movements and Contentious Politics*, 3rd rev. ed. (Cambridge: Cambridge University Press, 2011); Joachim Raschke, *Soziale Bewegungen: Ein historisch-systematischer Grundriß*, 2nd student ed. (Frankfurt am Main: Campus, 1988); Dieter Rucht, *Modernisierung und neue soziale Bewegungen:*

emphasizes the importance of the revolutions of the eighteenth to the mid-nineteenth centuries in the emergence of new means of political action. The revolutions brought about

> an extraordinary level of collective action, a politicization of all interests and thus of almost all the means of action . . . a frenzy of association and thus of action on the basis of associations, a promotion of the conditions for the development of capitalism and bourgeois hegemony and thus of a mounting threat to non-capitalist, non-bourgeois interests. If that summary is correct, the Revolution acted as a fundamental stage in the course of a transformation far longer and larger than the Revolution itself. Like the seventeenth-century consolidation of the national state, the changes of the Revolution led to a significant alteration of the prevailing modes of popular collective action . . . As the world has changed, so has its collective action.[37]

Tilly observes that the revolutions in Europe and the United States brought about new conflicts of interest and a high degree of politicization, association and collective action and thereby led to social transformations extending far beyond the revolutionary era in the narrow sense, especially with respect to collective action. His point is critically important for this book.

Historical sociologists explain the origin of such post-revolutionary means of action primarily in terms of the rise and dynamics of social movements. Traditional kinds of protest such as food riots and peasant revolts have limited, 'reactive' (Tilly) demands that are generally intended to defend or restore rights passed down through the generations. Such protest is distinguished from what one could analogously call 'proactive' demands of social movements, which formed for the first time in the late eighteenth century and especially in the nineteenth and sought to shape society in line with their own agenda. According to Dieter Rucht,

---

Deutschland, Frankreich und USA im Vergleich (Frankfurt am Main: Campus, 1994); and Roland Roth and Dieter Rucht (eds.), *Die sozialen Bewegungen in Deutschland seit 1945: Ein Handbuch* (Frankfurt am Main: Campus, 2008).

37 Tilly, *From Mobilization to Revolution*, 241–2.

A social movement is an action system consisting of networks of groups and organizations mobilized for a certain period and under-pinned by collective identity to induce, prevent, or reverse social change by means of protest – including the use of force if necessary. In this context social change means a fundamental alteration of the social order as an influence on what Touraine ... calls historicity. Ultimately, however, the movement refers to basic structures of economic regulation, political rule and sociocultural norming – though not necessarily in the specific issues it addresses.[38]

As a 'community of values' (Rainer Paris), social movements are thus characterized by the fact that they seek to bring about a change in the social order through action – sometimes even violent action – over a certain period of time. Accordingly, these movements are interventions in history. The members of social movements no longer view society as naturally given or God-given, but rather as something humans can shape. For this reason, sociologists consider social movements almost as trademarks of modernism.[39]

Historical sociologists and researchers studying social movements and protests are interested in the political means of action that large collectives choose. They investigate the genesis of social movements and the ensuing modes of political contention by examining the demonstra-tion, the strike and the revolution. Terrorism as a form of violence typi-cally engaged in by individuals or small groups is peripheral in their work, if it comes up at all.

However, sociological research lying at the intersection of studies on twentieth-century cases of movements and violence indicates the pivotal significance that movements and radical milieus have for the emergence of terrorism. As Donatella Della Porta observed in the late 1980s,

38 Rucht, *Modernisierung und neue soziale Bewegungen*, 76–7.
39 See Roland Roth and Dieter Rucht, 'Einleitung', in Roth and Rucht (eds.), *Die sozialen Bewegungen in Deutschland*, 9–36, 13–14; and Hans Haferkamp and Neil J. Smelser, *Social Change and Modernity* (Berkeley: University of California Press, 1992), Part 1. On the origins of social movements on the European continent, see Raschke, *Soziale Bewegungen*, Chapter 2; and Rucht, *Modernisierung und neue soziale Bewegungen*, 77–9. For the United Kingdom and the United States, see especially Tilly, *Social Movements*, Chapter 2; Tilly, *Contentious Performances*, Chapter 5; and Tarrow, *Power in Movement*, Part 1.

The social origins of terrorists vary with the organization and with the context. In our cases, political violence does not seem to depend on a subculture of violence among 'poor people' or on a frustrated reaction of bourgeois revolutionaries. Rather, the social origins of the militants of terrorist organizations reflect those of the protest movements in which they were recruited. Accordingly, we should examine the dynamics of those social movements . . . future terrorists can be described as small minorities within larger political subcultures and countercultures . . .[40]

According to della Porta, social movements convey the world view and political socialization that make the terrorist use of violence seem legitimate. These movements present the experiential realm for processes of political radicalization and the social context for the emergence of social networks vital to the survival of underground structures.[41] This understanding is consistent with Paris's analysis that terrorist provocations play a great role as 'strategic elements of collective action and basic patterns of symbolic practice' in the developmental dynamics of social movements.[42]

Terrorism researchers generally assume the existence of a modern society. When they speak about the causes of terrorist violence, they implicitly or explicitly take for granted the social framework and facilitating factors discussed above: the existence of social movements and the complexity of modern societies, urbanization, mass media and improved conditions of communication and transport. The researchers commonly begin where certain political factors within such a constellation may lay the ground for terrorist violence.

Martha Crenshaw has systematically studied and weighted the factors of modern society that can be regarded as causes of terrorist violence.

---

40 Donatella Della Porta, 'Introduction: On Individual Motivations in Underground Political Organizations', in Della Porta, *Social Movements and Violence*, 11–12. See also Richardson, *What Terrorists Want*, 48–9.

41 Della Porta, 'Introduction', especially 7–15; and Donatella Della Porta, *Social Movements, Political Violence, and the State: A Comparative Analysis of Italy and Germany* (Cambridge: Cambridge University Press, 1995). For analyses of interactions between and dynamics of terrorists, their supporters and sympathizers, and the state and society, see Stefan Malthaner and Peter Waldmann (eds.), *Radikale Milieus: Das soziale Umfeld terroristischer Gruppen* (Frankfurt am Main: Campus), 2012.

42 Paris, 'Der kurze Atem der Provokation', 57.

She finds the key ones to be the existence of social grievances and the awareness that they are undeserved and changeable, the lack of opportunities for political participation, insurgent traditions, and a dissatisfied social elite.

> Terrorism is essentially the result of elite disaffection; it represents the strategy of a minority, who may act on behalf of a wider popular constituency who have not been consulted about, and do not necessarily approve of, the terrorists' aims or methods . . .
>
> Perhaps terrorism is most likely to occur precisely where mass passivity and elite dissatisfaction coincide. Discontent is not generalized or severe enough to provoke the majority of the populace to action against the regime, yet a small minority, without access to . . . power . . . seeks radical change . . . Terrorism is the resort of an elite when conditions are not revolutionary.[43]

According to Crenshaw, then, terrorist violence is highly probable where an elite is pressing for change in society but finding that legal paths through political institutions are closed to it and that most of the population is unable or unwilling to rise up against the government.

Luigi Bonanate has called such polities 'blocked societies', which he describes as being stable enough to preserve themselves and ward off the citizenry's demands for change but incapable or unwilling to address these demands constructively.[44] In a blocked society, force is often used to foil undesired political solutions. 'The main goal of "individual terror" [that is, terrorism] is to prevent compromise,' observed Ze'ev Iviansky. 'And therein lies its greatest success. Terrorism tends to be most widespread in situations where a crucial political move is imminent, and at times of political chaos.'[45] But even in those kinds of political situation, according to Crenshaw, an additional trigger is necessary before conflict escalates to terrorist violence. In most cases, she asserts, government actions are such a catalyst. Typically, they involve an unusual and unexpectedly harsh use of force by state

---

43 Crenshaw, 'The Causes of Terrorism', 384.

44 Luigi Bonanate, 'Some Unanticipated Consequences of Terrorism', *Journal of Peace Research* 16/3 (1979), 197–211; on blocked societies, 205–6.

45 Iviansky, 'Individual Terror', 58.

authorities against the social movement. 'A regime thus encourages terrorism when it creates martyrs to be avenged,' writes Crenshaw, who believes that no emotion motivates individuals and groups to terrorist violence as much as the feeling of revenge does.[46]

At the second and third levels of analysis – the group and the individual – research on terrorism stresses that the political motivations of terrorists and their sympathizers can be understood only through the political ideologies, ideas and experiences giving rise to the motivations, for they justify the use of force: 'If terrorists perceive the state as unjust, morally corrupt, and violent, then terrorism may seem legitimate and justified.'[47] That is why Paul Wilkinson considers the philosophical and historical study of radical political ideologies to be the best way to understand terrorism and its dynamics.[48]

The fact that most of the individuals who turn to terrorist violence are seasoned political activists underscores the significance of political thinking. In many cases, they have already striven for a long time to achieve their goals non-violently. Through the experience they have gained and their unconditional commitment to their cause, they have developed a great willingness to take risks. Moreover, they have close ties to groups of like-minded people. Another motivation for carrying out political violence is the desire for transcendence – for a sense of purpose, recognition, even immortality – and the will for self-sacrifice. Fellow combatants of group members who have lost their lives through attacks or criminal convictions feel particularly strong survivor guilt, causing them to undertake increasingly hazardous operations.[49]

According to terrorism research, the organization (level 2 of analysis) usually does not opt for terrorist tactics until the failure of alternative ways to achieve the desired goal – such as mobilization of the majority to back the cause. In addition to the objectives in Waldmann's definition (to raise public awareness and to elicit sympathy or fear), Crenshaw, Iviansky and Paris maintain that the intent can also be to disrupt or discredit the government's work and to provoke inappropriate responses by the state. Other reasons for mounting terrorist attacks can include

---

46 Crenshaw, 'The Causes of Terrorism', 384.

47 Ibid., 390.

48 Paul Wilkinson, 'The Sources of Terrorism: Terrorists' Ideologies and Belief', in Kegley, *International Terrorism*, 139–40, 142.

49 Crenshaw, 'The Causes of Terrorism', 390, 393–5.

measures to enforce internal discipline, build morale, exert control or compete with other terrorist organizations.[50]

These results of research on terrorism have several implications for the historical study of the topic. First, it follows that societies undergoing rapid political, social and economic processes of modernization and whose populations are highly politicized and organized are generally more susceptible to the emergence of political violence than are societies not experiencing such transformations. Second, this violence assumes the form of terrorism particularly where social elites perceive grievances that they view as changeable but find that legal avenues for achieving such change through political institutions are blocked, or at least closed to them, and that collective violence is not an option. As the following historical study shows, the actual inventors of terrorism, Felice Orsini and John Brown, and the political situations of the societies in which they lived and politically operated met all these conditions to a remarkable degree.

Moreover, social-scientific research shows that social movements with proactive demands (such as for freedom or nation building) are crucial to the rise of terrorism, not least because terrorists are often experienced political activists who have gone through a long learning process and who choose terrorism as a tactic only when alternatives have failed or are blocked. Terrorists typically are quite willing to sacrifice themselves and have an intense desire for transcendence. Historical analysis has corroborated these observations especially for Orsini and Brown, but also for Becker, Booth and Karakozov.

The discussion above indicates that the inventors of terrorism should be taken seriously as rational actors. In this context, however, *rational* is not intended to mean pure rationality in the sense of universal reason free of social or cultural influences. Instead, rationality is understood to be tied to a historical social horizon of thought and action.[51] The thinking and actions of the five perpetrators in this study must be placed in their respective historical contexts and interpreted and explained on that basis, a stipulation underlying historiography but not met by many

---

50 Ibid., 390, 385–9. On the use of terrorism to prevent compromises (also known as the spoiler function), see Iviansky, 'Individual Terror'.

51 See the introduction in Ronald Wintrobe, *Rational Extremism* (Cambridge: Cambridge University Press, 2006).

biographical works on these five people (nor on terrorists in general). The historiographic approach is thus particularly well suited to meeting the requirements of terrorism research, namely to analyse political ideologies, ideas and experiences as well as socialization processes, models, legitimations and specific circumstances as precisely as possible in their historical contexts.

The aforementioned social framework, facilitating factors and points of departure bearing on the origins and practice of terrorism, as well as the organizational or group-level motivations and rationales that lead actors to choose terrorism as a tactic, suggest possible causes of terrorist acts of violence. They cannot explain terrorism's effect and conditions of success, however. The conditions for the tactic's effects and political success must be sought in the reactions to terrorist operations.

Effects

Terrorism needs responses, hence public display. That conclusion, too, follows from the analysis by Paris, who notes that 'a provocation that does not upset anyone is not a provocation.'[52] Accordingly, he defines provocation (including that by terrorists) in terms of dependence on reaction:

> Provocation makes sense only if the other is actually provoked, if that person reacts to the provocation . . . The interactive meaning of provocation depends entirely on the reciprocity of the actions and operations. The provocation is intended to provoke the other and is complete as an illocutionary act only if it succeeds in doing so.[53]

To prevent a provocation from dying 'the death of getting no reaction', as Paris explains, it must dramatize itself and, if necessary, further escalate the confrontation to force a reaction. Because the use of violence is the only way to ensure that the other responds, provocation inherently tends to escalate. In Paris's view, provocation has to entail the greatest possible assault, cross thresholds, and invade alien

52 Paris, 'Der kurze Atem der Provokation', 59.
53 Ibid., 62.

'territories of the self' to violate norms in a manner so drastic that it cannot be ignored.[54]

According to Paris, not just any reaction serves the purpose of the terrorist provocation. Only unmasking does that. 'If counterstigmatization [that is, if removing the stigma on the terrorist of having shed innocent blood and, at the same time, blaming the other as the real culprit] is to succeed, the other must betray himself. His response must expose him as the one whom the agitator wanted to expose. The provocation has torn the mask from his face and revealed him as the one who is actually guilty.'[55] In Paris's view, the demonstrative norm violation ultimately has the purpose of delegitimizing the norm itself. Because the agitator needs the immorality of the other, he must mistreat him so much that that party loses control. Such an overreaction lends itself best to exposing the other and justifying the provocateur's own norm violation. In a provocation, as Paris adds, counterstigmatization thus ensues by getting the other to stigmatize himself, with the exposure being a function of the reaction, not of the act that instigates it. The provocation is the cause and trigger of the process only to the extent that it elicits the desired behaviour. He observes that these dynamics often give rise to circular social conflicts in which provocation sparks reactions that, in turn, can be perceived as provocations to which one should react.[56] The powerful figure is suddenly put on the spot, is compelled to either avenge or condone the provocation. That actor has the choice between brutality and loss of face. In Paris's view, both the direct use of force and the revelation of de facto impotence jeopardize the legitimacy of his power, endorsing the agitator. The more public the action, the more 'objective' the reality that it creates and the more intense the inevitable social pressure to act. The emotional charge of the situation thereby polarizes the public and forces people to take sides.[57]

Communication is essential for bringing about revealing responses.[58] If a terrorist assault is intended primarily to discredit a powerful figure

54 Ibid., 58–9, referring to Erving Goffman, *Relations in Public: Microstudies of the Public Order* (New York: Basic Books, 1971), 28.

55 Paris, 'Der kurze Atem der Provokation', 63.

56 Ibid., 57, 64.

57 Ibid., 66, 69, 77–8.

58 See Waldmann, *Terrorismus*; Waldmann, 'Thesen: Terrorismus und Kommunikation', in Weinhauer and Requate (eds.), *Gewalt ohne Ausweg?*, 49–61; Hoffman, *Inside Terrorism*; Crenshaw, 'Thoughts on Relating Terrorism'; and Alex P. Schmid and Janny de Graaf, *Violence as Communication: Insurgent Terrorism and the Western News Media* (London: Sage, 1982).

and his established norms in the eyes of others and to sow fear and sympathy, the success of the action depends on ensuring that the public receives the message of violence and then absorbs and comprehends it. 'Without communication, there is no terrorism,' as Alex P. Schmid and Janny de Graaf write. Waldmann agrees: 'Terrorism, it must be said, is primarily a communication strategy.' For an attack to succeed, the importance of getting terrorist messages through to the population groups at which they are aimed 'cannot be overestimated.'[59]

The conditions for successful terrorist communication lie as much in the message of violence itself as in the sociopolitical circumstances in which it is conveyed. A polity's general level of violence can obstruct the message of violence. Where murder, kidnapping and other assaults are daily reality, terrorist attacks resulting in a small number of victims scarcely make an impression.[60] Hence political savvy, the ability to wait for the right moment, and the exact kind of violent act are crucial to the success of an attack.[61] Another key factor is the degree to which the terrorists are able to influence the interpretation and reception of their act. 'Terrorism is thus generated in anticipation of a public reaction and becomes part of an interactive process,' writes Martha Crenshaw. Precisely this interactive process determines whether the unmasking succeeds and whether the 'demonstrative norm violation' is in fact ultimately able to delegitimize the norm itself.[62] It is thus the intended population groups, the public and the state that contribute to the interpretation and reception of the violent act. The political success or failure of a terrorist attack hinges on their reactions.

If terrorism is primarily a communication strategy, then media have immense influence.[63] Media pass on the news of spectacular violent

---

59 Schmid and de Graaf, *Violence as Communication*, 9; Waldmann, *Terrorismus*, 15, 43.

60 Waldmann, *Terrorismus*, 39–40, 43.

61 See especially Bernd Weisbrod, 'Terrorism as Performance: The Assassination of Walther Rathenau and Hanns-Martin Schleyer', in Wilhelm Heitmeyer, Heinz-Gerhard Haupt and Andrea Kirchner (eds.), *The Control of Violence: Historical and International Perspectives on Violence in Modern Societies* (New York: Springer, 2011), 365–94.

62 Crenshaw, 'Thoughts on Relating Terrorism', 18; Paris, 'Der kurze Atem der Provokation', 59–60.

63 Building on Hans H. Hiebel, *Die Medien: Logik – Leistung – Geschichte* (Munich: Fink, 1998), 12, I regard the media in this context as 'material-mechanical or energetic (electric, electromagnetic, electronic, optoelectronic) purveyors of data and units of

events to the target groups: the public and the state. As Waldmann asserts, media are consequently an 'integral part of terrorist calculation and cannot be exchanged or factored out of this calculation without it and its underlying strategy collapsing'. They are 'the mechanism for connecting the isolated act and its sociopsychological impacts'.[64] Bruce Hoffman has spoken of a 'symbiotic relation' between terrorism and media, and Margaret Thatcher famously described the media as the 'oxygen' of terrorism.[65] That does not mean that the media are necessarily abettors or the terrorists' best friends, as is often claimed.[66] Media can also cooperate with government, and their coverage can help a horrified public mobilize its resources and disassociate itself from the perpetrators.

Because terrorists need the media in order to reach their target audience, they formulate their message in ways that the media cannot ignore. Unforeseen, spectacular acts of violence cannot be neglected by the media, for they contain all the main ingredients of a news flash or 'first

---

information and mechanical as well as electronic means of data-processing' in terms of 'the three basic medialogical phenomena of storage, transfer, and editing'. On the relation between media and terrorism, see particularly David L. Paletz and Alex P. Schmid, *Terrorism and the Media* (Newbury Park: Sage, 1992); and Odasuo A. Alali and Kenoye Kelvin Eke (eds.), *Media Coverage of Terrorism, Methods of Diffusion* (Newbury Park: Sage, 1991); Richard W. Schaffert, *Media Coverage and Political Terrorists: A Quantitative Analysis* (New York: Praeger, 1992); Isabelle Garcin-Marrou, *Terrorisme, medias et démocratie* (Lyon: Presses universitaires de Lyon, 2001); Brigitte Lebens Nacos, *Mass-Mediated Terrorism: The Central Role of the Media in Terrorism and Counterterrorism* (Lanham: Rowman & Littlefield, 2002); and Brooke Barnett and Amy Reynolds, *Terrorism and the Press: An Uneasy Relationship* (New York: Peter Lang, 2009).

64 Waldmann, *Terrorismus*, 83.

65 Hoffman, *Inside Terrorism*, 195, 184. Some terrorism researchers even go one step further, positing the mutual dependence of media and terrorism on each other. Ted Koppel, for instance, contends that 'the media, the press and TV, and the terrorists need each other. There is a symbiotic relationship among them. Without TV, terrorism loses its raison d'être. Without terrorism, TV is deprived of one of its most dramatic and popular objects.' 'Conference Report: Terrorism and the Media', in *Political Communication and Persuasion* 3/2 (1985), 185–90, 186. This is not to say that media have historically been spawned for terrorism as terrorism has been spawned for the media, but it cannot be denied that media profit from sales figures and viewership is boosted by terrorist attacks. On this aspect, see particularly Bruno S. Frey and Dominik Rohner, 'Blood and Ink! The Common-Interest-Game between Terrorists and the Media, Working Paper No. 285', *Public Choice* 133/1 (2007), 129–45.

66 Friedrich Hacker, *Terror: Mythos – Realität – Analyse* (Vienna: Molden, 1973), 290; Walter Laqueur, as cited in Hoffman, *Inside Terrorism*, 183.

news'. These arresting deeds penetrate daily routine, involve many elite actors, present villains and heroes, have a certain entertainment value, report current history, and potentially affect the lives of those to whom the news is directed. 'Violence is news; spectacular violence is big news,' as Kevin G. Barnhurst pithily remarks.[67] Nevertheless, there are various ways to formulate the terrorist message. According to Gabriel Weimann and Conrad Winn,

> The issue of comparative news value prompted many terrorists to contemplate ways of enhancing the newsworthiness of their actions ... The newsworthiness of an action could also be enhanced by symbolic content. Dramatic impact could be achieved by means of symbolism in the timing or location of actions and in the identity of the victims.[68]

This should be considered in the historical analysis.

The effect and perception of terrorist attacks is thus not least a function of the intensity, form and duration of their media presence. In reporting on terrorist acts of violence, media not only communicate information to a target audience but possess power to interpret it and produce feedback effects. The media's power to interpret begins with the decision whether to spread or repress news about a terrorist attack or to pass over it as unimportant. What is reported and how it is reported matter (what scope, context and significance). For example, the words

---

67 Kevin G. Barnhurst, 'The Literature of Terrorism: Implications for Visual Communications', in Alali and Eke, *Media Coverage of Terrorism*, 131. On the theory of newsworthiness, see Johan Galtung and Mari Holmboe Ruge, 'The Structure of Foreign News', *Journal of Peace Research* 2/1 (1965), 64–91; Hans Mathias Kepplinger, 'Theorien der Nachrichtenauswahl als Theorien der Realität', *Aus Politik und Zeitgeschichte* B15 (1989), 3–16; Hans Mathias Kepplinger, 'Der Ereignisbegriff in der Publizistikwissenschaft', *Publizistik* 46/2 (2001), 117–39; and especially Joachim Friedrich Staab, *Nachrichtenwert-Theorie* (Freiburg: Verlag Karl Alber, 1990); Christiane Eilders, *Nachrichtenfaktoren und Rezeption: Eine empirische Analyse zur Auswahl und Verarbeitung politischer Information* (Opladen: Westdeutscher Verlag, 1997); and Matthias Schulz, *Politische Kommunikation: Theoretische Ansätze und Ergebnisse empirischer Forschung* (Opladen: Westdeutscher Verlag, 1997). For a transmittal of this research to terrorism, see Bernard Johnpoll, 'Terrorism and the Mass Media in the United States', in Alexander and Finger, *Terrorism*, particularly 158–9.

68 Gabriel Weimann and Conrad Winn, *The Theatre of Terror: Mass Media and International Terrorism* (White Plains: Longman, 1993), 59–62 *passim*.

used to present what happened are crucial. Does a headline in a newspaper or a picture caption in a news programme label an attack as terrorism, or does it refer to guerrilla struggle, or rather to war?[69] Interpretations are perpetuated by the selection of images, comparisons, political commentaries, historical embedding, background reports and interviews with perpetrators or family members of the victims. It is through these interpretations that the events acquire political significance.[70]

Direct interactions between terrorism and media take place when newspapers and Internet pages publish calls for terrorist acts of violence, when terrorist organizations run their own media, when terrorists expressly target media organizations, and when media representatives voluntarily or involuntarily intervene in terrorist operations.[71] In addition, news about terrorist operations have repeatedly induced people to use similar methods – media coverage's copycat (or contagion) effect, which was highly significant for the perpetrators at the centre of this study.[72] The exact relation between terrorists, media and the public is

69 The media watchdog organization Fairness & Accuracy in Reporting (FAIR) criticized the media in the United States for readily speaking of terrorism or ecoterrorism when giving an account of a burning ski cabin, whereas violent acts against clinics and murders of doctors by anti-abortionist extremists are not usually called terrorism. Nacos, *Mass-Mediated Terrorism*, 104–5. See also Torsten Beermann, *Der Begriff 'Terrorismus' in deutschen Printmedien* (Münster: Lit, 2004); and Musolff, *Krieg gegen die Öffentlichkeit*. On ecoterrorism, see Keith Mako Woodhouse, 'In Defense of Mother Earth: Radical Environmentalism and Ecoterrorism in the United States, 1980–2000s', in Dietze and Verhoeven, *The Oxford Handbook of the History of Terrorism*.

70 See Weimann and Winn, *The Theatre of Terror*, 64–85; Odasuo A. Alali and Gary W. Byrd, *Terrorism and the News Media: A Selected, Annotated Bibliography* (Jefferson: McFarland, 1994), 12–13; and for an example, Christoph Weller, 'Das Fernsehen und die politische Deutung der Ereignisse am 11. September. Oder: die Kriegserklärung des Gerhard Schröder', in Martin Löffelholz (ed.), *Krieg als Medienereignis*, vol. 2: *Krisenkommunikation im 21. Jahrhundert* (Wiesbaden: VS Verlag für Sozialwissenschaften, 2003), 257–73.

71 Journalists have affected the course and outcome of terrorist acts by their own mediation efforts as well as by explicit calls for government representatives to respond and the conscious or unconscious transmittal of information and signs that give terrorists important clues during an attack. See Johnpoll, 'Terrorism and the Mass Media in the United States', 160–1; und Cornelia Glück, 'ETA und die Medien', in Sonja Glaab (ed.), *Medien und Terrorismus: Auf den Spuren einer symbiotischen Beziehung*, (Berlin: Berliner Wissenschaftsverlag, 2007), 24–5.

72 See, for example, Alali and Byrd, *Terrorism and the News Media*, 10–11; and the cases given by Jensen, *The Battle against Anarchist Terrorism*, 56–7.

complex, and its course and impacts can be studied only in light of an actual case.[73]

If the message of violence is successfully placed, terrorist attacks can become the departure point of a media event. The term 'media event' was originally coined for the 'high holidays of mass communication' – such as television broadcasts of royal weddings – and then transferred to the phenomenon of international terrorism as a 'coercive media event'.[74] The concepts of media event and coercive media event are best used to describe what was happening from the early 1970s to roughly the turn of the millennium, when television was the leading medium. In the main attributes and logic, however, they provide a framework for analysing the impact that terrorist acts of violence have on specific media and can be transferred to other media.

In that sense, spectacular terrorist attacks have all the essential features of a media event. Their media effect is precisely planned, the public cannot turn away, and they are characterized by drama and the priestly role of journalists who serve as mediators and sense makers.[75] Political leaders, too, play a prominent role, as do symbols that help society ensure its solidarity and the existing order. The social impacts as well are comparable. Terrorist attacks trigger intense collective feelings, whereby the content and kinds of coverage shape and direct the specific

---

73 The Red Army Faction (RAF) serves as a paradigmatic example of this point, as illustrated by Martin Steinseifer, 'Terrorismus' zwischen Ereignis und Diskurs: Zur Pragmatik von Text- Bild-Zusammenstellungen in Printmedien der 1970er Jahre (Berlin: de Gruyter, 2011).

74 Daniel Dayan and Elihu Katz, Media Events: The Live Broadcasting of History (Cambridge, MA: Harvard University Press, 1992), Chapter 1, 1; Weimann and Winn, The Theatre of Terror, Chapter 4; Friedrich Lenger, 'Einleitung: Medienereignisse der Moderne', in Lenger and Nünning, Medienereignisse der Moderne, 7–13; and the studies, including this one, which emerged out of the DFG-funded doctoral programme on Transnational Media Events of the Early Modern Period (Transnationale Medienereignisse von der Frühen Neuzeit bis zur Gegenwart) at the Justus Liebig University in Giessen, uni-giessen.de

75 The attacks on 11 September 2001 are an especially prominent case of extensive live coverage of terrorist strikes. But there have been many such examples since the 1960s, such as the broadcast of the attack that the Palestinian organization Black September carried out against the Israeli team in the Olympic Village during the 1972 Summer Olympics in Munich, Germany; the reporting of the RAF's occupation of the German embassy in Stockholm in 1975, and the kidnapping of the passengers and crew of TWA flight 847 in Beirut and Algiers by the members of Hezbollah and Islamic Jihad in 1985.

emotional and cognitive effects as media change their scheduled programming. Radio and television broadcast stations interrupt their regular broadcasts with news sequences to inform their public immediately and give an impression of the event's importance. They thereby cultivate a sense of contemporaneousness, of 'experienced history'. They simultaneously confer importance and status on the terrorists, who in turn are aware that they are playing their role on 'the world's greatest stage' and tailor their action to it.[76]

Violent acts of terrorism serve not only as the starting point for media events but also as triggers of historical events. Historical events are not defined by objective criteria, such as a particular intensity in the dynamics of change or an objectively measurable scale of grandness or monstrousness. Instead, actions or occurrences (past or expected, fictional or real) become historical events when people attribute significance to them, interpret them, talk or write about them, and react to them. The more people ascribe significance to something that has happened, and the greater that assigned significance is, the greater the event is. Meaning is attached to actions and occurrences that go beyond the boundaries of what is routinely expectable, beyond the 'space of experience' and the 'horizon of expectation' (Reinhart Koselleck) of contemporaries.[77]

Spectacular terrorist attacks admit of an especially wide range of explanations and need interpretation precisely because they lie outside the usual space of experience and horizon of expectation. As Rainer Paris puts it,

> Provocations can gain potential as brash challenges, as needling assaults, only because the agitator is doing something that runs counter to the 'normal' horizon of expectation ... Provocations suspend normality; indeed, they sometimes seek to void [and] disrupt it for a time ... Offensive norm violation pushes everyone involved to redefine the situation.[78]

---

76 Weimann and Winn, *The Theatre of Terror*, especially 91–108.

77 Reinhart Koselleck, ' "Space of Experience" and "Horizon of Expectation": Two Historical Categories', in Koselleck (ed.), *Futures Past: On the Semantics of Historical Time* (New York: Columbia University Press, 1985), 255–76. The present and following treatment of the relation between event and media event is based on ideas initially developed and supported with additional source information in Dietze, 'Von Kornblumen, Heringen und Drohbriefen'. See also p. 13, note 24, in this volume.

78 Paris, 'Der kurze Atem der Provokation', 58–9.

And because the interpretation of the actions and events is not inherent in them, they acquire meaning first through actions, direct and medially conveyed communication, and the use of symbols. Such attributions do not occur randomly, however. Their plausibility develops through evidence in a certain historical context framed by societal processes of negotiation that represent a battle for the redefinition of the spaces of experience and horizons of expectation as well as for the options opened or closed by them. Terrorist attacks are deliberate attempts to generate and choreograph events, to set them in motion and shape their interpretation in order to create new political, social and, hence, historical realities. Terrorists thus want to make a purposeful, surgical intervention in the course of history.[79]

In this attempt to bring about new historical realities, the 'terrorist' – at least that of the nineteenth century – corresponds entirely to someone who is 'a revolutionary'. Most of the inventors of terrorism who are the focus of this book saw themselves as 'revolutionaries'. From the perspective of conceptual history, it was Reinhart Koselleck who first traced the origin of the neologism 'revolutionary' (in the sense of a person) to the French Revolution and analysed this term's historical premises and philosophical background: the assumption is that 'history' and 'revolution' exist in the collective singular, with both perpetually

---

79 See Walther, 'Terror, Terrorismus', 385; Rucht, *Modernisierung und neue soziale Bewegungen*, 76–7; this volume, pp. 57–8; and Verhoeven, *The Odd Man Karakozov*, 6: 'Karakozov's factual propaganda suggests a model of political action . . . that . . . seeks to intervene in the historical process.' However, Verhoeven's substantiation and derivation of this proposition are problematic. They take one of Walter Benjamin's dictums – 'The awareness that they are about to make the continuum of history explode is characteristic of the revolutionary classes at the moment of their action' (Benjamin, 'Theses on the Philosophy of History', 261), which is a critique of the idea of progress in light of National Socialist terror – and freely transfer it to Dmitry Vladimirovich Karakozov and other Russian terrorists (see Verhoeven, *The Odd Man Karakozov*, 175). Applying the twentieth-century critique of progress to the nineteenth century is unhistorical and altogether unsupported by sources. Claudia Verhoeven, 'Time of Terror, Terror of Time: On the Impatience of Russian Revolutionary Terrorism (Early 1860s–Early 1880s)', *Jahrbücher für Geschichte Osteuropas* 58/2 (2010), 254–73, thus notes that at least some later Russian terrorists (members of the Narodnaia Volia group) adhered to the idea of progress that Benjamin criticized and did *not* embody his critique of progress (ibid., 262). In a chapter entitled 'Oh Times, There Is No Time (but the Time That Remains): The Terrorist in Russian Literature (1863–1913)', in Thomas Carl Austenfeld, Dimiter Daphinoff and Jens Herlth (eds.), *Terrorism and Narrative Practice* (Vienna: Lit, 2011), 117–35, she seems to have tacitly changed her initial stance (ibid., 133).

moving on – towards progress. There is also 'the conception that men could make revolutions, an idea that was previously unutterable'. In that regard the *'feasibility* of revolution' is a consequence of the fact that revolutionaries believe they recognize the laws of future revolutions. 'The transpersonal structures of Revolution, and Revolution's suscepti-bility to manipulation facilitated by knowledge of those structures, seem to elicit each other.'[80] In the context of the ideas about history and revo-lution outlined above, 'making' revolution thus means intervening in the course of history and propelling it forward. To that extent, the 'terrorist' has historically and conceptually in fact been a 'revolutionary' first, and in the subsequent course of the nineteenth century increas-ingly diverges from the emerging 'professional revolutionary' by choos-ing a different kind of tactic.

This idea of a perpetual revolution moving towards progress was fuelled by the demands arising from the great revolutions of the eight-eenth century. In his article on revolution, Koselleck mentions this connection only in passing:

> It lay in the unsurpassable universality of the revolutionary concepts
> – 'freedom', 'equality', 'fraternity' – that they could be measured against
> each other in various ways and, depending on new situations and
> interests, could be constantly redefined. That was why Robespierre
> could speak of the 'half revolution' not yet completed, a turn of phrase
> taken up again and again; that was why KANT could expect the revo-
> lution would not bring 'everything back to the previous track' in the
> sense of a return but would instead lead to the 'repetition of new
> efforts' that would bring the revolutionary principles closer to their
> fruition.[81]

---

80 'The transpersonal structures of Revolution and the growing susceptibility to its manipulation stemming from knowledge of it appear to have mutually self-sustained each other.' Reinhart Koselleck, 'Historical Criteria of the Modern Concept of Revolution', in Koselleck, *Futures Past*, 52. In addition, see the sections by Koselleck in Odilo Engels, Horst Gunther, Reinhart Koselleck and Christian Meier, 'Geschichte, Historie', in Brunner, Conze and Koselleck, *Geschichtliche Grundbegriffe*, vol. 2, 593–717; and Neithard Bulst, Jorg Fisch, Reinhart Koselleck and Christian Maier, 'Revolution, Rebellion, Aufruhr, Bürgerkrieg', in Brunner, Conze and Koselleck, *Geschichtliche Grundbegriffe*, vol. 5, 653–788.

81 Koselleck in Bulst et al., 'Revolution: Rebellion, Aufruhr, Bürgerkrieg', 761.

Indeed, the events constituting the invention of terrorism as a tactic represent such repeated attempts to bring the revolutionary principles closer to fulfilment or to preserve them, and they are actually efforts to meet the promises of key revolutionary concepts. However, as the following historical investigation shows, terrorism was not solely about the guiding concepts of the French Revolution but also those of the American Revolution. It was also about precise and explicit demands: personal and political freedom; that is, the demands for emancipation and nation. Such were the motives directing the actions of the five agents of violence studied in this book.

These considerations from social-science research and the literature on the philosophy of history make it clear that public and political reactions are an indispensable part of the historical analysis of terrorist violence because they decide on its success or failure. To Paris, the objective of a terrorist act of violence is to unmask, to challenge the legitimacy of a powerful opponent. Whether this aim is true of the first cases of terrorism is a question to be approached through examination of the historical evidence. The key to eliciting reactions and reaching the public is communication, and this communication takes place largely through the media. For historical investigation, it follows that the analysis of media reporting must receive close attention. Beyond that focus, a central interest in this book is to ascertain the copycat, or contagion, effects of media coverage, for they constitute the serial, cumulative learning process encompassing what I call the invention of terrorism. Another key facet of the historical analysis of public reactions is the great importance of the inherent dynamics and social logic of such media events – especially the role of symbols, politicians, journalists and collective feelings. A final goal of the historical analysis is to show the extent to which the five actors who made terrorism a potent weapon wanted and were able to unleash historical events with their acts of violence and thereby intervene in the course of history.

Contours of a history of terrorism: freedom, nation and violence

The theoretical perspectives offered by the social sciences and the history of philosophy in the preceding pages necessarily entail a certain level of abstraction to achieve their purpose. Turning now to the empirical examination of actual historical events, one finds that two revolutionary ideas have driven the invention of terrorism: the goal of personal freedom and the goal of political freedom; that is, the ideas of emancipation and nation. Terrorism as a political tactic was invented specifically in places where these ideas mattered to significant parts of the population and where their realization was particularly desirable but only partial, if at all. Such was the case with the idea of nationhood in Italy and Germany and with the idea of freedom in the United States and Russia.

Terrorist violence could take hold at two points in the process, for the realization of the idea of personal freedom and the idea of nationhood happened in two steps. In some cases, the two steps were taken together, but they must always be separated analytically: the first step is the political and legal implementation when the nation is founded or when emancipation is declared by law. The second step is much more difficult and takes longer because it involves realizing and acting on the ideas of freedom and nationhood in everyday life for the population as a whole. Political obstacles to both of these steps can arise. Perceiving such blockages was the precondition for the decision that each of this book's five central actors took to using the tactic of terrorism to overcome them. The purpose of the following sections is, first, to show that the first effective acts of terrorism aiming to achieve the objectives of freedom and nationhood occurred in Italy, the United States, Germany and Russia, and, second, to explain why they happened in those countries.

To build this argument effectively, it is not sufficient to document the sociopolitical obstacles in these four societies alone. It is also important to provide negative evidence; that is, at least some representative examples showing that the political challenges that led to the impasses in Italy, France, the United States, Germany and Russia were either handled differently in each of the other countries in that space of communication or did not yet exist there. Where these blockages also existed, the terrorist tactic was immediately taken up.[82]

---

[82] I concentrate on the brief span during which terrorism was invented and on its initial reception and relevant attempts to develop the tactic. The fact that terrorist tactics were used in certain societies with similar political blockages immediately after this period does not contradict the conclusions drawn here. For exact characterizations of the political blockages pivotal in the invention of terrorism, see this volume, pp. 78–81 and the final chapter.

This negative evidence is needed to ensure that this book's focus on spectacular acts of violence is not confined to societies in which blockages and terrorism coexisted. Such a restriction would lead one to overlook constellations in which there *were* political obstructions at that time but no ensuing terrorism, and would call into question the claim of a causal relationship between terrorism and political blockages. The theoretically conceivable opposite scenario (terrorism without political blockages) has not been found anywhere.

The examples of negative evidence also point to political alternatives that could inhibit the emergence of terrorism. These cases show how different societies succeeded in putting the ideas of freedom and nationhood into practice without political obstacles engendering terrorism in either the first step (that of politico-legal action) or the second step (that of the population's everyday life). Either political blockage was absent because the key actors used established political institutions of law or decree rather than force to introduce the ideas of freedom and nationhood, or political blockage was absent because the implementation of freedom and nationhood were achieved through the force of collective violence – revolution, civil war or both – within a manageable period and legally established under the new power structure.

In addition, there were societies in which political obstacles to freedom and nation did not emerge because these themes were not yet relevant. In the eight years under study in this book such cases usually mean that the ideas of freedom and nation were not yet anchored in significant parts of the population and that the public audience for the media had not yet developed to the necessary degree.

The idea of nation and its twofold implementation in Europe and the United States

Political freedom – meaning political participation and self-determination – was one of the great promises of the American and French revolutions. This promise was linked to the idea of nation, in and through which it was to be kept. The idea of nation and its realization in the process of building a nation and a nation state were historically new phenomena. Although the concept of 'nation' is older, it had long had other meanings. It originated from Latin, and since the fifteenth century had referred to the politically influential elite. Until the mid-eighteenth century throughout Europe, the nation meant the nobility and the cler-gy.[83] This early modern understanding of a nation based on feudal estates was reversed in the American and French revolutions.[84]

The new meaning of the idea of the nation was invented by enlightened intellectuals.[85] In France they declared the Third Estate, rather than the nobility and the clergy, to embody the *volonté générale* (general will). Hence they proclaimed the assembly of this estate's representatives (together with the majority of the clergy and a minority of the nobles who joined them) as the Assemblée nationale (national assembly). When they had thereby prevailed over King Louis XVI, who then commanded the rest of the nobil-ity and the clergy to join the Assembly of the Third Estate, the 'legal revolu-tion' – the first revolution in the French Revolution – was achieved. According to Eberhard Schmitt, it was a legal *coup d'état*, in which

the modern doctrine of national sovereignty, which until that point had only been discussed nonbindingly in the *République des lettres* (Republic of Letters) and in the flood of brochures about the conflict

83 On the genesis of the idea of the nation and the nation state in the world, see Bayly, *The Birth of the Modern World, 1780–1914*, 96–114 and Chapter 6; also Osterhammel, *The Transformation of the World*, Chapter 8. For the history of the term, see Fritz Gschnitzer, Reinhart Koselleck, Bernd Schonemann and Karl Ferdinand Werner, 'Volk, Nation, Nationalismus, Masse', in Otto Brunner, Werner Conze and Reinhart Koselleck (eds.), *Geschichtliche Grundbegriffe: Historisches Lexikon zur politisch-sozialen Sprache in Deutschland*, 8 vols. (Stuttgart: Klett-Cotta, 1972–97), vol. 7, 1992, 141–431; Miroslav Hroch and Jitka Malečková, ' "Nation": A Survey of the Term in European Languages', in Athena S. Leoussi (ed.), *Encyclopedia of Nationalism* (New Brunswick: Transaction Publishers, 2001), Chapters 2.1–2, 203–8; Hagen Schulze, *Staat und Nation in der europäischen Geschichte*, 2nd revised ed. (Munich: C. H. Beck, 1995), Chapters 2.1, 2.2; and Dieter Langewiesche, '"Nation", "Nationalismus", "Nationalstaat" in der europäischen Geschichte seit dem Mittelalter', in Langewiesche, *Nation, Nationalismus in Deutschland und Europa* (Munich: C. H. Beck, 2000), 14–34.

84 This reversal also applies partially to the Glorious Revolution in England. For more information on this point and on the relationship between the revolution in England and the revolutions in America and France, see, for example, Hans-Ulrich Wehler, *Nationalismus: Geschichte – Formen – Folgen* (Munich: C. H. Beck, 2001), Chapter 2.

85 See Gschnitzer et al., 'Volk, Nation, Nationalismus, Masse', 321–5; Schulze, *Staat und Nation in der europäischen Geschichte*, 168–72; Georges Lefebvre, *The Coming of the French Revolution* (Princeton: Princeton University Press, 1947), 49–60; Ernst Schulin, *Die Französische Revolution*, 4th ed. (Munich: C. H. Beck, 2004), 60–71; Rolf Reichhardt, *Das Blut der Freiheit: Französische Revolution und demokratische Kultur* (Frankfurt am Main: Fischer-Taschenbuch-Verlag, 2014), 115–16; and Timothy Baycroft, *Inventing the Nation: France* (London: Hodder Education, 2008), 14–15.

between the Estates, served for the first time on the European continent to legitimize the political will of the representatives of the majority of the nation as the will of the nation itself.[86]

This legal *coup d'état*, which proceeded non-violently in the French case, established the principle of political participation and self-determination in Europe for the first time. The sovereignty of the people as a nation replaced the monarchy-by-the-grace-of-God. That was the first step in the implementation of the idea of a nation, its politico-legal realization.

The second step in implementing the idea of a nation was its realization in the daily life of the population. The idea of the nation began to become an everyday reality for the whole French population in the further course of the French Revolution, the French Revolutionary Wars, and the Napoleonic Wars.[87] The Declaration of the Rights of Man and Citizen in August 1789 enshrined the conviction that the nation is essentially the source of all sovereignty and that all authority emanates directly from it.[88] In subsequent years, there were many ways in which this principle was symbolized, visualized, embodied, religiously exalted and transferred to other domains, such as the right of self-determination of nations.[89] The idea of the nation became especially real, however, for people drafted by the *levée en masse* (which involved the mass

---

86 Eberhard Schmitt, *Repräsentation und Revolution: Eine Untersuchung zur Genesis der kontinentalen Theorie und Praxis parlamentarischer Repräsentation aus der Herrschaftspraxis des Ancien régime in Frankreich, 1760–1789* (Munich: C. H. Beck, 1969), 281. See also Lefebvre, *The Coming of the French Revolution*, 89–90; Schulin, *Die Französische Revolution*, 69–70, which also contains the quotation from Schmitt, as well as Reichhardt, *Das Blut der Freiheit*, 119–20.

87 See Schulin, *Die Französische Revolution*, 216, 258, 267; Reichhardt, *Das Blut der Freiheit*, 224–56; and especially David Avrom Bell, *The Cult of the Nation in France: Inventing Nationalism, 1680–1800* (Cambridge, MA: Harvard University Press, 2001).

88 See 'Declaration of the Rights of Man and Citizen, 27 August, 1789', printed in John Hall Stewart, *A Documentary Survey of the French Revolution* (New York: Macmillan Company, 1951), 113–15, specifically Article 3; and also Schulin, *Die Französische Revolution*, 79–85.

89 See Schulin, *Die Französische Revolution*, 93, 115, 107, 118; Baycroft, *Inventing the Nation: France*, 15–16; Bell, *The Cult of the Nation*, Chapter 6; and Jörg Fisch, *The Right of Self-Determination of Peoples: The Domestication of an Illusion* (New York: Cambridge University Press, 2015), Chapter 7. On the creation of national languages and national historiographies in this process of the construction of a nation, see also Schulze, *Staat und Nation in der europäischen Geschichte*, 172–89.

conscription not only of soldiers but also of older men, women and children into service for the national defence) in 1793 and the Terror of 1793–4. For the first time in recent history, an entire population was unconditionally and totally pressed into service for national defence both external and internal, 'nationalizing' the Revolution.[90] Through such manifestation in the politico-legal sphere and daily life in France, the nation as a new idea became a beacon.

Subsequently, the idea of the nation's internal and external sovereignty, of the nation state and of nationalism was exported to the rest of the world and imported everywhere.[91] Unlike the course of events in France, where at least the first step of nation building was achieved non-violently because the king yielded and force was needed only in the second step (the expansion and implementation of the idea of a nation), that first step rarely happened peacefully elsewhere. As a rule, nations have been created and stabilized by means of massive collective violence – wars, revolutions and insurgencies. Where elites unconditionally seek to found a nation but eventually fail even despite repeated use of collective violence because of overwhelming resistance, the odds are great that one person or another among such elites will ultimately be willing to turn to individual violence as well; that is, to terrorism. The tactic of terrorism emerged as an innovation in the use of force to found a nation despite political blockages. It is thus part of the nation building processes in the modern era.

The emergence of the nation state and nationalism is one of the few research areas in historiography to have become a focus of theory building. Theories in this field treat nation building as a part of modernization processes.[92] Remarkably, the role of collective violence has generally not

---

90 See Schulin, *Die Französische Revolution*, 223, 230–1; and Baycroft, *Inventing the Nation: France*, Chapter 6. On the Terror see Hugh Gough, *The Terror in the French Revolution*, 2nd ed. (Houndmills: Palgrave Macmillan, 2010). On the significance of general conscription in this process of nation building, see Schulze, *Staat und Nation in der europäischen Geschichte*, 189–208.

91 See Bayly, *The Birth of the Modern World*, 106–7; Osterhammel, *The Transformation of the World*, 394–5; Wehler, *Nationalismus*, 15; Wolfgang Reinhard, *Geschichte der Staatsgewalt: Eine vergleichende Verfassungsgeschichte Europas von den Anfängen bis zur Gegenwart*, 3rd revised ed. (Munich: C. H. Beck, 2002); for an especially vivid account, see Reichhardt, *Das Blut der Freiheit*, 257–334.

92 See Ernest Gellner, *Nations and Nationalism* (Malden: Blackwell, 2006); John Breuilly, *Nationalism and the State* (Manchester: Manchester University Press, 1993); Eric John Hobsbawm, *Nations and Nationalism since 1780: Programme, Myth, Reality* (Cambridge: Cambridge University Press, 1992); and Benedict Anderson, *Imagined*

been included in that topic.[93] The significance of violence has been addressed more in typologies of nation building than in modernization theories about the nation.[94] The role of individual violence in particular has been completely ignored, although the significance of violence in the creation and stabilization of nations has been documented frequently in empirical historical studies. Nation states were begotten of wars (*Kriegsgeburten*), as Dieter Langewiesche has emphasized.[95] Violence was inherent in them. The finding that violence was already a key feature of the first political and legal step in becoming a nation holds for Europe, Russia and the United States for the entire 'long' nineteenth century.[96] On the whole, it meant collective violence: insurrection, revolution and war, or combinations thereof.

As far as the emergence of terrorism is concerned, three types of nation-building processes can be identified. In the first type, nation building was achieved through collective violence, at least in the

---

Communities: Reflections on the Origin and the Spread of Nationalism (London: Verso, 2006). On these theories, see Bayly, The Birth of the Modern World, 199–205; Anthony D. Smith, Nationalism and Modernism: A Critical Survey of Recent Theories of Nations and Nationalism (London: Routledge, 1998); and Miroslav Hroch, European Nations: Explaining Their Formation (London: Verso, 2015), Part 2, Chapter 5, 77–116.

93 Bayly, too, considers violence to be the decisive factor in processes of nation building and nationalism. See Bayly, The Birth of the Modern World, 204, 243.

94 Theodor Schieder distinguishes between a transforming nationalism in Western Europe (France and England), a unifying nationalism in Central Europe (Italy and Germany), and a secessionist nationalism in Eastern Europe (the Habsburg monarchy, Russia, Ottoman Empire). See Theodor Schieder, 'Typologie und Erscheinungsformen des Nationalstaats in Europa', in Otto Dann, Hans-Ulrich Wehler and Theodor Schieder (eds.), Nationalismus und Nationalstaat: Studien zum nationalen Problem im modernen Europa (Göttingen: Vandenhoeck & Ruprecht, 1991), 65–86. Breuilly, Nationalism and the State, presents a similar classification at the global level. Jürgen Osterhammel confirms transformation processes for Great Britain and France in his global typology. He also writes about types of revolutionary independence (for instance the United States, Greece and Belgium), hegemonial unification (e.g. Germany and Italy), evolutionary autonomization (such as Ireland) and the special cases of Japan and Siam (now Thailand). See Osterhammel, The Transformation of the World, 403–4, 407–17. The terms 'unification' and 'secession' and the categories of revolutionary independence, hegemonial unification and evolutionary autonomization usually imply the use of violence.

95 See, for example, Langewiesche, 'Nationalismus im 19. und 20. Jahrhundert', 45.

96 The term, coined by Eric John Hobsbawm, refers to the period from 1789 to 1914. See Eric John Hobsbawm, The Age of Revolution: Europe, 1789–1848 (London: Weidenfeld & Nicolson, 1962); Hobsbawm, The Age of Capital: 1848–1875 (London: Weidenfeld & Nicolson, 1975); Hobsbawm, The Age of Empire (London: Weidenfeld & Nicolson, 1987).

politico-legal step. When the use of collective violence was successful, there were no enduring political blockages and therefore no cause for terrorist violence in order to bring the nation into being. In the second type, external power relations made it impossible for nation building to be achieved with collective violence. Political blockages thwarted the creation of a nation, and when those blockages could not be overcome by political means, the reception of terrorist tactics was rapid and their use repeated. In the third type, too, all attempts to achieve a nation by political means or collective violence initially failed, but persons who believed in the idea of a nation saw the possibility of achieving their objective by committing individual violence.

The first type of nation-building process – success through collective violence – is illustrated by the two most significant examples of incipient nation state formation before the French Revolution: England and the United States. The use of collective violence was at first successful in the English Revolution and in the American Revolutionary War. In France the politico-legal foundations of the nation were established non-violently, but violence (civil war and war) was decisive for the diffusion and realization of the national idea. Two further examples of the successful use of collective violence for nation building are Greece and Belgium. The revolutionary war against the Ottoman Empire, which led to the creation of Greece as a nation, was won with the help of military intervention by Russia, Great Britain and France. In Belgium, the use of collective violence in the form of a revolutionary insurgency was victorious against the Netherlands within a few weeks without external help. The establishment of the nations of Greece and Belgium was successful because it did not threaten the European architecture of peace forged at the Congress of Vienna.[97] The significance of this factor will become evident when looking at the following cases.

Poland, Hungary and Ireland are the three most prominent cases of abortive national revolutions in the nineteenth century. They illustrate the second type. In Poland the national movement rose against Russia in 1830 and 1863; in Hungary, against the Habsburg monarchy in 1848; and, in Ireland, on a continuous basis against Great Britain. In all three cases the national movements fought against the strongest conceivable

---

97 See Matthias Schulz, *Normen und Praxis: Das europäische Konzert der Großmächte als Sicherheitsrat, 1815–1860* (Munich: Oldenbourg, 2009).

opponent: major powers that stood for the arrangements for peace in Europe negotiated at the Congress of Vienna. In all three cases they received little or no support from other major European powers. However, the Habsburg monarchy responded to the demand for political sovereignty in Hungary by agreeing on far-reaching rights of autonomy and thereby at least temporarily resolved the conflict by political means, whereas in Poland and Ireland the political blockages remained, leading to early reception and recurrent use of terrorist tactics.

The German and Italian states represent the third type of nation building. As in Poland, Hungary and Ireland, all attempts to found a nation with collective violence originally failed. The situation appeared to be externally and internally blocked in multiple ways. Unlike the circumstances in Poland, Hungary and Ireland, those in Central Europe offered the possibility of playing the major powers against each other. In Italy's case this meant Austria and France; in the German states it was Austria and Prussia. This book shows that individuals tried to take advantage of these conditions and took up violence. It was in this situation that terrorism emerged as an individual's use of violence to bring about the founding of a nation. It was the first time that the tactic was politically successful.[98]

The idea of freedom and its political and legal realization: the emancipation of slaves in the European colonies

Personal freedom and equality were the other great promises of the American and French revolutions, along with political participation and national self-determination. These promises were aimed at specific institutions of personal bondage, two forms of which existed in the mid-eighteenth century: serfdom and slavery.

Slavery had existed throughout most of the world since biblical times and was an institution considered both legitimate and necessary. China, Japan and Europe were exceptions. In Europe, slavery as it had been known in antiquity gave way to serfdom in the early Middle Ages. Even though the ancient form of slavery survived or reappeared in parts of Italy or the Iberian peninsula, it did not exist in the core European

---

98 Karl Ludwig Sand and his assassination of August von Kotzebue are discussed in the conclusion.

countries. With the founding of the Portuguese and Spanish colonies, and then especially the Dutch, French and British colonial empires, slavery was exported to the New World, where it was systematically established and vastly intensified as the plantation economy grew. A crucial factor in slavery's establishment was that the Europeans tried to develop the land masses of the New World for themselves without being able to draw on a reservoir of local labour. At the same time, they sought to raise and process certain agricultural crops in an industrial fashion (such as sugar cane, tobacco and rice) to serve the world market, which was growing rapidly in the seventeenth century. Sven Beckert uses the term 'war capitalism' to characterize this system that brought about the expansion of slavery.[99]

During the 1760s and 1770s, Europeans came to regard slavery as an injustice and a moral evil. This view, which John Brown later shared, resulted from a changing image of humans, a process that Hans Joas described as the embracing of the 'sacredness of the person'.[100] It became the basis for the formulation of the Declaration of Independence and the Declaration of the Rights of Man and Citizen in the American and French revolutions respectively. The rise of this view was spurred by the interaction of religious elements, such as the activities of the Quakers, the evangelical belief in conversion in British Protestantism, and a new ethic of benevolence, with philosophically secular developments,

---

99 Sven Beckert, *Empire of Cotton: A Global History* (New York: Alfred A. Knopf, 2014), xv. For a global perspective, see Bayly, *The Birth of the Modern World*, 402–10; Osterhammel, *The Transformation of the World*, 697–701; David Brion Davis, *Inhuman Bondage: The Rise and Fall of Slavery in the New World* (Oxford: Oxford University Press, 2006), Chapters 2–6; Seymour Drescher, *Abolition: A History of Slavery and Antislavery* (Cambridge: Cambridge University Press, 2009), Chapters 1–3; Norbert Finzsch, James O. Horton and Lois E. Horton, *Von Benin nach Baltimore: Die Geschichte der African Americans* (Hamburg: Hamburger Edition, 1999), Chapter 1; Jochen Meißner, Ulrich Mücke and Klaus Weber, *Schwarzes Amerika: Eine Geschichte der Sklaverei* (Munich: C. H. Beck, 2008), Chapter 2. On the replacement of slavery in the early Middle Ages and the continuity or reintroduction of the institution in the Mediterranean region, see Michael Mitterauer, *Warum Europa? Mittelalterliche Grundlagen eines Sonderwegs* (Munich: C. H. Beck, 2009), Chapter 2; also Alfred Haverkamp, 'Die Erneuerung der Sklaverei im Mitteelmeerraum während des hohen Mittelalters', in Elisabeth Herrmann-Otto (ed.), *Unfreie Arbeits- und Lebensverhältnisse von der Antike bis in die Gegenwart: Eine Einführung* (Hildesheim: Olms, 2005), 130–66. On the justification of slavery in European thinking, see David Brion Davis, *The Problem of Slavery in Western Culture* (Ithaca: Cornell University Press, 1966), Parts I, II.

100 Joas, *The Sacredness of the Person*.

including the Enlightenment idea of natural rights, according to which all people are born free. As a result, institutions of personal bondage increasingly came to be seen as emblems of backwardness, whereas emancipation stood for civilization. Within a few decades Europeans ceased to be the driving forces behind the worldwide expansion and intensification of the lucrative slave trade and the exploitation of slave labour and became the driving forces for their elimination.[101]

Slavery's abolition, which the European capitals carried out in their colonies, proceeded in two ways. The counterpart to the Continental model of emancipating slaves by decree was the Anglo-American process of broad public engagement in social movements. In France the National Convention under the leadership of Maximilien Robespierre declared all slaves of the French Empire to be citizens in 1794. Napoleon rescinded this emancipation, but it was reinstated after the February revolution of 1848, abolishing slavery in France and its possessions once and for all. Other European countries from Sweden to Portugal took similar paths. The public was only marginally involved in these decisions.[102]

Things were different in Great Britain and the United States, where the demands to emancipate the slaves became the focus of the first major

---

101 See Davis, *The Problem of Slavery in Western Culture*, Part 3; and David Brion Davis, *The Problem of Slavery in the Age of Revolution, 1770–1823* (Ithaca: Cornell University Press, 1975), Part 1. On the linking of freedom and civilization see Davis, *Slavery and Human Progress* (New York: Oxford University Press, 1984), Part 2; and Osterhammel, *Sklaverei und die Zivilisation des Westens* (Munich: Carl Friedrich von Siemens Stiftung, 2000).

102 For a comparison of the Continental and Anglo-American approaches, see Seymour Drescher, *Capitalism and Antislavery: British Mobilization in Comparative Perspective* (Basingstoke: Macmillan, 1986); and Drescher, *Abolition*, Chapters 6, 10, 12. For a comparison within continental Europe, see Olivier Pétré-Grenouilleau (ed.), *Abolir l'esclavage: Un réformisme à l'épreuve* (Rennes: Presses universitaires de Rennes, 2008). On France see Davis, *Inhuman Bondage*, Chapter 8: Frédéric Régent, *La France et ses esclaves: De la colonisation aux abolitions, 1620–1848* (Paris: Grasset, 2007), Chapters 8–9; also Lawrence C. Jennings, *French Anti-slavery: The Movement for the Abolition of Slavery in France, 1802–1848* (Cambridge: Cambridge University Press, 2000). On the Netherlands, see Gert Oostindie, *Fifty Years Later: Antislavery, Capitalism and Modernity in the Dutch Orbit* (Leiden: KITLV Press, 1995). On Portugal, see João Pedro Marques, *The Sounds of Silence: Nineteenth-Century Portugal and the Abolition of the Slave Trade* (New York: Berghahn Books, 2005). Latin America represents yet another paradigm for the emancipation of slaves, but it is not relevant for our discussion here.

social reform movement in history. The organizational form, objectives, strategies and effects of the British anti-slavery movement probably made it one of the biggest and most successful social movements of all time. It consisted of a network of groups and organizations that attempted to change society in a particular direction by involving large swaths of the population and by using various forms of protest and political influence over a long period.[103]

The British abolitionist movement began in the early 1770s. By the end of the 1780s it had reached a hitherto unknown degree of social engagement across classes, religions, genders and parties. Umbrella organizations such as the Society for Effecting the Abolition of the Slave Trade and the Society for the Mitigation and Gradual Abolition of Slavery proved to be extremely innovative in mobilizing nationally. They employed staff who conducted research, undertook an unprecedented level of public speaking as well as literary and journalistic writing, and supported a network of local groups even in remote provincial towns. They called on consumers, especially women, to boycott produce whose cultivation had involved slave labour. Above all, they used the legal system in new ways. In 1792 the British government received 519 petitions bearing the signatures of 390,000 people, or 13 per cent of the adult male population in England, Scotland and Wales. In 1833 Parliament received about 5,000 mass petitions signed by nearly 1.5 million people, including a petition that was a mile and a half long and signed by 350,000 women. Together, these activities still rank as the greatest such mobilization of the population for a political objective in the history of Great Britain.[104]

103 The British anti-slavery movement around 1800 thereby meets all of the criteria mentioned in the section of this chapter titled 'Causes' (p. 53) that are derived from sociological definitions of social movements. See Tilly, *Social Movements*, 33; Olivier Pétré-Grenouilleau, 'Abolitionisme et democratisation', in Pétré-Grenouilleau (ed.), *Abolir l'esclavage* (Rennes: Presses universitaires de Rennes, 2008), 7; and Herbert Aptheker, *Abolitionism: A Revolutionary Movement* (Boston: Twayne Publishers, 1989), Chapter 5. Margaret E. Keck and Kathryn Sikkink, in *Activists Beyond Borders: Advocacy Networks in International Politics* (Ithaca: Cornell University Press, 1998), speak of an initial form of a 'transnational advocacy network'. And yet, even though the anti-slavery movement meets all the criteria, German publications about social movements have not addressed it.

104 On the anti-slavery movement in Great Britain, see Davis, *Inhuman Bondage*, Chapter 12; Drescher, *Abolition*, Chapters 8–9; Meißner, Mücke and Weber, *Schwarzes Amerika*, 179–98; and Adam Hochschild, *Bury the Chains: The British Struggle to Abolish Slavery* (London: Pan, 2006). On the movement's public relations and political methods,

The abolitionist movement in Great Britain was successful because the country's political institutions responded to the public demand. The House of Commons set up public commissions that examined the slave trade and ways to emancipate slaves. Influential people in public life took up the subject and involved themselves in it for long periods. They convinced politicians they knew personally of their views. The movement advanced towards its goal on the strength of its intelligent arguments and tactics, sustained public pressure, and the support it gained from two slave revolts. In 1807 Parliament forbade British ships from participating in the transatlantic slave trade and followed up in 1833 by passing legislation that freed the approximately 800,000 slaves in British colonies in America and Africa.

In addition to the change in religious and philosophical ideas discussed above, the conditions paving the way for the emergence of this movement included the development of a political culture and a politically engaged public, which made it possible to rally the general population. With Parliament as the central representative institution, an advanced system of transport and communication, a high literacy rate, a well-developed market for books and other print media, numerous local and national newspapers, relatively liberal censorship rules, and active clubs and societies, Great Britain had all it needed for a sociopolitical movement by the end of the 1770s.[105]

It is true that contemporaries had, by that time, already begun criticizing the second step of implementing freedom, namely the actual processes of emancipation and its outcomes, for whereas slave owners

---

see John R. Oldfield, *Popular Politics and British Anti-slavery: The Mobilisation of Public Opinion against the Slave Trade, 1787–1807* (London: Frank Cass, 1998); and Sidney G. Tarrow, *Power in Movement: Social Movements and Contentious Politics* (Cambridge: Cambridge University Press, 2011), 47–51.

105 On the importance of a developed political public sphere as a precondition for the emergence of the abolitionist movement, see especially Drescher, *Abolition*, 208–9. On the development of the system of transport and communication, and of a politically interested public in Great Britain, and on the public's say in political matters, see Gottfried Niedhart, *Geschichte Englands im 19. und 20. Jahrhundert*, 3rd revised ed. (Munich: C. H. Beck, 2004), Chapter 1; Philip Sidney Bagwell, *The Transport Revolution from 1770* (London: Batsford, 1974), especially Chapters 1–3; Hannah Barker, *Newspapers, Politics, and Public Opinion in Late Eighteenth-Century England* (Oxford: Clarendon Press, 1998); and Joanna Innes, 'Legislation and Public Participation, 1760–1830', in David Lemmings (ed.), *The British and Their Laws in the Eighteenth Century* (Woodbridge: Boydell Press, 2005), 102–32.

received compensation for their lost property, former slaves had to work four more years without pay for their former masters. Receiving no support or training for starting a new life, they were then simply left to fend for themselves. Such objections did not result in outbreaks of political violence in Great Britain, however. People realized that abolition of the slave trade and of slavery was an unparalleled political process in which large swaths of the population had worked together with parts of the political elite for humanitarian reasons to end an institution that had contributed significantly to the development of power and wealth in the nation.[106]

The idea of freedom and its twofold implementation: the emancipation of serfs in Central and Western Europe

Is it possible to compare the emancipation of slaves and serfs? Where are similarities and differences between these two institutions of bonded labour? How did those characteristics influence the emancipation processes and, hence, the political dynamics and emergence of political blockages and political violence? Bonded labour – whether slavery or serfdom – has always been a regime with the primary purpose of forcibly ensuring the availability of a workforce despite a labour shortage. Yet serfdom, even in its rigid manifestations, cannot be equated with the institution of slavery as it was practised, say, in the United States. For example, slaves belonged only to their owner, whereas serfs were also subjects of their territorial princes. Slaves, at least in the first generation, were transported under inhumane conditions to a society utterly alien to them, where they constituted a minority and were differentiated by the way they looked. By contrast, serfs were indigenous and represented 70 to 90 per cent of the population.

What both institutions had in common was that serfs and slaves were compelled to provide manpower when it was scarce – especially for heavy labour (in sectors such as agriculture, forestry, mining and construction) without incentives like good pay and working conditions. Furthermore, both institutions established a regime to control

106 See Davis, *Inhuman Bondage*, Chapter 12; Drescher, *Abolition*, Chapters 8–9; Meißner, Mücke and Weber, *Schwarzes Amerika*, 179–98; Hochschild, *Bury the Chains*; and Oldfield, *Popular Politics and British Anti-slavery*.

labour according to a person's saleability, forced labour without pay, prevention of the freedom of movement, regulation of reproduction and personal attachments, manorial jurisdiction, and an almost unlimited monopoly on force. In other words, it encompassed the right to use slaves and serfs as labourers, to buy and sell them, to use them as security for loans or to gamble them away, to keep them from choosing their work and the place where they live, to permit or prohibit their marriage depending on the master's interest, and to judge and punish them.[107] Both institutions were incompatible with the ideals of civil society.

Around the mid-eighteenth century, personal bondage and coerced labour existed as serfdom in most of Europe. The reason lay in a clear lack of labour in most of Central Europe – as in America – since the mid-seventeenth century. This shortage owed to the devastation wrought by the Thirty Years War, which had decimated about a third of the population. The dearth of manpower occurred in Europe, as in the European colonies, at a time when the intensification of agriculture was becoming particularly lucrative for landowners. This development stemmed from a commercial revolution: the emerging world market for agricultural products. For example, trade with the Baltic region brought grain into the densely populated cities of the Netherlands, northern France, the south of England and Italy. In the German states east of the Elbe river, it led to the infamous practice of dispossessing peasants of agricultural tracts and buying up available farms (*Bauernlegen*), usually to increase the new landowner's income through direct management of the holdings. This process was coupled with a particularly strict form of serfdom

---

107 For contemporary eighteenth-century comparisons of serfdom and slavery, see, for example, Adolph von Knigge, *Über den Umgang mit Menschen* (Frakfurt am Main: Insel, 1977), 379 (the relevant chapter is not included in Peter Will's English translation, *Practical Philosophy of Social Life; Or the Art of Conversing with Men*, after the German of Baron Knigge (London: n.p., 1799), or Knigge, *Über Eigennutz und Undank*, in Knigge, *Sämtliche Werke*, 24 vols. in 6 divisions, ed. Paul Raabe (Munich: Saur, 1978–93), vol. 11 (1992), 181–2; and the writings of the Russian proponents of the Enlightenment, Alexandr Nikolayevich Radishchev and Nikolai Ivanovich Novikov. For comparisons in the historical literature, see the introduction by Stanley L. Engerman, 'Slavery, Serfdom and Other Forms of Coerced Labour: Similarities and Differences', in Michael L. Bush (ed.), *Serfdom and Slavery: Studies in Legal Bondage* (London: Longman, 1996), 18–41; Michael L. Bush, *Servitude in Modern Times* (Cambridge: Polity Press, 2000), Part 1; and Peter Kolchin, *Unfree Labor: American Slavery and Russian Serfdom* (Cambridge, MA: Belknap Press of Harvard University Press, 1987), 41–6.

that culminated in the second half of the seventeenth century and the early eighteenth.[108]

Like the abolition of slavery, however, the emancipation of serfs in Western and Central Europe was eventually achieved without political blockages. This holds true for both steps: that of legal emancipation and that of emancipation's subsequent realization in real life. That first step was accomplished either peacefully through established political institutions or in a limited period by means of collective violence in the French Revolution and as a result of the Napoleonic Wars.

Amid religious and intellectual changes similar to what had seeded the anti-slavery movement in England, petitions by serfs to their rulers and litigation initiated by peasants since the mid-eighteenth century unleashed a reform movement and a debate about serfdom in which the enlightened bourgeoisie, sovereigns, nobility, lawyers and clergy participated.[109] The developments in the North American colonies also left traces in these circles, one example being George Mason's *Virginia*

---

108 For a global perspective on the institution of serfdom, see Bayly, *The Birth of the Modern World*, Chapter 1, and 410–18; and Osterhammel, *The Transformation of the World*, 697–705. For a perspective on Europe as a whole, see Jerome Blum, *The End of the Old Order in Rural Europe* (Princeton: Princeton University Press, 1978), Part 1. On the history of serfdom in Germany, see Peter Blickle, *Von der Leibeigenschaft zu den Menschenrechten: Eine Geschichte der Freiheit in Deutschland* (Munich: C. H. Beck, 2006), Part 1; on Eastern Europe, Christoph Schmidt, *Leibeigenschaft im Ostseeraum: Versuch einer Typologie* (Cologne: Böhlau Verlag, 1997); on Russia, Jerome Blum, *Lord and Peasant in Russia: From the Ninth to the Nineteenth Century* (Princeton: Princeton University Press, 1961). On England, where serfdom had long since vanished by the eighteenth century, see Samuel Sugenheim, *Geschichte der Aufhebung der Leibeigenschaft und Hörigkeit in Europa* (St Petersburg: Eggers, 1861); and Mark Bailey, *The English Manor, c.1200–c.1500* (Manchester: Manchester University Press, 2002), 17–18; James A. Yelling, *Common Field and Enclosure in England 1450–1850* (London: Macmillan, 1977); and J. M. Neeson, *Commoners: Common Right, Enclosure and Social Change in England, 1700–1820* (Cambridge: Cambridge University Press, 1995).

109 The question of which factors were crucial in the emergence of reform movements against serfdom and in its abolition has been debated since the mid-nineteenth century. For a comparative summary of the debate, see Peter Kolchin, 'Some Controversial Questions Concerning Nineteenth-Century Emancipation from Slavery and Serfdom', in Bush, *Serfdom and Slavery*, 42–67. The argument presented above builds on work by Peter Blickle, who expanded the economic analysis to include the peasants themselves, the public and the state. Blickle, *Von der Leibeigenschaft zu den Menschenrechten*, 153–73. Lothar Gall, *Von der ständischen zur bürgerlichen Gesellschaft* (Munich: Oldenbourg, 1993), Chapter 2, underscores the significance of enlightened absolutism, an enlightened bourgeoisie and an enlightened civil service.

Declaration of Rights of 1776, which served as a model for the Declaration of Independence.[110] Freedom seemed to be the sign of the times.

Unlike the anti-slavery movement in England, the circles of the Central European elite who cared about the abolition of serfdom therefore did not even need to grow into a broad social movement. In the age of enlightened absolutism, revolution and the Napoleonic Wars, the sovereigns of Central Europe eventually responded, taking the political and legal path of decreeing the emancipation of people in servitude on their lands. The surge in population growth since the mid-eighteenth century helped prepare this step, which also strengthened and stabilized their rule, for freeing the serfs enhanced the control the prince could exercise over the population and stabilized the monarchy through 'defensive modernization'.[111]

The emancipation of serfs through legislation by sovereigns had started before the French Revolution and ended in 1833 when the manorial seigneurs in the south-west German principality of Hohenzollern-Sigmaringen released their serfs from hereditary subservience.[112] That act completed the emancipation of the peasants in Central Europe in the same year that Great Britain's Parliament freed the slaves in the remaining American colonies.[113]

In France, by contrast, the legal emancipation of the serfs came about through collective violence in a revolution. The Bastille was stormed on

---

110 See George Mason, *The Virginia Declaration of Rights, First Draft 1776*, from encyclopediavirginia.org. On the reception of the first constitutions of individual states by the enlightened elites in Europe, the classic resource remains Robert Roswell Palmer's *The Age of the Democratic Revolution* (Princeton: Princeton University Press, 1959), Chapter 9.

111 See Thomas Nipperdey, *Deutsche Geschichte 1800–1866* (Munich: C. H. Beck, 1998), Part 2; and Hans-Ulrich Wehler, *Deutsche Gesellschaftsgeschichte*, vol. 1 (Munich: C. H. Beck, 1987), Part 2, who emphasize this development differently.

112 See Dieter Langewiesche, *Europa zwischen Restauration und Revolution, 1815–1849* (Munich: Oldenbourg, 2007), section C.1; Sugenheim, *Geschichte der Aufhebung der Leibeigenschaft*; and Blum, *The End of the Old Order in Rural Europe*, Parts 2–3. For Germany and Austria, see Reinhard Rürup, *Deutschland im 19. Jahrhundert*, 2nd revised edition with an expanded bibliography (Göttingen: Vandenhoeck & Ruprecht, 1992), Chapter 2; Hans-Werner Hahn and Helmut Berding, *Gebhardt: Handbuch der deutschen Geschichte*, vol. 14: *Reformen, Restauration und Revolution 1806–1848/49*, 10. völlig neu bearbeitete Aufl. [des Gesamtwerks] (Stuttgart: Klett-Cotta, 2010), §3c; Christof Dipper, *Die Bauernbefreiung in Deutschland 1790–1850* (Stuttgart: Kohlhammer, 1980); and Karl Heinz Schneider, *Geschichte der Bauernbefreiung* (Stuttgart: Reclam, 2010).

113 On this see the previous section.

14 July 1789, as were palaces and cloisters in various parts of France thereafter, partly because of the Great Fear (*Grande peur*, mid-July to early August). These insurrections shocked the National Assembly. The fear of peasant rebellions was as great among European elites as was the fear of slave rebellions in the United States.[114] Instead of resorting to violent suppression, however, the representatives in the French National Assembly opted to make concessions. Working through the night from 4 to 5 August, in a sweeping gesture the representatives dissolved the society of the *Ancien Régime*. Georges Lefebvre described the consequences of that night: 'In a few hours on that occasion the Assembly had realized the juridical unity of the nation, destroying in principle, with the feudal regime, the ascendency of the aristocracy in rural life.'[115] On 11 August the National Assembly abolished the feudal regime and eliminated personal bondage unconditionally.[116] Two weeks later the assembly passed the Declaration of the Rights of Man and Citizen, codifying the freedom and equality of all people.[117] This declaration of human rights staked a universal claim,[118] but it did not initially apply to slaves in the French colonies (just as the rights introduced in the founding documents of the United States did not extend to slaves).[119] The legal

---

114 On the peasant revolution as a component of the French Revolution, see Lefebvre, *The Coming of the French Revolution*, Part 4; Schulin, *Die Französische Revolution*, 75–81; and the illustrative examples in Reichardt, *Das Blut der Freiheit*, 17–57. On the Great Fear, see Georges Lefebvre, *The Great Fear of 1789* (Princeton: Princeton University Press, 2016); and the sociological semantic study by Clay Ramsay, *The Ideology of the Great Fear: The Soissonnais in 1789* (Baltimore: Johns Hopkins University Press, 1992).

115 Lefebvre, *The Coming of the French Revolution*, 165; also see Reichhardt, *Das Blut der Freiheit*, 126–7.

116 See 'The August 4th Decrees, 4–11 August, 1789', in John Hall Stewart, *A Documentary Survey of the French Revolution* (New York: Macmillan Company, 1951), 106–10.

117 See again Stewart, *A Documentary Survey of the French Revolution*, 113–14. On the background and process of abolishing feudal rights and about the 'Declaration of the Rights of Man and Citizen', see especially Lefebvre, *The Coming of the French Revolution*, Part 5; and Schulin, *Die Französische Revolution*, 79–85.

118 See Schulin, *Die Französische Revolution*, 83.

119 On Saint Domingue the slaves themselves fought for their freedom in the Haitian Revolution. See Davis, *Inhuman Bondage*, Chapter 8; the classic study by Cyril Lionel Robert James, *The Black Jacobins: Toussaint L'Ouverture and the San Domingo Revolution* (1938), 2nd revised ed. (New York: Vintage Books, 1963); Laurent Dubois, *Avengers of the New World: The Story of the Haitian Revolution* (Cambridge, MA: The Belknap Press of Harvard University Press, 2004); and Jeremy D. Popkin, *You Are All Free: The Haitian Revolution and the Abolition of Slavery* (Cambridge: Cambridge University Press, 2010).

emancipation of the serfs was achieved in Western and Central Europe by collective violence or decree.

'What is freedom?' asked the future Republican US president James A. Garfield in a speech he gave in Ohio on 4 July 1865. 'Is it mere negation? Is it the bare privilege of not being chained, – of not being bought and sold, branded and scourged? If this is all, then freedom is a bitter mockery, a cruel delusion.'[120] The question, which Garfield posed this way shortly after the Civil War, represented one of the era's greatest challenges, and not only for American policy and the public. It also stood as a key problem of the times for the governments and populations of various European countries and Russia. Just as the politico-legal implementation of the idea of a nation by non-violent *coup d'état* in the French Revolution was only the first stride on the path to nation building, to be followed by that of becoming a reality for the population as a whole, the emancipation of the bonded population – slaves and serfs alike – also consisted of two steps: legal emancipation and then the definition, implementation and shaping of freedom for and by the emancipated people.

From Washington, DC to Paris, Berlin, Vienna and St Petersburg, this second step of emancipation raised essentially the same intricately interwoven questions about the legal, political, economic and social status of the freed people. The core issue to clarify in each society was which possibilities would be opened to the former slaves and serfs so that they could shape their lives, achieve economic independence and become citizens with equal rights and opportunities both socially and politically. The response, irrespective of whether it was serfdom or slavery that had been abolished, clearly depended on certain factors that were just as relevant in Europe and Russia as in the United States.[121] The

---

120 James A. Garfield, 'Suffrage and Safety. Oration Delivered at Ravenna, Ohio. July 4, 1865', in *The Works of James Abram Garfield*, ed. Burke A. Hinsdale, 2 vols. (Boston, MA: J. R. Osgood, 1882–3), vol. 1, 86.

121 See also Hugh Seton-Watson, who undertook a cursory comparison and already noted in 1967 that 'a detailed comparison of the two situations [in Russia and the United States] has yet to be made, and would be well worth undertaking'. Hugh Seton-Watson, *The Russian Empire, 1801–1917* (Oxford: Oxford University Press, 1967), 348. Studies that treat the processes of emancipation separately according to their different forms of bondage – slavery and serfdom – as Bush does in *Servitude in Modern Times*, Chapter 11, overlook these fundamental similarities. So do authors who overestimate the influence of differences in culture, tradition or mentalities between Russia and the United States (for example Kolchin, 'Some Controversial Questions', 55–6).

contemporary actors who were looking at and trying to learn from the solutions in other countries were aware of these parallels.

Differences between the measures taken were less a function of the type of servitude than of the societal conditions from which they sprang, the political system (especially the strength of a central political authority), the prevailing political and economic ideologies, and the way in which the emancipation process had emerged (for instance through legislated reform, revolution or imposition by the victor). Another important aspect was the extent to which the central authority engaged the aristocracy in Europe and Russia, the planter aristocracy in the United States, or other social groups in this process, and whether these groups accepted the emancipation.[122] With these factors in mind, it is possible to delineate a set of typical variations of the emancipation process. The set was not static but rather constantly developing because of changing power relations and continuing debates about the notion of freedom and what it entails. All these factors, in turn, were dominated by one variable, the significance of bonded labour as a resource for the economy in each of the societies. The high population density in Central Europe meant that bonded labour was less important there than in Russia and the United States.

The second step, shaping freedom, was usually as hotly contested as the first, the legal emancipation. The actual provisions of the reform legislation depended on whether it was moulded primarily by the nobility, the enlightened bureaucracy or revolutionary forces, for on continental Europe and in Russia the second step of emancipation gave rise to social movements that used collective violence (insurrection, revolution and war) to achieve their goals. Throughout Western and Central Europe collective violence – peasant unrest and especially the

---

122 The decisive role that absolute monarchy and its proponents played in the emancipation processes is underscored for Europe as a whole by Blum, *The End of the Old Order in Rural Europe*, Chapter 10; and for Russia by Seton-Watson, *The Russian Empire, 1801–1917*, 348; Field, *The End of Serfdom*; and Werner Eugen Mosse, *Perestroika under the Tsars* (London: I. B. Tauris & Co., St Martin's Press distributor, 1992), 35–6, 51–2. Bush's objection to Blum (*Servitude in Modern Times*, Chapter 11) and Bush's assertion that emancipation lay in the interest of the nobility as well (181–6) are unconvincing in light of the sustained resistance to it by most of the nobility on the European continent. The countervailing examples that Bush cites (such as Hungary) confirm the exception to the rule because in these cases a nationalistic nobility supported by the peasants tried to rise up against the monarchy.

revolutions of 1830 and 1848–9 – played a major role in the implementation of freedom. It was primarily about economic interests: land and compensation payments.[123]

Despite all the different ways of going about the second step of the emancipation process, they had several important characteristics in common in Western and Central Europe. First, many governments and authorities took part in the process and decided on numerous measures. In Prussia, for example, eighty-four laws and regulations were passed for purposes of agrarian reform, including the abolition of serfdom. Second, the process of defining freedom took a long time, up to half a century in the German-speaking realm, for instance. Third, the implementation of these laws (especially the instalments that the freed serfs had to pay) often lasted into the twentieth century. In Bavaria, for example, the high inflation that followed World War I helped many peasants clear their debts. Fourth, all agrarian reforms in Central and Western Europe were influenced by the fact that the freed serfs who ran a farm were permitted to take ownership of at least some of the land they cultivated and were thereby able to acquire their own economic base. Different approaches existed, with the outcome depending on the objective of the reform. It either strengthened peasant landownership and an egalitarian democratic tradition in the countryside (as in France) or promoted agro-capitalist structures and polarized differences between rich and poor (as in Prussia east of the Elbe river).[124] Nonetheless, both

---

123 See Schulin, *Die Französische Revolution*, 146–7; Rürup, *Deutschland im 19. Jahrhundert*, 36–46; and Hahn and Berding, *Gebhardt*, vol. 14, section §3c. The significance of collective violence in this process is also emphasized by Bush, *Servitude in Modern Times*, 178–9; and Blum, *The End of the Old Order in Rural Europe*, Chapter 15.

124 The economic and political effects and the assessment of the different modes of peasant emancipation and agrarian reform are still under discussion with regard to the German-speaking areas. The description here draws on Rürup, *Deutschland im 19. Jahrhundert*, 33–54; and on Hahn and Berding, *Gebhardt*, vol. 14, §3c, §10a, §11a, b. On the two models of socio-economic policy, see also Schneider, *Geschichte der Bauernbefreiung*, Chapter 2.3. For France, see Schulin, *Die französische Revolution*, 147; Georges Lefebvre, 'La Révolution française et les paysans', in Lefebvre, *Etudes sur la Révolution française* (Paris: Presses universitaires de France, 1954), 246–68; and Volker Hunecke, 'Antikapitalistische Strömungen in der Französischen Revolution', *Geschichte und Gesellschaft* 4/3 (1978), 291–323. For a comparison of these different modes and their political consequences, see Barrington Moore, *Social Origins of Dictatorship and Democracy: Lord and Peasant in the Making of the Modern World* (London: Penguin Press, 1967).

approaches to reform policy were so strongly oriented to securing basic economic livelihoods and social integration that it was possible to avoid consolidation of the divide between the formerly bonded and the freeborn.

Thanks to internal differentiation and the integrative – though by no means conflict-free – village culture, the stratum of serfs was soon no longer identifiable as such. From the mid-nineteenth century on, the former serfs were farmers and citizens. By contrast, the landless proletariat, which had grown significantly because of the population explosion and reforms, migrated in large numbers to the new industrial cities or to America.[125] These migration processes ensured the dissolution of serfs as a recognizable socio-economic part of society and thereby also resolved the problem of personal bondage and servitude.

Because the two steps of emancipation (its legalization and its implementation) came about in Western and Central Europe through collective violence or the established institutions, the topic elicited no political blockages or efforts to overcome such obstacles by individual violence under non-revolutionary conditions. In short, there were no grounds in Western and Central Europe for turning to terrorism to achieve the legal emancipation of the serfs or to advance or impede the realization of equality for them. However, in situations that offered no realistic prospects for successfully arriving at solutions by political means or collective violence, individual actors resorted to terrorist violence in the struggle to affect the further development of the emancipation process.

This was the case in the United States and Russia. In those two countries, the issue of emancipation remained highly contentious, particularly in its second phase as well. The United States and Russia thereby became arenas for assassinations, with terrorism being used to advance emancipation as well as to impede, undermine and reverse the implementation of measures conceived to facilitate, expand and enhance freedom and equality in everyday life.

John Wilkes Booth's assassination of Abraham Lincoln in 1865 and Dmitry Vladimirovich Karakozov's attempt on the life of Alexander II in 1866 are the first examples. Aware of John Brown's violence, Booth employed terrorism to stop the implementation and development of emancipation towards political, economic, legal and social freedom and

---

125 See Hahn and Berding, *Gebhardt*, vol. 14, 218–85.

equal opportunity, whereas Karakozov followed John Brown by using terrorism in an attempt to advance the process of emancipation. After the revolutionary principles had been successfully enacted by legal means – at least partly on account of revolutionary terrorism – counter-revolutionary or right-wing terrorism was added to social-revolutionary or left-wing terrorism, and nationalist terrorism continued. As already elaborated in the Introduction, this background marked terrorism's three political directions that came to have a powerful impact on the nineteenth and twentieth centuries: social-revolutionary, ethnic-nationalistic and right-wing radical terrorism.[126]

The differentiation and development of the history of terrorism in the nineteenth century, to the extent that it was directed at achieving personal freedom, can therefore be explained only by considering the different courses that emancipation processes took. These processes are crucial for understanding why, during the nineteenth century, there continued to be no terrorist violence regarding the issue of liberating the former serfs in Central and Western Europe, whereas in Russia social-revolutionary terrorism aimed at achieving emancipation was adopted, and right-wing terrorism was prevalent in the United States. The origin of the invention of terrorist violence, however, lay in the idea of the nation and Felice Orsini's attempt to create an Italian republic.

---

126 See also p. 51 above; and Waldmann, *Terrorismus*, Chapter 6, quotation at 99.

2

Bombs for the nation

Felice Orsini's assassination attempt on
Napoleon III and the emergence of Italy

The political blockage in the Italian states

Felice Orsini's violent act is only understandable against the backdrop of the political blockage to nation building in the Italian states around the middle of the nineteenth century. The plethora of little states was a decisive factor in this blockage: just like the German territories, the Apennine peninsula of the eighteenth century was fragmented into many small states as a legacy of the Holy Roman Empire. In addition, two major powers – Bourbon France and Habsburg Austria – had been fighting for pre-eminence in Italy since the dawn of the modern era. Tuscany and Milan had fallen to the Austrian Habsburgs, the French Bourbons had come to rule in Parma-Piacenza, and the Spanish Bourbons held dominion over Naples and Sicily as the Kingdom of the Two Sicilies. The only territory ruled by an Italian dynasty was the Duchy of Savoy-Piedmont, with Turin as its capital city.[1]

In the era of enlightened absolutism, political and economic reforms introduced in the Italian territories had afforded the local elites a certain amount of participation and public discussion. These reforms

---

1 See Angelica Gernert and Michael Groblewski, 'Ein Überblick: Die italienischen Staaten zwischen 1559 und 1814', and Gernert and Groblewski, 'Von den italienischen Staaten zum ersten *Regno d'Italia*: Italienische Geschichte zwischen Renaissance und Risorgimento (1559–1814)', both in Wolfgang Altgeld and Rudolf Lill (eds.), *Kleine italienische Geschichte* (Stuttgart: Reclam, 2002), 185–248; also Giuliano Procacci, *History of the Italian People* (Harmondsworth: Penguin Books, 1978), Chapters 7–8.

unwittingly paved the way for the ideas of the French Revolution to take hold. When the revolution took its course in France in 1789, the period of enlightened reforms was essentially over in Italy. It was for this reason that members of the Italian elite, influenced by the French Revolution, sought new ways and means of achieving societal change. They gathered in clubs and Freemason lodges to discuss, among other subjects, the national unification of Italy. No clear political programme emerged from these circles, however. Instead, it came from the Italian 'Republicans', or 'Jacobins' – supporters of the French Revolution in the Italian states. The greater the government restrictions and repressions in response to reforms, the stronger the Jacobins became.[2]

Young people were particularly enthusiastic about the revolutionary promises of political participation and self-determination. For example, the Jacobin student Filippo Buonarroti (a descendant of Michelangelo) moved to the island of Corsica in 1790, when the Italian-speaking island still belonged to France, and founded the newspaper *Giornale patriottico di Corsica*. It was the first publication of the Risorgimento ('resurgence', 'revival'), the era of building the Italian nation state. Students were also active leaders in organizing various revolutionary uprisings in Piedmont, Bologna and Palermo. The local authorities immediately suppressed these uprisings, however, so the Italian Jacobins pinned even greater hopes on France, which they regarded as a power capable of liberating Italy. To them, the aspirations of the Italian Revolution were identical to those of the French Revolution.[3]

And the Italian revolutionaries were not entirely wrong on this, at least as far as nation building was concerned, for France's victories brought within reach the unification for which the Italian Jacobins were hoping. Within a year (1796–7), the new commander of the French army in Italy, the Corsican Napoleon Bonaparte, brought all northern Italy under his control during the War of the First Coalition (1792–7). Under the sway of his advancing troops Jacobin republics were declared under a red, white and green tricolor. France conquered the Papal States

2 See Gernert and Groblewski, 'Von den Italienischen Staaten zum ersten *Regno d'Italia*', 250; Alexander Grab, 'From the French Revolution to Napoleon', in John Anthony Davis (ed.), *Italy in the Nineteenth Century, 1796–1900* (Oxford: Oxford University Press, 2000), 26; and an example in Reichardt, *Das Blut der Freiheit*, 315–17.

3 See Procacci, *History of the Italian People*, Chapter 9, especially 255–7; Grab, 'From the French Revolution to Napoleon', 26; and Reichardt, *Das Blut der Freiheit*, 317–18.

and helped to proclaim the territory as the Roman Republic in 1798. The following year France took over the Kingdom of Naples, establishing a republic there as well. With the annexation of Piedmont and the preventive occupation of Tuscany, the unification of Italy seemed palpably near for the first time. As self-appointed president of the Repubblica Italiana and (after being crowned emperor) as the king of the Regno d'Italia (Kingdom of Italy), Napoleon advanced the unification of Italy by repealing privileges, introducing and unifying civil codes, and modernizing state administration.[4]

However, this unity and unification of Italy by the grace of Napoleon was not what the Italian democrats had had in mind, as the states founded by Napoleon had an imperial and authoritarian character. France's 'sister republics' on the Apennine peninsula remained satellite states, organized to supply people, material and financial resources for their founder's wars. This fact meant the introduction of universal compulsory military service, high taxes and a reduction of the standard of living, particularly for the lower classes. Political sovereignty looked different.[5] The Napoleonic Wars therefore had two effects: they disseminated promises of political participation and national self-determination that, as the occupying power, they simultaneously denied; through this they strengthened the awareness of an identity distinct from that of the foreign ruler and intensified the demand for national unity and freedom.[6]

After the victory over Napoleon, the territorial order of the Italian states was restored at the Congress of Vienna – just as in the German-speaking realm. All the dynasties that Napoleon had driven out were reinstalled in their territories. By contrast, the old republics succumbed to the new order. Genoa became part of Piedmont, and Venice was

---

4 See Gernert and Groblewski, 'Von den Italienischen Staaten zum ersten *Regno d'Italia*', 250–4; Procacci, *History of the Italian People*, 258–67; and Grab, 'From the French Revolution to Napoleon'.

5 See Gernert and Groblewski, 'Von den Italienischen Staaten zum ersten *Regno d'Italia*', 253; Procacci, *History of the Italian People*, 258–62; Grab, 'From the French Revolution to Napoleon', 29–33, 37–9, 46; Reichardt, *Das Blut der Freiheit*, 315–21. On the counterrevolution in Naples as a reaction, see John Anthony Davis, *Naples and Napoleon: Southern Italy and the European Revolutions (1780–1860)* (Oxford: Oxford University Press, 2000), 87–93 and Chapter 1.6. On Italy in the European context, see David Laven and Lucy Riall, 'Restoration Government and the Legacy of Napoleon', in Laven and Riall, *Napoleon's Legacy: Problems of Government in Restoration Europe* (Oxford: Berg, 2000), 1–6.

6 For a global perspective see Bayly, *The Birth of the Modern World*, 112, 205.

combined with Lombardy to form the Kingdom of Lombardy–Venetia and was integrated into the Habsburg Empire.[7] As in the German-speaking realm, this state system was part of a sophisticated concept of checks and balances whose purpose was to assure peace in Europe and avoid the recurrence of the 'policy of dominion and hegemony of all of continental Europe as that of Napoleonic France'.[8]

In this system, the Italian and German states served as a buffer zone. Their territories were intended to be strong enough for them to protect themselves and the respective other side of Europe from the potential hegemonic ambitions of France or Russia, but too weak to develop and pursue hegemonic ambitions themselves. Italian unification was, there-fore, not in the interest of Europe as defined at the Congress of Vienna.[9] When the congress ended in 1815, the conception of a peace framework imposed 'from above', a static conception inimical to the idea of nation-hood, still appeared reasonable and feasible. But with the gradual growth of the German and Italian national movements, it was bound to become ever more difficult to maintain.[10]

For the Italian population, the decisions made at the Congress of Vienna were a setback in many ways. Some governments recognized that it would not be possible to ignore the social changes that had occurred under Napoleon. Others tried to revert to the old laws along with all their privileges and discrimination. In many cases governments wavered between concessions and repressions, between seeking to reach out to win the trust of the population and trying to put the people back in their traditional place. Every articulation of new political ideas was suppressed, and the more signs of dissatisfaction there were, the greater the repression became, stoking popular discontent with the restoration states. These disputes led to a political blockage that Felice Orsini tried to break with his attempt on the life of French emperor Napoleon III.

---

7 Procacci, *History of the Italian People*, 272–3; David Laven, 'The Age of Restoration', in Davis, *Italy in the Nineteenth Century*, 51–3.

8 Wolfgang Altgeld, 'Das Risorgimento (1815–1876)', in Altgeld and Lill, *Kleine italienische Geschichte*, 261.

9 See ibid., 262; Schulz, *Normen und Praxis*; Hannah Alice Straus, *The Attitude of the Congress of Vienna toward Nationalism in Germany, Italy, and Poland* (New York: Columbia University Press, 1949).

10 See Adolf M. Birke and Günther Heydemann (eds.), *Die Herausforderung des europäischen Staatensystems: Nationale Ideologie und staatliches Interesse zwischen Restauration und Imperialismus* (Göttingen: Vandenhoeck & Ruprecht, 1989).

An Italian revolutionary

Orso Teobaldo Felice Orsini was a typical member of the Italian revolutionary movement and the Risorgimento generation.[11] He was born in December 1819 in Meldola, which lies between Ravenna and Rimini in the Romagna region and belonged to the Papal States. His family came from an old aristocratic line with many branches. It harked back to the Roman Boboni, and over the centuries it had produced several popes and cardinals.

Figure 1. Felice Orsini. Lithograph by Ballagny.
Sailko via Wikimedia Commons.

---

11 The term 'Risorgimento generation' comes from Clara Maria Lovett, *The Democratic Movement in Italy, 1830–1876* (Cambridge, MA: Harvard University Press, 1982), 7. According to Lovett, the members of that political generation were born between 1800 and 1830, took part in the revolution of 1848, and typically came from the middle class or higher. Their fathers had either supported the Italian republics or fought for Napoleon, or both, and had joined secret organizations after Napoleon's defeat. See also Lovett, *The Democratic Movement*, 67–80. Ariana Arisi Rota and Roberto Balzani similarly speak of a 'first Mazzinian generation' in 'Discovering Politics: Action and Recollection in the First Mazzinian Generation', in Silvana Patriarca and Lucy Riall (eds.), *The Risorgimento Revisited: Nationalism and Culture in Nineteenth-Century Italy* (Basingstoke: Palgrave Macmillan, 2012), 77–96. On Orsini see ibid., 88–9.

Orsini's father, Andrea Orsini, had also belonged to the revolutionary movement. He had served as an officer in Napoleon's army and had been captured by the Russians. After his return from tsarist Russia, he became the manager of an estate for a noble who had also served under Napoleon.[12] Once the Papal States had been restored, Andrea Orsini joined the Carboneria, a secret society of opposition figures with Freemason and Jacobin roots. After the fall of Napoleon, this society attracted members especially from the Italian elite and middle classes of the Napoleonic period: civil servants, academics, liberal nobles and members of the rural bourgeoisie, as well as soldiers, officers and generals from the Napoleonic campaigns. They had either built their careers or prospered economically under French rule, then found themselves 'demoted, pensioned off and under surveillance, forced to witness the return of ineffective government, bigoted monarchs, scheming clerics and aristocratic émigrés bent on revenge'. In the secret societies, the opponents of restoration were organized in independent cells, and submitted themselves to rites of initiation and elaborate rituals, and when their commitment was evaluated favourably they could be gradually promoted many levels ahead into the inner circle. In exchange they were protected and could talk about their ideas because it was these societies that drew the people who desired to see Italy as an independent state based on the rule of law.[13]

It was these secret societies which began to practise collective violence in attempting to start insurgencies and revolutions in the kingdoms of Naples and Piedmont in 1820 and 1821. They demanded a constitution and the recognition of popular sovereignty, and, in Piedmont, they also

---

12 On Orsini's childhood and the political activities of his father, see Felice Orsini, *Memoirs and Adventures of Felice Orsini, Written by Himself* (Edinburgh: Thomas Constable, 1857), 1; and Orsini, *Memorie politiche scritte da lui medesimo e dedicate alla gioventù Italiana*, revised ed. (Turino: Presso La Liberia T. Degiorgis, 1858), 15; Luzio, *Felice Orsini*, 7–8; Michael St John Packe, *Orsini: The Story of a Conspirator* (Boston: Little, Brown & Co., 1958), Chapter 1.1.

13 This characterization of the secret societies is based on Altgeld, 'Das Risorgimento (1815–1976)', 272–3, quotation at 272. See also Procacci, *History of the Italian People*, 269; Lucy Riall, *Risorgimento: The History of Italy from Napoleon to Nation State* (Basingstoke: Palgrave Macmillan, 2009), 13. For a European comparison see Carlo Francovich, 'L'azione rivoluzionaria resorgimentale e del movimenti delle nazionalità in Europa prima del 1848', in Luigi Bulferetti and Walter Maturi (eds.), *Nuove questioni di storia del risorgimento*, 2 vols. (Milan: Marzorati, 1969) vol. 1, 457–512, especially sections 1–3.

wanted the restoration of the Kingdom of Italy as a nation. As a matter of fact, the rebels were initially successful in forcing the adoption of constitutions and, in Piedmont, the abdication of the king. But at the Congress of Laibach (a follow-up to the Congress of Vienna), the king of the Two Sicilies appealed to the European monarchs for military intervention, and the Holy Alliance authorized Austria to crush the insurgency. In March 1821, an Austrian expedition corps reinstated the pre-revolutionary conditions in Naples. Shortly thereafter, the heir to the throne in Piedmont succeeded, with help from Austria, in vanquishing the constitutionalists' army and restoring the king as an absolute monarch.[14]

The defeat of the insurgents was followed by a period of harsh repression. Trials were held in various cities around the country. In Naples alone, thirty insurgents were sentenced to death. Some revolutionaries managed to flee abroad, the first wave of political emigration from Italy. In the following years, the restoration's opponents were purged from the military and civil service, and the networks of secret societies were largely annihilated.[15] Andrea Orsini's conspiratorial activities also became known to the authorities. During a family outing to the theatre in Florence, the nine-year-old Felice Orsini witnessed his father being arrested, led out of the theatre in chains, and expelled from Tuscany 'for *political reasons*', as his mother explained to him.[16]

After his father's arrest, Felice Orsini was raised by a politically discrete uncle in Imola, thirty miles north of Meldola. There, the eleven-year-old Orsini experienced the revolution of 1831. The news of the successful July revolution of 1830 in Paris hit the Italian populace 'with the force of a bomb'. On 5 February of the following year, the Italian revolutionaries, including the remaining members of the secret societies, resumed the initiative, this time in the Papal States as well as in the small duchies of central Italy. At first, they again enjoyed rapid successes and set up a government of the 'United Provinces of Italy' in the rebel

---

14 On these insurgencies and their defeat, see Procacci, *History of the Italian People*, 275–7; Riall, *Risorgimento*, 13–15; Francovich, 'L'azione rivoluzionaria risorgimentale', sections 5, 6; Schulz, *Normen und Praxis*, Chapter A.2. On Naples, see Davis, *Naples and Napoleon*, Chapter 3.15.

15 Procacci, *History of the Italian People*, 277–8; Altgeld, 'Das Risorgimento (1815–1876)', 273; Francovich, 'L'azione rivoluzionaria risorgimentale', section 7.

16 Orsini, *Memoirs*, 1; see also Luzio, *Felice Orsini*, 8; and Packe, *Orsini*, Chapter 1.I.

areas. But again, they had little with which to counter Austria's intervention. By the end of March, the *status quo ante* had been re-established.[17]
It was thus not by chance that, for Felice Orsini, this revolution consisted
primarily of three key events: the raising of the Italian national flag over
his school, his uncle promptly removing the cockade displaying the
national colours of Italy that Felice had stuck onto his own hat during
the victorious days of the revolution, and the hard slaps that this same
uncle gave him after hearing Felice express enthusiasm for the imminent arrival of the Austrian army and its military bands.[18]

As a schoolboy, Felice Orsini experienced not only the politicization
and division of society into liberals and supporters of the Pope but also
the Terror of the Centurions (a counterrevolutionary militia in the
Papal States) that followed the revolution.[19] The English edition of his
memoirs contains a telling entry: 'Although young, my indignation was
extreme against the perpetrators of these barbarities.'[20] After Felice
Orsini completed his schooling, his uncle tried to persuade him to join
the Society of Jesus. The adolescent avoided it, however, pointing to
health problems. In 1840, he instead started to study law at the
University of Bologna, the centre of liberalism in Romagna. During the
three years he took to finish his doctoral studies there, Orsini read
widely, from the Latin classics and the literature of the Enlightenment
to the history of the French Revolution and Napoleon's writings. From
the classics, he picked up the legitimacy of killing a tyrant. His readings
about the French Revolution and the Napoleonic wars taught him
about the recent freedom movements, which deeply impressed him: 'So
much blood shed for liberty! So many sacrifices! And then – slavery!'
That had to change, and Felice Orsini was ready to fight for it. He joined
Mazzini's 'Young Italy' at the age of twenty-two while he was still at the
university.[21]

17 Procacci, *History of the Italian People*, 285–6, quotation at 285; Riall, *Risorgimento*,
15–16; Francovich, 'L'azione rivoluzionaria risorgimentale', section 10.

18 Orsini, *Memoirs*, 3; Luzio, *Felice Orsini*, 9–12; and Packe, *Orsini*, 27.

19 On the paramilitary militia organized by the papal Secretary of State Cardinal
Bernetti in the wake of the revolution of 1831 to defend the Papal State against revolution,
see Alan J. Reinerman, 'The Failure of Popular Counter-revolution in Risorgimento
Italy: The Case of the Centurions, 1831–1847', *Historical Journal* 34/1 (1991), 21–41.

20 Orsini, *Memoirs*, 6.

21 See ibid., Chapters 1–3, quotations at 6, 23; Orsini, *Memorie politiche*, Chapter 1.1;
also Luzio, *Felice Orsini*, 12–43; and Packe, *Orsini*, Chapter 1.2–5. Members of the

Figure 2. Giuseppe Mazzini. Wikimedia Commons.

The Young Italy movement was an important political factor in the revolutionary opposition in Italy at the time, and its leader, Giuseppe Mazzini, was an influential figure. He was born in 1805 in Genoa as the son of a professor sympathetic to Jacobin ideas.[22] He was reared in Jansenism, a Catholic reform movement that emphasized the importance of personal faith and personal mission and derived from it the right to challenge authority and the duty to act according to one's convictions. He started studying law at the age of fourteen. Shortly thereafter, he launched a career as a journalist and literary critic. Literature and literary criticism were the political arena of Mazzini's generation, which ascribed a social-revolutionary function to literature. In 1827, Mazzini

Risorgimento generation had typically attended secondary school and university, achieving a significantly above-average level of education, and entered national revolutionary movements at a young age. See Lovett, *The Democratic Movement*, 80–90.

22 On the life, thought, and work of Mazzini, see his autobiography, *Note Autobiografiche* (1861), ed. Mario Menghini, 2nd ed. (Florence: Felice le Monnier, 1944); also Denis Mack Smith, *Mazzini* (New Haven: Yale University Press, 1994); and Roland Sarti, *Mazzini: A Life for the Religion of Politics* (Westport: Praeger, 1997).

joined the Carbonari ('Charcoal-Burners', the members of the Carboneria secret political society), but he was soon betrayed and arrested. A few months later, he was released from jail for lack of evidence, and he went into exile in France, settling down in Marseille. In February 1831, he travelled from Marseille to Corsica, hoping to reach the Italian mainland and to participate in the revolutions. They were crushed, however, before he could arrive in Italy, so he returned to Marseille having achieved nothing. This experience persuaded him that the secret societies were unable to conduct successful revolutions and that revolutionaries would have to find new ways to achieve their goals.[23]

Mazzini analysed the problems of the Carboneria retrospectively in his autobiography, stating that the Carboneria had neither a 'positive, decisive belief' nor a programme of its own and therefore also lacked the power that comes from unity. In his view, the protection that the secret society had received from monarchs as it emerged had given an uncertainty to its direction and had bequeathed it a fatal tendency to draw its leaders from the topmost echelons of society. It therefore treated Italy's revival as a matter for the upper classes rather than as the responsibility of the people, whom Mazzini saw as the main actors in great revolutions. Furthermore, according to Mazzini, the leaders had dampened more than fired the enthusiasm and energy of the young people in its ranks. For all these reasons, he considered the secret societies to be nothing but a negative force.[24] Mazzini viewed the Carboneria as a huge and powerful body without a head, as a society with plenty of goodwill but few, if any, ideas and methods to turn its goals into successful action.

Mazzini wanted to remedy all these problems by founding Giovine (also Giovane) Italia (Young Italy). The movement took on some of the traits of the secret societies but was intended to agitate openly to make all its members, as well as the broader population, aware of its programme and goals: 'God and people and unity, power and liberty' was the motto. These goals were to be attained in a revolution by the people and for the people. To this end, in 1832, Mazzini founded the newspaper *Giovine Italia*, which was funded by Italian emigrants and smuggled into Italy. He opened the first issue with a sentence from Victor Cousin: 'The

---

23 Sarti, *Mazzini*, Chapters 1–3, provide the most detail.
24 Mazzini, *Note Autobiografiche*, 44–6.

young 20- to 35-year-olds grew up in the Revolution . . . They alone are our hope.'[25] Accordingly, he restricted membership to people under the age of forty; that is, to those who were born after 1791. What was formative for them was the autocracy of the Napoleonic regime rather than enthusiasm for the French Revolution, and they therefore relied on their own power, not on France, to achieve changes in the Italian states.

In terms of combat methods, Mazzini advocated the tactic of guerrilla warfare proposed by the officer Carlo Bianco di Saint Jorioz. Bianco had fought in Spain and Greece and had come to Marseille hoping for an Italian revolution. This was where he wrote a military treatise that appeared in 1830, *On National Insurrectionary War by Guerrilla Units, Applied to Italy* (*Della guerra nazionale d'insurrezione per bande, applicata all'Italia*), applied to national insurgency in Italy.[26] Bianco was also the head of a new secret society that the indefatigable Filippo Buonarotti had recently founded, Apofasimeni (plural of the modern Greek adjective ἀποφασισμένος, meaning 'resolute' or, as a noun, 'the resolute one', 'risk taker', which in the literature is also rendered in the sense of 'one who is condemned to death'). It was a particularly militant group that propagated guerrilla warfare and was intended not to shrink from poisoning food stocks and water if it served the objective of a unified, free and independent Italy. In 1831 Mazzini joined the Apofasimeni and met Bianco, from whom he adopted the notion of guerrilla warfare for the revolution. Given the counterrevolutionary violence perpetrated by the governments, Mazzini considered the use of revolutionary violence legitimate.[27]

25 Mazzini, 'Della Giovine Italia' (1832), in Commissione per l'edizione nazionale degli Scritti di Giuseppe Mazzini (ed.), *Scritti editi ed inediti*, vol. 2: *Politica 1* (Imola: Cooperativa tipografico-editrice Paolo Galeati, 1907), 85–113, quotation at 85; see also the (partial) translation in Mack Walter, 'Giuseppe Mazzini on "Young Italy"' (1832), in Mack Walter (ed.), *Metternich's Europe* (London: Macmillan, 1968), 160–9. On the founding of Giovine Italia, see especially Francovich, 'L'azione rivoluzionaria risorgimentale', section 11.

26 Carlo Bianco di St Jorioz, *Della guerra nazionale d'insurrezione per bande, applicata all'Italia: Trattato dedicato ai buoni Italiani da un amico del paese* (Malta: n.p., 1830, available as an e-book from liberliber.it). Translated in partial form as 'A Handbook for Revolutionary Bands', in Walter Laqueur (ed.), *Voices of Terror*, 258–67.

27 See Francovich, 'L'azione rivoluzionaria risorgimentale', 497. On trust in the potential of guerrilla warfare – a trust that Mazzini shared with other revolutionaries of the Risorgimento like Giuseppe Garibaldi and Carlo Pisacane, see Egidio Liberti (ed.), *Tecniche della guerra partigiana nel Risorgimento* (Florence: C. E. Giunti, G. Barbèra, 1972), Sections 4.1, 4.4–8, also 5.1, 5.2, 5.5.

Compared to the methods of the old secret societies, Mazzini's organizational and tactical innovations were indeed notable, but his decisive
innovation was a national ideology. Unlike the Italian Jacobins, Mazzini
was persuaded that France was no longer the vanguard of the revolution
in Europe. However, if France was no longer leading the way, every
people had the right and duty to seize the initiative. He viewed the
Catholic Church, with its rites, hierarchy and worldly authority of the
Pope, a supporter of the counterrevolutionary forces, as no longer being
in step with the times. Mazzini was convinced that a new belief in the
Italian nation and its mission in world history had to replace the church.
He was sure that he saw God showing the way in history, pointing to the
emergence of a divinely predestined Italian nation. Accordingly, he saw
Italy's God-given task to be that of overcoming the Catholic Church and
leading humanity into a new era of democracy. France had failed to do
so, for it had restored the monarchy. But Italy, as Mazzini saw it, with its
long-standing tradition of republican government from ancient through
to medieval and contemporary times, was chosen to make the idea of
popular sovereignty a reality. It was therefore Italy's mission, he asserted,
to achieve emancipation: the European question was to be decided in
Italy.[28]

Mazzini deliberately created a 'republican religion' by combining
religiosity with secularism, a fusion also reflected in his markedly religious manner of expression.[29] Young Italy was less an organization or a
party than 'an "apostolate," a quasi-religious movement that called its
members to a life of political conspiracy and self-sacrifice'. Its founder
was less a politician than a conspirator, prophet and martyr.[30] As in
parts of the German national movement, it was this amalgam of political and historical ideas and mythical religious exaltation, inspired by

---

28 On Mazzini's political ideology, see Sarti, *Mazzini*, 7–8 and especially Rosario
Romeo, 'Mazzinis Programm und sein revolutionärer Einfluß in Europa', in Birke and
Heydemann, *Die Herausforderung des europäischen Staatensystems*, 15–30; also Alberto
Mario Banti, 'Sacrality and the Aesthetics of Politics: Mazzini's Concept of the Nation', in
Christopher Alan Bayly and Eugenio F. Biagini (eds.), *Giuseppe Mazzini and the
Globalisation of Democratic Nationalism, 1830–1920* (Oxford: Oxford University Press,
2008), 59–74.

29 The term 'republican religion' comes from the text *Religious Republicanism:
Joseph Mazzini as a Religious Teacher* (Bath, 1871), written by Mazzini's English follower,
Emilie Ashurst Venturi.

30 Sarti, *Mazzini*, 60; Smith, *Mazzini*, 8, quotation at 5–6.

Romanticism, that so fascinated contemporaries about Mazzini. In Europe and beyond, it enabled him to reach many more people than would have been possible with purely political appeals. His concept of the nation was less democratic, however, compared to that in the French Revolution. It was no longer a country's population who created the nation but rather God, who also determined the national will and national purpose.[31]

Despite all these innovations, Young Italy was no more successful in practical political work than the old secret societies had been. One of Mazzini's first steps in 1831 had been to write a letter to the new king of Sardinia–Piedmont, Carlo Alberto, who himself was a member of the Carboneria. In this letter he asked the king to spearhead the Italian unification movement. When this request proved futile (as expected), Mazzini tried various forms of collective violence. In the spring of 1833, he attempted a rebellion against the royal house of Sardinia–Piedmont, an action whose main consequence was that Mazzini was sentenced to death *in absentia* and expelled from France. He moved from Marseille to Geneva. From there he planned an invasion of Savoy in February 1834, but it, too, failed from the outset because it had neither enough volunteers nor sufficient popular support. The logistical preparations and field communications were inadequate, too, and the authorities had advance knowledge of the plans, enabling them to nip the operation in the bud. This military activity led to Mazzini's expulsion from Switzerland as well. He then moved to London, where he continued to pursue the Italian cause through journalism and conceived a new plan to try and liberate the entire Apennine peninsula in the summer of 1843. But this seditious action never got off the ground, either.[32]

31 See especially Simon Levis Sullam, 'The Moses of Italian Unity: Mazzini and Nationalism as Political Religion', in Bayly and Biagini, *Giuseppe Mazzini*, 107–24. On the reception and effect of Guiseppe Mazzini, see in particular Romeo, 'Mazzinis Programm und sein revolutionärer Einfluß in Europa'; and Bayly and Biagini, *Giuseppe Mazzini and the Globalisation of Democratic Nationalism*, Part 3.

32 Mazzini's letter is printed under the title 'A Carlo Alberto di Savoja. Un Italiano', in Commissione per l'edizione nazionale degli Scritti di Giuseppe Mazzini, *Scritti editi ed inediti*, vol. 2, 17–41. For more information on the letter and about the activities in this period, see Francovich, 'L'azione rivoluzionaria risorgimentale', Sections 12–13; Smith, *Mazzini*, 5–44; Sarti, *Mazzini*, 62–126; and especially the detailed study by Franco Della Peruta, *Mazzini e i rivoluzionari italiani: Il 'partito d'azione' 1830–1845*

An especially brutal reaction, however, followed after this last failed revolutionary attempt by Mazzini and his followers: military courts sentenced twenty-one defendants to death and five to the galleys for life. The investigators spread their nets ever more widely in the course of continued investigations, and in late April 1844 they arrested Andrea Orsini and his son on the strength of a letter that Felice Orsini had sent to Nicola Fabrizi, Mazzini's right-hand man in Italy. It contained the younger Orsini's critique of the pan-Italian effort at emancipation in the summer of 1843, along with constructive suggestions for how to proceed in the future. Orsini had left a copy of the letter with a friend who was a co-conspirator, and it had fallen into the hands of the investigators when they had arrested the friend. Father and son Orsini were taken to San Leo castle, where the Papal States held political prisoners. Felice Orsini received a life sentence in the galleys for 'conspiring against all the governments of Italy' and was stripped of his doctorate. He remained jailed until an amnesty issued by the new Pope Pius IX freed him in June 1846.[33]

Being sentenced and imprisoned did not dissuade Felice Orsini from undertaking further political activities, however. On the contrary, after his release he first went to Meldola and Imola to recuperate from the effects of his confinement. Then in September 1846 he went to Florence, where he opened a law office, fought for freedom of the press, and wrote for the underground press. He ignored or circumvented all attempts to expel him from Tuscany. In the winter of 1847 he re-established contact with Fabrizi, who then visited him in Florence. In January 1848 Orsini was summoned to Rome in the name of a Young Italy committee, and was to proceed from there to southern Italy to support the revolts that had again broken out against the king of the Two Sicilies. Before Orsini

---

(Milan: Feltrinelli, 1974). On the attempted revolution in the summer of 1843 see Chapter 7 in the same publication. On Mazzini's exile in London in this period, also see the book by Marcella Pellegrino Sutcliffe, *Victorian Radicals and Italian Democrats* (Woodbridge: The Royal Historical Society, published by the Boydell Press, 2014), Chapter 1.

33 See Letter 13, 'A Nicola Fabrizi [Bologna, fine Settembre 1843]', published in Alberto Maria Ghisalberti (ed.), *Lettere di Felice Orsini* (Rome: Vittoriano, 1936), 13–28; also Della Peruta, *Mazzini e i revoluzionari italiani*, 400. See also Orsini, *Memoirs*, Chapter 4; Orsini, *Memorie politiche*, 23–43; and Packe, *Orsini*, Chapter 2.2–3. On the overall reaction to the attempted insurgency, see Packe, *Orsini*, Chapter 2.2–3, 52.

had arrived in the south, however, the king had granted a constitution and a liberal government.[34]

In the following weeks and months revolutions broke out all over Italy and continental Europe, and the realization of the goals of national movements throughout the continent by means of collective violence seemed to be within grasp. This was because something unbelievable happened: the March revolution in Germany. The opening phase of the revolution of 1848–9 in those lands spread to Austria–Hungary – to Budapest and to Vienna itself, the very centre of the Holy Alliance. When this news arrived in Lombardy–Venetia, the city populace of Milan and Venice forced the Austrian troops to withdraw. Venice was declared a republic, and Mazzini returned to Italy.[35] Felice Orsini volunteered immediately when the fighting broke out and participated as an officer of a volunteer unit in the battles for Venice.[36] In late November 1848 he returned to the Papal States, where the political situation had become acute, as on 15 November 1848 members of a radical republican group had killed the Roman prime minister, Count Pellegrino Rossi, because they feared (probably with good reason) that he was plotting a coup to repeal the constitution of the Papal States. The act was staged on the model of Caesar's assassination, as the murder of a tyrant. When Rossi entered the Roman parliament, he was encircled by a group of conspirators who stabbed him with daggers. It also served as a signal to revolt. The next day, revolutionaries opened fire on the Quirinale and demanded the appointment of a revolutionary government.[37]

34 On Orsini's return to political activity, see Orsini, *Memoirs*, Chapter 6; and Orsini, *Memorie politiche*, 62–3. See also Packe, *Orsini*, Chapter 2.4, especially 65.

35 For an introduction to the revolution of 1848–9 in Italy, see Procacci, *History of the Italian People*, 299–305; Simonetta Soldani, 'Approaching Europe in the Name of the Nation: The Italian Revolution, 1846–8', in Dieter Dowe, Heinz-Gerhard Haupt, Dieter Langewische and Jonathan Sperber (eds.), *Europe in 1848: Revolution and Reform* (New York: Berghahn Books, 2000), 59–88; Laven, 'The Age of Restoration', 65–73; Altgeld, 'Das Risorgimento (1815–1876)', 281–91; Riall, *Risorgimento*, 20–5; and specifically about the Republic of Venice and its defence, see Paul Ginsborg, *Daniele Manin and the Venetian Revolution of 1848–49* (Cambridge: Cambridge University Press, 1979), especially Chapter 5. On the Austrian situation, see Alan Sked, *The Survival of the Hapsburg Empire: Radetzky, the Imperial Army, and the Class War, 1848* (London: Longman, 1979).

36 See Orsini, *Memoirs*, Chapter 7; Orsini, *Memorie politiche*, 64–7; Luzio, *Felice Orsini*, 60–5; Packe, *Orsini*, 71–89; Ginsborg, *Daniele Manin and the Venetian Revolution*, 199.

37 On the political background and consequences of Rossi's assassination, and on its orchestration and reception as tyrannicide, the best account is still Harry Hearder, 'The Making of the Roman Republic, 1848–1849', *History* 60/199 (1975), 169–84.

Pope Pius IX fled for his life to Gaeta near Naples under the protection of the king of the Two Sicilies. Shortly after this, the members of parliament of the Papal States called for a national assembly to create a constitution. Felice Orsini was elected to represent his home district and took part in the constitutive assembly of 9 February 1849, which, dominated by Mazzini's supporters, deposed the Pope and proclaimed the Roman Republic. Mazzini also belonged to the triumvirate that was to rule the republic. Under his leadership, the Roman Republic became an exemplary democratic experiment in many ways. Orsini met the founder and leader of Young Italy for the first time in mid-April, when Mazzini appointed him envoy extraordinary of the Executive Committee and authorized him to end the machinations of renegade and counterrevolutionary militias in the provinces. Orsini returned to Rome at the end of June, just in time to experience the defeat of the volunteer army, which, with the help of the people of Rome, had defended the republic at the cost of many casualties and injuries.[38]

The military suppression of the Roman Republic was made possible by Louis Napoleon Bonaparte, of all people. The nephew of the first French emperor had returned to Paris from exile after the revolution in February 1848 and had been elected president of the Second Republic in December. Louis Napoleon, who named himself Napoleon III after his *coup d'état* in December 1851, had spent part of his childhood in Italy. When revolutions broke out there in February of 1831, he and his older brother Napoleon Louis assumed command of two revolutionary units in order to march on Rome and 'free the city from the papal yoke'. Napoleon Louis in particular had close contacts to the Carboneria, many of whose members had been Napoleonic officers. They had high hopes of him and his younger brother. Thus it was that the future Napoleon III came to be linked

---

38 For an introduction to the Roman Republic and Mazzini's role as the leading member of the triumvirate, see Riall, *Risorgimento*, 23–5; Smith, *Mazzini*, 64–76; Sarti, *Mazzini*, 138–47; also Hearder, 'The Making of the Roman Republic'; and Sutcliffe, *Victorian Radicals and Italian Democrats*, Chapter 2. On Felice Orsini's role in the revolution and the republic, see his written defence, *Memorie e documenti intorno al Governo della Repubblica Romana* (1850) (Rome: Edizioni dell'Ateneo, 1952); Orsini, *Memoirs*, 72–3, Chapter 7, and documents 35–9; Orsini, *Memorie politiche*, 67–76; Luzio, *Felice Orsini*, 65–77; Packe, *Orsini*, 89–111.

with the secret society and may have even become a member, although he later denied it.[39] Given this revolutionary past in Italy, the Italian Republicans had high expectations of the Second French Republic and its new president in the spring of 1849.

They were therefore particularly bitter when, as president of France, the former Italian revolutionary Louis Napoleon did not side with the revolution in Venice and Rome but rather with the counterrevolution. For reasons of state – most of the French population was Catholic – France, together with Austria and the Kingdom of the Two Sicilies, responded to the Pope's appeal for help after the revolution in Rome by sending an expeditionary corps of 14,000 soldiers under General Oudinot to Italy in late April.[40]

Mazzini had been proven right: the Italian revolutionaries had to rely on their own strength. The militia that had defended the Roman Republic and, in its heyday under the leadership of Giuseppe Garibaldi, had 15,000 volunteers from all of Italy – indeed from throughout Europe – succeeded in repulsing the first attack by Oudinot's corps on 30 April 1849. In early June, too, the volunteers managed to ward off the attack of the well-equipped French troops, which had swelled to 35,000 men. But the battles continued, and on 3 July 1849 the besiegers broke into the city.

---

39 The quotation comes from Johannes Willms, *Napoleon III: Frankreichs letzter Kaiser* (Munich: C. H. Beck, 2008), 26. Giuseppe Orsi, *Recollections of the Last Half-Century* (London: Longmans, Green and Co., 1881), 79, mentions Louis Napoleon's membership in the Carboneria, allegedly drawing on information from Louis Napoleon himself. Luzio, *Felice Orsini*, 10–11, 315, writes that Louis Napoleon later denied any membership in the Carboneria. There is still no agreement in the literature about this question. On this matter and Louis Napoleon's youth in Italy in general, see André Castelot, *Napoléon Trois*, 2 vols. (Paris: Perrin, 1973–4), vol. 1: *Des prisons au pouvoir*, Chapter 3, especially 116; Louis Girard, *Napoléon III* (Paris: Fayard, 1986), in particular 16–18; Pierre Milza, *Napoléon III* (Paris: Perrin, 2004), especially 46; Willms, *Napoleon III*, Chapter 1, which leaves the question open at 25 and note 24. On Louis Napoleon's election as president of the Second Republic and his *coup d'état*, see the relevant sections in the biographical literature and especially Sylvie Aprile, *La IIe République et le Second Empire 1848–1870: Du prince président à Napoléon III* (Paris: Pygmalion, 2000), Chapters 3–4; and Roger Price, *The French Second Empire: An Anatomy of Political Power* (New York: Cambridge University Press, 2001), Chapter 1.

40 On the contradictory political and military objectives of the corps (the president commanded it to remove the republic, which contradicted the parliament and the government without informing them) as well as the rationale of the domestic and foreign policy behind this decision, see Girard, *Napoléon III*, 105–6; Milza, *Napoléon III*, 169–71; and Schulz, *Normen und Praxis*, 179–200.

Figure 3. Napoleon III. After Lafosse, 1848. akg-images, Bildnr.AKG586379.

Protected by American or British passports, some of the republican politicians were able to escape. Many who could not flee were murdered. Garibaldi and the militiamen who felt they could weather the long march set out for Venice to help the republic there, which was under attack from Austrian troops. But, before he and his volunteers could reach the city, the Republic of Venice, too, had to capitulate.[41] The last bastion of the European revolutions of 1848–9 had fallen; the collective fight for an Italian nation had failed. Under protection by French or Austrian troops, the princes returned to their thrones in the Italian states.

---

41 For an introduction to the legendary defence of the Roman Republic by the volunteer army led by Garibaldi and others, and on the march to Venice, see Altgeld, 'Das Risorgimento (1815–1867)', 287–9; Riall, *Risorgimento*, 23–6; still useful is George Macaulay Trevelyan, *Garibaldi's Defence of the Roman Republic* (London: Longmans, Green and Co., 1907), Chapters 6–12; the account (not always reliable) by Frederike Hausmann, *Garibaldi: Die Geschichte eines Abenteurers, der Italien zur Einheit verhalf* (Berlin: Wagenbach, 1999), 60–4; and Lucy Riall, *Garibaldi: Invention of a Hero* (New Haven: Yale University Press, 2007), 75–97.

Among revolutionaries: in exile for Italy

After the fall of the republic, Felice Orsini succeeded in fleeing Rome. He first went to Florence, then to Genoa and onward to Nice, where many revolutionaries from all over Europe gathered when forced from their homelands. In Nice, Orsini met people such as the Russian opposition intellectual Alexander Ivanovich Herzen; the German poet of radical revolutionary verse George Herwegh, of whom he thought little; and Herwegh's wife, Emma Siegmund Herwegh, whom he held in such high esteem that he later dedicated the English version of his autobiography to her.[42] While in Nice, Orsini also tried to launch a small business trading in hemp, but with little success. Furthermore, he wrote about the military geography of Italy and, in response to charges brought by the Papal States, penned a justification for the approach he had taken as Envoy Extraordinary of the Roman Republic. Above all, however, he stayed in touch with his leader, Giuseppe Mazzini, and, to prepare himself physically and mentally for the next revolutionary task, he practised riding and shooting daily and systematically studied literature on military strategy.[43]

When Mazzini called him at last and asked him to collaborate on developing and executing the newest plans for insurrections, Orsini was only too happy to comply. However, their attempt to spark a revolution in Milan in February 1853 failed, as did a second attempt in September of that year in Lunigiana. The local elites distanced themselves from these undertakings; the number of insurgents did not grow as expected and needed. There was betrayal, and many lives were lost. Orsini was

---

42 On these encounters and the resulting entanglements, see Orsini, *Memoirs*, 98–9; Luzio, *Felice Orsini*, 48–51; Packe, *Orsini*, 118–26; for each of the other perspectives, see Ulrich Enzensberger, *Herwegh: Ein Heldenleben* (Frankfurt am Main: Eichborn, 1999), 252–60; Alexander Ivanovich Herzen, *My Past and Thoughts: The Memoirs of Alexander Herzen* (1924) (London: Chatto & Windus, 1968), vol. 2, 700, for the first meeting see 701.

43 Orsini, *Geografia militare della penisola italiana* (Turin: Cugini Pomba E.C. Editori, 1852); Orsini, *Memorie e documenti*. Orsini also planned to write a history of Italy since 1815, but he was unable to carry out this project. According to Packe, a synopsis of this work is said to have appeared in 1859 in *Eco d'Italia*, a newspaper published in New York. The bound volume of the newspaper in the Library of Congress (which is incomplete, however) does not contain this text. On Orsini's other activities in Nice, see especially Orsini, *Memoirs*, 98–101; Luzio, *Felice Orsini*, 7–84; Packe, *Orsini*, 115–18.

captured in the Kingdom of Piedmont and expelled from the territory. He followed Mazzini into exile in London, where he lived as Mazzini's attaché and was supported by him financially until the spring of 1854, at which point Mazzini had him return to Italy to support the outbreak of revolutions. However, all the various attempted insurgencies failed for the same reasons. In December 1854, Orsini was captured in Hermannstadt, Transylvania, where the Italian regiments of the Habsburg army were stationed. He was sent back to Italy, incarcerated in the Austrian fortress of San Giorgio, near Mantua, and after weeks of interrogation was sentenced to death. In March 1856, shortly before the sentence was to be carried out, he managed to escape and made his way through Switzerland to London, where he arrived in early May and went straight to Mazzini.[44]

The relationship between Mazzini, the master of the Young Italy movement, and Orsini, his hitherto unswervingly loyal follower, was no longer quite the same, however. The main reason for the change was that Orsini started to doubt Mazzini's leadership ability. He accused him of 'despotism' and 'establishing new religions'; that is, of pretentions to being a guru. In addition, 'the prophet' – the disparaging way Orsini always referred to Mazzini by late 1857 – might have been a genius with words but not as a man of deeds. 'We must put words aside and act with judgment,' Orsini explained in the English version of his autobiography. 'Let us cease talking, and act.'[45] Such calls implied that he considered himself more competent to plan and conduct successful and effective actions for the cause.

Moreover, Orsini increasingly had the impression that Mazzini was losing touch with the political situation and public opinion in Italy because of his long exile, and that he was therefore making poor decisions. When Orsini arrived in London, the master was in the process of

---

44 The best summary account of the attempted insurgencies by Mazzini and his followers after the revolution of 1848–9 is Procacci, *History of the Italian People*, 306–10. On Orsini's activities, imprisonment in the San Giorgio fortress and escape, see Orsini, *Memoirs*, Chapters 9–14; Orsini, *Memorie politiche*, Chapters 1.6–9, 2.1–11; also Luzio, *Felice Orsini*, 85–257; and Packe, *Orsini*, Chapters 3, 4.

45 Orsini, *Memoirs*, 219; and Letter 193, Felice Orsini to Ausonio Franchi, 15 September 1857, from London, reproduced in Ghisalberti, *Lettere di Felice Orsini*, 237–9, quotation at 238; and Orsini, *Memoirs*, 119, 191. On the use of 'the prophet' to refer to Mazzini, see the various references to him in Letters 201, 203, 204 in Ghisalberti, *Lettere di Felice Orsini*, 246–50.

planning the next revolt for the coming summer, in the Kingdom of Sardinia–Piedmont of all places – the only state with an Italian government, and also the only state that had begun to implement liberal policies after the revolutions in 1848–9 under its liberal prime minister, Camillo Benso, Count of Cavour. It was, moreover, precisely on Cavour and his government that nationally minded Italians and even former democratic revolutionaries were pinning all their hopes at this time.

Figure 4. Camillo Benso, Count of Cavour, by
Antonio Ciseri. Wikimedia Commons.

By involving Piedmont in the Crimean war, Cavour had succeeded in placing the Italian question onto the international agenda at the Paris peace conference in February and March 1856.[46] Orsini was therefore

---

46 For an introduction to Cavour and his Italian policy and about the Kingdom of Piedmont, public opinion and the founding of the Italian national society Società Nazionale specifically also by Mazzini's disillusioned followers, see Procacci, *History of the Italian People*, 310–13; Anthony Cardoza, 'Cavour and Piedmont', in Davis, *Italy in the Nineteenth Century*, 108–31, especially 112–25; Altgeld, 'Das Risorgimento (1815–1876)', 297–9; and Riall, *Risorgimento*, 25–8; also especially Paul Matter, *Cavour et l'unité italienne*, 3 vols. (Paris: Félix Alcan, 1922–7), vol. 2: *1848–1856*, Chapters 6–9; and Peter

certain that an attempted revolt against this government would be counterproductive for Mazzini's side. But Mazzini was not persuaded by
Orsini's arguments and expected his full support for the scheme. When,
in November 1856, Orsini told him that he had always been prepared to
take daring steps but that this action would have to be his last because
he did not want to appear ridiculous, Mazzini expelled him from the
movement. 'I was excommunicated,' Orsini later wrote in the Italian
version of his autobiography.[47]

The attempted revolt at the end of June 1857 failed again for the usual
reasons. In short, all attempts to achieve the national unification of Italy
with collective violence had failed for nearly forty years.[48] Given that
neither the secret societies nor Mazzini and his 'Young Italy' movement
had led a successful revolution, Orsini came to the conclusion that he
had to tread a new path himself.

Felice Orsini came well equipped for such a fresh start. He had experience as a leader, organizer and fighter, and his dedication to the cause
of the Italian democratic nation, which he had served over many years
under atrocious conditions, proved him to be a daring man of high
ideals.

Furthermore, Orsini had also gained some experience in dealing
with the media and the general public. His spectacular, unprecedented
escape from the fortress of San Giorgio had made him a celebrity and
the hero of all those who yearned for the unity and freedom of Italy.

Stadler, *Cavour: Italiens liberaler Reichsgründer* (Munich: Oldenbourg, 2001), 105–23.
For a pan-European perspective on the peace conference in Paris, see Schulz, *Normen
und Praxis*, Chapter B.2.

47 Orsini, *Memorie politiche*, 241, 242. Treatment of Orsini's criticism of Mazzini
and their break with each other is only cursory in the literature on Mazzini. See Smith,
Mazzini, 121–2; Sarti, *Mazzini*, 178. For a detailed description of the conflict from
Orsini's point of view, see Orsini, *Memoirs*, 96–8, 101–3, 118–19, 141, and especially
188–9; Orsini, *Memorie politiche*, 236, 239–45; Ausonio Franchi, 'Appendice alle
memorie di Felice Orsini', in Orsini, *Memorie politiche*, 351–464, Section I; Francesco
Sanvito (ed.), *Lettere edite ed inedite di Felice Orsini, Mazzini, Garibaldi e Guerrazzi
intorno alle cose d'Italia* (Milan: Libreria di Francesco Sanvito, 1862), especially 157–82;
and Packe, *Orsini*, 216–26. Orsini was not alone in criticizing Mazzini. On this point and
the choice between Cavour and Mazzini, which many members of the opposition in the
democratic camp felt they had to make, as well as the various arguments, see the
systematic studies by Lovett, *The Democratic Movement*, 182–6; and Sutcliffe, *Victorian
Radicals and Italian Democrats*, 84, 107–9.

48 See Procacci, *History of the Italian People*, 309.

While still in Zurich, Orsini had sent a report about his escape to Mazzini in London. Mazzini had handed this report to an English friend for translation and then published it in the *Daily News* on 8 June. The article was reprinted in newspapers all around England, including *The Times* of London.[49] After arrival in London, Orsini was courted by various circles of English society and by émigrés who wanted to hear the escape story first-hand.[50] Orsini took up Mazzini's recommendation to publish a report about his experiences. He wrote the manuscript within a few weeks in Italian, and an English woman who supported Young Italy translated it (closely following Mazzini's editorial suggestions). The book appeared in August 1856 and immediately became a bestseller, with 35,000 copies sold in the first year alone.[51] Lastly, Orsini memorized two lectures in English about his time in prison and his escape, and he travelled with them throughout England in the winter of 1856–7. The events were well attended, with Orsini impressing his public less with his lecture, which was difficult to follow, than with his good looks and the 'simplicity, sweetness, and soldierlike straightforwardness of his demeanour', as the Irish politician and journalist Justin McCarthy recalled. In some cities, Orsini even convinced his listeners to send petitions for the Italian cause to the English parliament.[52] In parallel with

49 'Escape of Felice Orsini from an Austrian Dungeon', *Daily News*, 27 May 1856, reprinted as Letter 161, 'A Giuseppe Mazzini [Zurigo], 20 Maggio 1856', in Ghisalberti, *Lettere di Felice Orsini*, 197–201. For reprints of the article under the same or slightly abbreviated title, see, for example, *The Times*, 29 May 1856, 10; *Glasgow Herald*, 30 May 1856; *Liverpool Mercury etc.*, 31 May 1856; *Lloyd's Weekly Newspaper*, 1 June 1856; *Reynold's Newspaper*, 1 June 1856; *Era*, 1 June 1856; *Hull Packet and East Riding Times*, 6 June 1856; and the section 'Foreign Intelligence', *Trewman's Exeter Flying Post or Plymouth and Cornish Advertiser*, 5 June 1856.

50 See especially Justin McCarthy, *Reminiscences*, 2 vols. (London: Chatto & Windus, 1899), vol. 1, 135–9; and Sutcliffe, *Victorian Radicals and Italian Democrats*, 104.

51 Felice Orsini, *The Austrian Dungeons in Italy: A Narrative of Fifteen Months' Imprisonment and Final Escape from the Fortress of St. Giorgio* (London: G. Routledge, 1856). After Orsini's assassination attempt translations appeared in other European languages as well. On the writing of the book and the reception of the text and its author, see Orsini, *Memoirs*, 185–7, 192–4; Orisini, *Memorie politiche*, 233, 237; Luzio, *Felice Orsini*, 3–7; Packe, *Orsini*, 216–21; Rota and Balzani, 'Discovering Politics', 88–9. On the sales numbers, see Letter 195 by Felice Orsini to Ausonio Franchi, 26 September 1857, from London, in Ghisalberti, *Lettere di Felice Orsini*, 239–41, 240.

52 McCarthy, *Reminiscences*, 137. On the lecture tours, see also Orsini, *Memoirs*, 187–8; Orsini, *Memorie politiche*, 237–8; Packe, *Orsini*, 221–2; and Sutcliffe, *Victorian Radicals and Italian Democrats*, 104–5.

these lecture tours, Orsini wrote his autobiography, of which an English translation appeared in May 1857.[53] By the end of the 1850s, all these activities had made Felice Orsini a public figure in Italy and England and beyond. He had made a name for himself.

Seeking alternatives to Mazzini's Young Italy, Orsini initially considered continuing with types of collective violence. With his lecture tour through England drawing to a close, he wrote a letter to Cavour on 31 March 1857 to offer his services to the Kingdom of Piedmont. As Orsini explained to the prime minister, experience had taught him that trifling operations were more likely to hurt than to advance the cause of Italy's unity. Strong force would thus be needed to rid Italy of such powerful and well-organized enemies as Austria and France. He expressed his readiness and willingness to serve any Italian government (except that of the Pope) that would put its means and army in the service of Italian national independence. Although he was a stalwart republican, as his letter lets Cavour know, Orsini maintained that, without independence, freedom was an empty dream and that independence had to rank first. As far as the political system was concerned, he wrote that he would bend to the national will.[54] Cavour later conceded, 'the letter that Orsini wrote to me was noble and emphatic' and 'a credit to Orsini.' Orsini never received a reply, however; the prime minister of the Kingdom of Sardinia–Piedmont believed it would be politically unwise to answer. He did not want to resort to any revolutionary means against Austria.[55] Thus Orsini's attempt to move into the realm of collective violence legitimized by the state came to naught.

---

53 Orsini, *Memoirs*. See also Orsini, *Memorie politiche*, 242. Rota and Balzani show that it was the success of Orsini's book and their personal and individual style that contributed to the dispute with Mazzini, for whom Orsini moved too far from the 'collective "cause"'. See Rota and Balzani, 'Discovering Politics', 88–9.

54 Letter from Felice Orsini to Camillo Benso di Cavour, 31 March 1857, from Edinburgh, reprinted in Camillo Benso conte di Cavour, *Epistolario*, 21 vols. (Florence: Leo S. Olschki, 1962–2008), vol. 14.1, 152–3; also in Ghisalberti, *Lettere di Felice Orsini*, Letter 182, 221–2. See also the similar explanations in Orsini, *Memoirs*, 191; and additionally Packe, *Orsini*, 223–4.

55 Camillo Benso di Cavour to Emanuele Tapparelli d'Azeglio and to Salvatore Pes di Villamarina on 1 March 1858 (n.p.), reprinted in Cavour, *Epistolario*, vol. 15.1, 208–9, 209–10; quotations at 208, 209. See these letters also for Cavour's explanation of why he did not respond to Orsini's letter.

In September, Orsini had a new idea. He wanted to start a new movement of his own with the Hungarian revolutionary Lajos Kossuth and
other Italian and French 'true and good republicans'. It would operate
from Italy. The movement would not exhaust itself in constantly trying
to initiate revolts but rather would engage – at the right moment and
when it was really worth fighting – in a strategically clever way by joining forces with others, such as the troops of the Kingdom of Piedmont.
He planned to take over a Turin newspaper called *La Ragione* (The Voice
of Reason) together with other 'excommunicated' former members of
Young Italy and thereby compete with Mazzini's Genoa-based newspaper *Giovine Italia*, the intention being to become the best organ for
presenting republican views: 'the republican *centre*'.[56] Substantively, the
new movement would draw on the books he had already published. To
this end he combined the original Italian versions of the two texts he
had published in English in a new volume, revising them in a more
programmatic, didactic style. He also added direct appeals to the Italian
youth, at whom his book was expressly targeted. The volume appeared
in Turin in January 1858.[57]

It was not easy to build a movement to rival Young Italy, however.
Financing turned out to be particularly difficult. Mazzini's last abortive
attempt at revolt had cost the Italian freedom fighters much sympathy in
England as well. In addition, the so-called Indian Rebellion against
British colonial rule had been preoccupying the public in England since
May 1857. The Italian cause was overshadowed, and the willingness to
donate to it declined. Orsini tried to deal with this problem by planning
a trip to New York in the autumn of 1857 to gather the funds he needed
to build up his new movement in the United States.

---

56 Letters 192, 193 from Felice Orsini to Ausonio Franchi on 1 and 15 September
1857 from Glastonbury (England) and London respectively, reprinted in Ghisalberti,
Lettere di Felice Orsini, 234–7, 237–9, quotations at 236, 238. See also Letter 195
from Felice Orsini to Ausonio Franchi, 26 September 1857, from London, in
Ghisalberti, *Lettere di Felice Orsini*, 239–41; Franchi, 'Appendice alle memorie di
Felice Orsini'; Packe, *Orsini*, 226–7; Sutcliffe, *Victorian Radicals and Italian
Democrats*, 105–6.

57 Orsini, *Memorie politiche*. On Orsini's programme and his appeals, see especially
Chapters 2.13–16 and the conclusion. For background on the making of the book, see
especially Franchi, 'Appendice alle memorie di Felice Orsini'; and Packe, *Orsini*, 219–24.
For the date of publication, see Letter 204 from Felice Orsini to Giuseppe Garibaldi,
26 November 1857, from London, in Ghisalberti, *Lettere di Felice Orsini*, 249–50, note 3.

Then a new and this time definitively insurmountable problem arose: Orsini was no longer allowed to enter Italy. In late September he had gone to the London embassy of the Kingdom of Sardinia–Piedmont and had submitted a request for a passport to visit his family in Turin. The application was rejected. Instead, he was permitted to travel to Nice only, and only by sea.[58] The embassy's decision to deny Orsini the right to enter Italy greatly increased the difficulties he faced in organizing the movement. The entry ban cut him off from his potential mass base and prevented him from undertaking any kind of collective action in the interests of Italian nation building.

The situation described theoretically in Chapter 1 had thus unfolded: the repeated use of different forms of collective violence had repeatedly encountered insurmountable resistance over a long period without achieving the desired goal – the creation of a nation state. Nevertheless, a member of the elite who was particularly engaged in this cause, Felice Orsini, still envisioned the national unification of Italy as a goal. When all further collective action became impossible, individual violence became an option to be taken seriously.

From political murder to terrorist tactic

Exactly when and how Felice Orsini decided to make an attempt on Napoleon III's life cannot be reconstructed with complete certainty. The literature agrees that the idea probably occurred to him no later than the autumn of 1856; that is, soon after his escape from the fortress of San Giorgio and his arrival in London. It is generally assumed that Orsini did not develop this idea alone, and that it actually emerged in conversations with other émigrés in the places where they met in Soho, such as Thomas Wyld's Reading Room or di Giorgi's Café Suisse.[59]

---

58 See especially Letters 195, 197 from Felice Orsini to Ausonio Franchi, 26 September, 15 October 1857, from London, reprinted in Ghisalberti, *Lettere di Felice Orsini*, 239–41, 242–4; also Packe, *Orsini*, 232–3.

59 For the topography of the Italian emigration in nineteenth-century London and the meeting places mentioned here, see Enrico Verdecchia, *Londra die cospiratori: L'esilio londinese dei padri del Risorgimento* (Milan: Tropea, 2010), 470; also Packe, *Orsini*, 228. Di Giorgi later helped prepare the assassination attempt. For example, he moved with his café to Brussels in December 1857, transporting parts of Orsini's bombs to the European mainland.

Bitterness about Napoleon III was generally high among the exiles in London. Democrats who had been forced to flee from Italy could not forgive 'the murderer of the Roman Republic', particularly because Louis Napoleon had so blatantly repudiated his earlier revolutionary beliefs and, as Felice Orsini and many other revolutionaries believed, had broken the oath he had sworn upon joining the Carboneria.[60]

Since Louis Napoleon's *coup d'état* on 2 December 1851, which heralded the end of the Second Republic and the restoration of the empire, Italian émigrés had been joined by vast numbers of refugees from France. In the days after the coup, they had witnessed the army's bloody suppression of the republic's supporters who had protested the dissolution of parliament. They fled the wave of repressions that threatened anyone indicating a critical stance towards the new political conditions. Months after the coup, French jails still held nearly 27,000 political prisoners without any prospect of a trial, and they had good reason to fear banishment or prison sentences as well as the loss of property, profession and reputation. The ' "legal terror" of this repression, which raged for weeks in some places, was of a brutality that had never been seen or imagined before', wrote Johannes Willms, a biographer who was otherwise well disposed to the emperor. 'The much-vaunted civility of the nineteenth century ended on this 2 December 1851, when there appeared for the first time something of the horror that would disfigure the face of the twentieth century.'[61] The democrats who remained in France and the republicans who had fled into exile in London agreed that Napoleon III was their worst enemy.

There had been several attempts on the life of Napoleon III since the *coup d'état*; others had been discovered in the planning stages. According to Sylvie Aprile, the very fact that the Second Empire was so profoundly a creation of Napoleon III and that power was so exclusively concentrated in him was bound to spawn assassination attempts by opponents wanting to overthrow the regime, for without this emperor (who had no

---

60 See Luzio, *Felice Orsini*, 10, 261.

61 Willms, *Napoleon III*, 104. On Louis Napoleon's *coup d'état* and the subsequent repression, see especially Aprile, *La IIe République*, 199–218 (the numbers are at 217); also Price, *The French Second Empire*, 27–37. Another worthwhile secondary resource is the analysis by Karl Marx, 'The Eighteenth Brumaire of Louis Bonaparte', in Karl Marx and Friedrich Engels, *Collected Works*, vol. 11: *Marx and Engels: 1851–53* (London: Lawrence & Wishart, 1979), 99–197.

heirs until 1856) the empire would have no future.[62] For this reason, plans to murder Louis Napoleon had existed in various quarters since 2 December, the *Deux-Décembre*. As early as 1852 the police had discovered a plot by workers in Paris in the affair of the Rue de la Reine Blanche. They had also found an 'infernal machine' in Marseille shortly before Louis Napoleon travelled through the city. In January 1853 there were rumours of an attempt to murder the newly proclaimed emperor on the day of his wedding as he was leaving the cathedral of Notre Dame. Half a year later, a group of students tried to take his life as he made his way from his palace to the horse races. In the same year, another attack was tried at the exit of the Opéra Comique in Paris. In March 1854, twenty-one people in Angers, and shortly thereafter forty-eight people in Tours, were accused of plotting a conspiracy against the emperor. In both cases, two well-known émigrés, Mazzini and the French republican Alexandre August Ledru-Rollin, were cast as the masterminds behind the plot. As Aprile comments, 'it is difficult to distinguish between the reality of illegal networks and the fictions manufactured by the authorities.'[63] In 1854, there was an attempt on Napoleon III's life as he journeyed by rail from Lille to Tournai. In 1855 another rebellion was tried in Angers, as was an assassination attempt by the Italian Giovanni Pianori en route to the Bois de Boulogne. Pianori had been a volunteer under Garibaldi in the battles to defend Rome and wanted to avenge the defeat of the republic. Acting with two accomplices two years later, another Italian, Paolo Tibaldi, tried to kill the emperor for the same reason. These acts, too, were attributed to Mazzini and Ledru-Rollin.[64]

There was clearly no lack of effort to take the life of Napoleon III and thereby bring down the empire. Nonetheless, all these attempted assassinations fall into the category of political murder.[65] Granted, they were undertaken (if these conspiracies ever really existed) by people who

---

62 Aprile, *La IIe République*, 282.

63 Ibid., 283. On the conspiracies and assassination attempts as well as the historiographic difficulties in assessing them, see ibid., 282–3; see also Price, *The French Second Empire*, 159–66; and Adrien Dansette, *L'attentat d'Orsini* (Paris: Del Duca Biarritz, 1964), 26–9.

64 On these attempted assassinations, see especially Aprile, *La IIe République*, 283; Dansette, *L'attentat d'Orsini*, 29–33; also Castelot, *Napoléon Trois*, vol. 2: *L'aube des temps modernes*, 275–7. On Tibaldi, see especially Luzio, *Felice Orsini*, 270–90.

65 For a discussion of the differences between political murders and terrorist attacks, also see the concluding discussion in this volume, 601–4.

belonged not to the political elite but to the politically engaged population – workers, students and members of Italian revolutionary movements. Moreover, they acted without legitimation from political or
church authorities. At best they had the backing of leaders of revolutionary movements. But the violence they engaged in was still primarily
instrumental. Killing Napoleon III would have achieved their objective,
such as revenge, the fall of the empire that depended on him, or both. At
least according to currently available research, these people were not
primarily interested in the psychological effect of violence, which was
then expected to achieve the intended political effects. Therefore these
assassination attempts do not yet qualify as terrorist acts. At most they
were violent phenomena on the way to terrorism.

It is generally assumed that the French émigré Dr Simon François
Bernard had a decisive influence on Orsini's assassination attempt.[66]
According to an anonymous article that appeared at the time of the
attempt, Bernard was born in Carcassonne to a family with republican
sentiments in 1817. He was thus two years older than Orsini. Bernard
had studied medicine, acquiring sound knowledge of the natural
sciences, including chemistry, and he became a follower of the early
socialist Charles Fourier. After working as a military doctor in the
French navy in South America, he returned to France and became the
editor of provincial democratic newspapers. Soon he also began to
lecture around the country on political, economic and social issues.
When the 1848 revolution broke out, he went to Paris, where he founded
the political club Bonne nouvelle (Good News), speaking there before
audiences of 4,000 to 5,000 people every evening. After the suppression
of the June insurrection, however, this club was closed, as were the
others Bernard started thereafter. After the 'semi-coup' and the parliament's self-dissolution in May 1849, he had to leave for Belgium to avoid
pursuit by the French authorities. From there he went into exile in
England. It was in London that he met Felice Orsini and offered to
become his coach and manager. Bernard organized lecture tours for
him, edited his speeches, accompanied him on his travels through Great
Britain, and arranged for the publication of the English edition of his
memoirs. Orsini and Bernard also worked together to prepare the

---

66 See especially Luzio, *Felice Orsini*, 286–7; and Dansette, *L'attentat d'Orsini*, 58–9,
62.

attempted assassination, with Orsini drawing on Bernard's expertise in chemistry, among other things.[67]

Other people supported them from the beginning or joined their endeavour later. The most important of these were Giuseppe Andrea Pieri, an émigré from Lucca in Birmingham; Thomas Allsop, a lawyer, follower of the Chartists, and one of Bernard's close associates; George Jacob Holyoake, a follower of Robert Owen's ideas and editor of various radical newspapers; and Joseph Cowen, a radical journalist and politician from Blaydon-on-Tyne, who is believed to have had long conversations with Orsini about the legitimacy of murdering a tyrant.[68]

Orsini and Bernard were of the same mind politically. They were both passionate republicans and endorsed national self-determination. Both men rejected Mazzini, his religiously tinged idea of the nation and his personality cult. They also agreed about Napoleon III. According to Bernard, the French emperor – with the help of his entourage – had used deceit and force to block all political progress, sown the seeds of hate, relentlessly exiled dissidents after his victory, and thereby subjugated France, Italy and Mexico to his will.[69] Orsini agreed: 'Italy finds herself at the present moment in the most deplorable condition that can be imagined.' But, he continued, this condition would not last much longer, for the Second Empire rested solely on Napoleon III; indeed, the restoration in all of Europe depended on the French emperor's policy. Orsini was convinced that this man and the despotic and treasonous government supporting him would not be tolerated for long.[70]

'But why does everything depend upon Napoleon?' asked Orsini rhetorically in his autobiography, to which he answered, 'Because he has

67 For Bernard's biography and his collaboration with Orsini, see Lancet, *Life of Dr. Bernard, with Portrait and Judgment of the Press on His Trial* (London: Holyoake, 1858); James Gordon Allan (ed.), *The Speech of Edwin James Esq, One of Her Majesty's Counsel, in Defence of Dr. Simon Bernard, Delivered at the Central Criminal Court, on Friday, the 16th of April, 1858* (London: Effingham Wilson, 1858); Felix Pyrax, *Sur la tombe du Docteur Simon Bernard* (London, 1862); Dansette, *L'attentat d'Orsini*, 59–62; and Packe, *Orsini*, 228–30.

68 About the accomplices and their recruitment, see Luzio, *Felice Orsini*, 290–308; Packe, *Orsini*, 230–2; Dansette, *L'attentat d'Orsini*, 58–63; and Sutcliffe, *Victorian Radicals and Italian Democrats*, 104. On the conversations with Cowen, see especially George Jacob Holyoake, *Sixty Years of an Agitator's Life*, vol. 2 (London: T. Fisher Unwin, 1892), 223. On the question of legitimacy in a broader theoretical and historical context, see Dietze, 'Legitimacy and Security from a Historical Perspective', especially 152–5.

69 See Pyrax, *Sur la tombe du Docteur Simon Bernard*, 6–7.

70 Orsini, *Memoirs*, 190.

a large army at his disposal.' With another European partner fighting alongside him, this military power would enable Napoleon to win any war – including one in coalition with an Italian state against Austria. Furthermore, according to Orsini, France was the linchpin in a pan-European chain reaction. As he saw it, a war of independence in Italy would unleash another revolution in France, which would lead to a European revolutionary war, as already indicated in 1848–9. 'A war of independence in Italy; a revolution in Paris; a war of principles and republicanism in continental Europe; these are the three great events which would rapidly follow each other.'[71] In Orsini's opinion, it was precisely because Napoleon III and the other European despots were aware of this fact that they viciously suppressed every independence movement in Italy. According to Orsini, the French emperor was thus pivotal for two reasons: France's military might and the country's political role in Europe, such that the future of revolutionary principles in France and all of Europe – political participation and national self-determination – hinged on Napoleon III's actions. In other words, as long as Napoleon III sided with reactionary forces in Europe, he would block every move towards national independence and self-determination in Italy and the rest of Europe.

What did Felice Orsini hope to achieve by assassinating Napoleon III? What political consequences could such an act of individual violence have in the political situation as he conceived it? As an experienced conspirator, Orsini gave no advance comment on this point in a way that could have been passed down. In the initial interrogation and at his trial, however, he did explain his intention. Together, these statements made on two separate occasions express Orsini's conviction that the chain reaction he had described in his memoirs – war of independence in Italy, revolution in France, European revolution – could just as well begin elsewhere, namely in Paris: 'We [Pieri and Orsini] were persuaded that the surest way of launching a revolution in Italy would be a revolution in France and that the surest way to get a revolution going in France would be to assassinate the emperor.'[72] The revolutions of 1830 and 1848

---

71 Ibid., 190. Similar statements appear in the Italian version; see Orsini, *Memorie politiche*, 249–50.

72 Felice Orsini in the first interrogation on 9 February 1858, read by the presiding official while questioning Orsini on 25 February 1858, in Constantin-Achille Dandraut (ed.), *Textuel: Procès Orsini, contenant par entier les débats judiciaires devant la Cour*

and the assassination of Prime Minister Rossi in 1848 in Rome were events that made this assumption seem justified. Orsini's assassination attempt was therefore an effort to put Metternich's observation into political practice: 'When Paris sneezes, the rest of Europe catches a cold.' Orsini sought to elicit a sneeze and thereby bring on the desired therapeutic cold.[73] Orsini also explained in the trial that his analysis of the political situation facing all the governments in Europe had revealed that only Napoleon III could end the occupation of Italy. The past political behaviour of the emperor, however, testified that Napoleon III 'did not want to do what only he could do'. As Orsini stated, 'I believed him to be an obstacle. And so, I told myself that he had to be removed. I acted as Brutus did. He has murdered my country; I wanted to murder him.'[74]

Orsini's intention in trying to assassinate Napoleon III was therefore to remove a political hurdle from Italy's path to independence and national self-determination. By removing this hurdle, he hoped to send the signal for a revolution in France, which would then incite a revolution in Italy. The assassination attempt had an element of revenge as well. Orsini wanted to kill the person who had put down the revolutionary movement in Italy. As emphasized by his comparison of his act with Brutus's conspiracy against Caesar, Orsini portrayed his assassination attempt as a tyrannicide.

Nevertheless, Orsini did not immediately act on the ideas he expressed in 1856. Allessandro Luzio considers Paolo Tibaldi's attempted murder of the French emperor in June 1857 to have been a key stimulus in Orsini's attack on Napoleon III. Luzio explains that Orsini, after breaking with Mazzini, found the idea of such an attack particularly attractive because it offered him the opportunity to achieve what his former chief appeared to have repeatedly failed to do. Orsini entered into 'a secret,

---

d'assises de la Seine et la Cour de cassation, le récit de l'exécution, de la commutation de peine, les lettres de Rudio et d'Orsini (Turin: Impr. nationale de G. Biancardi, 1857), 29.

73 The underlying certainty about the capacity to *make* revolutions has been systematically analysed by Reinhart Koselleck. See Neithard Bulst, Jorg Fisch, Reinhart Koselleck and Christian Maier, 'Revolution, Rebellion, Aufruhr, Bürgerkrieg', in Brunner, Conze and Koselleck, *Geschichtliche Grundbegriffe*, vol. 5, section 5.3.a. See also Koselleck, 'Historical Criteria of the Modern Concept of Revolution', in Koselleck, *Futures Past*, 54–5.

74 Felice Orsini at the trial on 25 February 1858, quoted in Dandraut, *Textuel*, 28, see also 34.

tacit contest' with Mazzini and his followers. Orsini wanted to prove that he, unlike Mazzini, was not only a man of words but also a man of action and a better conspirator. If he were to survive the assassination, the act should also become a rallying call to his alternative revolutionary national movement.[75] For that purpose, though, the attack would have to be spectacular and attract significant media attention. According to Luzio, Orsini considered the past attempts on the life of the French emperor by Mazzini, Ledru-Rollin and their supporters to have been the acts of 'common executors' (*volgari esecutori*), armed men who could not free themselves from the classical routine of political murders and who tried in vain with rusty daggers to carry out the grand act of tyrannicide. By contrast, he, Orsini, would use the infernal machine honed by Bernard to commit a 'modern, grand, and terrible' act ('io sarò moderno, grandioso, terribile applicando le macchinette infernali').[76] Orsini wanted to trump Mazzini and his followers. They were also, therefore, the indirect targets of the attempted assassination.[77]

The idea that he might not survive the attack on Napoleon III did not scare Orsini. The physically and psychologically demanding years he had spent in the revolutionary underground had familiarized him all too well with thoughts of suicide. His eighteen-month imprisonment in Mantua and his escape had not made his life any easier. He suffered frequently from severe headaches, fever, depression and anxiety. In these periods he feared he was losing his mind. He had also injured his leg during his escape, and the resulting pains never left him. To carry on despite all these problems, he regularly took strong medication or drugs. In addition to these hardships, he also had financial worries. To Orsini, death was therefore not particularly frightening, especially because he hoped his would serve a higher purpose, the national liberation of Italy.[78]

75 See Luzio, *Felice Orsini*, 269–79, quotation at 269, summary at 279. A similar interpretation appeared earlier in Holyoake, *Sixty Years of an Agitator's Life*, vol. 2, 222. See also Packe, *Orsini*, 227.

76 Luzio, *Felice Orsini*, 285–6.

77 It is not unusual for competition between political organizations and their leaders to escalate the use of violence, even to the point of terrorism. See Stephen Nemeth, 'The Effect of Competition on Terrorist Group Operations', *Journal of Conflict Resolution*, 20 (January 2013), jcr.sagepub.com.

78 See Orsini, *Memorie politiche*, 237; and Packe, *Orsini*, 224–8. For the human and social costs as well as the financial consequences of life in exile and in the revolutionary underground, see the systematic discussion in Lovett, *Democratic Movement*, 165–82.

The covert preparations for the assassination of Napoleon III began in mid-October 1857. First, Orsini, Pieri and Bernard recruited helpers, including Carlo Camillo de Rudio and Antonio Gomez, who had fought in all the arenas of the Italian revolution and were living in exile in London, and Outrequin, a businessman in Paris. They obtained the requisite chemicals from a pharmacy in London, allowing them to produce mercury fulminate (to be precise, mercury (II) fulminate, $C_2HgN_2O_2$), which at the time was often used in detonators and blasting caps. They bought three revolvers with all necessary supplies in Birmingham and commissioned the respected metal engineer Taylor to make them six grenades 'as large as a Dutch cheese'. Taylor was instructed to make them exactly according to a wooden model that they provided him, which they had copied from grenades that had been developed for use in the Crimean War, which had ended the year prior. With Bernard's help, Orsini had designed the bombs to explode on impact without priming, rendering them considerably more powerful than conventional models of this kind. George Jacob Holyoake tested two of these bombs with a colleague in Sheffield and Devon and reported satisfactory results back to London.[79] In late November Orsini applied for passports and visas for Brussels under the name of Allsop and withdrew 435 pounds in gold from the Bank of England, money he had earned from his lectures. On 28 November 1857 he left England for Brussels and travelled from there to Paris by train. It was a risky trip because Orsini was carrying the mercury fulminate under his arm in a package that had to be kept moist because otherwise it could explode even without being ignited or knocked. The other conspirators followed, joining him by early January. The London police later maintained that they had informed Paris of Orsini's date of departure, route and intentions, as well as those of his co-conspirators.

---

79 See the commissioning letter reprinted in Dandraut, *Textuel*, 59. The bombs and the way they functioned are best described in Dansette, *L'attentat d'Orsini*, 17–18. There are different accounts in the literature about how Felice Orsini had the idea of developing and using such bombs. Orsini's contemporary, Enrico Montazio (an alias of Enrico Valtancoli), believed that Bernard was covering up with an invented story that a bomb in a Belgian museum had served as a model (see Montazio, *Felice Orsini* [Turin: Dall'unione tipografico-editrice, 1862], 89), but Dansette, *L'attentat d'Orsini*, 29, thinks that the bomb in question was of the type used in the railroad attack in 1854. On the bomb tests, see Holyoake, *Sixty Years of an Agitator's Life*, vol. 2, Chapter 60, quotation at 21.

If that claim was indeed true, the matter was definitely not pursued further in Paris.[80]

Felice Orsini's tactical and strategic thinking and the clandestine character of the preparations, thus indicates that the design and intention of his plans for the assassination of Napoleon III no longer amounted to mere tyrannicide; they included all the essential features of terrorism. It was a carefully conceived act of violence by the underground against a political order, specifically the French Second Empire and the restoration governments in Europe. Napoleon III stood for both camps. The act was planned to be a surprise attack resulting in a shockingly spectacular and psychologically incisive break with societal norms. This effect was expected to trigger major political reactions and changes – revolutions in France and Italy and, consequently, throughout the rest of Europe. Achieving the political objective depended on the attack's effect on the public. It was an indirect tactic that relied on the public's reactions. Orsini's violence also had an instrumental and symbolic character, for he wanted the assassination of Napoleon III to eliminate the blockage in the political system of France and all of Europe, as well as to send a signal to sympathetic republicans that it was time to start the revolution. Thus Orisini's violence was aimed directly at Napoleon III as a victim and addressed indirectly to the democrats in France, Italy and the rest of Europe as the target. However, Orsini did not have a strategy of provocation. There is no recognizable evidence of an intention to escalate an existing conflict and to count on the opponent's overreaction.[81] Whether and to what extent these tactical and strategic ideas could successfully be put into practice had yet to be seen.

---

80 See Orsini's statements in Dandraut, *Textuel*, 29–34; Pierre François Gustave de la Gorce, *Histoire du Second Empire*, 7 vols. (Paris: Plon, 1894–1905), vol. 2, 216–18; Dansette, *L'attentat d'Orsini*, Chapter 4; Packe, *Orsini*, 238–50. For the reports by the London police to Paris, see especially Count Charles Frederick Vitzthum von Eckstädt, *St. Petersburg and London in the Years 1852–64: Reminiscences* (London: Longmans, Green and Co., 1887), vol. 1, 231–2; and, as a sequel, Luzio, *Felice Orsini*, 287–8. For a different view see Dansette, *L'attentat d'Orsini*, 58.

81 For a discussion about whether Orsini's assassination attempt on Napoleon III qualifies as terrorism, see above, p. 40, especially note 104. The analysis here corresponds with Martin Miller's judgement: 'The quantum leap into the modern age of terrorist theory made by Heinzen in his essay "Murder" was matched in deed by the daring attempt on the life of Napoleon III by Felice Orsini nine years later. Although there had been earlier assassination attempts on European rulers, Orsini's was the first to be carried out for explicitly political reasons as part of a secret and transnational conspiracy

The attempted assassination at the opera

After arriving in Paris, Orsini checked out the terrain. Every day he went riding in the Bois de Boulogne, where Napoleon III often appeared on horseback or in an open carriage. Usually, the emperor politely greeted the high society gathered there, chatting a bit with the locals and the foreigners. 'One day,' Orsini's landlord later testified at the trial, 'Mr Orsini told me that he had seen the emperor; he even added that the emperor showed no fear.'[82] Orsini now knew his intended victim by face, and Napoleon III's fearlessness apparently impressed him.

Orsini soon found a reliable way to locate the emperor. He learned that the illumination gala of the Le Peletier opera (known as the Italian opera) indicated on which day Napoleon III would attend a performance. Later, at the trial, he explained to the court, 'When I saw the preparations for the lighting on 14 January, I understood that the emperor would be going to the opera in the evening.'[83] That is why he, too, had gone over to the opera house that night. Ironically, the programme for that performance was full of insurgency and regicide, with a well-known Italian baritone singing in Rossini's *William Tell* to mark his final appearance. That work was to be followed by an act from Daniel Auber's *The Mute Girl of Portici* and another from Gaetano Donizetti's *Mary Stuart*, as well as the ballet from Auber's *Gustavus III, or the Masked Ball*, which staged the murder of King Gustav III of Sweden.[84] Whether Orsini specifically chose the opera house and this performance as a venue for his assassination attempt because of the themes of these operas and what they might say about his attempt has to remain an open question.

---

in the context of simultaneously creating an atmosphere of intimidation and fear in the general society.' Martin A. Miller, 'The Intellectual Origins of Modern Terrorism in Europe', in Crenshaw, *Terrorism in Context*, 36–7. Applying a different definition of terrorism, Marco Pinfari, 'Exploring the Terrorist Nature of Political Assassinations: A Reinterpretation of the Orsini Attentat', *Terrorism and Political Violence* 21/4 (2009), 580–94, comes to the same conclusion that Orsini's assassination attempt constituted terrorism, but he comes to this conclusion alone by virtue of what he calls the 'indiscriminate means with which it was undertaken' (ibid., 581).

82 Dandraut, *Textuel*, 47–8.

83 Ibid., 34.

84 See the announcement in 'Bulletin des Théâtres', *Le moniteur universel*, 13 January 1858, 51. Unlike the claims sometimes found in the literature, the announcement contains no indication that Napoleon III was to attend the performance.

Around 11 a.m. Orsini met with his accomplices and told them that their day had now come. He discussed matters with Pieri and, using a watch and a thermometer, began to dry the mercury fulminate carefully in front of the open fire in his apartment, fully aware that he 'and the whole house would be blown up' if a spark were to fall on it. After his co-conspirators had arrived at the apartment, Orsini distributed the freshly made bombs and at around 8 p.m. the group set out together for the opera.[85]

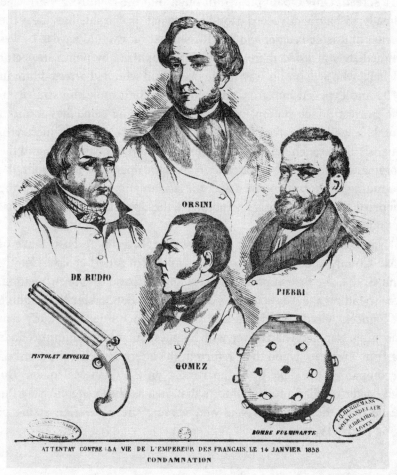

ORSINI

DE RUDIO

PIERRI

PISTOLET REVOLVER

GOMEZ

BOMBE FULMINANTE

ATTENTAT CONTRE LA VIE DE L'EMPEREUR DES FRANCAIS, LE 14 JANVIER 1858
CONDAMNATION

Figure 5. The assassins and their attempt on the life of Napoleon III, Paris, 14 January 1858. akg-images, Bildnr.AKG232041.

85 See Dandraut, *Textuel*, 30–1, 46–7; and Dansette, *L'attentat d'Orsini*, 70–1.

About a quarter of an hour later, Orsini and his co-conspirators arrived in the Rue Le Peletier and mingled with the crowd that had already gathered there. Napoleon III was not expected to arrive before 8:30 p.m., so there was still some time. At first, Pieri and de Rudio tried to position themselves in the emperor's private entryway, which had just been completed to help prevent attacks. They were soon sent away from this entry, however. They therefore went to the pavement in front of the main entrance and stood behind the first row of onlookers, using them as a screen. Only Orsini pushed through into the front row. Pieri, who already had a police record, stood somewhat on the sidelines, near the corner of Rue Le Peletier and Rue Rossini. As luck would have it, he was immediately arrested there after being recognized by police inspector Hébert, who was on his way to the opera and who had arrested him in 1852 and expelled him from the country. Hébert took him straight to the nearest police station, where, upon searching him, they found a bomb, a loaded revolver, knives and a considerable sum of money in English and French currency. By then it was already 8:30 p.m., and the commands called by the guards in front of the opera, the drum rolls, the pounding of horses' hooves and the acclamations of 'Long live the emperor' from the masses announced the approach of the imperial retinue.[86]

Napoleon III was hosting a state visitor. Ernst II August, Duke of Saxe-Coburg and Gotha, who was the brother of Albert of Saxe-Coburg and Gotha, the British prince consort and husband of Queen Victoria, was spending a few days in Paris on his way to London for the wedding of Princess Victoria and Prussian Crown Prince Friedrich. Early that morning, Napoleon had driven with his guest out to the hunting grounds of Fontainebleau. Upon their return in the afternoon, the emperor had accompanied the duke to his apartment on the Quai Malaquais. The duke later recalled in his memoirs that, just as they were crossing the Seine over the old Pont Neuf and passing the equestrian statue of King Henry IV, the

---

86 See Dandraut, *Textuel*, 30; de la Gorce, *Histoire du Second Empire*, vol. 2, 219–21; Packe, *Orsini*, 251–2; Dansette, *L'attentat d'Orsini*, 10, 72–3; Ernst II, Duke of Saxe-Coburg and Gotha, *Memoirs of Ernst II, Duke of Saxe-Coburg-Gotha*, 4 vols. (London: Remington & Co., 1888–90), vol. 3, 247–50, who gives an exact description of the private entrance built to protect the emperor.

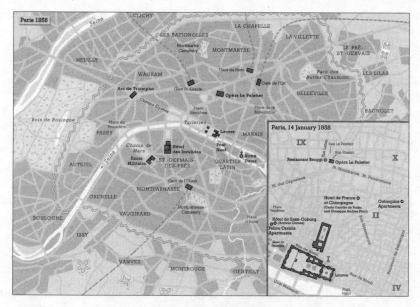

Map 1. Paris 1858.

emperor, after a short silence, made the following remark with reference to the statue of the King: Of all attempts at assassination, only
that with the dagger is dangerous, for the murderer surrenders his
own life in perpetrating it. In every other attempt on the life of a
sovereign, the traitor has still some hope of saving himself by flight.[87]

This observation, which Napoleon III is said to have made more than
once, was later to be considered prophetic.

The plan for the evening was to attend the opera. When the coaches
arrived in the courtyard, the members of the emperor's court entered
the first one, which was followed by an escort of mounted uhlans from
the imperial guard. Then came two mounted horsemen serving as the
vanguard (*avant-garde*), followed by the heavy, closed, iron-plated
coach in which Napoleon III, his wife, Eugénie de Montijo, and
Adjutant General Count Roguet took their places. It was flanked on
both sides by mounted officers, as well as a trumpeter on the right.
Behind it came an escort of lancers in rows of four as well as two

---

87 See Ernst II, *Memoirs*, vol. 3, 247–8. Packe, *Orsini*, 252–6, diverges widely from
the historical events insofar as they can be reconstructed.

Figure 6. Ernst II of Saxe-Coburg and Gotha.
Holzstich akg-images, Bildnr. AKG311364.

mounted rearguards (*arrière garde*). Napoleon's niece Mathilde
Bonaparte entered the next coach.[88]

As usual, the imperial procession set off a bit late. The Duke of Saxe-
Coburg and Gotha therefore waited with General Fleury, the court's
master of ceremonies, on the steps in the vestibule of the opera. To pass
the time, Fleury explained to the duke that due to 'the precautionary
measures which had lately been adopted here', 'the safety of the Emperor
was so great, that to perpetrate an attempt at this house, like the last one
at the Opera Comique, was scarcely possible'.[89] Shortly thereafter they
heard the first coach of the imperial entourage stop in front of the theatre and the members of the court exit the coach.

Behind them, the coachman of Napoleon III's vehicle reined in the
horses to turn into the brightly lit special entrance for the imperial

---

88 The most precise description of the procession of the imperial entourage is to be
found in *Le moniteur de l'armée*, 16 January 1858, 2. See also de la Gorce, *Histoire du
Second Empire*, vol. 2, 220–1; Packe, Orsini, 257; and Dansette, *L'attentat d'Orsini*, 10.

89 Ernst II, *Memoirs*, vol. 3, 249.

couple. At that very moment, Orsini gave the agreed signal and Gomez threw the first bomb. It exploded in front of the imperial coach with such force that the blast burst the windows and gas lamps of the opera house and the houses facing the opera, sending iron shrapnel raining down on the street. The lights went out. The startled horses of the uhlan escorts leapt forward so that the lancers surrounded the coach while the coachman whipped the horses in order to leave the danger zone quickly. At that instant the second bomb, hurled by de Rudio, landed directly in front of the coach, among the uhlan escorts. The detonation killed one of the coach's horses, bringing the heavy vehicle to an abrupt halt. The bomb also killed or injured twenty-four of the uhlans' horses and twelve soldiers. Chaos spread. The streets resounded with cries for help and screams of pain from the horrified and injured people, and with the neighing and clattering of hooves from the wounded and frightened horses. Despite the pandemonium, the uhlan escorts who were still at the ready managed to turn their horses back to the emperor's coach and surround it like a shield. Then Orsini threw his bomb directly under the vehicle. The explosion wounded still more horses and destroyed the outside of the coach. Shrapnel flew, injuring additional people and animals all around the vehicle, including Orsini, who had not tried to take cover. A fragment grazed his forehead, which bled so heavily that he momentarily could not see and was unable to wield either his revolver or his dagger. The people all around him fled in panic.[90]

Amidst this general confusion, a police officer made his way to the state coach. With some difficulty he managed to open the door of the emperor's carriage. Adjutant General Roguet clambered out, followed by Napoleon III. The emperor inquired about his niece and wanted to see the injured, but the empress stopped him and pulled him quickly into the entrance of the opera house – at least that is what she later reported to the assembled members of the diplomatic corps. The Duke of Saxe-Coburg and Gotha and Fleury stood transfixed by shock in the vestibule 'when the emperor and empress rushed in. They appeared to collapse . . . The emperor seemed dazed, moved shakily, and I thought

---

90 The description is based largely on the account in *Le moniteur de l'armée*, 16 January 1858, 2, which, though not impartial, is the most detailed one. See also Dandraut, *Textuel*, 31–2, 43, 51; Ernst II, *Memoirs*, vol. 3, 250; de la Gorce, *Histoire du Second Empire*, vol. 2, 222; Holyoake, *Sixty Years of an Agitator's Life*, 27; Pack, *Orsini*, 25–9; Dansette, *L'attentat d'Orsini*, 11.

he was wounded.' Behind the imperial couple surged a mass of people seeking cover, many of them injured. According to his memoirs, the duke dragged the empress away with him up the stairs to the theatre box. 'The emperor appeared at a loss to know in which direction to turn. Then he followed us up the stairs, and at last we all reached the box,' wrote Ernst II August in the somewhat self-serving pose of a lady-rescuer.[91]

In the theatre the performance had begun punctually. Napoleon III and Eugénie entered the box with the Duke of Saxe-Coburg and Gotha just as William Tell's oath on the Rütli was being rendered. Accounts of what happened next differ. Duke Ernst II August, who claimed to have stayed at the side of the imperial couple since meeting them in the vestibule, offers the only precise description: 'In the first *entr'acte*, during which the whole audience must have already heard of the attempt, as the wounded were receiving their first bandages in the corridors of the theatre, the Emperor and the empress stepped to the front of the box.' Louis Napoleon had a scrape on his nose and his hat had been riddled with shot and crushed; Eugénie's white dress was spattered with blood and her left eye had been injured by a shard of glass. Both were pale but otherwise well. According to Duke Ernst II August, however, the audience gave the imperial couple no sign of solidarity: 'But they met with no reception. Not a hand stirred, not a sound was raised. The Emperor said to me in German: "There you see the Parisians, – they are never treated harshly enough." '[92] According to later descriptions, the audience behaved as it ought to have towards its beloved sovereigns, greeting Napoleon III and his wife with enthusiastic applause while the orchestra struck up 'Partant pour la Syrie' (Departing for Syria), the unofficial national anthem of the Second Empire.[93] The vague and contradictory

---

91 Quotation from Ernst II, *Memoirs*, vol. 3, 250. For the empress's version, see Joseph Alexander Graf von Hübner, *Neuf ans de souvenirs d'un ambassadeur d'Autriche à Paris, sous le Second Empire, 1851–1859*, 2 vols. (Paris: Plon-Nourrit et cie, 1904), vol. 2, 91. See also Packe, *Orsini*, 258–9; Dansette, *L'attentat d'Orsini*, 11.

92 Ernst II, *Memoirs*, vol. 3, 250–1.

93 Without citing further sources, de la Gorce, *Histoire du Second Empire*, vol. 2, 222, reports that the audience remained silent, but he explains this silence as a reaction to the shock. Graf von Hübner, *Neuf ans de souvenirs d'un ambassadeur*, vol. 2, 89, who bases his description on later research into the events, simply states in general that the audience greeted the imperial couple enthusiastically. For descriptions that mention applause and the national anthem, but do without sources for the acclaim, see Castelot,

nature of these reports speaks for the accuracy of what Duke Ernst II August remembered, even if one considers that he was not particularly fond of the French emperor.

All the reports and various memoirs agree that many officials and family members appeared in the box over the course of the evening to congratulate the imperial couple for having survived the attack. To the Paris police prefect Pierre-Marie Pietri and the interior minister, visiting them at the opera that evening was like running the gauntlet, for it seemed at first that all the perpetrators had escaped unseen. When the two officials entered the box, the emperor is reported to have acknowledged them sarcastically with, 'The police did a fine job!'[94] According to Ernst II August, the emperor's insistent questioning was met by the police prefect's response, 'We know nothing at all.' In a second report an hour later, Pietri had to admit, 'We have made some arrests, but we are not yet further than before.' 'No names?' the emperor asked. Pietri: 'No!'[95] Before dawn of the next day, however, the police succeeded in apprehending all the accomplices in the assassination attempt.

Orsini and all his co-conspirators (except Pieri) had indeed managed to melt into the crowds after the attack. After Gomez had thrown his bomb, he sought refuge in Restaurant Broggi across the street from the opera. Many other people, too, had fled there to escape the bloodbath in the street, so he went unnoticed. De Rudio had flung himself face down to protect himself from the explosion of his bomb and then had slipped into a small cabaret, as did many others seeking safety. Later in the evening he walked back to his hotel, arriving there around ten o'clock. Orsini, by contrast, remained where he was and waited for Pieri's fourth bomb. When there was none, he walked up the Rue le Peletier to find a pharmacy, disposing of his weapons on the way. He found a pharmacy in the Rue Lafitte and had his head wound treated there. Then he took a fiacre back to his apartment, where he arrived around nine o'clock. The

Napoléon Trois, vol. 2, 286; Milza, *Napoléon III.*, 340; Dansette, *L'attentat d'Orsini*, 12–13; and Packe, *Orsini*, 259–60.

94 According to Graf von Hübner, *Neuf ans de souvenirs d'un ambassadeur*, vol. 2, 105, this was what Baron Georges-Eugène Haussmann overheard. Having hurried on foot to the theatre upon receiving the news at a dinner, he arrived at the box at the same time as the police prefect and the interior minister.

95 Ernst II, *Memoirs*, vol. 3, 251. The dialogues are reproduced there in French.

concierge later testified that Orsini had returned saying, 'I don't know what is going on. I will leave; the French wanted to kill me.' His land-lords helped clean the wound and called a doctor. After the doctor had left, Orsini lay down to sleep.[96] All the while, Pieri was being interro-gated at the police station and trying to lie himself to safety. By the end, however, he was so worn down that he divulged the name of his hotel. When police officers investigated the room he had rented there, they found de Rudio in bed. Meanwhile, people had noticed Gomez in the Restaurant Broggi. Further investigation about him revealed links to Orsini, whom the police also found in bed.[97]

At this point Orsini's attempted assassination was bound to seem like an utter failure. The French emperor had survived virtually unscathed, but 156 other people had been injured, including thirty-one policemen, and eight or even fourteen people died from the consequences of their injuries.[98] According to all available information, this is the highest number of killed and injured of any nineteenth-century terrorist attack. The political blockage persisted unchanged, the population remained calm, and there was no sign that a revolution was breaking out. Orsini's instrumental use of violence had proved useless or, worse still, counter-productive because it had killed the wrong people: soldiers on duty and people who had gathered to see the emperor, including tourists, women and children. But Orsini had succeeded in one aspect: he had produced an extremely spectacular, violent event. The very next day it began to become clear that this attack would attract a great deal of attention in the coming weeks and would produce a European media event, thanks to the sheer enormity of the violence perpetrated and the high symbolic value of the intended victim. Given the necessary political will, it thereby constituted the starting point of a historical event.

---

96 Dandraut, *Textuel*, 47, and, for the timing and the rest of the story, 48–9. See also Packe, *Orsini*, 261–2; Dansette, *L'attentat d'Orsini*, 15–17, 73.

97 Packe, *Orsini*, 261–4.

98 For the number of dead and injured, see the statements made by the medical experts at the trial as reprinted in Dandraut, *Textuel*, 45–6. The article 'Foreign Intelligence. France. Execution of Orsini and Pierri [*sic*]', *The Times*, 15 March 1858, 9, reports fourteen dead in mid-March. See also Tennyson, 'The Murder from Conviction, Orsini', 227–8; Dansette, *L'attentat d'Orsini*, 18.

Politico-symbolic failure

Orsini's attempt on Napoleon III's life was a sensation throughout Europe as far as Russia, as well as in the United States, and became head-line news.[99] Already on Friday, 15 January, the major Parisian newspapers such as *Le moniteur universel, Le Pays, La Patrie* and the *Journal des débats* published extensive articles about the previous evening's violent attack in the Rue Le Peletier.[100] Readers in London, too, would find the following report the next day in *The Times*:

> Attempt to Assassinate the Emperor Napoleon. (By Submarine and British Telegraph.) We have received the following telegram from our Paris correspondent dated Paris, Thursday, Jan. 14, 10 p.m. – The Emperor was fired at this evening at half-past 9 o'clock while he was entering the Italian Opera in the rue Lepelletier.

Another telegram on Friday morning supplemented the story: 'The *Moniteur* speaks of the attempt to assassinate the Emperor yesterday evening. The attempt was made with hollow projectiles. A considerable number of persons were injured . . . Neither the Emperor nor Empress was touched.'[101] The *Berliner Börsen-Zeitung* also gave an account in the Friday evening edition under the heading 'Telegraphic dispatches': 'An attack on the emperor took place as the emperor was about to enter the opera. His Majesty was fortunately saved. Some of the guards in his escort were wounded.'[102] The *Kölnische Zeitung* regarded this telegraphic

---

99 On the coverage in the United States, see pp. 177–84.

100 See, for example, 'Paris, le 14 janvier', 'Paris, le 15 janvier', and 'Liste des personnnes blessées dans la soirée du 14 janvier, dont les noms sont connus jusqu'à ce moment', *Le moniteur universel*, 15 January 1858, 57, and 16 January, 61 [1]. For newspapers using continuous pagination throughout the year, page numbers in square brackets are included hereafter to indicate the article's actual physical location in the issue if that detail is illuminating. See also 'France. Paris, 14 Janvier', *Journal des débats*, 15 January 1858, 1; 'Paris, 14 Janvier', *Le Constitutionnel*, 15 January 1858, 1; 'France. Paris – 15 Janvier 1858', *Le Siècle*, 1 January 1858, 1.

101 'Attempt to Assassinate the Emperor Napoleon. (By Submarine and British Telegraph)', and 'The Attempted Assassination of the Emperor Napoleon. (By Submarine and British Telegraph)', *The Times*, 15 January 1858, 7.

102 See 'Telegraphische Depeschen. Paris, 14. Januar. (W.T.B.)', *Berliner Börsen-Zeitung*, evening edition, 15 January 1858, 1.

bulletin as worth an extra.[103] Other major newspapers in Germany, Austria and Switzerland, such as the *Königlich privilegierte Berlinische Zeitung* (*Vossische Zeitung*), the *Neue Preußische Zeitung* (*Kreuzzeitung*), the Viennese *Morgen-Post* and Zurich's *Neue Zürcher Zeitung*, followed on Saturday, 16 January, with partially identical wording. Smaller papers and the Russian ones carried the news by Tuesday, 19 January.[104]

The European press unanimously condemned the assassination attempt. The *Kölnische Zeitung*, for instance, opined, 'It was a close call, a very close call; Emperor Napoleon almost fell victim to a heinous assassination yesterday evening.' The *Wiener Zeitung* referred to a 'catastrophe' and an 'odious attack'; the correspondent for *The Times* wrote of an 'atrocious attempt made by a few miscreants'. The *Neue Zürcher* characterized the conspirators as 'new-fangled regicides'; in Moscow, the *Moskovskie vedomosti* called it a 'criminal assassination attempt' that had shocked all of Paris and, of course, raised general outrage throughout the world. *L'Opinione* in Turin asserted, 'There is not a single political party that would not censure such an evil and cowardly attempted assassination,' but it was careful to add that a party which did not have the courage to express its disapproval would deserve to be discredited. In other words, it was known full well that the attack was welcomed in some quarters, but this officially excluded possibility was explicitly

103 See the note in the *Kölnische Zeitung*, 16 January 1858: 'We informed many of our readers with an extra this morning about the following telegraphic dispatch: "Paris, (Thursday) 14 February 12 o'clock at night. This evening an attempt was made on the life of the emperor at the entrance to the big opera. His majesty was fortunately unhurt, but some of the mounted guards in his entourage were injured."' 'Der Mordversuch gegen den Kaiser Napoleon. Köln, 15. Januar', *Kölnische Zeitung*, 16 January 1858, 1.

104 See, for example, 'Der Mordversuch gegen den Kaiser Napoleon', *Kölnische Zeitung*, 16 January 1858, 1; 'Wolff's Telegraphische Depeschen. Paris, 14. Januar, Mitternacht', *Königlich privilegierte Berlinische Zeitung*, 16 January 1858, 4; 'Paris, Freitag 15. Januar, Morgens. [Attentat auf den Kaiser]', *Neue Preußische Zeitung*, 16 January 1858, 2; 'Neuere Nachrichten. Paris, 14. Jan., Mitternacht (Telegraphische Depesche)', *Deutsche Allgemeine Zeitung*, 16 January 1858, 101 [4]; 'Attentat auf den Kaiser Napoleon', *Morgen-Post*, 16 January 1858, 1; 'Telegramme der Österreichischen Correspondenten. Paris, 16. Jänner', *Die Presse*, 16 January 1858, 1; 'Das neueste Attentat', *Neue Zürcher Zeitung*, 16 January 1858, 1; 'Politische Nachrichten. Paris, 15. Jan. (Attentat auf den Kaiser)', *Innsbrucker Nachrichten*, 17 January 1858, 93 [1]; 'Das Attentat vom 14. d.M. in Paris', *Wiener Zeitung*, 18 January 1858, 51 [3]; 'Frankreich', *Freiburger Zeitung*, 19 January 1858, 3; 'Das Attentat gegen den Kaiser Napoleon', *Berliner Gerichts-Zeitung*, 19 January 1858, 2–3; 'Parizh, Ianvariia 16-go', *Moskovskie vedomosti*, 7 January 1858, 46.

denounced.[105] Domestic- or foreign-policy considerations, such as the reminder of the *coup d'état*, the rivalry between Austria and France, or the rumour that Napoleon III wanted to annex the Rhineland for France did not curb the media's disapproval of the violent attack.[106]

The initial article in *Le moniteur universel*, the official French newspaper of the Second Empire, served as the factual basis for all the early reports. But even after the first correspondents wrote their own dispatches from Paris and the first editorial comments were published, topics and the reporting remained largely consistent. As in the French press, the journalist from *The Times* and the reporter for the *Kölnische Zeitung* detailed the course of events, the making of the bombs, the extensive damage caused to the opera and the surrounding structures, the security measures, the number of victims and their injuries (to the extent known), and the status of police investigations. The *Neue Zürcher Zeitung* added specifically that at the very moment 'the third projectile exploded . . . an act of William Tell was ending in the opera house'.[107] *Le*

---

105 'Der Mordversuch gegen den Kaiser Napoleon', *Kölnische Zeitung*, 17 January 1858, 1; 'Frankreich', *Wiener Zeitung*, 20 January 1858, 194 [2]; 'The Express from Paris. The Attempt to Assassinate the Emperor', *The Times*, 16 January 1858, 9; 'Das neueste Attentat', *Neue Zürcher Zeitung*, 16 January 1858, 1; 'Parizh, 15-go (3-go) Ianvaria', *Moskovskie vedomosti*, 14 January 1858, 21; 'Attentato contro Napoleone', *L'Opinione*, 18 January 1858, 1–2, quotation at 1; translation reprinted in French as 'Nouvelles étrangères', Piémont. Turin, 18 Janvier', *Journal des débats*, 21 January 1858, 2. See also 'Paris, 15 Janvier', *Le Constitutionnel*, 16 January 1858, 1; 'Partie politique. France. Paris – 15 Janvier 1858', *Le Siècle*, 16 January 1858, 1; and 'Das Pariser Attentat', *Die Presse*, 19 January 1858, 1. For the conclusion that 'the vast majority of the Swiss press [expressed] revulsion' about the attack in Paris, see *Neue Zürcher Zeitung*, 25 January 1858, 94.

106 The *Kölnische Zeitung* made this point explicit. See 'Der Mordversuch gegen den Kaiser Napoleon', *Kölnische Zeitung*, 17 January 1858, 1.

107 See especially 'Express from Paris. The Attempt to Assassinate the Emperor. The following is the letter of our Paris correspondent, dated yesterday (Friday), 6 p.m.', *The Times*, 16 January 1858, 9; 'Telegramme der Österreichischen Correspondenten. Paris, 16. Jänner', *Die Presse*, 16 January 1858, 1; 'Der Mordversuch gegen den Kaiser Napoleon . . . Unser pariser = Correspondent schreibt', *Kölnische Zeitung*, 17 January 1858, 1; 'Paris, 15. Januar', *Berliner Börsen-Zeitung*, 17 January 1858, 118 [2]; 'Zur politischen Geschichte des Tages. Ueber das Attentat', *Morgen-Post*, 17 January 1858, 1; 'Näheres über das Pariser Attentat', *Neue Zürcher Zeitung*, 18 January 1858, 67; the two articles 'Frankreich. Paris, 16. Januar' and 'Das Pariser Attentat', *Berliner Börsen-Zeitung*, 19 January 1858, 126, 126–7; 'Das Attentat auf den Kaiser Napoleon', *Deutsche Allgemeine Zeitung*, 19 January 1858, 115–16 [1–2]; 'Das Attentat in Paris. Verhaftung und Untersuchung', *Morgen-Post*, 20 January 1858, 1–2; 'Parizh, Ianvariia 16-go', and 'Parizh,

moniteur universel, as the official French source of news for all newspapers in Europe, retained its superior status, so the French government easily influenced the way the assassination attempt was portrayed in the European media.

The European press was conspicuously circumspect in its political interpretation of the assassination. The fact that it was Italians who had mounted the attack was generally mentioned, and Orsini's name appeared as early as 16 January in both London and Berlin. The media usually refrained from drawing political conclusions, however. For example, the correspondent's report in *The Times* of Friday, 16 January 1858, only stated,

> The number of persons taken into custody, I am told, amounted to 27 up to 2 o'clock this day, three or four of whom are believed to be the chiefs. They are most of them, if not all, Italians. One of them was a Colonel in the Roman (Republican) service . . . The Roman Colonel is named Pierri [*sic*] . . . The name of another of them is Orsini or Corsini . . . On this point it is difficult to say anything, as the reports are often contradictory, and it is certain that the examination of the prisoners is secret.[108]

Stating that the perpetrators were Italians and had served the Roman Republic will have sufficed to orient most readers of *The Times*. The *Kölnische Zeitung*, in its commentary on the attack, dared only to surmise that 'this attempted murder' had 'most probably . . . like all

---

Ianvariia 17-go', *Moskovskie vedomosti*, 9, 14, 16 January 1858, 32, 46–8, 56–7; 'Frankreich. Paris, 19. Januar', *Berliner Börsen-Zeitung*, 22 January 1858, 150; 'Francia. Del 17', *Gazzetta di Mantova*, 22 January 1858, 27; 'Parizh, 21-go Ianvariia', 'Parizh, 24-go Ianvariia', and '(Ind.B.)', *Severnaia pchela*, 18, 20 January 1858, 67, 73–4, whose reporting was largely based on German newspapers.

108 'Express from Paris. The Attempt to Assassinate the Emperor. The following is the letter of our Paris correspondent, dated yesterday (Friday), 6 p.m.', *The Times*, 16 January 1858, 9. Orsini's name is also mentioned in 'Telegraphische Depeschen. Paris, 15. Januar', *Berliner Börsen-Zeitung*, 16 January 1858, 1; 'Das Attentat auf den Kaiser Napoleon', *Deutsche Allgemeine Zeitung*, 19 January 1858, 115–16 [1–2]; 'Das Pariser Attentat', *Die Presse*, 19 January 1858, 1; 'Das Attentat in Paris', *Morgen-Post*, 21 January 1858, 1–2; 'Francia. Del 17', *Gazzetta di Mantova*, 22 January 1858, 27. Pieri was mentioned in 'Parizh, 15-go (3-go) Ianvariia', *Moskovskie vedomosti*, 7 January 1858, 21; and Pieri and Orsini, as well as Gomez and de Rudio, were mentioned in 'Näheres über das Pariser Attentat', *Neue Zürcher Zeitung*, 19 January 1858, 71.

earlier ones', been undertaken by 'fanatical parties'. The editors did not want to anticipate the outcome of the official investigation, but 'the deed hardly permits any guess other than political objectives.' They considered that the emperor surely had no personal enemies, given that he was a model of charitability and magnanimity.[109] This commentary and others like it enabled newspaper editors to provide their readership with initial leads about the background of the assassination attempt yet still put aside the symbolic dimension of the attack. Italian papers, such as *L'Opinione* in Turin, even tried to undermine any political reading by interpreting the attack as a selfish and antisocial atrocity committed purely for its own sake. Such presentations were intended to deny that the attack had any political significance.[110] Although Orsini had reached the European public with his act of violence, he could not control its reception, nor through it could he communicate a clear message or call to action.

The political reaction to the assassination attempt was not what Felice Orisini had hoped and expected, either. Instead of unleashing a revolution, it was followed by intensified repression in France, Italy and other European countries. The attack was used as an excuse to curtail civil rights and impose measures that would have been difficult to explain beforehand, particularly in France and the smaller states bordering it. In Switzerland, which had traditionally been a country that welcomed republican émigrés, the *Neue Zürcher Zeitung* reported as early as 20 January 1858 that, 'as a result of the assassination attempt, the cantons have been warned to monitor the behaviour of persons who have been granted asylum.'[111] This topic pervaded subsequent coverage, extending beyond Switzerland's asylum policy to include that of other European countries (especially England, France, Belgium and Sardinia–Piedmont), as well as articles published in those countries about Switzerland.[112]

109 'Der Mordversuch gegen den Kaiser Napoleon', *Kölnische Zeitung*, 17 January 1858, 1.

110 'Attentato contro Napoleone', *L'Opinione*, 18 January 1858, 1–2; the quotation at 1 was reproduced in French in 'Nouvelles étrangères, Piémont. Turin, 18 Janvier', *Journal des débats*, 21 January 1858, 2.

111 'Schweiz. Bundesstadt. (Korr.V.18.Jan.)', *Neue Zürcher Zeitung*, 20 January 1858, 75.

112 For examples of accounts of the developments of asylum policy in Switzerland and attempts by France to influence it, see *Neue Zürcher Zeitung*, 23 January 1858, 87; 27 January 1858, 1; 28 January 1858, 107; 31 January 1858, 118–19; 12 February 1858, 1;

After careful consideration of the question, the Swiss Federal Council in Bern decided to reduce cantonal influence on asylum law and to apply it more restrictively.[113]

In Belgium, where many members of the opposition had fled after Louis Napoleon's *coup d'état* of 2 December 1851, press laws were tightened and measures were taken against left-wing papers. The targets included radical papers like *Le Drapeau*, *Le Prolétaire*, and *Le Crocodile*, which had approved of Orsini's attack, and one had even drawn the parallel to Matthew 26:52: 'for all they that take the sword shall perish with the sword'. *Le moniteur universel* took up the subject in a short article right on the first page, expressing indignation 'that a paper printed in Belgium, *Le Drapeau* ... enthusiastically welcomed the attack on the emperor'. The official French paper demanded appropriate action. Yielding to the pressure that had been escalating over several years from Napoleon III's government, the Belgian parliament passed a law on 12 March 1858 empowering the government to impose harsh penalties on radical papers.[114]

---

15 February 1858, 179; 18 February 1858, 191; 1 March 1858, 235; 5 March 1858, 251; 11 March 1858, 275; 14 March 1858, 286; 15 March 1858, 291. On asylum policy in other countries, see, for example, *Neue Zürcher Zeitung*, 27 January 1858, 103; 30 January 1858, 115; 1 February 1858, 122; 4 February 1858, 135; 6 February 1858, 143; 7 February 1858, 147; 9 February 1858, 155; 13 February 1858, 170; 22 February 1858, 207. Examples of the observation of the reporting on Swiss asylum policy are the news about a report by the Berlin *Kreuzzeitung* (*Neue Preußische Zeitung*) on 7 February 1858, 147; and *La Patrie* in Paris on 19 February 1858, 195.

113 See especially the reprint of the relevant resolution in *Neue Zürcher Zeitung*, 21 February 1858, 203, and the report about the expulsions in the same newspaper on 16 March 1858, 295. Newspapers in other countries reported on Switzerland's stricter asylum policy. See, for example, 'Frankreich. Paris, 1. März' and 'Frankreich. Paris, 2. März', *Berliner Börsen-Zeitung*, 5 March 1858, 462; 'The Despatch of Count Walewski, dated 20 January, 1858', *The Times*, 13 March 1858, 9; 'Parizh, Ianvariia 21-go', *Moskovskie vedmosti*, 18 January 1858, 66; and 'Shveitsariia', *Severnaia pchela*, 20 February 1858, 186–7. Also see Dansette, *L'attentat d'Orsini*, 94. On Switzerland's asylum policy in this period, see, finally, Schweizerisches Bundesarchiv (ed.), *Zeitschrift des Schweizerischen Bundesarchivs, Studien und Quellen*, vol. 25: *Das Asyl in der Schweiz nach den Revolutionen von 1848* (Bern: Paul Haupt, 1999).

114 'Paris, le 19 Janvier', *Le moniteur universel*, 20 January 1858, 77 [1]; reprinted, for example, as 'France. Paris, 20 Janvier', *Journal des débats*, 21 January 1858, 1. For reporting on this, see, for example, 'Frankreich. Paris, 21. Januar', *Berliner Börsen-Zeitung*, 24 January 1858, 116, or 'Parizh, 20-ogo Ianvariia', *Severnaia pchela*, 18 January 1858, 67. On the incident, its background and the passage of the press Act in the Belgian parliament, see Dansette, *L'attentat d'Orsini*, 94; and Theo Luykx, 'Napoleon III. and the Belgian Press', *International Communication Gazette* 8/2 (1962), 133–42.

In the Kingdom of Sardinia–Piedmont, too, the government acqui-
esced to all French demands. When Cavour learned of the attack, he is
said to have cried out, 'Let us hope they are not Italians.'[115] After all, his
government had fully counted on an alliance with France. A few days
later the French foreign minister, Alexandre Collona-Walewski, menac-
ingly wrote to Turin that the Sardinian states and especially the city of
Genoa continued 'to offer protection to the enemies of European society',
and shortly thereafter Napoleon III himself spoke of Piedmont as 'a home
for agitators' that was 'dangerous for the whole world'. Everything was
immediately undertaken to mollify the big ally. The government in Turin
expelled émigrés, placed those who remained under strict surveillance,
condemned Mazzini yet again to death *in absentia*, and harassed the
editors of his newspaper, *L'Italia del popolo*, with prison sentences and
fines until they shuttered the paper.[116] On 20 January *La gazette piémontaise* reported the seizure of *La Ragione*, the newspaper that Felice Orsini
had wanted to develop with local democrats into the 'republican *centre*'
of Italy. The stated reason for this action against the newspaper was that
it 'had published an article from Paris about the iniquitous assassination
attempt of 14 January', a piece in which 'opinions were expressed that
crassly contradict the righteous and compelling disgust felt throughout
our country for the perverse theory of political assassination and for the
wretched people who made themselves its instrument'. When the editors
of *La Ragione* took the case to court and won against the government, the
parliament immediately tightened the press laws.[117]

---

115 A. J. Whyte, *Political Life and Letters of Cavour, 1848–1861* (London: Oxford
University Press, 1930), 245.

116 See Dansette, *L'attentat d'Orsini*, 118, quotations at 113, 117.

117 *La gazette piémontaise* quoted in 'Piémont. Turin, 21 Janvier', *Journal des débats*,
24 January 1958, 1. This report, too, was taken up by the press in other countries. See, for
example, 'Telgraphische Depeschen. Paris, 22. Januar', *Berliner Börsen-Zeitung*,
23 January 1858, 1; and '(N.Pr.Z.) Iz Turina, ot 21-go Ianvariia', *Severnaia pchela*,
18 January 1858, 68. For newspapers that described Orsini in the Kingdom of Sardinia–
Piedmont as 'a great man, one of the most significant figures in Italian history', and
celebrated the conspirators as 'strong personalities who live by austerity and self-
sacrifice, who die for their country and are exceptional men of action', see the report
'Sardinia. (From Our Own Correspondent)', *The Times*, 10 March 1858, 9. Specifically
on the events relating to *La Ragione* and Cavour's repressive policy in response to the
French demands, see Dansette, *L'attentat d'Orsini*, 114, 116, 118–19, as well as de la
Gorce, *Histoire du Second Empire*, vol. 2, Chapter 14, 11; and Matter, *Cavour et l'unité
italienne*, vol. 3: *1856–1861*, section 2.2–4.

The gravest impacts of the political reaction to Orsini's attack were felt in France itself. The attempted assassination gave Napoleon III's government the opportunity to spin sweeping conspiracy theories and to put repressive policies back on the agenda. According to Sylvie Aprile, the intention was less about repression than intimidation: 'Once again they purported to believe in a vast plot by the "reds"'. On 27 February 1858 a 'general security law' was announced, a state of emergency permitting the severe punishment of anyone who disturbed the peace in any way or who fomented disrespect of the imperial government. The law thereby defined a new kind of transgression, as a critic pointed out: 'the offence of holding a conversation'. More than 2,000 citizens were arbitrarily arrested; and 400 political prisoners of the period from 1848 to 1852 were suddenly sentenced to deportation to Algeria. A new interior minister was installed, General Espinasse, who had had a part in closing the national assemblies in 1849 in Rome and 1852 in Paris. In addition, there was a shake-up in the police force and a reorganization of the military. New passport and visa regulations were introduced for foreigners who wanted to travel to France. Lastly, newspapers critical of the government were forbidden, and the surveillance of the French press, wine bars and cafés increased.[118] The liberal press of other European countries analysed and commented on these measures critically, prompting *Le moniteur universel* and other French newspapers to push back. Moreover, the French ambassadors to Prussia, Austria and Switzerland requested the governments in those countries to intervene against such criticism.[119]

---

118 See Aprile, *La IIe République*, 284–5 (which includes both quotations); de la Gorce, *Histoire du Second Empire*, vol. 2, Chapter 13, section 2; Price, *The French Second Empire*, 147–53; and Dansette, *L'attentat d'Orsini*, 81–92. On the regulations for passports and visas, see the contemporary press reports, such as 'French Passports. To the Editor of the Times', *The Times*, 5 March 1858, 4; and the articles 'Austria. (From Our Own Correspondent)', *The Times*, 5, 8 March 1858, both at 7; *The Times*, 13 March 1858, 10; and 'Parizh, 23-go Fevralia' and 'Shveitsariia', *Severnaia pchela*, 20 February 1858, 186–7. On the press regulations, see, for example, 'Parizh, 21-go Ianvariia', 18 January 1858, 67.

119 For critical analyses from a liberal perspective, see, for example, the *Berliner Börsen-Zeitung*, 19 January 1858, 126; 22 January 1858, 150; the three articles on 'Frankreich. Paris, 20. Januar', *Berliner Börsen-Zeitung*, 23 January 1858, 158, 158–9, 159; 24 January 1858, 166; 4 February 1858, 246; 16 February, 330; 2 March 1858, 429. In *The Times*, see, for example, 5 March 1858, 7; 13 March 1858, 9. For the reprint or the satirical commentary of the counternarrative, see 'France', 'France (From Our Own Correspondent)' and 'Express from Paris', *The Times*, 18, 22 March 1858, 9, 7, 12. On the

All the while, Felice Orsini was sitting in Mazas prison in Paris. All access to the public was denied to him and he had no way of responding to the comments in the European press. Only Orsini's autobiographical books told the story in his own way, and they were discovered and analysed a few days later by various journalists. A few newspapers on the fringe approved of his attack,[120] but such voices were few and far between, and the repressive measures taken by the various governments soon silenced them. Under these circumstances the objectives that Orsini had pursued with his spectacular attack were, at best, to be intuited from the situation itself. If things had remained that way, the attack would have failed completely and would probably have been forgotten today, just like all the other attempts on Napoleon III's life. As paradoxical as it may sound, it was not until influential French politicians came to exploit the attempted assassination for their own political ends that they afforded Orsini the opportunity to achieve his.

The dialectics of defeat: cooperation makes a successful martyr

Orsini's act ultimately did succeed, because Napoleon III resolved to use the assassination attempt and the assassins to affect a shift in French policy towards Italy.[121] An initial attempt to instrumentalize the attack politically, albeit not by Napoleon himself, had already started on 16

---

attempts to exert diplomatic influence, see, for example, 'The Despatch of Count Walewski, dated 20, January, 1858', *The Times*, 13 March 1858, 9. For Prussia and Vienna see the articles 'Austria (From Our Own Correspondent)', *The Times*, 5 and 8 March 1858, 7; and 'Frankreich. Paris, 16. März', *Deutsche Allgemeine Zeitung*, 20 March 1858, 534–5 [2–3]; 'Ausland. Paris, 16. März', *Die Presse*, 20 March 1858, 2–3.

120 See p. 146 above; and, for example, 'On lit dans la Patrie: "La Revue des Deux Mondes", dans son numéro du 15 mars 1857, avait rendu compte d'une brochure publiée en Angleterre par Orsini', *Journal des débats*, 24 January 1858, 1; and the account of the positive reception given the assassination attempt in the Italian newspapers *Unione*, *La Ragione*, and *Gazetta del Popolo* in 'Sardinia (From Our Own Correspondent)', *The Times*, 10 March 1858, 9.

121 In the era of anarchist terrorism, 1880–1914, a number of politicians attempted to exploit terrorist violence for their own political goals. See Jensen, *The Battle against Anarchist Terrorism*, 44–52, especially 47. For contemporary examples illustrating the political instrumentalization of terrorism, see the chapters cited on p. 39 in Kassimeris, *Playing Politics with Terrorism*.

January 1858, when the imperial couple received members of the Senate and the Legislative Corps (Corps Législatif, the essentially powerless lower house of parliament), the diplomatic corps and the first emissaries from European courts to accept their congratulations on having survived the attack. On this occasion the lead was taken by the president of the Legislative Corps, Charles Demorny (who was usually referred to, with generous exaggeration, as Comte de Morny, to at least make it sound as though he had been raised to the nobility). He was Louis Napoleon's half-brother, a long-time companion of the emperor, one of the most important architects of the *coup d'état* and a proponent of rapprochement between France and Russia. He used the violent attack to criticize England because it had provided sanctuary to the attackers. With 'calculated aggression' he expounded that the French populace was wondering 'how it was possible that neighbouring and friendly governments were incapable of destroying these laboratories of assassination and how the sacred laws of hospitality could also extend to wild beasts'.[122] In the following days, official diplomacy added fuel to the fire, and the reproach against England for offering protection to assassins grew into the demand that Great Britain change its asylum law. The press was deployed as reinforcement. Along with the many congratulatory messages to the imperial couple, *Le moniteur universel* also published some messages from regiments that offered to lead an invasion of the British Isles.[123]

Politicians, the press and the general public in Great Britain reacted immediately to these offences. *The Times* reproduced the congratulatory speeches of 16 January word for word, commenting with understatement that such language was 'not calculated to win favour for any overtures of the French government' and reminding readers that every government was responsible for protecting itself. When the prime minister, Lord Palmerston, presented the House of Commons with a bill meeting the French demands, it was shot down. Palmerston resigned and France responded with an 'outburst of anger against the perfidious Albion', as the

---

122 Dansette, *L'attentat d'Orsini*, 77, and 'Partie non officielle. Paris, le 16 janvier', *Le moniteur universel*, 17 January 1858, 65 [1].

123 See, for example, 'Adresses présentées à l'Empereur', *Le moniteur universel*, 27 January 1858, 109 [1]. Other congratulatory messages printed in *Le moniteur universel* from 22 to 31 January 1858. For a contemporary political interpretation of these congratulations from the army, see Graf von Hübner, *Neuf ans de souvenirs d'un ambassadeur*, vol. 2, 95–6; and Dansette, *L'attentat d'Orsini*, 99.

Austrian ambassador Count (Graf) von Hübner wrote. For a brief moment the two countries appeared to be on the brink of war.[124] The press and public in the rest of Europe anxiously followed the escalation.[125] The situation did not ease until the French emperor, who had no interest in a war with Great Britain, struck a more conciliatory tone in mid-March. The whole conflict therefore proved to be a passing episode.

A key factor in the emergence of terrorism was that Napoleon III himself decided to use the attempted assassination to promote his own political goals. Contrary to all logic and expectations, he now began to plan a military intervention to free and unite Italy. In the context of these plans, he used Orsini to explain his intervention and to prepare the public for it.

124 The quotation is from 'London, Monday, January 18, 1858', *The Times*, 18 January 1858, 6. The reprint of a literal translation of Demorny's speech is also there. For a clear rejection of the French demands yet also for the renunciation of hostilities by the press, see, for example, 'The Despatch of Count Walewski, dated 20 January, 1858', *The Times*, 13 March 1858, 9; and 'The "Misconception" between France and England', *The Times*, 13 March 1858, 9. For observations of the British coverage and public opinion on this matter in French newspapers, see, for example, 'France. Paris, 19 Janvier' and 'On lit dans le *Globe* du 18 janvier', as well as 'France. Paris 24 Janvier', *Journal des débats*, 20, 25 January 1958, 1–2, 1 respectively. On the overall development of the conflict, see the contemporary documents by Graf von Hübner, *Neuf ans de souvenirs d'un ambassadeur*, vol. 2, 109–11, quotation at 109; and James Howard Harris, Earl of Malmesbury, *Memoirs of an Ex-minister: An Autobiography*, 3rd ed., 2 vols. (London: Longmans, Green, and Co., 1884), vol. 2, 92–104. On the escalation of the diplomatic conflict between France and England as well as its reception in the press and in public opinion in both countries, a general overview can be found in de la Gorce, *Histoire du Second Empire*, vol. 2, Chapter 13, Part 4; and Dansette, *L'attentat d'Orsini*, 94–109.

125 See, for example, *Berliner Börsen-Zeitung*, 'Telegraphische Depesche. Paris, 16. Januar', 17 January 1858, 1; 19 January 1858, 126; 20 January 1858, 137 [1]; 23 January 1858, 158–9; 24 January 1858, 166; 27 January 1858, 186; the two articles entitled 'Frankreich. Paris, 20. Februar', *Berliner Börsen-Zeitung*, 23 February 1858, 364, 364–5; the two articles entitled 'Frankreich. Paris, 22. Februar', *Berliner Börsen-Zeitung*, 25 February 1858, 400; 'Frankreich. Paris, 25. Februar', *Berliner Börsen-Zeitung*, 28 February 1858, 426; as well as the two articles 'Frankreich. Paris, 8. März', *Berliner Börsen-Zeitung*, 11 March 1858, 510. In *Die Presse* see, for example, 24 January 1858, 3; 27 January 1858, 1; 30 January 1858, 1; 6 February 1858, 3; 9 February 1858, 3; 12 February 1858, 3; 18 February 1858, 1–2; 26 February 1858, 3; 2 March 1858, 1; 11 March 1858, 1; 17 March 1858, 3; 18 March 1858, 1; and 19 March 1858, 2. In *Moskovskie vedomosti* the coverage began with the translation of Demorny's speech, 'Parizh, Janvaria 17-ogo', 16 January 1858, 56. Further see, in particular, 'London, Janvaria 18-go', 18 January 1858, 64; and the summarizing article entitled 'Imperator Napoleon III i Angliia', ibid., no. 30, 260–1, and no. 31, 266–9. See also *Severnaia pchela*, 18 January 1858, 67; 20 January 1858, 72.

The French emperor's decision to instrumentalize Orsini and his attack in this way was preceded by a change of mind that can be explained only indirectly; there is no explicit evidence of it. However, what appears to have been decisive is that the French emperor had basically always held onto his boyhood dream of contributing to the liberation and unification of Italy and had been waiting for a domestic and international situation that would permit such an intervention. These personal motives coincided with France's foreign-policy interests, for in Italy lay the opportunity to advance the revision of the European order that the Congress of Vienna had charted and that continued to restrict France's scope of action. According to Adrien Dansette, Orsini's attempt on the life of Napoleon III served as a kind of catalyst that provoked the French emperor into acting on long-standing political intentions.[126]

It was thus Orsini's intended victim, of all people, who helped in two ways to achieve the aims of his assassin and the attack he had mounted. First, Napoleon III reacted to the inherently provocative character of Orsini's spectacular, violent act (whether or not Orsini had planned and foreseen this reaction). Second, he helped Orsini to reach his target audience – the public media in France, Italy and Europe in general – with positive messages and to generate sympathy for himself and his objectives as well as understanding and approval of his violent act.

This constellation was not predictable and created a specific, new situation, for the only thing that made the tactic appear interesting and worth imitating was the success that crowned it through Napoleon's intervention. In that context, the unique factor to be observed in the emergence and invention of terrorism is the improbable cooperation between an extremely prominent and powerful victim and his heretofore comparatively unknown and unsuccessful assassin. This cooperation, and the success it made possible, gave an entirely new direction and dynamic to terrorism's further development.

126 For the initial responses of Napoleon III to the attempted assassination, his change of mind and the reactions of his environment, see Price, *The French Second Empire*, 148; Girard, *Napoléon III.*, 275–9; and Dansette, *L'attentat d'Orsini*, 155–6. For the available testimonies and the assessment that personal motives and statesmanship had a bearing on this decision, see Dansette, *L'attentat d'Orsini*, 147–50, 153–6. The salience of foreign-policy motives is also emphasized by Altgeld, 'Das Risorgimento (1815–1876)', 296.

The lack of direct sources precludes a detailed reconstruction of most aspects of the cooperation between Napoleon III and Orsini. Who took the initiative and pulled which strings at which point inevitably remains as unclear as the question 'whether the cooperation was implicit or explicit. It is certain, however, that two channels of interaction existed between Orsini and Napoleon III: three letters from Orsini to the French emperor, and Orsini's contact with the Paris police prefect Pierre-Marie Pietri, himself an Italophile Corsican and close confidant of Napoleon III. Pietri sought out Felice Orsini several times in his cell during his imprisonment and won his willingness to cooperate.

After arrest, Orsini initially denied everything, as was his habit whenever dealing with security authorities. However, confronted with overwhelming evidence against him and possibly persuaded by conversations with Pietri, he soon began to cooperate with the French investigators. It was probably also Pietri who encouraged Orsini to write a letter to Napoleon III on 11 February. Pietri may also have been helpful in persuading Jules Favre, one of the best and most eloquent lawyers in France, to take on Orsini's defence. In addition, Napoleon's police prefect provided Favre with a copy of Orsini's autobiography to help prepare the defence. At Favre's suggestion, Orsini wrote again to the emperor on 16 February, requesting permission for his lawyer to make use of the first letter in his defence plea. Permission was granted. After a few days in prison Orsini also asked for dark clothes and Barthold Georg Niebuhr's *Römische Geschichte* (The History of Rome) to help him prepare mentally for his trial. This wish, too, was granted. Upon official request following the trial, Orsini wrote a third letter to the French emperor. Like the first one, it ended up becoming crucial in the emperor's media and public policy.[127]

---

127 See Letters 211, 212, and 214 from Felice Orsini to Napoleon III, 11 and 12 February from the Mazas prison and 11 March 1858 from Grande Roquette prison, reproduced in Ghisalberti, *Lettere di Felice Orsini*, 254–5, 257–8. On these letters and other facets of the cooperation, see de la Gorce, *Histoire du Second Empire*, vol. 2, 351–2, Packe, *Orsini*, 268–9; and especially Dansette, *L'attentat d'Orsini*, 122, 150–3. Commenting on this situation, Favre later wrote only that Orsini had asked him for help and that he had accepted the case 'out of the free and poignant yearning' of his conscience to do justice to the assassin and patriot as well as to the greater interest of both nations. See M. Jules Favre, 'Préface', in Favre, *Discours du bâtonnat, défense de Félix Orsini, quatre discours prononcés au Corps Législatif dans la session de 1866* (Paris: J. Hetzel, 1866), iii.

Figure 7. Jules Favre. Wikimedia Commons.

Why did Felice Orsini agree to cooperate with Napoleon III and the French authorities in this manner? There are no direct sources available to answer this question, either. Presumably, Orsini was seeking the possibility of a pardon by cooperating and showing good behaviour, even if life was sometimes difficult for him to bear in his physical and mental condition. Aside from such personal motives, however, were there also political reasons for cooperating? The answer is quite probably that there were, and, unlike the French emperor, Orsini did not have to undergo a change of heart to arrive at them, for his readiness to cooperate was wholly consistent with his political assessments of previous years. As cited already above, Orsini had written in his memoirs in 1857, 'But why does everything depend on Napoleon?' and had answered his question by writing, 'Because he has a large army at his disposal' with which he can, in alliance with another European partner, win any war. Now that the assassination of Napoleon III had failed and no revolution was in sight, Orsini had only *one* final option for achieving his goal of national unity and independence for Italy: to persuade the French emperor and his large army to march with an Italian power – the Kingdom of Sardinia–Piedmont – in a war against Austria, or at least to support the preparation for such a war. Felice Orsini's cooperation with Napoleon III, in the weeks before his execution, became his last political act. It was at the trial that the cooperation between the assassin and his powerful victim first surfaced publicly.

The trial, which commenced on 25 February 1858, was a Parisian (media) event of European proportions. Approximately 6,000 people had sought entrance tickets to the courtroom, and on the opening day of the trial every available seat was taken. Correspondents from numerous leading French and other European newspapers attended, as did many well-known people close to the imperial couple, from the Senate and the Legislative Corps, as well as members of the diplomatic corps. When the defendants Orsini, Pieri, de Rudio and Gomez were ushered into the hall, many opera glasses were trained on them.[128] Orsini knew that he was bound to receive the death sentence, so he could go on the offensive by trying – to the extent allowed by the presiding official – to explain his attack to those present in the courtroom and to expound on the political objectives and rationale behind it.

He cut a good figure, at least in the eyes of the ladies of French high society: 'Orsini is the hero of this sad drama,' Count von Hübner commented disapprovingly in his diary. 'He looks good, has the manner of a man from high society . . . All the leading Russian and Polish ladies sitting on the courtroom benches rave about him. They admire his handsomeness, his courage, his resignation to his fate.' Tall and dignified, with a dark complexion, dark curly hair, black beard, black clothes,

---

128 See the contemporary coverage from the European press, such as the detailed and graphic report entitled 'The Attempt to Assassinate the Emperor of the French', *The Times*, 27 February 1858, 9; and 'Anklage-Act in Bezug auf das gegen den Kaiser Napoleon am 14. Jänner verübte Attentat', *Die Presse*, 27 February 1858, 2–4; 'Frankreich. Paris, 25. Februar', *Berliner Börsen-Zeitung*, 28 February 1858, 426; 'Der Attentats-Prozeß. Die Schwurgerichtssitzung vom 25. Febr.', *Morgen-Post*, 1 March 1858, 1; 'Aus Paris, 26. Februar, 6 Uhr Nachmittags', *Wiener Zeitung*, 1 March 1858, 190, [2]; 'Die schwurgerichtliche Verhandlung über das Attentat vom 14. Jänner in Paris', *Wiener Zeitung*, 191–2 [3–4]; 'Frankreich. Paris, 26. Febr.', *Deutsche Allgemeine Zeitung*, 2 March 1858, 410 [2]; 'Francia. Del 25', *Gazzetta di Mantova*, 5 March 1858, 73 [3]; 'Francia. Del 26', *Wiener Zeitung*, 73 [3]; 'Parizh, Fevralia 26-go' and 'Parizh, Fevralia 27-go', *Moskovskie vedmosti*, 25, 27 February 1858, 206–7, 213–17; 'Parizh, 26-go Fevralia' and 'Parizh, 27-go Fevralia', *Severnaia pchela*, 21, 24 February 1858, 191–2, 201–2. On the number of entrance tickets sought, see 'Frankreich. Paris, 26. Febr.', *Deutsche Allgemeine Zeitung*, 2 March 1858, 2. In the literature see especially Dansette, *L'attentat d'Orsini*, 121; and Packe, *Orsini*, 269–71.

Figure 8. The trial of Felice Orsini. Wikimedia Commons.

black gloves, a quick mind and good manners, Orsini perfectly fit the image of a noble, romantic, revolutionary hero. With his repeated expressions of admiration for France, the great Napoleon and the principles of the French Revolution, and with his steadfastly serious demeanour and aristocratic bearing, he won over many of the people in the courtroom despite all the aspersions by the presiding authority.[129]

Favre's defence plea the next day reinforced this positive impression. The speech is rightly described as a rhetorical masterpiece.[130] Favre was

---

129 Graf von Hübner, *Neuf ans de souvenirs d'un ambassadeur*, vol. 2, 117. On Orsini's reactions to the questions posed by the presiding official, see the section entitled 'Interrogatoire de l'accuse Orsini', in Dandraut, *Textuel*, 27–35. Orsini also made an impression on the journalists present from other European countries. See, for example, *The Times*, 27 February 1858, 9; *Berliner Börsen-Zeitung*, 28 February 1858, 426, and 2 March 1858, 428; *Morgen-Post*, 1 March 1858, 1; *Deutsche Allgemeine Zeitung*, 2 March 1858, 2, and 3 March 1858, 2–3; at least superficially in *Severnaia pchela*, 24 February 1858, 201–2; and initially *Neue Zürcher Zeitung*, 2 March 1858, 239. For contrasting views, see, for example, *Wiener Zeitung*, 1 March 1858, 190–2 [2–4]; and *Neue Zürcher Zeitung*, 3 March 1858, 242.

130 See Dansette, *L'attentat d'Orsini*, 129; also Packe, *Orsini*, 271–3. For a reprint of the defence plea, see Dandraut, *Textuel*, 67–76; and for an Italian translation of the court transcript, with an introduction, see Corte d'assise di parigi, *Il Processo Orsini* (Rome, 1944).

a republican who, as a representative in the national assembly in 1849, had fought for French support for the Roman Republic. Like Orsini, he went on the offensive in presenting his political persuasion, beginning his statement by staking out his political position and distancing himself from both the Second Empire and all forms of illegal political violence.[131] In doing so, Favre implicitly claimed for himself a position independent of the two parties to the conflict – Napoleon III and Orsini.

Favre's next step was to explain why he had agreed to take on Orsini's case although he loathed the act this client had perpetrated. Favre invited those present in the courtroom to identify themselves with him and his position towards Orsini: He, Favre, had sensed the significance of this defence and the 'nobility of the effort and its vanity', and had told Orsini that he understood his struggles and his suffering and that he would do the same if it were for France – with the exception of these murders, which his conscience repudiated.[132] Orsini had confessed to his crime, the assassin regretted it and was prepared to die in compliance with the law he had broken. He, Favre, had therefore promised Orsini that he would help him in this final hour. He would not do so with useless attempts at defence or glorification but rather with a quest to do justice to Orsini with regard to how he and his deed would be remembered. In this way Favre clearly defined the objective of his arguments: he was not about to excuse Orsini's misdeed but rather to explain it, 'to examine the meaning and the motive of the act'.[133] The defence plea thereby became political.

Favre then brought home to his Parisian public the legitimacy of Orsini's political objectives and their origin in the French Revolution, arguing that France had deviated from its path, whereas the assassins had remained true to the revolutionary principles. Using Orsini's biography, Favre showed that the assassin had spent his entire life in the service of the struggle for Italian national independence and self-determination. 'What did he want?' Favre asked his public, answering, 'To liberate his fatherland. He tells us himself . . . Do not deny the honesty of his statement, we have his whole life as a guarantee.' This goal, the realization of the unity and independence of Italy, was completely

131 See Dandraut, *Textuel*, 68.
132 Ibid., 68.
133 Ibid., 68.

legitimate – after all, the great Napoleon had also pursued it.[134] What
had Napoleon Bonaparte done to attain it? He had broken the worldly
power of the Pope. That is precisely what Orsini had done with his
contribution to the attempted insurrection in 1843 and in the revolutions of 1848–9 as well. Those revolutions had managed to topple the
papal government, and Orsini had been elected as a representative in
the constituent assembly, an election based on universal suffrage, just as
in France. Who was responsible for this institution's demise? 'France's
cannons'. Driven out of his country by French arms, he continued,
Orsini had begun to conspire. None of this, Favre reminded his audience, was alien to recent French history. The court was looking at an
Italian who wanted to do for Italy exactly what one would also do for
France.[135]

To the general astonishment of the courtroom, Favre then started to
read out Orsini's first letter to Napoleon III. It contained quite specific
foreign-policy considerations about why the creation of an Italian nation
was necessary for France – indeed for all of Europe – and prophesied
darkly about what would happen should this not be permitted to take
place:

> To preserve the current balance in Europe, Italy must be given back its
> independence . . . Italy calls upon France not to intervene against it, it
> calls upon France not to allow Germany to support Austria in the
> struggles that may soon begin. Now, this is precisely what Your
> Majesty can do, if you so wish. The well-being or misfortune of my
> fatherland depends on this will . . . I implore Your Majesty to restore
> to Italy the independence that its children lost in 1849 through the
> fault of these very same French. That your Majesty . . . realize that
> Europe's calm and your own are no more than a chimera as long as
> Italy is not independent.[136]

These words were Orsini's last, Favre explained, and they were consistent with his whole life. 'From the edge of the grave, he is directing this
solemn request to the one against whom he held no personal hate, to the

---

134 Ibid., 69.
135 See ibid., 70–1, quotation at 70.
136 Ibid., 71–2.

one who was the enemy of his country but who can also be its saviour.'[137] Favre concluded with a suggestive rendition of Orsini's appeal to Napoleon III in his own words. It was a direct appeal to the French emperor to take his own beliefs seriously and to free Italy.

Favre's defence speech for Orsini became – with explicit permission from the emperor – a speech of accusation against Napoleon III. Nevertheless, the jury declared Orsini, Pieri, de Rudio and Gomez guilty that same evening and sentenced the first three to death for patricide (implying that Napoleon III was the father of the French people) and Gomez to life imprisonment at hard labour.[138] Apart from this decision, though, the court case had become a kind of affirmative show trial, a variety of the type famously used by twentieth-century totalitarian regimes for the vilification of political opponents, only with the negative charge turned to positive.

From the time Felice Orsini was sentenced on 26 February 1858 until his execution on 13 March of that year, his case occupied French politics and the public more intensely than any other topic. On the morning after the proceedings, the general demand for information was so great that the French newspapers permitted to cover the trial were sold for three to four times more money than usual.[139]

Orsini's performance, Favre's defence and the public reading of the letter to Napoleon III turned the legal proceedings into a peculiarly explosive political event, eliciting amazement and manifold speculation. 'What attracted the most attention during the whole trial was Orsini's letter to the emperor,' the correspondent for the *Berliner Börsen-Zeitung* reported about the reactions in the courtroom.

> Among the diplomats who were present when it was read aloud, the greatest possible astonishment became apparent, to the extent that diplomats show it at all; one finds it beyond comprehension how the

---

137 Ibid., 72.

138 For a summary of the sentence, see Dansette, *L'attentat d'Orsini*, 135. The fact that Favre had permission for his defence plea is mentioned by the empress in her recollections. See Georges Maurice Paléologue, *The Tragic Empress: Intimate Conversations with the Empress Eugénie, 1901 to 1911* (London: Thornton Butterworth, 1928), 159.

139 See 'Express from Paris. The Attempt to Assassinate the Emperor of the French', *The Times*, 27 February 1858, 12.

emperor, as Favre explicitly explained, could allow the letter to be made public before the court, to oblige Orsini and permit such a demonstration against Austria. One searches in vain for a solution to the riddle.[140]

The search was bound to appear even more pressing because it was known that the French reporting of the trial had been minutely orchestrated in advance, a fact in itself worthy of comment. 'Directors of the Parisian newspapers were summoned to the ministry of the interior,' reported the *Deutsche Allgemeine Zeitung*, 'and they were instructed to reprint the trial as recorded in the court press organs, the *Gazette des Tribunaux* and *Droit*, which would adopt the text after it had been carefully read and vetted by the court's presiding official.' The newspaper added an explanation: 'In higher circles it is not considered advisable to make public everything that will be said on this matter.'[141] In light of such measures, the fact that *Le moniteur universel* reproduced the censored court proceedings, including all of Favre's defence plea and Orsini's letter, must have been interpreted as a sign of official approval.[142]

Through the correspondents who attended the trial and through the reprint in *Le moniteur universel*, Orsini's statements, the indictment, Favre's defence plea and the letter to Napoleon appeared, at least in excerpts, in the other European newspapers as well,[143] except in

140 'Paris, 27. Februar', *Berliner Börsen-Blätter*, 2 March 1858, 429. Similarly, 'Frankreich. Paris, 28. Febr.', *Deutsche Allgemeine Zeitung*, 3 March 1858, 2.

141 'Frankreich. Paris, 24. Febr.', *Deutsche Allgemeine Zeitung*, 28 February 1858, 3. On this procedure see also 'Express from Paris. The Attempt to Assassinate the Emperor of the French', *The Times*, 27 February 1858, 12. For an overview of the reactions by the French media and public, see also Dansette, *L'attentat d'Orsini*, 135.

142 See 'Cour d'assises de la Seine. Audience du 25 février 1858' and 'Cour d'assises de la Seine. Audience du 26 février 1858', *Le moniteur universel*, 26, 27 February 1858, 245–9 [1–5], 25–6 [2–4] respectively. Orsini's letter is at 255, marked by the heading 'To Napoléon III., Emperor of the French'. The *Wiener Zeitung* reported 'that Favre's defence plea, which contains Orsini's letter to the emperor, was reprinted in the "Moniteur" on the express order from the Tuileries' (that is, by order of the emperor). 'Frankreich. Paris, 28. Februar', *Wiener Zeitung*, 4 March 1858, 671–2 [1–2], 672 [2].

143 See, for example, *The Times*, 27 February 1858, 9, 12; *Berliner Börsen-Zeitung*, 2 March 1858, 429; *Deutsche Allgemeine Zeitung*, 2 March 1858, 2–4; *Neue Zürcher Zeitung*, 3 March 1858, 1–2, and 4 March 1858, 246; *Moskovsie vedomosti*, 27 February, 213–17 (Orsini's letter is at 216); and *Severnaia pchela*, 24 February 1858, 201–2.

Austria.[144] The coverage of the assassination attempt in France and the political signals it implied were met with incomprehension, or anger and fear, or sometimes with enthusiasm in various European countries, depending on the receiver's political position. In that sense, the official response to Favre's defence plea and to Orsini's letter in particular had just the impact that terrorist acts of violence are intended to achieve: strong psychological effects, both negative and positive.

The incomprehension in countries that were not directly affected can be read as an indicator of the novelty of the phenomenon. 'Everywhere people are preoccupied with considering, with probing Orsini's letter to the emperor, turning it this way and that in every possible way without gaining any clarity', the correspondent of the *Börsen-Zeitung* reported to Berlin after the trial, eloquently alluding to a scientific examination of a new, as yet unknown object to express his perturbation. This disorientation of an otherwise alert journalist suggests that Napoleon III had engaged in a political manoeuvre for which neither a model nor any experience or interpretation yet existed.[145]

In Vienna, which was directly affected by Napoleon III's press policy, people felt only too clearly which way the wind was blowing. Their reactions reflected anger and concern. The *Wiener Zeitung*, for instance, branded Favre's defence plea an 'out-and-out glorification of the Brutus theory' and 'absolutely revolutionary'.[146] The government and the public responded to it differently. 'This Government professes to believe that the Emperor Napoleon had no *arrière pensée* [ulterior motives] when he gave orders that the letter addressed to him by Orsini should be inserted in the *Moniteur*, but the public, both of high and low degree, is of a very

---

144 The trial was widely reported in the Austrian press as well (see especially *Die Presse*, 27 February 1858, 2–4; and the *Wiener Zeitung*, 27 February, 1 March, 2 March 1858). In Austria, however, only the indictment was translated in its entirety, whereas Orsini's letter and Favre's defence plea were merely summarized and interpreted. For an article that discusses Favre's plea at length, see 'Aus Paris, 3. März (Jules Favre und der Attentats-Prozeß)', *Wiener Zeitung*, 8 March 1858, 214–15 [2–3]. The fact that other Austrian papers – except the *Volksfreund* – avoided the topic of Orsini's letter and Favre's defence plea at the request of the government is documented in an article about Austria in *The Times*. See 'Austria. (From Our Own Correspondent)', *The Times*, 8 March 1858, 7.

145 'Frankreich. Paris, 28. Februar', *Berliner Börsen-Zeitung*, 3 March 1858, 446.

146 'Aus Paris, 3. März (Jules Favre und der Attentats-Prozess)', *Wiener Zeitung*, 8 March 1858, 214–15 [2–3], quotation at 215 [3].

different opinion', as the correspondent from *The Times* summarized the responses in Austria. The reporter continued that the publication of the letter offended the Austrians deeply, that the French emperor was accused of inconsistency, and that it could 'not be denied, that the charge is perfectly well founded'. Napoleon III, he wrote, was demanding that the Austrian government issue new regulations for passports and repressive measures for the inhabitants of Lombardy–Venetia, yet at the same time was permitting the publication of such a document in an official newspaper and thereby possibly inciting them 'to imitate the detestable example of a man whom they will henceforth regard as a political martyr'.[147] What could be the objective of such a policy? According to *The Times*, the prevailing impression was that Napoleon III had published the document so that the Italians would see Austria as the decisive barrier on the way to national unity and freedom. However, the Austrian government had prohibited the publication of such conjectures and interpretations in the press in order not to antagonize the French government. 'The total silence of the other papers [except for the aforementioned newspaper *Volksfreund*] on a topic of such significance to Austria is caused by the strict orders they have received to avoid giving offence to the French Government.'[148] The government in Vienna, according to the *Times* correspondent, was clearly intimidated by the actions of the French state.

In Italy, too, the symbolic salience of the publication of Orsini's letter to Napoleon III was immediately understood. The 'effect produced here is immense', Cavour wrote in early March to Sardinia–Piedmont's ambassador to Paris, adding that this was as true or even more so in the rest of Italy. In Cavour's estimation, the letter put Orsini on a pedestal from which it would be impossible to remove him. In his opinion it transformed the assassin into a martyr, attracting the sympathy of all Italians and the admiration of many people who were far from being followers of Mazzini's sect. Like the Austrian public, Cavour, too, was clearly aware that Orsini's letter and the official form of its publication converted stigma into charisma and transformed the assassin into a

---

147 'Austria. (From Our Own Correspondent)', *The Times*, 12 March 1858, 7. The articles in the Austrian press confirm this assessment. See, for example, 'Aus Paris, 1. März. (Orsini und Jules Favre)', *Wiener Zeitung*, 5 March 1858, 688 [2].

148 'Austria. (From Our Own Correspondent)', *The Times*, 8 March 1858, 7.

martyr with whom broad swathes of the population in the Italian states sympathized. The king and the government in Sardinia–Piedmont were not at all pleased about their subjects' sympathizing with Orsini. As Cavour saw it, the position that the French emperor personally granted to Orsini made things much more difficult for the government in Piedmont. How should anyone intervene against justifications for regicide if in France it were made out to be more interesting than ever, through measures much more effective than the scattered bad newspaper articles against which the French government was forcing him to take action? King Vittorio Emanuele II, wrote Cavour, was extremely unhappy about the publication and the trouble it would still cause his government.[149]

It was not only in Italy but also in France itself that Orsini suddenly met with interest and understanding, sometimes even rapturous acclaim from important quarters of leading society, including the empress. Years later she recalled, 'In spite of the fact that Orsini, far from excusing himself, actually glorified his crime, I was deeply moved by the nobility of his language, the heroism of his attitude, the supreme dignity of his bearing before the assize courts. Would you believe that I wept over it?'[150] The empress was so taken by her attacker that she even wished to visit him in prison and personally received his wife Assunta Orsini and their children, until the emperor made the ironic comment one day, 'And now all that is missing is for us to invite them to dinner.'[151]

149 Letter 151 from Camillo Benso di Cavour to Salvatore Pes di Villamarina, 4 March 1858, n.p., reprinted in Cavour, *Epistolario*, vol. 15.1, 218–19; English translation in Whyte, *Political Life and Letters of Cavour*, 251; see also de la Gorce, *Histoire du Second Empire*, vol. 2, 350–1; and Matter, *Cavour et l'unité italienne*, Vol. 3, 72–3. As Villamarina reported to Turin, he informed the French foreign minister that reading out and publishing the letter 'had made the attack interesting and had disseminated the idea of regicide'. Letter 168 by Salvatore Pes di Villamarina to Camillo Benso di Cavour, 13 March 1858, from Paris, reprinted in Cavour, *Epistolario*, vol. 15.1, 239–40, quotation at 240.

150 Paléologue, *The Tragic Empress*, 159.

151 On the empress's admiration for Orsini, see Graf von Hübner, *Neuf ans de souvenirs d'un ambassadeur*, vol. 2, 117; and Packe, *Orsini*, 274–5. The press reported on Assunta Orsini's trip and published Felice Orsini's letters to his children. See, for example, *Neue Zürcher Zeitung*, 13 March 1858, 283; and 'Orsini and His Children', *The Times*, 17 March 1858, 5. On the remark Napoleon III is said to have made, see Dansette, *L'attentat d'Orsini*, 156. On the admiration for Orsini in France 'as a kind of William Tell', see de la Gorce, *Histoire du Second Empire*, vol. 2, 352.

The empress did not waver, however, and fought to have Orsini pardoned: 'Further, after the condemnation, I begged the emperor to grant an immediate pardon,' she remembered later. 'I kept on repeating to him: "No, you can't send this man to the guillotine! You cannot do it, you of all men!" '[152] The emperor was not disinclined to listen to his wife, and large parts of French society speculated as to whether or not the execution would take place. 'Sometimes they say the empress, at other times Princess Mathilde, is taking an active interest in getting Orsini pardoned,' the correspondent of the *Börsen-Zeitung* explained to his German readers, 'and given that even those closest to the emperor very rarely know in advance about his decisions, there is plenty of room for even the wildest conjectures until the axe falls.'[153] But for all Louis Napoleon's sympathy for Orsini, the members of the government in the Conseil privé (privy council) refused to consider commuting the sentence. On 12 March the decision was finalized to reduce Rudio's punishment but to execute Orsini and Pieri, who bore the primary responsibility.[154] Whether or not Orsini learned of his status as martyr and, if so, how he reacted to it, is not known.

The executions took place on 13 March 1858 on the Place de la Roquette. When the trial ended, Orsini, Pieri and de Rudio were transferred to Grande Roquette, the prison in front of which all public executions in Paris were conducted. The guillotine was set up on a scaffold about fifteen steps in front of the prison gate. The prominent prisoners in Grande Roquette were under watch by the inhabitants of the nearby quarters of workers and artisans, in which it is said that word went around 'to gather at the Place de la Roquette on the day of Orsini's execution and to appear collectively the moment *the martyr* mounted the scaffold'.[155] When the rumour circulated that Orsini was to be secretly executed already on 4 March, 10,000 people persevered all night

152 Paléologue, *The Tragic Empress*, 159. On people's rumours about pardons, see, for example, 'Express from Paris', *The Times*, 8 March 1958, 7.

153 'Frankreich. Paris, 8. März', *Berliner Börsen-Zeitung*, 11 March 1858, 510.

154 See the minutes of the meeting in Dansette, *L'attentat d'Orsini*, 160–6. See also Packe, *Orsini*, 276–7. On the institution of the Conseil privé, which was created after Orsini's attack and which conferred official status on the meetings of Napoleon III's advisers, see Price, *The French Second Empire*, 47.

155 Letter 154 from Salvatore Pes di Villamarina to Camillo Benso di Cavour, 7 March 1858, from Paris, reprinted in Cavour, *Epistolario*, vol. 15.1, 221–3, quotation at 222.

outside the prison.[156] During the two nights before the execution date, 'the Place de la Roquette and the streets contiguous were covered with a multitude, who braved the intense cold and wet to witness the execution.' The 'crowds that held vigil the whole of last night were almost beyond calculation', *The Times* reported.[157]

Figure 9. Felice Orsini at the guillotine. akg-images, Bildnr.AKG415085.

It had snowed that night, and fog hung over the square at 5 a.m. when, accompanied by drums and bugles, several companies of infantry marched up, accompanied by a few echelons of cavalry units as well as police officers and *sergens de ville*, making for more than 5,000 men under arms. They pushed the crowds of people to the edge of the square and ensured their safe distance from the scaffold. At six o'clock the prison director woke Orsini and Pieri. In the straitjackets that they had had to wear since their conviction, they were led to the so-called *chambre de la toilette*. There, the prisoners condemned to death were prepared for their fate by the Paris executioner and two colleagues who had arrived from Rouen and Caen specifically to assist him in his awesome

---

156 See 'Foreign Intelligence. France (From Our Own Correspondent)', *The Times*, 4 March 1858, 9; 'Express from Paris', *The Times*, 5 March 1858, 7, and 'Frankreich, Paris, 12. März, *Wiener Zeitung*, 16 March 1858, 836 [2].

157 'Foreign Intelligence. France. Execution of Orsini and Pierri [*sic*] (From Our Own Correspondent)', *The Times*, 15 March 1858, 9.

responsibility. They shaved Orsini's and Pieri's necks so that their hair would not affect the guillotine's blade, removed their shoes, and pulled over their heads the hoods which were reserved for patricides. When the prison clock struck seven times, the door to the Place de la Roquette opened and Pieri began to sing 'Mourir pour la patrie' (To Die for the Fatherland), the national hymn of the Second French Republic of 1848. Led by the prison chaplains, Orsini and Pieri ascended the steps of the scaffold. On the platform they waited barefoot in the snow while the court usher read out the sentence. Then the executioners seized Pieri and strapped him to the plank of the guillotine. The moment they removed the hood from his head, he called out 'Long live Italy! Long live the republic!' Then the blade fell. Now it was Orsini's turn. He is said to have turned to the distant crowd and called 'Long live Italy! Long live France!' before he was bound to the plank. At five minutes after seven, his head, too, fell into the guillotine's basket.[158]

Once more, newspapers throughout Europe reported on the execution, except *Le moniteur universel*.[159] In Italy Felice Orsini was celebrated as a martyr. The Austrian correspondent of *The Times* wrote from Milan that 'anonymous letters were a few days ago sent to the ladies of the Lombard capital' to request their presence at the Corso (the name of a main street) and 'to wear black veils in honour of Orsini'. In addition, posters called the Italian public to pray for the soul of Orsini, the martyr. The correspondent of *The Times* in Turin reported that the previous day's *Unione* had presented its pages under a headline calling for a 'subscription to present a gold medal or some other testimonial of respect to Jules Favre, Orsini's advocate . . . To-day, the *Ragione* declares that it had conceived the same idea before the *Unione* put it forth, and it also opens a subscription.'[160] Such gestures were not confined to Italy; in

---

158 Ibid. See also Packe, *Orsini*, Chapter 5.6.

159 In addition to the detailed report in *The Times*, see, for example, 'Exécution d'Orsini et de Pieri', *Journal des débats*, 14 March 1858, 2; *La Presse*, 14 March 1858, 1; *Le Constitutionnel*, 14 March 1858, 1; *Wiener Zeitung*, 15 March 1858, 237 [1]; *Neue Zürcher Zeitung*, 15, 16, 17 March 1858, 291, 295, 299; *Deutsche Allgemeine Zeitung*, 16 March 1858, 503 [3]; *Gazzetta di Mantova*, 16 March 1858, 3; *Morgen-Post*, 16 March 1858, 1; *Die Presse*, 17 March 1858, 2–3; *Severnaia pchela*, 3, 11 March 1858, 231, 262–3; and *Moskovskie vedomosti*, 4, 11 March 1858, 236, 259.

160 'Austria. (From Our Own Correspondent)', *The Times*, 26 March 1858, 10; and 'Sardinia. (From Our Own Correspondent)', *The Times*, 10 March 1858, 9. On the 'Orsini cult', also see, for example, 'Italien', *Neue Preußische Zeitung*, 4, 7 April 1858, both on 2.

Great Britain, too, there were gatherings at which Orsini was enthusiastically honoured.[161]

Orsini owed his status as a martyr primarily to Napoleon III. Provoked by the spectacular and mediagenic character of the attack on his person, the French emperor had decided to use the assassin to inaugurate a shift in his policy towards Italy, to signal this change to the French and the broader European public alike, and to generate support for his new policy especially among the French and Italian populations. He wanted to obtain this support partly by arousing sympathy for the assassin as a person and understanding for that man's objective – to make people realize the moral and political necessity of French engagement in the creation of a sovereign Italian nation state. The key to instilling sympathy and understanding in France and Italy was Orsini's letter to Napoleon III and the enactment of the court proceedings as a positive show trial. As observed by *Die Presse* in Vienna as early as April 1858, 'The formally staged Orsini trial was a hand grenade flung over the Alps, igniting the Orsini cult.'[162] The rapt fancy for Orsini and the martyr cult that enveloped him prove that the manoeuvre was successful. How far the sympathy extended, into which sections of the population, and whether it would really be convertible into a willingness to support the new policy on Italy are other questions. Moreover, the reactions to the cooperation between the French emperor and Orsini may have developed a momentum that Napoleon III neither had foreseen nor could control. What is certain, however, is that, after Orsini's death, he continued pursuing the course on which he had embarked while preparing the trial.

Orsini's attack and the founding of Italy

Ten days after the execution, the French emperor had Orsini's third letter sent to Cavour with express permission to use it. This letter amounted to a political testament: Orsini thanked Napoleon III for having permitted him to publish his first letter and informed him that it consoled him in the hours before his death to know that the French

---

161 See 'Vermischte Nachrichten', *Morgen-Post*, 9 April 1858, 2.
162 'Wien, 6. April', *Die Presse*, 7 April 1858, 1.

emperor held true feelings for Italy. Then he explained to the world that murder, in whichever form, still did not belong to his principles, even if he had allowed himself 'by a disastrous mental mistake' to organize the attack of 14 January. And he called upon his countrymen to listen to the voice of a dying patriot and to repudiate assassination as a tactic because emancipation and deliverance must be achieved through one's own dedication and virtue, as well as by a constant unity of efforts and sacrifices. Only with such gifts would Italy become free and worthy of the glory of its ancestors. He himself would die 'in peace and honour', and he hoped that his memory would not be sullied by his crime. He offered his blood as 'expiatory sacrifice' for the victims of 14 January.[163]

Cavour well understood the political implications of this third letter. He foresaw 'that its publication would anger Austria to an even greater extent' and wrote to Piedmont's ambassador to Paris, Salvatore Pes di Villamarina, 'It is a direct assault upon Austria, not only on the part of Piedmont but also of the Emperor.' He nevertheless had Orsini's third letter published on 31 March 1858 in the *Gazette piémontaise*, 'introduced by a few lines intended to intensify the effect', and encouraged *L'Opinione* to add that the emperor regarded Italy as his second home and hated the tyrants and foreigners who kick it around. 'He fought for Italian freedom against theocratic despotism.'[164] The French newspapers kept silent on the matter. Neither the Austrian nor the Russian press reprinted the wording of the letter but did discuss the policy behind it exhaustively. The English and the German press reproduced Orsini's letter from the *Gazette piémontaise* and commented on it extensively.[165]

---

163 Letter 214 from Felice Orsini to Napoleon III on 11 March 1858, from Grande Roquette prison, reprinted in Ghisalberti, *Lettere di Felice Orsini*, 257–8.

164 Letter 202 from Camillo Benso di Cavour to Salvatore Pes di Villamarina on 31 March 1858, n.p.; *L'Opinione*, 1 April 1858; and Ghisalberti, *Lettere di Felice Orsini*, 257–8; also see the partial translation in Whyte, *Political Life and Letters of Cavour*, 251–2. On the publication of this letter and the related political implications, see Dansette, *L'attentat d'Orsini*, 180; and Frank J. Coppa, *The Origins of the Italian Wars of Independence* (London: Longman, 1992), Chapter 6, especially 79.

165 The author has not been able to find a reference to this letter in *Le moniteur universel* or *Le Constitutionel*, *Le Siècle*, or *Journal des débats*. For Austria, see, for example, the *Wiener Zeitung*, 4, 6 April 1858, 1137, 305 [1]; *Die Presse*, 4, 7, 20 April 1858, 1–2; *Morgen-Post*, 4 April 1858; and for Russia, 'Italia (N.Pr.Z.)', *Severnaia pchela*, 29 March 1858, 326. For Great Britain, see, for example, 'Orsini's Will, and His Second Letter to the Emperor Napoleon', *Leeds Mercury*, 6 April 1858, 1; 'Italian Comments on the Last Letter of Orsini', *Daily News*, 6 April 1858, 5; 'News of the Day' and 'Italian

Fully in keeping with the French emperor's new foreign policy, the diplomatic relations between Paris and Turin subsequently intensified. In late May or early June, before Napoleon III went to spend the summer in the small spa town of Plombières-les-Bains in the Vosges, he invited Cavour to visit him there to 'chat on the state of Italy' with him (likely punning intentionally – 'de causer avec moi l'état de l'Italie'), as Cavour wrote to his ambassador to Paris.[166] The meeting took place on 21 July 1858. During an eight-hour conversation in the Pavillon des princes and on a coach ride in the forests of the Vosges, they came to a preliminary understanding on the joint future policy.

Just as Orsini had wished, Napoleon promised Cavour military assistance in a war against Austria. The condition was that Piedmont would bear the costs and that the military intervention could be presented to the public as necessary and just. In other words, Austria would have to be seen as the aggressor and declare war, and the confrontation was not allowed to have any revolutionary causes. The war's objective was to be to evict Austria and the Habsburg rulers from northern Italy, with Lombardy–Venetia, Modena and the northern part of the Papal States falling to Piedmont. In exchange, the Kingdom of Piedmont would cede its provinces of Nice and Savoy to France. Only general agreements were made about central and southern Italy: the other parts of the Papal States (except Rome and its direct surroundings) would pass to a sovereign yet to be determined, and the Kingdom of the Two Sicilies and Tuscany would be maintained but would go to another dynasty. In January 1859 the agreement was sealed in a secret agreement between France and Piedmont.[167]

Comments on the Last Letter of Orsini', *Birmingham Daily Post*, 6, 7 April 1858, both on 1; 'The Last Will and the Last Letter of Orsini Are Now before the World', *The Times*, 7 April 1858, 8. For the German states, see 'Italien', *Königlich privilegierte Berlinische Zeitung*, 7 April 1858, 8, or 'Italien' and 'Italien. Turin, 3 April', and 'Von Orsini', *Neue Preußische Zeitung*, 7, 9 April 1858, each on 2.

166 Letter 301 from Camillo Benso di Cavour to Salvatore Pes di Villamarina, 2 June 1858, n.p., reprinted in Cavour, *Epistolario*, vol. 15.1, 416. See also Whyte, *Political Life and Letters of Cavour*, 255. On the diplomacy surrounding the publication of Orsini's third letter to Napoleon and in preparation of the meeting between Napoleon III and Cavour, see Dansette, *L'attentat d'Orsini*, 178–81; Coppa, *The Origins*, 80; and especially Matter, *Cavour et l'unité italienne*, vol. 3, 74–6 and section 2.5.

167 This description of the secret meeting in Plombières and the alliance between France and Piedmont is based largely on Altgeld, 'Das Risorgimento (1815–1876)', 300. But also see Procacci, *History of the Italian People*, 315–16; Coppa, *The Origins*, 80–2;

Immediately after the secret meeting in Plombières-les-Bains, France and Piedmont started using every means at their disposal to provoke Austria and isolate it internationally. 'Napoleon unleashed the official and semiofficial French press, Cavour readied the Piedmont army and equipped thousands of refugees with weapons.' He even tried to foment rebellions against the Habsburg rulers in central Italy, and when all that failed to help, he 'was desperate enough to be willing . . . to stake everything on revolutionary uprisings!' When Great Britain and then also Russia offered to mediate, the plan for a joint war against Austria temporarily seemed seriously jeopardized. But precisely at this moment the Austrian government, given the unrest in its Italian territories, overreacted and presented Piedmont with an ultimatum: the Italian state was to order demobilization within three days, dismiss the newly recruited troops, and disband the volunteer forces. When Piedmont stood firm, Austria finally declared the desired war.[168]

As a state-sanctioned form of collective violence, the war claimed a great many casualties. In late April 1859 Field Marshall Count Ferencz Gyulai crossed the frontier, entering Piedmont with Austria's 100,000-man army in Italy. On 4 June 1859 the first major clash of the war took place east of Milan, the 'monstrous' Battle of Magenta, which was fought solely between Austrian and French armies, with Austria suffering defeat. In this battle alone 5,000 soldiers were killed, 12,000 wounded and 8,000 captured on the Austrian side; the French suffered 6,000 dead and wounded. On 24 June 1859 the second major action of the war took place south of Lake Garda – the twin battles of Solferino and San

---

Cardoza, 'Cavour and Piedmont', 126; Riall, *Risorgimento*, 30; see, too, the detailed treatment of the topic by de la Gorce, *Histoire du Second Empire*, vol. 2, Chapter 14, section 12; Matter, *Cavour et l'unité italienne*, vol. 3, 74–6 and section 2.6; and Stadler, *Cavour*, 124–5.

168 On the preparations for war, see Altgeld, 'Das Risorgimento (1815–1876)', 300–1, from which the quotations are taken; also Cardoza, 'Cavour and Piedmont', 126; Riall, *Risorgimento*, 30–1; and the detailed presentation in de la Gorce, *Histoire du Second Empire*, vol. 2, Chapter14, 13; also Matter, *Cavour et l'unité italienne*, vol. 3, section 2.8 and Chapter 3. On the international diplomatic preparations that consisted of France seeking (unsuccessfully) to win over Russia for the war against Austria and trying (successfully) to keep Prussia from becoming involved, on the British and Russian attempts to mediate, and on the inflexible Austrian escalation policy, see especially Coppa, *The Origins*, 93–8; Schulz, *Normen und Praxis*, 449–96; and Arnold Blumberg, *A Carefully Planned Accident: The Italian War of 1859* (Selinsgrove: Susquehanna University Press, 1990).

Martino, in which approximately 120,000 Austrians faced just as many French and Piedmontese troops. By the end of the day, the Austrian army again had to withdraw from the field, leaving 5,000 dead and 25,000 wounded on both sides.[169]

After the heavy losses in the twin battles of Solferino and San Martino, Napoleon III and Franz Josef I signed the preliminary peace of Villafranca, initiated by the French emperor. According to this agreement, Austria 'only' had to relinquish Lombardy, with the status quo remaining unchanged on all other matters. Both emperors were under the pressure of international developments, as most of the governments and public opinion in the German states called for the German Confederation to intervene in the war, the intention being to defend 'the Rhine at the Po' (Friedrich Engels) by attacking across the Rhine with Prussia's help. Such plans constituted a direct threat to France and an indirect one to the position of the Habsburg Empire in the German realm. Because the preliminary peace of Villafranca clearly contravened the Plombières agreement, Cavour resigned in bitterness two days after the agreement between France and Austria.[170]

The process of Italian unification that Napoleon III and Cavour had set in motion with this 'second war of independence' could no longer be stopped, however. The war had reignited the national movement, which now successfully employed political means that were non-violent and plebiscitary: spontaneous demonstrations as well as demonstrations controlled by Cavour and his national society ousted the Habsburg rulers from central Italy and drove the papal government representatives out of the northern parts of the Papal States. National liberals took their places. They conducted referenda in these territories, in which 98 or 99 per cent of the population voted for annexation to the Kingdom of Sardinia–Piedmont. Nonetheless, the arrangements made in the preliminary peace agreement of Villafranca, including the maintenance of the

---

169 This description is based on Altgeld, 'Das Risorgimento (1815–1876)', 301–2. See also Coppa, *The Origins*, 93–8; Cardoza, 'Cavour and Piedmont', 127; Riall, *Risorgimento*, 31; and the detailed descriptions in Stadler, *Cavour*, Chapter 9; and Matter, *Cavour et l'unité italienne*, vol. 3, Chapter 4.

170 Friedrich Engels, 'Po and Rhein', in Karl Marx and Friedrich Engels, *Collected Works*, vol. 16: *Marx and Engels 1858–60* (London: Lawrence & Wishart, 1980), 211. The description is based, in turn, on Altgeld, *Das Risorgimento (1815–1876)*, 302–3. On the preliminary peace of Villafranca and its international premises, see Schulz, *Normen und Praxis*, 496–9.

status quo ante in central Italy, were reaffirmed in the Treaty of Zurich at the end of 1859. However, Great Britain now entered the scene. The British government supported Cavour's return to office in January 1860 and stressed that it would no longer allow foreign interventions against the unification of northern and central Italy.[171]

As of that point the national unification of Italy was only a matter of time. The war had added impetus to the cause of the national liberals as well as democrats like Giuseppe Mazzini and Giuseppe Garibaldi. They did not content themselves with the unification of central and northern Italy under the Piedmontese king; they aimed to unify all of Italy, including the symbolically significant city of Rome. That intent contradicted not only the policy of France, whose troops still protected the secular power of the Pope, but also that of Cavour, who was counting on France. Cavour had been able to keep Garibaldi in line during the war by giving him control of a volunteer commando unit. When Cavour ceded Nice – Garibaldi's home town – along with Savoy to France and social unrest broke out in Sicily in April, Garibaldi again seized the initiative. With his legendary 'thousand' volunteers between the ages of eleven and seventy, mostly Italians but also many Germans, English, French, Poles and Hungarians, he set out from Genoa for Sicily by sea. They achieved what no one believed they could do: on 11 May 1860 they landed in Sicily, defeated the armies of the king of the Two Sicilies with the help of rebellious peasants and other volunteers, captured the capital city of Palermo, and marched into Naples on 7 September. The king withdrew to the fortress of Gaeta and then went into exile in Rome. Naples became a magnet for democrats and national revolutionaries throughout Europe, and Cavour began to fear that Garibaldi would march on Rome next and trigger a war with Napoleon III. But at a meeting with Vittorio Emanuele II in Teano, Garibaldi yielded. To avoid an Italian civil war, he placed the fate of Italy in the hands of the Piedmontese king. On 7 November 1860 Vittorio Emanuele II entered Naples, and the Kingdom of the Two Sicilies, too, merged with Sardinia–Piedmont. In February

---

171 For an introduction to the Zurich Peace Treaty and the integration of the central Italian states into the Kingdom of Sardinia–Piedmont, see Procacci, *History of the Italian People*, 316–17; Coppa, *The Origins*, 98–100; Cardoza, 'Cavour and Piedmont', 126–8; Riall, *Risorgimento*, 31. For a detailed treatment see Stadler, *Cavour*, 134–8; Matter, *Cavour et l'unité italienne*, vol. 3, Chapters 5, 6; and Schulz, *Normen und Praxis*, 499–503. The presentation above follows Altgeld, 'Das Risorgimento (1815–1876)', 304–5.

1861 Italy was officially united, with Turin as the capital and Vittorio Emanuele II as the first 'king of Italy'.[172]

Felice Orsini was not forgotten during these events. On the contrary, many reprints and translations of his autobiography, biographies (some of which were written by friends and acquaintances) and editions of his letters and other documents marked the months immediately after the attempted assassination of Napoleon III and the years after the official unification of Italy.[173] The fact that one of the objectives of these publications was to position Orsini as a national hero and martyr for Italy is especially apparent in the lavish new edition of his autobiography, whose format and layout resemble a family Bible.[174] These efforts at canonization succeeded, in the sense that Orsini and his attempted assassination of Napoleon III have remained key moments in the history of the Risorgimento to this day.

Nevertheless, Orsini's canonization remained precarious. As the writer Giancarlo de Cataldo notes, there is no Via Felice Orsini in Rome, only in Milan and small towns like Imola, Forli, Modena and Molfetta. He concludes from this finding that these toponomastics, or patterns of place names, transformed the 'only real terrorist' of the Risorgimento into a 'rural and peripheral hero'. And yet, de Cataldo continues, one ought to grant 'to poor Orsini a position in the pantheon of the heroes who, albeit with questionable methods, created Italy'. After all, Cavour granted Orsini's widow a pension.

---

172 See especially Altgeld, 'Das Risorgimento (1815–1876)', 305–10; and the vivid description by Procacci, *History of the Italian People*, 317–21; also Coppa, *The Origins*, 101–9; Cardoza, 'Cavour and Piedmont', 128–31; and Riall, *Risorgimento*, 32–3. For a detailed account, see Matter, *Cavour et l'unité italienne*, vol. 3, Chapters 7, 8.

173 See especially Felice Orsini, *Memorie politiche*, which dedicates a great deal of space to the conflict with Mazzini and the history of the attempt on the life of Napoleon III; the edited volume of letters, Sanvito, *Lettere edite ed inedite*; and the biographies by Felice Venosta, *Felice Orsini: Notizie Storiche* (Milan: Presso Carlo Barbini, 1862), and Montazio, *Felice Orsini*.

174 Anonymous, *Vita e memorie di Felice Orsini precedute dalla storia dell'attentato del 14 gennaio 1858 e seguite dagli interrogatori e documenti del processo* (Florence: A spese dell'editore, 1863). In addition to Orsini's autobiography, the volume contains a description of the attack on Napoleon III, a biography that positions Orsini in the history of Italy, the transcript of the trial, a letter by Orsini's wife, and numerous other letters and documents. For a general discussion of the culture and policy of remembering the heroes of the Risorgimento, see Alberto Mario Banti, 'The Remembrance of Heroes', in Patriarca and Riall, *The Risorgimento Revisited*, 171–90.

But the thought of placing Orsini among the 'great fathers of the Risorgimento' clearly makes de Cataldo uneasy. Would such status not be historical proof that terrorism works? Can and may one concede that a terrorist, that terrorism, made a considerable contribution to the emergence of Italy as a nation?[175] Whereas de Cataldo leaves open the question he poses about the effectiveness of terrorism, the historical literature on this topic tends to stress 'the unforeseeable' and the 'dramatic', but 'largely unintended . . . consequences' of Orsini's act.[176]

Taken on their own, statements about the unforeseeable and unintended consequences of the attempt on Napoleon III's life are undoubtedly correct. To leave the matter at that, however, is misleading. Such statements suggest that unintended and unforeseeable consequences of actions are unique to Felice Orsini and his act of violence and thereby divest the attacker and his deed of their historic import. It is like saying that an action by Orsini cannot be credited with an effect he did not plan and foresee. As Anthony Cardoza stresses, the unintended and unforeseeable in the Risorgimento are pivotal not only with respect to Orsini's attack but throughout the entire process of Italian nation building: 'There is little question that the new nation which emerged in 1861 was a largely unplanned product of war, diplomacy, and popular revolution carried out against all odds by a large cast of often mutually hostile forces that ranged from Bonapartists to Mazzinian democrats.' According to this view, the creation of the Italian nation state – contrary to what the nationalist and fascist historiography of the nineteenth and twentieth centuries suggests – is actually not 'a striking example of how exceptional individuals can have a profound impact on the course of history'. It is not the result of the continual and deliberate agency of a few superhuman figures. Instead, 'the campaign for the unification of Italy was an extremely contingent and unpredictable process' that even powerful conspirators like Napoleon III and Cavour could not control. It was instead a process in which they, their objectives and their political actions always had to adapt to contingencies and the unforeseeable and unintended consequences of war, diplomacy and revolution.[177] If, then,

---

175 Cataldo, *Il Maestro, Il Terrorista, Il Terrone*, 69, 95–6. For the diagnosis of precarious canonization (and the attempt to change it), also see Manzini, *Avventure e morte de Felice Orsini*.

176 Procacci, *History of the Italian People*, 315; Riall, *Risorgimento*, 29.

177 Cardoza, 'Cavour and Piedmont', 131.

the significance of the unforeseeable – of goal-oriented action, which must remain flexible and ever responsive to new, unforeseen conditions – also extends to other protagonists of the Risorgimento, then Orsini and terrorism must be included along with war, diplomacy, revolution and the brisk jockeying between innumerable adversarial actors that, in sum, brought Italy forth as a nation.

In the case of Felice Orsini, the use of terrorist violence as a tactic did indeed lead to the desired result in the medium term. His attack was the point of departure for historical events that gave rise to the creation of the Italian nation. His act of violence thereby vitally contributed to the fact that a united and independent Italy emerged. This outcome owed less to Felice Orsini's strategic and tactical planning than to the response by Napoleon III. He made the political goals of his attacker his own. Among many other things, he used the perpetrator and that person's spectacular act to achieve those goals – as he, Napoleon, understood them. Terrorism and its success were, hence, the result of cooperation between the attacker and his victim as they pursued different goals.

The example of Felice Orsini does not yet constitute historical evidence of terrorism's successful use – defined as the use of terrorism as a tactic that achieves its political aims. Nevertheless, the combination of Orsini's bomb attack exceeding all expectations in its brutality, the cooperation between the assassin and the French emperor, and Napoleon III's media policy set a precedent for what spectacular violence can trigger when it is subsequently stage-managed in the mass media and politically instrumentalized. This lesson did not pass unnoticed – either within Europe or beyond that continent.

3

Transatlantic communication

*Reporting in the United States of America on
Orsini's attempted assassination of Napoleon III*

At 10:20 a.m. on 16 January 1858, the three-masted paddle steamer *Canada* left the port of Liverpool under the command of Captain Lang. The steamship of the British and North American Royal Mail Steam-Packet Company founded by Samuel Cunard (also called the Cunard Line) sailed around the north coast of Wales, continued along the south coast of Ireland, and reached the port city of Cork on the morning of 17 January, where it stopped to pick up additional mail and passengers. At midday, it raised anchor and set course for British North America (soon to be known as Canada), a passage that lasted eleven days. When the ship arrived at Halifax harbour at 4 a.m. on 28 January, the ship's crew had already thrown a package of newspapers overboard for the New York Associated Press ninety miles from Cape Race, the eastern tip of Newfoundland. Wrapped in watertight packaging and marked by a signal flag, the parcel was fished from the water by the crew of a small yacht and taken to St John's. There, the Associated Press had set up a telegraph station about a year and a half earlier to collect news from ships coming from Europe as they approached the eastern coast of North America. The most important bulletins were then telegraphed from St John's to New York City, which the steamships reached on their route several days later.[1]

---

1 On the transportation of the news, see 'Three Days Later from Europe. Arrival of the Canada at Halifax . . . Attempt to Assassinate the Emperor Napoleon' and 'News of the Day', *New York Times*, 29 January 1858, 1, 4. On the *Canada* and the British and North American Royal Mail Steam-Packet Company, see the item entitled 'Canada 1848/

The regular transatlantic shipping that brought newspapers, correspondents' reports and telegraphic dispatches from Europe to the United States was a new phenomenon. The Cunard Line had been operating only since 1840, and most of the other Atlantic shipping lines had not been created until the 1850s, such as the Allan Line (1854) and the Galway Line (1858). Key technical innovations in the use of steam engines on ocean-faring vessels, the increase in foreign trade and the international competition between government-funded shipping companies all contributed to the decade's increase in the number and speed of ships used for Atlantic crossings.[2]

Mississippi', accessed 7 January 2016, 'The Ships List', Ship Descriptions, 11 July 2012, theshipslist.com; Thomas Alexander Bushell, *Royal Mail: A Centenary History of the Royal Mail Line, 1839–1939* (London: Trade and Travel Publications Ltd, 1939); and especially Stephen Fox, *Transatlantic: Samuel Cunard, Isambard Brunel, and the Great Atlantic Steamships* (New York: Oxford University Press, 2003). See also Janette McCutcheon, *Cunard: A Photographic History* (Stroud: Tempus, 2004); and the introduction in Peter Pigott, *Sailing Seven Seas: A History of the Canadian Pacific Line* (Toronto: Dundurn Press, 2010). For an introduction to the competition for the freshest news from Europe and the Associated Press's station on St John's, see Jenny Higgins and Luke Callanan, '19th Century Communications and Transportation', in *Newfoundland and Labrador Heritage Web Site*, heritage.nf.ca; Menahem Blondheim, *News over the Wires: The Telegraph and the Flow of Public Information in America, 1844–1897* (Cambridge, MA: Harvard University Press, 1994), Chapter 4 and 110–13, 128–9; and the vivid description in Victor Rosewater, *History of Coöperative News-Gathering in the United States* (New York: D. Appleton and Company, 1930), 32–3.

2 The first steam-aided transatlantic crossing by ship took place in 1819, when the *Savannah* used its steam engine on four of thirty days at sea. In 1838 two ships, the paddle-wheel steamers *Sirius* and *Great Western*, crossed the Atlantic solely under steam power for the first time. On these crossings, the transport revolution involving steam engines and the shipping companies cited here, see the classic work by George Rogers Taylor, *The Transportation Revolution, 1815–1860* (New York: Rinehart, 1951), 112–22; Bushell, *Royal Mail*, Chapters 1–2; the overview by John Haskell Kemble, 'Mail Steamers Link the Americas, 1840–1890', in Adele Ogden and Engel Sluiter (eds.), *Greater America: Essays in Honor of Herbert Eugene Bolton* (Berkeley: University of California Press, 1945), 475–97; Fox, *Transatlantic*; and the introduction in Pigott, *Sailing Seven Seas*. Richard Bach Jensen points to 'the first great globalization boom' at the end of the nineteenth and beginning of the twentieth centuries, a boom labelled as such by the economists Kevin H. O'Rourke and Jeffrey G. Williamson, in order to explain the spread of anarchism and anarchist terrorism throughout the world (Jensen, *The Battle against Anarchist Terrorism*, especially 58). This is certainly convincing. However, it was not so much the globalization of the economy that was necessary for the invention of terrorism, but rather the internationalization to a certain degree of transportation, communications, the media and the public. These had already been achieved by the mid-nineteenth century.

The connection between the transport revolution and the revolution in communications and the media acquires concrete definition in the transatlantic realm, as the development in steam-powered navigation is supplemented by other innovations in media and communication technologies in the United States. The emergence of the penny press and the use of the telegraph to gather and report news are two important examples of this. Penny papers were dailies that people could buy spontaneously from newspaper boys on the street rather than having to pay expensive annual subscriptions or purchase a copy for six pence at selected newspaper stands. The first successful paper of this kind, the *Sun*, had been founded by Benjamin H. Day in New York in 1833. The new concept permitted Day to attract new strata of readers, for, until then, the high price of newspapers had made them a preserve of the economic and political elite. Day actively targeted the general population. His bet paid off, and the *Sun* soon had competitors to contend with. In 1834 the *New York Transcript* and the *Man* followed up with the same business model. In 1835 James Gordon Bennett founded the *Morning Herald*, which, under the name *New York Herald* and with a print run of 12,000 copies, became the most popular US daily by 1845.[3]

The competition between these penny papers fundamentally changed the newspaper business in the United States. To reach the new strata of readers, the articles in the penny press were written in clear, simple and lively language. New topics, such as local news, crime reporting, court trials, sports, human-interest stories and serial novels were included in

---

3 See James L. Crouthamel, *Bennett's New York Herald and the Rise of the Popular Press* (Syracuse: Syracuse University Press, 1989), 4; Gerald J. Baldasty, *The Commercialization of News in the Nineteenth Century* (Madison: University of Wisconsin Press, 1992), Chapter 2; William Huntzicker, *The Popular Press, 1833–1865* (Westport: Greenwood Press, 1999), Chapters 1–2; Susan Thompson, *The Penny Press* (Northport: Vision Press, 2004), prologue and Chapters 1–2; and James L. Crouthamel, 'The Newspaper Revolution in New York, 1830–1860', *New York History* 45/2 (1864), 91–113. In 1924 the *New York Herald* was bought by its competitor, the *New York Tribune*, and was renamed the *New York Herald Tribune*. The European edition, once named the *International Herald Tribune*, is known today as the *New York Times* international edition. Richard Bach Jensen argues in a similar way that the beginning of the age of mass media was crucial to the generation of anarchist terrorism. He refers to the emergence of a 'new journalism' in the 1880s in order to make his point (Jensen, *The Battle against Anarchist Terrorism*, especially 52–4). I argue here that it was even earlier, in the 1830s and 1840s, that the rise of the popular press, the invention of the telegraph and the development of the news agencies enabled the invention of terrorism to occur.

the reporting.[4] Most important, it suddenly became paramount to report news more quickly than the competition did, for a newspaper's well-to-do subscribers, too, bought a penny paper on the street if its news was more current. The time factor thereby began to play an important role in collecting and transmitting news, and publishers like Day and Bennett were willing to pay a considerable sum for the timeliness of their papers. They used carrier pigeons, their own pony express and, later, a private locomotive express between Washington and New York City. To receive European news earlier than their competitors, these entrepreneurs also sent boats into the Long Island Sound to meet the ships arriving from Europe.[5]

The invention of the telegraph complemented this development, with Samuel F. B. Morse patenting the electrical telegraph in the United States in 1837. After the first connection between Washington and Baltimore was inaugurated in 1844, his coverage of the Democratic Party convention persuaded politicians and the public alike of the invention's viability and utility. The newspaper publishers recognized this technology as crucial for their operations. Several of them jointly created the Magnetic Telegraph Company, which helped advance the expansion of the telegraph network in the United States. By 1846 the lines from Washington, DC to New York, Boston, Albany and Buffalo were up and running. Connections southward towards New Orleans and westward into the Mississippi valley were under construction. New York became the hub of this telegraph network.[6]

The establishment of the American news agency was linked to this development. After the Mexican–American war broke out in 1846, six major New York newspapers (the *Sun*, *Herald*, *Tribune*, *Express*, *Journal of Commerce* and *Courier and Enquirer*) banded together to organize an express news service from Mexico to the southernmost telegraph post in the United States. It was the birth of the New York Associated Press. The six papers soon deepened their collaboration, jointly acquiring news from Washington and Boston, where the ships of the Cunard Line

---

4 See, for example, Thompson, *Penny Press*, prologue; and Huntzicker, *Popular Press*, Chapter 1.

5 On these early systems for transmitting news, see Rosewater, *Coöperative News-Gathering*, Chapters 1–4; Richard Allen Schwarzlose, *The Nation's Newsbrokers*, 2 vols. (Evanston: Northwestern University Press, 1989), vol. 1: *The Formative Years, from Pretelegraph to 1865*, Chapter 1; and Blondheim, *News over the Wires*, Chapter 1.

6 See Kenneth Silverman, *Lightning Man: The Accursed Life of Samuel F. B. Morse* (New York: Alfred A. Knopf, 2003), Chapters 7–12; Schwarzlose, *The Nation's Newsbrokers*, vol. 1, Chapter 2; and Blondheim, *News over the Wires*, Chapter 2.

originally arrived with the most recent reports from Europe. New York thereby also became the country's communications hub.[7] In the early 1850s the telegraph network in the United States greatly expanded, connecting ever more distant regions and adding ever more branch lines to the main network.[8] The New York Associated Press pursued and used this expansion of the network, transforming itself into a national news agency to which essentially all the country's newspapers belonged: 'By 1859 the New York Associated Press had created a truly national system for the transmission of public information,' as Menachem Blondheim characterizes this development.[9]

Technologically and organizationally, the nation was ready in 1858 to receive the news of Orsini's violent act and transmit it into the furthest regions with unprecedented speed. The packages that the *Canada* had taken on board in Liverpool and Cork on 16 and 17 January 1858 and had delivered at Cape Race contained newspapers from London and Paris dated 14, 15 and 16 January, which contained accounts of Orsini's attempted assassination of Napoleon III. These reports became front-page news in the United States, too, and were immediately transmitted in detail by telegraph from Cape Race to New York City on 28 January along with the London stock exchange figures and the most important political news from Europe and China. They appeared in the *New York Times* and the *New York Herald* on 29 January – two weeks after Orsini's attack.[10] On the following two days, these first telegraphic reports were already supplemented by reprints of articles from British and French newspapers and by the commentaries of New York City's own newspapers.[11] On 3 February, the propeller steamship *Edinburgh* arrived in New York harbour. It had left Glasgow on 16 January,

---

7 See Rosewater, *Coöperative News-Gathering*, Chapter 5; Schwarzlose, *The Nation's Newsbrokers*, vol. 1, Chapters 2 and 3; Blondheim, *News over the Wires*, Chapters 3 and 4.

8 See Rosewater, *Coöperative News-Gathering*, Chapters 7–11; Blondheim, *News over the Wires*, 65–7; Silverman, *Lightning Man*, Chapter 14.

9 Blondheim, *News over the Wires*, 117.

10 'Three Days Later from Europe. Arrival of the Canada at Halifax . . . Attempt to Assassinate the Emperor Napoleon' and 'News of the Day', *New York Times*, 29 January 1858, 1, 4; 'Another Attempt on the Life of the Emperor Napoleon', *New York Herald*, 29 January 1858, col. D.

11 See the compilation of articles under 'Interesting from Europe. Further Particulars of the Attempted Assassination of Napoleon', *New York Times*, 1 February 1858, 2; and 'Attempt to Assassinate the Emperor Napoleon', *New York Herald*, 30 January 1858, col. A, as well as the commentary entitled 'The Gospel of Murder', *New York Times*, 30 January 1858, 4.

the same day that the *Canada* had embarked, but not until evening, so it carried the evening newspapers, which were a few hours more up to date than those that the *Canada* had brought from Liverpool. The New York press once again published the full reports from these papers, which had also been taken from the major newspapers in London and Paris.[12]

The pivotal news package reached the United States four days later with the Cunard Line steamer *Arabia*, which had left Liverpool on 23 January carrying the previous week's reports from the French and British papers as well as the original accounts written by American correspondents in Paris.[13] Drawing on all this input, the newspaper editors filled the columns on 8 and 9 February with detailed descriptions of the events, the background and the reactions in France and around Europe. They also composed more recent and more extensive commentary on the situation. The demand for such news persisted, and over the following weeks other ships delivered further reports about the police investigations and the trial, keeping the story highly topical until well into May 1858.[14]

The news about Orsini's attempt on the life of Napoleon III found an interested and well-informed readership in the United States. Ever

---

12 See 'Arrival of the Edinburgh ... Further Particulars of the Attempted Assassination of Napoleon' and 'News of the Day', *New York Times*, 4 February 1858, 1, 4; 'Arrival of the Edinburgh ... The Attempted Assassination of Napoleon', *New York Herald*, 4 February 1858, col. A.

13 'One Week Later from Europe. Arrival of the Arabia. Details of the Attempted Assassination of the French Emperor', *New York Times*, 8 February 1858, 1; and 'Our Foreign Files by the Arabia Contain the Following Additional Particulars Relative to the Feeling Pervading the Mind in Europe on the Subject of the Late Attempt on Napoleon's Life', *New York Herald*, 8 February 1858, 2.

14 'One Week Later from Europe. Arrival of the Arabia. Details of the Attempted Assassination of the French Emperor'; 'France and the Emperor'; 'The Attempted Assassination of the Emperor of the French. Complete History of the Plot and Its Denouement. Antecedents of the Conspirators. From Our Own Correspondent. Paris, Thursday, Jan. 21, 1858', and 'News of the Day', *New York Times*, 8 and 9 February 1858, 1, 4; 'The Attempted Assassination of Napoleon. Additional Interesting Particulars. Six Killed, and Nearly One Hundred and Fifty Wounded. Demands on the English Government to Expel the Refugees'; 'Interesting from France. Opening the French Chambers. Napoleon's Speech. What Is Thought of the Attempted Assassination'; and the commentary 'The News from Europe. Effect of the Attempted Assassination of Louis Napoleon'; 'Napoleon's Escape from Assassination. The Projectiles. General Rejoicing of the Continental Monarchs. Official and Popular Congratulations'; and 'Our Foreign Files by the Arabia Contain the Following Additional Particulars Relative to the Feeling Pervading the Mind in Europe on the Subject of the Late Attempt on Napoleon's Life', *New York Herald*, 8 and 9 February 1858, cols. B, D, F 2, and 4.

since the mid-1840s, many Americans, especially abolitionists, had been quite favourably disposed towards the European revolutionary movements, especially the struggle for an Italian republic. In Italy – as in the United States in 1776 – the conflict was about achieving political freedom and national independence, a fact that 'caused the Italian question to come perhaps nearer to America's sympathy than any other European exigency'.[15] The publication of Margaret Fuller Ossoli's letters from the Roman Republic in the *New York Tribune*, the coverage in daily newspapers and journals, the traditional study tours in Italy by the upper middle classes, Italian literature and speeches all served as important sources of information. In addition, there was the agitation by the Giovine Italia, which had its own offshoots in the United States. Giuseppe Mazzini had many prominent followers in America, including the abolitionist William Lloyd Garrison, who frequently allotted space in the *Liberator* to the Italian struggle for freedom. Furthermore, the government reactions to the revolutions of 1848–9 had led many political refugees from Italy and other European countries to the United States. These refugees had personal experience with the revolutionary struggles in Europe, and their reports and stories shaped the American image of the political situation in Europe. Moreover, the refugees from Europe were themselves a well-informed public interested in news about how the struggles were developing. There had already been extensive reporting in the United States both on the attempted insurrection in Milan, in which Felice Orsini had participated, and on Mazzini's effort to foment a revolution in Sardinia–Piedmont in 1857, which Orsini had refused to join.[16]

---

15 Howard Rosario Marraro, *American Opinion on the Unification of Italy, 1846–1861* (New York: Columbia University Press, 1932), 305. See also Mischa Honeck, *We Are the Revolutionists: German-Speaking Immigrants and American Abolitionists after 1848* (Athens, GA: University of Georgia Press, 2011), 13–15.

16 See Marraro, *American Opinion*, especially ix, 205–14, 305. On the Italian Forty-Eighters, see Stefano Luconi, 'Gli Stati Uniti come meta', *Archivo Storico dell'Emigrazione Italian*, 2014, asei.eu/it; and Patrizia Audenino, 'Esuli risorgimentali: esploratori della libertà o naufraghi della rivoluzione', *Archivo Storico dell'Emigrazione Italian*, 2013, asei.eu/it. Both sources are reprinted in Emilio Franzina and Matteo Sanfilippo, *Risorgimento ed emigrazione* (Viterbo: Sette Città, 2014). On German Forty-Eighters, see Carl Frederick Wittke, *Refugees of Revolution: The German Forty-Eighters in America* [1952] (Westport: Greenwood Press, 1970); Charlotte Lang Brancaforte, *The German Forty-Eighters in the United States* (New York: P. Lang, 1989); Bruce C. Levine, *The Spirit of 1848: German Immigrants, Labor Conflict, and the*

In short, the revolutionary struggles in Europe, including Italy, were on people's minds in the United States.

Coverage of Orsini's assassination attempt was extensive and lively in the US dailies,[17] and it drew a reaction from many people. The news of Orsini's execution in Paris was followed in New York by a torchlight procession of French, Germans, Italians, Hungarians and other foreigners on 22 April. According to the *New York Times*, an estimated 20,000 'red republicans' participated, making it the largest political demonstration that the country had ever witnessed among recently arrived immigrants. Many of these immigrants gave speeches, emphasized Orsini's noble sacrifice, and quoted the last words he was said to have spoken. During the march, the Steuben House, the seat of the organizing committee, was illuminated and emblazoned with the names of 'martyrs for freedom'.[18] In cities such as Boston, Cincinnati and Chicago, similar, smaller demonstrations took place. Just as in some European countries, Orsini was celebrated as a martyr in the United States.

And just as in Europe, Felice Orsini and his act of violence radicalized and polarized politics in America. Whereas radical immigrants and inveterate radical segments of the population in the US's northern and southern states celebrated the attack by Orsini as an act perpetrated to help secure universal rights of freedom, liberals and conservatives insisted that he was simply a criminal and a murderer. Considering the influence on American policy, the German scholar of American studies Mischa Honeck has described Felice Orsini as an outright 'transatlantic revolutionary',[19] and, as such, Orsini especially left his mark on history through the impression his act made on John Brown.

Coming of Civil War (Urbana: University of Illinois Press, 1992); and Honeck, *We Are the Revolutionists*.

17 For more on this, see Marraro, *American Opinion*, 215–18; Mischa Honeck, ' "Freemen of All Nations, Bestir Yourselves": Felice Orsini's Transnational Afterlife and the Radicalization of America', *Journal of the Early Republic* 30/4 (2010), 587–615, 591–2; and pp. 263–75 in this volume.

18 See Janine C. Hartman, 'Transatlantic Spartacus', in Andrew Taylor and Eldrid Herrington (eds.), *The Afterlife of John Brown* (New York: Palgrave Macmillan, 2005), 150–1; Honeck, 'Freemen of All Nations', 593–5; Mark A. Lause, *A Secret Society History of the Civil War* (Urbana: University of Illinois Press, 2011), 88–9.

19 Honeck, 'Freemen of All Nations', especially 589–90; quotation at 590. On this period of radicalization in the United States, see also Lause, *A Secret Society History*, 87–92.

4

Hostages for emancipation

John Brown's raid on Harpers Ferry and the end of slavery in the United States

The political blockage in the United States

With their seizure of the federal armoury and arsenal in Harpers Ferry, John Brown and his volunteers sought to break the political blockage that had arisen from the prolonged dispute about the abolition of slavery. For in the United States, unlike in Europe, all attempts to emancipate the slaves either peacefully by decree or through public engagement had failed.[1]

This divergence occurred despite a political culture and public sphere similar to that in Great Britain having developed in the former British colonies. Since 1791, the freedoms of speech, press, assembly and petition had been anchored in the Constitution through the Bill of Rights.[2] The literacy rate among men and women was high. After the end of the British–American War of 1812, in 1815, the Union, soon to have twenty

---

1 See pp. 81–6.

2 The First Amendment of the Constitution states, 'Congress shall make no law . . . abridging the freedom of speech, or of the press; or the right of the people peaceably to assemble, and to petition the Government for a redress of grievances.' In Jack N. Rakove (ed.), *The Annotated US Constitution and Declaration of Independence* (Cambridge, MA: Harvard University Press, 2009), 223. Facsimile available on the website for the National Archives and Record Administration, hereafter NARA, archives.gov. On the similarity of the American and British political cultures and public spheres, see Jürgen Heideking and Christof Mauch, *Geschichte der USA*, 4th revised and expanded ed. (Tübingen: Francke, 2006), 20–2.

states and already territorially quite extensive, experienced a transport and communication revolution. These dramatic developments were driven by the construction of road and canal networks, the invention and use of steamboats, the systematic expansion of the postal system, and the adoption of innovations in paper production and the printing industry. Such advances allowed the country to grow together. By 1822, more newspapers were being read in the United States than in any other country worldwide (regardless of population), with over 160 newspapers based in New York City alone by 1828. A national market for printed matter had developed by 1830, and the emergence of the penny press in the 1830s meant that newspapers reached not only the elite, but also the general population.[3] A national public sphere – the prerequisite for a broad-based social movement – existed by this time at the latest.

The conflict over slavery began in North America in the early 1770s with a debate about the British abolitionists' first courtroom victories. In Britain's North American colonies, the anti-slavery coalition initially resembled its counterpart in the mother country: Quakers, Puritan ministers, intellectuals from Boston to Philadelphia and African Americans. It was slaves who in 1773 first petitioned the Massachusetts legislature and Quakers who in 1775 founded the first anti-slavery society, which would soon include prominent members such as Benjamin Franklin and Alexander Hamilton.[4]

---

3 On the transport and communication revolutions see pp. 177–85 in this volume. See also Daniel Walker Howe, *What Hath God Wrought: The Transformation of America, 1815–1848* (Oxford: Oxford University Press, 2007), Chapter 6 and 227; George Rogers Taylor, *The Transportation Revolution, 1815–1860* (New York: Rinehart, 1951); and Richard R. John, *Spreading the News: The American Postal System from Franklin to Morse* (Cambridge, MA: Harvard University Press, 1995). On the connection between nation building, political culture, participation and the press in the United States, see Thomas C. Leonard, *The Power of the Press: The Birth of American Political Reporting* (New York: Oxford University Press, 1986), 54–96; Richard D. Brown, *The Strength of a People: The Idea of an Informed Citizenry in America, 1650–1870* (Chapel Hill: University of North Carolina Press, 1996); Trish Loughran, *The Republic in Print: Print Culture in the Age of US Nation Building, 1770–1870* (New York: Columbia University Press, 2007); and Robert A. Gross and Mary Kelley (eds.), *A History of the Book in America*, vol. 2: *An Extensive Republic: Print, Culture, and Society in the New Nation, 1790–1840* (Chapel Hill: University of North Carolina Press in association with the American Antiquarian Society, 2010).

4 See Drescher, *Abolition*, 106–14; James Brewer Stewart, *Holy Warriors: The Abolitionists and American Slavery* (New York: Hill and Wang, 1996), Chapter 1; Merton Lynn Dillon, *Slavery Attacked: Southern Slaves and Their Allies, 1619–1865* (Baton Rouge: Louisiana State University Press, 1990), Chapter 2; Stanley Harrold, *American*

But, with the outbreak of the Revolutionary War, the question of slavery in North America receded for the time being into the background, with the Euro-American population now having other priorities. Yet the contradiction between the rebels' struggle against Britain's supposed attempts to 'enslave' them and their holding of slaves was not lost on the European colonists in America, their slaves or the British public. Many of the United States' founding fathers, such as George Washington, Thomas Jefferson, James Madison, John Adams and the aforementioned Benjamin Franklin and Alexander Hamilton, saw slavery as a great burden for the new state, regardless of whether they themselves held slaves or not. Numerous slaves were freed during or immediately following the Revolutionary War by their owners, while others seized the chance during the War of Independence to flee or join the ranks of the armies in hopes of gaining their freedom after surviving the battlefield. The abolition of slavery, however, did not occur during the American Revolution. After United States independence was recognized with the Treaty of Paris in 1783, some 700,000 slaves and almost 60,000 free African Americans lived in the newly founded country.[5]

The contradiction between the promise of freedom and equality for all people and the perpetuation of slavery found its way into the United States' founding documents and was stipulated there. Although slaveholder Thomas Jefferson had so brilliantly formulated the ideals of

---

Abolitionists (Harlow: Longman, 2001), Chapter 2; Finzsch et al., *Von Benin nach Baltimore*, 119–24; and especially Winthrop D. Jordan, *White over Black: American Attitudes toward the Negro, 1550–1812* (Chapel Hill: University of North Carolina Press, 1968), parts 3–4; and James D. Essig, *The Bonds of Wickedness: American Evangelicals against Slavery, 1770–1808* (Philadelphia: Temple University Press, 1982). For the perspective of social-movement research, see Michael P. Young, *Bearing Witness against Sin: The Evangelical Birth of the American Social Movement* (Chicago: The University of Chicago Press, 2006).

5 For an introduction to the American Revolution, see Heideking and Mauch, *Geschichte der USA*, Chapter 2; and Robert Middlekauff, *The Glorious Cause: The American Revolution, 1763–1789* (New York: Oxford University Press, 2005). On slaves and the question of slavery, see Middlekauff, Chapter 21.5; Davis, *Inhuman Bondage*, Chapter 7; Drescher, *Abolition*, Chapter 5; Finzsch, Horton and Horton, *Von Benin nach Baltimore*, 119–42; Jordan, *White over Black*, 289–304, 349–56; the still-valuable analysis by Edmund S. Morgan, *American Slavery, American Freedom: The Ordeal of Colonial Virginia* (New York: W. W. Norton, 1975); and Ira Berlin, *Slaves without Masters: The Free Negros in the Antebellum South* (New York: New Press, 1974), Chapter 1. On the numbers of slaves, see Morgan, *American Slavery*, 45–50, 396–7.

freedom and equality in the Declaration of Independence from 1776 –
'We hold these truths to be self-evident: that all men are created equal;
that they are endowed by their Creator with certain unalienable rights;
that among these are life, liberty, and the pursuit of happiness'[6] – the
Constitution of 1787 supported the institution of slavery by protecting
slaveownership, leaving the decision to abolish slavery up to the individual states, and stipulated with the 'three-fifths-clause' that five slaves were
to be counted as three free persons when assessing taxes owed the Union
and apportioning seats in the House of Representatives.[7] Through their
high numbers, the disenfranchised slaves thus involuntarily strengthened
the mandate of those campaigning for their continued enslavement.

To resolve the contradiction between the promises of the American
Revolution and the reality of life in the United States, between the
Declaration of Independence and the Constitution, the states north of
the Mason–Dixon Line (where slaves constituted less than 10 per cent of
the population) began to introduce emancipation measures after the War

6 Thomas Jefferson et al., 'July 4, 1776, Copy of Declaration of Independence', the
Thomas Jefferson Papers at the Library of Congress, -07-04, 1776, Manuscript/Mixed
Material, loc.gov/resource/mtj1.001_0556_0559; a downloadable high-resolution scan
and transcription is available at archives.gov. An interesting facsimile of a broadside
printed on 4 July 1776 can be found at research.history.org.

7 Signed Copy of the Constitution of the United States; Miscellaneous Papers of the
Continental Congress, 1774–1789; Records of the Continental and Confederation
Congresses and the Constitutional Convention, 1774–1789, Record Group (hereafter
RG) 360; National Archives Building Washington, DC (hereafter NAB), archives.gov,
NARA, ourdocuments.gov, reprinted in Rakove, *The Annotated US Constitution and
Declaration of Independence*, 103. On regulations pertaining to slavery see Finzsch,
Horton and Horton, *Von Benin nach Baltimore*, 150–3; and specifically Paul Finkelman,
Race and the Constitution: From the Philadelphia Convention to the Age of Segregation
(Washington, DC: American Historical Association, 2010), Chapter 1; Jürgen Heideking,
*The Constitution before the Judgment Seat: The Prehistory and Ratification of the American
Constitution, 1787–1791*, ed. John P. Kaminsky and Richard Leffler (Charlottesville:
University of Virginia Press, 2012), 128–32; David Waldstreicher, *Slavery's Constitution:
From Revolution to Ratification* (New York: Hill and Wang, 2009); and George William
van Cleve, *A Slaveholders' Union: Slavery, Politics, and the Constitution in the Early
American Republic* (Chicago: The University of Chicago Press, 2010), Part 2. In contrast
to older literature, which treated the topic of slavery in the negotiations in Philadelphia
as incidental and viewed the Constitution as neutral in this question, these authors
detail the crucial significance of the slavery question at the convention and point out the
character of the Constitution as 'politically, economically, and legally favoring slavery'
(Van Cleve, *A Slaveholders' Union*, 270), even if the terms 'slave', 'slavery' and 'race' do not
appear in the text.

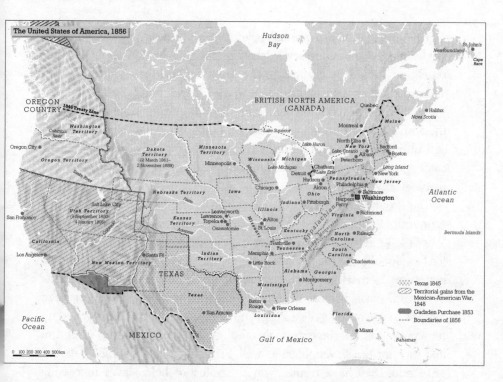

Map 2. The United States of America, 1856.

of Independence. By 1804 legislatures and courts in Vermont, New Hampshire, Massachusetts, Connecticut, Rhode Island, Pennsylvania, New York and New Jersey had ratified an immediate or gradual abolition of slavery. These bodies, however, also instituted laws discriminating against the freed African Americans at all levels of political, economic and social life. Nevertheless, these emancipation processes were generally considered successful. Thus the expectation had become widespread by the end of the War of 1812 in 1815 that other states would pass similar emancipation laws over time, with the 'peculiar institution' of slavery dying out and the United States living up to its own revolutionary claims.[8]

---

8 See Finzsch, Horton and Horton, *Von Benin nach Baltimore*, 138–42; the classic account by Arthur Zilversmit, *The First Emancipation: The Abolition of Slavery in the North* (Chicago: Doubleday, 1967); Leon F. Litwack, *North of Slavery: The Negro in the Free States: 1790–1860* (Chicago: The University of Chicago Press, 1961); and Joanne Pope Melish, *Disowning Slavery: Gradual Emancipation and 'Race' in New England, 1780–1860* (Ithaca: Cornell University Press, 1998). On the expectation that slavery would die out with time in the United States, see, for instance, Drescher, *Abolition*, 142.

This anticipation of a gradual, peaceful ending of slavery was, however, not fulfilled. On the contrary, a debate in Congress in 1819 about whether statehood should be granted to the Missouri Territory, which allowed and protected slavery, first brought to the broader public's attention that the part of the Union allowing slavery was expanding more rapidly with the admission of Kentucky, Tennessee, Louisiana, Mississippi, Alabama and ultimately Missouri than the part prohibiting it, with slavery advocates growing stronger economically and going on the offensive ideologically.[9]

The grounds for the aggressive expansion of slavery were primarily economic. Rapid expansion of the world economy after the end of the War of 1812 in the United States and the Napoleonic Wars in Europe had led to a doubling of the price of cotton within a year. The invention of the cotton gin, a machine to remove seeds from the cotton fibres, and the opportunity arising from the forced resettlement of the Native American nations to cultivate fertile acreage in the new southern states opened up new prospects for the extremely labour-intensive cultivation of cotton and thus for the slaveholders as well. Prices for slaves doubled between 1814 and 1819 as a result, with the value of held slaves increasing accordingly.[10]

The economic incentives were augmented by power-political and racist motives. The Euro-American elite in the states with plantation-based economies south of the Mason–Dixon Line had been confronted since the founding of the United States with the question of how to maintain supremacy and racial segregation in a democracy when slaves made up between one-third and nine-tenths of the population in their regions. Emancipating the slaves and accepting them as social and political equals was out of the question for this white population:

---

9 For introductory information, see Heideking and Mauch, *Geschichte der USA*, 91–2, 109–10; Finzsch, Horton and Horton, *Von Benin nach Baltimore*, 188–90; Howe, *What Hath God Wrought*, 4; and Drescher, *Abolition*, 139–40.

10 See Finzsch, Horton and Horton, *Von Benin nach Baltimore*, 160–4; and specifically Jordan, *White over Black*, 315–21; Drescher, *Abolition*, Chapter 5 and 308–9; Howe, *What Hath God Wrought*, Chapter 4; and in a global historical context, Beckert, *Empire of Cotton*, especially 101–20. On the formation of an ideology defending slavery as a positive good, see George M. Fredrickson, *The Black Image in the White Mind: The Debate on Afro-American Character and Destiny, 1817–1914* (New York: Harper & Row, 1972), Chapter 2.

We are told it is cruel and disgraceful to keep them in slavery. There is
no doubt of it. But would it not be more cruel to place them in a situation where we must in self-defence – gentlemen will understand me –
get rid of them in some way. We must get rid of them, or they of us;
there is no alternative . . . Not one of them would be left alive within a
year.

The often repeated threat – here in the words of Peter Early, a congressman from South Carolina – was that the inevitable outcome of emancipation would be a war of extermination between whites and blacks, just
as in French Saint-Domingue.[11]

Euro-Americans critical of slavery therefore supported the American
Colonization Society founded in 1816. This organization, which was
influential in both the South and North in the 1820s, propagated the
emigration of free African Americans to Haiti or Africa as a solution to
the slavery issue. In this way, according to the society's concept, slaveholders could free their slaves without contributing to the dreaded proliferation of the population of free African Americans in the United States.[12]

The political resistance faced by the abolitionist movement in North
America was disproportionately greater than that encountered in

11 Speech by Peter Early on 17 December 1806 on the topic of the slave trade, in *The
Debates and Proceedings in the Congress of the United States in the Congress of the United
States; with an Appendix Containing Important State Papers and Public Documents and
All the Laws of a Public Nature; with a Copious Index, Ninth Congress – Second Session,
Comprising the Period from December 1, 1806, to March 3, 1807, Inclusive* (The Library
of Congress, American Memory, Lawmaking Home, Annals of Congress, Washington:
Gales and Seaton 1852, memory.loc.gov), 174.

12 There are many examples from this period of the idea held by European
Americans that the United Sates was 'a country of the white man', of the notion that
blacks and whites could not live together in one society, of the fear and evocation of race
wars, and of the resultant demand that free African Americans leave the country.
Particularly prominent is Thomas Jefferson, 'Notes on the State of Virginia', in Thomas
Jefferson, *Writings*, ed. Merrill D. Peterson (New York: Viking Press, 1984), Query 14,
264–70. On that topic and the American Colonization Society, see Drescher, *Abolition*,
Chapter 5; Davis, *Inhuman Bondage*, 256–8; Finzsch, Horton and Horton, *Von Benin
nach Baltimore*, 176–7, 183–7; Fredrickson, *The Black Image in the White Mind*,
Chapter 1; and Berlin, *Slaves without Masters*, Chapter 6. See also Eric Burin, *Slavery
and the Peculiar Solution: A History of the American Colonization Society* (Gainesville:
University Press of Florida, 2005), 5, in which he judges the American Colonization
Society to be an emancipatory movement. On Jefferson specifically, see Jordan, *White
over Black*, Chapter 12.

England or continental Europe because of this economic and political situation. For the decision made in the European capitals to abolish slavery was made for distant colonies, whose needs had to take a back seat to those of the mother country should interests diverge. The colonial elite's fears about the possible consequences of freeing the slaves ultimately hardly interested the elites and populations of the European centres of government.

The situation was different in the colonies that had just won the struggle for independence from Great Britain, with the slaveholding plantation owners and the merchants and industrialists economically dependent on them representing a significant portion of the political elite. Their interests, fears and prejudices directly determined the politics of the republic. Conflicts, which in Europe were largely carried out between the capitals and the overseas colonial elites and could be settled without major damage to the former and to the detriment of the latter, were contested in the United States within the now autonomous Union.[13] Unlike Europe, in the United States the debate about the first step of emancipation – the judicial act of freeing the slaves, as it was ultimately executed through the Emancipation Proclamation and the Thirteenth Amendment – led to political deadlock. John Brown sought to break this blockage with individual violence.

An American revolutionary

Just as Felice Orsini was a typical representative of the Risorgimento generation, John Brown was, in many respects, a typical member of the abolitionist movement. He was born in 1800 into a family of tanners, shoemakers and farmers in Connecticut that proudly traced its roots back to the earliest Puritan settlers. Both of Brown's grandfathers had fought in the American War of Independence. This family history imbued Brown with an elite consciousness and a strong sense of responsibility for the polity of the United States. Raised as an orthodox Calvinist, he believed in the doctrine of predestination, according to which the destiny of the world and humankind is pre-determined by God, and the task of all persons is to recognize and fulfil their

---

13 See also Drescher, *Abolition*, 299–303.

Hostages for emancipation

destiny in the course of their lives.[14] John's father, Owen Brown, was influenced during his youth by theologians sharply critical of slavery. He thus taught John and his five siblings from an early age to respect people of all races and to see slavery as a 'sin in the sight of God'.[15] As various African Americans have confirmed, John Brown was indeed one of the few Euro-Americans of his time who was free of racism in both thought and deed.[16] In 1805, the family moved west in an ox-drawn wagon to settle in Hudson, Ohio. The area had only recently been opened for settlement to citizens of Connecticut under the name Western Reserve. It would become both famous and infamous as a stronghold of abolitionism, and it was this environment that shaped John Brown.[17]

John Brown was deeply religious. After a brief sceptical phase – which was practically obligatory in orthodox Calvinism – he experienced the equally obligatory conversion as a young adult and memorized the Bible, later remarking self-confidently that he 'possessed a most unusual

14 See Gerald McFarland, *A Scattered People: An American Family Moves West* (New York: Pantheon Books, 1985), 3–17; Oates, *To Purge This Land with Blood*, 3–12; Louis A. DeCaro Jr, 'Fire from the Midst of You': A Religious Life of John Brown* (New York: New York University Press, 2002), Chapters 1–2; and McGlone, *John Brown's War*, Chapters 2.2–2.4, 3.1–3.2. On reformed orthodoxy, its doctrines and its social significance in the United States, see Michael Hochgeschwender, *Amerikanische Religion: Evangelikalismus, Pfingstlertum und Fundamentalismus* (Frankfurt am Main: Verlag der Weltreligionen, 2007), Chapters 1–2; or E. Brooks Holifield, *Theology in America: Christian Thought from the Age of the Puritans to the Civil War* (New Haven, CT: Yale University Press, 2003), especially Part 1; and the classic study by Sacvan Bercovitch, *The Puritan Origins of the American Self* (New Haven: Yale University Press, 1975).

15 Jonathan Edwards Jr, 'The Injustice and Impolicy of the Slave Trade, and of Slavery', in *The Works of Jonathan Edwards, D.D. Late President of Union College, with Memoir of His Late Character*, ed. Tryon Edwards (Andover: Doctrinal Tract and Book Society, 1842), 90. The works of the Calvinist theologian Jonathan Edwards Jr, especially this sermon, were very important to Owen and John Brown throughout their lives.

16 See Quarles, *Blacks on John Brown*, ix–xi; and Benjamin Quarles, *Allies for Freedom* [1974] (Cambridge: Da Capo Press, 2001), 13–14 and Chapter 2.

17 See McFarland, *A Scattered People*, 43–7, 68–77; and James F. Caccamo, *The Story of Hudson, Ohio* (Hudson: Friends of the Hudson Library, 1995), 10. On the settlement of the Old Northwest, the social structure of the Western Reserve, and abolitionism's influence on it, see ibid., Chapters 1 and 4; and Howe, *What Hath God Wrought*, Chapter 4.3. On the impact of the Western Reserve on John Brown's character, see Mary Land, 'John Brown's Ohio Environment', *Ohio Archaeological and Historical Quarterly* 57 (1948), 24–7; and Quarles, *Allies for Freedom*, Chapter 2.

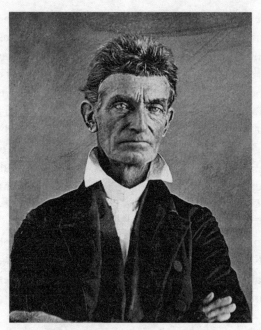

Figure 10. Half-length portrait of John Brown with his
arms folded, *c*.1856. Wikimedia Commons.

memory of its entire contents'.[18] Brown initially felt a calling to the
ministry, but had to abandon his college-preparatory studies at the
academy because of financial difficulties and a chronic eye
infection.

Brown returned to the Midwest, where he married and as a typical
frontier settler practised diverse trades, including tanner, livestock
dealer, surveyor, postmaster, church founder, lay preacher and teacher.[19]

---

18 John Brown writing to Henry L. Stearns on 15 July 1857 and George Luther
Stearns on 8 August 1857 from Red Rock, Iowa and Tabor, Iowa respectively; Record ID
65, MS02-0013, Boyd B. Stutler Collection (hereafter BBStColl), West Virginia State
Archives, Charleston, WV (hereafter WVStA), published as 'John Brown's Autobiography,
Written by Him to Henry L. Stearns, Son of George L. Stearns, and Bearing Date Red
Rock, Iowa, July 7, 1857', in Richard L. Hinton, *John Brown and His Men: With Some
Account of the Roads They Traveled to Reach Harper's Ferry* (New York: Funk & Wagnalls,
1894), 651. For general information on the vocation experience, see Hochgeschwender,
Amerikanische Religion, 37; or Holifield, *Theology in America*, 42.

19 On living conditions in the rural United States after the turn of the century,
especially on the frontier, see Howe, *What Hath God Wrought*, Chapter 1.2.

Of his twenty children from two marriages, eleven survived childhood.[20] Brown, like many of his fellow citizens, went bankrupt in the Panic of 1837, which triggered the worst economic crisis in US history prior to 1929. In the following years he succeeded in re-establishing himself as a horse and sheep breeder, but again faced financial ruin as the head of a wool cooperative. He understood too little about the capitalist economic system that was being established in the northern United States at the time. And, ultimately, he was dubious of worldly goods.[21] As a result, Brown and his family persistently lived in precarious economic circumstances.[22] But neither his poverty nor his frontier life prevented him from dedicating himself to the betterment of African Americans.

Figure 11. American abolitionist William Lloyd Garrison (1805–79). Daguerreotype, 1852. ullstein bild – Granger, New York.

---

20 On John Brown's second wife Mary Ann Brown and his daughters, see Bonnie Laughlin-Schultz, *The Tie That Bound Us: The Women in John Brown's Family and the Legacy of Radical Abolitionism* (Ithaca: Cornell University Press, 2013).

21 See Oates, *To Purge This Land*, Chapters 3–5; and McGlone, *John Brown's War*, Chapters 2.1, 3.4. On the breakthrough of capitalism in the northern states around 1840, see Howe, *What Hath God Wrought*, Chapter 14. On the depression from 1837 to 1843, see ibid., Chapters 10, 13.

22 These experiences – education through parents shaped by evangelicalism, conversion feeling called to the ministry, and economic uncertainty – were typical of those who campaigned from 1830 for the immediate abolition of slavery. See Donald M. Scott, 'Abolition as a Sacred Vocation', in Lewis Perry and Michael Fellman (eds.), *Antislavery Reconsidered* (Baton Rouge: Louisiana State University Press, 1979), 51–74.

Abolitionism as a social movement emerged in the United States in the early 1830s. It built on the activities of free African Americans who felt threatened by the American Colonization Society because they did not want to be deported to Africa, a place completely foreign to them. Many African Americans could point to a much longer line of ancestors living in America than many of the immigrants from Europe, and some had fought in the American Revolution. Instead of deportation, they demanded equal participation in American society. *Freedom's Journal*, the first newspaper published by African Americans in the United States, was thus founded in New York in 1827 and campaigned for equality. And David Walker, a free African American living in Boston, published an *Appeal to the Colored Citizens of the World*, in which he demanded an immediate abolition of slavery and the end of discrimination against free African Americans and predicted slave rebellions if the nation continued to practise slavery.[23]

Influenced by Walker's text and thanks to his contacts with the African American communities in Baltimore, Philadelphia and Boston, printer William Lloyd Garrison began to publish the newspaper *Liberator* in 1831. In its pages he advocated the abolition of slavery in the United States and the equitable integration of African Americans into American society. Garrison was also the driving force behind the founding of the New England Anti-Slavery Society in 1832 and the American Anti-Slavery Society the following year. The establishment of these societies, which operated according to the British model and initially with the support of personnel from England as well, set off an 'explosion' of abolitionist activity that soon surpassed the engagement seen in Great Britain. The Anti-Slavery Society employed seventy persons

---

23 David Walker, *Appeal to the Coloured Citizens of the World*, ed. Peter P. Hinks (University Park: Pennsylvania State University Press, 2000). On the *Appeal* and *Freedom's Journal* and their significance for the emergence of the abolitionist movement, see Finzsch, Horton and Horton, *Von Benin nach Baltimore*, 230–1; Timothy Patrick McCarthy, '"To Plead Our Own Cause": Black Print Culture and the Origins of American Abolitionism', in Timothy Patrick McCarthy and John Stauffer (eds.), *Prophets of Protest: Reconsidering the History of American Abolitionism* (New York: W. W. Norton, 2006), 114–44; Grey Gunmaker , 'Give Me a Sign: African Americans, Print, and Practice', in *A History of the Book in America*, vol. 2 (Chapel Hill: University of North Carolina Press in association with the American Antiquarian Society, 2010), 483–95. On the reaction of African Americans to the American Colonization Society, see Berlin, *Slaves without Masters*, 199–214.

full-time, and within five years its 1,346 local chapters would have some
100,000 members. Following the integrated model of the British abolitionist movement, Euro-American and African American men and
women worked side by side in the United States. The movement in the
United States was thus also able to quickly move the topic of slavery to
the political agenda.[24]

Yet, even if the American abolitionist movement did actively learn
about organization and strategy from its sister movement in Great
Britain and draw on its experience for orientation, it remained deeply
American in character. In the United States the anti-slavery movement
represented an important part of the Second Great Awakening, an evangelical revivalist movement that inspired extensive reform efforts and
countless reform associations with the goal of divinely perfecting the
United States. Degrading to slaves people created by God as equals had
to be the work of the Devil and led people to stray from the path of
righteousness in numerous ways. The country must free itself from this
source of sin, or face God's punishment. This applied all the more to the
United States, which according to Puritan beliefs was to be a community
established exemplarily according to God's commandments, as 'a Citty
vpon a Hill [sic]'.[25] American abolitionism was thus a moral movement

24 See Drescher, *Abolition*, Chapter 11 (for the term 'explosion', see 304); Davis,
Inhuman Bondage, Chapter 13; Stewart, *Holy Warriors*, Chapter 3; Harrold, *American
Abolitionists*, Chapter 3; and Finzsch, Horton and Horton, *Von Benin nach Baltimore*,
231–4. On Garrison's life with African Americans and their influence on him, and on
the founding of the *Liberator* and the abolitionist societies, see Henry Mayer, *All on Fire:
William Lloyd Garrison and the Abolition of Slavery* (New York: Martin's Press, 1998),
Chapters 6–9. On the significance of journalism to the abolitionist movement, see Trish
Loughran, *The Republic in Print: Print Culture in the Age of US Nation Building, 1770–
1870* (New York: Columbia University Press, 2007), Chapter 6, especially 328–44; Ford
Risley, *Abolition and the Press: The Moral Struggle against Slavery* (Evanston:
Northwestern University Press, 2008); and Robert Fanuzzi's analysis *Abolition's Public
Sphere* (Minneapolis: University of Minnesota, 2003), which was inspired by Jürgen
Habermas's study of the public sphere.

25 John Winthrop employed this allegory, which is contained in the Sermon on the
Mount (Matthew 5:14), in a sermon he held aboard the *Arbella*, a ship bringing Puritan
immigrants to North America in 1630. In this homily he cautioned the future settlers of
Massachusetts Bay that their community would be as a city upon a hill, which was
watched by the entire world. John Winthrop, 'A Model of Christian Charity', in *Winthrop
Papers*, ed. Stewart Mitchell, Allyn Bailey Forbes and Malcolm Freiberg (New York:
Russell & Russell, 1968), 295. On the self-image of the Puritans' founding colonies as
model communities allied with God, see Hochgeschwender, *Amerikanische Religion*,

inspired by messianic Protestantism, a community of values with political goals.

At the same time, the American Anti-Slavery Society understood itself as a revolutionary movement intent on continuing and completing the American Revolution. 'More than fifty-seven years have elapsed since a band of patriots convened in this place to devise measures for the deliverance of this country from a foreign yoke,' reads the Declaration of Sentiments, the founding document of the American Anti-Slavery Society named after the Declaration of Independence. The seminal text formulated by Garrison was ratified at the society's founding convention in Philadelphia in 1833: 'The corner-stone upon which they founded the Temple of Freedom was broadly this – "that all men are created equal . . ." . . . We have met together for the achievement of an enterprise, without which that of our fathers is incomplete.'[26] The actions and thinking of those who signed the Declaration of Sentiments were based explicitly on the Bible and the United States Declaration of Independence: 'We plant ourselves upon the Declaration of our Independence and the truths of Divine Revelation as upon the Everlasting Rock.'[27] The signatories vowed to free the country of the deadly curse of slavery and to secure for the African American population of the United States all the rights and privileges due them as men (people) and as Americans. They committed themselves to this 'holy cause' with their entire person and assets,

---

Chapter 1; Bercovitch, *The Puritan Origins of the American Self*, Chapter 3; Edmund S. Morgan, *The Puritan Dilemma: The Story of John Winthrop* (New York: Pearson Longman, 2007), Chapter 6; and Perry Miller, *The New England Mind: The Seventeenth Century* (New York: The Macmillan Company, 1939), Part 4. On the Second Great Awakening, the large reform movements it inspired, and its significance to the abolitionist movement, see Hochgeschwender, *Amerikanische Religion*, Chapter 4; Howe, *What Hath God Wrought*, Chapter 5; Robert T. Handy, *A History of the Churches in the United States and Canada* (Oxford: Clarendon Press, 1976), Chapter 6; and Robert H. Abzug, *Cosmos Crumbling: American Reform and the Religious Imagination* (New York: Oxford University Press, 1994).

26 Declaration of Sentiments, ratified at the National Anti-Slavery Society founding convention in Philadelphia on 6 December 1833, in Wendell Phillips Garrison and Francis Jackson Garrison, *William Lloyd Garrison: 1805–1879: The Story of His Life Told by His Children* (New York: Century, 1885–1889), 408. On the abolitionist movement's revolutionary self-image, see especially Aptheker, *Abolitionism*, Chapter 3.

27 Garrison and Garrison, *William Lloyd Garrison*, 412. The formulation draws on the biblical verse Isaiah 26:4, which in the Revised Standard Bible reads, 'Trust ye in the LORD for ever: for the LORD GOD is an everlasting rock.'

'whether we live to witness the triumph of Liberty, Justice and Humanity, or perish untimely as martyrs in this great, benevolent, and holy cause'.[28] The founders of the Anti-Slavery Society saw themselves symbolically and substantively as following in the footsteps of Christ and the revolutionaries of 1776, whose work they strove to complete – whatever the cost.

However, fundamental differences existed between the Anti-Slavery Society and the founding fathers of the nation, as Garrison pointed out in the Declaration of Sentiments. The grievances of the revolutionaries from 1776 against the British Crown, for instance, paled in comparison 'with the wrongs and sufferings of those for whom we plead ... Our fathers were never slaves'.[29] Another difference, which stemmed from the importance of the revivalist movement for leading members of the anti-slavery movement, was the commitment to non-violence. The principles that allowed the revolutionaries of 1776 'to wage war against their oppressors, and to spill human blood like water, in order to be free' were, according to Garrison, unacceptable to the movement:

> Ours forbid the doing of evil that good may come, and lead us to reject, and to entreat the oppressed to reject, the use of all carnal weapons for deliverance from bondage; relying solely upon those which are spiritual, and mighty through God to the pulling down of strong holds.[30]

With the Declaration of Sentiments, Garrison and the Anti-Slavery Society founders proclaimed a non-violent, revolutionary crusade based on moral suasion, the appeal to people's sense of morality.

John Brown initially moved intellectually, socially and in his choice of media within the sphere of this abolitionist movement. He, too, was

---

28 Garrison and Garrison, *William Lloyd Garrison*, 412.

29 Ibid., 409. With this formulation the founders revealed their understanding of the organization as a white initiative, by ignoring the three African Americans (who represented the free blacks of Boston, New York City and Philadelphia) among the some sixty delegates. According to Harrold (*American Abolitionists*, 33) it was remarkable and courageous that any African Americans (and also four women) participated in the conference at all.

30 Garrison and Garrison, *William Lloyd Garrison*, 409. This formulation follows 2 Corinthians 10:4: 'For the weapons of our warfare are not carnal, but mighty through God to the pulling down of strong holds.'

certain that the enslavement of a person by another blatantly violated the basic principles of the American republic and the core ideas of Christianity – the Declaration of Independence and the Golden Rule, the precept stating, 'And as ye would that men should do to you, do ye also to them likewise.'[31] Slavery was the Devil's doing, 'the sum of all villanies'.[32] Here he was in complete agreement with the Declaration of Sentiments and the sentiments of other abolitionists. His father, Owen Brown, was an early subscriber to the *Liberator* and other radical abolitionist publications, so John Brown, according to family accounts, became aware of Garrison's newspaper at his father's house as early as 1833 or 1834. The younger Brown subscribed as well to the *Liberator* and later on also to the *New York Tribune*, a high-circulation newspaper with abolitionist tendencies published by Horace Greeley as of 1841. In addition, he received the various newspapers by Frederick Douglass, an escaped slave who had fled to the North and was considered the 'unofficial president' of the African Americans. Brown was thus well informed about national developments regarding slavery and emancipation, as well as about the assessments and opinions of black and white abolitionists.[33]

---

31 The Gospel according to Luke, 6:31. See also the Gospel according to Matthew, 7:12, 'Therefore all things whatsoever ye would that men should do to you, do ye even so to them: for this is the law and the prophets.'

32 William A. Phillips, 'Three Interviews with Old John Brown', quoted in Louis Ruchames (ed.), *John Brown, The Making of a Revolutionary: The Story of John Brown in His Own Words and in the Words of Those Who Knew Him* (New York: Grosset & Dunlap, 1969), 220.

33 On John Brown's subscription to newspapers published by Garrison, Greeley and Douglass, see Oswald Garrison Villard, *John Brown 1800–1859: A Bibliography Fifty Years After* (Boston: Houghton Mifflin, 1910), 49; Oates, *To Purge This Land*, 30; and the entries in the notebook for 28 January 1858 and the undated entry on the payment of the subscriptions for himself and his oldest son. Memoranum (*sic*) book of John Brown, Franklin Mills, Portage Co. Ohio, vol. 2: 1855–1859; Boston Public Library, Boston, MA (hereafter BPL), n.p. On Frederick Douglass see the classic work by William S. McFeely, *Frederick Douglass* (New York: W. W. Norton, 1991). On his newspapers, see especially Frankie Hutton, *The Early Black Press in America: 1827 to 1860* (Westport: Greenwood Press, 1993); Patrick Scott Washburn, *The African American Newspaper: The Voice of Freedom* (Evanston: Northwestern University Press, 2006); and Ford Risley, *Abolition and the Press: The Moral Struggle against Slavery* (Evanston: Northwestern University Press, 2008), 112–19, 135. For the term 'unofficial president', see, for example, Jules Abels, *Man on Fire: John Brown and the Cause of Liberty* (New York: Macmillan, 1971), 26. The idea is implied in John Stauffer, *Giants: The Parallel Lives of Frederick Douglass and Abraham Lincoln* (New York: Twelve, 2008).

Frederick Douglass

Figure 12. Frederick Douglass (c.1817–95), American reformer.
Steel engraving, 1854. ullstein bild – Granger, New York.

In addition, John Brown participated in the abolition movement's
activities, speaking at gatherings calling for an end to slavery and the
discriminatory special laws for African Americans in the northern
states, signing corresponding petitions, and personally confronting
discrimination against African Americans in churches and restaurants. John Brown repeatedly entertained plans to found a school for
blacks and to adopt a black youth to afford him a good education.
For – as he wrote to his brother in 1834 – he wished 'to devise some
means whereby I might do something in a practical way for my poor
fellow-men who are in bondage'.[34] The last two endeavours, however,

---

34 John Brown to Frederick Brown, 21 November 1834, from Randolph, PA,
wvculture.org/history/jbexhibit/oldsouthbrownletter.html, West Virginia Division of
Culture and History, Archives and History, 'His Soul Goes Marching On'. The Life and
Legacy of John Brown, A West Virginia Archives and History Online Exhibit, reprinted in
Sanborn, *The Life and Letters*, 40. On Brown's commitment, see Oates, *To Purge This Land*,
15, 19, 30–3, 41–2, 53, 58; Quarles, *Allies for Freedom*, 16–17; and McGlone, *John Brown's
War*, Chapter 3.3. Such activities were typical of rank-and-file members of the movement
in the 1830s and 1840s. See especially Drescher, *Abolition*, 294–6, 302–7; Aptheker,
Abolitionism, especially Chapters 4–5; and Stewart, *Holy Warriors*, Chapters 2–4.

failed because Brown often had barely enough money to feed his own family.

Although he participated in a broad range of activities to emancipate the slaves and achieve equality for African Americans, Brown never joined the Anti-Slavery Society or one of its local chapters. Despite his sympathy for the cause, he did not think much of Garrison's programme of moral suasion or the endless talk against slavery: 'Talk, talk, talk! That will never free the slaves,' he is supposed to have said after attending an anti-slavery meeting in Boston in the late 1850s.[35] Direct action had been important to him in younger years as well, when, for instance, he worked on the Underground Railroad, a network of free African Americans in the northern United States that hid escaped slaves along their difficult and dangerous journey to Canada, where slavery had been abolished in 1833 by the British parliament's Slavery Abolition Act. John Brown – whose father served as the first Underground Railroad 'stationmaster' in Hudson, OH – helped by harbouring escaped slaves, caring for injured fugitives and acting as a 'conductor', repeatedly travelling hundreds of miles in his wagon to bring runaway slaves concealed under furniture to the next safe house. He maintained this commitment throughout his life and developed a certain degree of daring in the process.[36]

All of these activities – holding abolitionist lectures, organizing meetings, circulating petitions, developing plans for African American education and supporting escaped slaves – were carried out within the framework of civic engagement and Christian

---

35 Sanborn, *The Life and Letters*, 131. See also Land, 'John Brown's Ohio Environment', 29, 33.

36 On the Underground Railroad, see Harrold, *American Abolitionists*, 67–9; Finzsch, Horton and Horton, *Von Benin nach Baltimore*, 244–50; and the still especially valuable account from Larry Gara, *The Liberty Line: The Legend of the Underground Railroad* (Lexington: University Press of Kentucky, 1996), who critically examines myth and reality and emphasizes that the Underground Railroad network was an 'important example of the successful nonviolent action'. See also David W. Blight (ed.), *Passages to Freedom: The Underground Railroad in History and Memory* (Washington, DC: Smithsonian Books, 2004); and Fergus M. Bordewich, *Bound for Canaan: The Underground Railroad and the War for the Soul of America* (New York: Amistad, 2005). On Owen and John Brown's commitment, see Quarles, *Allies for Freedom*, 16–19; Caccamo, *The Story of Hudson*, 19–20; and James F. Caccamo, *Freedom Seekers: Ohio and the Underground Railroad* (Columbus: Friends of Freedom Press, 2004), Chapter 2.

assistance in the belief that change could be achieved through peaceful political means and reforms.[37] The question therefore arises as to which events, experiences and influences radicalized John Brown's thought and actions to the extent that over time he not only justified, but even deemed necessary, using force to emancipate the slaves and that he also planned and executed such violence himself. Answering this question is not easy.[38]

Initially, it was the reactions of the Anti-Slavery Society's adversaries that radicalized John Brown (and many other opponents of slavery), for the very methods that had led the British anti-slavery campaign to success merely revealed that political work on this issue in the United States faced serious limitations. Whereas, in Great Britain, the activities of the abolitionists were considered an expression of British civilization and English conscience that Parliament was not allowed to impinge upon, the activities of the anti-slavery movement in the United States were declared un-American because they had been inspired by Great Britain and threatened the Union.[39]

---

37 Villard sums it up similarly in *John Brown*, 49.

38 Of the various Brown biographers, Villard and Abels pose this question most clearly. Villard, *John Brown*, even dedicates an entire chapter (Chapter 2) to answering it, with the resulting narrative profoundly influencing subsequent portrayals, not least because Villard convincingly identifies several significant signs of the radicalization process Brown went through. This evidence found its way into later depictions and has also been incorporated here. Villard, though, follows an explanatory approach based on individual psychology (see ibid., 42–3, where he contrasts the sciences of psychology and history, but in doing so reveals his preferred line of thought). According to his reasoning, the 'secret of this riddle [of John Brown's radicalization]' is ultimately rooted in Brown's 'Puritan inheritance', his 'iron will', his power of imagination, and especially in the 'driving force of a mighty and unselfish purpose, and the readiness to devote life itself to the welfare of others' (ibid., 78). In contrast, Villard seldom incorporates political contexts, adding to a sometimes unconvincing dating and insufficient scrutiny of sources that leaves him only able to make rather vague statements on the question of Brown's radicalization (see ibid., 49, 54–5). Abels, on the other hand, writes about the question of John Brown's radicalization process, 'that seems to be an unanswerable question', and only refers very broadly to the political context shaped by the heated anti-slavery atmosphere in the North and the 1850 Kansas–Nebraska Act. Abels, *Man on Fire*, 24, 35, 38.

39 See the remarks in this volume, pp. 82–4; Davis, *Inhuman Bondage*, Chapter 12; Drescher, *Abolition*, Chapters 8–9; Jochen Meißner, Ulrich Mücke and Klaus Weber, *Schwarzes Amerika: Eine Geschichte der Sklaverei* (Munich: C. H. Beck, 2008), 179–98; Hochschild, *Bury the Chains*; Oldfield, *Popular Politics and British Anti-slavery*; and Tarrow, *Power in Movement*, 47–51.

Instead of eliciting political answers, as in Great Britain, the abolitionist movement in the United States called forth repressive and violent countermeasures. When the anti-slavery movement sent large quantities of abolitionist writings into the South in hopes of convincing slaveholders with rational and moral arguments, groups of whites broke into post offices at night and burned the shipments to prevent them falling into the hands of free blacks or slaves. The Postmaster General responded by ordering that mail being sent to the South from the North be censored in advance. When the first petitions from opponents of slavery reached the House of Representatives and the Senate, pro-slavery members of Congress implemented the 'gag rule', which prohibited Congress from either accepting or debating abolitionist petitions. And in the North as well, the proverbial 'gentlemen of property and standing' – the traditional, male, political and economic elites – responded with violence to collaboration between European and African Americans and to abolitionist activity (especially by women). They organized mobs specifically targeting founding meetings of anti-slavery groups, abolitionist gatherings and prominent opponents of slavery, such as William Lloyd Garrison, as well as free African Americans and their neighbourhoods, with the perpetrators certain of unspoken consent by the police and judges. Against this background of violence tolerated or even endorsed by the state, Garrison, who narrowly escaped a lynch mob, spoke of a 'reign of terror'.[40]

A particularly spectacular case of such mob violence was the murder of Elijah P. Lovejoy, a Presbyterian minister, who published the *St Louis Observer* in St Louis, Missouri. A group of whites had tied the free African American Francis J. McIntosh to a tree in the middle of the city and burned him alive. Elijah Lovejoy protested vehemently in his newspaper against this lynching and the perpetrators' subsequent acquittals, with the result that he and his paper became the target of violence. Lovejoy subsequently moved his business to Alton, located on the other

---

40 On the gag rule, mail censuring and other repressive countermeasures, see Davis, *Inhuman Bondage*, 263; Stewart, *Holy Warriors*, 70–1, 83–5; and Harrold, *American Abolitionists*, 34–5. On the wave of violence against abolitionists and free African Americans, see preferably Leonard L. Richards, *'Gentlemen of Property and Standing': Anti-abolition Mobs in Jacksonian America* (New York: Oxford University Press, 1970). On the role of the media, see Loughran, *The Republic in Print*, 344–54. On the persecution of Garrison, see Mayer, *All on Fire*, 196–207, quotation at 196.

side of the Mississippi river in Illinois, a state prohibiting slavery. But abolitionists such as Lovejoy were also unwelcome in Alton, and his printing presses were destroyed three times. He was then shot dead as he and fellow combatants tried to defend a fourth press with rifles on 7 November 1837. The anti-slavery movement now had a martyr.[41]

The murder of Lovejoy acted as a wake-up call to the general public and radicalized John Brown, as it did many other opponents of slavery. The national press carried and disseminated the news of the brutal act, with passions flaring across the United States, for many Americans felt the mob violence also threatened a fundamental principal of democracy, the freedom of expression.[42] After reports of Lovejoy's murder reached Hudson, Laurens Hickok, a theologian and philosopher at the local Western Reserve College (now Case Western Reserve University), rode through town, spreading the news and inviting people to a memorial prayer service the following evening. 'The crisis has come,' he said in his speech to assembled townspeople: 'The question now before the American citizens is no longer alone, "Can slaves be made free?" but, "Are we free, or are we slaves under Southern mob law?"' And he continued, 'I propose that we take measures to procure another press and another editor. If a like fate attends them, send another, till the whole country is aroused; and if you can find no fitter man for the first victim, send me.'[43] The conviction that the system of slavery and its violent supporters threatened political freedom in America and that the conflict

41 On the lynching of McIntosh and the expulsion and murder of Lovejoy, see Merton Lynn Dillon, *Elijah P. Lovejoy: Abolitionist Editor* (Urbana: University of Illinois, 1961), Chapters 8–13; and Charles van Ravenswaay, *Saint Louis: An Informal History of the City and Its People, 1764–1865* (Urbana: University of Illinois Press, 1991), Chapter 15.

42 On this radicalization, see Dillon, *Elijah P. Lovejoy*, Chapter 14; Stewart, *Holy Warriors*, 89–96; Harrold, *American Abolitionists*, Chapter 6; Aileen S. Kraditor, *Means and Ends in American Abolitionism: Garrison and His Critics on Strategy and Tactics* (New York: Pantheon Books, 1969); and Stanley Harrold, *The Rise of Aggressive Abolitionism: Addresses to the Slaves* (Lexington: University Press of Kentucky, 2004).

43 J. Newton Brown, 'The Beginning of John Brown's Career: To the Editor of the Nation', *Nation* 98/2537 (12 February 1914), 157, quotes here from the memoirs of Rev. Edward Brown (John Brown's cousin and a student at Western Reserve College at the time), who published these on 21 October 1892 in the *Northwestern Congregationalist* (John Brown Pamphlets, vol. 24, unbound), BBStColl., WVStA, wvculture.org, West Virginia Division of Culture and History, Archives and History, West Virginia Memory Project, John Brown/Boyd B. Stutler Collection Database (hereafter JB/BBStColl. Db).

had to be further aggravated in order for a majority of the citizenry to become active in protecting the republic characterized John Brown's thinking as well. He, too, was ready to sacrifice his life in this struggle. Brown attended the memorial service with his father, sitting silently in the back of the church, listening to the speeches, and joining in the prayers. Shortly before the gathering dispersed, he stood up, raised his right hand, and vowed before those present and before God that he would dedicate his life from then on to ending slavery. John Brown had found his calling in life – one chosen by God.[44]

Following the murder of Lovejoy most members of the abolitionist movement remained largely faithful to its pacifist founding principles; solely the use of force for self-defence was now being justified by more and more abolitionists.[45] This did not satisfy John Brown, who increasingly saw the *offensive* use of force as a legitimate means in the struggle to eliminate slavery. The questions of when, exactly, he began to endorse the offensive use of force and how it came to that are again not easy to answer. For Brown – in contrast to Garrison and many members of the Anti-Slavery Society, who often were also active in the American Peace Society and the New England Non-Resistance Society – had not been a pronounced pacifist since the late 1820s or early 1830s, when he began carrying a weapon in response to threats by Freemasons because of his criticism of their secret lodges. He had also long regarded force as a legitimate means of self-defence.[46] In addition, no immediate action followed his public vow in the Hudson church. Brown had his hands full in the years after 1837 just securing his family's economic survival and therefore continued as usual, employing peaceful means to oppose

---

44 According to J. Newton Brown the oath was: 'Here, before God, in the presence of these witnesses, from this time, I consecrate my life to the destruction of slavery!' J. Newton Brown, 'The Beginning of John Brown's Career', 157. A neighbour who had also been one of John Brown's bible students passed on the wording: 'I pledge myself with God's help that I will devote my life to increasing hostility towards slavery'. Lora Case, *Hudson of Long Ago: Progress of Hudson during the Past Century, Personal Reminiscences of an Aged Pioneer: Reminiscences Written in 1897* (Hudson: Hudson Library and Historical Society, 1963), 53–4.

45 On the pacifism of the first generation in the abolitionist movement in particular, see p. 198 in this volume; and Lawrence Jacob Friedman, *Gregarious Saints: Self and Community in American Abolitionism, 1830–1870* (Cambridge: Cambridge University Press, 1982), Chapter 7. On the dispute about the use of force, see Friedman, 200–2.

46 DeCaro, *'Fire from the Midst'*, 93–4.

discrimination against blacks and helping fugitive slaves escape to the North.[47]

The first indication that John Brown's thinking had further radical-ized and that he was considering using not only defensive, but also offensive, violence in the anti-slavery struggle is found in a letter from his oldest son, John Brown Jr. In it he writes that John Brown was sitting around the open kitchen hearth in his Hudson farmhouse one evening in 1839 with his wife; his oldest sons John Jr, Jason and Owen; and possi-bly an African American theology student from Western Reserve College who lived with the family, when he announced to his family that he 'wanted to make war on slavery . . . by force and arms'. In John Brown Jr's account, his father powerfully described the hopeless plight of the slaves and then asked his wife and each of his sons individually if they were ready to join him in doing everything in their power to break 'the jaws of the wicked' and tear 'the spoil out of his teeth' (Job 29:17). After he had received an affirmative reply from each of them, John Brown knelt down, followed by his family, and they prayed together. This was the first time John Jr had seen his father kneel to pray, which lent this prayer particular significance in his eyes. After praying, Brown asked his wife and sons to raise their right hands and swear to fight slav-ery in any way possible, even with weapons, and to reveal their covenant to no one.[48]

John Brown is thought to have been convinced since that time, at the latest, that God had predestined him to free the American slaves, with the struggle to end slavery then becoming a personal, holy duty imposed on him by God.[49] John Brown was not alone in this conviction. His world view, along with its religious concepts and self-images – including the acceptance of a mission from God – was typical of radical abolition-ists who put their thinking into practice by going into the South to free

---

47 See Oates, *To Purge This Land*, 42–50.

48 John Brown Jr, after consulting his brother Jason, gave this account to Franklin B. Sanborn, reprinted in Sanborn, 'John Brown's Family Compact: Concord Mass, December 20', *Nation* 51/1330 (25 December 1890), 500. Franklin Sanborn, *The Life and Letters*, 121, adopted this dating, as does DeCaro, *'Fire from the Midst'*, 45. Villard, *John Brown*, 46, also calls this incident significant for Brown's radicalization but supplies a date that is neither plausible nor supported by available sources.

49 On this conviction, see especially DeCaro, *'Fire from the Midst'*, 89, 95, 139, 189, 239–40. On the time, see 106.

the slaves there.[50] A special feature in John Brown's case was that he could count on his family's support from now on, for he had made the militant struggle against slavery a family concern.

Events surrounding the *Amistad* formed the background for the radicalization of John Brown described above. In August 1839 a schooner named *La Amistad* dropped anchor off the tip of Long Island. It had left Havana in June carrying fifty-three Africans, who had been kidnapped in the area of present-day Sierra Leone and taken to Cuba in contravention of all laws banning the slave trade. The sailing ship had originally left Havana for Puerto Príncipe (now Camagüey), a city several hundred miles to the south-east where the Africans were to be sold as slaves. On that sea journey, however, one of the Africans, Sengbeh, also known as Cinqué, managed to open his iron shackles with a nail and free his fellow captives. Together they overpowered the crew without excessive bloodshed and took control of the ship. Cinqué ordered that it be sailed back to Africa, but one of the slave traders, a former captain, reset the ship's course each evening for the United States, in hopes he might still be able to sell the Africans there. They thus reached Long Island in the state of New York, where the authorities decided to tow the *Amistad* to Connecticut, where slavery was still permitted (unlike in New York). Once there, the Africans were imprisoned in New London. A legal battle ensued about whether they were to be extradited to Cuba, as demanded by President Martin van Buren in an attempt to gain votes in the South for his re-election, or were free men and could return to Africa, as called for by former president John Quincy Adams, whom the anti-slavery movement had won over to represent the Africans. After several appeals, the case ultimately reached the Supreme Court, which ruled the Africans be freed.[51]

Similar to the murder of Elijah Lovejoy, the *Amistad* case polarized public opinion and radicalized many members of the anti-slavery movement. It, too, involved issues fundamental to the national self-understanding, namely the importance of natural law enshrined in

---

50 See Stanley Harrold, *The Abolitionists and the South, 1831–1861* (Lexington: University of Kentucky Press, 2004), 71–3.

51 See Davis, *Inhuman Bondage*, Chapter 1; Finzsch, Horton and Horton, *Von Benin nach Baltimore*, 250–1; and Howard Jones, *Mutiny on the Amistad: The Saga of a Slave Revolt and Its Impact on American Abolition, Law, and Diplomacy* (New York: Oxford University Press, 1987).

the Declaration of Independence in relation to positive law, which protected slavery, and the right to use force in the struggle for 'the recovery of personal liberty'. Members of the anti-slavery movement increasingly thought it legitimate for slaves to use force to free themselves.[52]

John Brown, too, was impressed by Cinqué and his revolt. 'How often,' wrote one of his daughters, 'have I heard him speak in admiration of Cinques' [sic] character and management in carrying his points with so little bloodshed!'[53] Brown's analysis of the rebellion aboard the *Amistad* and the conclusions he drew from it for his fight against slavery can be discerned in his *Words of Advice*, which he wrote for an African American self-defence group he had co-founded. He commences his advice, 'Nothing so charms the American people as personal bravery. Witness the case of Cinques [sic], of everlasting memory, on board the *Amistad*.' The American nation showed more concern for this 'bold and to some extent successful man', who earnestly defended his life and rights, than for the accumulated wrongs and sufferings of more than 3 million of its submissive colored population.[54] In this interpretation, written ten years after the Supreme Court's acquittal, Brown certainly benefited from knowing the outcome of the *Amistad* trial. Yet he might have believed as early as 1839 that many Euro-Americans were impressed by African rebel Cinqué despite his use of force, although they cared

52 See Friedman, *Gregarious Saints*, 202; Stewart, *Holy Warriors*, 112–13; and Harrold, *American Abolitionists*, 63–4.

53 Quoted in Redpath, *The Public Life of Captain James Brown: With an Autobiography of His Childhood and Youth* (Boston: Thayer and Eldridge, 1860), 38–9.

54 John Brown, 'Words of Advice. Branch of the United States League of Gileadites. Adopted Jan. 15, 1851, as Written and Recommended by John Brown', in Sanborn, *The Life and Letters*, 124–6; William Wells Brown published a slightly different version: 'John Brown and the Fugitive Slave Law', *New York Independent*, 10 March 1870, 6 (Boyd B. Stutler Scrapbook, vol. 4, BBStColl., WVStA). There are differing opinions in the literature about whether Brown's interpretation of the reactions to the *Amistad* revolt was factually correct. DeCaro, 'Fire from the Midst', 192, describes Brown's belief that whites could admire blacks for fighting other whites as 'naïve'. Mayer, *All on Fire*, 308–9, argues that the American public could more easily accept the revolt because it was carried out by Africans on the open sea against Catholic Spanish authorities and not against Protestants in the United States; and Stewart, *Holy Warriors*, 113, also states the *Amistad* rebellion was surprisingly well received by whites in the North, even if they rejected equality for African Americans or the emancipation of the slaves. On the public response see also Jones, *Mutiny on the Amistad*.

little for the plight of millions of peaceful slaves in the country, because abolitionist newspapers commonly held this position.[55]

John Brown thus inferred from the *Amistad* revolt not only that violence – if correctly used – is an effective and publicity-generating means in the fight against slavery, but also that many people empathize more easily with an individual who dramatically embodies injustice than with massive, anonymous daily suffering.[56] This lesson about the great public impact of individual symbolic violence was an important step on John Brown's path to the invention of terrorism.

A guerrilla war to free the slaves: the emergence of a plan

How, though, could force be effectively used to free the American slaves? In the following years, John Brown developed a plan for a guerrilla war, but not yet for terrorism, and by 1846 that plan had taken on a concrete form.[57] The basic idea behind his plan was inspired by African American and Euro-American abolitionists who went into the South to help slaves escape. Their names and activities became known in the early 1840s when some of them were captured and put on trial.[58]

Decisive for the specific nature of John Brown's plan was his hiring by Oberlin College in spring 1840 to survey a land endowment in western Virginia. His father had close links to the Ohio college – the first in the United States to ignore skin colour on principle as an acceptance criterion. Brown spent a month in Virginia and became familiar with the Allegheny Mountains, whose highest peaks were almost 5,000 feet tall, and the Appalachians, which extend as far as Georgia. To Brown, these mountains seemed God-given for his project of freeing the slaves. 'He

---

55 Jones, *Mutiny on the Amistad*, Chapter 2.

56 This is also stated by Evan Carton, *Patriotic Treason: John Brown and the Soul of America* (New York: Free Press, 2006), 135–6.

57 Sanborn reports (though without evidence) that Brown discussed his plan in 1846 with Thomas Thomas (*sic*), a former slave and employee at his wool collective. See Sanborn, *The Life and Letters*, 133; Villard, *John Brown*, 55; and Oates, *To Purge This Land*, 61.

58 On these actions as the result of the radicalization of a part of the anti-slavery movement in the early 1840s, see Harrold, *The Abolitionists and the South*, Chapter 4. On the connection with Brown's plans, see ibid., 82–3; and Richard Owen Boyer, *The Legend of John Brown: A Biography and a History* (New York: Alfred A. Knopf, 1973), 87.

called my attention to a map of the United States, and pointed out to me the far-reaching Alleghenies, which stretch away from the borders of New York, into the Southern States,' recounted Frederick Douglass about a meeting with John Brown in 1847 at which he had laid out his plans. 'These mountains,' Brown had said, 'are the basis of my plan. God has given the strength of the hills to freedom, they were placed here for the emancipation of the negro race; they are full of natural forts, where one man for defense will be equal to a hundred for attack.' Douglass reported Brown had said he 'kn[e]w these mountains well, and could take a body of men into them and keep them there despite of all the efforts of Virginia to dislodge them.'[59] Brown's idea was to begin with twenty or twenty-five carefully selected and well-armed men, deploying them in the mountains in bands of five to go down into the plantation fields to invite the most courageous slaves to join their ranks. Once the group had grown in this fashion to around a hundred men it would begin to free the slaves on a large scale and flee with them into the mountains. The strong and courageous slaves were to stay with the force in the mountains and the others would be smuggled to the North with the help of the Underground Railroad. The liberation army would steadily grow in numbers and continue to advance south.[60]

Brown, therefore, did not actually plan an uprising, which he considered counterproductive, although he endorsed the use of force when it was needed to help slaves escape or to defend themselves in the mountains. According to him, the operation's most urgent objective was rather to destroy the market value of the held slaves. He thought this could be achieved by making this form of ownership unreliable. And even if his action failed and the group was decimated in the mountains, he 'had no better use for his life than to lay it down in the cause of the slave', as he told Douglass.[61] This, then, was John Brown's Subterranean Pass Way

---

59 Frederick Douglass, 'Life and Times', in *Autobiographies*, Frederick Douglass, 717–18. See also his report, F. D. [Frederick Douglass], 'Editorial Correspondence. Lynn, Mass. Feb. 5, 1848', *North Star*, 11 February 1848, 2; in which he could not mention the plans because it would endanger their execution. See also McFeely, *Frederick Douglass*, 186–7.

60 Douglass, 'Life and Times', 718. See also Villard, *John Brown*, 48, 55; and Oates, *To Purge This Land*, 61–4.

61 Douglass, 'Life and Times', 718–19, 754–5. It was a common complaint by slavery supporters that helping slaves escape would depress the price of slaves. See Harrold, *The Abolitionists and the South*, 154.

scheme, which essentially was an offensive and organized expansion of the Underground Railroad. His code name for the endeavour, 'a Rail Road business on a somewhat extended scale', indicates this.[62]

To discover models for his undertaking, to develop it, and to train himself in military thinking, Brown read in the following years everything he could find about military tactics and armed insurgency. He was primarily interested in how people in various historical situations had succeeded in standing up to an enemy superior in numbers, equipment and training. He studied ancient warcraft, with his favourite books including Plutarch and Josephus's works, as well as the French historian Charles Rollin's *Ancient History*. His focus was on ancient warfare and slavery, for instance, Leonidas's stand against a far larger Persian army at Thermopylae, the Spartacus Revolt, the life of Quintus Sertorius, the resistance of the Lusitanians and Numantians against Roman troops in the mountains of the Iberian peninsula, and probably Agathocles of Syracuse's war against Carthage as well.[63] In Josephus's *The War of the Jews*, Brown could find descriptions of the Maccabean Revolt, the Jewish rebellion against Rome and the tactics of the Sicarii, as well as their last warriors' collective suicide at the fortress of Masada.[64]

---

62 See Gara, *The Liberty Line*, 87–8. On the codenames, see, for instance, Brown's letter to Higginson from 12 February 1858, quoted in Oates, *To Purge This Land*, 227.

63 On John Brown's favourite books, see the information from his daughter Ruth Thompson (Sanborn, *The Life and Letters*, 38). Contemporary American editions were Charles Rollin, *The Ancient History of the Egyptians, Carthaginians, Assyrians, Medes and Persians, Grecians and Macedonians* (New York: Andrus & Judd, 1843); Plutarch, *Plutarch's Lives: Translated from the original Greek, with Critical and Historical Notes and a New Life of Plutarch* (Baltimore: W. & J. Neal, 1834); and Flavius Josephus, *The Genuine Works . . . Containing Twenty Books of Jewish Antiquities, Seven Books of the Jewish War, Two Books in Answer to Apion, the Martyrdom of the Maccabees, and the Life of Josephus, Written by Himself* (Boston: S. Walker, 1833). On Brown's interest in these books, see his letter to Franklin Sanborn on 26 February 1858 from Brooklyn, NY, in Sanborn, *The Life and Letters*, 443–4, 449–50; the mentions of them to Phillips ('Three Interviews', 226); the witness testimony of Richard Realf in United States Congress, *Report*, 90–113, 96; and Phil Milhous, 'A Footnote to John Brown's Raid', *Virginia Magazine of History and Biography* 67/4 (1959), 396–8. On the Spartacus revolt and resistance on the Iberian peninsula, see Barry Strauss, *The Spartacus War* (New York: Simon & Schuster, 2009); and the classic study by Helmut Simon, *Roms Kriege in Spanien, 154–133 v. Chr.* (Frankfurt am Main: V. Klostermann, 1962).

64 On the Sicarii in the standard account of the history of terrorism, see in this volume the introduction, pp. 15, 18, 25; and the conclusion, pp. 605–6.

John Brown also dedicated himself to studying more recent history's rebellions, guerrilla wars and revolutions, along with corresponding contemporary events. It is known that he was familiar with George Washington's leadership in the American War of Independence and Toussaint L'Ouverture's defence of the young Haitian republic against Spanish, French and British troops. He read Headley's *Napoleon and His Marshals* and Stocqueler's biography of Wellington, with his notebook entries indicating his particular interest in Francisco Javier Mina and the guerrilla war against Napoleon's troops in the mountainous regions of Spain.[65] He studied everything he could get his hands on about slave rebellions, for example about the plans undertaken by Gabriel Prosser and Denmark Vesey, the Nat Turner insurrection in Virginia, and the conspiracy on the Cumberland river in Tennessee. Brown is supposed to have known 'by heart' the history of the Maroons, slaves who fled into the mountains of Jamaica and Surinam, where they established their own societies, sometimes defending them for over a century against European colonial armies. He also followed the Seminole Wars, in which the United States fought a coalition of Native Americans and Maroons in the Florida swamps.[66] Brown was well informed about the Swiss

---

65 See Memoranum book, vol. 2; BPL, n.p., archive.org; and Oates, *To Purge This Land*, 213. On the importance of these books for Brown, see also his letter to Franklin Sanborn on 26 February 1858 from Brooklyn, NY, and the information from Ruth Thompson (Sanborn, *The Life and Letters*, 443–4, 38). On Brown's knowledge of the revolution on Haiti, see Realf in United States Congress, *Report*, 96. For contemporary accounts of the revolution on Haiti see Brown, *St. Domingo*; and the literature listed in footnote 119 on p. 90 in this volume. On the guerrilla war in Spain, see Charles Esdaile, *Fighting Napoleon: Guerrillas, Bandits and Adventurers in Spain, 1808–1814* (New Haven: Yale University Press, 2004).

66 On Brown's knowledge about the aforementioned insurrections, wars, and so on, see Hinton, *John Brown and His Men*, 66; and Alexander Boteler, 'The John Brown Raid: Recollections by a Virginian Who Witnessed the Fight', in *Century* 26/3 (1883), 402. For contemporary accounts of the slaves' history and tactics, see Bryan Edwards, 'Observations on the Disposition, Character, Manners, and Habits of Life, of the Maroon Negros of the Islands of Jamaica; and a Detail of the Origin, Progress and Termination of the Late War between those People and the White Inhabitants', in *The History, Civil and Commercial, of the British Colonies in the West Indies* (London: John Stockdale, 1801); Robert Charles Dallas, *The History of the Maroons, from Their Origin to the Establishment of Their Chief Tribe at Sierra Leone: Including the Expedition to Cuba for the Purpose of Procuring Spanish Chasseurs and the State of the Island of Jamaica for the Last Ten Years, with a Succinct History of the Island Previous to the Period* (London: T. N. Longman and O. Rees, 1803); and Jon Gabriel Stedman, *Narrative, of a Five Years' Expedition, against the Revolted Negros of Surinam, in*

independence movement; the Greek Revolution; the Italian, Polish, Hungarian and Irish rebellions; and the revolutions of 1848–9. He also occupied himself intensively with the resistance of the Muslim mountain peoples of Chechnya and Dagestan in the Caucasus, where the legendary Imam Shamil succeeded in forming a resistance movement and a state as of 1840 and in decimating a Russian army.[67] Brown even claimed to have visited several sites connected with these struggles while on a trip to Europe to sell sheep's wool, an assertion verifiable at least in the case of Waterloo.[68] John Brown thus acquired extensive in-depth knowledge of military history, especially regarding guerrilla warfare.[69]

Guiana, on the Wild Coast of South America, from the Year 1772 to 1777 (London: J. Johnson & T. Payne, 1806). For modern perspectives, see Jordan, *White over Black*, Chapter 10; Meissner, Mücke, and Weber, *Schwarzes Amerika*, Chapter 6; Howe, *What Hath God Wrought*, 98–107, 516–17; the classic account by Herbert Aptheker, *American Negro Slave Revolts* (New York: International Slave Revolts, 1943); Richard Price (ed.), *Maroon Societies: Rebel Slave Communities in the Americas* (Baltimore: Johns Hopkins University Press, 1996), 7–10; and Alvin O. Thompson, *Flight to Freedom: African Runaways and Maroons in the Americas* (Kingston: University of the West Indies Press, 2006).

67 See Memoranum book, vol. 2; BPL, n.p., archive.org; the references in Brown, 'Words of Advice', 124; Brown to John Brown Jr, 24 April 1848, from Springfield, MA, in MSS 47 John Brown Jr Papers, Ohio Historical Society, Columbus, OH; Brown to Mary Brown, 22 December 1851, from Boston, MA, in Ruchames, *John Brown*, 86–7; Realf in United States Congress, *Report*, 96; and Alexander Milton Ross, *Recollections and Experiences of an Abolitionist, from 1855 to 1865* (Toronto: Rowsell and Hutchison, 1875), 22. See also Oates, *To Purge This Land*, 244; and on the events, Bayly, *The Birth of the Modern World*, Chapters 1.3, 2.4; Osterhammel, *The Transformation of the World*, Chapters 4.5, 10; and David Armitage and Sanjay Subrahmanyam, *The Age of Revolutions in Global Context, c.1769–1840* (Basingstoke: Palgrave Macmillan, 2010).

68 See Realf in United States Congress, *Report*, 96; and Oates, *To Purge This Land*, 68, 244.

69 Timothy M. Roberts has written ('The Relevance of Giuseppe Mazzini's Ideas of Insurgency to the American Slavery Crisis of the 1850s', in Bayly and Biagini, *Giuseppe Mazzini and the Globalization of Democratic Nationalism*, 313–14, especially 314) that Brown was familiar with Carlo Bianco di St Jorioz's *Della guerra nazionale d'insurrezione per bande* (1830), and that Brown's plans were influenced by Bianco's writings (on Bianco di St. Jorioz see p. 107 in this volume). Roberts assumes that Brown became aware of Bianco's ideas through his contact with Hugh Forbes. But Forbes first joined Brown in January 1857 (see Oates, *To Purge This Land*, 200). It is thus unlikely that Brown's plans prior to 1857 (in this case, the planning until 1846) had already been directly influenced by Bianco's writings, especially because there is no evidence that Brown read Italian. On Brown's possible knowledge of events in Italy, see pp. 263–75 in this volume.

His plan to use the Appalachians as a haven and a springboard for advances into the southern states bore detailed similarity to the examples from Spain, the Caribbean and the Caucasus.

Yet the texts most important to John Brown's plan to free the slaves were the Bible and Joel Tyler Headley's *The Life of Oliver Cromwell*, which stood right next to the Bible on his bookshelf. Oliver Cromwell, the devout Calvinist, who on God's behalf with his Ironsides regiment and the New Model Army ended the tyranny of Charles I, had the king executed after a show trial, and bloodily repressed the Irish Rebellion, was regarded as a regicide and dictator following the restoration of the English monarchy in 1660. However, in the 1840s, the historian Thomas Carlyle, who came from a Scottish Calvinist family, reinterpreted the Lord Protector as the embodiment of faith and heroism.[70] The American author Joel Tyler Headley adopted this interpretation and, moreover, declared the divinely guided Calvinist the founder of the democratic spirit that led to the American Revolution. This triggered a veritable Cromwell cult in the United States. The mixture of Calvinism, republicanism and political violence presented by Headly was so attractive to John Brown that he took the Lord Protector as a role model and strove to embody him. The saying attributed to Cromwell, 'trust in God and keep your powder dry', became his motto.[71]

John Brown, however, found the decisive inspiration for his project to free the slaves in the Bible. God's command to Moses to return to Egypt to liberate his people from bondage, God's support for the Israelites during their desert wandering in the war with the Amalekites, and the story of Samson, who slew thousands of Philistines with a donkey jawbone, were evidence in Brown's eyes that it was possible to overcome a much superior power, if it suited God's will and plan. A particularly important example of this for him (as well as for William Lloyd Garrison and other opponents of slavery) was the case of Gideon, who as God's chosen one routed an

---

70 See Thomas Carlyle, *On Heroes, Hero-Worship and the Heroic in History* (London: Chapman and Hall, 1872); and Thomas Carlyle (ed.), *Oliver Cromwell's Letters and Speeches with Elucidations* (New York: Wiley & Hall, 1845); and on that subject, Jens Nordalm, 'Der gegängelte Held: 'Heroenkult' im 19. Jahrhundert am Beispiel Thomas Carlyles und Heinrich von Treitschkes', *Historische Zeitschrift* 276/3 (2003), 647–75.

71 See Reynolds, *John Brown, Abolitionist*, 164–5, 230–1.

entire Midianite army with only 300 men. According to the biblical account, Gideon positioned his comrades-in-arms around the enemy encampment, where they suddenly brought forth their torches, blew their trumpets, and shouted, 'The sword of the LORD, and of Gideon.' They thus surprised the enemy and 'the LORD set every man's sword against his fellows, even throughout the host: and the host fled.'[72] Divine psychological warfare made up for military might and led to the holy outcome. John Brown firmly believed that God even in his – Brown's – presence also determined all events occurring in the world. He was, therefore, convinced that God would also ensure that the freeing of the slaves, which, after all, was *His* work, would turn out well.[73]

The media and violence: lessons from the Kansas–Missouri Border War

Like many other abolitionists, John Brown saw the existence of slavery in the United States not only as evidence of the hypocrisy of American society, but also as the cause of an ever more pervasive erosion of the foundations of the American republic, that experiment in democracy of global importance. When the slaveholding state of Texas applied for admission to the Union in 1837, even John Quincy Adams warned of a slave-power conspiracy. Texas nevertheless entered the Union in December 1845. After the war by the United States against Mexico from 1846 to 1848, Mexico was forced to cede its entire north-west to the United States in return for compensation. This once again threw into question the balance between slaveholding states and free states. Tough negotiations led to the Compromise of 1850, which stipulated that

---

72 Authorized King James Bible, Exodus 3:15, Exodus 17:8–16, Judges 13–16, Judges 7, quotations from verses 20, 22.

73 On the religious basis of Brown's political thought, see pp. 192–4 in this volume; in general, Oates, *To Purge This Land*; DeCaro, *'Fire from the Midst'* (on Gideon as a role model, see Chapter 15); and Ted A. Smith, *Weird John Brown: Divine Violence and the Limits of Ethics* (Redwood City: Stanford University Press, 2014), especially 59–60. See also Carola Dietze, 'Religious Teleologies, Modernity and Violence: The Case of John Brown', in Henning Trüper, Dipesh Chakrabarty and Sanjay Subrahmanyam (eds.), *Historical Teleologies in the Modern World* (London: Bloomsbury Academic, 2015), 253–73.

California and the Oregon Territory would be free states, but New
Mexico and Utah would remain open to slavery.[74]

The effect of the Compromise of 1850 on American society, and
especially on John Brown, was one of further radicalization. This
was mainly due to one section of the Compromise, the Fugitive Slave
Act, a law intended to make capturing fugitive slaves easier. After its
passage free African Americans could no longer feel safe in the
United States. For persons accused of being a runaway slave had no
legal means to mount a defence, which the anti-slavery movement
denounced as a fundamental breach of the principle of the rule of
law and of the biblical commandment, 'Thou shalt not deliver unto
his master the servant which is escaped from his master unto thee.'[75]
After the law took effect, more than 20,000 African Americans fled
to Canada out of justified fear that they could be abducted and forcibly returned to the South. Many critics of slavery took to the streets,
and some even tried to actively resist the rendition of blacks to the
slaveholders.[76] 'It now seems,' wrote Brown to his wife, 'that the
Fugitive Slave Act was to be the means of making more Abolitionists
than all the lectures we have had for years. It really looks as if God
had His hand on this wickedness also.'[77] With black friends and
acquaintances he organized the United States League of Gileadites,

74 For a pragmatic characterization of the United States society in the late 1840s, see
Richard H. Sewell, *A House Divided: Sectionalism and Civil War, 1848–1865* (Baltimore:
Johns Hopkins University Press, 1988), Chapter 1. On the expansion of the United States
and the questions it raised about slavery, see ibid., Chapter 2; Heideking and Mauch,
Geschichte der USA, Chapter 3.4; Howe, *What Hath God Wrought*, Chapters 17–20;
Drescher, *Abolition*, 317–25; the classic account by David Morris Potter, *The Impending
Crisis, 1848–1861*, ed. Don E. Fehrenbacher (New York: Harper & Row, 1976),
Chapters 1–5; and James McPherson, *Battle Cry of Freedom: The Civil War Era* (New
York: Oxford University Press, 1988), Chapter 2.

75 Authorized King James Bible, Deuteronomy 23:16, continues, 'He [the slave]
shall dwell with thee, *even* among you, in that place which he shall choose in one of thy
gates, where it liketh him best: thou shalt not oppress him.' Brown cited this verse in his
criticism of the law in a letter to Douglass.

76 On the law and the reactions to it, see Finzsch, Horton and Horton, *Von Benin
nach Baltimore*, 262–5; Potter, *The Impending Crisis*, Chapter 6; McPherson, *Battle Cry*,
Chapter 3.1; Stanley W. Campbell, *The Slave Catchers: Enforcement of the Fugitive Slave
Act, 1850–1860* (Chapel Hill: University of North Carolina Press, 1970); and Morris,
Free Men All.

77 Letter written on 28 November 1850 from Springfield, MA, in Ruchames, *John
Brown*, 79–80.

named after the Gilead Mountains, the site where, according to the Bible, Gilead selected his warriors.[78]

Moreover, the Fugitive Slave Act also had an indirect polarizing effect on American society. Outrage about the law led the author Harriet Beecher Stowe to write the novel *Uncle Tom's Cabin*, which was serialized in an abolitionist newspaper beginning in summer 1851 and appeared as a book the following year, eliciting an unusually powerful response in the United States as well as in Europe.[79] In the same period, the first novel ever published by an African American in the United States appeared – *Clotel, or, The President's Daughter* – which was written by escaped slave William Wells Brown and told the story of Thomas Jefferson's illegitimate daughter from his relationship with a slave. Other books included slave autobiographies, for instance the biographies of William Wells Brown and Frederick Douglass, as well as Salomon Northup's *Twelve Years a Slave* and Harriet Jacobs's *Incidents in the Life of a Slave Girl*. Collectively, these publications injected an emotional charge into the slavery question.[80]

---

78 On the league, see also 'Words of Advice', pp. 209–10 in this volume; Villard, *John Brown*, 50; Oates, *To Purge This Land*, 72–5; and Quarles, *Allies for Freedom*, 25–7. On the name Gilead see the Authorized King James Bible, Judges 7:3: 'Now therefore go to, proclaim in the ears of the people, saying, Whosoever *is* fearful and afraid, let him return and depart early from Mount Gilead. And there returned of the people twenty and two thousand; and there remained ten thousand.'

79 An estimated 1.5 million copies of the book were sold in England and its colonies by April of that year, with some 300,000 copies being sold in the United States by the end of 1852. Translations in various European languages also appeared that year. Only the Bible exceeded the book's total print run in the nineteenth century. See Finzsch, Horton and Horton, *Von Benin nach Baltimore*, 269–70; and also Friedrich Lenger, 'Im Vorfeld des Bürgerkriegs: 'Uncle Tom's Cabin' by Harriet Beecher Stowe (1851/52)', in Dirk van Laak (ed.), *Literatur, die Geschichte schrieb* (Göttingen: Vandenhoeck & Ruprecht, 2011), 43, 53.

80 William Wells Brown, *Clotel, or, The President's Daughter: A Narrative of Slave Life in the United States*, ed. Robert S. Levine (1853) (Boston: Bedford Cultural Edition, 2011); Douglass, 'Narrative of the Life of Frederick Douglass, an American Slave [1845]', in Yuval Taylor (ed.), *I Was Born a Slave: An Anthology of Classic Slave Narratives*, vol. 1: *1772-1849* (Chicago: Lawrence Hill Books, 1999), 523–99; William Wells Brown, 'Narrative of William W. Brown, a Fugitive Slave', in *I Was Born a Slave*; Solomon Northup, 'Twelve Years a Slave: Narrative of Solomon Northup, a Citizen of New York, Kidnapped in Washington City in 1841, and Rescued in 1853, from a Cotton Plantation Near the Red River, in Louisiana', in Yuval Taylor (ed.), *I Was Born a Slave: An Anthology of Classic Slave Narratives*, vol. 2: *1849-1866* (Chicago: Lawrence Hill Books, 1999), 159–317; Harriet Jacobs (pseudonym for Linda Brent), 'Incidents in the Life of a Slave

With the once regionally structured public sphere in the United States now encompassing the entire nation by the early 1850s, these texts and other books and writings received attention countrywide. In the process, they exposed the political and societal differences between the free and slave states all the more,[81] and thus contributed decisively to polarization between the two sections.

In spring 1854, the passage of the Kansas–Nebraska Act further escalated the dispute between the North and the South. The law provided for the creation of two new territories west of Missouri and Iowa – Kansas in the south and Nebraska in the north – and allowed their residents to decide on the basis of the newly declared principle of popular sovereignty whether or not slavery would be allowed in their state. The Act thus violated the Missouri Compromise of 1820, which banned slavery in that area. The Kansas–Nebraska Act was therefore seen by many opponents of slavery as proof that the slave powers intended ultimately to spread slavery across the entire United States.[82]

John Brown reacted with great alarm: 'I have thought much of late of the extreme wickedness of persons,' he wrote to Frederick Douglass shortly after the bill had been introduced into the Senate, 'who use their influence to bring law and order, and good government, and courts of justice into disrespect and contempt with mankind.' What punishment by God or man can be too severe in the face of such malignance? It was high time to curb the 'undermining of our truly republican and democratic institutions' by wicked supporters of slavery.[83]

The need to prevent further subversion of the United States must have appeared all the more urgent when it soon became apparent that

---

Girl [1861]', in Taylor, *I Was Born a Slave*, vol. 2, 533–681. On the use of autobiographies by the abolitionist movement, see, for example, Catherine Clinton, '"Slavery Is War": Harriet Tubman and the Underground Railroad', in David W. Blight (ed.), *Passages to Freedom* (Washington, DC: Smithsonian Books, 2001) especially 202. On the charging with emotion see Lenger, 'Im Vorfeld des Bürgerkriegs', 57.

81 See Loughran, *The Republic in Print*, Chapter 7.

82 See Finzsch, Horton and Horton, *Von Benin nach Baltimore*, 273–6; Potter, *The Impending Crisis*, 160–77; Sewell, *A House Divided*, Chapter 3; McPherson, *Battle Cry*, 121–9, 136; and Drescher, *Abolition*, 325–7.

83 Letter from Akron, OH on 9 January 1854. Douglass published it in *Frederick Douglass' Paper* (Rochester, NY), 27 January 1854, 3, col. B; and it is reprinted in Ruchames, *John Brown*, 92. On Douglass's newspaper, see McFeely, *Frederick Douglass*, 167–9.

the passage of the Kansas–Nebraska Act would unleash a long conflict. For even before the law took effect, politicians in Missouri began organizing pro-slavery settlers to ensure that Kansas could be won for the expansion of slavery. What the South could do, the North could also do, with, for example, several wealthy New Englanders founding the New England Emigrant Aid Company, which recruited and assisted settlers who wanted to keep the territory free of slaves.[84] John Brown's sons were also infected by pioneer fever, not least because of this organization's advertising efforts. In autumn 1854, Owen, Frederick and Salmon Brown set out with their livestock and possessions, arriving in spring 1855 in the Kansas Territory (KT), where they staked a claim to land near Osawatomie on Pottawatomie Creek and founded 'Brownsville', also known as 'Brown's Station'. Jason and John Brown Jr later followed with their families.[85]

John Brown initially refused to join the move to Kansas. He had no objection if his sons wanted to go 'with a view to defeat Satan and his legions', he wrote to the oldest one, '*but I feel committed to operate in another part of the field*'.[86] At the time Brown wrote this, he had just wound up the financial disaster of the wool cooperative and was finally free to dedicate himself to the Subterranean Pass Way plan and the North Elba settlement in the Adirondack mountains in northern New York State. The wealthy philanthropist Gerrit Smith had made land grants available there to African American settlers. Most of them, however, were town or city dwellers who struggled with their subsistence existence in the sparse heights of the Adirondacks, especially because the area's harsh climate hindered productive agriculture and the long-established settlers were hostile towards their new neighbours.[87]

84 For an introduction to the struggle for Kansas, see McPherson, *Battle Cry*, Chapter 5, especially 145–6; and Potter, *The Impending Crisis*, Chapter 9. The interpretation of the proto-civil war in Kansas in the literature remains controversial. For a more recent interpretation, see, for instance, Nicole Etcheson, *Bleeding Kansas: Contested Liberty in the Civil War Era* (Lawrence: University Press of Kansas, 2004).

85 See Oates, *To Purge This Land*, 84–8; and McGlone, *John Brown's War*, Chapter 4.5.

86 John Brown to John Brown Jr, 21 August 1854, from Akron, OH, in Ruchames, *John Brown*, 94.

87 See Finzsch, Horton and Horton, *Von Benin nach Baltimore*, 240–1; and the classic works by Ralph Volney Harlow, *Gerrit Smith, Philanthropist and Reformer* (New York: H. Holt, 1939), Chapter 11; and Alfred L. Donaldson, *A History of the Adirondacks* (New York: Century, 1921), vol. 2, Chapter 30.

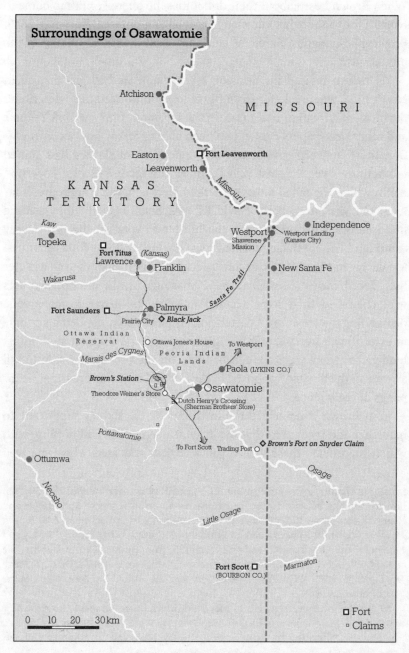

Map 3. Surroundings of Osawatomie.

When Brown heard about their difficulties, he offered Smith to come to North Elba to share his knowledge gained as a pioneer. By spring 1849, Brown had bought a parcel of land and moved with his family to the mountains.[88]

Yet Brown revised his decision a year later. He had just arrived in North Elba, where a letter from his oldest son awaited him, describing the brothers' situation in Kansas. In the *Liberator*, the *New York Tribune* and other newspapers Brown had been able to follow how a confrontation there between supporters and opponents of slavery had gained momentum over the past year.[89] For as the territory's first governor, Andrew Reeder, called on its settlers to elect congressional representatives, the Missouri senator David Rice Atchison responded by leading hundreds of Missourians over the border to vote for the pro-slavery candidate. The spectacle repeated itself during elections for a territorial legislature in March 1855, despite precautionary measures such as voter lists. Faced with the heavily armed Missourians, the election workers who cherished their lives decided it would be better to let anyone demanding to vote do so. An Atchison employee commanded his people to exterminate 'every scoundrel' showing even the slightest abolitionist tendencies; there were enough of them on the pro-slavery side to kill anyone in the territory opposed to slavery and now was not the time for pangs of conscience.[90]

John Brown Jr described the invasions by the slavery supporters to his father and recounted that the 'friends of freedom' had nothing with which to counter these well-organized and paid men who were well

---

88 See Quarles, *Allies for Freedom*, 22–5; and Harlow, *Gerrit Smith*, 246, 393. On Brown's deciding between Kansas and North Elba, see his letters to Ruth Brown and Henry Thompson on 30 September 1854 from Akron, OH in Ruchames, *John Brown*, 94; and to them on 3 January and 13 February 1855 from Akron, OH; on 7 May and 4 June 1855 from Rockford, IL; and on 18 June 1855 from Hudson, OH, in Sanborn, *The Life and Letters*, 191–3. On this decision see also Villard, *John Brown*, 54; Oates, *To Purge This Land*, 75–9, 85–6; Quarles, *Allies for Freedom*, 29–30; and McGlone, *John Brown's War*, Chapter 4.4, 4.6.

89 See, for example, *Liberator*, 11 May 1855, which quotes an article from the *New York Tribune*; 'More Trouble in Kansas', *Daily National Intelligencer*, 10 May 1855, col. A; 'The Kansas Difficulties', *North American*, 10 May 1855; and 'The Kansas Outrage', *Kansas Herald of Freedom*, 12 May 1855.

90 A special committee later ruled that 1,700 votes in the November election and 4,908 votes in the March election were invalid. See Potter, *The Impending Crisis*, 201–2; and McPherson, *Battle Cry*, 146–7.

supplied with arms and whisky and had thus acted very cowardly while these 'lawless bands' trampled on their 'dearest rights'. In his view the only solution was to organize a self-defence force. His brothers and he were ready, but they needed weapons: could their father acquire and ship arms to them (a detailed list followed)?[91] John Brown was more than willing and several days later he set out to attend a convention of the Radical Abolitionist Party, co-founded by Frederick Douglass, where he had his son's letter read to the audience. Many were moved to tears and made donations for Brown's sons and the opponents of slavery in Kansas. In early August, John Brown left with his son-in-law Henry Thompson for Ohio to collect more weapons and donations, which they immediately brought to Kansas, arriving in Brown's Station in early October with John's son Oliver, who had joined them in Chicago.[92]

The proto-civil war, whose violence increased the next year and would become known in history as the Border War and Bleeding Kansas, was a proxy war between the North and the South. During and on account of this conflict, John Brown would become not only a wanted murderer but also a national celebrity. At first, it seemed as if the conflict could still be resolved peacefully. For while the state legislature in Leavenworth elected with southern assistance was adopting slave state Missouri's statutes, instituting draconian punishments for any statements critical of slavery, and filling all sheriff and judge posts with slavery advocates, opponents of slavery, now a majority of the population, were beginning to organize themselves politically. They founded the Free State Party, declared their rejection of the pro-slavery 'bogus legislature', held new (this time correctly run) elections for a legislature, and ratified their own constitution.[93]

The Brown clan initially trusted in these political processes and actively participated in them. John Brown Jr was elected captain of the local militia and representative of his district to the new legislature in

---

91 John Brown Jr to John Brown, 20, 24 and 26 May 1855, from Brownsville, Kansas Territory, quoted in Boyer, *The Legend of John Brown*, 524–5.

92 On proceedings at the convention, see John Brown to his wife and children, 28 June 1855, from Syracuse, NY, in Sanborn, *The Life and Letters*, 193. On the convention, travel and additional donations, see also Oates, *To Purge This Land*, 90–3; and Quarles, *Allies for Freedom*, 31–2. On the Radical Abolition Party, see Finzsch, Horton and Horton, *Von Benin nach Baltimore*, 281.

93 See Heideking and Mauch, *Geschichte der USA*, 135–6; Potter, *The Impending Crisis*, 204–7; and McPherson, *Battle Cry*, 147–8.

224 The Invention of Terrorism

Topeka. His father wrote home optimistically that the South had apparently conceded the Kansas Territory and there were no grounds 'to doubt a favorable result, if the Free State folks will hold on patiently'.[94] The situation escalated again in December 1855, when slavery supporters murdered two free-staters, and Missouri senator Atchison turned up on the outskirts of Lawrence, the stronghold of the abolitionists, accompanied by the Kansas Territory's new governor, William Shannon, and several hundred Missourians. (Andrew Reeder, the former governor, had been dismissed by President Franklin Pierce for refusing to recognize the legislature elected with the South's help.) The siege, however, was resolved through negotiation.[95] On that occasion, John Brown, who had rushed to the aid of the town with his sons, was also made a captain, and given command of a small group named the Liberty Guards.[96]

A hard winter with considerable snowfall then set in, and Brown wrote to his wife that they would 'have no general disturbance' until the weather warmed.[97] His appraisal proved right, but as the snow began to melt and Brownsville's residents once again received news from the outside world, they had to recognize that they had been overly optimistic politically.

Rather than conceding Kansas, those in favour of expanding slavery had won over the federal government in Washington. In speeches to Congress in late December 1855 and late January 1856, President Pierce had positioned himself unequivocally on the side of pro-slavery forces. He described the free-staters' political initiatives as 'treasonable insurrection' against government authority and declared that the executive branch would suppress such revolutionary acts with all means available under the Constitution. To this end, Pierce placed the US troops stationed in the region's forts at the disposal of the slavery-friendly

---

94 John Brown to Owen Brown, 19 October 1855, from Brownsville, Kansas Territory, in Ruchames, *John Brown*, 95–6, quotation at 96. On John Brown Jr's activities, see Oates, *To Purge This Land*, 112–14, 116–17.

95 See Potter, *The Impending Crisis*, 207–8; and McPherson, *Battle Cry*, 147–8. On Brown's role, see Oates, *To Purge This Land*, 103–11; and McGlone, *John Brown's War*, Chapter 5.1.

96 Oates, *To Purge This Land*, 108.

97 John Brown to 'Dear Wife and Children, Every One on 1 February 1856 from Osawatomie, Kansas Territory', in Sanborn, *Life and Letters*, 222; reprinted in Ruchames, *John Brown*, 101.

governor of the Kansas Territory.[98] Shortly thereafter slavery supporters attacked a captain of a free-state militia with knives and an axe and dumped him, mortally wounded, in front of his log cabin.[99]

Threatened by the federal and territorial authorities as well as by neighbouring pro-slavery settlers and their allies in the South, Brown turned to Joshua H. Giddings, Ohio's abolitionist congressman. He wrote to him that he feared that the anti-slavery settlers could soon be forced to fight against US soldiers, and asked 'in the name of Almighty God', 'in the name of our venerated fore-fathers' and 'in the name of all that good or true men ever held dear; will Congress suffer us to be driven to such "dire extremities"? *Will anything be done*?'[100] Giddings replied that he was doing what he could, but that he had limited influence as a member of the minority in Congress. He found it inconceivable that President Pierce would deploy US troops against settlers in Kansas.[101] The congressman's reply showed that no help could be expected from that side; the opposition at the federal level was too powerless and naive to protect its supporters.

Meanwhile the threat on the ground was moving closer and becoming more concrete. In early May, for example, members of the free-state government were charged with insurrection. John Brown Jr had to fear that he, too, could face similar charges as a member of the free-state legislature. In addition, a group of armed men from Georgia had set up their camp in the immediate vicinity of Brown's Station. Pro-slavery neighbours contacted the new arrivals immediately and also began to blatantly threaten the free-staters on the Pottawatomie Creek that they would be killed if they did not depart at once.[102]

---

98 Franklin Pierce, 'Third Annual Message' and 'Special Message to the Senate and House of Representatives', in James D. Richardson (ed.), *A Compilation of the Messages and Papers of the Presidents* (Washington, DC: Government Printing Office, 1896–1899), 358. See in addition Boyer, *The Legend of John Brown*, 470–1.

99 See McGlone, *John Brown's War*, 102–4.

100 Letter, 20 February 1856, from Osawatomie, Kansas Territory, in Villard, *John Brown*, 131.

101 Giddings to Brown, 17 March 1856, from the Hall of Representatives, Washington, Kansas Historical Society (hereafter KSHS), Series B: John Brown, Personal Papers, 1839–1924, Microfilm reel MS 1245, reprinted in Robert Penn Warren, *John Brown: The Making of a Martyr* (New York: Payson & Clarke, 1929), 137–8. On Giddings, see especially James Brewer Stewart, *Joshua R. Giddings and the Tactics of Radical Politics* (Cleveland: Press of Case Western Reserve University, 1970).

102 See Oates, *To Purge This Land*, 119–25; and McGlone, *John Brown's War*, Chapters 5.3–5.4, 6.2.

The deadly conflict was escalating and little was needed to bring it to a head. The necessary impetus came soon enough. On the afternoon of 21 May a messenger arrived on horseback at Brown's Station to report that a large pro-slavery force had reappeared outside Lawrence, this time with a cannon. The Browns and their free-state militias were called to the city's aid and departed that same day. Early the next morning, another messenger galloped up to say that the free-staters had decided not to defend Lawrence since mercenaries from Missouri were ransacking the town. The Browns were best advised to turn back, for there was nothing left for them to do in Lawrence. However, reports coming in shortly thereafter that the Missourians had regathered prompted them to await further developments.[103] The following morning a messenger arrived at their camp with news from Washington that Charles Sumner, a prominent abolitionist and Massachusetts senator, had been beaten nearly to death in the Senate by a South Carolina congressman because of a speech he had held denouncing slavery.[104]

For John Brown, who had previously expressed his aggravation at the 'cowardice' of the free-staters in Lawrence, these last developments were more than he could accept. He is reported to have said, 'something must be done, to show these barbarians that we, too, have rights,' and gone about recruiting volunteers for a 'secret mission' that would include 'some killing'. He felt it was time to 'fight fire with fire' and 'to strike terror in the hearts of proslavery men'. In his opinion it would be better for a few bad men to die than to have the free-staters driven out of the Kansas Territory. That evening he set out with seven men to return to Osawatomie. The group included four of his sons (Frederick, Oliver, Owen and Salmon), his son-in-law Henry Thompson, and Theodore Weiner, a Jew and free-stater from Vienna, Austria. Weiner had a small store in the area and had been threatened by the Sherman brothers, immigrants from Oldenburg, Germany, who also owned a local shop and advocated slavery.

With his band of volunteers, John Brown crossed the line to the active use of violence once and for all by engaging in premeditated killings. By this time six free-staters had been murdered by slavery supporters in the

---

103 See Oates, *To Purge This Land*, 126–8.
104 See David Herbert Donald, *Charles Sumner and the Coming of the Civil War* (New York: Alfred A. Knopf, 1960), Chapters 11–12.

Kansas Territory. Acting on the principle of 'an eye for an eye, a tooth for a tooth' (Exodus 21:24), the self-proclaimed Northern Army led by Brown killed five pro-slavery men living along Pottawatomie Creek on the night of 24 May. Those killed had actively participated in the formation of the 'bogus legislature' and efforts to have slavery introduced in the Kansas Territory and had threatened Brown's family or other free-staters in the area. Using swords donated to Brown on his way to Kansas, the Northern Army men split open their victims' skulls, hacked off their arms, or slit their throats so that the mutilated corpses were indeed apt to spread fear and terror.[105] This was murder and it was political, and therefore it may seem to have been Brown's first act of terrorism. But I will discuss a little later why this act of violence does not completely qualify for such a designation. That Brown was aware of his guilt before men can be inferred from his not daring to openly tell his wife about it, instead writing cryptically, 'We feel assured that He who sees not as men see, does not lay the guilt of innocent blood to our charge.' Brown was convinced he had murdered for a higher purpose; God, he hoped, would acknowledge this.[106]

The destruction of Lawrence and especially the political murders along Pottawatomie Creek provoked an escalating proto-civil war in the Kansas Territory and further polarized society in the rest of the United States. While organized opponents of slavery in the North intensified their efforts to send armed settlers to the Territory and continued to be successful even in face of the violence there, slavery advocates in the South recruited mounted volunteers for the fight.[107] The Osawatomie area was now swarming with US marshals and troops with orders to arrest John Brown and his men. Many Missourians and their helpers joined the hunt, searching free-staters' farms and often pilfering anything they deemed valuable. They razed Brown's Station and took John Brown Jr prisoner, despite his not having participated in the murders, treating him so brutally that he temporarily lost consciousness and suffered symptoms throughout his life that now would be

105 Oates, *To Purge This Land*, Chapter 10; Quarles, *Allies of Freedom*, 33–5; and especially McGlone, *John Brown's War*, Part 2. On the course of events, see Chapter 6.1, 6.3.

106 John Brown to Mary Ann Brown, June 1856, from 'Near Brown's Station, K.T.', in Ruchames, *John Brown*, 105. See Quarles, *Allies for Freedom*, 34.

107 See Potter, *The Impending Crisis*, 213–14; and McPherson, *Battle Cry*, 153.

associated with post-traumatic stress disorder. The men also shot and killed Brown's son Frederick.[108]

But they were unable to track down the Northern Army, which hid out with the help of Brown's friend John Tecumseh Jones (usually referred to as Ottawa Jones), who was part Native American. Additional volunteers, on the other hand, managed to find their way to the group, including several who had participated in the 1848–9 revolutions in Europe and been forced to leave the continent after the suppression of those political upheavals. The revolutionaries had immigrated to the United States and come to the Kansas Territory in the belief that the decisive battle for the liberation of humankind would be fought there. Brown's radicalism was entirely in line with their convictions.[109]

Hardly a week after Pottawatomie the captain of a free-state militia, Samuel T. Shore, also located the Northern Army camp and asked its commander to support his troops in their fight against approaching Missourians. Brown agreed, and together they mounted a surprise dawn attack on the foe's camp. After wild exchanges of fire, during which Brown cleverly used the local terrain to his advantage, the free-staters succeeded in forcing the numerically superior Missourians to surrender. This Battle of Black Jack was – as Brown proudly wrote home to his wife and children – 'the first regular battle fought between Free-State and proslavery men in Kansas'.[110] Two months later Brown again played a leading role in the battle for the town of Osawatomie. Although he and his group, now numbering some thirty-five men, could not prevent the Missourian force of several hundred from burning down the town, Brown was able to inflict significant losses on the pro-slavery force by once more shrewdly exploiting the elements of surprise and geography. Regardless of the battle's concrete military benefit, its symbolic

---

108 Oates, *To Purge This Land*, Chapters 11–13. On the efforts to arrest Brown, see ibid., Chapter 12.

109 Among the volunteers were Bavarian social democrat Charles Kaiser and Viennese Jew August Bondi, both of whom had both fought in the Hungarian Revolution under Lajos Kossuth. See Frank Baron, 'German Republicans and Radicals in the Struggle for a Slave-Free Kansas: Charles F. Kob and August Bondi', in *Yearbook for German-American Studies* 40 (2005), 3–26. On criticism of Garrison and his supporters characteristic of the Forty-Eighters and on their sympathy for the radical abolitionists, see Honeck, 'Freemen of All Nations', 608–9.

110 John Brown to his wife and children, June 1856, from 'Near Brown's Station', in Ruchames, *John Brown*, 105. On the battle, see Oates, *To Purge This Land*, Chapter 12.

importance lay in the fact that Osawatomie (in contrast to Lawrence) had not surrendered without a fight. It was with this armed encounter, at the latest, that Brown became a hero in the eyes of many free-staters. The next time he rode into the rebuilt town of Lawrence he was received with loud cheers, 'as if the President had come to town', according to a subsequent eyewitness account.[111]

In Kansas, Brown gained experience in the use of violence as well as in dealing with journalists and the media, for the proxy war in and about Kansas was being waged not only locally, but also in the national media and polarized public sphere.[112] Even before Brown joined his sons in Kansas, his texts and letters were being published in abolitionist newspapers, for instance his 'Sambo's Mistakes', in the style of Benjamin Franklin's satirical pieces, or the aforementioned letter to Frederick Douglass about the Kansas–Nebraska Act.[113] Those, however, were more random or occasional publications.

In Kansas, Brown began to deliberately engage in public relations work. Initially, this involved the common practice of sharing information by copying and passing along letters. He contacted, for example, the publisher of the local newspaper in Akron, Ohio, with the request to print his letter so that each of the town's many donors of weapons and ammunition received a report from him, as a 'substitute', for he was unfortunately not able to write to each one individually. Brown explicitly asked his family to copy his extensive report to them about the Battle of Black Jack and send it to the abolitionist philanthropist Gerrit Smith, because it was the only way he knew to 'get these facts, & our situation before the world'. And in mid-December 1855 he sent a letter detailing the fighting at Lawrence to Douglass, who then published it in his

---

111 Villard, *John Brown*, 253. On the battle for Osawatomie, see Oates, *To Purge This Land*, Chapter 13. On the broad acceptance of militant abolitionism in Kansas as a result of the battles against the pro-slavery forces, see Karl Gridley, ' "Willing to Die for the Cause of Freedom in Kansas": Free State Emigration, John Brown, and the Rise of Militant Abolitionism in the Kansas Territory', in McCarthy and Stauffer, *Prophets of Protest*, 147–64.

112 See especially Lorman Ratner and Dwight L. Teeter, *Fanatics and Fire-Eaters: Newspapers and the Coming of the Civil War* (Urbana: University of Illinois Press, 2003), Chapter 4.

113 Brown, 'Sambo's Mistakes', in the African American newspaper *Ram's Horn*, reprinted in Ruchames, *John Brown*, 69–72. On this text, see Quarles, *Allies for Freedom*, 21–2; Carton, *Patriotic Treason*, 113–15; and Reynolds, *John Brown*, 119–21. On the letter to Douglass, see pp. 219–20 in this volume.

newspaper.[114] The transition, therefore, from letters as a message to friends and relatives to their use as newspaper articles for communication with a larger audience was seamless.

Brown's prominence resulting from the battles in Kansas opened new ways for him to reach the public. Following the murders on the Pottawatomie, the Scottish journalist James Redpath, a correspondent for the Missouri *Democrat* and various newspapers in the Northeast, came to the Northern Army hideout, where he spoke for an hour with the men, in particular John Brown. When he left he 'was thoughtful, and hopeful for the cause', as he wrote later, for he 'had seen, for the first time the spirit of the Ironsides . . . the predestined leader of the second and holier American Revolution'.[115] The captain of the Northern Army obviously understood how to convey his self-image to others.

John Brown began to reach out to the media and journalists more proactively. He got to know Augustus Wattles and George W. Brown, the publishers of the *Kansas Herald of Freedom* from Lawrence; visited William Addison Phillips, a correspondent for the *New York Tribune*; and befriended Richard J. Hinton, a writer for the *Boston Traveller* and *Chicago Tribune*.[116] Brown responded to an account of the Battle of Black Jack published by the Missourians' commander with a correction printed in the *New York Tribune* and possibly in the *Republican* from St

---

114 John Brown to the editor of the *Summit Beacon* newspaper (Akron, OH), 20 December 1855, from Osawatomie, KS, in Ruchames, *John Brown*, 97; John Brown to his wife and children, June 1856, 'near Brown's Station', in Ruchames, *John Brown*, 105; and Brown to Frederick Douglass, *Frederick Douglass' Paper*, 11 January 1856. It has not been possible to date to find an original copy of the edition containing this article. For help in the search I thank Jerome Brooks from the Library of Congress's Serial and Government Publications Division; Vincent Golden from the American Antiquarian Society, Worcester, MA; and the staff at the Moorland-Springarn Research Center, Howard University, in Washington, DC.

115 Redpath, *The Public Life*, 85. On Redpath and the encounter see John R. McKivigan, *Forgotten Firebrand: James Redpath and the Making of Nineteenth-Century America* (Ithaca: Cornell University Press, 2008), 28–9.

116 See George Washington Brown, *The Truth at Last: History Corrected. Reminiscences of Old John Brown: Thrilling Incidents of Border Life in Kansas* (Rockford: Abraham E. Smith, 1880), 7; Hinton, *John Brown and His Men*, especially 40–1, 47; Phillips, 'Three Interviews', especially 216–17; Oates, *To Purge This Land*, 159, 175, 177; Carton, *Patriotic Treason*, 215–16; and McGlone, *John Brown's War*, 99 and Chapter 9.1. On the role of journalists in the Kansas conflict generally, see Ratner and Teeter, *Fanatics and Fire-Eaters*, Chapter 4.

Louis as well.[117] After the attack on Osawatomie he immediately wrote a
report about the events for the press in the East.[118] He also carefully
observed the 'different stories' the press published about him. Brown cut
out the articles and sent them to his family in North Elba, pointing out
with a certain coquetry that 'none of them tell things as I tell them,' thus
maintaining his interpretive prerogative.[119]

In the literature the murders along Pottawatomie Creek have sometimes been described as terrorism or as a preliminary form of this type
of violence.[120] Such a classification is based on definitions of terrorism
that conceive of this type of violence as 'a mutual exchange of intimidating violence' or the 'use of violence or the threat of violence by an organized group to attain political objectives'. Such broad definitions, however,
would denote not only the murders along the Pottawatomie as terrorism, but also war, revolution and rebellion.[121] The Pottawatomie murders

---

117 Report by John Brown to the editors of the *New York Tribune*, 1 July 1856, from
Lawrence, KT, reprinted in the article 'Another Feature of the Conspiracy. *From Our
Special Correspondent. Lawrence, K.T.*, Tuesday, July 1, 1856', *New York Daily Tribune*,
11 July 1856, 6. The information in the report was also published in a version of the
Missouri Republican – Daily, Weekly or *Tri-weekly* could not be verified, at least not on
the basis of a search of the July 1856 issues of the *Daily Missouri Republican*, whose
articles usually appeared in the other editions. For assistance in this search I thank Lukas
Keller, Vincent Golden from the American Antiquarian Society, Worcester, MA, and
Sean D. Visintainer from the St Louis Mercantile Library, St Louis, MO. An undated
entry in Brown's notebook reads 'Capt. H. Clay Pates statement of Black Jack affair is in
New York Tribune of June 19th 1856', which indicates he had followed the press coverage
of the conflict in Kansas. Memoranum book, vol. 2; BPL, n.p., archive.org.

118 John Brown, 'The Fight of Osawatomie, Lawrence, Kansas, Sept. 7, 1856', in
John Brown Collection, 299, Box 1, Folder 17, KSHS, republished in Sanborn, *The Life
and Letters*, 318–20; 'Interesting from Kansas . . . Statement of Captain John Brown
concerning The Battle of Ossawatomie', *New York Times*, 20 September 1856; 'Details of
Kansas News; Border Ruffians Defy Gov. Geary and Gen. Smith. (News) John Brown',
Cleveland Daily Herald, 22 September 1856, col. C.

119 John Brown to Mary Ann Brown, 6 March 1857, in the John Brown Collection,
KSHS, kansasmemory.org.

120 See, for example, Lutz and Lutz, *Terrorism in America*, 48–9, 53; Fellman, *In the
Name of God and Country*, Chapter 1, 18–19, 28–9; and Reynolds, *John Brown*, 149,
165–6. McGlone writes that 'in some respects the slayings anticipated latter-day
terrorism – acts of violence designed to produce political change by inspiring widespread
fear.' He considers it basically anachronistic to speak of terrorism in antebellum United
States, however – 'if terrorists are individuals or groups who use clandestine violence to
gain political objectives, then Brown and others who followed his example in Kansas
may be seen as among their precursors.' McGlone, *John Brown's War*, 134–5, 136.

121 Fellman, *In the Name of God and Country*, 2; and Lutz and Lutz, *Terrorism in
America*, 2. McGlone's definition – conspiratorial violence to achieve political objectives

did involve politically motivated 'shocking acts of violence' that were primarily intended to 'spread insecurity and horror', but also 'to generate sympathy and a willingness to provide support', thus fulfilling a number of important criteria underlying the sociological definition of terrorism laid out in the introduction to this volume.[122] The symbolic value of the murders lay in their retaliatory character, as well as in their intention to mark the limits of what slavery opponents would tolerate, to demonstrate that not all free-staters were 'pacifistic cowards', and to show that involvement in slavery was not without risk either.[123]

Figure 13. James Redpath. Kansas State Historical Society.

These violent acts along the Pottawatomie, however, lacked other key characteristics of terrorism. The murders were directed not bottom-up against representatives of the slavery-friendly governments in Leavenworth or Washington, but against politically active opponents

by spreading fear – is too general as well. On the problem of overly broad definitions of terrorism, see pp. 29–30 in the introduction to this volume.

122 Waldmann, *Terrorismus*, 12. See also Chapter 1, p. 47, in this volume.

123 Tony Horwitz, for instance, also emphasizes this in *Midnight Rising: John Brown and the Raid That Sparked the Civil War* (New York: Henry Holt, 2011), 54–5.

among the population. Instead of ensuring that news of the killings spread as widely as possible, John Brown and his accomplices sought to keep them a secret. The murders had not been planned long beforehand, but occurred spontaneously. In addition, they also had a strongly instrumental character, with Brown and the others ultimately acting to eliminate a threat in the immediate vicinity of their settlements. Moreover, the murders did not occur in peacetime, but rather in a situation fraught with threats and violence in which all peaceful political means appeared to have been exhausted. And finally, the violent acts were intended more as retaliation than as provocation, even if they had the latter effect.

In view of this the murders carried out by the Northern Army are rather to be counted as acts of deliberately staged cruelty and judged as ostentatiously gruesome political murders – an archaic kind of violence typical of unregulated war. There are countless examples of this type of warfare throughout history.[124] In the United States, settlers from Europe associated conspicuous brutality primarily with slave uprisings and the violence practised by the Native Americans. This form of violence, however, was used by both sides in the conflicts between European and Native Americans and in the suppression of slave revolts, with settlers dealing similarly with adversaries they considered uncivilized and unworthy. Both parties in the proto-civil war in Kansas were aware of such violent practices and mentioned them specifically in the political disputes about the murders along Pottawatomie Creek. William A. Phillips, for example, deliberately attempted to mislead his readers into thinking that the Pottawatomie victims were victims of the Comanche Indians, and George W. Brown commented about the murders that such 'savage barbarity and demoniac cruelty' were 'certainly characteristic of North American savages'.[125] John Brown appropriated these attributions

---

124 David Reynolds has previously called attention to the ethnic and 'primitive' character of the violent act, although he was thinking solely of 'the spirit of the retaliatory savagery of two minority groups'. Reynolds, *John Brown*, 167. On ostentatious cruelty and its long history, see, for example, Trutz von Trotha, Jakob Rosel and Rainer Geißler (eds.), *On Cruelty = Sur la cruauté = Über Grausamkeit* (Cologne: Köppe, 2011).

125 See William A. Phillips, *The Conquest of Kansas by Missouri and Her Allies: A History of the Troubles in Kansas, from the Passage of the Organic Act until the Close of July, 1856* (Boston: Phillips, Sampson, 1856), 317; and George Washington Brown, *The Truth at Last: History Corrected: Reminiscences of Old John Brown: Thrilling Incidents of Border Life in Kansas* (Rockford: Abraham E. Smith, 1880), 14. On the use of cruelty as a deterrent by European Americans in violent confrontations with slaves and Native

and attempted to exploit them by taking on a Native American *nom de guerre*, calling himself John Brown of Osawatomie, Osawatomie Brown, or simply Old Osawatomie (the place name traces back to a Native American language). Just two weeks after the murders, a play with the title *Osawatomie Brown* was in production on Broadway.[126]

Even if the murders on Pottawatomie Creek were more characteristic of an archaic form of violence, John Brown's experience of exercising that violence nonetheless represented another important step for him along the path towards the invention of terrorism as a specific tactic. For through those murders he came to understand both the effectiveness and the functioning of the logic of violent provocation. Through the targeted killing of five pro-slavery settlers, John Brown succeeded in escalating the tense situation in Kansas into a proto-civil war, and in the process became familiar with the psychological impact of violent acts.

Among the New England elite: supporters and theories of violence

John Brown set out for the East in early October 1856, to finally dedicate himself to the Subterranean Pass Way plan. There was nothing more for him to do in Kansas at the moment, because John W. Geary, who had become governor after Shannon resigned, had succeeded in suppressing the guerrilla war through his impartial and uncompromising approach – without, however, having solved the underlying political problems.[127] Brown assumed that the implementation of his plan would resolve the slavery question in the United States once and for all. 'God sees it,' he had said,

---

Americans in this specific period, see also the introduction and the contributions of Evan Haefeli, Sally E. Hadden and Junius P. Rodriguez in Michael A. Bellesiles (ed.), *Lethal Imagination: Violence and Brutality in American History* (New York: New York University Press, 1999); and James W. Clarke, *The Lineaments of Wrath: Race, Violent Crime, and American Culture* (New Brunswick: Transaction Publishers, 1998), especially Chapter 2. On Native Americans' guerrilla tactics from the perspective of US troops, see Robert Marshall Utley, *Frontiersmen in Blue: The United States Army and the Indian, 1848–1865* (New York: Macmillan, 1967).

126 See Paul Finkelman, 'John Brown and His Raid', in Paul Finkelman (ed.), *His Soul Goes Marching On: Responses to John Brown and the Harpers Ferry Raid* (Charlottesville: University Press of Virginia, 1995), 5.

127 See Potter, *The Impending Crisis*, 214–15; and McPherson, *Battle Cry*, 161–2.

according to his son Jason, while having to stand by and watch as the southern volunteers burned Osawatomie to the ground after the battle for the settlement: 'There will be no more peace in this land until slavery is done for. I will give them something else to do than to extend slave territory. I will carry the war into Africa [that is, into the slave states].'[128] Brown knew of his reputation as a hardened Kansas fighter and wanted to profitably invest this valuable symbolic capital in his project as quickly as possible. He headed east carrying letters of recommendation from a leading free-state politician; collecting additional such letters on his way through Nebraska, Iowa and New York; and noting the names of people he thought would support his long-cherished and most important, indeed holy, mission.[129]

John Brown reached Boston in early January 1857 and went to the Massachusetts State Kansas Committee, which coordinated support for the free-state settlers. There he hoped to receive funds and weapons for equipping and training a small troop of abolitionists that he could deploy if the civil conflict in Kansas reignited – or perhaps elsewhere. He was greeted at the committee's office by its twenty-five-year-old secretary, Franklin Benjamin Sanborn. A native of New Hampshire, to the north of Boston, Sanborn had devoured Carlyle's Cromwell book, Byron's poems and Sir Walter Scott's historical novels as a student. An admirer of the American Transcendentalists, he had then made the acquaintance of the famous philosophers and authors Ralph Waldo Emerson, Henry David Thoreau and Amos Bronson Alcott during his studies at Harvard. Now a teacher, he instructed their children in Concord. Over the course of the previous year Sanborn had read much about John Brown in the newspapers. Now that the man stood before him, with his 'tall, slender, and commanding' figure, his military bearing, his 'severe and masculine' facial features that also showed a 'latent tenderness', and his 'piercing blue-gray' eyes, he was impressed, subsequently writing of this first encounter, 'a Puritan soldier, such as were common in Cromwell's day, though not often seen since'.[130] Sanborn was willing to make this Kansas veteran's cause his own and to support him in any way he was able.

---

128 Villard, *John Brown*, 248.

129 The testimonials are found in Franklin B. Sanborn, *Recollections of Seventy Years*, vol. 1 (Boston: Richard G. Badger, 1909), 84–91. On Brown's return east, see Oates, *To Purge This Land*, 175–7.

130 Sanborn, *The Life and Letters*, 247, 627–8. See also Sanborn, *Recollections*, vol. 1, 75–84; and Oates, *To Purge This Land*, 181–4.

And Sanborn was able to do a lot, acting from then on, at least inter-mittently, as John Brown's private secretary. He possessed enormous organizational talent, drive, tact, creativity and perseverance when it came to helping John Brown achieve his goal – and thus attain a promi-nent position in Boston society as well. Sanborn immediately activated his networks in New England and brought the notorious Kansas fighter into contact with Garrison and Amos A. Lawrence, the most important sponsor of the New England Emigrant Aid Company and eponym of the free-state town in Kansas.[131]

Above all, however, he introduced Brown to a key circle of Boston's intellectual elite, whose members had known each other for years and shared many connections, including their illustrious descent from the first Puritan settlers and heroes of the American Revolution, their educa-tion at Harvard, their partiality for Transcendentalism, their friendships, mentorships, occasional disputes among themselves and with the bludg-eoned Senator Charles Sumner. Another bond was their anti-slavery activities in the Kansas Committee and the Boston Vigilance Committee, a Boston militia formed to prevent rendition of fugitive slaves and kidnapped free African Americans. This Boston elite included Theodore Parker, a Unitarian minister, who had been banned from the pulpit because of controversy surrounding his radical views but nonetheless filled a Boston concert hall weekly; Thomas Wentworth Higginson, also a Unitarian minister, who after enactment of the Fugitive Slave Act had fought battles with the Boston police to prevent an African American from being carried off to the South; Dr Samuel Gridley Howe, who as a physician had aided the Greeks in their War of Independence against the Ottoman Empire and spent three weeks in an East Prussian prison on his way to the Polish November Uprising; and the wealthy businessman George Luther Stearns, who hid runaway slaves in his mansion and donated generously to diverse reform causes. Completing this group were Franklin Sanborn and Gerrit Smith, the affluent philanthropist who had made land available in the Adirondack mountains and actively fought the rendition of fugitive slaves to the South as well.[132]

---

131 Oates, *To Purge This Land*, 185–6.

132 See ibid., 186–92; and Jeffery S. Rossbach, *Ambivalent Conspirators: John Brown, the Secret Six, and a Theory of Slave Violence* (Philadelphia: University of Pennsylvania Press, 1982). Otto J. Scott's *The Secret Six: John Brown and the Abolitionist Movement* (New York: NY Times Books, 1979) is an erudite work, but it is not based on his own

It was these Boston businessmen and intellectuals – the Secret Committee of Six, as they would soon call themselves, or simply the Secret Six – who made it possible for John Brown to enact his Subterranean Pass Way plan. In John Brown they recognized one of their own and took him into their midst. Brown, like them, was a descendant of Puritans and revolutionaries who felt responsible for the American Revolution and republic. He, too, was a profoundly religious person who applied high moral standards to himself and others and embodied great self-control. Brown also advocated the very same values the Secret Six held and admired. He was well groomed, courteous and disciplined; preached hard work, ambition and thrift; praised 'moral fiber'; and upheld the institution of the family as well as the republic and the freedoms won in the American Revolution. Parker remarked, for instance, that Brown had achieved 'a superior culture' despite not having studied at Harvard. In contrast to Brown, who was ready to act, the prominent New Englanders (with the exception of Higginson) continued in early 1857 to shy away from the use of force.[133]

These different standpoints existed although the Secret Six had undergone the same radicalization process as John Brown during the past decades. Educated as law-abiding citizens, Howe, Stearns and Smith, in particular, had long wrestled with the question of the use of force as members of the first generation of abolitionists. Unlike Brown, they considered the New Testament's pacifism the cornerstone of Christianity and were convinced the world could only be lastingly changed through the non-violent means of moral appeals. However, political developments since the mid-1840s and their experiences in the context of their political activities had led them to doubt ever more strongly the effectiveness of such appeals and to increasingly accept and

research and has a perspective distinctly slanted to the southern states. On the individual persons, see Dean Grodzins, *American Heretic: Theodore Parker and Transcendentalism* (Chapel Hill: University of North Carolina Press, 2002), which, however, only covers the period until 1846; Tilden G. Edelstein, *Strange Enthusiasm: A Life of Thomas Wentworth Higginson* (New Haven: Yale University Press, 1968); the in many ways outdated biography by Harold Schwartz, *Samuel Gridley Howe: Social Reformer, 1801–1876* (Cambridge, MA: Harvard University Press, 1956); Charles E. Heller, *Portrait of an Abolitionist: A Biography of George Luther Stearns, 1809–1867* (Westport: Greenwood Press, 1996); and Harlow, *Gerrit Smith*; on their collaboration on the Boston Vigilance Committee, see Stanley W. Campbell, *The Slave Catchers*, Chapter 6.

133 See Rossbach, *Ambivalent Conspirators*, 89.

GEORGE L. STEARNS

GERRIT SMITH

FRANK B. SANBORN

T. W. HIGGINSON

THEODORE PARKER

SAMUEL G. HOWE

JOHN BROWN'S NORTHERN SUPPORTERS

Figure 14. The 'Secret Committee of Six', Brown's primary financial sponsors. West Virginia State Archives, Boyd B. Stutler Collection.

practise the use of force for self-defence. They, too, perceived the decisive stages in this process to be the Mexican–American War, which had been called for by the South and provoked by the United States; the mob attacks, which also targeted them personally; the *Amistad* case; their experiences with the Underground Railroad; their involvement in freeing African Americans following the entry into force of the Fugitive Slave Act; their support (with weapons as well) for the free-staters in Kansas; and the attack on their friend Charles Sumner.

The Secret Six had also progressively lost trust in the Union's institutions as well as in hope for a political solution. For too long they had experienced how the South's power in Congress was perpetuated under the Three-Fifths Clause based on, of all things, the increasing number of slaves and how the government in Washington as a result persistently sided with the slaveholder party, while the founding of abolitionist parties (the Liberty Party and Radical Abolitionist Party) never got beyond modest beginnings. Higginson, together with Garrison, thus turned into 'disunionists': they began calling on anti-slavery forces to boycott congressional elections and campaigned for the dissolution of the United States under the slogan 'No union with slaveholders'. Garrison even went so far as to burn the US Constitution, to great publicity effect, because of its one-sided support of slaveholder interests. The Pierce administration's partisan policies in Kansas additionally strengthened the Secret Six in their conviction that the law stood on 'the wrong side', making it seem ever more plausible that the 'slavocracy' could only be overcome with force.[134]

The Supreme Court decision in the *Dred Scott v. Sanford* case in 1857 brought this radicalization to its logical outcome by casting doubt on the highest court as well in the eyes of the abolitionists. For the Supreme Court, with its majority of judges from the South, some of whom owned slaves, sought to use the case – against the opinion of two judges from the North – to definitely settle the slavery question in the interest of the slaveholders. To this end the court undertook to rule on the contradiction between the American Constitution and the Declaration of

---

134 On the radicalization of the Secret Six and other abolitionists, see Aptheker, *Abolitionism*, 126–8; Friedman, *Gregarious Saints*, Chapter 7; Rossbach, *Ambivalent Conspirators*; and the biographies mentioned above. On Higginson's and Garrison's efforts to disband the Union, see Edelstein, *Strange Enthusiasm*, 197–203; and Mayer, *All on Fire*, especially 313–16, 452–3, quotation at 328.

Independence in favour of the Constitution. Referring to the Declaration of Independence, the Supreme Court stated 'that the enslaved African race were not intended' to be afforded its protections, for if that had been the case 'the conduct of the distinguished men who framed the Declaration of Independence would have been utterly and flagrantly inconsistent with the principles they asserted.'[135] America's highest-ranking justices maintained that if the Declaration of Independence had applied to coloured people, the document's authors would have acted accordingly; any other course of action would be inconsistent. The fact that the founding fathers had not emancipated the slaves could only be interpreted to mean that the right to 'life, liberty, and the pursuit of happiness' did not apply to them, which is why they were now being excluded once and for all from such rights. The court furthermore determined that African Americans were 'beings of an inferior order . . . altogether unfit to associate with the white race either in social or political relations' and thus 'had no rights which the white man was bound to respect'.[136] The Supreme Court thus adopted the view that African Americans could not become citizens of the United States. The court ultimately also concluded that prohibiting slavery in the new western territories was unconstitutional.[137]

This court decision outraged abolitionists in general and the Secret Six too, for they understood all too well that its intention was to formalize slavery as an institution and spread it across the entire United States. The court action thwarted all of their efforts to have Kansas become a free state and made it obvious once and for all that the political paths to abolishing slavery in the United States were blocked because all federal institutions were committed to its perpetuation. This is highly

---

135 C. J. Taney, Opinion of the Court, US Supreme Court, *Scott v. Sandford*, 60 US How. 393 (1856), Nolo Law for All, supreme.nolo.com.

136 Ibid.

137 See Finzsch, Horton and Horton, *Von Benin nach Baltimore*, 282–3; Sewell, *A House Divided*, 56–61; in particular Don Edward Fehrenbacher, *The Dred Scott Case: Its Significance in American Law and Politics* (New York: Oxford University Press, 1978); Earl M. Maltz, *Dred Scott and the Politics of Slavery* (Lawrence: University of Kansas Press, 2007); and David Thomas Konig, Paul Finkelman and Christopher Alan Bracey (eds.), *The Dred Scott Case: Historical and Contemporary Perspectives on Race and Law* (Athens: Ohio University Press, 2010). On the historical consequences, see especially Finkelman, 'Scott v. Sandford: The Court's Most Dreadful Case and How It Changed History', *Chicago-Kent Law Review* 82/3 (2007), 3–48.

significant in view of the later turn to terrorism, because the painful loss of all faith in the initially so highly esteemed political institutions actually made the use of force as a form of extra-institutional 'self-help' seem attractive and plausible. Added to this was the fact that the Secret Six had not only lost hope of abolishing slavery using political institutions in the late 1850s, but also begun to develop theories in discussions with John Brown and among themselves about why the use of force was desirable, even necessary. These considerations rested on their interpretation of the American Revolution.

John Brown had long felt that moral appeals and political action would not lead to the abolition of slavery. He had told Frederick Douglass this during their conversation about the Subterranean Pass Way plan in 1847 and stated his opinion that 'the practice of carrying arms would be a good one for colored people to adopt, as it would give them a sense of manhood. No people . . . could have self-respect or be respected who would not fight for their freedom.'[138] Only in this way could African Americans empower themselves to a life in freedom while also overcoming the racist contempt they experienced everywhere. Brown thus attributed cathartic affects to the use of force.

Brown's conviction was founded on his analysis of the *Amistad* rebellion as well as on his examination of the opinions of radical African American abolitionists. Henry Highland Garnet, a slave who had fled to the North, spoke in 1843 at the National Convention of Colored People and Their Friends, calling in his Address to the Slaves for the slaves of the United States to rebel: 'LIBERTY OR DEATH. Oh what a sentence was that!' he had exclaimed in a direct reference to Patrick Henry's famous proclamation 'Give me liberty or give me death.'[139]

However much you [the slaves in the United States] and all of us may desire it, there is not much hope of redemption without the shedding of blood. If you must bleed, let it all come at once – rather *die freemen, than live to be slaves* . . . No oppressed people have ever secured their liberty without resistance.[140]

---

138 Douglass, 'Life and Times', 717.
139 Patrick Henry, 'Give Me Liberty or Give Me Death. March 23, 1775', Yale Law School, the Avalon Project, avalon.law.yale.edu.
140 Henry Highland Garnet, *A Memorial Discourse Delivered in the Hall of the House of Representatives, Washington, D.C. on Sabbath, February 12, 1865* (Philadelphia:

242 The Invention of Terrorism

Slavery, according to Garnet, was an undignified condition, which was why men who accepted this station were afforded no respect. No people had ever gained its liberty without resistance; freedom had to be won. A real man risked everything to achieve that goal, even his life. Brown was impressed by Garnet's speech and agreed with him. He contacted Garnet and other radical African American abolitionists and decided to republish Garnet's speech together with David Walker's *Appeal* at his own expense.[141]

The respect was mutual. As of this time Garnet and the other radical African American abolitionists supported John Brown and his plans to free the slaves, even if they gauged the chances of success more cautiously and realistically. Common among them, however, was the conviction that there were many courageous men among the slaves ready to fight. John Brown wanted to provide these men the opportunity to prove themselves in the struggle for liberation. He viewed his activity as helping the slaves to help themselves.[142]

The Secret Six shared Brown's belief in the productive, cathartic effect of violence. For they, too, were permeated with the fundamental American political experience, whose key premise was that their personal freedom and the free society in the northern United States were based on their grandparents' willingness to fight for this freedom. 'Justified political violence and the willingness to fight for freedom were keystone virtues among righteous Anglo-American men,' according to Jeffrey Rossbach.[143] From this experience, the Secret Six now concluded,

J. M. Wilson, 1865), 46, 49, 51. For Garnet's biographical details see Finzsch, Horton and Horton, *Von Benin nach Baltimore*, 256–7; and Martin B. Pasternak, *Rise Now and Fly to Arms: The Life of Henry Highland Garnet* (New York: Garland, 1995). On his speech and its reception, see ibid., Chapter 6.

141 On this intention, see Pasternak, *Rise Now*, 52. The reprint is probably of the following edition: David Walker and Henry Highland Garnet, *Walker's Appeal, with a Brief Sketch of His Life: And Also Garnet's Address to His Slaves of the United States of America* (New York: J. H. Tobitt, 1848). On this see also, Finzsch, Horton and Horton, *Von Benin nach Baltimore*, 261. On Brown's establishing contact with Garnet, see Boyer, *The Legend of John Brown*, 366.

142 See J. Sella Martin's account of a conversation between Garnet and Brown in 'Speech of Rev. J. Martin', *Liberator*, 9 December 1859, 194; reprinted in Quarles, *Blacks on John Brown*, 25–31, 29–30; and Pasternak, *Rise Now and Fly to Arms*, 94. On the interpretation of the undertaking as help to self-help, see Rossbach, *Ambivalent Conspirators*, 155.

143 Rossbach, *Ambivalent Conspirators*, 194, 268, quotation at 194.

conversely, that a struggle for freedom was the prerequisite for the appropriation of those values and attitudes necessary to succeed in the North's competitive society.

In contrast, however, to John Brown, the thinking of the Secret Six was marked by romantic racism,[144] a version that preferably consigned the aggression needed for such a freedom struggle to the Anglo-Saxons. 'We are the most aggressive, invasive, and exclusive people on the earth. The history of the Anglo-Saxon, for the last three hundred years, has been one of continual aggression, invasion, and extermination,' declared Theodore Parker in a speech to slavery opponents. In contrast, the African, according to him, was 'the most docile and pliant of all races of men; none has so little ferocity: vengeance, instantial with the Caucasian, is exceptional in his history'. Parker was convinced, 'No race is so strong in the affectional instinct . . . none so easy, indolent, confiding, so little warlike'.[145] Unlike the supporters of slavery, who also attributed these characteristics to Africans, Parker did not conclude, however, that the African race was predestined to slavery, but instead interpreted these supposed characteristics as evidence of a higher form of Christianity.[146] Parker's friend and colleague Higginson attributed the same qualities to Africans, but deemed them environmental and the result of slavery rather than innate. 'We see among us the African as he is crushed by social institutions, overwhelmed by ignorance, kept back and down by poverty . . . we do not see what has been, or may be again.'[147] Both men, however, agreed that the slaves' temperament had to undergo a transformation if they were to succeed in the free society of the North.

They hoped that this transformation would result from an act of violence. 'By the act of insurrection, slaves would exchange docility and group consciousness for a more assertive and individualistic outlook,' is how Rossbach has summarized the ideas of the Secret Six. 'Violent acts

144 See Fredrickson, *The Black Image in the White Mind*, Chapter 4.

145 See Theodore Parker, 'Some Thoughts on the Progress of America, and the Influence of Her Diverse Institutions. An Address Prepared for the Anti-Slavery Convention in Boston, May 31, 1854', in *The Collected Works of Theodore Parker*, vol. 6: *Discourses on Slavery*, ed. Frances Power Cobbe (London: Trübner, 1864), 4; and Parker, 'The Present Aspect of Slavery', 289.

146 See Fredrickson, *The Black Image in the White Mind*, especially 45–64, 119–21.

147 Mr. Yerrinton, 'New York Anti-Slavery Society. Speech of Rev. T. W. Higginson', *Liberator*, 28 May 1858, 86, col. D. See on this speech Fredrickson, *The Black Image in the White Mind*, 119.

were first steps to responsible participation in a democratic wage-labor society, first steps to assimilation of Anglo-Saxon culture, and first steps to a respected place in northern social life.'[148] John Brown, 'a real American who embodied the ideals of Bunker Hill', was in their eyes the appropriate person to initiate, supervise and channel this transformation.[149] For this reason, the Secret Six supported John Brown.

From guerrilla war to terrorist tactics

In the two years following his return from Kansas in January 1857, John Brown, supported by the Secret Six, went about organizing his 'Kansas militia'; in other words, his force for a guerrilla war in the South. Sought by US marshals, he used diverse aliases such as Nelson Hawkins or Shubel Morgan while travelling through the north-eastern United States to collect money and arms. He solicited funds for the struggle in Kansas, which was to be a step along the path to freeing the slaves, at meetings of various Kansas committees, at numerous widely reported talks about his fighting in the West (doing his best to omit the Pottawatomie murders), at the Massachusetts Legislature, and in appeals published in newspapers and made personally to selected prominent individuals. He contacted people he hoped would support his cause, approaching, in particular, African Americans, such as Frederick Douglass and Henry Highland Garnet, who as escaped slaves and through their activities with the Underground Railroad had experience in the South and were also convinced that slavery in the United States could only be ended with force. Brown recruited volunteers and organized their military training at a Quaker settlement, of all places. He had special weapons made – long pikes that inexperienced fighters could use more easily than rifles in combat – and stashed donated arms with friends. He studied demographic data and maps, marking the towns and regions where the slaves made up a particularly high proportion of the population, and established a route for the liberation campaign with information garnered from former slaves

---

148 Rossbach, *Ambivalent Conspirators*, 269.
149 Ibid., 157.

who had fled from those areas.[150] To accomplish and coordinate all this, he travelled tirelessly and enlisted Sanborn, the Secret Six, and his own family – insofar as they allowed it.

Brown's preparations, though, included more than just practical and tactical arrangements. He drew up founding documents defining public life to pre-empt accusations that the society emerging in the course of his slave liberation would be a 'lawless and unorganized' horde, unable to govern itself. To draft these texts, he moved into Frederick Douglass's home as a paying guest from late January to mid-February 1858.[151]

There he composed the Provisional Constitution and Ordinances for the People of the United States, which explicitly rejected the Supreme Court's *Dred Scott* decision and declared slavery in the United States to be irreconcilable with the Declaration of Independence and a 'most barbarous, unprovoked, and unjustifiable war of one portion of its citizens upon another portion'. The citizens of the United States and all people who according to the Supreme Court had no rights temporarily granted themselves this constitution, 'the better to protect [their] persons, property, lives, and liberties, and to govern [their] actions'.[152] The document also had a moral character. In it John Brown stipulated

150 The best evidence of these activities is Brown's notebook, in which he recorded donations, expenses and keywords regarding correspondence. Memoranum book, vol. 2; BPL, n.p., archive.org. See also Oates, *To Purge This Land*, Chapters 14–16; Carton, *Patriotic Treason*, Chapter 10; and McGlone, *John Brown's War*, Chapter 9.2. On the training in Springdale, see Irving Berdine Richman, *John Brown among the Quakers, and Other Sketches* (Des Moines: The Historical Department of Iowa, 1894). On support by African Americans, see Quarles, *Allies for Freedom*, Chapters 3–4; McFeely, *Frederick Douglass*, 190–5; and Pasternak, *Rise Now and Fly to Arms*, 94.

151 Martin R. Delany in Frank A. Rollin, *Life and Public Services of Martin R. Delany, Sub-assistant Commissioner, Bureau Relief of Refugees, Freedmen, and of Abandoned Lands, and Late Major 104th U.S. Colored Troops* (Boston: Lee and Shepard, 1868), 89. See also Douglass, 'Life and Times', 755; McFeely, *Frederick Douglass*, 191; and Oates, *To Purge This Land*, 224–7.

152 Pamphlet, John Brown's 'Provisional Constitution and Ordinances for the People of the United States' from records relating to John Brown's raid at Harpers Ferry, Virginia (now West Virginia) in October 1859, 1859–1859, 15; Letters Received by the Office of the Adjutant General (Main Series), 1822–1860 (hereafter Letters Received); Returns of Military Organizations, compiled ca. 1800–12/1916 (National Archives Microfilm Publication M567, Roll 618, frames 411–20); Records of the Adjutant General's Office, 1762–1984, RG 94; NAB, catalog.archives.gov, NARA, Online Public Access, John Brown's 'Provisional Constitution', partially reprinted in Ruchames, *John Brown*, 119–21.

his social values and, in anticipation of the second American revolution, devised his ideal United States as a counterproject to the actually existing society.[153] Moreover, he penned a 'Declaration of Liberty by the Representatives of the Slave Population of the United States of America', which was oriented to the original Declaration of Independence and set forth the political principles that were to govern the society in the Appalachians.[154]

In addition, John Brown, with the help of African American physician and writer Martin R. Delany (an early proponent of black nationalism), convened a constitutional convention attended by some fifty people in Chatham, Canada, where many former slaves who had fled from the United States lived. The participants discussed Brown's project and his proposed constitution for a reformed American republic that was finally to live up to its founding principles, ratified the document, elected a government (postponing the election of a president), and appointed Brown commander-in-chief of the armed forces.[155] This marked the conclusion of preparations for implementing the Subterranean Pass Way plan. This was a plan for a guerrilla war.

The liberation action should have begun at this point, but further postponement became necessary. A conflict broke out between Brown and his drillmaster, Hugh Forbes, an Englishman and follower of Giuseppe Mazzini who had fought in defence of the Venetian Republic in 1848 and later under Garibaldi.[156] Brown had hired him to train his volunteers in warfare and tactics, but the two clashed when Forbes

153 See also Carton, *Patriotic Treason*, 263. Perplexed or condescending statements about the overtly moral tone of Brown's constitution have appeared since 1859. This characteristic of the document, however, seems only logical if it is considered within the context of the anti-slavery movement understood as a community of values.

154 'A Declaration of Liberty by the Representatives of the Slave Population of the United States of America', in Hinton, *John Brown and His Men*, 637–43. See McGlone, *John Brown's War*, 213–16.

155 See the minutes 'Journal of the Provisional Constitutional Convention, held on Saturday, May 8, 1858', in United States Congress, *Report*, 45–7; and the reports by Delany in Rollin, *Life and Public Services*, 85–93; and by Osborne P. Anderson, *A Voice from Harper's Ferry* (1861) (Atlanta: World View, 1980), 37–9. See also Oates, *To Purge This Land*, 242–7; and McGlone, *John Brown's War*, 213–16.

156 See Ginsborg, *Daniele Manin*, 214, 216. On Forbes and his activities for radical democratic and abolitionist objectives in the United States, see Marraro, *American Opinion*, 207; and Lause, *A Secret Society History*, 84–5, 147–8.

questioned his plans and leadership abilities and also probably tried to squeeze money out of Brown and the Secret Six. Failing at the latter, Forbes then began to inform various high-ranking members of the abolitionist movement and politicians in Washington by letter or in discussions about Brown's plans and his supporters.[157]

Upon hearing about Forbes's betrayal, most of the Secret Six got cold feet and decided that Brown should return to Kansas in summer 1858 as a diversionary tactic. The proto-civil war had broken out again there and they hoped that Brown's presence in the area would discredit Forbes's information about plans for a rebellion in the East. Brown thus once again headed west with his group of volunteers. That December in Missouri, they freed eleven slaves who had asked them for help because they feared their families were to be torn apart by sale. Despite being pursued by a superior force trying to recapture the stolen slaves, Brown and his men safely transported the fugitives more than a thousand miles in a horse-drawn wagon in the middle of winter across Iowa and Illinois to Chicago, and then from there by train to Detroit. There, the freed slaves were able to board a ship for Windsor, Canada. This diversionary manoeuvre was spectacular and had the desired effect, with the newspapers reporting on it in detail for two months.[158] This undertaking allowed Brown to consolidate his reputation as an unyielding freedom fighter, increase his celebrity, and gain further experience in dealing with the media.

The decisive moment finally came just a few months later, in summer 1859. Twenty-one volunteers between the ages of twenty and forty-eight – five African Americans and sixteen Euro-Americans, including three

157 See, for instance, Oates, *To Purge This Land*, 248–50; and Lause, *A Secret Society History*, 87–8.

158 On Forbes's betrayal, the freeing of the slaves and the media echo, see John Brown, 'Old Brown's Parallels, Trading Post, January 1859', in John Brown Collection, 299, Box 2, Folder 1, KSHS, initially published in the *New York Daily Tribune*, 11 February 1859, republished in 'From the New York Tribune. Old Brown's Parallels', *Anti-slavery Bugle* (New-Lisbon, OH), 12 February 1859, 1; and in Villard, *John Brown*, 375–6; and see, for instance, 'Kansas. Old Brown . . . From Our Special Correspondence, Lawrence, K.T., Feb. 3, 1859', 'Later', 'Catching Old Brown – How to Do It – Montgomery. From Our Special Correspondence, Lawrence, K.T., Feb. 4, 1859', *New York Daily Tribune*, 12 February 1859, 6; and in this regard Villard, *John Brown*, 285–396; Sanborn, *The Life and Letters*, 425–64; Thomas Wentworth Higginson, *Cheerful Yesterdays* (Cambridge, MA: Houghton, 1898), 221; Oates, *To Purge This Land*, 200–1, 247–68; and McGlone, *John Brown's War*, 210–12.

of Brown's sons – arrived one after the other over a period of several weeks at the Kennedy farm in Maryland, a property Brown had rented in July under the alias Isaac Smith.[159] While making final preparations and waiting to begin their operation, John Brown and his force of radical abolitionists lived out their common ideal and the utopia of a community free of racism and discrimination enshrined in Brown's Provisional Constitution for several weeks on this farm in the slave state of Maryland. 'There was no milk and water sentimentality – no offensive contempt for the negro, while working in his cause,' was how the African American printer Osborne P. Anderson, an immigrant to Canada, would subsequently describe the group's life together. He also expressed his gratitude to God for having been allowed to experience to the 'furthest, fullest extent, the moral, mental, physical, social harmony of an Anti-Slavery family, carrying out to the letter the principles of its antetype, the Anti-Slavery cause. In John Brown's house, and in John Brown's presence', thus voicing his reverence for his captain in what is perhaps one of the most beautiful tributes Brown has ever received: 'men from widely different parts of the continent met and united into one company, wherein no hateful prejudice dared intrude its ugly self – no ghost of a distinction found space to enter.'[160] With racist prejudice and discrimination still present around the world, the extraordinary and precious nature of this experience – whether idealized or not – survives to this day.

The Kennedy farm lay just five miles north of Harpers Ferry, Virginia (now West Virginia), the site Brown had chosen as the starting point for his action to end slavery in the United States. Here and in the following, the currently employed spelling, 'Harpers Ferry', is used, although the spelling common at the time, 'Harper's Ferry', is taken over in quotations. The choice of this location had to do with tactical decisions John Brown had made while further developing his original Subterranean

---

159 There are biographical studies on some of the volunteers. See, for instance, Steven Lubet, *John Brown's Spy: The Adventurous Life and Tragic Confession of John E. Cook* (New Haven: Yale University Press, 2012); and Steven Lubet, *The 'Colored Hero' of Harpers Ferry: John Anthony Copeland and the War against Slavery* (New York: Cambridge University Press, 2012).

160 On the Kennedy farm and the preparations in the final months preceding the raid, see Anderson, *A Voice from Harper's Ferry*, Chapters 4–9, quotation at 58; and Oates, *To Purge This Land*, Chapter 18.

Pass Way plan. Harpers Ferry lies in the midst of the Blue Ridge Mountains on a spit of land at the confluence of the Shenandoah and Potomac rivers. In the mid-nineteenth century, the town was home to arms factories and a US arsenal and had almost 5,000 inhabitants. Although set in rural surroundings, Harpers Ferry was (and is) well connected via the Baltimore & Ohio and Winchester & Potomac Railroads with New York, Baltimore, Washington, the commercial centres to the north-west (such as Cincinnati and St Louis), and western Virginia.[161]

John Brown's decision to launch the armed liberation of the slaves in Harpers Ferry represented a crucial alteration of the Subterranean Pass Way plan,[162] a change that becomes most apparent in Douglass's account of a conversation: 'The taking of Harper's Ferry, of which Captain Brown had merely hinted before, was now declared as his settled purpose,' Douglass recalled about a discussion with Brown just a few weeks before the action. 'To me, such a measure would be fatal to running off slaves (as was the original plan), and fatal to all engaged in doing so.' For in Douglass's view, 'It would be an attack upon the federal government, and would array the whole country against us.' But Brown, according to Douglass,

> did not at all object to rousing the nation; it seemed to him that some-thing startling was just what the nation needed. He had completely renounced his old plan, and thought that the capture of Harper's Ferry would serve as notice to the slaves that their friends had come, and as a trumpet to rally them to his standard.

As Douglass recounted, neither was able to convince the other:

> We spent the most of Saturday and a part of Sunday in this debate – Brown for Harper's Ferry, and I against it; he for striking a blow which

---

161 See James Biser Whisker, *The United States Armory at Harper's Ferry, 1799–1860* (Lewiston: Edwin Mellen Press, 1997); Craig H. Miner, *A Most Magnificent Machine: America Adopts the Railroad, 1825–1862* (Lawrence: University Press of Kansas, 2010), Chapter 1; and John F. Stover, *History of the Baltimore & Ohio Railroad* (West Lafayette: Purdue University Press, 1987), Chapters 1–6.

162 This is also stated by Sanborn, *The Life and Letters*, 418; McGlone, *John Brown's War*, Chapter 10; and Horwitz, *Midnight Rising*, 70–1, 235.

should instantly rouse the country, and I for the policy of gradually and unaccountably drawing off the slaves to the mountains, as at first suggested and proposed by him.[163]

According to Douglass, Brown now planned to seize the unprotected US government arsenal and arms factories in a surprise raid with his volunteers. Once he had captured Harpers Ferry, its geographical location would make it impossible to dislodge him. He and his men would distribute the pikes and rifles they had brought along and weapons from the arsenal to the slaves and sympathizers and then withdraw into the mountains. There, they would begin their guerrilla-style liberation operation, pushing ever deeper into the South.[164]

Based on his knowledge of the original Subterranean Pass Way plan, Douglass had agreed to come with Brown and support him in freeing the slaves and setting up the community in the mountains, but withdrew his promise after Brown told him about the new plan, considering it to be an entirely different undertaking.[165] Douglass had recognized the changed character of the operation and correctly assessed its poor chances of military success.

Brown's new plan entailed deciding *against* an operation that was militarily feasible, but with little publicity impact, and *for* an action that was militarily risky, but immediately spectacular. This decision to shift the focus from the undertaking's chances of military success to its potential for publicity represents the transition from guerrilla warfare to terrorism. This change of the Subterranean Pass Way plan primarily involved two specific elements: launching the action with a raid on the goverment facilities at Harpers Ferry and taking the public impact of such a raid into account. The objective of producing a psychological effect through the use of violence was not entirely new to Brown. He had observed that violence could have a strong psychological effect during

---

163 Douglass, 'Life and Times', 759–60; McFeely, *Frederick Douglass*, 195–7; and William S. King, *To Raise Up a Nation: John Brown, Frederick Douglass and the Making of a Free Country* (Yardley: Westholme, 2013), Chapter 6.

164 Robert McGlone, who has critically examined the most important available sources, came to the conclusion that 'the gist of his reminiscence was doubtless true', even if Douglass had retold the story numerous times on his lecture tours, and it had become slightly altered as a result. McGlone, *John Brown's War*, 231.

165 Douglass, 'Life and Times', 760.

the *Amistad* case and experienced the same in Kansas with the murders on Pottawatomie Creek. In addition, his original Subterranean Pass Way plan had pursued the psycho-economic goal of making the commercial value of slaveownership – and thus of slavery itself – uncertain. In his new plan, however, the psychological impact advanced from being a side effect of the use of violence to being its primary goal, in the sense both of *first* and of *most important*.

How did this revised plan come about? When and why did Brown change the Subterranean Pass Way plan he had been contemplating for twenty years? These questions are, again, not easy to answer, because Brown, like Orsini, was a cautious conspirator. During preparations for his operation, he never wrote down his plans. Brief consultations with supporters and volunteers or his family, often in code words, can be found in letters he used to organize and coordinate the project. He liked to use formulae and metaphors, such as 'to deliver the slave', 'his greater work', 'to go to war', 'to carry the war into Africa' (that is, into the South) or 'to disturb Israel', a common analogy to the Israelites as slaves in Egypt.[166] Furthermore, Brown only discussed his plan with selected people, and these insiders generally remained discreet and did not commit what they knew to paper. Also, following the raid on Harpers Ferry, many who had had contact with Brown before the raid destroyed anything that could associate them with John Brown. The few who had records or created them and risked keeping or even publishing them remained deliberately vague regarding key points in order to protect themselves and others from prosecution. Added to this was the fact that Brown seldom fully revealed his plans to those he shared them with.[167] On the contrary, he generally seems to have communicated concrete information in carefully measured doses; some did not want to know all that much.[168] Robert McGlone therefore comes to the conclusion that 'Brown's strategy is still disputed because evidence of his intentions is

166 See, for instance, ibid., 743; and Villard, *John Brown*, 248.

167 See, for example, the directions in Brown's letter to John Brown Jr, 4 and 5 February 1858, from Rochester, NY, Record ID 70, MS02-0018 AB, BBStColl., WVStA, wvculture.org, JB/BBStColl. Db; and Sanborn, *The Life and Letters*, Chapter 12, especially 418, 424, 466; Higginson, *Cheerful Yesterdays*, 223; Rollin, *Life and Public Services*, 87, 90; and, in this regard, for example, Villard, *John Brown*, 56.

168 'I do not wish to know Captain Brown's plans; I hope he will keep them to himself', wrote, for example, Gerrit Smith, 26 July 1858, from Peterboro to F. B. Sanborn, reprinted in Sanborn, *The Life and Letters*, 466.

variously unclear, incomplete, or unreliable.'[169] Nevertheless, careful analysis of the available material can reveal crucial information about the development of Brown's strategy and tactics that has not yet been seen as such in the literature and therefore requires detailed argumentation.

John Brown turned to the concrete planning of his Subterranean Pass Way plan in summer 1857.[170] It was during that time that Harpers Ferry as a town with a federal arsenal and armoury first caught his attention. This knowledge stems from the only contemporary report about Brown's plans, which is contained in a letter from the disloyal drillmaster Hugh Forbes to Samuel Gridley Howe, one of the Secret Six.[171] Forbes and Brown had lived together from August to November 1857 and discussed military planning issues. As an expert from the Italian revolutionary wars, Forbes was, after all, supposed to train Brown's volunteers, refine the strategy and tactics, and help execute the operation,[172] so it can be assumed that Brown disclosed his plans to him.

---

169 McGlone, *John Brown's War*, 221.

170 See Villard, *John Brown*, 297.

171 Villard (ibid., 54–6), writes that John Brown had named Harpers Ferry as the target as early as 1854. This assertion, however, is based on interviews and letters from the years 1894 to 1908 – more than fifty years after the events – stemming from Brown's children, who were about ten years old during the period in question. It is likely, therefore, that those memories were influenced by subsequent knowledge. This, however, does not mean that those memories contradict my statement above, if one assumes that the name Harpers Ferry was mentioned along with other locations before 1857. The town was, after all, located within the area Brown had focused on from the beginning. However, in the absence of any contemporary evidence, it is not plausible to assume that prior to 1857 Brown was already pursuing the plan regarding Harpers Ferry that he subsequently enacted, as Villard suggests in places. Horwitz, on the other hand, notes in agreement with my reconstruction that Brown first mentioned Harpers Ferry in the period referred to in the text above (that is, summer 1857). But he surmises that the plan had already undergone the decisive revision by that time. He suggests Brown was inspired by the actions of the Filibusters from the southern United States (Horwitz, *Midnight Rising*, 70–1). This point, however, fails to convince, because (1) the tactical elements of the plans passed on by Forbes did not diverge qualitatively in their tactical elements from the original Subterranean Pass Way plan and (2) the *coups d'état* by the Filibusters in South and Central America differed too much from Brown's plans.

172 On Brown and Forbes's collaboration in Tabor, see Richman, 'John Brown among the Quakers', 15–20; Villard, *John Brown*, 285–7; and Oates, *To Purge This Land*, 210–18.

In his letter to Howe, Forbes passed on Brown's ideas, presenting them as inadequate in order to recommend himself instead of Brown. Forbes communicated to Howe that John Brown wanted to attack slave quarters in Virginia with a force of some twenty to twenty-five well-armed men and ample surplus weapons, free the slaves, and then 'make a dash at Harper's Ferry manufactory, destroying what he could not carry off', before withdrawing together with the freed slaves into the Alleghenies.[173] He also reported that Brown had argued that 'were he pressed by the United States troops, which after a few days might concentrate, he could easily maintain himself in the Alleghenies.' According to Forbes, Brown also assumed 'that his New England partisans would in the meantime call a Northern Convention to restore tranquility and overthrow the pro-slavery administration'.[174] In Forbes's account, Brown included Harpers Ferry in his deliberations as early as late summer and autumn 1857. At that time, however, the raid on the arsenal still had a primarily instrumental character, with Brown's aim being to procure weapons for the freed slaves and prevent the enemy from arming itself from the arsenal. The fact that Brown produced a list of the arsenals and forts from Pennsylvania to Florida and Texas in summer 1857 also speaks to the importance of this instrumental character.[175] He hoped to seize weapons from these arsenals along the march route of his guerrilla army through the South to arm newly joining slaves.

---

173 Hugh Forbes to Samuel Gridley Howe from Washington [DC], 14 May 1858, reprinted in 'The Harper's Ferry Outbreak . . . Important Revelations of Col. Forbes', *New York Herald*, 27 October 1859, 4; and 'The Virginia Rebellion. The Forbes Revelations', *New York Times*, 28 October 1859. See in this regard Schwartz, *Samuel Gridley Howe*, 227–32; and for a critical assessment of these sources, McGlone, *John Brown's War*, 235–7.

174 Hugh Forbes to Samuel Gridley Howe from Washington [DC], 14 May 1858, reprinted in 'The Harper's Ferry Outbreak . . . Important Revelations of Col. Forbes', *New York Herald*, 27 October 1859, 4; and 'The Virginia Rebellion. The Forbes Revelations', *New York Times*, 28 October 1859.

175 Fayetteville, NC (Fayetteville Arsenal); Pittsburgh, PA (Fort Pitt); Bridesburg, PA, near Philadelphia, where an arsenal was located; Pikesville, MD (Garrison Fort); Augusta, GA (Fort Gordon); St Louis, MO (St Louis Arsenal); Baton Rouge, LA (Baton Rouge Arsenal); Mount Vernon, AL (Mount Vernon Arsenal); Charleston, SC (Fort Sumter and Fort Moultrie); Washington [DC] (Fort Washington); Little Rock, AR (Little Rock Arsenal); San Antonio, TX (Alamo); Chattahoochee, FL (Apalachicola Arsenal) and St Augustine, FL (Castillo De San Marcos). Harpers Ferry is missing. See Memoranum book, vol. 2; BPL, n.p., archive.org. On dating to summer 1857, see Oates, *To Purge This Land*, 214, note 10.

Forbes's letter indicates as well that Brown in summer and autumn 1857 was already expecting substantial public political reaction as soon as US troops moved against him and his slave army. Forbes wrote in his letter that Brown was counting on 'his New England partisans', in other words the Secret Six, to use and channel these reactions by convening a constitutional assembly in the North that would declare the secession of slave-free states from the Union and overthrow the pro-slavery government in Washington. Forbes expressed himself somewhat derisively, especially about Brown's trust in the Secret Six and their ability to separate the free states from the Union. He wrote to Howe, for instance, that he did not think the other conspirators capable of such revolutionary acts. Yet a letter from Sanborn to Higginson suggests that at least those two members of the Secret Six actually did see Brown's guerrilla war as the beginning of a process of secession from the Union by the northern states. So Brown and the Secret Six were indeed thinking early on in larger political dimensions.[176]

Reports from people informed by Brown about his plans in the following months essentially confirm Forbes's information. They all say that Brown's objective was a guerrilla war to free the slaves that was to begin in Virginia and involve a raid on the Harpers Ferry arsenal to obtain weapons, followed by a subsequent withdrawal into the Alleghenies and gradual advance into the South. Force was to be used less offensively, for fighting the slaveowners, than defensively, for self-defence and the defence of slaves who wanted to flee into the mountains.[177] John Brown also discussed his plans with Frederick Douglass, while composing his constitution at the man's home from late January to mid-February 1858, 'first thing in the morning and the last thing at

---

176 See Villard, *John Brown*, 303.

177 See Realf in United States Congress, *Report*, 90–113; John Edwin Cook, 'Statement of his Connection with Captain John Brown', in Richard J. Hinton (ed.), *John Brown and His Men* (New York: Funk & Wagnalls, 1894); L. F. Parsons, 'Statement, Salina, Kan., October 7, 1908, to the Author', quoted in Villard, *John Brown*, Chapter 9; and Ross, *Recollections*, 22. Alexander Milton Ross used the term 'guerrilla war' when quoting Brown's words. These accounts should be taken with caution because they date from long after the events or emerged in the course of government inquiries. It is nonetheless significant that they do not diverge in their content from Forbes's descriptions. For a critical assessment of these texts as sources, see McGlone, *John Brown's War*, 233–5. See generally also Villard, *John Brown*, 313–14; and Oates, *To Purge This Land*, 221–3.

night, till I confess it began to be something of a bore to me', as Douglass recounted.

> Once in a while, he [John Brown] would say he could, with a few resolute men, capture Harper's Ferry, and supply himself with arms belonging to the Government at that place, but he never announced his intention to do so. It was, however, very evidently passing in his mind as a thing he might do.[178]

According to Douglass, Brown was pondering the idea of a raid on Harpers Ferry in early 1858 but had not yet decided on it. A letter Brown wrote to John Brown Jr on 4 February confirms the veracity of this impression.[179] These plans, however, also still agreed with the version of the Subterranean Pass Way plan Frederick Douglass had known for some ten years. This follows from Douglass's description and is confirmed by his later surprise at the change in tactics. It can therefore be concluded from all available sources that John Brown continued to consider a plan like the one described by Forbes until early February 1858.

The only deviation from Forbes's descriptions that exists for this period in other sources casts no doubt on this conclusion. The discrepancy is found in the Provisional Constitution, which Brown wrote while staying with Douglass. Article XLVI of this constitution for the new society in the Alleghenies stipulates, 'The foregoing Articles shall not be construed so as in any way to encourage the overthrow of any State Government, or of the General Government of the United States: and look to no dissolution of the Union, but simply to Amendment and Repeal.'[180] Accordingly, the Provisional Constitution and the society it

---

178 Douglass, 'Life and Times', 756.

179 See John Brown to John Brown Jr, 4 and 5 February 1858, from Rochester, NY, record ID 70, MS02-0018 AB, BBStColl., WVStA, wvculture.org, JB/BBStColl. Db. In this letter Brown asked his oldest son to scout out and find supporters in the area around Bedford, Chambersburg, Gettysburg and Uniontown in the free state of Pennsylvania. All were located in the Appalachians or their footlands directly north of that state's border to the slave states of Virginia and Maryland and thus on a large arc around Harpers Ferry (map, 277). See John Brown Jr's answer to Dear Father [John Brown], 13 February 1858, from Lindenville, OH, John Brown Collection, 299, Box 1, Folder 17, Item Folder 31, 102692, KSHS, kansasmemory.org.

180 Pamphlet, John Brown's 'Provisional Constitution'.

was to underpin, as well as John Brown's entire plan, had the explicit aim of improving the American government, not overthrowing it.

The political objective of improving the United States conflicted with the expectations and estimations shared by Forbes, Sanborn and Higginson in summer and autumn 1857 regarding the secession of the North, but concurred with John Brown's long-standing political convictions. John Brown wanted to destroy slavery precisely in order to preserve and perfect the American republic in its free and democratic spirit. His constitution thus included the highly symbolic wording 'and our Flag shall be the same that our Fathers fought under in the Revolution', which was the only article hotly contested at the constitutional convention in Chatham but one defended by Brown and his fellow campaigners.[181] For, unlike in the case of Orsini, who faced numerous monarchical territories on the Apennine peninsula and first had to fight for the formation of a democratic nation of Italy, the democratic nation state had already been established legally and politically with the victory of the American Revolution and the founding of the United States. For Brown and other abolitionists, however, this American republic was marred by the retention of slavery and the partial or complete exclusion of African Americans from the polity. In Brown's opinion, this defect could not be remedied by creating a new, smaller nation through secession, but only by perfecting the existing republic as a whole, thus also protecting it from divine retribution.[182] Brown's concern, therefore, was the preservation of the United States.

Significant changes to the version of the Subterranean Pass Way plan as described by Forbes, Brown's recruits and Douglass first appear in the sources for the end of February 1858. At the invitation of Gerrit Smith, the philanthropist who had made the land available in the Adirondack mountains, John Brown travelled to Peterboro, New York, to inform the Secret Six about his plans in the seclusion of Smith's stately home. Of those from Boston, only Sanborn could attend. Brown presented his undertaking in detail to him, the Smith couple and their private tutor

---

181 See the 'Journal of the Provisional Constitutional Convention, held on Saturday, May 8, 1858', in United States Congress, *Report*, 46; Delany's comments in Rollin, *Life and Public Services*, 88–9; and Oates, *To Purge This Land*, 246.

182 See Oates, *To Purge This Land*, for instance, 247; and on the theological foundations of this position, DeCaro, 'Fire from the Midst', and in this volume, pp. 192–4, 215.

for the first time.[183] As Sanborn would later write in his memoirs, this plan 'was very different from the plan he [John Brown] had unfolded to Thomas and to that other Maryland freedman Frederick Douglass, at Brown's own house in Springfield in 1847'.[184] It was 'an amazing proposition – desperate in its character, wholly inadequate in its provision of means, and of most uncertain result,' recollected Sanborn some fifty years later. 'Such as it was, Brown had set his heart on it as the shortest way to restore our slave-cursed republic to the principles of the Declaration of Independence; and he was ready to die in its execution – as he did.'[185] In his Brown biography, Sanborn also recalled that Brown had presented not only his ideas about methods of organization, fortification and settlement creation in the South or withdrawal to the North, but also 'his theory of the way in which such an invasion would be received in the country at large'. Sanborn recounted that Brown had no doubt 'that the enterprise would *pay*',[186] and that he had not mentioned Harpers Ferry.

A week and a half later, on 4 March 1858, John Brown arrived in Boston, where he stayed until 8 March, during which time he shared his plans – to a greater or lesser extent – with Higginson, Parker, Stearns and Howe.[187] All that has been conveyed about these talks lasting several days is that Brown concluded his remarks with the assurance that 'the whole country from the Potomac to Savannah would be ablaze' if he could sustain his planned rebellion for even just a few days. Brown also asked Sanborn in private and seemingly at random what he thought about a raid on Harpers Ferry. 'He spoke of it [Harpers Ferry] to me

183 On this topic and the conversations with the Smith couple, Sanborn and Edwin Morton, see Sanborn's unfinished letter to Higginson dated 23 February 1858 from Peterboro, NY (copy), record ID 913, MS07-0045 AB, BBStColl., WVStA, wvculture. org, JB/BBStColl. Db; Sanborn, *The Life and Letters*, 436–40; Sanborn, *Recollections*, vol. 1, 144–7; Higginson, *Cheerful Yesterdays*, 216–19; Villard, *John Brown*, 319; Oates, *To Purge This Land*, 229–32; Rossbach, *Ambivalent Conspirators*, 135–43; Harlow, *Gerrit Smith*, 395–9; and Ralph Volney Harlow, 'Gerrit Smith and the John Brown Raid', *American Historical Review* 38 (1932), 39–41.

184 Sanborn, *The Life and Letters*, 418.

185 Sanborn, *Recollections*, 145. See also Villard, *John Brown*, 321.

186 Sanborn, *The Life and Letters*, 438–9; and almost identically in Sanborn, *Recollections*, vol. 2, 146.

187 See Sanborn, *The Life and Letters*, 447–51; Higginson, *Cheerful Yesterdays*, 219–21; Schwartz, *Samuel Gridley Howe*, 226–7; Heller, *Portrait of an Abolitionist*, 95–9; Rossbach, *Ambivalent Conspirators*, 144–7; and Oates, *To Purge This Land*, 233–8.

beside his coal-fire in the American House [a Boston hotel], putting it as a question, rather, without expressing his own purpose. I questioned him a little about it; but it then passed from my mind,' wrote Sanborn about the conversation in his Brown biography.[188] Brown explained to Alexander Milton Ross, an abolitionist who had travelled into the South several times to instruct and equip slaves for their escape, and whom he met daily in Boston during his stay there, that he would cause 'fear and trembling' and 'terror' in the slave states; on 31 May he also spoke of 'terror' to Higginson.[189]

How did the plan known to Forbes, Brown's recruits and Douglass as the Subterranean Pass Way plan differ from the undertaking John Brown presented to the Secret Six in Peterboro on 23 February and in Boston as of 4 March 1858? And what significance did this shift have for the emergence of terrorism? The idea of a raid on Harpers Ferry was not the crucial element, for in conversation with his supporters Brown only mentioned the arsenal privately to Sanborn, and then only in the form of an apparently offhand question. The quoted comments from the sources instead point to something else: a new calculation of the operation of violence. Until mid-February 1858, all reports about the planning indicate that Brown thought he would have to achieve everything he sought to accomplish with his allies; that is, going down into the fields and freeing the slaves, defending the emerging society in the mountains, advancing into the South, and perhaps also convening a constitutional convention for the North that would declare the secession of the free states from the Union.

Yet, a few weeks later, in late February and early March 1858, he had a plan that would lead more quickly to the desired result – the end of slavery in the United States. This new scheme included a theory about the national public's reception of the intended violent action and was no longer geared to the activities of sympathizers in the North, but, rather,

---

188 Sanborn, *The Life and Letters*, 450; and Sanborn, *Recollections*, vol. 1, 151.

189 Higgins recounted Brown having said, 'The knowledge that Forbes could give of his plan would be injurious, for he wished his opponents to underrate him; but still . . . the increased terror produced would perhaps counterbalance this, and it would not make much difference.' Higginson, memorandum from 1 June 1858, quoted in Sanborn, *The Life and Letters*, 464; and Higginson, *Cheerful Yesterdays*, 222. See in this regard Oates, *To Purge This Land*, 250, 401, endnote 26. On Ross's account of Brown, see Ross, *Recollections*, Chapter 3, quotation at 50–1.

to the reactions of the opponents in the South.[190] The key target group of the violence had shifted from the North to the South, a strategy of struggle had become one of provocation and escalation, instrumental violence had become symbolic violence to be conveyed through the media, and the planned guerrilla war had become planned terrorism. Harpers Ferry thus also obtained a different function. The town went from being a source of arms to being a place where Brown believed his use of violence would have a symbolic potential capable of eliciting the psychological reaction he sought in the South. It became a deeply symbolic victim of the political violence.[191] In contrast to Orsini, all elements of the social logic of terrorism were thus reflected in John Brown's modified planning – including the strategy of provocation.

It can safely be assumed that, in early March in Boston, Brown's co-conspirators encouraged him to stage the liberation of the slaves and the beginning of his guerrilla war in a way that attracted maximum publicity. They were, after all, seasoned Bostonian and New York abolitionists, who over the years had perfected the high art of dealing with audience, press and public and proven their mastery of it (also as a team).[192] As their letters to each other illustrate, they saw Brown's plan to free the slaves less in its military than in its symbolic dimension. They measured the value of the undertaking primarily in terms of its effect on public opinion and the abolitionist movement. Among themselves, Higginson, Sanborn, Howe and Smith expressed clearly that an important goal of the raid was to arouse emotions, to spread panic and 'terror' in the South and to awaken moral sentiment in the North. In their view the success of this effect depended on the element of surprise. They were convinced that even an insurrection with some *temporary* success would lead to the desired result. Just as with the actions they had participated in to stop the rendition of the former slaves to the South, they felt it was not so much the rescue of one African American, more or less, that mattered in the medium and long term, but rather the event, which was

---

190 McGlone also comments on the shift from the military to the political and asserts that Brown ultimately was mostly interested in gaining national attention and spreading panic in the South. McGlone, however, only describes these elements, without analysing them as terrorist tactics or differentiating them from guerrilla warfare. See McGlone, *John Brown's War*, 245, 249, 278–9.

191 On the social logic of terrorism, see Chapter 1, pp. 49–53 in this volume.

192 See Rossbach, *Ambivalent Conspirators*, Chapter 1.

to demonstrate the strength of public opinion and reveal the need for political change.[193] Thus, from the very beginning, Brown's circle of supporters had a contingency plan – the psychological and political exploitation of a spectacular event that included violence – in case the slaves proved too peaceable for battle or the small force too ineffectual militarily.

During the following period, from spring 1858, when the shifts in planning became evident, to autumn 1859, when the action began, certain discrepancies can be identified between reports about Brown's plans and his practical preparations.[194] Descriptions by persons who had newly learned of the plans or discussed them with Brown – with regard to the process of the violent operation – thus still matched the reports by Douglass, Forbes and the Kansas recruits, except that the plans now involved principles of provocation. This nuance is evident in an account by John Kagi, a teacher in Virginia who went as a journalist to Kansas, where he joined the free-staters and became John Brown's closest confidant and right-hand man among the recruits. He disclosed the scheme to Richard J. Hinton in June 1858 in its prior form, explaining that the first manoeuvres were to have the appearance of a local uprising: 'Harper's Ferry was mentioned as a point to be seized, but not held – on account of the arsenal.' Brown's men planned to take the weapons from the arsenal and go into the mountains with the slaves who would join their insurrection. Hinton, however, also learned from Kagi 'that in no point was the system [of slavery] so vulnerable as in its fear of a slave-rising'. The movement would, therefore, 'strike terror into the heart of the Slave States by the amount of organization it would exhibit, and the strength it gathered . . . In their terror they [the oligarchs of the southern states] would imagine the whole North was upon them pell-mell, as well as all their slaves.'[195] The plan Kagi described to the new recruit Hinton was based on a strategy of provocation, whose fear-inducing elements were to be the high level of organization, the growing strength of the

193 See ibid., 81, 89, 98, 137, 164, 168, 187, 208.

194 Sanborn pointed out this divergence earlier (see *The Life and Letters*, 450), but it has not received any attention in the literarture until now.

195 [Richard J. Hinton], 'A Talk with John Brown and Kagi', in Redpath, *The Public Life*, 144–5. On Kagi's special position of trust, see Delany, quoted in Rollin, *Life and Public Services*, 87.

guerrilla army, and the participation of the Euro-Americans from the North.

Diverse reports indicate that the vast majority of Brown's supporters were convinced to the end that this or similar versions constituted his plan, including the members of the constitutional convention in Chatham, most of the Secret Six, and John Brown Jr, who because of his mental condition participated in the planning of the violent action, but not in its execution.[196] Martin Delany formulated this discrepancy quite clearly when he subsequently emphasized that 'the idea of Harper's Ferry was never mentioned, or even hinted at in that convention [in Chatham].' He also named a likely reason for Brown's reticence: 'Had it been intimated, it is doubtful of its being favorably regarded.'[197] John Brown and his closest comrades-in-arms thus generally continued to communicate the Subterranean Pass Way plan, sometimes including more strategy of provocation, sometimes less. Of those who wanted to join the operation, only a few, among them Frederick Douglass, learned that a spectacular initial phase was planned for Harpers Ferry – and then only shortly before the action was to begin. Others seem to have been ignorant of this aspect right up to the end, as Osborne Anderson's report, for instance, suggests.[198]

Information available about the operation's practical preparation, however, points to Harpers Ferry as of early March. John Brown, for example, requested in a letter to John Brown Jr dated 4 March 1858 (the day Brown arrived in Boston and prior to his discussions with the Secret Six) that he include Harpers Ferry in his reconnaissance. A month later, he repeated this request and in June 1858 he sent John Cook to the town to scout out conditions there.[199] The arsenal in Harpers Ferry thus seems

196 See, for example, Higginson's memorandum from 1 June 1858 about his conversation with John Brown, 31 May 1858, in Higginson, *Cheerful Yesterdays*, 220–2; Sanborn's letter to Higginson, 4 June 1859; John Brown Jr's testimony in 1867; Edwin Coppoc's testimony, reprinted in Sanborn, *The Life and Letters*, 524, 452–3, 425; and the reports about the Chatham convention in April 1858 (for a summary, see Oates, *To Purge This Land*, 244). Horwitz, *Midnight Rising*, 111, also states that Brown did not reveal his exact plans until summer 1859.

197 Delany, quoted in Rollin, *Life and Public Services*, 88.

198 See Anderson, *A Voice from Harper's Ferry*, especially 67–9, 75, 79, 98.

199 See John Brown to John Brown Jr, 4 March 1858, from Boston, MA, Ohio Historical Society, Columbus, OH, John Brown Jr Papers, Box 2, Folder 3, MSS 47; and John Brown to John Brown Jr, 8 April 1858, from St Catherine's, Canada, BBStColl., WVStA, wvculture.org, JB/BBStColl. Db. On Cook, see Lubet, *John Brown's Spy*.

to have had more significance in Brown's plans as of March 1858 than he divulged to the recruits, supporters and closest friends. Up to now, this circumstance has complicated the dating of the change of plans in the historical literature.

The sources provide no direct references to John Brown's reasons and motives for altering the Subterranean Pass Way plan, giving rise to various assumptions. Sanborn, for instance, wrote, 'There can be no question that what Brown saw and did in Kansas gave a new tone to his scheme.'[200] It can, in fact, be assumed that his experiences with provocation in the proto-civil war in Kansas and especially with the murders on Pottawatomie Creek shaped John Brown's subsequent thinking about violence. This evolution, however, will have been shaped not only by the aforementioned experiences in dealing with the media and publicity and the psychological effects of violence, but also by the idea of arming his men with weapons from forts and arsenals. For this had been practised by pro-slavery forces who had taken weapons from a US military depot in Missouri during the proto-civil war in Kansas. Brown, however, could not infer from that example that this style of attack would produce a powerful symbolic and psychological effect because the Kansas attack had developed no particular symbolic power in that civil-war-like situation.[201] Another suggestion stems from Robert McGlone, who surmises that John Brown changed his plan because not enough volunteers had joined his operation.[202] This interpretation, however, is contradicted by the fact that John Brown planned from the start to begin with a small group of twenty to twenty-five men, which is the number who actually arrived at the Kennedy farm. In addition, it only became clear in October

---

200 Sanborn, *The Life and Letters*, 421.

201 On the raid on the US Army Missouri Depot in Liberty, Missouri, see Don M. Jackson and Jack B. Wymore, *The Heritage of Liberty: A Commemorative History of Liberty, Missouri* (Liberty: R. C. Printing Service, 1976), 17; and 'January 29, 1861 – Lawrence, Kansas, Celebrates Statehood with a Bang', Douglas County Law Library, *This Month in Legal History Archive* (2011), douglascolawlibrary.org. The idea, however, could just as well have been inspired by Brown's reading. Denmark Vesey, for instance, had planned to supply rebels with weapons taken from an arsenal near Charleston, and during the Bussa Rebellion on Barbados slaves seized an arsenal and armed themselves. See Davis, *Inhuman Bondage*, Chapter 11. These rebellions also developed little significant symbolic or psychological impact, with Vesey's rebellion failing to materialize, and the raid in Barbados happening within an ongoing insurgency.

202 See McGlone, *John Brown's War*, Chapter 10, especially 239–41.

1859 how many volunteers had actually come. By then, however, Brown was already following his modified plan. McGlone's hypothesis can also not explain the postponements verifiable in the sources from late February and early March 1858.

Orsini as a role model? Arguments for a transatlantic inspiration

A different explanation that has not yet been discussed in research on John Brown is possible.[203] If one considers the timing of changes to the Subterranean Pass Way plan, another influence, surprising only at first glance, seems obvious: the coverage of Orsini's attempted assassination of Napoleon III that filled the columns of American's East Coast newspapers as of 8 February. Their main reporting of Orsini's attack on Napoleon III coincided exactly with John Brown's further development of his Subterranean Pass Way plan from the version previously known to Douglass into a strategy of provocation that Brown more or less openly presented to some of the Secret Six and, shortly before the raid, to Douglass as well.

That Brown took note of the news about the assassination attempt in Paris cannot be proven beyond doubt. For no source has yet been found (such as remarks by Brown in his journals or letters) that definitely prove such acknowledgement – but then written comments about an aspect so central to his tactics would have been entirely uncharacteristic of Brown.

---

203 This same also applies to Lause (*A Secret Society History of the Civil War*, 88), who in his book describes Orsini's attack immediately after portraying John Brown's conflict with Forbes, but fails to establish a connection between the events. Yet contemporaries had already likened Brown and Orsini, among others the radical German immigrant Karl Heinzen and Abraham Lincoln, who in his speech on 27 February 1860 stated that 'Orsini's attempt on Louis Napoleon, and John Brown's attempt at Harpers Ferry were, in their philosophy, precisely the same.' Abraham Lincoln, 'Address at the Cooper Institute, New York City, February 27, 1860', in *The Collected Works of Abraham Lincoln*, ed. Roy P. Basler, Lloyd A. Dunlap and Marion Dolores Pratt (New Brunswick: Rutgers University Press, 1953), 541; on Heinzen see Honeck, *We Are the Revolutionists*, 148. On the basis of Heinzen's and Lincoln's observations, Mischa Honeck has also suggested Brown may have known about Orsini. To support this hypothesis, he generally points to the keen interest in Orsini among political émigrés and abolitionists in the United States, but does not present a line of reasoning regarding John Brown. See Honeck, 'Freemen of All Nations', 587–8, 598, 611–12.

It is, nevertheless, highly likely that Brown closely studied coverage of Orsini's act of violence in detail. He regularly read not only the
abolitionist press but also the major New York papers. In addition,
he was a guest at Frederick Douglass's house during the time news of
Orsini's assassination attempt first reached the United States.
Douglass, as the publisher of his own newspaper, received copies of
all US newspapers of relevance to him postage-free through a professional exchange procedure, and recounted in another instance that
Brown read these newspapers and drew corollaries between their
reports and his plan.[204] Brown had also followed the political struggle to unify and liberate Italy and news reports about the various
attempts at revolution on the Apennine peninsula and in Europe and
analysed these with regard to his own plans. Furthermore, a number
of revolutionaries from the European revolutions of 1848–9 had
joined and fought with his Northern Army during the proto-civil
war in Kansas. Through these men, Brown would have at least
received assessments of the events in the Italian states that in many
ways were illustrative and so important to the outcome of the revolutions. If Brown had not at least been rudimentarily informed about
those processes he would hardly have hired Hugh Forbes, a Mazzini
follower who had fought for the 1848 Venetian Republic and later
alongside Garibaldi, to be his drillmaster. Forbes, in turn, would
surely have informed Brown on these topics during their collaboration and sensitized him to the cause of the Italian independence
struggle. Therefore Brown may even have been familiar with the
name Felice Orsini as early as 1857.[205]

Moreover, in spring 1858, when the news of the attempt to assassinate
Napoleon III broke in the United States, prominent leaders in the

---

204 The Postal Act of 1792 established that 'every printer of newspapers may send
one paper to each and every other printer of newspapers within the United States, free
of postage.' See John, *Spreading the News*; and Richard Burket Kielbowicz, *News in the
Mail: The Press, Post Office, and Public Information, 1700–1860s* (New York: Greenwood
Press, 1989), Chapter 8, quotation at 145. On Brown's reception of a report about the
1857 Indian Rebellion during his stay in Rochester in February 1858, see Douglass, *John
Brown*, 25; and the reprint in *Frederick Douglass: Selected Speeches and Writings*, ed.
Philip S. Foner (Chicago: International, 1999), 646.

205 See pp. 105–114 in this volume. For information on Forbes, who came to the
United States in 1851 and lectured on the Italian struggle for freedom, see pp. 252–4 in
this volume.

abolitionist movement whom Brown deeply admired sympathized publicly with Orsini.[206] William Lloyd Garrison had received an invitation to the meeting 'in honor of Orsini and Pierri [sic], the noble martyrs of Liberty',[207] in Boston, but was not able to attend in person. So he wrote a letter explaining,

> I deem it an honor to have received an official invitation to be present, this evening, at the meeting at Nassau Hall, to commemorate the memories of Orsini and his associates ... because it implies that you believe my sympathies and aspirations are with the oppressed throughout the world, without regard to race, color or clime. You rightly judge my character. I am not only an abolitionist for the chatelized slave, but an emancipationist for the whole human race. I am no advocate for one-sided liberty, or mere national independence; but, wherever tyranny exists, I loathe and execrate it, and proclaim liberty to be the inalienable right of every human being – liberty of person, of locomotion, of thought, or speech, of the press – liberty in all things, at all times, under all circumstances, in all lands, for all peoples, through all time, and to all eternity. Therefore it is that I deeply sympathize with your gathering, this evening, because it is a heartfelt protest against the cowardly, perfidious, bloodstained usurper who has crushed the liberties of France, perpetrated innumerable crimes and atrocities, and is seeking to aid every form of European despotism.[208]

Garrison equated Orsini's attempt to trigger a revolution in France and open the path for the liberation of Europe with the abolitionist movement's fight for the liberation of slaves in the United States. According to him, both were identical in their goals; they were two different manifestations in the great struggle for liberty. For all these reasons it seems implausible that Brown was unaware of or uninterested in Orsini's attack on Napoleon III.

---

206 On the interest in Orsini in the United States see especially Marraro, *American Opinion*, 215–18; and Mischa Honeck, 'Freemen of All Nations', 591 f.

207 'Orsini and Pierri [sic] Meeting', *Liberator*, 7 May 1858, 74.

208 Ibid.

Which ideas for his undertaking could Brown have won from the American coverage of Orsini's assassination attempt? What could someone seeking to destroy slavery in the United States learn from the Paris attack carried out in hopes of precipitating a nationalist revolution? Which elements of the news coverage had the potential to convince Brown to revolutionize his plan and switch from guerrilla warfare to a new tactic? The first news reports in late January and early February based on the message packets from the *Canada* and *Edinburgh* steamships were primarily factual, and condemned the violent act.[209] But interesting tie-ins for Brown first surfaced in the coverage gleaned from message packets brought across the Atlantic by the *Arabia* that appeared in newspapers as of 8 February.

John Brown was able to infer from the American coverage and correspondents' reports as of 8 February, first, that the act of violence immediately attracted maximum attention. 'As quick as lightning the news flew to every part of the city' and 'the whole city was thrown into commotion,' the *New York Herald* and the *New York Times* reported about the reactions in Paris, with the reader also learning that the events were quickly magnified by the public imagination: 'It was known that the Emperor had been fired at, and rumors flew about of something more disastrous.'[210] Not only Paris, but all of Europe was upset by the act, as American correspondents repeatedly emphasized, not least to make the domestic audience aware of the true magnitude of the event. Reporters described, for instance, the emissaries sent by all European courts to Paris to congratulate the French emperor on his survival, the representatives of the diplomatic corps, and the many other 'personages, high functionaries and dignitaries' who arrived at Napoleon's palace.[211]

209 'The Gospel of Murder', *New York Times*, 30 January 1858, 4.

210 'One Week Later from Europe. Arrival of the Arabia. Details of the Attempted Assassination of the French Emperor', *New York Times*, 8 February 1858, 1; and 'Napoleon's Escape from Assassination. The Projectiles – General Rejoicing of the Continental Monarchs – Official and Popular Congratulations, etc. Our Paris Correspondence. Paris, Jan. 21, 1858', *New York Herald*, 9 February 1858, col. F.

211 'One Week Later from Europe', *New York Times*, 8 February 1858, 1. See also especially 'France and the Emperor', *New York Times*, 9 February 1858, 4; and 'The Conspiracy against Napoleon. Extended Ramifications of the Plot', *New York Times*, 18 February 1858, 2.

Second, John Brown could at this point already learn from the American newspapers that many correspondents sympathized with Felice Orsini – despite their emphatic repudiation of his violent act. Orsini was portrayed in news reports as a noble and heroic personality, although his failed attempt to assassinate Napoleon had killed or injured many uninvolved people. The American press initially saluted his technically sound and well-planned preparations. 'This conspiracy is one of the most remarkable on record,' wrote, for instance, the *New York Times* on 9 February 1858: 'The assassins were determined men, who had been hatching their plots in another land for months and months. They had given themselves up, body and soul, to the work, and were resolved, at all hazards, to see it executed. No possible measure of precaution was neglected.'[212] The American media were fascinated by the masterminds of the attack – especially Orsini – by their adventurous biographies, dedication to the cause, determination, stamina, daring, discretion and technical inventiveness, making their condemnation of the violence sound comparatively dull and formulaic. Brown, who planned the violent end of slavery with a similar dedication and tenacity, could identify with Orsini and probably noted the respect shown the Italian revolutionary.

In a similar vein Brown could have learned another important lesson from the reactions to Orsini's letter to Napoleon III. It was also printed in the United States, where it gained the revolutionary enormous sympathy and respect, with people assuming that any man who could write so elegantly must be morally upstanding and honourable. Even newspapers that previously had condemned the assassination attempt now took Orsini's side. 'Atrocious as his crime undoubtedly was,' commented, for instance, the *New York Times*, 'it is impossible not to draw a broad distinction between Felice Orsini and the ruffians who deal in political assassination as an ordinary incident in their career.'[213] John Brown could observe from the reactions of the American press to Orsini's attack that it was possible to win over large sections of the public to a cause with well-formulated,

---

212 'News of the Day', *New York Times*, 9 February 1858, 4.

213 On the debate surrounding the attempted assassination and the fundamental importance of Orsini's letter, see Marraro, *American Opinion on the Unification of Italy*, 216, where this quotation is also cited.

moral–political explanations, even after the use of violence against innocents.

Third, from the news reports, John Brown could garner that the assassination attempt had elicited fear, repression and conflict disproportionate to the act of violence. It became clear that the public agitation quickly activated amazing theories of an international conspiracy: 'It seems to be the general opinion on the Continent that the attempt on the life of Louis Napoleon was connected with a plan for a general revolutionary movement in France, Italy and Spain,' wrote the *New York Herald*, for instance, and reported in this context on sweeping demands for repressive domestic and foreign policy measures:

> The late attempt to assassinate the French Emperor has not only given a great shock to Europe, but it has produced a remarkable effort, which is evidently participated in by several of the Continental Powers, to obtain such a modification of the English laws as will authorise the arrest of political refugees in England, or at least drive them out of that kingdom.[214]

In the following days and weeks the American press, too, intently followed how these demands increasingly strained British–French relations and the situation threatened to escalate into war.

Exposed to that coverage, an attentive, suitably interested reader could identify the elements constituting the logic of escalation provoked by terrorism: the agitation and fear that a highly symbolic and mediagenic act of violence triggers among the adversaries; the assumption of rife conspiracies, which are apt to seem increasingly plausible in that state of apprehension; the magnification of the threat the perpetrators allegedly pose and, in turn, of the fear stoked by such conspiracy theories; the demand for countermeasures proportional to the supposed symbolic power of the violent act, the general climate of fear and the insinuated level of danger – measures that must have similar symbolism and public impact; and the logic of political escalation that follows from these demands. There is reason to believe that such reports about the political and psychological repercussions of the assassination attempt, about the attention, sympathy and fear it had

---

214 'The News from Europe – Effect of the Attempted Assassination of Louis Napoleon', *New York Herald*, 8 February 1858, 4.

generated and the repression and escalation that it had ensured, could have been the crux that moved Brown to recalculate the dynamics of a violent act and to modify his plans.

This terrorist logic of escalation would have impressed John Brown not least by the speed and breadth of the political response to the violent provocation. For not only did he now sense that time was running short; he also did not fear the possible consequences of a provocation strategy; on the contrary, he yearned for them. Both the impression that he had little time left to successfully implement his action and his endorsement of escalation and its consequences were based on Brown's interpretation of the political situation and the mission he ascribed to his violent intervention. Brown explained these aspects to certain comrades-in-arms and sympathizers between spring 1858 and autumn 1859. This was a form of communication not reflected in sources for previous periods and a further indication that Brown had now definitively opted for terrorist tactics and was interested in elucidating them with a view to posterity.

Brown's interpretation of the political situation was shaped by several factors, the first being the election of a new US president to take place in 1860. In the election campaign, the Republican Party, founded in 1854 and advocating 'the reestablishment of liberty and the overthrow of the Slave Power', challenged the Democrats, who represented the interests of the South's plantation-owning elite and commercial interests associated with them in the North.[215] In the presidential election of 1856, the Republican candidate had lost against Democrat James Buchanan, not least because southern politicians threatened to secede if the Republican won. But political developments since that election – the Supreme Court *Dred Scott* decision, the resurgence of the proto-civil war in Kansas because of the Buchanan administration's partisan policies, Buchanan's plans to expand and strengthen slavery by annexing the Spanish colony of Cuba, and his economic policies ignoring the interests of small farmers and growing industry – had brought Democrats in the North under pressure. In addition, there had been a demographic shift in favour of the North, as the censuses of 1850 and 1860 would clearly show, with the majority of European immigrants arriving in the country in the 1840s

---

215 'What Is to Be Done?', *National Era*, 25 May 1854, 83; and McPherson, *Battle Cry*, 126.

and 1850s (especially from Ireland and Germany) settling mainly in the free states. Their votes counterbalanced the more slowly growing population of slaves, whose numbers had previously insured the South's dominance. For the first time in US history, the election of a president who won with a majority based in the North and who was opposed to slavery became possible.[216] The election thus represented a new chance for a political and institutional solution to the slavery question in the United States.

Important to John Brown's assessment was the fact that an insecurity complex, an atmosphere of crisis, based on rational as well as irrational fears, had long prevailed among the politically influential class of the plantation owners and their representatives, despite 'their' states having largely dominated the Union politically up to then.[217] While the population, cities and educational institutions in the slavery-free states grew rapidly and transport and communication systems, agriculture and industry expanded, the South remained primarily agricultural and had reached the limits of its growth. Each year, it became more apparent that the competition with the North would eventually end poorly for the South and that the North would soon hold sway in the Union. At the same time, the South's political class saw itself surrounded by enemies. Millions of abolitionists in the North agitated against the peculiar institution, Central and South America (with the exception of Brazil) had abolished slavery in the course of their independence struggles, and Great Britain was intervening against slavery and the slave trade on the world's oceans and in the Caribbean. The notion of being the victim of a worldwide abolitionist conspiracy thus had a tradition in the South. In addition, those supporting slavery had to constantly defend its continuation in the United States against attacks by a world public ever more sharply denouncing the practice as backward and barbaric. Intellectuals, writers and members of the clergy from the slave states did regularly

---

216 McPherson, *Battle Cry*, Chapters 4–6. Contemporary awareness of this shift is stressed especially by Adam Goodheart, *1861: The Civil War Awakening* (New York: Alfred A. Knopf, 2011), 222.

217 Comer Vann Woodward, 'John Brown's Private War', in Comer Vann Woodward (ed.), *The Burden of Southern History* (Baton Rouge: Louisiana State University Press, 2008), 62; and Oates, 'God's Stone in the Pool of Slavery', in Stephen B. Oates (ed.), *Our Fiery Trial: Abraham Lincoln, John Brown, and the Civil War Era* (Amherst: University of Massachusetts Press, 1979), sec. 2.

campaign against this viewpoint, but, to avoid debate on the topic, other measures had been taken, primarily the limitation of free speech and the militarization of society.[218]

The main reason for an insecurity complex among the members of the white elite in the slave states, however, stemmed from their concern for their safety in their own country, with demographics continuing to play a crucial role. In many regions of the Deep South (mainly South Carolina, Georgia, Alabama, Mississippi and Louisiana) slaves outnumbered all categories of free people combined – the slaveowners, Euro-Americans without slaves and free African Americans. Every southern state was home to three times as many non-slaveholders (the slaves themselves, free African Americans and Euro-Americans without slaves) as slaveholders. Members of the 'planter families', those holding more than twenty slaves, represented only 4.1 per cent of the population, even in South Carolina and Mississippi. The plantation owners, who politically dominated the South (and the Union), were a tiny minority within a minority. Although slave owners liked to idealize their relationship with their slaves as patriarchal care for satisfied servants, they also had to explain flight, sabotage and insurrection. In this respect, all sides were aware that neither the slaves themselves nor the free African Americans living in the South could be regarded as supporters of the peculiar institution and of the few families who profited from it. As if that were not enough, some whites without slaves also rejected slavery, whether on religious and humanitarian grounds or because it suppressed their wages and they were constantly being called upon to perform militia duties that primarily served the interests of slaveholders. The planter elite thus viewed the groups consisting of the slaves, free African Americans and non-slaveholding Euro-Americans as a considerable potential threat in their own right. Even greater was the fear among the southern elite that these groups might unite – possibly even with abolitionists from the North. Waves of

---

218 See Woodward, 'John Brown's Private War', 62–3; Oates, 'God's Stone in the Pool of Slavery', sec. 2; McPherson, *Battle Cry*, Chapter 3; Davis, *Inhuman Bondage*, Chapter 14; Drescher, *Abolition*, Chapter 11; and Davis, *The Slave Power Conspiracy*. For an example of this awareness, see *'From the Chicago Times, (Home Organ of Judge Douglas.) Are All Republicans Enemies of Their Country?'*, *Southern Argus*, 7 November 1859, 2; and 'The North and the South', *Charleston Courier, Tri-weekly*, 15 December 1859, col. D.

panic precipitated by rumours that gripped the region at regular intervals were an expression of these tensions.[219] In view of such deep fears
and conflicts of interest, the political atmosphere in the United States
was charged.

John Brown was deeply sceptical of the newly formed Republican
Party. According to F. M. Arny, he declared in late 1858 in Kansas that
the abolitionists would not achieve anything with their 'do-nothing
policy' and 'milk-and-water principles', and '[a]s for the Republicans,
they were of no account, for they were opposed to carrying the war
into Africa [into the slaveholding states]; they were opposed to
meddling with slavery in the States where it existed.' Which was why
he wanted to free the slaves with the sword.[220] Other reports corroborate this depiction. The journalist James Redpath, for example, was in
close contact with John Brown in the last months before the raid on
Harpers Ferry and discussed objectives and strategies with him, not
least so he could maintain the Secret Six's allegiance when Brown was
not in Boston. 'The inevitable coming triumph of the Republican
Party . . . was the most powerful reason for the precipitate movement,'
wrote Redpath in a newspaper article he published immediately after
Brown's violent action. 'The old man distrusted the Republican leaders; he said that their success would be a backward movement to the
anti-slavery enterprise. His reason was that the masses of the people
had confidence in these leaders; and would believe that by their action
they would ultimately and peacefully abolish slavery.' And Redpath
expanded on this: 'That the people would be deceived, that the
Republicans would become as conservative of slavery as the Democrats
themselves, he sincerely – may I add, *and with reason* – believed?
Apathy to the welfare of the slave would follow; hence it was necessary
to strike a blow at once.'[221]

Foreign policy considerations also come into play. For instance, in a
conversation Brown had with the journalist William Addison Phillips

219 See Woodward, 'John Brown's Private War', 62–3; and Peter Wallenstein,
'Incendiaries All: Southern Politics and the Harpers Ferry Raid', in Finkelman, *His Soul
Goes Marching On*, 149, 153–6.

220 Sanborn, *The Life and Letters*, 421.

221 Redpath, 'Notes on the Insurrection', *Boston Atlas & Daily Bee*, 21 October 1859,
1. On Redpath's function as a middleman to the Secret Six, see McKivigan, *Forgotten
Firebrand*, 44.

in Kansas several months prior to his action he conveyed a kind of political testament for posterity: ' "And now," [Brown] went on,' recalled Phillips,

> we have reached a point where nothing but war can settle the [slavery] question . . . If the republican party elects its president next year, there will be war. The moment they [the slaveholding states] are unable to control they will go out [of the Union], and as a rival nation along-side they will get the countenance and aid of the European nations, until American republicanism and freedom are overthrown . . . We are on the eve of one of the greatest wars in history, and I fear slavery will triumph, and there will be an end of all aspirations for human freedom.[222]

Brown, according to Arny, Redpath and Phillips, feared that the Republicans – should they win the election – would act exclusively within the framework provided by the Constitution. That document's protection of slavery in states where it was established meant the Republican Party would not abolish the institution there. The opponents of slavery would end their activities and no longer consider force an option; they would deradicalize their thought and action in the belief that the Republicans would find a political, institutional path to peaceful emancipation. The slaveholders, however, would never agree voluntarily to emancipation. If the slave states remained in the Union, slavery would survive in the United States and slowly but surely erode all freedoms the nation had once set out to realize. If the slaveholding states seceded from the Union, they would gain the support of the European monarchies and be able to defeat the free states. The great experiment in democracy and freedom would be doomed in any case.

Brown's reasoning was to use provocation to trigger a violent resolution of the slavery question in order to pre-empt the Republicans' assumption of power in the White House and forestall both possible responses by the slave states as well. To this end the display of force had not only to precede presidential elections in autumn 1860, but also to have yielded results by then.[223] Similarly to Orsini, Brown was interested

---

222 Phillips, 'Three Interviews', 224–5.
223 Stephen B. Oates also states this in 'God's Stone in the Pool of Slavery', 19–21.

in using provocation to escalate a situation he considered latently revolutionary into one that was manifestly so. Yet, while Orsini had misjudged the social situation in 1858 as corresponding to the situations existing in 1830 and 1848, Brown had accurately analysed the political situation in the United States.

In view of tensions between the northern and southern states, Brown was convinced that the only possible outcome of a strategy of provocation could be an escalation into war. He had already gained experience with such escalation in Kansas and condoned the consequences:

> I believe in the Golden Rule and the Declaration of Independence. I think they both mean the same thing; and it is better that a whole generation should pass off the face of the earth, – men, women, and children, – by a violent death, than that one jot of either should fail in this country. I mean exactly so, Sir.[224]

In Brown's understanding, the United States should serve as a role model and pioneer for humanity. There could be no slavery in such a nation. He was prepared to sacrifice his own life and those of others to put an end to the constant violations of the biblical commandment of equality and of human rights in the United States.[225] Villard wrote of one of Brown's granddaughters telling him in 1902 that her father, Salmon Brown, had repeatedly spoken of hearing discussions between his older brother, John Brown Jr, and his father, during which the elder Brown said he wanted to solve the slavery question by provoking a civil war.[226] The account, though most likely coloured by later events, proves correct, at least for the one and a half years between the US coverage of Orsini's assassination attempt and the raid on Harpers Ferry. It could, therefore, have made sense to Brown,

---

For concise consideration of the accuracy of this appraisal see Mark Graber, 'John Brown, Abraham Lincoln, Dred Scott, and the Problem of Constitutional Evil', in Konig, Finkelman and Bracey, *The Dred Scott Case*, 49–67.

224 Brown speaking to Sanborn, *The Life and Letters*, 122.

225 For a general perspective, see Oates, *To Purge This Land*; DeCaro, 'Fire from the Midst'; and Smith, *Weird John Brown*, Chapter 4; and for more detail and additional citations, Dietze, 'Religious Teleologies, Modernity and Violence: The Case of John Brown', 253–73.

226 Villard, *John Brown*, 56.

in many respects, to learn from Orsini and to adapt his Subterranean Pass Way plan to the newest tactical developments and ideas of European revolutionaries.

This is all the more true because subsequent events in Europe showed that Felice Orsini's strategy worked. So it can be assumed that Brown also followed in the American press the outbreak of the second Italian war of independence in April 1859 and the French and Piedmontese troops' victories in Magenta and Solferino in June of that year. It is likely he was able to draw conclusions for his own planning from that coverage, although this needs to be researched and verified. Whatever the outcome of that research: just as was also clearly the case in Orsini's attempt, Brown's plans and the reasoning behind them demonstrate once again that the invention of terrorism as a specific tactic of political violence does not have to do with psychopathic acts carried out by lunatics, but with rational and targeted interventions in politics and history.

Nevertheless, Brown did not abandon his plan completely. With the decision to launch the operation at Harpers Ferry, Brown sought to merge his old idea of an Appalachians-based guerrilla war to free the slaves with a high-publicity event, perhaps not least to retain the loyalty of his volunteers. But he as he would find out, the logic of a successful guerrilla war, which depends on withdrawal into impenetrable terrain, and the logic of a publicity-making act of violence, which depends on visibility and easy access by the media and public, are mutually exclusive in one and the same operation. For, even if Harpers Ferry was well connected, it was nothing like Paris, in terms of either the public stage or the density of media. This difference had to affect John Brown's action as well as his opponents' reactions.

The raid on Harpers Ferry

John Brown called his recruits together for a worship service early in the morning of Sunday, 16 October 1859. Osborn Anderson wrote how Brown read a section of the Bible 'applicable to the condition of the slaves, and our duty as their brethren, and then offered up a fervent prayer to God to assist in the liberation of the bondmen in that slaveholding land'.[227] The men reassembled after breakfast for a briefing, during which Brown read the Provisional Constitution for those unfamiliar with it and led the men in an oath on the document. That afternoon each of them received his written orders and around eight o'clock that evening Brown gave the marching order: 'Men, get on your arms; we will proceed to the Ferry.'[228] Soon thereafter he left the Kennedy farm with eighteen of the twenty-one volunteers. The other three men, whose health excluded them from combat, were to stay behind with the weapons, blankets, garments, tents and food left at the farm and deliver them the next morning.

At first everything went according to plan. In a light rain the commander-in-chief of the Provisional Army of the North, as Brown called himself in accordance with the Provisional Constitution, guided the wagon heavily laden with a sledge hammer, crowbar, pikes, 100 pine fagots (easily ignitable bundles of brush), punk sticks, 250 pounds of black powder and over 1,000 rifle cartridges down the narrow unpaved road from the Kennedy farm to the main road to Harpers Ferry. John Cook and Charles P. Tidd went ahead to cut telegraph wires, while the

227 Anderson, *A Voice from Harper's Ferry*, 65. There are countless reports about the Harpers Ferry raid by contemporary witnesses in magazines and newspapers. But, as Abels has observed, many of these only reiterate what had been printed elsewhere. Exceptions are especially the reports by Boteler, 'The John Brown Raid'; Joseph G. Rosengarten, 'John Brown's Raid: How I Got Into It, and How I Got Out of It', *Atlantic Monthly* 15/92 (June 1865), 711–18; Rayburn S. Moore, 'John Brown's Raid at Harpers Ferry: An Eyewitness Account by Charles White', *Virginia Magazine of History and Biography* 67/4 (1959), 387–95; and Cecil D. Eby, 'The Last Hours of the John Brown Raid: The Narrative of David H. Strother', *Virginia Magazine of History and Biography* 73/2 (1965), 169–77. On Strother and his role during the raid on Harpers Ferry, see Cecil D. Eby, *'Porte Crayon': The Life of David Hunter Strother* (Chapel Hill: University of North Carolina Press, 1960). The monographs among the secondary literature do not usually draw on their authors' research but on biographical literature on John Brown. Recommended are especially Allan Keller, *Thunder at Harper's Ferry* (Englewood Cliffs: Prentice-Hall, 1958); and Jonathan Earle, *John Brown's Raid on Harpers Ferry: A Brief History with Documents* (Boston: St Martin's, 2008). For a military-historical depiction see Bernard C. Nalty, *The United States Marines at Harper's Ferry and in the Civil War* (Washington, DC: Historical Branch, G-3 Division, Headquarters, 1966). On the exact course of events of the raid, see Anderson, *A Voice from Harper's Ferry*, Chapters 11–15; Oates, *To Purge This Land*, 290–301; McGlone, *John Brown's War*, Chapters 11–12; and Horwitz, *Midnight Rising*, Chapters 8–9.

228 Anderson, *A Voice from Harper's Ferry*, 69; on the briefing, ibid., 65; on Brown's orders, ibid., 67–8. See Oates, *To Purge This Land*, 288–9; and McGlone, *John Brown's War*, 260.

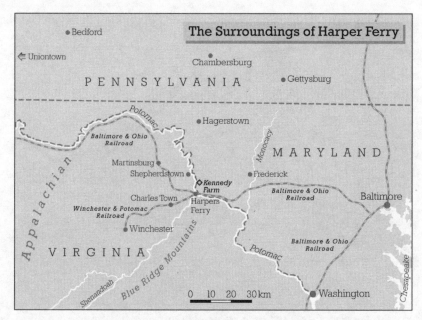

Map 4. The surroundings of Harpers Ferry.

others followed quietly in two loosely spaced two-man columns. A nightwatchman they encountered on the bridge over the Potomac was taken prisoner by Aaron Stevens and John Kagi. The group continued together to the US Armory, where they broke open the gate, seized its watchman, and locked their prisoners in the site's small fire engine house. Several men then proceeded to the rifle works and captured it as well. Brown and his volunteers had thus managed to take over all militarily significant buildings in the town in a very short period of time without bloodshed.[229]

The insurrectionists, according to Anderson, now gathered for a brief discussion in the engine house. Stevens, Tidd, Cook, Shields Green, Lewis Sheridan Leary and he then rode out to the surrounding communities with orders to take the area's influential slaveholding citizens hostage, bring the liberated male slaves back to Harpers Ferry, and tell the female slaves to spread news of the revolt.

---

229 See Anderson, *A Voice from Harper's Ferry*, 70–1; Oates, *To Purge This Land*, 290–1; and McGlone, *John Brown's War*, 261–2, 280–1.

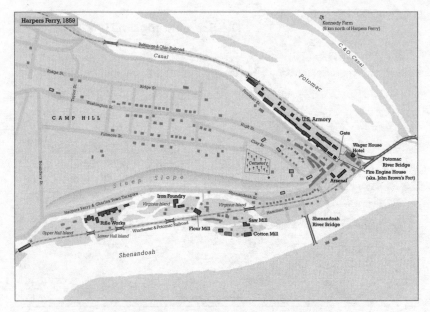

Map 5. The gate to the US Armory, with the Fire engine house on
the left. West Virginia State Archives, Boyd B. Stutler Collection.

Brown had given special instructions for the hostage-taking of the
planter and slaveowner Colonel Lewis W. Washington to transform his
capture into a symbolic act and piece of political theatre. The great-
grandnephew of President George Washington, who acted as a military
adviser to Virginia's governor and who was one of the region's most
prominent citizens, possessed a dress sword Frederick the Great had
given the first president of the United States and a pair of pistols the
Marquis de Lafayette had used during the Revolution and presented to
General Washington as a memento. Brown ordered that Lewis
Washington was to hand over these weapons personally to Osborne
Anderson: 'Anderson being a colored man, and colored men being only
things in the South, it is proper that the South be taught a lesson upon
this point.'[230] Lewis Washington and the other prominent slaveholders
were brought to the other prisoners in the fire engine house, where John
Brown lectured them – under guard of their own slaves – on the evils of
slavery and explained his plans to free the slaves. As dawn broke, there

---

230 Anderson, *A Voice from Harper's Ferry*, 68. On the interpretation, see Carton,
Patriotic Treason, 299.

were forty hostages in the fire engine house and up to ten freed slaves cooperating with the insurrectionists.[231]

But as of Monday morning, nothing was going according to plan any more. Brown ordered breakfast for his prisoners from a nearby hotel and had the proprietor informed that he 'want[ed] dinner at three o'clock for perhaps 200 men', and he would pay for everything then.[232] Instead of the region's slaves and anti-slavery Euro-Americans, it was militias from surrounding towns who turned up in the course of the day at the scene of the insurrection. These militias, who had been promptly alarmed by Harpers Ferry residents, were not willing under any circumstances to negotiate with the insurrectionists: even the most prominent of hostages did not change that. So, while Brown was having breakfast brought to his hostages, making repeated attempts to arrange a cease-fire, and, in the process, bitterly realizing that the other side was not abiding by the rules of civilized warfare, the town's inhabitants were recapturing the arsenal and rifle works with the aid of the militias. These forces killed any of Brown's comrades-in-arms who did not flee in time and mutilated the corpses of African Americans by slicing off the ears as trophies and leaving the bodies for the hogs to devour.[233] In the early afternoon, Brown was left with only the fire engine house, four of his volunteers and the hostages.

But things got even worse, in just the manner Frederick Douglass had predicted. By eleven that evening, 120 marines under the command of Colonel Robert E. Lee (the future commander of the Confederate Army of Northern Virginia) had already arrived in Harpers Ferry by train from Washington. To avoid endangering the hostages, Lee decided to postpone all military action until the next morning. Around 7 a.m., when it had become light, he sent Lieutenant J. E. B. Stuart (who later became a general in the South's cavalry) to the fire engine house with written surrender conditions. Brown refused to lay down his arms and

---

231 See Anderson, *A Voice from Harper's Ferry*, 71–2; Oates, *To Purge This Land*, 291–2; and McGlone, *John Brown's War*, 266–8. The numbers stem from McGlone, *John Brown's War*, 273, 277.

232 'The Insurrection in Virginia: The Statement of W. W. Throckmorton', *New York Herald*, 21 October 1859, 2; quoted in McGlone, *John Brown's War*, 274.

233 On the taking of trophies see Cora Bender, '"Transgressive Objects" in America: Mimesis and Violence in the Collection of Trophies during the Nineteenth Century Indian Wars', *Civil Wars* 11/4 (2009), 502–13.

tried one last time, in vain, to negotiate a retreat from Harpers Ferry. With this out of the question for Lee, twelve marines under the command of Lieutenant Israel Green stormed the building, stabbing two of the insurrectionists to death with bayonets while Green went after Brown, slashing and wounding him. Brown's injuries, however, were not fatal because the marine had left his standard-issue sword at the barracks and was armed only with his light dress saber.[234]

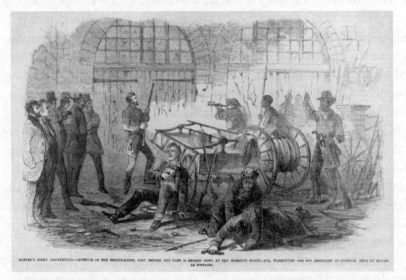

Figure 15. Harpers Ferry insurrection. Interior of the engine-house, just before the gate is broken down by the storming party. Col. Washington and his associates as captives, held by Brown as hostages. Library of Congress, Prints and Photographs Division, LC-USZ62–132541.

---

234 See the report by Colonel Robert E. Lee to the adjutant general dated 19 October 1859 from Headquarters, Harper's Ferry, Letters Received (M567, Roll 618, frames 399–406), RG 94, NAB, NARA, especially frames 402–3; Lee's surrender conditions from 18 October 1859 from Headquarters, Harper's Ferry, Letters Received (M567, Roll 618, frame 408), RG 94, NAB, NARA; the description in J. E. B. Stuart's letter to his mother on January 1860 from Fort Riley, partially reprinted in Henry Brainerd McClellan, *The Life and Campaigns of Major-General J. E. B. Stuart, Commander of the Calvary of the Army of Northern Virginia* (Boston: Houghton Mifflin, 1885), 29–30; Boteler, 'The John Brown Raid', 409; Anderson, *A Voice from Harper's Ferry*, Chapters 11–15; Oates, *To Purge This Land*, 300–2; and McGlone, *John Brown's War*, Chapter 12.

Brown's long-cherished and well-prepared modified Subterranean Pass Way plan had already failed militarily and tactically after only thirty-six hours. Seventeen people had lost their lives since the operation began on Sunday evening: ten volunteers, three Harpers Ferry residents (including a free African American), two slaves, one slaveholder and one marine. The number of slaves freed is unknown, but Virginia authorities were still searching for and pursuing runaway slaves days after the event.[235]

Attempts in the literature to explain John Brown's tactical failure have primarily focused on why he did not withdraw with his group and the freed slaves into the mountains in time on Monday morning. Through his hesitation Harpers Ferry became a trap for him and his insurrectionists. 'Had he gathered his scattered men at that early hour and withdrawn into the mountains, he might have done so unopposed by any organized force,' was how McGlone, for example, put it. 'But as crucial hours passed, he seemed paralyzed by indecision. He tarried far too long and was finally trapped.'[236]

In the literature published so far, various authors have offered different answers as to why Brown remained in Harpers Ferry, ranging from waiting for resupply with arms and other equipment left at the Kennedy farm to psychological illnesses; Brown's 'monomania'; his inability to take aggressive action; the lack of a precise plan; a secret desire for self-sacrifice, martyrdom and death; and a fear of his own courage – that is, a fear of the bloody consequences of a slave revolt.[237] A number of

---

235 McGlone, *John Brown's War*, 273–4.

236 Ibid., 277. Villard, *John Brown*, 438, speaks of John Brown's 'indecision' and writes, 'Just why it was that the commander-in-chief let slip the golden hours when escape was possible will never be wholly explained.' Oates, *To Purge This Land*, 293, remarks, 'the old man had mysteriously delayed'; Reynolds, *John Brown*, 310, 315, adopts this formulation as 'Mysteriously, he delayed', and 'Brown dallied'. Ken Chowder, 'The Father of American Terrorism', *American Heritage* 51/1 (2000), 84, quotes the writer Russell Banks: 'The question is, why didn't John Brown attempt to leave? Why did he stay in Harpers Ferry?'; and Horwitz, *Midnight Rising*, 236, writes, 'Even more mysterious, and disastrous, was Brown's failure to budge from his position at Harpers Ferry.'

237 See, for example: on 'monomania', McGlone, *John Brown's War*, 277–8; on Brown's inability to use violence and his lack of a plan, Villard, *John Brown*, 438; and on Brown's yearning for martyrdom, Lacey Baldwin Smith, 'John Brown. "Let them Hang Me"', in *Fools, Martyrs, Traitor: The Story of Martyrdom in the Western World* (New York: Alfred A. Knopf, 1997), 250–1; and Russell Banks, quoted in Chowder, 'The Father of American Terrorism', 84.

reasons for Brown's remaining in Harpers Ferry can be listed, however, without having to resort to assumptions unfounded in the historical sources.

Brown had expected large numbers of slaves and whites critical of slavery to join his forces and was also firmly convinced that holding prominent hostages would allow him to negotiate conditions for his withdrawal at any time. None of this transpired. In this respect, his failure initially stemmed from two erroneous assumptions regarding the reactions of the local population.[238] Various people had tried to convince Brown prior to the raid that he had miscalculated these reactions, but in the end he had always countered such doubts by saying that he could be sure of God's support in his holy war against slavery because it was God's war: 'If God be for us, who can be against us?' (Romans 8:31).[239] With God on his side – his response seemed to imply – he need not concern himself with the reactions locally or with their impact on his plan.

The question of why the majority of slaves stayed away is the subject of controversy in the literature. Many authors mention the structure and demography of the region (where there were no large plantations) and emphasize that slaves generally were allowed to go out on Sunday evenings,

238 See Douglass's ('Life and Times', 759) account of his conversation with Brown, quoted on pp. 249–50 in this volume, and Brown's statements in the interviews immediately after his capture (pp. 289–91, 298 in this volume). Douglass's conversation is cited repeatedly in the John Brown literature, but it is seldom enlisted to explain Brown's behaviour in Harpers Ferry. Only Abels, *Man on Fire*, 277–8, refers to the conversation; he speaks of two incorrect assumptions and goes in detail into Brown's false expectations regarding the reactions of the slaves and the whites. Carton and Reynolds also mention this misconception, which they see as the reason for Brown's hesitation. Reynolds writes that Brown had 'a sudden revelation in the early morning hours of October 17' and 'the reality of the situation had hit him'. Reynolds, *John Brown*, 313, 315; see also Carton, *Patriotic Treason*, 302–3. Villard, *John Brown*, 438; and McGlone, *John Brown's War*, 278, also assume that Brown waited in Harpers Ferry for more slaves to arrive. Drawing on other sources DeCaro, 'Fire from the Midst', 333, endnote 2, surmises that Brown expected reinforcements. The second misconception that Abels, *Man on Fire*, 277–8, like Villard, *John Brown*, 437, writes about is Brown's erroneous assumption that Harpers Ferry residents were poorly armed and would offer little resistance. But Brown's conversations with Douglass show he had no such misconceptions.

239 See Sanborn's accounts of the meeting with Brown and Smith in Peterboro and J. Sella Martin on a conversation between Brown and Garnet. Sanborn, *The Life and Letters*, 439; Sanborn, *Recollections*, vol. 1, 146; and 'Speech of Rev. J. S. Martin', *Liberator*, 9 December 1859, 194; reprinted in Quarles, *Blacks on John Brown*, 29–30. On this self-conception of Brown see also DeCaro, 'Fire from the Midst', Chapter 19.

so they would not have been home, but off visiting friends and family or, in mid-October, collecting chestnuts (an activity actually mentioned several times in the sources).[240] However, African American authors, in particular, point out that life had taught slaves one thing above all else: to be sceptical of whites, especially when they made fine promises, and to take a cautious, wait-and-see approach because any unwanted action could result in severe sanctions, including torture and death. 'The horror lying at the bottom of that attempt [John Brown's plan] is more than I could describe,' was how Harrison Berry, a slave from Georgia, formulated this fear of retaliatory measures.

> I can imagine that I can see gibbets all over the Slave-holding States, with Negroes stretched upon them like slaughtered hogs, and pens of light-wood on fire! Methinks I hear their screams . . . I can see them chained together . . . and shot down like wild beasts. These are but shadows to what would have been done, had John Brown succeeded.[241]

With Brown's limited troop strength no indication he would prevail, most slaves preferred not taking any risks.[242]

As for local Euro-American critics of slavery, there were indeed many people living in and around Harpers Ferry who disliked slavery. It was

---

240 On the agricultural structure and the proportion of slaves in the population, see Villard, *John Brown*, 427–8; and Oates, *To Purge This Land*, 274. Lewis Washington's testimony (United States Congress, *Report*, 35) is generally cited in the discussion about whether so few slaves were present at the farms because they were permitted to be away on Sundays. Abels, *Man on Fire*, 277, writes that many slaves were out collecting chestnuts on the Sunday evening in question because it was chestnut season.

241 Harrison Berry, The Property of S. W. Price, Covington, Georgia, *Slavery and Abolitionism as Viewed by a Georgia Slave* (Atlanta: M. Lynch, 1861), 15–16. On the interpretation see Clarence L. Mohr, *On the Threshold of Freedom: Masters and Slaves in Civil War Georgia* (Athens: University of Georgia Press, 1986), 57–63.

242 On the discussion about why the majority of slaves did not join Brown and the cooperation that nonetheless took place, see Anderson, *A Voice from Harper's Ferry*, Chapter 19; and Quarles, *Allies for Freedom*, 104–5; and subsequently DeCaro, 'Fire from the Midst', 329, endnote 1; Carton, *Patriotic Treason*, 304; and Reynolds, *John Brown*, 314–15. See also the careful reconstruction of the cases of cooperation in McGlone, *John Brown's War*, 268–74; Hannah Geffert, 'John Brown and His Black Allies: An Ignored Alliance', *Pennsylvania Magazine of History and Biography* 126/4 (2002), 591–610; and Hannah Geffert and Jean Libby, 'Regional Black Involvement in John Brown's Raid on Harpers Ferry', in McCarthy and Stauffer, *Prophets of Protest*, 165–79.

not without reason that the town belonged to the part of Virginia that seceded from the Old Dominion and joined the Union as West Virginia during the Civil War. Yet it was a major step from generally rejecting slavery to spontaneously participating in an act of violence.[243]

Brown was surprised by the unexpected course of events and unsure how to respond. Anderson, in any case, later noted, 'Capt. Brown was all activity, though I could not help thinking that at times he appeared somewhat puzzled.'[244] Perhaps Brown was no longer entirely clear about God's plan because of unanticipated developments. In such situations he usually waited for a hint from the Lord showing him the way forward.[245] Added to Brown's indecision was the unforeseen effect the hostages had on him. As it turned out, the commander of the small guerrilla force held people like Lewis Washington in high esteem and went to great lengths to gain the understanding and respect of George Washington's great-grandnephew and the other illustrious hostages. Brown looked after his prisoners attentively and was perplexed about what to do with them when he retreated into the mountains. He spent valuable time on Monday morning formulating terms for their release and, according to Anderson, responded to his men's pressure to withdraw from Harpers Ferry by saying, 'Hold on a little longer, boys … until I get matters arranged with the prisoners.' His volunteers rightfully considered this a 'bad omen' for, as Anderson put it, it 'was no part of the original plan to hold on to the Ferry, or to parley with prisoners.'[246] It was, in fact, during these hours that Brown's offensive lost crucial momentum, while the militias from Harpers Ferry and surroundings succeeded in gaining the upper hand.

Added to such difficulties associated with John Brown's personality was an entirely objective, tactical dilemma, for he was walking a fine line with his altered Subterranean Pass Way plan. How much public

---

243 Carton states this as well in *Patriotic Treason*, 303–4.

244 Anderson, *A Voice from Harper's Ferry*, 73.

245 John Brown wrote to Franklin Sanborn from Chatham, 14 May 1858, 'it is an invariable rule with me to be governed by circumstances, or, in other words, not to do anything while I do not know what to do.' Reprinted in Sanborn, *The Life and Letters*, 456–7. This behaviour can indeed be seen repeatedly – for example, in Kansas in 1858. See Oates, *To Purge This Land*, Chapter 17.

246 Anderson, *A Voice from Harper's Ferry*, 75. See as well McGlone, *John Brown's War*, 285. On Brown's friendly and respectful treatment of the prisoners, see McGlone, *John Brown's War*, 284, 292–5.

attention was enough to fulfill the plan's terrorist logic? How much would be too much to still allow the use of guerrilla war tactics? Harpers Ferry was not Paris, where reactions had become immediately visible in various ways. Yet without a reaction the provocation was pointless and threatened to become embarrassing, if not tragicomic. If Brown's objective with the capture of the rifle works and arsenal in Harpers Ferry had, above all, been to attract the nation's attention, he now faced the problem of having to determine on the ground in Harpers Ferry whether he had been successful and could retreat into the mountains with his group. How long did the temporary success have to last to have the desired effect?[247]

This question soon emerged very concretely, namely in the form of a train that – according to the Baltimore & Ohio schedule – reached Harpers Ferry on its way to Baltimore at 1.21 a.m. and forced Brown to weigh up his alternatives. Having heard reports of armed insurrectionists, the crew stopped the train outside firing range, just short of the station, as a precaution. When Brown heard this, he had the train staff brought to him and initially informed them no trains could pass Harpers Ferry. At dawn, however, he personally accompanied the same train across the bridge, knowing full well that this would assure dissemination of news about his raid. The conductor did telegraph a message from the next station, Monocacy, Maryland, to the master of transportation in Baltimore, who – after finally accepting the truth of the report – informed the president of the Baltimore & Ohio Railroad. He, in turn, warned President Buchanan, Virginia governor Henry A. Wise, and Maryland volunteers major general George H. Stewart, who then called out the Marines and the state militias.[248] Soon, news of events in Harpers Ferry also reached the national press. In this respect, John Brown's decision to let the train pass represented the crucial pivot away from guerrilla warfare towards terrorism.

John Brown failed militarily and tactically measured against the guerrilla warfare objectives of the original Subterranean Pass Way plan and its surviving elements. The beginning of the fighting mission was also its

247 McGlone, John Brown's War, 249, also sees a conflict of objectives here.
248 See Stover, History of the Baltimore & Ohio Railroad, 99–100; and McGlone, John Brown's War, 263–5. On the arrival time see Daniel Appleton and Co. (ed.), Appletons' Railway and Steam Navigation Guide (New York: Daniel Appleton, 1859), 148.

end. But this failure arising from Brown's incorporation of terrorist elements into the Subterranean Pass Way plan – launching the fighting in Harpers Ferry and seeking to elicit a strong moral reaction in the North and fear and terror in the South – was a foregone conclusion. Brown continued to pursue this terrorist logic in Harpers Ferry, by persevering in the town and allowing the train to pass.[249] The elevated military risk of terrorist logic immediately took its toll, and, if Brown had been killed during the storming of the fire engine house, his violent action would have had no further political consequences. The action would have been a complete failure.

John Brown, though, was lucky: he survived. He knew it was now a matter of exploiting the opportunities presented by his choice of the terrorist logic of violence. The state authorities had admittedly had an easy time with him tactically and militarily. But it was by no means clear who would emerge victorious strategically and politically. The prerequisite for such a victory by Brown was that he reach the public, both the potentially sympathetic public in the free states and the presumably hostile public in the slaveholding states. Whether this would succeed depended first and foremost on the immediate reception of the violence itself.

This act of violence was above all a brutal spectacle attracting public and media attention, meaning that news of the event was immediately given priority, simply because of its sensationalist character and even before it had attained any clear political significance. In contrast to Paris, however, this attention only became perceptible with a delay because of the provinciality of the place, with the concrete conditions of spatiality, time and available transport all playing an important role. As of Monday morning, crowds of excited people had gathered at the train stations in

249 Horwitz, *Midnight Rising*, 235–9, also emphasizes the discrepancy between the plan and the operation, concluding that Brown 'had a second plan', according to which he emulated the biblical figure of Samson. Louis A. DeCaro Jr, in particular, rejects classifying Brown's violence as terrorism: 'Had he been a murderer and terrorist as many presume today, the Harper's Ferry incident would have had an entirely different result, much to the disadvantage of the community [Harpers Ferry]. Certainly a terrorist would not be charged by his own men with erring "in favor of the families of the prisoners," as was John Brown.' DeCaro, *'Fire from the Midst'*, 268, instead characterizes slavery as institutionalized terrorism. He does not employ an analytical concept of terrorism or terror, but rather reacts mainly to the normative meaning of the term as it is commonly used today.

the nearby towns to hear the latest news and rumours,[250] and by early Tuesday approximately 2,000 people had assembled in a wide circle around the fire station to witness the Marines' storming of the insurrectionists' last bastion. In addition to some 1,200 militia members, there were many politicians, newspaper reporters and onlookers from surrounding counties and towns, as well as other people who had come from further away. Alexander R. Boteler, for instance, a US congressman for the Harpers Ferry district who lived about ten miles away near Shepherdstown, had been alerted by a messenger on Monday morning. He had immediately had his horse saddled and ridden to Harpers Ferry, where he arrived around noon, as the militias were pushing the insurrectionists back to the fire station. News of the raid on Harpers Ferry was also received on Monday morning in Baltimore, which was almost seventy miles away, when the train's staff and passengers recounted what they had heard and seen and telegraph reports arrived from the towns near Harpers Ferry. Reporters from the *Baltimore American, and Commercial Advertiser* then set out for Virginia to cover events directly from the scene. They managed to switch to a military train just arriving from Washington at the Relay House railway junction and succeeded in reaching Harpers Ferry that Monday evening.[251]

The spectacle that presented itself there was brief but worthwhile. 'The firing from the interior was rapid and sharp,' wrote a reporter from Baltimore. 'They [the insurrectionists] fired with deliberate aim, and for a moment the resistance was serious and desperate enough to excite the spectators to something like a pitch of frenzy.' But it was over in just a few minutes. 'The next moment the marines poured in, the firing ceased, and the work was done; while cheers rang from every side, the general feeling being that the Marines had done their part admirably.'[252] Accompanied by raucous shouting from the onlookers and loud demands for a lynching, the soldiers carried the dead and wounded

---

250 Eby, 'The Last Hours of the John Brown Raid', 171–2.

251 See Boteler, 'The John Brown Raid', 400, 406; 'Insurrection at Harper's Ferry. Conflicting Reports and Statements', *Baltimore American, and Commercial Advertiser*, 18 October 1859, 1; and E. F., 'The Very Latest. [From Our Special Correspondent.]', *Baltimore American, and Commercial Advertiser*, 18 October 1859, 1. One of the journalists from Baltimore was C. W. Tayleure. See Quarles, *Allies for Freedom*, 104; and Abels, *Man on Fire*, 298.

252 Report from the *Baltimore American*, quoted in the *New York Tribune*, 19 October 1859, 5.

fighters out of the building, laid them on the grass in front of the arsenal
and freed the hostages. They now also had the task of keeping the
onlookers back, for many people wanted to get a closer look at the insurrectionists. John Brown was bleeding profusely from sabre wounds to
his head and body. To protect him from the aggressive crowd and its
calls for vigilante justice, Robert E. Lee had him brought into the arsenal
paymaster's office, where he was laid on blankets – along with Aaron
Stevens, who also had deep wounds on his head and chest.[253]

As it turned out, Brown and his comrades-in-arms had achieved the
temporary success the Secret Six deemed necessary to gain national attention and attract political and journalistic notables to Harpers Ferry.
Charles J. Faulkner, until recently a member of the House of Representatives
and soon to be Buchanan's ambassador to France, and James M. Mason,
one of Virginia's two senators, lived near Martinsburg and Winchester.
They had heard about the insurrection on Monday and set out immediately, reaching Harpers Ferry on Tuesday, around noon. Arriving at about
this time were also the prosecuting district attorney, Andrew Hunter; the
governor, Henry A. Wise; and a journalist from the *Richmond Enquirer*,
Wise's house organ. Wise and the reporter had arrived in Harpers Ferry
from Washington on the same train as Clement L. Vallandigham, a
congressman from Ohio who would become one of Abraham Lincoln's
toughest opponents during the Civil War. The congressman had heard by
chance on Tuesday morning about Brown's raid while waiting for his train
to Ohio at the station in Washington. His travel route passed by the scene
of events anyway so he decided to deboard in Harpers Ferry and have a
look around for himself, before continuing west with the evening train. A
little later, the reporters from the *New York Herald* and the *New York Times*
finally also arrived in Harpers Ferry by train.[254] The town's good rail
connections had served their purpose.

253 See the report by Colonel Robert E. Lee to the adjutant general dated 19 October
1859 from Headquarters, Harper's Ferry, Letters Received (M567, Roll 618,
frames 399–406), RG 94, NAB, NARA, frames 403–4; Boteler, 'The John Brown Raid', 410;
'Insurrection at Harper's Ferry. Authentic Details. [Reported for the Baltimore American]',
Baltimore American, 19 October 1859, 1; and Oates, *To Purge This Land*, 302.

254 See Robert W. Young, *Senator James Murray Mason: Defender of the Old South*
(Knoxville: University of Tennessee Press, 1998), 88; Barton Haxall Wise, *The Life of
Henry A. Wise, 1806–1876* (New York, 1899), 245; Craig M. Simpson, *A Good Southerner:
The Life of Henry A. Wise of Virginia* (Chapel Hill: University of North Carolina Press,
1985), Chapter 11; Andrew Hunter's testimony in United States Congress, *Report*,

With the arrival of these politicians and journalists the national stage opened for John Brown, for in their efforts to understand recent events in Harpers Ferry they turned to, of all people, John Brown. The first to visit the insurrection leader was Congressman Alexander Boteler, who crouched next to Brown's improvised bed and asked him about his motives and objectives.[255] Shortly thereafter the politicians Mason, Faulkner and Vallandigham queried Brown about the background and aims of the operation in the presence of the illustrator David H. Strother and the reporters for the *Baltimore American*, the *Baltimore Sun*, the *New York Herald* and the *Cincinnati Gazette*, as well as Lewis Washington, J. E. B. Stuart the physician, and several officers and local residents. The reporters took down the questions and answers verbatim.[256] Wise spoke afterwards to Brown for two to three hours in the presence of David H. Strother, Lewis Washington, Robert E. Lee, district attorney Hunter, the reporter from Richmond and about ten other people, with this exchange having 'more the character of a conversation than a legal examination', since, according to Strother, 'the Governor treated the wounded man with a stately courtesy.'[257] Finally, the *New York Times* correspondent

59–67; James L. Vallandigham, *A Life of Clement L. Vallandigham* (Baltimore: Turnbull Brothers, 1872), 120–4; Frank L. Klement, *The Limits of Dissent: Clement L. Vallandigham & the Civil War* (New York: Fordham University Press, 1998), 3–4; 'The Harper's Ferry Outbreak', *New York Herald*, 21 October 1859, 1; and Q., 'The Negro Insurrection . . . Postscript – 5 O'Clock A.M. Full and Succinct Narrative of the Whole Affair. From the Special Correspondent of The New York Times, Harper's Ferry, Tuesday, Oct. 18 – P.M.', *New York Times*, 19 October 1859, 1; and the Baltimore & Ohio Railroad schedule in *Appletons' Railway and Steam Navigation Guide*, 148.

255 See Boteler, 'The John Brown Raid', 410–11.

256 'The Virginia Conspiracy – Revelations of Capt. Brown – Full Verbatim Report of His Conversations', *Cincinnati Daily Gazette*, 21 October 1859, col. A; 'A Conversation with "Old Brown"', *Baltimore American*, 21 October 1859, 1; and 'The Harper's Ferry Outbreak', *New York Herald*, 21 October 1859, 1; reprinted in Robert M. De Witt, *The Life, Trial, and Execution of Captain John Brown, Known as 'Old Brown of Ossawatomie', with a Full Account of the Attempted Insurrection at Harper's Ferry* (New York: R. M. De Witt, 1859), 44–9. See also Strother's description in Eby, 'The Last Hours of the John Brown Raid', 176–7.

257 D[avid] H. Strother [alias Porte Crayon], 'The Late Invasion at Harper's Ferry. – [From Our Own Artist Correspondent.]', *Harper's Weekly: A Journal of Civilization*, 5 November 1859, 714. See also Strother's engraving 'Portrait of Ossawattomie Brown, Wounded and Prisoner. – [Sketched by Porte Crayon during His Examination by Governor Wise]', *Harper's Weekly*, 5 November 1859, 712. For the conversation with Wise, see 'Important from Harper's Ferry. Confession of Brown', *Daily Richmond Enquirer*, 20 October 1859, 2; and 'Captain Brown's Interview with Governor Wise', *Baltimore American*, 21 October 1859, 1.

also used the opportunity to have a brief conversation with Brown and other volunteers.[258]

Figure 16. 'Gouverneur Wise, from Virginia, and the district attorney Ould [*sic*] questioning the wounded prisoners in the presence of officers, the N.Y. Herald reporter, and our special artist.' *Frank Leslie's Illustrated Newspaper*, 29 October 1859. West Virginia State Archives, Boyd B. Stutler Collection.

During these conversations, Brown showed remarkable stamina, although he had good reason to be exhausted, for he had last eaten a meal on Sunday evening, not slept for forty-eight hours and lost two sons in the fighting, and he was severely wounded as well. Yet when Lee offered to clear the room of visitors to give Brown some quiet, he responded that they were not disturbing him; on the contrary, he was glad to be able to explain himself and his motives.[259] All accounts report that he was in a cheerful mood and acted in a friendly and courteous manner. Speaking without notes, he used the opportunity to present the background and goals of his undertaking and asked the governor to read his Provisional Constitution out loud so that everyone in the room could become familiar with it. Governor Wise, a fair and fearless man who was presumably curious to learn more about Brown's ideas, kindly

---

258 Q., 'The Negro Insurrection', *New York Times*, 19 October 1859, 1.
259 'The Harper's Ferry Outbreak', *New York Herald*, 21 October 1859, 1.

obliged. District attorney Hunter later remarked he had never experienced such openness and talkativeness on the part of a prisoner. It was only by questions about his supporters and financing that Brown quick-wittedly became evasive with carefully weighed answers. The newspaper reporters were unable to detect any signs of anxiety or fear on the part of Brown or Aaron Stevens.[260] Brown's perseverance would pay off, for with these conversations he laid the groundwork for his subsequent politico-symbolic success.

Politico-symbolic failure

As happened with reports about Orsini's assassination attempt, the news of the raid on Harpers Ferry was given highest priority countrywide. The first telegraph dispatches about the event reached editorial departments on the East Coast and in the Midwest on Monday. The newspapers printed these still contradictory telegrams in the Tuesday editions, often accompanied by sceptical commentaries in view of the incredible information. Some accounts were truly exaggerated, telling of an insurrection by 500 to 600 armed Negroes accompanied by 200 to 300 whites. Yet, in addition to such rumours, there were the first substantial reports about the extent, course of events and intention of the raid.[261] As of

260 Ibid.; 'A Conversation with "Old Brown"'; Strother, 'The Late Invasion at Harper's Ferry'; Andrew Hunter's testimony in United States Congress, *Report*, 60–1.

261 For examples of the first reports for the North, see 'Riot at Harper's Ferry', *Lowell Daily Citizen & News*, 18 October 1859, col. C; 'By Telegraph to the Post. The Insurrection at Harper's Ferry', *Providence Daily Post*, 18 October 1859, 2; 'By Magnetic Telegraph for the N. American & US Gazette. Insurrection at Harper's Ferry. All the Public Offices Seized by a Mob', *North American and United States Gazette*, 18 October 1859; for the District of Columbia and the slave states, see 'Reported Insurrection and Capture of the Arsenal at Harper's Ferry', *Daily National Intelligencer*, 18 October 1859, 3; 'Insurrection at Harper's Ferry. Conflicting Reports and Statements', *Baltimore American*, 18 October 1859, 1; 'A Desperate Riot at Harper's Ferry' and 'Reported for the Richmond Enquirer. Riot at Harper's Ferry – Military Called Out, etc.', *Daily Richmond Enquirer*, 18 October 1859, 2; 'Reported for the Richmond Enquirer. Latest from Harper's Ferry', 'Additional Details' and 'Capture of Sharpe's Rifles, Tents, Ammunition Blankets, etc.', *Daily Richmond Enquirer*, 19 October 1859, 2; 'Riot at Harper's Ferry – Troops Ordered from Fortress Monroe' and 'Negro Insurrection at Harper's Ferry. Headed by 250 Abolitionists', *Southern Argus*, 18 and 19 October 1859, 2; 'Latest by Telegraph', *Charleston Mercury*, 18 October 1859, col. D; 'By Telegraph. Terrible Insurrection at Harper's Ferry', *Daily Morning News*, 18 October 1859, 1; and 'Great Excitement at Harper's Ferry – The Place

Wednesday, 19 October 1859, the correspondents who had travelled to Harpers Ferry began to publish detailed, well-researched reports from the scene that were nuanced in tone and substance.[262] These reports reached the majority of the country's newspaper editors through the system of mutual newspaper exchange. By the end of the week, most of the newspaper editorial departments – in both the North and South – had printed abbreviated versions of the comprehensive reports from Baltimore and New York, sometimes supplementing them with additional information and references of local interest, as well as their own political commentaries.[263] The newspapers on the West Coast first

in Possession of Rioters – Seizure of the United States Arsenal and Stoppage of the Railway Trains', *Memphis Morning Enquirer*, 19 October 1859, 3; and for the Midwest, see 'Further Particulars of the Negro Insurrection' and 'This Afternoon's Report. The Insurrection at Harper's Ferry. Several Men Killed, Further Particulars of the Riot', *Daily Cleveland Herald*, 18 October 1859, col. G.

262 See especially 'Insurrection at Harper's Ferry', *Baltimore American*, 19 October 1859, 1; 'Sketch of Captain John Brown, the Leader of the Insurrection', *Baltimore American*, 20 October 1859, 1; 'Fearful and Exciting Intelligence. Negro Insurrection at Harper's Ferry. Extensive Negro Conspiracy in Virginia and Maryland. Seizure of the United States Arsenal by the Insurrectionists . . . Special Despatches to the Herald' and 'Startling News from Virginia and Maryland – Negro Insurrection at Harper's Ferry – Strange and Exciting Intelligence', *New York Herald*, 18 October 1859, 3, 6; 'The Harper's Ferry Outbreak', *New York Herald*, 20 October 1859, 3; Q., 'The Negro Insurrection ', *New York Times*, 19 October 1859, 1; 'The Harper's Ferry Rebellion. Northern Abolitionists Apparently Implicated . . . From the Special Correspondent of The New York Times', *New York Times*, 20 October 1859, 1; 'Harper's Ferry – The Scene of the Late Insurrection', 'Harper's Ferry', and 'Extraordinary Insurrection at Harper's Ferry', *Harper's Weekly*, 29 October 1859, 692, 694–5; and the series of six pictures by D[avid] H. Strother [alias Porte Crayon], *Harper's Weekly*, 5 November 1859, 705, 712–14.

263 For the North see, for example, 'Troubles at Harper's Ferry', *Lowell Daily Citizen*, 19 October 1859, 2; and 21 October 1859, cols. C and E; *Boston Daily Advertiser*, 21 October 1859, col. B; 'The Riot at Harper's Ferry. "Osawatomie Brown," of Kansas Notoriety, the Leader of the Desperadoes. The Rebel Brown Shot!!!', *Providence Daily Post*, 19 October 1859, 2; 'The Irrepressible Conflict' and 'From the New York Times of Wednesday. Reliable Narrative of the Affair at Harper's Ferry', *Providence Daily Post*, 20 October 1859, 2; 'Slave Insurrection! Startling News', *Hartford Weekly Times*, 22 October 1859, 2; 'The Virginia Insurrection', *New York Tribune*, 19 October 1859, 4–5; 'Extraordinary Insurrection at Harper's Ferry', *Harper's Weekly*, 29 October 1859, 694–5; for the South: 'Insurrection at Harper's Ferry' and 'The Conspiracy at Harper's Ferry', *Daily National Intelligencer*, 19 and 20 October 1859, both 2; 'Insurrection at Harper's Ferry', *Southern Argus*, 21 October 1859, 2; 'Startling News from Virginia', *Fayetteville Observer*, 20 October 1859, col. A; 'The Insurrection', *Charleston Mercury*, 19 October 1859, col. D; *Charleston Mercury*, 20 and 22 October 1859, 1; 'Telegraphic. The Harper's Ferry Insurrection', *Daily Morning News*, 20 October 1859, 1; 'The Harper's Ferry Riot',

reported on the Harpers Ferry insurrection some three weeks later, referring in their coverage to newspapers from the Midwest, which had been brought to California by stagecoach. The fact that Midwestern papers based their coverage on the extensive reporting from Baltimore and New York meant that accounts in the West Coast newspapers also stemmed indirectly from those dispatches.[264] The raid on Harpers Ferry had thus become headline news across the entire United States.

John Brown's violent act was initially perceived and interpreted as instrumental violence, both by sympathizers and by those the Harpers Ferry raid was intended to provoke. The first newspaper reports in both the North and South were characterized by repudiation across the entire political spectrum,[265] with the only difference being how they evaluated the threat represented by the raid.

The potential danger was originally considered to be low in the slave-holding states. The Washington *Daily National Intelligencer*, for instance, dismissed the story as a 'phrenzied [*sic*] movement, conducted without any definite plan of operations', and found it inconceivable anyone would get involved 'in an enterprise so foolhardy' with only twenty-one people. The *Sun* from Baltimore came to a similar conclusion, writing, 'The whole affair dwindles into utter insignificance as the literal facts are brought out from the uncertainty.' Both papers were convinced that the quick suppression of the insurrection would serve as a lasting warning to other

---

Memphis Morning Enquirer, 23 October 1859, 3; 'Harpers Ferry Insurrection' and 'Additional from Harpers Ferry', *Jacksonville Republican*, 27 October 1859, 2; for the old Northwest and the Midwest: 'The Scene Changed from Kansas to Virginia' and 'Black Republican Insurrection in Virginia', *Daily Cleveland Herald*, 19 October 1859, col. A; 'Investigate the Matter', *Daily Cleveland Herald*, 22 October 1859, col. B; and 'Attempted Negro Insurrection in Maryland. Harper's Ferry Captured by Abolitionists and Negroes', *Freedom's Champion*, 22 October 1859, col. A.

264 Examples of early articles are 'Terrible Abolitionist Riot at Harper's Ferry, VA', 'The News' and 'The Rebellion', *Daily Alta California*, 11 November 1859, 1–2; with reference to St Louis newspapers from 18 October 1859; and 'Insurrection at Harper's Ferry', *Los Angeles Star*, 12 November 1859, 1–2; with reference to the *Missouri Democrat*.

265 Public perception at the time also agreed with this view. See, for example, 'The Revolt at Harper's Ferry', *National Era*, 27 October 1859, 2. For an overview of the key positions taken by the American press following the Harpers Ferry raid, see also the source compilation in Trodd and Stauffer, *The Tribunal: Responses*; Villard, *John Brown*, 471–3; Merrill D. Peterson, *John Brown: The Legend Revisited* (Charlottesville: University of Virginia Press, 2002), 11–18; and Ratner and Teeter, *Fanatics and Fire-Eaters*, Chapter 5.

'abolitionist criminals'.[266] It was repeatedly emphasized that the slaves had remained loyal and the insurrection had therefore been a slave revolt without slaves.[267] However, South Carolina's leading newspaper, the *Charleston Mercury*, pointed out that, 'While we can see no cause for present alarm, none can blind their eyes to the audacity of the attempt.' The affair proves 'that there are at the North men ready to engage in adventures upon the peace and security of the southern people, however heinously and recklessly', with the raid indicating what was to be expected 'of the future of the Union with our sectional enemies' if the Republicans' success continued.[268] The tenor of first assessments out of the South was that the raid had involved a poorly thought-out, miserably executed and easy-to-suppress attempt at insurrection carried out by a few lunatics and fanatics from the North and therefore posed no further threat. If the matter deserved further attention, then it was as proof of the enmity in the North towards the South and as a bad omen for a future in which the power could lie in the hands of the North.

The press in the North also unanimously denounced the raid on Harpers Ferry, although opinion was divided over its threat potential. Some of the governing, pro-slavery Democrats and the media close to them immediately sought to politicize the event and exploit it for campaign purposes by blaming Brown's act of violence on the aspiring, anti-slavery Republicans and presenting their prospective leading

266 'The Conspiracy at Harper's Ferry', *Daily National Intelligencer*, 19 October 1859; and 'The Insurrection at Harper's Ferry', *Sun*; quoted from the reprint in *Daily National Intelligencer*, 20 October 1859, col. D. An exception was the *Richmond Whig*, which reported a 'wide-spread, deliberately planned and most diabolic conspiracy on the part of these Northern Abolitionists against the peace and safety of the Slaveholding States' and claimed that 'hundreds and perhaps thousands' were engaged in it. *Richmond Whig*, 20 October 1859; quoted in 'The South and the Insurrection', *New York Times*, 22 October. 1859.

267 See, for example, 'The Abolition Invasion of Harper's Ferry – A Lesson from the Slaves', *New York Herald*, 27 October 1859, 6; J. M. Mason, 'Letter from Senator Mason' and 'The Riot at Harper's Ferry. To the Editors of the Richmond Enquirer', *Daily Richmond Enquirer*, 27 October and 8 November 1859, both 2; 'How the Slaves Received Brown's Proposition', *Southern Argus*, 31 October 1859, 1; 'The Insurrection', *Charleston Mercury*, 31 October 1859, 1; 'A Detailed Account of the Harper's Ferry Outrage, & c.', *Weekly Raleigh Register*, 2 November 1859, 1. But some abolitionist newspapers also emphasized that slaves took practically no part in the action, e.g. *National Era*, 27 October 1859, 2.

268 'The Harper's Ferry Insurrection', *Charleston Mercury*, 19 October 1859, 1; and 'The Insurrection', *Charleston Mercury*, 21 October 1859, col. A.

candidate, William H. Seward, as the true mastermind behind the operation. 'The first overt act in the great drama of national disruption which has been plotted by that demagogue, Wm. H. Seward, has just closed at Harper's Ferry,' wrote the Democrat-friendly *New York Herald* on Wednesday, 19 October 1859. 'It opened in treason, robbery and murder, and has appropriately closed in the blood of the misguided fanatics.'[269] In their attempt to enduringly handicap the Republicans, the Democrats portrayed the danger posed by the raid as being as great as possible: 'This is altogether the most alarming and daring insurrectionary demonstration that ever has been made in the United States,' was the wording in the 18 October edition of the Washington newspaper the *States*, the mouthpiece of Democrat Stephen A. Douglas, architect of the Kansas–Nebraska Act and rival of Abraham Lincoln.[270] And the Democratic congressman from Ohio, Clement Vallandigham, who tried to make his Republican rival Joshua Giddings partially responsible for the raid on Harpers Ferry, described the insurrection in a letter to the editor of the *Enquirer* as 'one among the best-planned and executed conspiracies that ever failed'. Brown had organized his undertaking across thousands of miles and various states, was outstandingly equipped, with weapons in reserve for more than 50,000 insurrectionists, and planned, like Napoleon, to nourish war with war. In Vallandigham's view Brown as a person was courageous and strong-willed, steadfast and patient, earnest and practical. In short, he embodied all of the character traits of a perfect commander, but had simply fought on the wrong side. The congressman, therefore, did not want to see Brown as the real culprit, but rather 'the false and cowardly prophets and teachers of Abolition' who preached what he

---

269 'The "Irrepressible Conflict." Wm. H. Seward's Brutal and Bloody Manifesto. The True Issue for our November Election. Proposed Total Destruction of the Southern States and their Institutions. Seward's Black Republican Programme for 1860', *New York Herald*, 19 October 1859, 2. See also 'The Outbreak at Harper's Ferry – Complicity of Leading Abolitionists and Black Republicans', *New York Herald*, 20 October 1859, 6; 'The Harper's Ferry Abolition Outbreak and the Republican Party', *New York Herald*, 21 October 1859, 4; '*From the Chicago Times (Home Organ of Judge Douglas)*. Are all Republicans Enemies of Their Country?', *Southern Argus*, 7 November 1859, 2. On attempts by politicians to exploit terrorism for their own political goals, see also chapter two, page 149 and footnote 121.

270 *The States*, 18 October 1859, quoted in 'From the States of Tuesday, Oct. 18. The Insurrection at Harper's Ferry', *National Era*, 27 October 1859, 2.

had put into practice – here taking a dig at leading abolitionists and Republicans.[271]

Newspapers critical of slavery that sympathized with the Republicans distanced themselves from the operation and tried to depict the raid as totally insignificant and harmless. 'A most extraordinary telegraphic bulletin startled the whole country yesterday – one importing that *an Insurrection had just broken out at Harper's Ferry, Virginia, and that it was the work of negroes and Abolitionists!*' wrote, for example, the editor of the *New York Tribune*, Horace Greeley, in the Tuesday edition of his newspaper, initially in an incredulous and ironic tone. 'That some sort of a disturbance has taken place in that locality is manifest . . . but, as negroes are not abundant in that part of Virginia, while no Abolitionists were ever known to peep in that quarter, we believe the nature of the affair must be grossly misapprehended.'[272] After reports of the insurrection increased, he acknowledged the following day, '*The Insurrection*, so called, at Harper's Ferry, proves a verity,' but dismissed the action as the 'work of a madman.'[273] William Lloyd Garrison agreed in the *Liberator* that Brown's action appeared to be 'misguided, wild, and apparently insane', even if it was well intentioned.[274] Abolitionist commentators explained Brown's alleged insanity with his experiences in Kansas, the brutal treatment of his son John Brown Jr and the shooting of his son Frederick.[275] They declared, however, 'No humane or reasonable man will for a moment sympathize with this effort to incite servile insurrection.'[276] And the *New York Times* determined, 'The insurrection

271 Vallandigham, *A Life of Clement L. Vallandigham*, 123–4.

272 'A Most Extraordinary Telegraphic Bulletin Startled the Whole Country Yesterday', *New York Daily Tribune*, 18 October 1859, 4.

273 'The Insurrection, So Called, at Harper's Ferry, Proves a Verity', *New York Daily Tribune*, 19 October 1859, 4.

274 'The Virginia Insurrection', *Liberator* 29/42, 1503 (21 October 1859), 166. It was thus initially the pro-abolitionist press in the North that declared Brown insane, rather than the pro-slavery press in both the North and South, as is sometimes stated in the literature.

275 Frederick Douglas strongly rejected claims that Brown was insane or had carried out the Harpers Ferry raid in reaction to the murder of his son Frederick in Kansas, because these explanations obscured the substantive reasons that had actually motivated the raid. See 'Capt. John Brown not Insane', *Douglass' Monthly*, November 1859, 161, col. A.

276 'Old John Brown', *Freedom's Champion*, 22 October 1859, col. A. See also 'John Brown's War', *Lowell Daily Citizen & News*, 21 October 1859, col. C: 'Only a monomaniac

at Harper's Ferry turns out to have been practically a very harmless affair.'[277] With the assessment of the raid on Harpers Ferry as well meant and courageous, but insane, unwise, wrong and harmless, the anti-slavery and Republican newspapers followed a pattern that had proven itself since the 1840s with regard to abolitionists helping slaves escape. The strategy allowed the newspapers to distance themselves from the escape helpers and depoliticize their efforts while nonetheless supporting them with concrete assistance.[278] With this approach they also sought to deflect suspicions of co-responsibility from the Republican Party and to generally rid the violence of its political explosiveness.

The anti-slavery press immediately saw through the Democratic Party's exploitation of the events and agreed in their criticism of the party's approach with some journalists from the South. 'Two classes of men will rejoice at this deplorable folly,' wrote, for example, the editor of the *National Era*, Margaret L. Bailey, with political foresight, 'the misguided men who set them upon the bloody work, and the Democratic demagogues who, at any sacrifice of the peace of the South they profess to love so well, are ready to turn it into political capital.' And she continued,

> The hue and cry they now raise, pretending to believe that the Republican party are responsible for Brown's schemes, is gotten up in a spirit of unmitigated demagogueism. The Washington *States*, the *Constitution* newspaper, the New York *Herald*, *Express*, *Day Book*, and other kindred sheets, are persistently charging this affair to the Republican party. They know that their assertions are false, libelous, and incendiary; but they have caught at it like a drowning man at a straw, and they will persist in it, though they know its tendency is to produce the very consequences they pretend to deprecate.[279]

Bailey's analysis in one of the most important abolitionist newspapers in the United States was shared by some newspaper editors – in the slave

---

would be capable of such an expedition as that of Brown. The planters may therefore dismiss their fears on that score, for monomaniacs are not very plenty at the north, and most of them are securely confined.'

277 'The South and the Insurrection', *New York Times*, 22 October 1859, 4.

278 See Harrold, *The Abolitionists and the South*, 77–8.

279 'The Revolt at Harper's Ferry', *National Era*, 27 October 1859, 2. On this newspaper and its publishers, see Risley, *Abolition and the Press*, 101–12.

states as well. 'The Democratic journals of the North are adroitly attempting to cast upon the Republican party the damnable odium of having incited the Harper's Ferry insurrection; and they will attempt to make political capital out of it, for the coming campaign for the Presidency', wrote, for instance, the *Memphis Morning Enquirer* from Tennessee: the raid on Harpers Ferry 'was a sad affair, begun in madness, stained with blood, and now to end upon the scaffold. There it ought to rest, and there it would have rested, if the Democracy [that is, the Democratic Party] had not been in need of something to sustain their sinking fortunes.'[280] Both newspapers criticized the cynical political exploitation of John Brown's violence by leading northern Democrats and their newspapers, who for the sake of maintaining power were even willing to put the good of the South at risk with false assertions.

The initial reactions to the Harpers Ferry raid were marked less by an opposition between the northern free and the southern slaveholding states than one between the northern Democrats, who attempted to exploit and politically magnify John Brown's violence for their own purposes, and the Republicans in the North and the Democrats in the South, who warned against just such a politicization. The editors of the *Memphis Morning Enquirer* hoped that the country after 'sober second thought' would 'place the blame where it rightly belongs.'[281] These hopes would not be fulfilled. All efforts to have the raid viewed in its military, instrumental dimension rather than a political, symbolic one in order to limit its political implications failed sooner or later, with the spontaneous common ground established between the North and South in their condemnation of the violence forgotten all too soon. Initially this was taken care of by John Brown himself, who – in contrast to Felice Orsini – was not denied access to the public.

Self-elevation through the media: from stigma to charisma

John Brown had no interest in seeing his person or his violent act marginalized or depoliticized and he knew how to prevent this through

---

280 'The Irrepressible Conflict – The Slavery Agitation' and 'Harper's Ferry Riot', *Memphis Morning Enquirer*, 26 and 27 October 1859, both 2.

281 *Memphis Morning Enquirer*, 26 October 1859, 2.

the clever use of calculated publicity for himself and his cause. 'I have been whipped as the saying is,' he wrote to his wife on 10 November 1859,

> but am sure I can recover all the lost capital occasioned by that disaster; by only hanging a few moments by the neck; & I feel quite determined to make the utmost possible out of a defeat. I am dayly & hourly striving to gather up what little I may from the wreck.[282]

Brown fretted over his military mistakes and the defeat in Harpers Ferry and was therefore all the more interested in extracting the maximum from his loss for the cause of the slaves and the abolitionist movement on the symbolic level. He did this by explaining his actions, ideals and world view to as many people as possible and trying to win them over to his cause. Mass media, although not the sole factor, did play the decisive role in that process.

A first step in this publicity work was the conversations John Brown held in the Harpers Ferry paymaster's office following his military defeat. He was aware of the opportunity presented by the questions of the politicians and journalists, and he used it to explain his ideas to them in detail. His priority was to convey certain points to his listeners: slavery was a 'great wrong against God and humanity' and anyone who interfered with it was right to do so; the injustice of slavery could not be settled peacefully, so arguments other than moral appeals were necessary; he himself acted in accordance with the Golden Rule of 'doing unto others as you would that others should do unto you' (Luke 6:31) and respected 'the rights of the poorest and weakest of colored people, oppressed by the slave system, just as much as . . . those of the most wealthy and powerful'; and he was not a ruffian, but rather a conscientious, principled, moral person, who treated his prisoners well and only used force for self-defence. Indeed, if he had not acted so responsibly towards his prisoners his operation would not have ended this way. Brown also emphasized that the slavery question would soon confront the South and it would do well to prepare itself for the settlement of the matter. 'You may dispose of me very easily, – I am nearly disposed of

---

282 John Brown to Mary Ann Brown, 10 November 1859, reprinted in Villard, *John Brown*, 540.

now; but this question is still to be settled, – this negro question I mean; the end of that is not yet.' Asked whether he considered his undertaking a religious movement, he replied that it was indeed the greatest service one could render to God; the question whether he considered himself an instrument of God he answered affirmatively.[283] In these conversations, Brown succeeded in effectively conveying his view of slavery as a sin, his conviction that the time for peaceful emancipation initiatives was past, and his self-image as a human emissary sent by God to fight for the poorest of the poor in the United States. He thus sought to portray his breach of the norm as legitimate and sanctioned by God and the norm of legalized slavery as illegitimate.

The reporters' verbatim publication of the conversation transcripts made the questioning of John Brown into one of history's first interviews. The text genre of the interview became established in the United States after the Civil War, with the style taking hold in France at approximately the same time in 1866. In the rest of Europe it was long scorned as 'American barbarity' and only hesitantly accepted in the late nineteenth century.[284] The interview and the rendering of other conversations appeared in time for the weekend editions of the large East Coast newspapers.[285] Via the newspaper exchange, it found its way into

283 'The Harper's Ferry Outbreak. Verbatim Report of the Questioning of Old Brown by Senator Mason, Congressman Vallandigham, and Others', New York Herald, 21 October 1859, 1, reprinted in Ruchames, John Brown, 126–33.

284 On the history of the interview, see Michael Schudson, 'Question Authority: A History of the News Interview in American Journalism, 1860–1930s', Media, Culture & Society 16/4 (1991), 565–6; reprinted in Schudson, The Power of News, 72–3; and Leonard, The Power of the Press, 79–80. On Europe, see Martin Kött, Das Interview in der französischen Presse: Geschichte und Gegenwart einer journalistischen Textsorte (Tübingen: Niemeyer, 2004).

285 'A Conversation with "Old Brown"', 'A Speech to the Reporters', and 'Captain Brown's Interview with Governor Wise', Baltimore American, 21 October 1859, 1; 'The Harper's Ferry Outbreak. Verbatim Report of the Questioning of Old Brown by Senator Mason, Congressman Vallandigham, and Others', New York Herald, 21 October 1859, 1; 'Captain Brown's Statement to Gov. Wise', Baltimore American, 20 October 1859, 1; 'The Governor's Interview with Old Brown', Daily Dispatch, 21 October 1859, 1; 'Interview between Gov. Wise and Brown', New York Times, 22 October 1859, 1; 'Our Richmond Correspondence – The Interview between Gov. Wise and Old Brown Misrepresented', New York Herald, 1 November 1859, 10; and Strother, 'The Late Invasion at Harper's Ferry'; which also quoted District Attorney Hunter's notes on the conversation and presents verbatim conversations Strother had with Brown and Stevens.

newspapers throughout the entire republic in the following days and weeks.[286] Brown's words thus found the widest possible dissemination.

In the following weeks, oral or written statements by or about John Brown were highly sought after by the media. Brown had left a sack of documents behind at the Kennedy farm that J. E. B. Stuart discovered as he inspected the property with some marines after the fighting had ended.[287] The sack contained the 'Vindication of the Invasion, Etc.' (Brown's handwritten defence of his actions), his Declaration of Liberty, an autobiographical essay titled 'History of John Brown, Otherwise "Old Brown" and his Family', his written orders to the recruits, stacks of the Provisional Constitution, the minutes of the Chatham conference that had ratified the Provisional Constitution, and the guerrilla war manual Brown had commissioned from the drillmaster, Forbes.[288] Lee handed these documents over to Governor Wise, who studied them on Tuesday evening by reading them aloud in the presence of militiamen sitting and lying on the floor at a Harpers Ferry hotel, and interjecting amused commentary.[289] As the governor wanted the public to understand the specific threat posed by John Brown and his group, he then released them for publication, with the result that most of these documents soon appeared in prominent East Coast newspapers and were subsequently reprinted in other newspapers around the country.[290]

286 For complete or shortened reprints in the North, see, for example, *Liberator*, 28 October 1859, 1–2; *Harper's Weekly*, 29 October 1859, 694–5; and *Douglass' Monthly*, November 1859, 165–7; for the South: *Daily National Intelligencer*, 20 and 25 October 1859, 2, 3 respectively; *Southern Argus*, 23 October 1859, 2; *Memphis Morning Enquirer*, 23 and 25 October 1859, both 2; *Charleston Mercury*, 24 October 1859, col. A; *Mississippian*, 2 November 1859, col. F; for the Midwest: *Anti-slavery Bugle*, 29 October 1859, col. 2; and for the West Coast: *Oregon Sentinel*, 3 December 1859, 1.

287 See the report by Colonel Robert E. Lee to the adjutant general dated 19 October 1859 from Headquarters, Harper's Ferry, Letters Received (M567, Roll 618, frames 399–406), RG 94, NAB, NARA, frames 403, 406; J. E. B. Stuart's letter to his mother in McClellan, *The Life and Campaigns*, 29; Boteler, 'The John Brown Raid', 410; and Oates, *To Purge This Land*, 300–2.

288 See J. E. B. Stuart's letter to his mother in McClellan, *The Life and Campaigns*, 30; Oates, *To Purge This Land*, 301; and McGlone, *John Brown's War*, 216.

289 Rosengarten, 'John Brown's Raid', 716–17.

290 See, for instance, 'Insurrection at Harper's Ferry. Additional and Interesting Details. Constitution of the Provisional Government. [Reported for the Baltimore American]', *Baltimore American*, 20 October 1859, 1; 'The Abolition Invasion at Harper's Ferry . . . The Constitution of the Provisional Government', *Daily Dispatch*, 21 October 1859, 1; 'Insurrection at Harper's Ferry . . . The Provisional Government of the

Brown could not have wished for a better way to disseminate his ideas and ideals.

Then – just as in the case of Orsini – the trial of John Brown became a historic and media event in its own right, with the court proceedings being the first in American history to receive extensive daily coverage in the national press.[291] The courtroom at the Jefferson County courthouse in Charles Town (then named Charlestown), some seven miles west of Harpers Ferry, was filled to capacity with reporters from domestic and foreign newspapers, lawyers and onlookers throughout the entire trial.[292] A telegraph line solely for the coverage of the trial was installed from Harpers Ferry to Charles Town to connect the town with the national telegraph network. Day after day the columns of broadsheet East Coast newspapers were filled with journalists' reports and verbatim renderings or detailed summaries of the stenographic records of court proceedings and witness examination. The technical arrangements and scale of coverage were themselves of news value.[293] The press presented detailed discussions of legal questions, with the hunt for Brown's fugitive comrades-in-arms, their capture or escape, their extradition or its obstruction, and their trials also proving to be fruitful topics.[294] In this

Insurrectionists ', *Daily Richmond Enquirer*, 21 October 1859, 2; 'Disclosures by the Conspirators', *Daily National Intelligencer*, 20 October 1859, 3; 'The Harper's Ferry Outbreak', *New York Herald*, 20 October 1859, 22 October 1859, 3, 1 respectively; 'The Virginia Rebellion', *New York Times*, 22 October 1859, 1.

291 See Robert A. Ferguson, *The Trial in American Life* (Chicago: The University of Chicago Press, 2006), Chapter 4, 117; Zoe Trodd and John Stauffer, 'Introduction', in Zoe Trodd and John Stauffer (eds.), *Meteor of War: The John Brown Story* (Maplecrest: Brandywine Press, 2004), 20; and Brian McGinty, *John Brown's Trial* (Cambridge, MA: Harvard University Press, 2009), 6–7.

292 For an unsurpassed description of the atmosphere, see 'The Invasion of Virginia. Public Feeling, Sentence of Brown, State of the Prisoners', *New York Daily Tribune*, 5 November 1859, 5; see also the engravings by Porte Crayon [Strother] in *Harper's Weekly*, 12 November 1859, 721, 728.

293 On the connection to the telegraph network and other 'arrangements' by the Associated Press, see 'Line Extended from Harper's Ferry to Charlestown', *New York Herald*, 10 November 1859; 'The Virginia Trials', *New York Times*, 25 October 1859; and in this regard McGinty, *John Brown's Trial*, 6–7. De Witt (*The Life*) offers a contemporary summary of the court reporting. On the trial generally see also Oates, *To Purge This Land*, 324–7.

294 See, for instance, the continuous coverage as of 19 October 1859 in the *Lowell Daily Citizen*, *New York Herald*, *Daily National Intelligencer*, *Daily Richmond Enquirer*, *Southern Argus*, *Memphis Morning Enquirer*, *Cleveland Daily Herald*, *Cleveland Morning Leader* and, in particular, also the *Bangor Daily Whig & Courier*, 26 October 1859,

way, the raid on Harpers Ferry remained a main subject in the American press until around Christmas.

John Brown initially participated actively in the trial. But, with the judge not paying him much heed, he soon resigned himself to his fate, following the proceedings quietly from a cot. It was only when his lawyer, without consulting him, attempted to have Brown declared legally insane to avert the death penalty that he vehemently protested. After all, such a finding would have denied the intentionality of his violent act, thus robbing it of its political and symbolic substance. His protest was successful and the court ruled him sane.[295]

John Brown also gave a short speech on 2 November 1859, the day of his sentencing. Asked by the court 'whether he had anything to say why sentence should not be pronounced upon him', Brown stood up and speaking without notes said calmly, if somewhat hesitantly, that his death penalty was unjust, for if he had acted similarly 'in behalf of the rich, the powerful, the intelligent, the so-called great . . . it would have been all right, and every man in this court would have deemed it an act worthy of reward rather than punishment'. Brown accused the court of double standards and restated the biblical principles behind his actions. 'This Court acknowledges, too, as I suppose, the validity of the law of God,' he began rhetorically.

> I see a book kissed, which I suppose to be the Bible, or at least the New Testament, which teaches me that all things whatsoever I would that men should do to me, I should do even so to them. It teaches me, further, to remember them that are in bonds as bound with them.

Here Brown again made reference to the Golden Rule (Luke 6:31) and the teaching of Hebrews (13:3) to 'continue to remember those in prison as if you were together with them in prison'. He stressed his unwavering

---

col. A; *Charleston Tri-weekly Courier*, 1 November 1859, col. E; *New York Daily Tribune*, 5 November 1859, 6; and *Harper's Weekly*, 5 November 1859, 710–11. On this subject see also McGinty, *John Brown's Trial*.

295 See Oates, *To Purge This Land*, 324–34. On the discussion about Brown's possible mental illness, see also McGlone, *John Brown's War*, Chapters 7–8, who at 200 comes to the conclusion that if Brown 'suffered from mental illness or personality disorder, it eludes classification. He was not psychotic. In Kansas, to be sure, he found a new sense of vocation and a new persona. What old friends in Ohio saw in him as obsession, Brown saw as mission.'

belief that he had behaved correctly by virtue of these commandments and felt no guilt: 'I endeavored to act up to that instruction . . . I believe that to have interfered as I have done, as I have always freely admitted I have done in behalf of His despised poor, is no wrong, but right.' Brown reiterated the morality and legitimacy of his actions, while denying the court both. He concluded by accepting the verdict:

> Now, if it is deemed necessary that I should forfeit my life for the furtherance of the ends of justice, and mingle my blood further with that blood of my children and with the blood of millions in this slave country, whose rights are disregarded by wicked, cruel, and unjust enactments, I say let it be done.[296]

In Brown's eyes, the sentence of death by hanging to be carried out on 2 December 1859 was part of the illegitimate system of slavery. He, too, became a victim of this system, just like the millions of African Americans living in the United States. Brown's speech, which was widely printed and commented on in the newspapers, became an instant classic.[297]

In another parallel with Felice Orsini, John Brown's courtroom speech elevated him to the status of martyr in the eyes of the abolitionist movement, transforming stigma into charisma.[298] Brown willingly accepted the attribution of being the one who sacrificed himself to emancipate the slaves. He himself interpreted the course of the Harpers Ferry raid, his

---

296 'Speech and Sentence of Brown', in De Witt, *The Life*, 94–5. On the situation and presentation, see 'The Invasion of Virginia. Public Feeling, Sentence of Brown, State of the Prisoners', *New York Daily Tribune*, 5 November 1859, 5; and on the interpretation of the speech, McGlone, *John Brown's War*, 314–17. On the question of legitimacy in a broader theoretical and historical context see Dietze, 'Legitimacy and Security from a Historical Perspective', especially 156–9.

297 James M. McPherson, *Ordeal by Fire: The Civil War and Reconstruction* (New York: Random House, 1982), 116. For reprints and commentaries, see such different newspapers as 'Trial of John Brown. Convicted and Sentenced to Be Hung. Brown's Address to the Court', *Douglass' Monthly*, Nov. 1859, 171; 'Trial of the Harper's Ferry Insurgents. Trial of Coppoc – Sentence of Death passed on Brown – His Speech to the Court' and 'Brown's Speech before Sentence', *Daily Richmond Enquirer*, 4 and 7 November 1859, both 2; and 'Trial of the Harper's Ferry Rioters. Brown's Speech Previous to his Sentence', *Memphis Morning Enquirer*, 6 November 1859, 3.

298 See especially Smith, 'John Brown'; and Paul Finkelman, 'Manufacturing Martyrdom: The Antislavery Response to John Brown's Raid', in Finkelman, *His Soul Goes Marching On*, 41–66.

imprisonment, and the imminent execution through the lens of the Bible, the history of Christianity (particularly of English Protestantism), and the history of the American Revolution. These sources provided Brown with ample role models who had been imprisoned and executed for faith and freedom. In substance this fate is what defines a martyr. The early Christian martyrs of Rome, like the Protestant martyrs of England, stood firm even at the price of persecution and death and remained true to their faith. In this respect they were 'figures of suffering', a suffering, however, 'whose course and meaning they sought to take into their own hands'. They re-enacted Christ's sacrificial death. In this *Imitatio Christi* (imitation of Christ) they were witnesses to the Passion of Christ, followers of 'this archetype of a "sacrifice *for*"' manifested by Christ.[299]

Brown also claimed to be a follower of Christ and to make the 'sacrifice *for*', with the readiness to die for the emancipation of the slaves conveyed by the 'law of God' identical with the readiness to die for Christ. 'To me it is given in behalf of Christ, not only to believe in him, but also to *suffer* for his sake,' he wrote in a letter answering an Ohio pastor unknown to him. 'I went against the laws of men, it is true; but "whether it be right to obey *God* or *men*, judge ye."'[300] He also attempted to communicate this self-interpretation to his respective listener and to the public. Brown constantly compared himself directly or indirectly with those who fought in the American Revolution, with the martyrs of Protestantism, with biblical figures such as Moses and Samson, and ultimately with Christ. 'You cannot have forgotten *how*; *& where our Grand Father* Capt (John Brown [John Brown's namesake and grandfather]:) fell in 1776; & *that he too*; might have perished on the Scaffold had circumstances been but *very little* different,' he wrote to a relative. '*The fact* that a man dies under the hand of an executioner (or otherwise) has but little to do with his true character, as I suppose. John Rogers [the first Protestant martyr in England] perished at the stake *a great & good*

---

299 Sigrid Weigel, 'Schauplätze, Figuren, Umformungen: Zu Kontinuitäten und Unterscheidungen von Märtyrerkulturen', in Sigrid Weigel (ed.), *Märtyrer-Porträts: Von Opfertod, Blutzeugungen und heiligen Kriegern* (Munich: Wilhelm Fink, 2007), 12. See also Silke-Petra Bergjan and Beat Näf, *Märtyrerverehrung im frühen Christentum: Zeugnisse und kulturelle Wirkungsweisen* (Stuttgart: Kohlhammer, 2014).

300 John Brown to Reverend McFarland, 23 November 1859, from Charlestown, VA, reprinted in Redpath, *The Public Life*, 258. Brown quotes the apostle story of Luke (Acts 4:19): 'Whether it be right in the sight of God to hearken unto you more than to God, judge ye.'

man.'[301] Beyond the self-image as martyr, such statements by Brown in turn question the legitimacy of the state whose laws were to condemn him to death, thus expressing his belief that a death penalty could be unjustified and therefore a matter of religious and political power relations.

In the four weeks between his conviction and execution, Brown did everything possible to expand his martyr role. John Avis, the jailer in Charles Town, who had been fighting with a local militia against Brown's force as recently as Monday, gave the prisoner a free hand. Brown and his fellow prisoners were allowed to correspond by letter and to receive any visitors they wished. The sensation surrounding the insurrectionists did not abate, and curiosity seekers came in droves, from Governor Wise to militiamen, soldiers, newspaper reporters, clergymen, towns-people and old acquaintances and friends. Brown's comrade-in-arms Edwin Coppoc wrote on 22 November that they had probably had around a thousand visitors in the last two days, some out of sympathy, but most out of animosity. With the exception of clergy from the slave states who wanted to pray with the men condemned to death, for the salvation of their souls, Brown welcomed all visitors into his cell, shook their hands, talked to them, complimented the militiamen and soldiers, and 'preached' (as he referred to it to a *New York Tribune* reporter) patiently about the monstrous nature of slavery. Such statements found their way yet again into the newspapers.[302]

---

301 John Brown to Reverend Luther Humphrey, 19 November 1859, from Charlestown, VA, Record ID 101, MS02-0049 AB, BBStColl., WVStA, A, wvculture.org, JB/BBStColl. Db; reprinted in Villard, *John Brown*, 543. John Brown modelled himself right down to the level of individual formulations in the spirit of John Rogers. See McGlone, *John Brown's War*, 321.

302 See Villard, *John Brown*, 544–5. Edwin Coppoc's statement is in his letter to 'friends in Iowa' that is excerpted in Hinton, *John Brown and His Men*, 487–90, 489–90. For interviews or reports about visitor conversations, see especially 'Old Brown's History of Himself. Special Despatch to the Herald', *New York Herald*, 22 October 1859, 1; 'Our Special Despatch from Charlestown' and 'The General Newspaper Despatch', *New York Herald*, 31 October 1859, 1; partially reprinted as 'Visit of the Military to Old Brown', *Douglass' Monthly*, Nov. 1859, 168–9; 'The Invasion of Virginia. Public Feeling, Sentence of Brown, State of the Prisoners', *New York Daily Tribune*, 5 November 1859, 5; 'The Trial of the Conspirators. [From Our Own Artist Correspondent]', *Harper's Weekly*, 12 November 1859, 729–30; Theodore Tilton, 'Interviews with Brown and His Wife', *New York Times*, 18 November 1859; 'John Brown's Invasion. Correspondence of The NY Tribune. Charlestown, VA, Monday, Nov. 21, 1859' and 'From the Correspondence

Figure 17. Front page of *Frank Leslie's Illustrated Newspaper* with a
picture of John Brown. Caption under Brown's portrait: 'John Brown,
now under sentence of death for treason and murder, at Charlestown,
Va. From a photograph one year ago by Martin M. Lawrence,
381 Broadway, N.Y.' Library of Congress, Prints and Photographs
Division, LC-USZ62-137591, Photographer: Martin M. Lawrence.

Just as with Felice Orsini, letters also played a central role in the
public's positive perception of John Brown. But in contrast to Orsini,
Brown was able to influence this perception, even without the cooperation of powerful politicians. Innumerable people from around the country wrote to Brown, and he attempted to answer as many as possible –
friends as well as strangers.[303] He was still answering mail on the morning

of *The Baltimore American*: . . . Interviews with the Prisoners . . . Interview with Capt.
Brown', *New York Daily Tribune*, 24 November 1859, 6; 'John Brown in Prison. His State
of Mind. His Principles on Slavery', *Harper's Weekly*, 26 November 1859, 758; 'A Visit to
Brown in Prison', *Harper's Weekly*, 3 December 1859, 774–5; 'The Harper's Ferry Affair;
Our Special Despatch from Charles-Town', *New York Herald*, 4 November 1859, col. D;
'The Brown Conspiracy', *Frank Leslie's Illustrated Newspaper*, 5 November 1859, col. A;
and 'John Brown's Counsel', *New York Daily Tribune*, 9 November 1859, 7.

303 For collections of these letters, see the Boyd B. Stutler Collection in the West
Virginia State Archives and the Library of Virginia, Brown, John (1800–1859). Transcript
of Letters, 1830–1859 [microfilm]. Miscellaneous reels 875, 999. Accessions 31218,

of his execution because he was convinced: 'Christ the great Captain of *liberty*; as well as of salvation; . . . *saw fit* to take from me a sword of steel after I had carried it for a time but he has put another in my hand: ("The sword of the Spirit;").'[304] Here Brown referred to Ephesians 6:16–17: 'Above all, take the shield of faith, wherewith ye shall be able to quench all the fiery darts of the wicked. And take the helmet of salvation, and the sword of the Spirit, which is the word of God.' Brown's idea that he was spreading the word of God is to be taken literally, for he was convinced that God spoke through him, just as through Paul, with whom he strongly identified.[305] His letters are written in an unconventional language informed by the Bible and permeated with biblical quotes, a language that does not conform to the rules of grammar and spelling (even those customary at the time) but has lost none of its expressive impact.

Brown knew about the peculiar power of his letters. Many recipients, aware of their significance, passed them on to newspapers for publication, with other newspapers subsequently reprinting them.[306] In this way they became known to a broad public and were frequently the subject of commentaries. This form of dissemination, which Brown had practised earlier in Kansas and which blurred the boundaries between personal and public utterance, between letter and newspaper report, suited his purposes quite well. He expressly wrote to some of his correspondence partners that they 'may make such use of' his letters as they saw fit, effectively releasing them for publication.[307] Brown was thus able

32561. Some are reprinted in James Redpath, *Echoes of Harper's Ferry* (Boston: Thayer and Eldridge, 1860), Chapter 6; Redpath, *The Public Life*, Chapter 8; Sanborn, *The Life and Letters*, 578–620; Ruchames, *John Brown*, 135–67; and Earle (whose account draws on Sanborn's), *John Brown's Raid*, Chapter 3.

304 John Brown to Reverend H. L. Vaill from Charlestown, VA, 15 November 1859, reprinted in Ruchames, *John Brown*, 143.

305 See especially McGlone, *John Brown's War*, 322–6.

306 See, for instance, 'Capt. Brown's Letter to Judge Tilden', *Daily National Intelligencer*, 29 October 1859, 3; 'Brown's Letter to His Wife. Charlestown, Jefferson Co., Va, 16th Nov. 1859', *Liberator*, 16 December 1859, 197; 'John Brown in Prison, to His Old Schoolmaster. His Views of Death, and Religious Hopes – An Interesting Letter . . . The Rev. H. L. Vail [sic]', *New York Daily Tribune*, 24 November 1859, 6; 'Letter from John Brown', *New York Times*, 28 November 1859, 1; 'Letter from John Brown in Prison', *Liberator*, 2 December 1859, 190.

307 John Brown to Lydia Maria Child from Charlestown, 4 November 1859, WVStA, BBStColl., record ID 97, MS 02-0045AB, B, reprinted in Ruchames, *John*

to consolidate his reputation as an abolitionist martyr and convert and radicalize many of his pacifist critics, who like much of the abolitionist public in the North under the sway of the religious revivalist movement were very receptive to this self-interpretation as a martyr. Brown himself also seemed increasingly convinced of the historical value of his letters, for he increasingly directed them not only at the recipients and the nation, but also at posterity.

Regardless of how successful John Brown was in his publicity campaign from prison, he alone could not have succeeded in transforming the assessment of his violent action from failed, insignificant and ridiculous into admiration for the act and respect for the perpetrator. This required the support of people more versed in the field of interpretation and meaning who already enjoyed broad public attention in the United States. He needed the support of intellectuals who sympathized with him.

American icon: apotheosis through the intellectuals in the North

The sociologist Pierre Bourdieu described intellectuals as 'specialists in dealing with symbolic goods'[308] whose classic function was to 'enter the political arena in the name of values and truths'.[309] Although this characterization stems from the French context, it also applies to the group of anti-slavery intellectuals, authors, artists and clergymen from the North who contributed most to Brown's symbolic and political victory. Contrary to expectations, the Secret Six were temporarily unable to perform this task. Their absence was an indirect consequence of the military defeat at Harpers Ferry, for the sack of documents that fell into

---

Brown, 140; published as, for instance, 'Jno [*sic*] Brown's Letter to Lydia Maria Child', *Memphis Morning Enquirer*, 18 November 1859, 3; and 'Mrs. L. Maria Child: My dear Friend', *Anti-slavery Bugle*, 17 December 1859, 2.

308 Pierre Bourdieu, 'Une interprétation de la théorie de la religion selon Max Weber', *Archives européennes de sociologie* 12/1 (1971), 3–21, quoted in Christophe Charle, *Les intellectuels en Europe au XIXe siècle: Essai d'histoire comparée* (Paris: Seuil, 1996), 16.

309 Pierre Bourdieu, *The State Nobility: Elite Schools in the Field of Power*, trans. Lauretta C. Clough (Stanford: Stanford University Press, 2010), 339; and Charle, *Les intellectuels en Europe au XIXe siècle*, 16.

J. E. B. Stuart's hands at the Kennedy farm contained not only writings by John Brown but also letters and cheques he had received from the Secret Six and other supporters such as Frederick Douglass. Governor Wise released these letters as well for publication.[310] In addition, Hugh Forbes turned over the letters in his possession to the press. These sources revealed Brown's plans, along with the complicity of prominent figures from the North, with the press only too glad to reprint the documents.[311] The authorities and public were therefore immediately aware of the full extent of the conspiracy.

---

310 As an example, see the particularly active *New York Herald*: 'The Outbreak at Harper's Ferry – Complicity of Leading Abolitionists and Black Republicans' and 'The News', 20 October 1859, 6; 'Brown's Magazine' and 'The Harper's Ferry Abolition Outbreak and the Republican Party', 21 October 1859, 1, 4 respectively; 'Gov. Wise's Speech on the Insurrection', 23 October 1859, 1; 'The Abolition Conspiracy of Treason – The Revelations and Their Consequences' and 'The Exposure of the Nigger Worshipping Insurrectionists', 28 October 1859, 4. For reprints of the letters or texts of their contents, see, for instance, *New York Herald*: 'Letter from Gerrit Smith to Captain Brown', 21 October 1859, 1; 'The Harper's Ferry Outbreak . . . Correspondence of the Conspirators . . . Letters, Documents and Memoranda Found in John Brown's House Telling Many of the Secrets of the Conspiracy', 25 October 1859, 4; 'Insurrectionary Correspondence of Ossawatomie Brown and His Confederates', 25 October 1859, 6, and 'The Rise and Progress of the Bloody Outbreak at Harper's Ferry', 27 October 1859, 8. See also the published letters, reports on this practice of publishing letters, and analyses of the Brown network in the *New York Times*, *Daily Dispatch*, *Daily Exchange*, *Daily National Intelligencer*, *Daily Richmond Enquirer*, *Southern Argus* and *Memphis Morning Enquirer*; 'Incendiary Letters', *Douglass' Monthly*, Nov. 1859, 164; and 'More Letters of the Conspirators' and 'A Further Installment of Documents from Capt. Brown's Carpet Bag', *Daily National Intelligencer*, 26 October and 3 November 1859, both 2. See in addition Oates, *To Purge This Land*, 312; and McFeely, *Frederick Douglass*, 198.

311 See 'Colonel Hugh Forbes and His Connection with Ossawatomie Brown – A Chance of Further Disclosures', *New York Herald*, 26 October 1859, 1; 'More Disclosures from Harper's Ferry – Two Years' Secret History of Abolitionism', *New York Herald*, 27 October 1859, 6; 'Most Important Disclosures. Further Documentary Testimony Involving Seward, Sumner, Hale, Lawrence, Chase, Fletcher and Other Prominent Abolitionists – Correspondence between Colonel Forbes and His Abolitionist Friends – His Interviews with Seward, Sumner and Hale', *New York Herald*, 27 October 1859, 3; and 'More of the Forbes Correspondence', *New York Herald*, 28 October 1859, 2. For reprints of these letters, as well as reports and commentaries on them, see 'Practical Abolitionism', *New York Times*, 28 October 1859; 'Startling Revelations. Seward, Hale, Sumner and Other Republicans Implicated – Colonel Forbes' Correspondence Published', *Daily Richmond Enquirer*, 2 November 1859, 2; 'Senator Hale and Colonel Forbes', *Southern Argus*, 7 November 1859, 2; 'The Harper's Ferry Difficulty' and 'The Plan of the Insurrectionists', *Memphis Morning Enquirer*, 28 October and 1 November 1859, 3, 2 respectively.

This probably was part of John Brown's calculus. The fact that he did not destroy the letters from the Secret Six before heading to Harpers Ferry would, therefore, not have been the result of carelessness or naivety, but because he wanted – following Orsini's example – to create the impression of the greatest possible conspiracy in order to ensure political reactions. This is also supported by his advice as early as 1851 to the African American self-defence group the United States League of Gileadites, when he told its members they should immediately contact their most prominent white friends in the eventuality of a confrontation with slave hunters and US marshals, because 'that will effectually fasten upon them the suspicion of being connected with you, and will compel them to make a common cause with you, whether they would otherwise live up to their profession or not'. This, Brown had told the embattled African Americans at the time, 'would leave them no choice in the matter'.[312] Brown now heeded his own advice of taking the most influential patrons at their word. In the medium term his plan proved successful, as is shown by the many texts by Brown's supporters explaining and defending him – and thus themselves as well.[313] Initially, though, this approach had the opposite effect.

Because none of the Secret Six had expected public incrimination, they panicked, with the co-conspirators fearing that they, too, would be prosecuted in Virginia. Sanborn, Stearns and Howe fled temporarily to Canada and published denials in American newspapers; Smith had himself committed to the Utica Lunatic Asylum. Only Higginson and Parker (abroad in distant Europe because of tuberculosis) stood by their word.[314] The press and public followed the exculpation attempts and escape efforts of these New England public figures and the recurring appearance of new evidence against them with great

---

312 Brown, 'Words of Advice', 85.

313 This was also stated by Carton, *Patriotic Treason*, 296. For corresponding works by the Secret Six, see Sanborn, *The Life and Letters*; Sanborn, *Recollections*; Higginson, *Cheerful Yesterdays*; and by others Redpath, *The Public Life*; Hinton, *John Brown and His Men*; and Douglass, 'Life and Times'. For a critical view of these 'worshipful biographies', see Stephen B. Oates, 'John Brown and His Judges: A Critique of the Historical Literature', *Civil War History* 17 (1971), 5–7.

314 See Rossbach, *Ambivalent Conspirators*, Chapter 8; Higginson, *Cheerful Yesterdays*, 224–5; Schwartz, *Samuel Gridley Howe*, Chapter 15; Edelstein, *Strange Enthusiasm*, Chapter 13; Heller, *Portrait of an Abolitionist*, 106–8; Harlow, *Gerrit Smith*, 407–14; and Harlow, 'Gerrit Smith and the John Brown Raid', 51–4.

interest.[315] On the day after Brown's defeat an arrest warrant was issued for Frederick Douglass, who, as a fugitive slave and now famous civil rights champion and intellectual, had immediately become a person of particular interest to Governor Wise. Douglass only narrowly managed to escape arrest. As a precaution he, too, left for Canada, from where he set off on a lecture tour to England that had already been planned long since.[316]

Other abolitionist opinion makers stepped in to fill the gap left by the Secret Six. Initially, it was Brown's companions who responded, with the first being journalist James Redpath, who had visited Brown and his troop in Kansas.[317] An article by him appeared as early as Friday, 21 October 1859 (thus still in the week that began with the raid on Harpers Ferry), in the Republican-friendly *Boston Atlas & Daily Bee*, with additional ones following at short intervals. In them, he supported Brown's portrayal of himself in the interviews: John Brown was 'a man of the sternest integrity of character' who did not tolerate people 'of unprincipled or unworthy character' around him, 'a puritan in the Cromwellian sense of the word', and even 'the American Moses, predestined by Omnipotence' to lead the slaves in the southern states to

315 For reports about, for instance, Gerrit Smith, see, for example, 'Gerrit Smith's Guests', *Daily Richmond Enquirer*, 7 November 1859, 2; 'Personal', *New York Daily Tribune*, 14 November 1859, 5; 'Gerrit Smith Insane', *Harper's Weekly*, 19 November 1859, 742, and 26 November 1859, 758; and under this or a similar headline in the *Southern Argus*, 14 November 1859, 2; *Lowell Daily Citizen & News*, 10 November 1859, col. B; *Daily National Intelligencer*, 12 November 1859, col. B; *Daily News and Herald*, 16 November 1859, col. A; *Virginia Free Press*, 17 November 1859, col. D. For denials, see, for example, J. R. Giddings, 'Card from Joshua R. Giddings', *New York Herald*, 26 October 1859, 1; following the publication in the *North American*, 24 October 1859; and reports about the topic in *Memphis Morning Enquirer*, 25 October 1859, 3; and *Liberator*, 4 November 1859, 174. For further denials, see, for instance, Charles Bickley, 'Card from a "K. G. C."' To the Editor of the Herald', *New York Herald*, 30 October 1859, 1; John P. Hale, 'Senator John P. Hale's Card', *New York Herald*, 3 November 1859, 3; and 'Hon. John P. Hale and the Harper's Ferry Insurrection', *New York Herald*, 1 November 1859, 3. For commentaries, see, for example, 'The Object, the Design of the Expected Insurrection', *Lowell Daily Citizen*, 2 November 1859, col. A; and 'The Trial of Brown', *Daily Evening Bulletin*, 17 November 1859, col. D.

316 See Quarles, *Allies for Freedom*, 114–15; and McFeely, *Frederick Douglass*, 198–203. Douglass's explanation of his actions also made it into the press: 'Letter from Fred Douglass', *New York Herald*, 4 November 1859, col. D; and under a similar title in the *New York Daily Tribune*, 4 and 9 November 1859, both 6; *Liberator*, 11 November 1859, col. E; and the *Boston Daily Advertiser*, 4 November 1859, col. B.

317 See pp. 230–2 in this volume; and Rossbach, *Ambivalent Conspirators*, 175–6.

freedom, 'if necessary through the Red Sea of a civil war'. Redpath also distanced Brown from the Republican Party, writing that Brown despised Republicans: 'When the Republicans cried, Halt; John Brown said FORWARD, *march!* He was an Abolitionist of the Bunker Hill school. He had as little sympathy with Garrison as Seward.' Here Redpath contrasted Brown with the most famous advocate of non-violent abolitionism and the most prominent representative of the Republican Party in order to reclaim the legacy of the American Revolution for John Brown because Brown 'admired Nat Turner as well as George Washington. He could not see that it was heroic to fight against a petty tax on tea . . . and a crime to fight in favor of restoring an outraged race to every birthright.'[318] Brown became for Redpath the true heir to the American Revolution precisely because he did not shy away from the use of force to assert its ideas. Redpath thus supplied crucial catchwords for the interpretation and legitimization of the violent act.

The next person to take the floor was the former slave Henry Highland Garnet, who in 1843 had called for rebellion in his 'Address to the Slaves', a speech that at the time had greatly influenced Brown.[319] On Sunday, 23 October 1859, he preached to his congregation at the Shiloh Presbyterian Church in New York about slavery and liberty. According to the newspaper report, the church was full to overflowing, whereby the regular African American churchgoers were joined by many European Americans, including a number of prominent citizens. After his reading from the books of Moses and the biblical precepts on the treatment of slaves, Garnet came around to speaking about Brown. He stressed the selfless nature of the Harpers Ferry raid and pointed out the extraordinary fact that nineteen men were managing to preoccupy the entire nation, including the president. Like Redpath, Garnet justified the act of violence by the American Revolution. 'If John Brown was wrong in trying to secure liberty to the oppressed, then George Washington was wrong in giving liberty to this continent . . . The man

---

318 James Redpath, 'Notes on the Insurrection', *Boston Atlas & Daily Bee*, 21 October 1859, 1; reprinted in McKivigan, *Forgotten Firebrand*, 48–50. For republications, see, for instance, *New York Times*, 22 October 1859, 1; *Bangor Daily Whig & Courier*, 24 October 1859, col. B; *Liberator*, 28 October 1859, 1; *Charleston Tri-weekly Courier*, 1 November 1859, col. E; *Holmes County Republican*, 3 November 1859, 1; *Daily Evening Bulletin*, 17 November 1859, col. D; and *Kansas Herald of Freedom*, 19 November 1859, col. H.

319 See pp. 241–2 in this volume.

who condemns Brown must also condemn Washington.' As Brown had
done in his letters and speech before the court, Garnet pointed out that
the judgement of an action was all too often only a question of its success
and thus of power and the contingency of history. 'Brown is condemned
because he failed, and Washington would have been hanged if he had
failed in the good work he attempted so successfully.' Brown's motives,
hower, were pure. 'Brown obeyed the Divine command in endeavoring
to release the oppressed . . . Where was the man who could find fault
with him for so doing?' Moreover, Garnet included Brown and his
African and European American comrades-in-arms in the history of
the blacks' struggle for freedom in the United States. He judged the
outcome of the raid 'a blessing to the slaves' because thousands of whites
now stood on the side of the slaves. Garnet was certain that Brown's
work would meet with success and that the end of slavery in North
America was near.[320]

Garnet was not the only one who preached that Sunday about John
Brown and the Harpers Ferry raid. Other ministers in the North who
did not know Brown also dealt with the conflict between freedom and
slavery in their homilies, referring directly or indirectly to his violent
act. With their efforts to interpret and make sense out of the event, the
clergymen were responding to an urgent need for orientation within
their congregations. Extensive coverage of these church services by the
press transformed them into important contributions to the national
discussion.[321]

The first among New England's elite to step forward was Wendell
Phillips. Like Brown, he was an orthodox Calvinist. The offspring of
one of Boston's best families, Phillips had ancestors who had come to
America together with John Winthrop on the *Arbella* and shaped
public life in Massachusetts since 1630. He attended Boston Latin

---

320 'The "Irrepressible Conflict" in the Pulpit', *New York Herald*, 24 October 1859, 2.
321 See, for instance, the article, 'Service at Hope Chapel', on the sermon by
George F. Noyes at the 'Independent Church', Hope Chapel, 720 Broadway, New York, in
New York Herald, 24 October 1859, 2; the report on Henry Ward Beecher's sermon to his
congregation on Orange Street, Brooklyn NY, 'Beecher on the Harper's Ferry Outbreak',
Douglass' Monthly, November 1859, 167; the article '"The Murder at Harper's Ferry."
Discourse by the Rev. Mr. Remington at Brooklyn', *New York Daily Tribune*, 14 November
1859, 5; and commentary on these sermons titled 'The Pulpit and the Rebellion', *Daily
Richmond Enquirer*, 26 October 1859, 2; and in the *Charleston Mercury*, 27 October
1859, 1. Many sermons on the following Sunday also dealt with the Harpers Ferry raid.

School as well as Harvard University and Law School with Senator Charles Sumner and belonged, like the Secret Six, to Boston's abolitionist, intellectual elite.[322] Phillips was among those who had met Brown in 1857 just after his return from Kansas and introduction into the networks of the New England elite by Sanborn. Phillips had aided Brown with some money and met him several times during his preparations for the Subterranean Pass Way plan, so he was informed about the general gist of the undertaking. Unlike the Secret Six, however, Phillips had maintained a certain distance from Brown, but he now became active because his friends and colleagues were faltering and paralyzed by public exposure. Together with the unshakable Higginson he organized help for Brown's family, and with John A. Andrews, a Republican lawyer who would soon be elected governor of Massachusetts, he arranged legal counsel for Brown and his volunteers. Moreover, the three of them made plans for Brown to be kidnapped from the jail or gallows, with the liberation to fall to German Forty-Eighters, who were to be armed with 'Orsini bombs'. Brown, however, rejected all plans to free him.[323]

Phillips's decisive contribution to the John Brown cause, though, was his lectures. The handsome and elegant Bostonian, who was known as a brilliant speaker, had, since the murder of Lovejoy, been travelling throughout the northern states on behalf of the anti-slavery movement. He now placed his talent at the service of John Brown because he, like Garnet, was convinced that the raid on Harpers Ferry had heralded the end of slavery in the United States. He held his first lecture, titled 'The Lesson of the Hour', at the Plymouth Church in Brooklyn on Tuesday, 1 November 1859. The church of Henry Ward Beecher was filled far beyond capacity on this occasion. Phillips subsequently toured with this lecture through New England and the Northwest.[324]

---

322 See Irving H. Bartlett, *Wendell Phillips: Brahmin Radical* (Boston: Beacon Press, 1961); and James Brewer Stewart, *Wendell Phillips: Liberty's Hero* (Baton Rouge: Louisiana State University Press, 1986).

323 See Bartlett, *Wendell Phillips*, Chapter 12; Stewart, *Wendell Phillips*, 201–8; Higginson, *Cheerful Yesterdays*, 226–8; Edelstein, *Strange Enthusiasm*, 227–30; and Horwitz, *Midnight Rising*, 228.

324 See 'The Virginia Rebellion . . . Wendell Phillips on the Outbreak', *New York Times*, 2 November 1859, 1; reprinted slightly changed as 'Harper's Ferry' in Wendell Phillips, *Speeches, Lectures, and Letters* (Boston: James Redpath, 1863), 263–88. On the lecture tour see Stewart, *Wendell Phillips*, 206; and the reports ' "The Lesson of the

Phillips began with the words, 'The Lesson of the Hour? I think the lesson of the hour is insurrection,' sparking wild excitement among the audience. He then took co-responsibility for Brown's violence: 'Insurrection of thought always precedes the insurrection of arms. The last twenty years have been insurrection of thought. We seem to be entering on a new phase of the great moral American struggle.'[325] Phillips clearly placed the Harpers Ferry raid in the tradition of the American Revolution.

Phillips also pointed out that it was not Brown who embodied the insurgent principle, but rather the state of Virginia, for any entity that calls itself a government, but does not fulfill the responsibilities of a government – protecting its citizens and ensuring justice – is not a government. It was the machinations of the 'barbarous horde who . . . imprison women for teaching children to read, prohibit the Bible, sell men on the auction-block, abolish marriage, condemn half their women to prostitution, and devote themselves to the breeding of human beings for sale' that represented the true 'chronic insurrection', the insurrection against all morality. John Brown, therefore, had the right to hang Governor Wise and not vice versa.[326] Phillips thus denied the slaveholding states any claim to legitimacy, with John Brown's act of violence becoming the morally legitimate act, or for that matter the only, legitimate act. 'Resistance to tyrants is obedience to God,' he said, applying a remark originally attributed to Thomas Jefferson to Brown.[327]

The newspaper articles, sermons and lectures by radical abolitionists, such as Redpath, Garnet and Phillips, had their audience and reached a broad public through printing and reprinting. This, however, should not

Hour": Address of Wendell Phillips on the Insurrection at Harper's Ferry', *Douglass' Monthly*, Dec. 1859, 182–4; 'Wendell Phillips at Brooklyn (News)', *Boston Daily Advertiser*, 4 November 1859, col. B; 'The Following Is a Sketch of the Remarks of Wendell Phillips upon Insurrection, Delivered in Brooklyn (N.Y.) on Wednesday Evening . . . (News)', *Boston Daily Advertiser*, 4 November 1859, col. C; 'Extraordinary Address of Wendell Phillips on the Insurrection; Eulogy on Mad Brown – The Plot the Legitimate Fruit of Anti-slavery Doctrines – Brown a Martyr to Law, Justice and Humanity, &c. (News)', *New York Herald*, 2 November 1859, col. B.

325 'The Virginia Rebellion', *New York Times*, 2 November 1859, 1; and Phillips, 'Harper's Ferry', 263.

326 'The Virginia Rebellion', *New York Times*, 2 November 1859, 1; and Phillips, 'Harper's Ferry', 272.

327 'The Virginia Rebellion', *New York Times*, 2 November 1859, 1; and Phillips, 'Harper's Ferry', 271. On the question of legitimacy in a broader theoretical and historical context, see Dietze, 'Legitimacy and Security from a Historical Perspective', especially 157–8.

obscure the fact that these were only isolated voices, which remained the exception in comparison to the general repudiation of the violence initiated by John Brown. With their arguments the radical abolitionists were able to express the thoughts and feelings of those who already sympathized with Brown's positions. By encouraging and reinforcing such sympathizers in their convictions, the abolitionists made an important contribution to Brown's cause, which was also theirs. Their ability to influence the opinions of the moderate public in order to persuade new segments of the population was limited. In this context greater weight should be given to interpretations by intellectuals and writers who had only met Brown a few times and until then had hardly been visible as abolitionists, but who had for some time enjoyed the attention and admiration of the American reading public.

First and foremost among these latently anti-slavery intellectuals were the Transcendentalists. They comprised a group of philosophers and writers influenced by German idealism who lived in and around Concord, near Boston, among them Henry David Thoreau and the 'sage of Concord' and 'Plato of America', Ralph Waldo Emerson.[328] 'No one shaped the John Brown image more strongly than the Transcendentalists, the nation's most prominent intellectuals. Their admiration of him [John Brown] laid the basis for the later widespread deification of him in the North,' was the assessment of English and American studies specialist David S. Reynolds. Without the Transcendentalists' public statements of support for John Brown, he might easily have remained a 'forgettable oddball', a laughable, albeit tragic, figure.[329] Not only were these

328 See Philip F. Gura, *American Transcendentalism: A History* (New York: Hill and Wang, 2008); and Lawrence Buell, *The American Transcendentalists: Essential Writings* (New York: Modern Library, 2006). On Thoreau specifically, see Walter Roy Harding, *The Days of Henry Thoreau* (New York: Alfred A. Knopf, 1965); on Emerson, see Robert D. Richardson, *Emerson: The Mind on Fire: A Biography* (Berkeley: University of California Press, 1995), xi; and Ronald A. Bosco and Joel Myerson (eds.), *Emerson in His Own Time: A Biographical Chronicle of His Life, Drawn from Recollections, Interviews, and Memoirs by Family, Friends, and Associates* (Iowa City: University of Iowa Press, 2003), 111.

329 Reynolds, *John Brown*, 214–15. See also Harold K. Bush, 'Emerson, John Brown, and "Doing the Word": The Enactment of Political Religion at Harpers Ferry, 1859', in T. Gregory Garvey (ed.), *The Emerson Dilemma* (Athens: University of Georgia Press, 2001), 197–217; Andrew Taylor, 'Consenting to Violence: Henry David Thoreau, John Brown, and the Transcendent Intellectual', in Taylor and Herrington, *The Afterlife of John Brown*; Stoneham, *John Brown and the Era of Literary Confrontation*; and Janet

intellectuals responsible for the fact that Brown was soon celebrated as a martyr and hero in the North, but they were also the first to attempt to understand his act of violence and to place it in a larger context. Their statements are therefore significant in two respects – as relevant contributions to John Brown's politico-symbolic victory and as commentaries by the first analysts of this new form of political violence.

As with John Brown and the Secret Six, the Transcendentalists' remarks and assessments resulted from a process of political radicalization that began in the 1830s. For both groups the stages of this process can be outlined: the murder of Lovejoy, the expulsion of the Cherokees, the Mexican–American War, the Fugitive Slave Act, the kidnapping and rendition of African Americans from the North to the South, *Uncle Tom's Cabin*, Kansas, and the Supreme Court's *Dred Scott* decision. Thoreau, for example, withheld a portion of his taxes in 1846 in protest against a state that protected slavery, spent a night in jail as punishment, and explained the intentions of his act in the lecture 'The Relation of the Individual to the State'. In the address, which would later become famous as 'On the Duty of Civil Disobedience', he asserted the right of the individual to follow the higher law of personal conscience.[330] Thoreau thus demonstrated a clear sense for symbolic acts and their interpretation as early as the mid-1840s.

In contrast to the Secret Six, the Transcendentalists cultivated a marked individualism and refrained from commenting on political topics and getting actively involved. Moreover, Emerson, if not others as well, was not free of racism. So it was initially the women in Concord – especially Lidian Emerson, Henry's mother Cynthia Thoreau, and his sisters Sophia and Helen – who became active and gradually persuaded their men or sons or brothers that they could no longer stand idly by. Cynthia Thoreau involved her son quite directly. She ran a private boarding house where she regularly hid slaves fleeing to Canada, and it was up to her son to make sure they reached their destination safely.[331]

Kemper Beck, *Creating the John Brown Legend: Emerson, Thoreau, Douglass, Child and Higginson in Defense of the Raid on Harpers Ferry* (Jefferson: McFarland, 2009).

330 Henry David Thoreau, 'On the Duty of Civil Disobedience', in *Thoreau: Collected Essays and Poems*, ed. Elizabeth Hall Witherell (New York: Library of America, 2001), 203–24.

331 On Thoreau's and Emerson's political thought and their relationship to the antislavery movement, see Gura, *American Transcendentalism*, 243–8; and Beck, *Creating*

Thoreau, Emerson and the Transcendentalist reformer and educator Amos Bronson Alcott had met John Brown for the first time in March 1857. In his quest to help John Brown establish connections in New England, Sanborn had also introduced him to his circle in Concord and organized a speaking opportunity for him to tell about his experiences in Kansas. Sanborn, who lived across from the Thoreaus and usually joined them for the midday meal, had brought Brown along to dine with them and left him immersed in conversation with Thoreau while he attended to his afternoon teaching duties at the school. Ralph Waldo Emerson had happened to come by Thoreau's later, and the three of them had gone over to his house to continue the discussion. That evening Thoreau and Emerson had attended Brown's talk with Alcott. This was repeated in May 1859 when Brown spoke after returning from his second Kansas trip. On this visit Emerson had even invited Brown to stay as a guest at his home.[332]

Emerson, Thoreau and Alcott were impressed by Brown, as their journal entries indicate. Alcott emphasized his 'courage and religious earnestness'; Thoreau considered him a 'man of rare common-sense and directness of speech as of action, a Transcendentalist above all, a man of ideas and principles'; and Emerson wrote, 'Captain John Brown of Kansas gave a good account of himself in the Town Hall, last night, to a meeting of Citizens. One of his good points was, the folly of the peace party in Kansas.'[333] The authors of 'Nature', 'Self-Reliance', 'On the Duty of Civil Disobedience' and 'Slavery in Massachusetts' found in Brown the principled soldier, the Cromwell, the embodiment of the hero, whom they, too, admired because of the Cromwell biographies by Headley and by Carlyle (a personal friend of Emerson's). In their view

---

the *John Brown Legend*, Chapters 3–4. On Emerson, see also Len Gougeon, *Virtue's Hero: Emerson, Antislavery, and Reform* (Athens: University of Georgia Press, 1990); and Garvey, *The Emerson Dilemma*. On the Thoreau household's involvement and the famous night in jail, see Harding, *The Days of Henry Thoreau*, especially 21, 73–4, 119–20, 175–6, 195–6, 200–8, 314–19.

332 See Sanborn, *Recollections*, 163–4; Harding, *The Days of Henry Thoreau*, 415–16, Oates, *To Purge This Land*, 196–7; and Beck, *Creating the John Brown Legend*, 40–1.

333 Amos Bronson Alcott, *The Journals of Bronson Alcott* (Port Washington: Kennikat Press, 1966), 315; Thoreau, 'Oct. 22', 420; and an 'undated entry' by Ralph Waldo Emerson in *Journals and Miscellaneous Notebooks of Ralph Waldo Emerson*, ed. Susan Sutton Smith and Harrison Hayford (Cambridge, MA: Belknap Press, 1978), 125.

Brown epitomized the ideas of their philosophy and enacted what they wrote and talked about.[334]

The Transcendentalists were profoundly affected by Brown's raid on Harpers Ferry. Emerson wrote to his brother, 'We are all very well, in spite of the sad Harpers Ferry business, which interests us all who had Brown for our guest twice.'[335] And Louisa May Alcott, daughter of A. Bronson Alcott and well-known author of children's books, noted to a friend in early November,

> What are your ideas on the Harpers Ferry matter? If you are *my* Dolphus [a figure from Dickens's *The Haunted Man and the Ghost's Bargain: A Fancy for Christmas*] you are full of admiration for old Brow[n]s courage & pity for his probable end. We are boiling over with excitement here for many of our people (Anti Slavery I mean) are concerned in it. We have a daily stampede for papers, & a nightly indignation meeting over the wickedness of our country, & the cowardice of the human race. I'm afraid mother will die of spontane-ous combustion if things are not set right soon.[336]

For an entire week Thoreau read all the articles by and about John Brown in any newspaper he could obtain. What he read occupied him so much that he slept poorly and kept paper and pen nearby to note down his thoughts in the dark.[337]

---

334 See Ralph Waldo Emerson, 'Nature' and 'Self Reliance', in *Emerson: Essays and Lectures* (New York: Viking Press, 1983), 9–12, 257–82 respectively; and Thoreau, 'On the Duty of Civil Disobedience' and 'Slavery in Massachusetts', in *Thoreau: Collected Essays*, 203–24, 333–48 respectively. On their relation to Brown, see Reynolds, *John Brown*, Chapter 9; and Beck, *Creating the John Brown Legend*, Chapters 3–4.

335 Ralph Waldo Emerson to his brother William Emerson, 23 October 1859, from Concord, reprinted in Ralph L. Rusk and Eleanor M. Tilton (eds.), *The Letters of Ralph Waldo Emerson*, 6 vols. (New York: Columbia University Press, 1939–95), vol. 5, 178.

336 Louisa May Alcott to Alfred Whitman, 8 November [1859], from Concord, in Joel Myerson, Daniel Shealy and Madeleine B. Stern (eds.), *The Selected Letters of Louisa May Alcott* (Athens: University of Georgia Press, 1995), 49.

337 Thoreau, 'A Plea for John Brown', in *Thoreau: Collected Essays*, 396, 401, 404. Thoreau's journal entries from 19 to 22 October 1859 comprise 10,016 words on the topic of John Brown. See Henry David Thoreau, *The Writings of Henry David Thoreau: Journal*, vol. 12: *March 2–November 30, 1859*, ed. Bradford Torrey (Boston: Houghton Mifflin, 1906), 400–39; and in that regard Bradley P. Dean and Ronald Wesley Hoag, 'Thoreau's Lectures after *Walden*: An Annotated Calendar', *Studies in the American Renaissance* (1996), 310–11; and Harding, *The Days of Henry Thoreau*, 416–17.

Moved by his need to share his view of events, Thoreau discussed the matter with his family and then sent a boy around town to invite the townspeople to a talk on John Brown he would hold that Sunday evening. Members of the Abolition Committee and the Republican Party attempted to dissuade him from speaking, considering it premature to make a statement. Sanborn also advised him to wait 'until there was a better feeling among the people' because a defence of John Brown could be dangerous. To such objections Thoreau responded, 'I did not send to you for advice, but to announce that I am to speak.'[338] With his talk on 30 October 1859 at the well-filled First Parish House in Concord he became the first Transcendentalist to side with Brown. In the next few days he gave the same lecture to an audience of 2,500 people at the Tremont Temple in Boston as part of the Fraternity Lectures initiated by Theodore Parker and again in Higginson's home city of Worcester, not far from Boston.[339]

Thoreau pursued two goals with his lecture 'The Character and Actions of Capt. John Brown', which later appeared as 'A Plea for John Brown'. Similarly to Jules Favre in his defence of Orsini, he wanted to portray Brown in a manner that did the man justice. He was concerned as well with correcting 'the tone' of the news coverage of the raid on Harpers Ferry.[340] To this end he invoked several typical images – John Brown as a New England farmer in the tradition of Lexington Common

---

338 Ralph Waldo Emerson, 'Thoreau', in *Lectures and Bibliographical Sketches* (1883) (Boston: Houghton Mifflin, 1904), 460.

339 On the lecture in Concord, see Dean and Hoag, 'Thoreau's Lectures', 308–14. Thoreau held the lecture in Boston on 1 November 1859, substituting for Frederick Douglass, who was scheduled to speak that evening but was unable to because he had fled the United States. See Dean and Hoag, 'Thoreau's Lectures', Lecture 66, 314–20; Harding, *The Days of Henry Thoreau*, 418–20; the extensive coverage in the *Boston Daily Advertiser*, 2 November 1859, 1; *Liberator*, 4 November 1859, 174; and *New York Herald*, 5 November 1859, 2; and Kenneth Walter Cameron, *Transcendental Log: Fresh Discoveries in Newspapers Concerning Emerson, Thoreau, Alcott, and Others of the American Literary Renaissance, Arranged Annually for Half a Century from 1832* (Hartford: Transcendental Books, 1973), 134. On the lecture in Worcester, see Dean and Hoag, 'Thoreau's Lectures', Lecture 67, 320–4; and Sanborn, *The Life and Letters*, 506.

340 Thoreau, 'A Plea for John Brown', 396; and even more emphatically in 'Fraternity Lectures: "Captain John Brown of Ossawatomie," by Henry D. Thoreau', *New York Herald*, 5 November 1859, 2. See in this regard also Stoneham, *John Brown*, Chapter 4; and Jack Turner, 'Performing Conscience: Thoreau, Political Action, and the Plea for John Brown', *Political Theory* 33/4 (2005), 448–71.

322   The Invention of Terrorism

and Bunker Hill, as the spartan Puritan and Cromwellian soldier – but also made several original observations garnered from his conversation in Concord, such as Brown's faith in the Union and the United States Constitution, which were hindered solely by slavery, and his fundamental aversion to militarism.[341] Thoreau, similarly to the Secret Six, was impressed by Brown as a person with strength of character, common sense and life experience, and as an autodidact who knew what counts in life: 'He did not go to the college called Harvard, good old Alma Mater as she is. He was not fed on the pap that is there furnished.' And he quoted Brown, '"I know no more of grammar than one of your calves."' But,' continued Thoreau, 'he went to the great university of the West, where he sedulously pursued the study of Liberty,' and 'he finally commenced the public practice of Humanity in Kansas, as you all know. Such were his humanities, and not any study of grammar. He would have left a Greek accent slanting the wrong way, and righted up a falling man.'[342] For Thoreau, Brown was a counterintellectual, a doer who effected change through his actions and deeds.

Following these characterizations Thoreau analysed and commented on the press coverage of the raid on Harpers Ferry, noting that, with the exception of one article in the *Boston Atlas & Bee* (by Redpath), he had not been able to find 'a single expression of sympathy' for Brown and his recruits.[343] He criticized the condemnation of Brown in the Republican and abolitionist newspapers (the Democratic press was not worth the effort) and the denials and exculpation attempts by those caught in the judiciary's spotlights. They were all only concerned with their little egotistical interests and blind to the grandeur of what was occurring right in front their eyes. 'When a man stands up serenely against the condemnation and vengeance of mankind ... [T]he spectacle is a sublime one, – didn't ye know it, ye Liberators, ye Tribunes, ye Republicans? ... Do yourselves the honor to recognize him [John Brown]. He needs none of your respect.'[344] With his choice of words

---

341 Thoreau, 'A Plea for John Brown', 396–400, 396, 397, recollection of conversation with Brown, 396.

342 Ibid., 397–8.

343 Ibid., 404. The reference to the *Boston Atlas & Daily Bee* is found in the report 'Fraternity Lectures. "Captain John Brown of Ossawatomie", by Henry D. Thoreau', *New York Herald*, 5 November 1859, 2.

344 Thoreau, 'A Plea for John Brown', 407.

Thoreau also rebuked the efforts of the anti-slavery press and the Republicans to distance themselves from Brown simply because of attacks from Democratic newspapers, for in doing so they disregarded the symbolic dimension of his actions.

In Thoreau's view, this negative coverage also ignored the existence of considerable support in the North for Brown and his act: 'There are at least as many as two or three individuals to a town throughout the North, who think much as the present speaker does about him and his enterprise. I do not hesitate to say that they are an important and growing party.'[345] And it was precisely this sympathy for Brown and his violent act that counteracted all attempts to marginalize and depoliticize the raid on Harpers Ferry, for 'anxious politicians' could claim 'that only seventeen white men and five negroes were concerned in the late enterprise, but their very anxiety to prove this might suggest to themselves that all is not told'. According to Thoreau, they were 'so anxious because of a dim consciousness of the fact, which they do not distinctly face, that at least a million of the free inhabitants of the United States would have rejoiced if it had succeeded. They at most only criticise the tactics.'[346] In his analysis Thoreau analysed and verbalized what Brown and the Secret Six had anticipated, namely that the violent act was an event that would reveal the sympathy for a slave revolt and articulate public opinion in the North. And it was precisely in this sympathy for the violent perpetrators that they had seen the actual significance of the raid.

Thoreau had carefully observed the importance and effect of the interviews, whose content and reproduction in the press had deeply affected him, with the immediacy of the still unfamiliar text form having a noticeable impact. He repeatedly drew on the interviews to counter the judgement that Brown was insane. Explaining their role in Brown's cause, he noted that John Brown 'could afford to lose his Sharps' rifles, while he retained his faculty of speech, a Sharps rifle of infinitely surer and longer range. And *The New York Herald* reports the conversation "*verbatim*"! 'It does not know of what undying words it is made the vehicle.'[347] To reinforce his appraisal, Thoreau cited several of Brown's statements that in his opinion put the interviewers on a par with the

---

345 Ibid., 401.
346 Ibid., 401.
347 Ibid., 408–9.

The Invention of Terrorism

inglorious likes of Pontius Pilate, the Inquisition and Hermann Gessler, the Habsburg baliff in the William Tell legend.

Thoreau also analysed the functioning of the violent provocation in detail. Just as the conversations with the captured Brown revealed the Washington and Virginia politicians as tyrants, the raid on Harpers Ferry exposed the character of the American government: 'I regard this event as a touchstone designed to bring out, with glaring distinctness, the character of this government. We needed to be thus assisted to see it by the light of history.' For Thoreau the raid on Harpers Ferry was the provocation that forced the United States government to reveal its true self to the light of history through its response. What emerged was a government that defended bondage and injustice and sentenced to death those who acted in the name of freedom and justice – an illegitimate, tyrannical government no better than the European monarchies that subjugated freedom-loving peoples:

> When a government puts forth its strength on the side of injustice, as ours to maintain Slavery and kill the liberators of the slave, it reveals itself a merely brute force, or worse, a demoniacal force . . . It is more manifest than ever that tyranny rules. I see this government to be effectually allied with France and Austria in oppressing mankind.[348]

For Thoreau, it was John Brown's revolt against this tyranny that made him 'the most American of us all' and even ranked him above the heroes of the American Revolution, for they had fought against an external foe of the republic, whereas he had dared to confront his own country, a task that by implication was infinitely more difficult.[349] Just as Orsini, in Favre's opinion, had remained true to the legacy of the French Revolution, Thoreau felt Brown had remained faithful to the ideas and legacy of the American Revolution.

In his lecture, Henry David Thoreau declared violence to be a legitimate means in the struggle to free the slaves. 'It was his peculiar doctrine,' he said in recounting one of his conversations with Brown, 'that a man has a perfect right to interfere by force with the slaveholder, in order to rescue the slave.' And referring to what the Harpers Ferry

---

348 Ibid., 410.
349 Ibid., 407, 397.

raid had revealed to him, Thoreau added, 'I agree with him,' for Brown's form of 'philanthropy' was the only promising path.[350] Violence, in addition, was not as unusual in America as all sides would claim and was omnipresent in everyday life in the 'peaceful' society: 'We preserve the so-called peace of our community by deeds of petty violence every day. Look at the policeman's billy and handcuffs! Look at the jail! Look at the gallows!' Even the use of many forms of deadly force was socially sanctioned. John Brown, on the other hand, had for once employed violence for a cause approved of by Thoreau, who gauged violence according to its purpose: 'The question is not about the weapon, but the spirit in which you use it.'[351] In Thoreau's eyes, there was good and bad, legitimate and illegitimate, violence, distinguishable by its intention. John Brown's act of violence was good because it had exposed the tyrannical nature of the US government and promised an increase in freedom.

Finally, Thoreau defended John Brown against the disparaging judgement that his group had been too small, an assessment often cited as proof of Brown's insanity. In Thoreau's opinion the low number of insurrectionists was inherent to the undertaking: 'When were the good and the brave ever in a majority? Would you have had him wait till that time came? – till you and I came over to him?'[352] In this way Thoreau confronted his listeners with their own lack of courage and readiness to sacrifice. He emphasized that Brown's force consisted of a chosen few:

> His company was small indeed, because few could be found worthy to pass muster. Each one who there laid down his life for the poor and oppressed was a picked man, culled out of many thousands, if not millions; apparently a man of principle, of rare courage, and devoted humanity; ready to sacrifice his life at any moment for the benefit of his fellow-man.[353]

Thoreau doubted an equal number of worthy men could be found anywhere in the country.

---

350 Ibid., 413.
351 Ibid., 413.
352 Ibid., 412.
353 Ibid., 412.

From chosenness and self-sacrifice, Thoreau came to compare John Brown and his volunteers with Jesus Christ. In his lecture he repeatedly evoked Christian associations, pointing out, for instance, that Brown was to have had 'as many at least as twelve disciples' or by referring to him as the 'redeemer' of the slaves.[354] Towards the end of his talk, he became explicit: 'You who pretend to care for Christ crucified, consider what you are about to do to him who offered himself to be the savior of four millions of men.'[355] And even before Brown had been condemned to death, he proclaimed, 'Some eighteen hundred years ago Christ was crucified; this morning, perchance, Captain Brown was hung. These are the two ends of a chain which is not without its links. He is not Old Brown any longer; he is an Angel of Light.'[356] Thoreau placed responsibility for the legacy arising from that in the hands of his audience. He, like Jules Favre in the case of Orsini, did not want to plead for John Brown's life, but for 'his character – his immortal life';[357] it was no longer Brown who was responsible for his legacy, but rather the people of the United States. If his audience had neither the courage nor the commitment to fight actively against slavery, they should at least do Brown justice and stand up for his legacy and cause.

Thoreau's plea for John Brown impressed his audience in Concord, and the newspapers reported on the lecture's enthusiastic reception in Boston and Worcester as well. Emerson wrote that Thoreau's 'earnest eulogy of the hero was heard by all respectfully, by many with a sympathy that surprised themselves', and his son Edward observed that many 'who had come to scoff remained to pray'. Emerson warmly recommended the speaker and his lecture to the organizer of the Fraternity Lectures in Boston.[358]

In the following week, Emerson then also expressed his opinion of Brown and continued the apotheosis. He initially used his speaking

---

354 Ibid., 408, 415, 413.
355 Ibid., 415.
356 Ibid., 416.
357 Ibid., 416.
358 On the reception of the lecture, see Dean and Hoag, 'Thoreau's Lectures', 312–13, 316–20, 321–4. The quotation from Edward Waldo Emerson is in Dean and Hoag, 'Thoreau's Lectures', 313; the quotation from his father in Emerson, 'Thoreau', 460–1. The recommendation is from Ralph Waldo Emerson to Charles Wesley Slack, 31 October 1859, from Concord, reprinted as Appendix A in Stoneham, *John Brown*, 165.

invitation at the Fraternity Lectures on the Tuesday after Thoreau's appearance to underscore his friend's remarks. Emerson asked that people recognize virtue when they saw it and 'not cry with the fools, "*Madman!*" when a hero passes'.[359] He told of courageous men who stood up against tyranny and inquisition, and ranked Brown among them as 'that new saint, than whom none purer or more brave was ever led by love of man into conflict and death'.[360] Emerson ultimately also continued Thoreau's likening of Brown to Christ, describing him as 'a new saint, waiting yet his martyrdom', who, should he suffer this martyrdom, would make the 'gallows glorious like the cross'. This latter formulation, which Emerson had borrowed from abolitionist Mattie Griffith, met with prolonged applause. It struck home, received wide coverage in the press, and subsequently inspired many comparisons between the cross and the gallows.[361]

Ten days later, Emerson made his own contribution to the reflection on John Brown at a meeting to raise aid for the Brown family. Two thousand people had come to the Tremont Temple for the event. In his talk Emerson began by stressing Brown's roots in the Puritan faith and American fight for independence, his ties to Plymouth Rock and the Revolution and his belief in the Golden Rule and Declaration of Independence.[362] This characterization served him as the starting point for describing Brown as an idealist, an idealist for whom there was a unity of idea and action, of

359 'Emerson on Courage', *Liberator*, 18 November 1859, 1; and Cameron, *Transcendental Log*, 136. For the venue, time and title, see the announcement 'Fraternity Lectures. Sixth Lecture this (Tuesday) Evening', *Boston Daily Advertiser*, 8 November 1859, 2. On the lecture see also Gougeon, *Virtue's Hero*, 242; Stoneham, *John Brown*, 123–4; and Beck, *Creating the John Brown Legend*, 121.

360 'Emerson on Courage', *Liberator*, 18 November 1859, 1.

361 On Emerson's use of Griffith's subsequently well-known formulation, see Gougeon, *Virtue's Hero*, 242. For the exact quotation of this formulation, see, for instance, 'Personal . . . Ralph Waldo Emerson, in His Lecture at the Tremont Temple, Boston', *New York Daily Tribune*, 14 November 1859, 5; 'In the Course of His Brilliant Lecture on Courage', *Anti-slavery Bugle*, 19 November 1859, 3; 'Communications', *Anti-slavery Bugle*, 17 November 1859, 2.

362 Emerson, 'Speech at a Meeting to Aid John Brown's Family', in *Transcendental Log*, 137; and Ralph Waldo Emerson, *Emerson's Antislavery Writings*, ed. Len Gougeon and Joel Myerson (New Haven: Yale University Press, 1995), 118. See Gougeon, *Virtue's Hero*, 243–6; Stoneham, *John Brown*, 125–40; and Beck, *Creating the John Brown Legend*, 122. For an account, see 'The John Brown Fund', *New York Daily Tribune*, 21 November 1859, 7; and on other similar initiatives 'Boston Caring for Brown's Family. Public Meeting for Their Relief', *New York Daily Tribune*, 21 November 1859, 7.

thought and deed: 'He believed in his ideas to that extent, that he existed to put them all into action.'[363] Brown was also an idealist in Emerson's eyes because he discerned ideas and substance behind the forms: 'He saw how deceptive the forms are.' Emerson related this ability to political life: 'We fancy, in Massachusetts, that we are free ... Great wealth, great population, men of talent in the executive, on the bench – all the forms right, – and yet, life and freedom are not safe,' said Emerson, alluding to the Fugitive Slave Act and the kidnapping of African Americans. 'Why? Because the judges rely on the forms, and do not, like John Brown, use their eyes to see the fact behind the forms,' because these judges did not understand they were not serving the law and justice by merely complying with forms when dealing with infringements of the spirit and idea of law, trial and procedure, but rather doing 'substantial injustice'. For example, they enforced the Fugitive Slave Act, which retained the semblance of a hearing, but provided African Americans no opportunity to defend themselves against false accusations. Thus the very application of the law and procedures resulted in a perversion of justice. The task of a good judge was 'to secure good government', according to Emerson.[364] 'If judges cannot find law enough to maintain the sovereignty of the State, and to protect the life and freedom of every inhabitant not a criminal,' then they are 'of no more use than idiots,' in spite of all their learnedness and respectability.[365]

The lectures of Thoreau and Emerson illustrate the impact of John Brown's public outreach. Thoreau's lecture also represents an early analysis of the form of violence practised by John Brown that contains key elements of current findings in contemporary terrorism research. First, Thoreau analysed at this early stage the social logic of provocation as an unexpected breach of norms that drew the slaveholding states into open conflict and caused them to react in ways that morally discredited them.[366] Second, he recognized the fundamental importance of communication and the media, which allowed Brown to convey his message to

---

363 Emerson, 'Speech', in *Antislavery Writings*, 119.

364 Ibid., 119.

365 Ibid., 120.

366 This formulation draws on Rainer Paris's definition of provocation as 'a deliberate, surprising norm violation intended to draw the other into an open conflict and prompt a reaction that morally discredits and exposes that party in the eyes of third parties'. Rainer Paris, 'Der kurze Atem der Provokation', in *Stachel und Speer*, 58.

the nation. Third, he realized that a positive reception of Brown's act of violence by the population would decide the success of the Harpers Ferry raid and he saw that such sympathy existed and understood the explosive power it harboured for the political conditions in the United States. He knew that awakening and maintaining this sympathy was an interactive process that he could contribute to. His interpretation of the violence in Harpers Ferry contributed to the success or failure of the action.[367] Fourth, Thoreau recognized (and justified) the individual character of John Brown's violence. With his admiration of the man of action who courageously acts to change society in desired and necessary ways, with his differentiation between good and bad violence, and with his reverence for the martyr Brown, who sacrificed himself for the oppressed, he informed patterns of interpreting terrorist violence that are still present today. Emerson, like Thoreau, severely criticized his country's political institutions. But, in his analysis, he focused less on the violence and more on its structural causes – in other words, on the failure of the political institutions, which he thought had caused Brown's raid on Harpers Ferry and driven devout patriots such as Brown to use violence to enforce the spirit of the law. For Brown's courage to do this, Emerson declared him 'a representative of the American Republic', thus adding him to the ranks of his Representative Men.[368]

As of mid-November more and more preachers, writers, poets and painters in the North joined the group of Brown supporters, regardless of whether they had met Brown personally.[369] To give but a single example, John Greenleaf Whittier, one of the most respected literary figures of his day, grappled with the question of violence in his poem 'Brown of

---

367 On these elements in the sociology and political science literature, see pp. 63–73 in this volume, especially 65 and 70.

368 Ralph Waldo Emerson, 'Representative Men', in *Essays and Lectures* (New York: Library of America, 1983), 611–761. For Emerson this exemplary group included the philosopher Plato, the mystic Swedenborg, the sceptic Montaigne, the bard Shakespeare, the worldly Napoleon and the writer Goethe. See also Stoneham, *John Brown*, 129–40.

369 On the reactions of people in the cultural sphere and on the creation of the John Brown legend in literature, theatre, film, visual arts, music, historiography and politics in the nineteenth and twentieth centuries, see especially Victor Vincent Verney Jr, 'John Brown: Cultural Icon in American Mythos', dissertation (Buffalo: State University of New York at Buffalo, 1996); Russo and Finkelman, *Terrible Swift Sword*; Taylor and Herrington, *The Afterlife of John Brown*; Peterson, *John Brown*; and R. Blakeslee Gilpin, *John Brown Still Lives! America's Long Reckoning with Violence, Equality, & Change* (Chapel Hill: University of North Carolina Press, 2011).

Osawatomie' and concluded that although Brown's tactics did not merit commemoration, his goal did:

> Perish with him [John Brown] the folly
> That seeks through evil, good;
> Long live the generous purpose
> Unstained with human blood!
> Not the raid of midnight terror,
> But the thought which underlies;
> Not the outlaw's pride of daring,
> But the Christian's sacrifice.[370]

Whittier's criticism of Brown's violence led to a long controversy because Garrison, of all people, accused him in the *Liberator* of being too harsh on Brown, whom Garrison thought deserved just as much respect as the biblical military leaders Joshua and Gideon and the American Revolution commanders George Washington and Joseph Warren. Whittier defended himself against Garrison's criticism in the *Liberator*, Redpath intervened, and the discussion about a poem turned into a public debate about the ethics of violence.[371] The genres of literature and journalism interacted similarly to the genres of private correspondence or sermon and journalism.[372] A comparable process can be observed in other areas of intellectual and cultural life, for example painting.

Public opinion had already shifted in favour of the perpetrator of the violence at Harpers Ferry by the time Emerson held his second lecture on

---

370 J. G. W. [John Greenleaf Whittier], '*From the New York Independent*. Brown of Osawatomie', *Liberator*, Friday, 13 January 1860, 8; reprinted as 'Brown of Ossawatomie', in John Greenleaf Whittier, *The Poetical Works* (Boston: Houghton Mifflin, 1888), 188–9. On the abolitionist poet Whittier see especially Roland H. Woodwell, *John Greenleaf Whittier* (Haverhill: Trustees of the John Greenleaf Whittier Homestead, 1985). On Whittier's thinking about John Brown and his poem about him, see Woodwell, *John Greenleaf Whittier*, 288–9.

371 'Poem on John Brown, by John G. Whittier; and his Controversy with William Lloyd Garrison thereon', in Redpath, *Echoes of Harper's Ferry*, 303–15. See also Woodwell, *John Greenleaf Whittier*, 289; and William Keeney, 'Hero, Martyr, Madman: Representations of John Brown in the Poetry of the John Brown Year, 1858–60', in Russo and Finkelman, *Terrible Swift Sword*, 154–5.

372 On the Harpers Ferry raid as a 'literary event', see Keeney, 'Hero, Martyr, Madman', 143.

John Brown on 18 November 1859. Sanborn wrote to Theodore Parker in Europe on 14 November, 'the feeling of sympathy with Brown is spreading fast over all the North, and will grow stronger if he is hanged.' According to him this change of mood had been brought about by the advocacy of Phillips, Thoreau and Emerson.[373] How had it been possible to redirect the discourse and transform the initial repudiation into sympathy?

Every Boston newspaper, as well as the larger party organs on the East Coast and many abolitionist papers, covered the lectures by Emerson and Thoreau with more or less comprehensive summaries and quotations. In this way their remarks were widely disseminated in interested circles and beyond.[374] Thoreau's attacks on the anti-slavery press not necessarily won him any friends in its editorial offices, and many newspaper editors published amused, critical or disparaging commentaries about his lecture.[375] This, however, did not hinder the spread of his words or opinions, for the newspaper readers could identify with his statements despite the editorial comments: 'I wish to thank you for the utterance of

373 Franklin Benjamin Sanborn to Theodore Parker, 14 November 1859, quoted in Beck, *Creating the John Brown Legend*, 135. Sanborn and other European American supporters of Brown hardly noticed Garnet's contribution and the activities of other African Americans – perhaps with the exception of Frederick Douglass. See also McFeely, *Frederick Douglass*, 191.

374 See, for instance, *Boston Daily Evening Traveller*, 2 November 1859; *Boston Daily Journal*, 2 November 1859; *Boston Daily Advertiser*, 2 and 4 November 1859, 1; *Boston Semi-weekly Advertiser*, 2 November 1859; *Boston Daily Messenger*, 2 November 1859; *Boston Daily Courier*, 2 November 1859; *Boston Atlas & Daily Bee*, 2 and 3 November 1859; *Springfield Republican*, 3 November 1859; *Liberator*, 4 November 1859, 174; *Worcester Daily Spy*, 4 November 1859; *New York Daily Tribune*, 4 November 1859; *Boston Press and Post*, 4, 5, and 9 November 1859; *New York Herald*, 5 November 1859, 2; *Freedom's Champion*, 5 November 1859, col. B; *New York Daily Tribune*, 9 November 1859; *New York Daily Tribune*, 14 November 1859, 5; *Liberator*, 18 November 1859, 1; *Anti-slavery Bugle*, 17 and 19 November 1859, 2, 3 respectively; *New York Herald*, 20 November 1859, 1; *New York Times*, 21 November 1859; *New York Daily Tribune*, 21 November 1859, 7; *Ashtabula Weekly Telegraph*, 26 November 1859, 2; *Cleveland Morning Leader*, 23 November 1859, 2; and *Anti-slavery Bugle*, 3 December 1859, 2. Newspapers in the slave states, on the other hand, reported only the occurrence of the assemblies and their speakers; see, for instance, *Memphis Daily Appeal*, 30 November 1859, 2; and *Daily News and Herald*, 19 November 1859, col. A.

375 See, for example, *New York Daily Tribune*, 9 November 1859; *Boston Daily Advertiser*, 2 November 1859; *Boston Press and Post*, 5 November 1859; and *Springfield Republican*, 3 November 1859. See also Michael Myers, 'Thoreau's Rescue of John Brown from History', *Studies in the American Renaissance* (1980), 309; and Dean and Hoag, 'Thoreau's Lectures', *Studies in American Renaissance* (1996), 316–18, 321–3.

332 The Invention of Terrorism

those brave, true words in behalf of the noble Saint and self-forgetting hero of Harpers Ferry,' wrote, for instance, Mary Jennie Tappan from Bradford, New Hampshire to Thoreau on 7 November, they were

> just *the* words I so longed to have some living voice speak, *loud*, so that the world might hear – In the quiet of my home among the hills I read them tonight and feel that my thought has found a glorified expression and I am satisfied, and through the distance I reach forth my hand to thank you.[376]

Thoreau's and Emerson's ideas and interpretations resonated in abolitionist circles and gave expression and intellectual legitimacy to latent emotions and thoughts there.

For many in the audience critical of slavery, this response to the lectures triggered a radicalization process like the one observable among radical abolitionists such as Brown, Garnet, the Secret Six and Phillips as early as the 1840s and undergone by intellectuals such as Thoreau and Emerson in the face of John Brown's violent action and his statements in Harpers Ferry. John Brown's act of violence thus indeed acted as a catalyst, albeit less for the slaves in the South than for the portion of the population in the North critical of slavery. Many residents of the northern states rejected slavery and were alarmed and appalled by the political turn their country had taken. Some had joined the anti-slavery movement and tried to achieve emancipation peacefully. Up to this point many people had been critical of political developments but not got involved. The raid on Harpers Ferry changed that. Brown's attempt to carry the violence into the southern states lay so far outside the everyday space of experience and horizon of expectation (Reinhart Koselleck) that many who previously had followed political events disapprovingly, but silently and without intervening, had now taken a stand. In doing so they began to ask about the motivation behind the violence, to take a position on the question of violence, and to question the political foundations of the state, with some – for instance, Henry Thoreau – who had previously considered themselves pacifists suddenly endorsing the use of violence if it served the cause of freedom.

---

376 Mary Jennie Tappan to Henry D. Thoreau, 7 November 1859, from Bradford, NH, quoted in Dean and Hoag, 'Thoreau's Lectures', 319.

Sanborn attributed this change in public opinion primarily to the women: 'The women everywhere are on his side – the failure is a success, – it has done more for freedom than years of talk could,'[377] he wrote to Parker. Sanborn thus expressed what John Brown himself had predicted and written about to Theodore Parker in March 1858 during preparations for the Subterranean Pass Way: 'Females are susceptible of being carried away entirely by the kindness of an intrepid and magnanimous Soldier, even when his bare name was a terror but the day previous.'[378] This may also explain why Brown sought to play the fearless yet magnanimous soldier and stated in the interviews immediately following his capture that he should have left Harpers Ferry for the mountains, but he had 'thirty odd prisoners, whose wives and daughters were in tears for their safety', and he 'felt for them'.[379] Whether women – as Graf von Hübner claimed of the 'women from the Russian and Polish upper middle class' in Orsini's case – were indeed primarily impressed by the image of the noble soldier Brown projected in romantic, male chauvinist manner and possibly also following American reporting on the trial in Paris must remain open at this point.[380]

In this process of gaining legitimization and acceptance for John Brown's political violence the Bible and American Revolution played key argumentative roles. Redpath, Garnet, Phillips, Thoreau and Emerson invoked American history and the American self-image in their justification of Brown, glorifying him as the personification of the key Christian precept of the Golden Rule and the founding formulation of the American republic, the preamble of the Declaration of Independence, whose values Brown practised and was willing to die for. In this way they lent the raid on Harpers Ferry a legitimacy that they

377 Franklin Benjamin Sanborn to Theodore Parker, 14 November 1859, quoted in Beck, *Creating the John Brown Legend*, 136.

378 John Brown to Theodore Parker, 7 March 1858, from Boston, the Massachusetts Historical Society, Theodore Parker Papers 1826–1862 [microfilm], Ms N-661, P-175, vol. 9, 287–9, reprinted in 'The Harper's Ferry Outbreak', *New York Herald*, 21 October 1859, 1; and John Weiss, *Life and Correspondence of Theodore Parker* (New York: Da Capo, 1970), vol. 2, 164–5.

379 'The Harper's Ferry Outbreak', *New York Herald*, 21 October 1859, 1; and De Witt, *The Life*, 44.

380 On this question, see Wendy Hamand Venet '"Cry Aloud and Spare Not": Northern Antislavery Women and John Brown's Raid', in Finkelman, *His Soul Goes Marching On*, 98–115.

denied the state. According to Harold Bush, Emerson, Thoreau and all those who followed them looked to Brown's example in formulating 'the root paradigm of the distinctly American political religion,' according to which Americans should be 'doers of the word' (James 1:22), and declared John Brown the embodiment of this political religion. By repeatedly emphasizing Brown's morally impeccable character, referring to biblical examples of the use of violence, and portraying Brown as a Christian hero, Cromwell, man of action, idealist, representative American, American Moses, martyr and Christ, they positioned John Brown as a hero at the centre of the nation's moral self-conception and transformed him into an American icon.[381]

With the raid on Harpers Ferry John Brown achieved what he and the Secret Six had hoped for in terms of influencing political and intellectual culture and awakening moral sentiment in the North. John Brown's ability and skill in presenting himself and his cause, the backing of radical abolitionists, the supportive arguments of intellectuals and artists, and the positive resonance of Brown's deed among the population critical of slavery in the North – possibly from women in particular – helped Brown achieve a politico-symbolic victory following a military and tactical defeat. More important, however, than the stirring of moral sentiment in the North were the reactions in the South, a perspective Brown may have gained from Orsini's attempted assassination of Napoleon III. The response in the South determined whether his strategy of provocation would bring about the abolition of slavery in the United States.

An American demon: speechlessness and terror in the South

The reactions south of the Mason–Dixon Line to John Brown's violence reflected those in the northern states, but from an opposite standpoint. In the South, too, the objective assessment and rational view of the raid as instrumental violence yielded to an emphasis on its symbolic dimension. Yet here, the shift in interpretation did not lead to radicalization in terms of moral resolve and an affirmation of targeted violence, but rather to widespread panic that extended into the election year 1860, with some contemporary witnesses and

---

381 Bush, 'Emerson, John Brown, and "Doing the Word"', 213.

historians comparing the atmosphere to the Great Fear in France in 1789.[382]

Many contemporary witnesses and also historians often blamed Virginia governor Henry A. Wise's crisis management for the escalation of public feeling to the level of a moral panic. This assessment is not entirely wrong, for Governor Wise became John Brown's opponent in the actual event and in the media event surrounding the raid on Harpers Ferry. Nevertheless, assigning responsibility in this way is too simple, for it follows the idea of provocation as something that 'prompt[s] a reaction that morally discredits and exposes' the other and drives the protagonists to '*personalize* the conflict'. This viewpoint does not adequately take into account that provocation contains 'an implicit program of action', which 'often also prevails over the participants' other intentions' and determines the course of events in a specific way.[383]

Figure 18. Henry A. Wise. Library of Congress, Prints and Photographs Division, LC-DIG-cwpb-06502.

---

382 See Ollinger Crenshaw, *The Slave States in the Presidential Election of 1860* (Baltimore: Johns Hopkins University Press, 1945), 107; Woodward, 'John Brown's Private War', 67; McPherson, *Battle Cry*, 212–13; and Oates, *To Purge This Land*, 322–3. On the *grande peur* specifically, see p. 90 in this volume. On the interaction between anarchist terrorism and moral panics in the late nineteenth century, see Jensen, *The Battle against Anarchist Terrorism*, especially 39–44.

383 Paris, 'Der kurze Atem', 83, 57.

Rather, the inarticulateness of the slave states, that is to say, the inability of moderate circles in the South to come up with an adequate intellectual and symbolic answer to counter northern abolitionists' iconization of John Brown, must be regarded as decisive for the escalation. Brown 'was more than a match for all the Wises, Masons, Vallandighams and Washingtons', stated Frederick Douglass correctly in 1881: 'They could kill him, but they could not answer him.'[384] Virginia's governor was of significance regarding this inability, for he was one of the few slave-state politicians who perceived the problematic nature of the South's politico-moral position and, therefore, one of the few people who would even have been able to find such an answer. The fact that he failed to do so is a serious indication that such an answer did not exist within the context of the moderate or conservative unionist thought in the South at that time.

Simply in terms of his biography, Henry Alexander Wise was a southern counterpart to Brown, Phillips and the Secret Six. Just a few years younger than Brown, he also came from a family that had set out for the New World in the seventeenth century, but settled on Virginia's Eastern Shore. His ancestors had helped shape the political fortunes of their colony from early on, and Wise was inspired by a sense of responsibility for the American experiment in democracy and the state in which he lived similar to that of Brown, Phillips and the Secret Six. Wise, though, was more worldly wise than they were. He had studied at Washington College in Pennsylvania and in Winchester, Virginia, after which he moved to Nashville, Tennessee, to be near his future wife. There he practised law and became acquainted with President Andrew Jackson, whose plantation he frequented in the role of a 'surrogate son'. Back in Virginia he was elected at age twenty-six to the US House of Representatives, where he served from 1833 until 1844. He subsequently went to Brazil as US minister. After his return from Rio de Janeiro in 1855, he was elected governor of Virginia. In the late

---

384 Frederick Douglass, *John Brown: An Address by Frederick Douglass, at the Fourteenth Anniversary of Storer College, Harper's Ferry, West Virginia, May 30, 1881* (Dover: Morning Star Job Printing House, 1881), 18; reprinted in Foner, *Frederick Douglass*, 641. Similarly, but with entirely different points of departure and a broader timeframe, Robert Penn Warren wrote in 1961, 'After the debates in the Virginia legislature in 1831 . . . public discussion was at an end.' Robert Penn Warren, *The Legacy of the Civil War*, 35.

1850s, he fostered ambitions to run for president as the Democratic Party candidate in 1860.[385]

Henry A. Wise had an ambivalent relationship with slavery. He basically rejected the institution and considered it a burden on the states of the Upper South – Virginia, Delaware, Maryland, North Carolina, Kentucky and Tennessee – where slaves represented a smaller proportion of the population than in the Deep South and the economy was not dependent on slavery. Wise explained Virginia's increasing backwardness within the Union through slavery and its associated social structures. Yet he saw no means of safely abolishing the institution. Wise did not belong to one of the Virginian planter families with large holdings and was not respected by them. As younger son, he had inherited only some land and a few slaves; he purchased more as soon as he could afford it. Shortly after his return from Tennessee, he witnessed the shock waves of the Nat Turner slave rebellion. Wise later lost his wife, house and farm in an arson fire set by one of his slaves. Not least because of this experience, he turned his efforts as congressman to drafting and vehemently supporting the gag rule that prevented Congress from dealing with abolitionist petitions. Wise fathered a child with one of his slaves. He emancipated the woman, who moved to Washington, where their son – whom Wise is said to have loved deeply – served his father as a constant helper and companion and listened to all his speeches in Congress. After the Civil War, this son became a gifted preacher. As the US minister to Brazil, much to the displeasure of both the American and the Brazilian governments, Wise fought to abolish the slave trade with Africa, an enterprise, as he bitterly noted, run mainly by shipowners from the northern US states. Yet, if anyone questioned his loyalty to slavery by referring to that activity or the emancipation of his slave, he would fly into one of his legendary fits of rage. His speeches were full of racist statements.[386]

Wise was a full-blooded antebellum politician. Charismatic in an odd, rakish way, he wore his hair long and let his clothing go for the sake of effect. He was one of the South's best rhetoricians and one of very few politicians from the slave states able to inspire the general

---

385 See Simpson, *A Good Southerner*, Chapters 1–10, quotation at 10.
386 See ibid., Chapters 1–10.

public. He took politics seriously, understanding it as a responsibility
for the future of his state and the nation, performed at his best in difficult and hard-nosed confrontations, and had consistently showed
good political sense in critical situations. Wise was used to success in
dealing with the media and the public. There were, of course, the ongoing feuds with his political opponents, the representatives of the rich
plantation-owing families. With his charisma as orator and his oldest
son as coeditor of the *Richmond Enquirer*, Wise had previously always
been able to count on his persuasiveness and impact even in thorny
issues, especially among the broader public. He therefore saw no
reason to shy away from moving assertively against a handful of
desperados in Harpers Ferry.

Yet although the governor of Virginia was a high-calibre politician,
the situation following the raid in Harpers Ferry slipped from his
grip. There were several reasons for this: like Demorny and
Napoleon III in France in the case of Orsini or the Democrats
Douglass and Vallandigham from the northern states in the case of
Brown, he had no interest in John Brown's act being minimized. Wise
wanted to exploit the violent incursion by northern abolitionists to
distinguish himself as the protector of the South in advance of the
Democratic Party convention. Again, the more dangerous the violence
seemed, the more heroic his role appeared. Just as Napoleon III had
played into Orsini's hands, Wise now unwittingly played into Brown's.
Wise, however, was not able to control and channel the exploitation
of the violence as effectively as the French emperor because of political divisions in the United States, his less influential position as governor, and the more pluralistic and ultimately uncontrollable media
coverage. In addition, he had professional adversaries in the northern
abolitionists, who knew how to capitalize on compelling symbols and
also how to utilize Wise's actions and statements as propaganda for
their cause.

Wise was impressed by Brown precisely because of his sense of political symbolism, and even went so far as to imitate Brown at the beginning of the Civil War. In April 1861, he organized a conspiratorial
scheme by which a pro-slavery force captured Harpers Ferry with the
aim of driving Virginia to secede and securing the federal government's
weapons for the South. And in June, in the early days of the Civil War,
he called on the population of Richmond: 'Get a spear – a lance. Take a

lesson from John Brown.'[387] Wise thus damned Brown's violence in the matter, but was moved out of a mixture of chivalrous integrity and disinterest in depoliticization to praise the plan and its perpetrators – except the African Americans – even publicly. 'He is a man of clear head, of courage, fortitude, and simple ingenuousness,' said Wise in an impromptu speech upon his return to Richmond, countering the widespread opinion of Brown's craziness:

> He is cool, collected and indomitable, and it is but just to him to say, that he was humane to his prisoners, as attested to me by Col. Washington and Mr. Mills; and he inspired me with great trust in his integrity as a man of truth. He is a fanatic, vain and garrulous, but firm, and truthful, and intelligent. His men too, who survive, except the free negroes with him, are like him.[388]

This speech appeared in the Richmond press and was subsequently published and discussed in newspapers across the country.[389] By emphasizing that Brown was a misguided fanatic, but certainly not a madman or criminal, Wise played into the hands of his opponents, with northern abolitionists soon fond of citing his speech as a testimony for Brown.[390]

Wise's publication of his correspondence with the writer and abolitionist Lydia Maria Child is another example of his miscalculation, one that also illustrates the veritable speechlessness of moderate circles in the

---

387 When Wise returned home after the Civil War, he discovered that one of Brown's daughters had set up a school for African American children in his house. To the surprise of his companions, he is reported to have declared, 'John Brown! John Brown was a great man, Sir. John Brown was a great man!' See Villard, *John Brown*, 466; and Wise, *The Life of Henry A. Wise*, 247, endnote 1.

388 Governor Henry A. Wise, speech to the Virginia militia in Richmond, 21 October 1859, in Wise, *The Life of Henry A. Wise*, 246–7, quotation at 246.

389 See 'The Return of Governor Wise' and 'Speech of Governor Wise on His Return to Richmond from Harper's Ferry', *Daily Richmond Enquirer*, 22 and 25 October 1859, both 2; *Daily Evening Bulletin*, 23 November 1859, col. D; *New York Herald*, 23 and 26 October 1859, both 1; *Charleston Mercury*, 24 October 1859, col. A; *Southern Argus*, 24 and 27 October as well as 8 November 1859, in each case 2; *Vermont Chronicle*, 1 November 1859, 175; *Weekly Raleigh Register*, 2 November 1859, col. A; and *Liberator*, 4 November 1859, 1.

390 See, for instance, Wendell Phillips's lecture in Brooklyn, 'The Virginia Rebellion', *New York Times*, 2 November 1859; *Liberator*, 2 December 1859, 190; and *Douglass' Monthly*, November 1859, 164.

slaveholding states when confronted by the arguments and symbolism of northern abolitionists. The exchange of letters began harmlessly enough on 26 October 1859, with Child inquiring whether she could come to Virginia to nurse the wounded Brown and openly stating her support of abolition and non-violence. She included a letter written to Brown containing the same question.[391] Wise replied diplomatically three days later, pointing out her constitutional right to travel to Virginia and promising to do everything in his power to enable her to exercise that right. At the same time, he could not resist declaring abolitionists such as Child jointly responsible for Brown's violence, writing that Brown's raid on Harpers Ferry 'was a natural consequence of your sympathy'.[392] Child responded with a lengthy letter in which she described the familiar stages of the process of radicalization in the North that had resulted from federal government policies favouring the southern states. She concluded, 'You may believe it or not, Gov. Wise, but it is certainly the truth that, because slaveholders so recklessly sowed the wind . . . they reaped the whirlwind at Harper's Ferry'.[393] Wise or his office must have passed on this correspondence to the *New York Tribune*, because it appeared in that paper's weekly edition and from there found its way into the national press.[394] In the South, however, Child's reply to Governor Wise was excluded.[395] Upon

---

391 'Letter to Gov. Wise, Wayland, Mass., Oct. 26th, 1859' and 'Mrs. Child to John Brown. Wayland, Mass., Oct. 26th, 1859', in Lydia Child, Henry Alexander Wise and Maria Jefferson Carr Randolph Mason, *Correspondence between Lydia Maria Child and Gov. Wise and Mrs. Mason, of Virginia* (Boston: the American Anti-Slavery Society, 1860), 3–4, 14. See on this topic Deborah Pickman Clifford, *Crusader for Freedom: A Life of Lydia Maria Child* (Boston: Beacon Press, 1992), Chapter 17; Carolyn L. Karcher, *The First Woman in the Republic: A Cultural Biography of Lydia Maria Child* (Durham, NC: Duke University Press, 1994), Chapter 17; Peterson, *John Brown*, 19–20; and Beck, *Creating the John Brown Legend*, 122–5.

392 'Reply of Gov. Wise. Richmond, VA. Oct. 29th, 1859', in Child, Wise and Mason, *Correspondence*, 4–6, quotation at 5.

393 'Mrs. Child to Gov. Wise', n.p., n.d., in Child, Wise and Mason, *Correspondence*, 6–12, quotation at 12.

394 See Karcher, *The First Woman*, 420; and 'Mrs. Child, Gov. Wise, and John Brown' and 'Lydia Maria Childs Reply to Gov. Wise', *New York Weekly Tribune*, 12 and 26 November 1858, 7, 4 respectively.

395 See, for instance, the *Richmond Enquirer*, where the wording is: 'Some imperfect extracts from the annexed letters have been published, we have thought it advisable, to a correct understanding of the subject, to give the entire correspondence'. 'Mrs. Child and the Insurgent Brown', *Daily Richmond Enquirer*, 5 November 1859, 2. But the paper only published the initial letters from Child to Wise and Brown and Wise's reply to Child.

seeing the letters in the newspaper, Child wrote to the editor of the *Tribune*, explaining that she was not responsible for their dissemination and including Brown's reply, in which he informed her that he was well and asked that she tend to the needs of his wife and children instead of nursing him. These letters were also published in the *Tribune*.[396]

Maria Jefferson Carr Randolph Mason, Senator James Mason's wife, then joined in the correspondence, beginning her letter, 'Do you read your Bible, Mrs. Child?' instead of a salutation and continuing with a line from Matthew 23:27: 'Woe unto you, Hypocrites.'[397] She wrote that Child wanted to care for the murderers from Harpers Ferry, but wondered if she would do the same for 'an old negro, dying of a hopeless disease', or 'soften the pangs of maternity' of her servants. Mrs Mason claimed that women in the South would care for their servants because 'we endeavor *to do our duty in that state of life it has pleased God to place us*. In his revealed word we read our duties to them – theirs to us are there also – "Not only to the good and gentle, but to the froward." '[398] In closing she expressed the South's hope that it would at least gain the sympathy of those in the North who deserved to be called women. The press promptly published the letter.[399]

Asking an abolitionist such as L. Maria Child if she read the Bible was a risky manoeuvre. In her reply Child countered the biblical verse cited by Mason (1 Peter 2:18), 'the favorite text of slaveholders', with eighteen biblical verses often invoked by abolitionists. She also cited laws, newspaper articles and other sources from the slave states, as well as the words of Thomas Jefferson and John Randolf (Mason's illustrious

---

396 *New York Weekly Tribune*, 19 November 1858, 6; reprinted as 'Letter of Mrs. Child. Explanatory Letter. To the Editor of the New York Tribune. Boston, Nov. 10th, 1859', and 'Reply of John Brown', n.p., n.d., in Child, Wise and Mason, *Correspondence*, 13, 15 respectively. Child complied with Brown's request and set up a relief fund for his family. See 'Boston Caring for Brown's Family. Public Meeting for Their Relief', *New York Daily Tribune*, 21 November 1859, 7; and in this regard, Karcher, *The First Woman*, 426–7.

397 'Letter of Mrs. Mason. Alto, King George's Co., Va., Nov. 11th, 1859', in Child, Wise and Mason, *Correspondence*, 16–18, quotation at 16.

398 Child, Wise and Mason, *Correspondence*, 16-17. Mason quoted from 1 Peter 2:18: 'Servants, *be* subject to *your* masters with all fear; not only to the good and gentle, but also to the froward [harsh]'.

399 See, for instance, 'Virginia and Massachusetts; Interesting Correspondence. (News) L. Maria Child', *Liberator*, 31 December 1859, col. A; and with a similar title, *New York Daily Tribune*, 24 December 1859, 8.

ancestors and family members), to drive home the brutality of slavery in the United States, a practice clearly in conflict with the biblical commandments. She noted the right of citizens in the free states to express their opinion about slavery and to be consulted about the issue as well. In answer to Mason's questions, she describes how difficult it would be to find a woman in villages of the North who did not help the poor or sick, yet 'here at the North, after we have helped the mothers, *we do not sell the babies*.'[400] Child reminded Mason that in an enlightened age all moral and rational means should be employed to depose despots, but 'if they resist such agencies, it is in the order of Providence that they *must* come to an end by violence. History is full of such lessons.'[401] Thus, with this reference to the Bible and history, Child also turned her back on non-violence.

Child struck a deep vein of sympathy in the North with this correspondence. Maria Mason published her letter in Virginia, leading Child to send her response to the *Tribune*.[402] The following year the Anti-Slavery Society published a compilation of the letters as a brochure that quickly attained an extremely high print run of 300,000 copies. 'Gov. Wise, by publishing our correspondence, secured me a very large audience; and I siezed [*sic*] the opportunity to impress some powerful facts on their minds,' she wrote to a friend in late November.[403] With regard to the different reactions in the North and South to John Brown's violence, the correspondence shows above all that dialogue and debate, or even communication between the two sections, had become impossible. In the South there were no intellectuals who could have stood by Wise or Mason and answered Child's letter and no statements that could have been ranked alongside the sermons and speeches of a Garnet, Phillips, Thoreau or Emerson and whose words could have found a place in the canon of debate on the legal or illegal, legitimate or illegitimate, use of violence. This deficit may partially have been due to

---

400 'Reply of Mrs. Child. Wayland, Mass., Dec. 17th, 1859', in Child, Wise and Mason, *Correspondence*, 18–28, quotation at 26.

401 Child, Wise and Mason, *Correspondence*, 26.

402 Karcher, *The First Woman*, 422.

403 Lydia Maria Child to Dear Friend [Anne Warren Weston?], Wayland, 28 November 1859, archive.org. See also Beck, *Creating the John Brown Legend*, 125. For information about the edition, whose sales equalled those of the original edition of *Uncle Tom's Cabin*, see Karcher, *The First Woman*, 423; or Peterson, *John Brown*, 19.

the nature of slavery as an institution, which was already considered threatened by public discussion and justification. Nonetheless, the successful assertion of a narrative about guilt and innocence like the one presented by Child influenced whether a position retained or lost legitimacy.[404] In this matter it would be Child – and not Wise – who had the last word.

Governor Wise merely responded again from an official perspective to Brown's action and its reception in the North, countering such interpretations with a legal positivist position. In his address to the Virginia General Assembly, which took place shortly after the execution of John Brown, he took the standpoint that the raid on Harpers Ferry was not the act of common criminals, but rather 'an extraordinary and actual invasion, by a sectional organization, specially upon slaveholders and upon their property in negro slaves'.[405] But even such an event, however sad, was hardly worth mentioning if one could assume that the punishment of the perpetrators would restore social peace. But that was not the case, because an 'evil spirit of fanaticism . . . has seemed to madden whole masses of one entire section of the country' and incited the perpetrators.[406] This fanaticism, according to Wise, was based on a belief in 'a "higher law" than that of a regular government bound by constitutions and statutes'. Inherent in this conviction was 'the doctrine of absolute individual rights' – the right of every individual 'to set up his conscience, his will and his judgment over and above all legal enactments and social institutions'.[407] Wise argued against that point of view, defending the assumption that the individual is embedded in a society through its institutions, conventions and norms. Since the raid on Harpers Ferry, the 'evil spirit of fanaticism' had proclaimed that 'that "*insurrection is the lesson of the hour*" – not of slaves only, but all are to be free to rise up against fixed government', he said, in a reference to Wendell Phillips. Wise asked, 'What does it mean but "confusion worse confounded," and

404 See Paris, 'Der kurze Atem', 67.

405 Henry A. Wise, 'Message 1. To the Senate and House of Delegates of the General Assembly of the Commonwealth of Virginia', in *Governor's Message and Reports of the Public Officers of the State, of the Boards of Directors, and of the Visitors, Superintendents, and Other Agents of Public Institutions or Interests of Virginia* (Richmond: William F. Richie, 1859), 3.

406 Ibid., 4–5.

407 Ibid., 5.

the overthrow of all rights, of all property, of all government, of all religion, of all rule among men?'[408] The belief that each member of a society has the prerogative to call for insurrection against the legitimate government on the basis of individual conscience can only lead to the end of governability, to civil war. The raid on Harpers Ferry therefore represented a new form of crime that was even worse than the murder of the peaceful citizens of the town: 'the death of a state.'[409] Wise's speech was covered in the press nationwide.[410]

Wise understood clearly that Brown, Phillips and other radical abolitionists sought to use the Harpers Ferry raid and its aftermath to delegitimize Virginia as a state and himself as its governor. He responded by questioning the legitimacy of such intentions and in doing so pinpointed a key problem in the argumentation of radical abolitionists such as John Brown, Wendell Phillips and David Henry Thoreau. But Wise had little to offer in the way of constructive solutions to the fundamental political problems. He called upon conservative forces in the North to finally bring their weight to bear and declared that the relationships between the states could not be sustained without slavery either being abolished throughout the entire United States or defended by force of arms.[411] Wise did not mention the possibility of emancipation again in his speech. His efforts to improve cooperation among the slave states or to gain better protection from the Union had – as he reported himself – produced no results. So there remained only the third path: 'we are clearly thrown on our self dependence. *We must rely on ourselves, and fight for peace! I say then – To your tents! Organize and arm!*'[412] The political situation

----

408 Ibid., 6. The quotation 'confusion worse confounded' is from John Milton. See *Paradise Lost* (London: Penguin Books, 2003), 50.

409 Wise, 'Message 1', 7. For a resumption of this argumentation (without reference to Wise), see Robert Penn Warren, *The Legacy of the Civil War: Meditations on the Centennial* (New York: Random House, 1961), 20–33, in which the author designates the positions contrasted by Wise as 'higher law' and 'legalism'.

410 See, for instance, *New York Herald*, 6 December 1859, 5; *Daily News and Herald*, 10 December 1859, col. C; *Memphis Morning Enquirer*, 10 December 1859, 2; *Ripley Bee*, 10 December 1859, col. B; and *Mississippian*, 16 December 1859, col. B.

411 Wise, 'Message 1', 7, 15, 17. On the questions of legitimacy in a broader theoretical and historical context, see Dietze, 'Legitimacy and Security from a Historical Perspective'.

412 Ibid., 23. Wise quotes here from 1 Kings 12:16: 'To your tents, O Israel: now see to thine own house, David!'

and a review of the arguments available to a politician in Wise's position left the use of force in defence of the state and of slavery as the
only option. This very recourse to the use of force as the only possible
response was the self-unmasking on the part of his adversaries that
John Brown had hoped to achieve with his violent act. At this point,
the distance to secession was not long any more, and Wise himself
soon followed the logical consequence and went in this direction. The
escalation logic of provocation potentially inherent in the Harpers
Ferry raid and indicative of this violent act's terrorist character could
thus run its course practically unchecked.

This provocation began with the publication of the documents found
at the Kennedy farm. The many letters and evidence of financial donations from well-known abolitionists and politicians from the North
represented in some ways a greater provocation for the South than John
Brown's violent act itself. For these documents served to convince many
in the South that the Harpers Ferry raid was not a dilettantish action by
a small group of crazy fanatics, as had initially been assumed, but rather
the outcome of a conspiracy that had been planned long beforehand and
had prominent supporters in all of the northern and north-western
states and Canada.[413] Rumours soon circulated that influential citizens
and a 'powerful organization' in the North still backed Brown and his
men and were now planning to free them from jail.[414] As the number of
these supporters grew, so did the political significance of the raid – and
the feeling of fear.

The maps found in John Brown's sack of documents were also a
source of particular alarm. On them he had marked the towns and
regions with a high proportion of slaves among the population and
noted the demographic data for whites and slaves and for men and

413 See, for example, 'The Harper's Ferry Invasion', 'Important Disclosures
Respecting the Harper's Ferry Plot', and 'Latest from Charlestown, VA', *Charleston
Tri-weekly Courier*, 1 November 1859, 1; *New York Herald*, 24 October 1859, 4; *Charleston
Mercury*, 25 October 1859, col. F, and *Semi-weekly Mississippian*, 28 October 1859,
col. A.

414 See, for instance, 'The Irrepressible Conflict Movement in New York', *Semi-
weekly Mississippian*, 2 November 1859, col. F (with reference to the *New York Sun*);
Charleston Mercury, 1 November 1859, 1; and *Weekly Raleigh Register*, 2 November
1859, 1. On the rumour that free African American reporters in New York had informed
the *New York Evening Post* about a riot, see *Daily Richmond Enquirer*, 28 October 1859,
2.

women on the basis of the 1850 census. On 21 October the Baltimore *Daily Exchange* published a meticulous description of these maps and each of their marks in four states of the Deep South. Many newspapers, especially in the southern and western states, subsequently reprinted the information.[415] These 'peculiar marks' were interpreted by the *Charleston Mercury* as seeming to 'indicate that the points of attack, and the course of an insurrectionary movement through the South, had already been carefully determined upon by this well-organized and confident league of traitors'.[416] On the basis of these maps, the slave-holding population in the marked regions could already see itself as the victim of the long-invoked race war, which had almost befallen them. 'This "method in their madness" shows whence sympathy was to be expected, and that the ball of insurrection was to gather strength entirely from the Slave States,' concluded the *Daily Cleveland Herald* in an interpretation also shared by the *Charleston Mercury*, which, however, chose to veil it in Latinized language as a precaution.[417] The realization that John Brown intended to recruit slaves in the South for his insurrection made the comparatively moderate beginnings in Virginia with twenty-two persons seem anything but ridiculous. There was ever less talk of a 'phrenzied [*sic*] movement, conducted without any definite plan of operations',[418] with the raid instead being described as a well-organized group of traitors.

The publication in mid-November of a letter from Lawrence Thatcher, an alleged Brown collaborator, further fuelled the fear and anger. Chances are it was penned by James Redpath, who intended it as

---

415 See, for example, 'The Abolition Invasion at Harper's Ferry ... Startling Revelation – The Points of Attack', *Daily Dispatch*, 21 October 1859, 1; *New York Times*, 22 October 185, 1; *Daily Cleveland Herald*, 24 October 1859, col. A; *Charleston Mercury*, 24 October 1859, col. A, and 25 October 1859, col. B; *Fayetteville Observer*, 27 October 1859, col. C; *Semi-weekly Mississippian*, 4 November 1859, col. F; *Newark Advocate*, 11 November 1859, 1; *Daily Mississippian*, 14 November 1859, col. D; *Southern Argus*, 28 December 1859, 2; and *New York Herald*, 31 December 1859, 6.

416 'The Virginia Insurrection. Additional Details', *Charleston Mercury*, 25 October 1859, col. B. This sentence was included in almost all articles drawing on the original.

417 'The Insurrection – Its Aim and Its Causes', *Daily Cleveland Herald*, 24 October 1859, col. A; 'The Virginia Insurrection. Additional Details', *Charleston Mercury*, 25 October 1859, col. B.

418 'The Conspiracy at Harper's Ferry', *Daily National Intelligencer*, 19 October 1859.

yet another provocation.[419] In a letter dated 22 October, 'A Traveller'
wrote to Governor Henry Wise that he had observed how a suspicious-
looking person on the Philadelphia–New York train had lost two letters
and a memorandum out of his coat pocket. The writer had tried to
locate the person, but too late, for the train was already moving again.
While attempting to identify the addressee or sender of the letters,
which had been mailed in Memphis, Tennessee, he had noticed that
they were addressed to John Brown. The traveller was now turning the
documents over to Wise, in case they might shed some light on the
Harpers Ferry raid. After examining them, Wise sent the documents to
Tennessee governor Isham G. Harris as a precaution. Harris in turn
concluded that much spoke for their authenticity. On 10 November the
entire correspondence, including the letter from the anonymous traveller and the allegedly found letter from Thatcher, was published verbatim in the *Memphis Morning Enquirer*, and subsequently taken over by
other newspapers. The official letter from the state of Virginia and the
response of Tennessee seemed to vouch for the credibility of the entire
correspondence.

According to the letter to 'Dear Capt.', Lawrence Thatcher was an agent
who travelled through the slave states on Brown's behalf to scout out the
conditions for uprisings. The findings of his – fictional – research were
that 'of all the States of the South, Tennessee and Arkansas [were] the best
fitted to make the first strike in.' Two slave states were thus included in
the supposed insurrection planning for which there were no markings
on Brown's maps. According to the letter there were many slaves in both
states who were willing to join the fight for their freedom at the first sign,
'while the large mass of the whites' rejected slavery and would immediately come to their aid. The letter writer also refers to teachers who
worked secretly for the abolitionist movement but were in a good position to win the trust and confidence of the local community, and sums
up, 'We must send out more well qualified men to the South as school
teachers, and work them in everywhere.' Mention was also made in the

---

419 Redpath had undertaken three trips through the slave states beginning in 1854
and chronicled his experiences and impressions in a book he dedicated to John Brown,
so he would have had the necessary practical and local knowledge of the southern states
and the needed insight into Brown's plans. See James Redpath, *The Roving Editor or,
Talks with Slaves in the Southern States* (New York: A. B. Burdick, 1859); and McKivigan,
Forgotten Firebrand, 44–5.

letter of a Dr Palmer, who owned slaves only to avoid raising the suspicions of his neighbours and was preparing a revolt with his slaves and
their friends and relatives at other plantations. At a signal from Brown,
Palmer could easily mobilize a thousand armed slaves. Thatcher closed
by saying he had to be cautious and often changed aliases, sometimes
impersonating a travelling preacher and sometimes a businessman from
New Orleans, surmising that 'Southern people are easily gulled.'

The letter specifically targeted the slaveholding elite's fear of abolitionists and southern whites critical of slavery and raised the spectre
that these groups might collaborate with the slaves and help them
prepare for rebellion. It sought to extend this mistrust into the slaveholding elite's inner circle of the planter families and goaded southerners by representing them as naive.

The letter and its publication had an immediate effect, with Governor
Harris actually having a Dr W. R. Palmer, who superficially fit the letter's
description, arrested and jailed. This official act, which was reported in
the press together with a reprint of the official correspondence, gave
Thatcher's letter added authority.[420] The next day the *Memphis Morning
Enquirer* questioned the authenticity of the letter, subjected it to a
detailed analysis, and exposed it as a forgery.[421] These findings, however,
did not make their way into the national press.[422]

420 See 'Arrest of Dr. W. R. Palmer' and 'Arrest of Dr. Wm. R. Palmer! His
Examination and Committal! Others Suspected! Great Excitement!!', *Memphis Morning
Enquirer*, 9 and 10 November 1859, both 3; and the reprinting as 'An Abolition Agent at
Memphis', *Charleston Mercury*, 14 November 1859, col. A; 'Arrest of Dr. Wm. R. Palmer',
Charleston Courier, 15 November 1859, col. E; 'Slave-Holding Gullibillity. Tennessee
Alarmed. Fears of an Insurrection', *Daily Cleveland Herald*, 15 November 1859, col. B;
'Arrest of One of the Harper's Ferry Conspirators in Tennessee', *New York Herald*,
16 November 1859, 5; 'Arrest of Dr. Wm. R. Palmer', *Daily News and Herald*, 16 November
1859, col. C; 'Harper's Ferry Excitement Spreading', *Boston Daily Advertiser*, 18 November
1859, col. D; 'Preliminary Examination of Dr. Wm. R. Palmer', *Southern Argus*,
19 November 1859, 2; 'More of Harper's Ferry', *Dover Gazette & Strafford Advertiser*,
26 November 1859, col. A; 'Arrest of Dr. Wm. R. Palmer! . . . Thatcher's Letter. Memphis,
Tenn., Oct. 3, 1859. To Capt. A. [*sic*] Brown, Gen'l Commander-in-Chief of the
Provisional Gov't U.S.A.', *Memphis Morning Enquirer*, 10 November 1859, 3.

421 See 'W. R. Palmer' and 'The Daily Enquirer', *Memphis Morning Enquirer*,
11 November 1859, 1, 3; and J. C., 'Correspondence of the Enquirer. Huntsville, Nov. 12,
1859', *Memphis Morning Enquirer*, 15 November 1859, 2.

422 The only mention the author could find in this regard left the case up in the air.
See *Dover Gazette & Strafford Advertiser*, 26 November 1859, col. A; and *Ashtabula
Weekly Telegraph*, 26 November 1859, 2.

What most incensed many southerners was the iconic status John
Brown enjoyed in the North. They found this apotheosis all the harder
to bear because southern newspapers had declared the reactions in the
North to the Harpers Ferry raid to be a litmus test for the continued
existence of the Union. The *Richmond Whig*, for instance, had reas-
sured its readers on 20 October 1859, 'we believe that the great body of
the Northern people look upon these Abolition conspiracies with
almost as much horror as we do,' but the newspaper had also admitted
it awaited the northern responses 'with no little anxiety' and demanded
firm evidence that its assumption was correct. If the Union was to
survive, and civil war to be averted, the people in the North had to
stand up in a show of commitment to public safety and condemn 'these
bold, bad men, and their dangerous, incendiary counsels'. If they did
not, 'the Harper's Ferry conspiracy [would] constitute the beginning of
an "irrepressible conflict" between the North and South, which [could]
only end in an utter destruction of the Federal Government, and in
oceans of fraternal blood'.[423] The *Whig* saw little alternative: reject
abolitionism and commit to the Union or there would be civil war. The
raid on Harpers Ferry, according to the *Whig* and other newspapers,
had to finally open the northerners' eyes to the fact that abolitionism
could only lead to violence, rebellion and race war and thus to an acute
endangerment of the white population – men, women and children –
in the South. The *Whig* therefore called on the North's citizenry to
assemble in every city, town and county to 'unite before the country
and the world in bold and manly denunciation of the Abolition faction
and their incendiary doctrines, aims and projects'.[424] It was thus not
only Brown and the Secret Six who thought public opinion was decisive, but also this Richmond newspaper, which was equally interested
in revealing it.

The more visible the sympathy in the North for John Brown began to
become, the more alarmed were the responses in the slave states. People
were well informed about the evolving apotheosis of Brown,[425] a

423 'Comments of the Richmond Press ... From the Richmond Whig, 20th', *New
York Times*, 22 October 1859.

424 Ibid. Similar is, for instance, *Weekly Raleigh Register*, 2 November 1859, 1; and
col. A; *Semi-weekly Mississippian*, 2 November 1859, col. C.

425 The pro-slavery press in the North and South informed its readership using
correspondents' letters, press analyses, republished newspaper articles and reprints of

development that ran counter to what the *Whig* had demanded. Brown and his volunteers were consequently increasingly vilified in the South as 'proto-martyrs', 'demons' and 'diabolical miscreants', with their raid on Harpers Ferry disparaged as 'machinations of the fanatical devils at the North' or a 'diabolical attempt to array the slaves against their masters'.[426] Wendell Phillips's public preaching of high treason in Brooklyn – to applause no less – and similar sermons and speeches and the press critical of slavery endorsing the traitors and their bloody deeds, 'either by glorying in it, like Phillips, and exalting "old Brown" to the rank of a demi-god, or by expressing regret, not for what has been done, but that it has been done so badly, and that so little success has attended the performance', were no longer seen simply as 'portentous signs of the times' or 'the rapid progress of revolutionary principles in the North',[427] but rather represented ever more painfully the actual

---

letters to Brown about the appearance, upsurge and reception of hagiographic interpretations. See, for instance, *Daily Richmond Enquirer*, 8 November 1859, 2; *New York Herald*, 16 November 1859, 5; *Liberator*, 25 November 1859, col. E; and *New York Herald*, 25 November 1859, 4.

426 'John Brown' and 'Startling Developments. The Bloody Insurrection of Harper's Ferry Only a Premature Explosion of a General Conspiracy', *Southern Argus*, 20 and 22 October 1859, both 2; 'Harper's Ferry Outbreak – Important Disclosures' and 'A Detailed Account of the Harper's Ferry Outrage, &c.', *Weekly Raleigh Register*, 2 November 1859, 1; and 'Let It Be Remembered', *Daily Mississippian*, 9 November 1859, col. C. In a similar vein, see, for instance, *Daily Morning News*, 22 October 1859, col. A; *Charleston Mercury*, 1 November 1859, 1; *Semi-weekly Mississippian*, 2 November 1859, col. C; *New York Herald*, 6 November 1859, 1; and *Fayetteville Observer*, 7 November 1859, 1.

427 'Alarming Condition of the Country', *New York Herald*, 3 November 1859, 6; reprinted in *Daily Morning News*, 8 November 1859, 1. See, for instance, the reprint of the speech '[From the New York Times, November 1] Wendell Phillips in Brooklyn' and the commentary 'Wendell Phillips' Lecture', *Daily Richmond Enquirer*, 5 November 1859, 2; 'The Pulpit and the Rebellion', *Charleston Mercury*, 27 October 1859, 1; 'The Conflict between Freedom and Slavery. Discourse of the Rev. Geo. F. Noyes', *Charleston Mercury*, 2 November 1859, col. C; 'Sympathy and Compromise', *Daily Richmond Enquirer*, 9 November 1859, 2; 'Old Brown a Hero' and 'From Our New York Correspondent. Abolition Lecturers – The Gun Will Recoil – Agitation a "Paying" Game at Present. New York, Nov. 14th, 1859', *Southern Argus*, 8 and 17 November 1859, both 2; 'Treason in the Pulpit', *New York Herald*, 19 November 1859, 1, 4; reprinted shortened in *Daily Morning News*, 24 November 1859, 1; 'Another Insurrection in Preparation at the North', *New York Herald*, 20 November 1859, 4; and 'The New Era of the Anti-slavery Agitation', *New York Herald*, 25 November 1859, 4. For a systematic analysis of the northern press, see, for instance, 'The View of the Press upon the Beginning of the Irrepressible Conflict at Harper's Ferry', *Southern Argus*, 25 October 1859, 2; 'A Detailed Account of the Harper's

affront and sense of scandal felt by the southerners. 'Have you seen Wendell Phillips speech in H. Ward Beechers [*sic*] church?' wrote, for instance, Charles White, the Presbyterian minister from Harpers Ferry to his brother-in-law in Massachusetts. 'It is the most atrocious – treasonable & murderous piece of villa[i]ny I have ever read . . . I do not know that the Devil would display such malignity.'[428] It was the assumed and the actual level of sympathy and support for John Brown in the North before and after the Harpers Ferry raid that truly provoked the southerners – just as Brown and the Secret Six had anticipated.

This escalation was highly welcomed by the secessionist movement in the South – the 'fire-eaters' – who did all they could to ratchet it up. Just as many abolitionists in the North had long been convinced that freedom had no chance in a union with slaveholders, the fire-eaters believed the institution of slavery and dignity of the southern states could no longer be guaranteed in a union with the free states. They therefore campaigned for the slave states to secede from the North. With this position they had represented the extreme fringe of the political spectrum prior to the Harpers Ferry raid, but now saw their chance to win over a large majority of the voting population to their standpoint. They pretended to be neither surprised nor impressed by Brown's violent act, but instead proclaimed that there probably was 'not a thoughtful man in the South who has not been anticipating, for years past, such events as those which lately transpired at Harper's Ferry', as Robert Barnwell Rhett, an old warhorse of the secessionists in South Carolina, wrote in the *Charlestown Mercury*. For him the raid was simply 'fact, coming to the aid of logic'.[429] Something similar had to happen sooner or

Ferry Outrage, &c', *Weekly Raleigh Register*, 2 November 1859, 1. On the reprinting of letters written to Brown with the aim of presenting the mood in the North to the newspaper's own readership, see, for example, 'Letters to John Brown while in Prison. A Bloody Letter. Copied from the Originals for Publication in the Southern Argus', *Southern Argus*, 6 January 1860, 2; reprinted as 'Letters to John Brown while in Prison – A Bloody Letter', *Charleston Tri-weekly Courier*, 10 January 1860, col. C.

428 Moore, 'John Brown's Raid at Harpers Ferry', 391.

429 Robert Barnwell Rhett, 'The Insurrection', *Charleston Mercury*, 31 October 1859, 1; *New York Herald*, 5 November 1859, 2; and on this topic Wallenstein, 'Incendiaries All', 166; and William C. Davis, *Rhett: The Turbulent Life and Times of a Fire-Eater* (Columbia: University of South Carolina Press, 2001), 380–2. On the Fire-Eaters, see the classic account by Ulrich Bonnell Phillips, *The Course of the South to Secession: An Interpretation* (New York: Appleton-Century, 1939), Chapter 6; and Eric H.Walther, *The Fire-Eaters* (Baton Rouge: Louisiana State University Press, 1992), on Rhett, Chapter 4.

later; the secessionists had been saying so for a long time. The Fire-
Eaters thus quickly recognized that this fact was superbly suited to
represent and illustrate their logic.

Unlike moderates such as Henry A. Wise, the secessionists had no
difficulty finding symbolic answers. In their eyes the fact of the raid
on Harpers Ferry symbolized the acute threat the North posed to the
South, with the pikes commissioned by John Brown for arming the
slaves having the greatest symbolic value. Edmund Ruffin, a tried and
tested Fire-Eater from Virginia, managed to obtain one of the pikes.
He had it inscribed with 'Samples of the favors designed for us by our
Northern Brethren' and travelled with it to Washington, to show to
the congressmen from the southern states. Satisfied with their reactions, he acquired additional pikes, had them inscribed with the said
text, and sent one to each of the slave-state governors. He kept a pike
for himself and took it with him wherever he went – just like another
political activist, who had become a disunionist from the North,
Wendell Phillips, who also was aware of the weapon's symbolic significance. He, too, armed himself with a pike and pistol, while additionally surrounding himself with a bodyguard of muscular, radically
democratic German gymnasts to protect against renewed attacks by
the anti-abolitionist mob.[430] Contemporaries noticed and commented
on the significance of the fact that these two political activists, in
particular – the Fire-Eater Ruffin and the radical abolitionist Phillips
– no longer went out without a pike. Many a journalist even suspected
secret collaboration between the secessionists and the abolitionist
disunionists because the cooperation between the two radicalisms on
either side of the Mason–Dixon Line functioned so perfectly
together.[431]

In response to the growing fear, militias and extralegal vigilance
committees formed in many southern communities in the weeks and
months after John Brown's raid. These armed groups were soon
pursuing anyone and anything they thought could be connected with

---

430 See Walther, *The Fire-Eaters*, Chapter 7; and Betty L. Mitchell, *Edmund Ruffin:
A Biography* (Bloomington: Indiana University Press, 1982), Chapter 10. On the use of
pikes by Ruffin and Phillips, see Mitchell, *Edmund Ruffin*, 145–6, 149–50; and Stewart,
Wendell Phillips, 203, 215.

431 See, for instance, *North American and United States Gazette*, 6 and 8 December
1859, col. A.

John Brown, abolitionism or the North. Thus the delivery of newspapers such as the *New York Tribune* to subscribers was prevented in the slave states. In South Carolina, Kentucky, Mississippi, Alabama and Texas abolitionist literature was publicly burned. Dozens of letters were sent to Governor Wise denouncing strangers and local people as Brown collaborators. A teacher who had lived in the Deep South states for ten years was given thirty-six hours to leave Arkansas. The newly appointed president of a college in Alabama, a native of New York, had to hastily leave his new place of employment. Kentucky expelled an entire thirty-nine-person community critical of slavery from its territory. Labourers, seafarers and haulers, as well as travelling booksellers, preachers, salesmen and northerners on journeys through the South were arrested, interrogated and imprisoned or beaten, whipped, tarred, feathered and banished from the slave states. As late as four months after the raid on Harpers Ferry a northerner was lynched in South Carolina as 'one of Brown's associates'. Many plantation owners intensified their security measures and threatened to whip or hang any slave who even appeared to be insubordinate. Throughout the South there were calls for free African Americans to be re-enslaved or expelled because they per se represented incitement to rebellion. In Texas a sixty-year-old minister, a Democrat who believed in the biblical justification of slavery, was given seventy lashes across his back because he had called for better treatment of slaves in a sermon. In addition, during the election year of 1860, wild rumours circulated there about arson, abolitionists planning insurrections with slaves, and slaves with large quantities of strychnine for poisoning wells. Across the South, people boycotted products from the North, thus returning to a form of political and economic pressure practised during the American Revolution.[432]

These and other occurrences were covered in turn countrywide in the press, with the newspapers in the North describing them under the headline 'Reign of Terror'. William Lloyd Garrison compiled a corresponding column every week in the *Liberator* and published a collection

---

432 See Woodward, 'John Brown's Private War', 64–7; Oates, *To Purge This Land*, 320–3; and Wallenstein, 'Incendiaries All', 152–6. On Georgia see Mohr, *On the Threshold of Freedom*, Chapter 2. For denunciatory letters to Wise, see, for instance, LOV, RG-3, Governor Henry A. Wise Executive Papers (hereafter Wise Exec. Papers) 1856–60, Microfilm 4193–4220, MF 4218–4220, frames 233, 244, 304–5.

of these articles as a brochure in 1860.⁴³³ The North was kept well
informed about the violence against its citizens in the slave states.
Whereas the southerners were incensed by the reactions in the North to
the raid on Harpers Ferry, the northerners were outraged by the restrictions on civil liberties and the violent assaults in the South. A further
polarization was the result.

These radicalization processes in both parts of the Union did not go
unchallenged within each of the sections, with large gatherings actually taking place in the North to express solidarity with Virginia as
well as a commitment to the Constitution and the Union – just as the
Richmond Whig had called for. Many of the rallies were spectacularly
orchestrated and much larger than the events in support of John
Brown, with the one in Philadelphia reportedly the largest to have ever
occurred in the United States.⁴³⁴ In that respect, they represented
impressive articulations of public opinion in the North *opposed* to the

433 William Lloyd Garrison, *The New 'Reign of Terror' in the Slaveholding States,
for 1859-60* (New York: American Anti-Slavery Society, 1860). For coverage in the
North, see, for instance, 'Miscellaneous News Items', *Douglass' Monthly*, November
1859, 176; 'The Reign of Terror in the South', *Douglass' Monthly*, December 1859,
178–9; *New York Herald*, 21 November 1859, 2; 'Miscellaneous News Items', *Douglass'
Monthly*, December 1859, 185; 'Reign of Terror in Virginia', *Daily Cleveland Herald*,
2 December 1859, col. D; 'Conflict of Laws', *Lowell Daily Citizen*, 28 December 1859,
col. A; 'Dastardly Outrages upon Northern Citizens at the South', *Liberator*,
30 December 1859, 205–6; 'The Reign of Terror Approaching in the United States' and
'The Reign of Terror in the South', *New York Herald*, 4 January and 24 February 1860,
6, 4 respectively; 'Espionage in the South', *Liberator*, 4 May 1960, 1; and 'The Rev. Daniel
Worth', *Ripley Bee*, 17 May 1860, 1. For reporting in the South, see, for instance, 'A
Traitor Tarred and Feathered', *Southern Argus*, 5 December 1859, 2; 'Lynch Law in
Savannah, Georgia', *Memphis Morning Enquirer*, 16 December 1859, 1; or 'Case of Rev.
Daniel Worth', *Milwaukee Daily Sentinel*, 5 May 1860, col. B. On the demand that all
free African Americans be expelled, see, for example, 'Free Negroes in Our Midst',
Southern Argus, 19 November 1859, 2.
434 On the particularly spectacular rallies in Philadelphia, Boston and New York,
see, for example, 'A Conservative Union Mass Meeting' and 'The Union Meeting', *North
American and United States Gazette*, 6 and 8 December 1859, both col. A; 'Union
Meeting in Faneuil Hall', *Boston Daily Advertiser*, 9 December 1859, col. C; 'The Crisis
– The Great Conservative Elements of the North Beginning to Move' and 'E Pluribus
Unum. Immense Conservative Demonstration at the Academy of Music', *New York
Herald*, 8 and 20 December 1859, 4, 3 respectively. Assemblies also took place in other
cities, such as Harrison, PA, Newark, NJ, Hartford and New Haven, CT, and Washington,
DC.

radical abolitionists, and were also understood as such in the South.[435] These 'Union meetings', however, first occurred as of mid-December 1859, in reaction to the mobilization of the abolitionists, therefore only after a significant portion of the population had long since been convinced of the necessity and legitimacy of using force to abolish slavery in the United States. These rallies, as well as the mob attacks on abolitionists and their meetings, which became increasingly frequent once again, only served to show that the free-states' population was divided and that the tensions were also profound within the North. This evidence of disagreement, however, offered little reassurance to the population in the slave states.

In the South, criticism was therefore often directed against Governor Wise and his handling of the crisis. The events in Harpers Ferry should have 'been treated and represented either in its best light as the mad folly of a few deluded cranks branded fanatics or, more truly, as the vulgar crime and outrage of a squad of reckless desperate Ruffians', wrote, for instance, James A. Seddon, a former Virginia congressman, to his friend Robert M. T. Hunter, a Virginia senator and Wise opponent. The abolitionists 'should have been accordingly tried and executed as execrable criminals in the simplest and most summary manner. There should not have been the chance offered of elevating them to political offenders or making them representatives and champions of Northern Sentiment'.[436] The *Richmond Enquirer* followed suit, advising that the 'whole gang of outlaws' should have been executed without delay and

---

435 See, for instance, the article about Philadelphia: 'Union Demonstration Meeting', *Southern Argus*, 12 December 1859, 2; 'Enthusiastic Union Meeting in Philadelphia' and 'The Union Meeting in Philadelphia', *Memphis Morning Enquirer*, 10 and 13 December 1859, 3, 2 respectively; 'The Grand Union Mass Meeting of Citizens, Irrespective of Party, Was Held to Night at Jayne's Hall, the Object Being to Re-affirm Allegiance to the Union and the Constitution, and Condemn All Fanaticism', *Charleston Mercury*, 12 December 1859, col. C; 'The Union Mass Meeting at Philadelphia', *Daily Morning News*, 12 December 1859, col. D; 'Mass-Meeting in Philadelphia', *Fayetteville Observer*, 12 December 1859, col. F; 'Great Union Demonstrations at the North!', *Weekly Raleigh Register*, 14 December 1859, col. D; and also the press survey on the union meetings under 'Southern Sentiment', *Liberator*, 6 January 1860, 1.

436 James A. Seddon to Robert M. T. Hunter, 26 December 1859, from St James Parish, LA, reprinted in Charles Henry Ambler (ed.), *Correspondence of Robert M. T. Hunter* (Washington, DC: Government Printing Office, 1918) vol. 2, 280–4, quotation at 281. See also Wallenstein, 'Incendaries All', 166–7.

that exactly this should be done in the event of a repetition of such attacks: 'Let the "higher law" of abolitionism be met by the "higher law" of self-preservation.'[437] By treating the abolitionists in accordance with constitutional procedures and elevating them to political perpetrators and leaders of a northern conspiracy, Wise, according to Seddon and the *Enquirer*, had given them the chance to be recognized as representatives of public opinion in the North in the first place.

Two weeks before his execution, Brown indicated his satisfaction with the effect he and his volunteers had brought about with their Harpers Ferry raid in a letter to his former teacher at the academy, Reverend Herman L. Vaill:

> As I believe most firmly that God reigns; I cannot believe that any thing I have *done suffered or may yet suffer will be lost*; to the *cause of God or of humanity*: & before I began my work at Harpers Ferry; I felt assured that in the *worst event*; it would certainly PAY. I often expressed that belief; & I can now see no possible cause to alter my mind.

Even if Brown had initially been disappointed by his military failure in Harpers Ferry, he meanwhile had come to terms with it:

> I am not as yet in the *maine* at all disappointed. I have been *a good deal* disappointed as it regards *myself* in not keeping up *to my own plans*; but I now feel entirely reconciled to that even: for Gods plan, was Infinitely better; *no doubt*; or I should have kept to my own . . . But 'Gods will *not mine* be done.'[438]

As a reporter from the *New York Tribune* reported, Brown knew during his confinement 'almost as well as any person in the country' of the

---

437 Quoted in 'Refuge of Oppression. The Fate of Brown', *Liberator*, 11 November 1859, col. A. See also *Ashtabula Weekly Telegraph*, 26 November 1859, 2; *Daily Richmond Enquirer*, 2 November 1859, 2; 'Refuge of Oppression. The Fate of Brown' press survey, *Liberator*, 11 November 1859, col. A; *New York Herald*, 27 November 1859, 4; and 'The Charlestown Excitement', *Weekly Raleigh Register*, 30 November 1859, col. A.

438 John Brown to Reverend Herman L. Vaill, 15 November 1859, from Charlestown, VA, reprinted in Ruchames, *John Brown*, 144. Brown quotes here from Luke 22:42: 'Nevertheless not my will, but thine, be done.'

impact of his act and of 'the extent of the shock he ha[d] given'.[439] Brown
wrote to Vaill that he had been convinced since devising the plan to raid
Harpers Ferry and presenting it to the Secret Six in Peterboro and
Boston that the violence would pay off politically, even if it failed militarily. This conviction had proved correct.

Execution and martyr cult

John Brown's execution was set for 2 December 1859, and similar to
Orsini's case in France, the question whether Governor Wise should
– and would – pardon Brown or let him hang roused tempers across
the country. Especially in the North there were many people who
hoped their hero would be pardoned, and appealed to Governor Wise
in countless letters and petitions to show himself to be a merciful
Christian and make use of his right of pardon.[440] However, for most
people in the South – but also for many in the North – a pardon was
unacceptable.

The question of how the execution of Brown would affect his public
standing – that is, his status as martyr – played a greater role in this
debate in the United States than similar considerations in the case of
Orsini in France. 'To Hang a Fanatic is to make a martyr of him, and
fledge another brood of the same sort,' pointed out, the pro-slavery
newspaper the *New York Journal of Commerce* in early November:
'Better send these creatures to the penitentiary, and so make of them

---

439 'What Brown Has Accomplished [Correspondence of the NY Tribune]',
Douglass' Monthly, December 1859, 184.

440 See, for example, George P. Edgar, New York, 18 November 1859, LOV, RG-3,
Wise Exec. Papers MF 4219, frames 501–3; J. C. Hathaway, New York, 22 November
1859; LOV, RG-3, Wise Exec. Papers, frame 510; W. Emmons, Boston, MA,
19 November 1859, LOV, RG-3, Wise Exec. Papers, frame 518; C. Sophias, n.p.,
2 December 1859, LOV, RG-3, Wise Exec. Papers; J. J. Hamilton, PA, 6 December
1859, LOV, RG-3, Wise Exec. Papers, frame 1201. As a petition, see, for instance,
Marise of Laprairie, Montreal, Canada, 10 December 1859, Wise Exec. Papers, MF
4220 frames 76–7; and author unknown, n.p., n.d., Wise Exec. Papers, frames 120–4.
For press articles see, for example, 'Will Brown Be Executed? – The Abolitionists
Preparing to Celebrate the Day' and 'A Suggestion to Governor Wise about Old Brown',
New York Herald, 5 and 27 November 1859, both 4; and 'Execution of Capt. John
Brown', *Liberator*, 18 November 1859, 182.

miserable felons.' This idea convinced thoughtful minds in the South and many in the North who sympathized with the South and observed Brown's glorification with concern.[441] Governor Wise constantly received letters attempting to convince him of the political wisdom of this proposal, letters that in turn became the subject of the news coverage.[442] Propaganda-savvy abolitionists agreed with the analysis but advocated execution precisely for that reason. 'Let no man pray that Brown be spared,' preached, for instance, Henry Ward Beecher on 30 October in Brooklyn: 'Let Virginia make him a martyr. Now, he has only blundered. His soul was noble; his work miserable. But a cord and a gibbet would redeem all that, and round up Brown's failure with a heroic success.'[443] Some from the Secret Six agreed with Beecher – even Brown himself, who received a copy of Beecher's sermon on the initiative of the *New York Herald* with the request that he comment on it. Brown consented and made several critical or favourable notes along its margins. Next to the passage in which Beecher calls for his hanging, he wrote 'good!'[444] In opposition to conservative and moderate voices in the North and South,

441 Quoted in 'To Hang a Fanatic Is to Make a Martyr of Him, and Fledge Another Brood of the Same Sort', *Liberator*, 4 November 1859, col. B. The suggestion was discussed in both the North and South. For supportive commentaries, see, for instance, 'How Shall Brown Be Punished?', *Fayetteville Observer*, 7 November 1859, col. D; 'Capt. John Brown to Be Hung', *Cleveland Morning Leader*, 7 November 1859, 2; 'Another Southern Press [*Frankfort Yeoman*] Speaking Out', *Cleveland Morning Leader*, 23 November 1859; 2. For critical commentaries, see 'The Presidency for a Pardon', *Daily Richmond Enquirer*, 3 November 1859, 2; 'The Law of Virginia Forbids the Pardon of Brown', *Daily Richmond Enquirer*, 7 November 1859, 2; reprinted in *Southern Argus*, 9 November 1859, 2; *New York Observer*, titled 'The Religious Press on Old Brown', *Southern Argus*, 15 November 1859, 1; 'Clemency to the Harper's Ferry Criminals', *Memphis Daily Appeal*, 30 November 1859, 2.

442 See, for example, Benjamin D. Harvey to Governor Wise, 9 December 1859, from Euston, PA, LOV, RG-3, Wise Exec. Papers, MF 4220, frame 63; and, for instance, 'Threatening and Appealing Letters to Gov. Wise [*Richmond Dispatch*]' and 'Interesting Letters', *Daily Richmond Enquirer*, 3 November 1859, 2; 'Threatening and Appealing Letters to Gov. Wise', *North American and United States Gazette*, 3 November 1859, col. E; and 'Letters Received by Gov. Wise – Force Organizing to Rescue Old Brown', *Weekly Raleigh Register*, 30 November 1859, col. D. See in this regard also Warren, *John Brown*, especially 414–18.

443 Henry Ward Beecher, 'The Nation's Duty to Slavery', in John Raymond Howard (ed.), *Patriotic Addresses in America and England* (New York: Fords, Howard & Hulbert, 1887), 207.

444 'Beecher on Brown, and Brown on Beecher. Old Brown's Commentaries on Beecher's Harper's Ferry Sermon – A Curious and Highly Interesting Document', *New York Herald*, 23 November 1859, 1.

radical pro-slavery advocates, like radical abolitionists, called for an execution. In choosing their stance, they took the public effect of an execution into account. Their thinking followed the logic of self-sacrifice and martyrdom, which only an execution could fulfil, although they may also have been swayed by Orsini's glorification as martyr in some parts of Europe, where this logic and its impact had already been demonstrated.[445]

The execution was yet another major (media) event in its own right, which all involved parties realized and responded to accordingly. National attention was focused on the officials and people of Virginia, as well as Charles Town and its surroundings, with the level of apprehension rising as the execution date neared. The appearance of a heavenly sign – an unusually large meteor clearly visible across much of the eastern United States on 15 November 1859 – charged the situation with still more significance and expectation.[446]

The region had lived in an atmosphere of unrest and fear since the raid on Harpers Ferry, with false alarms causing troops and militias to mobilize to put down insurrections and attacks, only to find the scene peaceful and the residents asleep.[447] In the weeks following Brown's conviction, several barns and outbuildings burned down near Harpers Ferry, primarily at farms belonging to people involved in the guilty verdicts handed down for Brown and his volunteers. At other farms, all livestock suddenly died. The culprits were never found, but the general belief was that slaves had set the fires and poisoned the animals to show their solidarity with John Brown and his group and to take revenge for his conviction. In response, Governor Wise increased the number of troops stationed in Charles Town. All of these events became the subject of national news coverage, with the press also covering Governor Wise's receipt of hundreds of threatening letters as well as ones mentioning potential attempts

---

445 See pp. 149–67 in this volume.

446 See R. P. Greg, 'A Catalogue of Meteorites and Fireballs, from A.D. 2 to A.D. 1860', in *Report of the Thirtieth Meeting of the British Association for the Advancement of Science* (London: John Murry, 1861); 'The Meteor in New Jersey', *New York Daily Tribune*, 21 November 1859, 7; and Reynolds, *John Brown*, 383–4.

447 See the report by Colonel Robert E. Lee to the Adjutant General dated 19 October 1859 from Headquarters Harper's Ferry, Letters Received (M567, roll 618, frames 399–406), RG 94, NAB, NARA.

to free John Brown from jail or the gallows.[448] Believing at least some of the letters to be credible, Wise gathered even more military in Charles Town on the day of Brown's execution, prohibited civilians from entering a mile-wide exclusion zone around the execution site, and forbade Brown from speaking at the gallows. It was only after a lengthy dispute that a few newspaper reporters were accredited to cover the execution.[449]

Brown knew his conduct before and during the execution would decide his future public image and, therefore, the success or failure of his entire violent undertaking – of his life's work. He rose at dawn on the day of execution and read his Bible, marking all the passages in the Old and New Testaments that had always been particularly important to him throughout his life. Brown then wrote a short letter to his wife, enclosing his will and giving her instructions about the inscriptions for himself and his sons Oliver and Watson that she was to add to the gravestone of his grandfather, who had died in the Revolutionary War, as an enduring reminder that he and his sons had at last completed the revolution of his ancestors with their action.[450] He then answered one last letter. When jailer Avis opened the cell door, Brown was ready. For their kindness towards him he gave Avis his silver watch and his prison guard his Bible, and said farewell to his fellow fighters. Dressed in the torn clothes he had worn during the raid on Harpers Ferry and with his Kansas hat on his head, he walked out of the prison onto the street, surveyed the rows of soldiers, and commented wryly, 'I had no idea that Governor Wise considered my execution so important.' He then handed one of the guards a note with his last message to the nation:

448 On the letter threats see, for instance, Simeon Suredeaths, n.p., 21 November 1859, LOV, RG-3, Wise Exec. Papers, MF 4219, frame 493; Jais. M. P., Richmond, IN, December 1859, LOV, RG-3, Wise Exec. Papers, frames 1174–6; anon. n.p., n.d., LOV, RG-3, Wise Exec. Papers, frame 1185; anon., Baltimore, MD, 14 December 1859, LOV, RG-3, Wise Exec. Papers, frame 145; and Jas. M. Pheason, Greeneville, OH, 16 December, LOV, RG-3, Wise Exec. Papers, frame 159. For a press report see 'Threatening Letters', *Southern Argus*, 29 November 1859, 2.

449 Reynolds, *John Brown*, 392–3.

450 See 'John Brown to My Dear Wife and Children, Every One', 12 May 1858, from Chatham, Canada, reprinted in Sanborn, *The Life and Letters*, 455–6; and Villard, *John Brown*, 278–9.

Charlestown, Va, 2d, December, 1859

I John Brown am now quite *certain* that the crimes of this *guilty, land:*
will never be purged *away*; but with Blood. I had *as I now think: vainly*
flattered myself that without *very much* bloodshed; it might be done.[451]

Then, with his arms bound behind his back, he climbed onto an open
wagon, where he sat down on his coffin between Avis and the sheriff of
Charles Town.[452]

Accompanied by an escort the vehicle set off for a field just outside
Charles Town where the gallows stood, guarded by 1,500 cavalry soldiers
and militiamen. A mild wind came from the south, and the Blue Ridge
Mountains rose in the distance behind the hilly landscape. 'This *is* a
beautiful country,' Brown is said to have commented to Avis. 'I never
had the pleasure of seeing it before.' Major Thomas L. Jackson, who was
to become famous during the Civil War under the name 'Stonewall
Jackson,' was present as a professor of the Virginia Military Institute and
stood with his cadets directly adjacent to the gallows. He reported later
how John Brown had climbed the stairs with 'unflinching firmness.'

On the platform above, Avis removed Brown's hat, placed the noose
around his neck, and put a linen sack over his head. The Charles Town
sheriff guided Brown onto the trapdoor and tied his legs together at the
ankles. Brown was ready, but it took another ten minutes for the last
soldiers to take their assigned places. During that time Edmund Ruffin,
the Fire-Eater so intrigued by Brown's pikes, observed John Brown
intently and later admitted the extraordinary courage of the man who
stood motionless up on the gallows platform. The last troops finally
indicated their readiness. Avis and the sheriff descended from the
gallows. Brown stood alone on the platform, and a great stillness
descended over the scene.

The sheriff opened the trapdoor, Brown fell into the void, and the
crowd watched silently as his body twisted in the throes of death. When
this movement had ceased, Major J. T. L. Preston from the Virginia

---

451 Brown's 'last note' and his Bible with his markings are preserved at the Chicago
Historical Society. See Chicago Historical Society, John Brown papers, 1842–1928,
NUCMC MS 62–1410. The wording and unusual punctuation of the original last note
are given as quoted in Oates, *To Purge This Land*, 351.

452 Oates, *To Purge This Land*, 349–51.

Figure 19. 'The Execution of John Brown, in a Stubble Field, near
Charlestown [W.] Va.' In the foreground are men on horseback. Library
of Congress, Prints and Photographs Division, LC-USZ62-11424.

Military Academy called out, 'So perish all such enemies of Virginia! All
such enemies of the Union! All such foes of the human race!' After
thirty-eight minutes Brown's pulse had ceased, and his corpse was
removed from the gallows.[453]

The cult surrounding John Brown reached its climax at the time of his
hanging in Virginia. In the towns and cities of the North and Northwest
thousands of people came out to pay him their last respects. The American
Anti-Slavery Society had called on all 'friends of impartial freedom' at the
beginning of November to observe the day in whatever way they felt
appropriate, 'whether by public meetings and addresses, the adoption of
resolutions, private conferences, or any other justifiable mode of action –
for the furtherance of the Anti-Slavery cause.'[454] Opponents of slavery
followed this call everywhere, with memorial services for Brown combining prayer with revolutionary songs such as the Marseillaise taking place
in Hudson, Concord and almost every town in the North and Northwest.
In Lawrence, Kansas, free-state settlers assembled, and in Detroit and

453 Ibid., 351–2.
454 'Execution of Capt. John Brown', *Liberator*, 4 November 1859, 174.

Pittsburgh the African American communities gathered to declare Brown a hero, patriot and martyr; to praise his raid on Harpers Ferry; and to proclaim he had died for the freedom of humanity. In Akron, Ohio, and other cities, businesses, banks and public institutions remained closed. The city fathers of Albany, New York, honoured Brown with a hundred-gun salute at the hour of his death, and the sound of bells was heard from Kansas to Cape Cod, with the fire bell at City Hall in Syracuse, New York, tolling the entire day. In Cleveland, Ohio, 1,400 citizens attended a memorial service at which Reverend J. C. White declared, 'The great and sinful system of American slavery will never be overthrown by pacific means. "Without the shedding of blood, there can be no remission of such a sin." '[455] The radical credo that Brown had once again formulated in his last message to the nation had long since arrived there.

The news that Brown had been hanged in Charles Town arrived in Boston by telegraph around 4 p.m., bringing public life to a standstill. Many people closed their businesses and wore mourning ribbons and a rosette with his portrait. The co-founder of the American Anti-Slavery Society and publisher of the *Liberator* newspaper, William Lloyd Garrison, and the abolitionist writer L. Maria Child, who had corresponded with Governor Wise, had announced that an assembly honouring Brown would take place at the Tremont Temple on that evening. Half an hour before the scheduled start of the event, the hall was already overflowing, while another 3,000 people wanting to attend waited outside. Garrison and Child had hung the walls with banners bearing Bible verses alongside quotations from John Brown and pronouncements by Virginia's prominent sons, for example Jefferson's preamble to the Declaration of Independence and Patrick Henry's 'Give Me Liberty, or Give Me Death'. A cross with a wreathed picture of Brown adorned the pulpit. Resplendent above it hung the great seal of Virginia with its motto '*Sic semper tyrannis*' ('Thus always to tyrants'), words Brutus supposedly uttered during the murder of Caesar.[456] Virginia's revolutionary tradition was held up to the Old Dominion as a mirror.[457] During

---

455 Oates, *To Purge This Land*, 354–5; Mayer, *All on Fire*, 500–1; Quarles, *Blacks on John Brown*, 120–31. On Concord see 'Brown Meeting in Concord', in Cameron, *Transcendental Log*, 138–40.

456 On the hall's decoration, see Mayer, *All on Fire*, 501.

457 See 'Great Meeting in Boston on the Day of the Execution of Captain John Brown', *Liberator*, 9 December 1859, 194.

the gathering speakers read from the Bible, held speeches and recited poetry. Garrison read Brown's speech to the court. The high point of the event was Garrison's own address. The veteran of the anti-slavery movement, who with the Declaration of Sentiments had composed one of the Anti-Slavery Society's founding documents in 1833, declared that the struggle against slavery remained a struggle to complete the American Revolution.[458] Although he had stated almost thirty years earlier that abolitionists' principles forbade doing evil to achieve good and had himself remained a consistent advocate of non-violence, he now, on the day of John Brown's death, for the first time publicly acknowledged violence as a means of emancipation.[459] Most of those present recognized that this was a significant and memorable moment for the abolitionist movement.

All of these events were recounted in the press, with coverage in the North and Northwest surging yet again. Newspapers covered the last days, hours and minutes of John Brown's life in detail. Their readership was intensely interested in the execution preparations, information about possible liberation attempts, Brown's actions before his execution, his words to his fellow insurrectionists, his behaviour on the way to the execution site, his steadfastness on the gallows, and the proclamations of the commanding officers. John Brown's perseverance in his role to the end and unwavering conduct, even in the face of death, earned him broad respect.[460] The press also provided detailed reports about the

458 'Speech of Wm. Lloyd Garrison. At the Meeting in Tremont Temple, Dec. 2d, relating to the Execution of John Brown', *Liberator*, 16 December 1859, 198.

459 Ibid. Mayer, *All on Fire*, 502–4; and Oates, *To Purge This Land*, 355.

460 See, for instance, 'Friday, the Second of December', 'Movements for the Rescue of Brown', 'The Remains of Brown', *Southern Argus*, 2 December 1859, all 2; 'The Execution of Brown', 'Personal Bearing of the Charlestown Prisoners', *Southern Argus*, 3 December 1859, 2; 'The Execution of Brown' and 'Sketch of John Brown', *Southern Argus*, 6 December 1859, 2; 'The Remains of John Brown' and 'Will of John Brown', *Southern Argus*, 8 December 1859, 1; 'John Brown Hung', 'Incidents Connected with John Brown . . . A Fresh Excitement. Military Arrangement. The Remains of Brown. The Latest', 'The Execution of Brown', *Memphis Morning Enquirer*, 6, 7, and 11 and 18 December 1859, 2, 2, 1–2 respectively; 'The Execution of Brown. On the Gallows. Brown's Interview with His Fellow-Prisoners . . . His Wishes about His Property. About His Death. Mrs. Brown's Opinions. Proclamation by Governor Wise', *Harper's Weekly*, 10 December 1859, 794; 'John Brown's Will. Correspondence between Governor Wise and Mrs. Brown', in *Harper's Weekly*, 17 December 1859, 807; 'Execution of the Harper's Ferry Insurgents. John Brown's Autograph. A John Brown Meeting', *Harper's Weekly*, 24 December 1859, 823.

demonstrations of sympathy and counter-rallies on 2 December, as well as their speeches, sermons and resolutions.[461] This coverage was supplemented by human-interest stories from Brown's life and the lives of those involved in the fighting at Harpers Ferry.[462] The journey of the coffin to North Elba in upstate New York developed into a procession, which the press covered meticulously along with Brown's burial. Obituaries appeared,[463] and people sent countless letters, essays and occasional poems to newspapers. Garrison had to publish an extra edition of the *Liberator* for the first time in its history in order to accommodate everything.[464] More and more writers, artists, intellectuals and poets felt moved to take a stand. Walt Whitman, for instance, considered John Brown in his poem 'Year of the Meteors (1859–60)', and Herman Melville wrote his ominous poem 'The Portent'.[465] John Brown as a meteor, harbinger and signal of war became a *topos*, for Melville was not the only one who saw a war coming.[466]

461 See, for instance, 'John Brown Meeting in Boston. Meeting at Tremont Temple – Praying and Speech. Making by Members of the Abolition Society – Addresses by Garrison, Sewall and Others – Action of the Legislature, &c.', *New York Herald*, 5 December 1859, col. F; 'Not the Sentiment of the North' and 'An Anti-Brown Meeting', *Southern Argus*, 7 December 1859, 2; 'Hung in Effigy [Wise and Brown]', *Southern Argus*, 8 December 1859, 2; 'Brown Prayer Meetings at Montreal' and 'Incidents Connected with John Brown . . . One Hundred Guns in Albany. Prayers in Philadelphia. Colored Men Praying in Boston. The Bells Tolled, *Memphis Morning Enquirer*, 6 and 7 December 1859, 3, 2 respectively; 'Sympathy for John Brown', *Charleston Tri-weekly Courier*, 7 December 1859, col. D; 'Speech of Wm. Lloyd Garrison' and 'John Brown Meeting on the Cape', *Liberator*, 16 December 1859, 198–9; and 'John Brown Meeting. Mogadore, Dec. 6th, 1859', *Anti-slavery Bugle*, 17 December 1859, 2.

462 See, for example, 'John Brown's Firmness', 'Very Interesting Letter from Miss Fouke of Harper's Ferry' and 'Old Brown's Homestead', *Memphis Morning Enquirer*, 9, 15, and 20 December 1859, 2, 1 and 1 respectively.

463 See, for instance, 'The Body of John Brown in New York' and 'Old Brown's Body', *Southern Argus*, 7 and 10 December 1859, both 2. For positive as well as negative obituaries, see, for example, *New York Herald*, 5 December 1859, 7; *Boston Investigator*, 7 December 1859, 262; *Liberator*, 9 December 1859, col. F; *New York Tribune*, 10 December 1859, 4; *Hinds County Gazette*, 28 December 1859, col. E; *Vermont Patriot and State Gazette*, 31 December 1859, col. E.

464 See Oates, *To Purge This Land*, 355–8; and Mayer, *All on Fire*, 504.

465 Walt Whitman, 'Year of Meteors (1859–60)', in *Walt Whitman: Complete Poetry and Collected Prose*, ed. Justin Kaplan (New York: Library of America, 1982), 380; and Herman Melville, 'The Portent', in *Herman Melville: Moby-Dick, Billy Budd, and Other Writings* (New York: Library of America, 2000), 931. Melville dated the poem 1859, but first published it in 1866.

466 See Trodd and Stauffer, 'Introduction', in Trodd and Stauffer, *Meteor of War*, 1–4.

In the political arena as well, the topic of John Brown was still far from being buried following his execution. The 36th United States Congress convened in Washington for its first session on 5 December 1859 – three days after Brown had been executed. Yet the House of Representatives remained incapacitated for eight weeks because the election of the Speaker of the House sparked a fierce debate about who was responsible for Brown's raid. Soon the entire House of Representatives were bringing with them to the chamber both weapons and people, also armed, who sat in the public galleries as reinforcements in case it came to a fight. Many people thought the proxy conflict between the North and South would eventually be fought out with armed force in the halls of Congress.[467] The press covered the dispute and highlighted the link to the raid on Harpers Ferry.[468] In the Senate James Mason and Jefferson Davis, the subsequent president of the Confederate States of America, were appointed along with other senators to a select committee to find out, among other things, whether proof existed that the Republican Party was involved in the violence. The committee's findings were inconclusive, but the proceedings were followed through to the presentation of its report in June 1860 with great interest by the press.[469] John Brown also remained an important topic in the presidential campaign, for the Republicans had to repeatedly clarify their position on him and distance themselves from his violence. Abraham Lincoln, for example, declared in a speech in Kansas that Brown's raid was wrong for two reasons: 'It was a violation of law and it was, as all such attacks must be, futile as far as any effect it might have on the extinction of a great evil.' He stated that the United States Constitution provided for a non-violent means to express one's opinion about slavery, namely 'through the ballot box'. John Brown had showed 'great courage' and 'rare unselfishness', as even Governor Wise had testified. 'But no man, North or South, can approve of

467 See McPherson, Battle Cry, 198–201; and Ollinger Crenshaw, 'The Speakership Contest of 1859–1860: John Sherman's Election a Cause of Disruption?', Mississippi Valley Historical Review 29/3 (1942), 323–38.

468 See, for instance, Lowell Daily Citizen, 23 December 1859, col. A; Weekly Raleigh Register, 4 January 1860, col. D; North American, 5 January 1860, col. C; New York Times, 10 and 14 January 1860.

469 See United States Congress, Report. The Virginia General Assembly held its own investigation.

violence or crime.'[470] In this way John Brown and his violence remained present and relevant in the political process.

Brown's raid on Harpers Ferry and the end of slavery in the United States

The history of events that led to the abolition of slavery in the United States is well known. On 6 November 1860 the very thing happened that the South's political elite had feared: a Republican, Abraham Lincoln, was elected president. Lincoln's victory exclusively through votes from the North was tantamount to a revolution in the minds of his contemporaries.[471] The counterrevolution followed promptly, with the South Carolina legislature unanimously resolving just four days later to hold elections to a state assembly that was to define the future relationship between South Carolina and the Union. In February representatives from the states of the Deep South met and drafted a new constitution for the Confederate States of America. On 4 March 1861 Abraham Lincoln was inaugurated president. One month later he decided Navy ships should bring urgently needed resupply to Fort Sumter in the harbour at Charleston, South Carolina. As the Union fleet approached the mouth of the harbour on 12 April 1861, Confederate troops opened fire on Fort Sumter. The American Civil War had begun.[472]

This civil war was a war about slavery. Although there was frequent talk of the states' right to self-determination, the political elite of the slave states began this war because they insisted on their right to hold African Americans as slaves and to settle the new western territories

---

470 Abraham Lincoln, 'Speech at Elwood, Kansas, December 1 [November 30?], 1859', in *The Collected Works of Abraham Lincoln*, 496; see also the mention of Brown in Lincoln, 'Address at the Cooper Institute', in ibid., 319; Lincoln, 'Speech at Hartford', in ibid., 335–7; and Lincoln, 'Speech at New Haven', in ibid., 358.

471 See Heideking and Mauch, *Geschichte der USA*, 138–9; McPherson, *Ordeal by Fire*, 125–6; McPherson, *Battle Cry*, 232–3; and David Herbert Donald, *Lincoln* (New York: Simon & Schuster, 1995), 256. On the Civil War as a revolution, see also Aptheker, *Abolitionism*, Chapter 10.

472 For an introduction to the South's secession, Buchanan's reactions, the beginning of Civil War, and the characterization of these responses as a counterrevolution, see, for example, Heideking and Mauch, *Geschichte der USA*, 139; McPherson, *Ordeal by Fire*, Chapter 9; McPherson, *Battle Cry*, Chapter 8; and Aptheker, *Abolitionism*, Chapter 10.

with these slaves. In addition, they feared losing their power in the federal institutions and having their interests there marginalized. What they feared most, however, was that the government in Washington would do nothing more to stop abolitionist invasions: 'Now that the black Republicans have the power I suppose they will Brown us all,' shouted a man in South Carolina after hearing that Lincoln had been elected president.[473] In the North, the abolitionists and many Republicans saw the Civil War as a revolutionary war between two social systems, as a 'glorious second American Revolution' to end slavery and ensure 'Life, Liberty, and the Pursuit of Happiness' for every person in the United States – in short, as an opportunity to create a new Union that would actually deliver on the promises of the American Revolution of 1776.[474]

Abraham Lincoln did not begin the Civil War as a war to end slavery, but as a war to preserve the Union. He was reported to have told the *New York Herald* in December 1861 that 'emancipation would be equivalent to a John Brown raid, on a gigantic scale.'[475] But the Civil War continued. A war fought in traditional formations but conducted with modern weapons, it developed into the bloodiest war the United States ever waged.[476] It became a total war calling for the total mobilization and destruction of people and resources, a war that could only be ended with unconditional surrender. This radicalization of the war led as well to a radicalization of its official aims, with Lincoln and many of his officers viewing the freeing of the slaves as a militarily necessary means to conquer the Confederacy as of summer and autumn 1862. On 22 September 1862, five days after Union

---

473 Mary Boykin Miller Chesnut, *A Diary from Dixie* (New York, 1905), 1. On the Civil War as a war about slavery, see Sewell, *A House Divided*, Introduction and Chapters 5–8; Ira Berlin, Barbara J. Fields, Steven F. Miller, Joseph P. Reidy and Leslie S. Rowland, 'The Destruction of Slavery, 1861–1865', in Berlin, Fields, Miller, Reidy and Rowland (eds.), *Slaves No More* (Cambridge: Cambridge University Press, 1992). On the South's war objectives see also McPherson, *Ordeal by Fire*, 129–32; and McPherson, *Battle Cry*, especially 284, 308–12.

474 See Berlin et al., 'The Destruction of Slavery, 1861–1865', especially 3–4, 17–19; McPherson, *Ordeal by Fire*, 149–50; McPherson, *Battle Cry*, especially 308–12, 358, 452.

475 *New York Herald*, 10 December 1861. See McPherson, *Battle Cry*, 246–8, 284–307.

476 More than 620,000 soldiers died in this war, more than in all other wars involving the United States combined, from the Revolutionary War, the War of 1812, the Mexican–American War, and the Spanish–American War, the two World Wars, the Korean War, the Vietnam War, to the wars in Iraq and Afghanistan. See McPherson, *Ordeal by Fire*, vii–viii; and McPherson, *Battle Cry*, 471–7.

troops had repelled Lee's invasion at the Battle of Antietam or Sharpsville, Lincoln's Cabinet decided, on his initiative, to announce an Emancipation Proclamation on 1 January 1863.[477] This proclamation turned the Union Army into a liberation army. Lincoln had also decreed that African Americans be admitted into the Union Army as of 1 January 1863, so the freed slaves could now become liberators themselves. Thomas Wentworth Higginson, Brown's steadfast conspirator from the Secret Six who was still convinced of the transformational effect of violence, became colonel of one of the first African American regiments, the 1st South Carolina Volunteers. These regiments earned the respect of the northern public during the war campaigns of 1863. Attacks by Democrats in the North on Lincoln's emancipation policies thus became attacks on the Union war effort.[478]

In this war, John Brown became a symbol for the Union Army and gave meaning to the mass deaths of soldiers. The best-known example of this is the song 'John Brown's Body', which was likely sung by soldiers from Massachusetts to the tune of the Methodist hymn 'Say, Brothers Will You Meet Us', which was a favourite at Evangelical revivalist camp meetings. The first verse is:

John Brown's body lies a-mouldering in the grave;
John Brown's body lies a-mouldering in the grave;
John Brown's body lies a-mouldering in the grave;
But his soul goes marching on.
(chorus)
Glory Hally, Hallelujah! Glory Hally Hallelujah!
Glory Hally, Hallelujah! His soul's marching on![479]

---

477 The Emancipation Proclamation, 1 January 1863; General Records of the United States Government, RG 11; NAB, NARA, Washington, DC, ourdocuments.gov.

478 On the Emancipation Proclamation and the origin and effect of this measure, see Heideking and Mauch, *Geschichte der USA*, 144–6; and Berlin et al., 'The Destruction of Slavery, 1861–1865', 43–53; Sewell, *A House Divided*, 167–80; and McPherson, *Battle Cry*, Chapters 16–18, especially 564–5, 686–8. On the experiences and activities of the African Americans in the Union Army, see Ira Berlin, Barbara J. Fields, Steven F. Miller, Joseph P. Reidy and Leslie S. Rowland, 'The Black Military Experience, 1861–1867', in Berlin et al., *Slaves No More*, 187–233; and Finzsch, Horton and Horton, *Von Benin nach Baltimore*, 297–313. On Higginson's activities see Finzsch, Horton and Horton, *Von Benin nach Baltimore*, 300–3; and Edelstein, *Strange Enthusiasm*, Chapters 15–16.

479 George Kimball, 'Origin of the John Brown Song', *New England Magazine* 7/4 (1890), 373. On the origins of the song, see James Fuld, 'Battle Hymn of the Republic – (Say, Brothers, Will You Meet Us? – John Brown – Glory Hallelujah – John Brown's Baby

This song, for which there are many verses and versions, became one of the favourite hymns of the Union Army, especially among the African American regiments. Julia Ward Howe, wife of Secret Six conspirator Dr Samuel Gridley Howe, drew inspiration from this song and used its melody when she wrote the 'Battle Hymn of the Republic', one of the United States' most popular and best-known patriot songs. Other versions followed.[480] In the popular, military and political culture of the time, John Brown's raid on Harpers Ferry, the Union's war effort, and the abolition of slavery in the United States remained closely linked.[481]

When Lincoln was re-elected in 1864, he understood his election as a mandate to pursue the emancipation of the slaves as an end in itself and not just as a means to achieve victory for the Union. In his second term, he campaigned actively for a constitutional amendment that was to resolve the slavery issue in the United States once and for all.[482] The Thirteenth Amendment to the US Constitution simply states, 'Neither slavery nor involuntary servitude, except as a punishment for crime whereof the party shall have been duly convicted, shall exist within the United States, or any place subject to their jurisdiction.'[483] This constitutional amendment was adopted in the House of Representatives by

---

Has a Cold upon His Chest)', in James Fuld (ed.), *The Book of World-Famous Music: Classical, Popular, and Folk*, 5th ed. (New York: Dover Publications, 2000), 131–5; and Steven Cornelius, *Music of the Civil War Era* (Westport: Longman, 2004), 26–9, which also includes several verses from African American and German-speaking regiments. For other versions of the song reaching up to the 1960s civil rights movement, see 'Various Versions of the John Brown Song Spanning More than a Century', trans-video. net.

480 See also especially the version by the abolitionist theologian and later president of the African American Howard University, Reverend William Weston Patton: 'John Brown was John the Baptist of the Christ we are to see / Christ who of the bondmen shall the Liberator be /And soon thruout the Sunny South the slaves shall all be free / For his soul is marching on. 'Various Versions of the John Brown Song Spanning More Than a Century'. For a slightly modernized performance, see youtube.com.

481 See McPherson, *Ordeal by Fire*, 265.

482 See Heideking and Mauch, *Geschichte der USA*, 146–7; Berlin et al., 'The Destruction of Slavery, 1861–1865', 69–70; Sewell, *A House Divided*, 181–5; and McPherson, *Battle Cry*, 838–9.

483 Constitutional Amendment 13, Section 1, Constitution of the United States of America, from the House Joint Resolution proposing the Thirteenth Amendment to the Constitution, January 31, 1865; Enrolled Acts and Resolutions of Congress, 1789–1999; General Records of the United States Government, RG 11: NAB, NARA, ourdocuments. gov; also in Rakove, *The Annotated US Constitution and Declaration of Independence*.

119 votes to 56 on 31 January 1865. While cheering broke out in
Congress and representatives and spectators wept for joy and embraced,
a hundred rounds were fired from cannons in the streets of Washington
to honour the historic vote.[484] Lincoln signed the Thirteenth Amendment
the very next day. By 6 December 1865 the necessary number of states
had ratified it, and slavery in the United States of America was
abolished.[485]

What contribution did John Brown make to the emancipation of the
slaves in the United States with his raid on Harpers Ferry? This question,
which is at the same time a question about Brown's political success and
about the effectiveness of the form of political violence he co-invented
and practised, is the subject of controversial debate in American historiography. Revisionist and Marxist historians long assumed that the
Civil War would have broken out even without Brown's violent provocation and that slavery as an institution was already in its final stages and
would soon have been abandoned. In that case both Brown's violence
and the Civil War would have been in vain and superfluous.[486]

In recent decades, however, various historians have strongly questioned these interpretations. According to them, the raid on Harpers
Ferry provoked the majority of citizens in the South so much that any
compromise between them and the Republicans in the North became
impossible. This inability to compromise and cooperate was what led to
secession and war after the election of a Republican as president in
1860.[487] Qualified specialists in this epoch therefore now agree that 'the
act for which Brown and sixteen of his followers, including two of his
sons, paid with their lives ... did much to bring on that war,'[488] a war

484 See George Washington Julian, 'George W. Julian's Journal – the Assassination
of Lincoln', *Indiana Magazine of History* 11/4 (1915), 327.

485 See McPherson, *Battle Cry*, 840; and Henry Wilson, *History of the Antislavery
Measures of the Thirty-Seventh and Thirty-Eighth United-States Congresses, 1861–65*
(Boston, 1865), Chapter 13.

486 For a brief overview of the authors who came to the conclusion that the war was
either avoidable or unavoidable, see Warren, *The Legacy of the Civil War*, 93–100. For a
discussion about the different positions and their prerequisites and implications, see
Edward Ayers, 'Worrying about the Civil War', in Perry Halttunen and Lewis Perry
(eds.), *Moral Problems in American Life* (Ithaca, 1998), 145–67.

487 Oates, 'God's Stone in the Pool of Slavery', especially 12, 19, 21.

488 James McPherson, 'Escape and Revolt in Black and White', in *This Mighty
Scourge: Perspectives on the Civil War* (Oxford: Oxford University Press, 2007), 29; and,
almost identically worded, Wallenstein, 'Incendiaries All', 170.

that led to the abolition of slavery being enshrined in the Constitution. In addition, recent research suggests that slavery in the United States was by no means at an end and could have persisted into the twentieth century in the absence of violent intervention. 'It required a war to end American slavery in the nineteenth century,' according to Gary J. Kornblith.[489] 'In one sense the Harpers Ferry raid was a tragic, wretched failure,' notes, therefore, James M. McPherson, 'But in a larger sense, perhaps, if Brown's goal was to provoke a violent confrontation and liberate the slaves, he succeeded beyond his dreams.'[490] As the reconstruction of Brown's strategic considerations has shown, his aim – should the freeing of the slaves by guerrilla warfare fail – was precisely that: by raiding Harpers Ferry to provoke the South to such an extent that the election of a Republican as the next president would inevitably lead to civil war, the war that was necessary to abolish slavery in the United States. The raid on Harpers Ferry must therefore be seen as a decisive contribution to the emancipation of the slaves in the United States. John Brown had attained his goals and thus achieved politico-symbolic victory much more clearly and independently than did Orsini. The raid on Harpers Ferry was successful, and Brown's contemporaries also perceived it as such.

Such intentionalist argumentation and interpretation must, however, not lose sight of contingency. The success of the raid on Harpers Ferry was not automatic, despite the great tractive force of the implicit action programme of provocation that John Brown set in motion with his violence. The act of violence could have failed at many moments, also, and especially, in its politico-symbolic dimension: if Lieutenant Green had had his sword that day and killed John Brown with it during the hostage rescue, if Governor Wise had decided to suspend usual legal procedures and have Brown and his volunteers court-martialled and shot, if the American press had neglected the story or consistently dismissed it as the tragicomical undertaking of a few madmen, if politicians and journalists in the North and South had not sought to extract political capital from the affair, if radical abolitionists and prominent

---

489 Gary J. Kornblith, 'Rethinking the Coming of the Civil War: A Counterfactual Exercise', *Journal of American History* 90/1 (2003), 102; whose assessment draws on, among other sources, works by David Eltis, Seymour Drescher and William W. Freehling.

490 McPherson, *Ordeal by Fire*, 116.

intellectuals had not commented on the violence at all or only in order to disassociate themselves from it – John Brown's provocation would have failed entirely. Conversely, this shows how dependent on preconditions a successful terrorist act is, and how many shoulders bear responsibility for the politico-symbolic success of such violence.

This reality was to be first experienced by the three people who during the 1860s sought to imitate the strategy enacted by Orsini and Brown and to reproduce their success. All three attempts at imitation failed, which is precisely why they are so informative regarding the conditions for the success of terrorism, a new form of political violence that would soon become an integral part of the repertoire of insurgent violence in the United States as well as Europe. The transmission of news and its reception played a key role in the further spread of terrorist tactics – just as they had in John Brown's reception of Orsini's assassination attempt.

5

Transatlantic communication

European and Russian coverage of the raid on Harpers Ferry

'A true Michael Kohlhaas': John Brown as a liberation hero and a Bible-thumping Christian

Like the news of Orsini's attempt on the life of Napoleon III, the reports of John Brown's raid on Harpers Ferry were a sensation that sparked international interest: they provoked comparisons to both real and fictional folk heroes, such as Heinrich von Kleist's *Michael Kohlhaas* in German-speaking lands, and served as the inspiration for both real and fictional revolutionary heroes in Russia. The news of Brown's act of violence arrived in Europe on 27 October 1859 with the steam clipper *Circassian*, which had left New York ten days earlier on Monday, 17 October, passing St John's on the coast of Newfoundland at midnight on 18 October. News of the raid thus reached the Old World by sea some two weeks earlier than it did the US West Coast, travelling by land, even though the *Circassian*, which regularly plied the route between Galway on the west coast of Ireland and New York for the Royal Atlantic Steam Navigation Company (or Galway Line), had been delayed on this Atlantic crossing by severe easterly storms.[1]

---

1 On the transportation of the news, see 'The United States', *The Times*, 29 October 1859, col. F. On the Royal Atlantic Steam Navigation Company and the *Circassian*, see Timothy Collins, *Transatlantic Triumph and Heroic Failure: The Story of the Galway Line* (Cork: Collins Press, 2002); and 'Circassian 1857', 'The Ships List', theshipslist.com.

From Galway, the news was immediately passed by telegraph to newspapers across Great Britain on 27 October. As in the United States, the use of the telegraph in Great Britain, allowing for the prompt transmission of news even to the provincial press, was a recent phenomenon. It had not been until the autumn and winter 1858–9 that German émigré Paul Julius Reuters – an 1848 revolutionary and the founder of the Reuters Telegraphic Company – had been successful in delivering news from abroad to all of Great Britain's cities. His telegraph network rapidly improved the access that newspapers had to such reporting.[2]

Before embarking to cross the Atlantic, the *Circassian* had taken the New York newspapers from 18 October 1859 on board. That was the day when Lee's marines had stormed the fire engine house and when the first telegrams, still contradictory and often exaggerated, appeared in East Coast newspapers. The main US news item that appeared in newspapers across Great Britain on 28 and 29 October sounded accordingly vague:

A fearful insurrection was reported to-day at Harper's Ferry. Negroes seized the United States Arsenal, and were sending cartloads of muskets into Maryland and elsewhere . . . The object of the outbreak is unknown. The details are very confused. All telegraph wires leading to Harper's Ferry were cut . . . Later despatches say that all the railroad trains were stopped. The insurrectionists number from 500 to 700.[3]

---

2 See Michael Palmer, 'The British Press and International News, 1851–99: Of Agencies and Newspapers', in George Boyce, James Curran and Pauline Wingate (eds.), *Newspaper History* (London: Constable, 1978), 206; Donald Read, *The Power of News: The History of Reuters, 1849–1989* (Oxford: Oxford University Press, 1992), 22–3; and Roland Wenzlhuemer, *Connecting the Nineteenth-Century World: The Telegraph and Globalization* (Cambridge: Cambridge University Press, 2013), especially Chapters 4.3 and 7. On *The Times*'s own network of correspondents, see Palmer, 'The British Press and International News', 205–6; *The History of* The Times: *The Tradition Established, 1841–1884* (London: The Times, 1939), Chapters 7, 13; and Philip Howard and Jack Lonsdale, *We Thundered Out: 200 Years of* The Times, *1785–1985* (London: Times Books, 1985), 18, 22–4. On the correspondents in the United States, see ibid., 53.

3 'The United States', *The Times*, 29 October 1859, col. F. Identical reports were published, for example, in *Belfast News-Letter*, 28 October 1859; *Glasgow Herald*, 28 October 1859; *Liverpool Mercury*, 28 October 1859; *Caledonian Mercury and Daily Express*, 29 October 1859; *Manchester Examiner and Times*, 29 October 1859; *Leeds Mercury*, 29 October 1859; *Hampshire Telegraph and Sussex Chronicle*, 29 October 1859; *Morning Chronicle*, 29 October 1859; and *Lloyd's Weekly Newspaper*, 30 October 1859.

The alarmist tone and negative assessment reflect the initial coverage in the United States.

Newspapers in France, Russia and the German-speaking world reran this account in their own languages, passing on its assessment as well. The coverage appeared in the press of the capital cities throughout Europe and in prominent German-language newspapers from 29 October to 1 November 1859 and was reprinted in the provincial newspapers in the days following. Just as in Great Britain, the raid on Harpers Ferry was considered the most important news from North America on the European continent. French newspapers immediately put it on the front page.[4] Newspapers with a readership across Germany, such as the *Kölnische Zeitung* and the Augsburg *Allgemeine Zeitung*, carried it on the front page under the headline 'Negro Rebellion in Virginia' and then provided more in-depth coverage in the international news section.[5] The initial reception of this abolitionist violence was uniform in all other European countries as well because their coverage all depended on the same source. In the following days, some newspapers supplemented this summary of events by reprinting, verbatim, the first telegrams of 17 October from Baltimore and Washington, DC – telegrams that had been published in East Coast newspapers on

---

Ipswich Journal, 29 October 1859; and *Reynolds's Newspaper*, 30 October 1859, ran abridged versions of the report.

4 For an example of a summary version by the French news agency Havas-Bullier, see 'Télégraphie privée. Le steamer *Circassian* apporte les nouvelles suivantes de New-York', *Journal des débats*, 29 October 1859, 1; and 'Télégraphie privée. Londres, 28 octobre. Galway (Irlande), 26 octobre', *Le Constitutionnel*, 29 October 1859, 1. For the verbatim rendition, see, for example, 'On racontait le jour même qu'une terrible insurrection avait eu lieu à Harper's ferry', *Journal des débats*, 31 October 1859, 2; and 'Le vapeur *Circassian* est arrivé à Galway', *Le Constitutionnel*, 30 October 1859, 2. For the Russian translation, see 'N'iu-Iork, 18/6 okt.', *Sankt Peterburgskie vedomosti*, 18 October/30 October 1859, 993; or 'Novosti zagranichnie – telegrafnie depeshi', *Severnaia pchela*, 19 October/31. October 1859, 905.

5 'Vereinigte Staaten von Nordamerika', *Allgemeine Zeitung*, 1 November 1859, 4980. See the almost identical article entitled 'America', *Kölnische Zeitung*, 1 November 1859, 5; and 'Nachtrag. Telegraphische (Privat-) Depeschen. New-York, 18. Oktober', *Wiener Zeitung*, 29 October 1859, 8; 'Newyork, 18. October', *Die Presse*, 29 October 1859, 5; 'Nord-Amerika. New York, 28. October. [Neger-Aufstand]', *Neue Preußische Zeitung*, 30 October 1859; and the reprints of this article as 'Aus Nord-Amerika', *Görlitzer Anzeiger*, 1 November 1859, 1; 'Zu Harpers-Ferry', *Innsbrucker Nachrichten*, 4 November 1859, 2191.

18 October.[6] This perhaps served to keep the topic current until more recent news became available.

The reporting had already improved by the next week: with the arrival of the *Canada* in Liverpool early on 31 October 1859, more diverse accounts became available. The three-masted paddle-wheel steamer, which covered the New York–Liverpool route for the Cunard Line, brought the newspapers of 18 October from New York; the newspapers from 19 October from Boston; the newspapers from Halifax, Novia Scotia, published on 21 October; and a report for *The Times* from its own correspondent in New York.[7] Three days later the steamer *Indian* from the Montreal Ocean Steamship Company (also known as the Allan Line) reached Liverpool with the news of 22 October from Quebec, and this was followed three days later by the Cunard Line's *Africa* with the news of 26 October from New York.[8] Subsequent arrivals continued at similar intervals.

The press in Great Britain remained the gold standard for news from the United States: continental European newspapers received most of their information about North America from the ships sailing to England and Ireland (then still part of the British Empire), once the news reports brought by those ships spread to the British papers.[9] This dependence is apparent in the introductory comments to the articles, for instance: 'The *Africa* arrived from New York with news up to the 26th of last month . . . *The Globe* writes.'[10] Russian newspaper coverage

---

6 For France, see, for example, 'On écrit de New-York, le 18 octobre, au *Times*', *Journal des débats*, 5 November 1859, 1.

7 See 'America. (By Electric and International Telegraph)', *The Times*, 31 October 1859, 7; and on the *Canada*: 'Canada 1848/Mississippi', 'The Ships List', theshipslist.com.

8 See 'America', *The Times*, 4 and 6 November 1859, 7, 9. On the *Montreal Ocean Steamship Company* and the *Indian* see 'The Allan Line', 'The Ships List', theshipslist.com, and 'Allan Royal Mail Line – Passenger Lists and Historical Documents Archives', Gjenvick-Gjonvik Archives, gjenvick.com. On the *Africa* see the relevant sections in Fox, *Transatlantic*.

9 Similarly in the case of the *National Zeitung*, see Jürgen Wilke, 'The Telegraph and Transatlantic Communication Relations', in Norbert Finzsch and Ursula Lehmkuhl (eds.), *Atlantic Communications: The Media in American and German History from the Seventeenth to the Twentieth Century* (Oxford: Berg, 2004), 121, which, however, refers primarily to the period beginning in 1875. Volker Depkat came to the same conclusion for the period 1789 to 1830. See his *Amerikabilder in politischen Diskursen: Deutsche Zeitschriften von 1789 bis 1830* (Stuttgart: Klett-Cotta, 1998), Chapter 2.1, especially 71.

10 'Télégraphie privée . . . L'*Africa* est arrivé de New-York', *Journal des débats*, 10 November 1859, 1.

of the United States was based on reports in continental European newspapers, so indirectly it, too, depended on the British press.[11]

This reliance on the British press occurred even when countries had their own maritime communications. For instance, Augsburg's *Allgemeine Zeitung* reported on 4 November 1859 that the three-masted steamship *Teutonia*, which sailed between Hamburg, Southampton and New York for the Hamburg-Amerikanische Packet-Actien-Gesellschaft (also called the Hamburg America Line, or HAPAG), had arrived in Hamburg from New York with outdated reports.[12] The reports that the North German Lloyd line's three-masted steam clipper *Newyork* brought from the United Stated in mid-December came to German newspapers first through the British press. Even steamships travelling from the United States to Germany deposited their newspapers and telegraphic dispatches with news agencies in Southampton. Articles could therefore already be published while the ships continued on their way to Hamburg or Bremerhaven.[13]

The geographical source of the news was another crucial factor in European coverage. The *Circassian*, the *Canada*, the *Indian*, the *Africa*, the *Teutonia*, the *Newyork* and other steamships that brought newspapers from the United States across the Atlantic in the subsequent weeks and months connected Europe with ports in the northern US and Canada. Hence the European press drew its information almost exclusively from correspondence and media based in the north: New York City, Boston,

11 For articles that mention the ship that transported the news, see, for example, 'Amerika', *Severnaya pchela*, 14 December 1859, 1096, and 24 December 1859, 1131–2.

12 'Vereinigte Staaten von Nordamerikar', *Allgemeine Zeitung*, 4 November 1859, 8. On the HAPAG, founded in 1847, see Bodo Hans Moltmann, *Geschichte der deutschen Handelsschiffahrt* (Hamburg: Hanseatischer Merkur, 1981), 120–2; and Susanne Wiborg and Klaus Wiborg, *1847–1997: The World Is Our Oyster: 150 Years of Hapag-Lloyd* (Hamburg: Hapag-Lloyd, 1997), 18–52; on the *Teutonia*, see 'Heritage-Ships: Emigrant Ship Images', heritage-ships.com.

13 See 'America', *The Times*, 9 December 1859, 9; and 'Vereinigte Staaten von Nordamerika', *Allgemeine Zeitung*, 12 December 1859, 5668. On the Norddeutsche Lloyd, founded in 1857, see Moltmann, *Geschichte der deutschen Handelsschiffahrt*, 124–6, Adolf E. Hofmeister, 'Bis 1857: Vorgeschichte und Gründung', in Dirk Peters (ed.), *Der Norddeutsche Lloyd* (Bremen: H. M. Hauschild, 2007); and Christian Ostersehlte, '1857–1918: Aufstieg zur Größe', in Peters, *Der Norddeutsche Lloyd*, 21–36. On the *Newyork*, see Arnold Kludas, *Die Seeschiffe des Norddeutschen Lloyd* (Herford: Koehler, 1991), 10.

Quebec and Halifax.[14] Because the European newspapers rejected slavery as an institution – even *The Times*, which did not have a very friendly position towards abolitionism – they were substantively more in tune with the reporting from the northern states than with the coverage and analysis coming from the southern states.[15] It seems that the European papers and their correspondents saw no need to actively seek out papers or articles from the South. The perspectives of the southern states, meanwhile, usually only reached European editors and their readers indirectly, by way of select reprints in the northern press or through what US correspondents had read. The European newspapers received the positions and assessments of supporters of slavery only from the big northern democratic papers (especially the *New York Herald*) and the verbatim transmission of speeches such as President James Buchanan's State of the Union Address.[16] The

14 See also Seymour Drescher, 'Servile Insurrection and John Brown's Body in Europe', *Journal of American History* 80/2 (September 1993), 499–524, reprinted in Finkelman, *His Soul Goes Marching On*, 256, 266. He analysed primarily the reactions in Great Britain and France.

15 For Prussia and Saxony, see Michael Löffler, *Preußens und Sachsens Beziehungen zu den USA während des Sezessionskrieges, 1860–1865* (Münster: Lit, 1999), 35–6. For England and France, see Drescher, 'Servile Insurrection', although he incorrectly describes *The Times* as taking a pro-slavery stance. See also the analysis by Martin Crawford, *The Anglo-American Crisis of the Mid-Nineteenth Century: The Times and America, 1850–1862* (Athens: University of Georgia Press, 1987), Chapter 4, which states, 'For *The Times* during the 1850s to have adopted any other attitude toward southern slavery but that of severe moral condemnation would have been unthinkable . . . In the view of *The Times*, slavery was "an abomination in the sight of man and God".' Ibid., 56–7. All that the conservative editors rejected was any kind of violence and, therefore, radical abolitionism. The journalist who reported from the United States for *Le Constitutionnel* took a similar position.

16 See, for example, 'Amérique. (Correspondance particulière du *Siècle*). New-York, le 18 octobre' and 'Amérique. (Correspondance particulière du *Siècle*). New-York, le 26 octobre', *Le Siècle*, respectively 4 and 9 November 1859, 2; 'Le paquebot Canada est arrivé à Liverpool', 'On écrit de Harpers-Ferry au même journal', and 'On lit dans le *New-York Herald*', *Journal des débats*, respectively 18 and 28 December 1859, 1; 'Amerika', *Sankt Petersburgskie vedomosti*, 14 November 1859, 1100–1, and 19 November 1859, 1124–5; 'Novosti zagranichnie', *Severnaya pchela*, 30 December 1859, 1142; and 'Die americanische Präsidenten-Botschaft. Köln, 11. Januar' and 'America', *Kölnische Zeitung*, 12 and 13 January 1859, 1, 3; Z 63 Köln [Julius Faucher?], 'Ein Putsch in den Vereinigten Staaten. Köln. 10. November', and 'America', *Kölnische Zeitung*, 11 and 15 November 1859, 1, 2. On the correspondents' codes, see the relevant explanatory pages in Karl Buchheim, *Die Geschichte der Kölnischen Zeitung, ihrer Besitzer und Mitarbeiter*, 4 vols. (Cologne: M. DuMont Schauberg, 1930). A conclusive attribution of the correspondent's code Z 63 is missing. In ibid., vol. 2, 196, Buchheim identifies the correspondent with

means and routes of transport thus shaped the content of the news and reporting.

Important similarities and common denominators in fundamental political positions, as well as in the sources and use of information, resulted in reporting that was largely consistent across Europe. This is evident from the fact that the European papers not only presented the change in John Brown's image from 'madman' to martyr but also carried out this change themselves.[17] For example, the *Kölnische Zeitung* initially wrote of the 'insurgents' and 'ruffians of Harper's Ferry', but soon respectfully referred to 'Captain John Brown', the 'slave-freer', and the 'hero of Harper's Ferry'. In France 'these wretched people [*ces misérables*] of Harper's Ferry' became 'genuine heroes', and John Brown himself was transformed from 'a hapless fool' to an 'energetic defender of freedom for the Negroes'.[18] Another common denominator among

---

this code as Julius Faucher, who lived in London until 1861 and worked in the foreign-policy section of the *Morning Star*. Buchheim's conclusion that Faucher ceased working as a correspondent for the *Kölnische Zeitung* in 1851 is not definitively supported by the sources he cites. Instead, it is likely that Faucher continued reporting from London until he returned to Germany in 1861, especially given that his code was not reassigned. On Faucher generally, see 'Julius Faucher', in *Meyers Konversations-Lexikon*, 19 vols., 4th ed. (Leipzig: Bibliographisches Institut, 1885–92), vol. 6, 70–1.

17 'Madman' was for instance the epithet used by Horace Greeley in his initial reaction to John Brown and his raid of Harpers Ferry. See Greeley's 'A Most Extraordinary Telegraphic Bulletin Startled the Whole Country Yesterday', *New York Daily Tribune*, 18 October 1859, 4; and on this above, p. 296; while the Transcendentalist American poet Ralph Waldo Emerson in his Fraternity lecture in mid-November asked that people 'not cry with the fools, "Madman!" when a hero passes'. See 'Emerson on Courage', *Liberator*, 18 November 1859, 1; and above, p. 327.

18 'Correspondance particulière du Constitutionnel. New York, 26 octobre 1859', *Le Constitutionnel*, 9 November 1859, 2; as well as 'Amérique. (Correspondance particulière du Siècle) New York, le 1 novembre 1859', and 'Amérique. (Correspondance particulière du Siècle) New York, le 5 novembre 1859', *Le Siècle*, 16 and 21 November 1859, both on p. 2. For an analysis of this process, see 'États-Unis. (Correspondance particulière du Siècle.) New York, 1 novembre 1859', *Le Siècle*, 16 November 1859, 2. On the terms 'insurgents' (*Aufständische*) and 'ruffians' (*Tumultanten*), see 'America', *Kölnische Zeitung*, 4, 6 and 9 November 1859, 2, 3, 5 respectively. For 'Captain John Brown' (*Capitän John Brown*) see 'America', *Kölnische Zeitung*, 18 December 1859, 3. For 'slave freer' (*Sclaven-Befreier*), see, for example, Roderich Arndt, 'America. Köln, 2. Dezember', *Kölnische Zeitung*, 3 December 1859, 1; and 'America im Jahre 1859', *Kölnische Zeitung*, 9 January 1859, 1. For 'Hero of Harper's Ferry' (*Held von Harper's Ferry*), see 'America', *Kölnische Zeitung*, 16 and 19 November 1859, both on p. 5. On the identification of Roderich Arndt as the correspondent, see Buchheim, *Die Geschichte der Kölnischen Zeitung*, vol. 4, 106; for Arndt's biography, see Buchheim, *Die Geschichte der Kölnischen*

the European papers was their critical reporting on the response to the attempted insurrection within the United States. On the question whether the rules of fairness and due process were being upheld in the US, discussion in the German-speaking lands sometimes revealed a competitiveness and arrogance vis-à-vis the New World. Usually, however, this question was motivated by a desire to understand the advantages and disadvantages of American democracy in order to draw conclusions for the writer's or newspaper's own political demands.[19] This interest in comparing systems of governance was less pronounced in Great Britain and France.[20]

The topic that attracted the most attention throughout Europe was the terror in the slave states. The diplomat Friedrich Freiherr von Gerolt – the Prussian ambassador in Washington – reported on acts of violence against Germans suspected of being abolitionists: one was 'thrown out of a railroad carriage while the train was travelling at full speed because

---

Zeitung, vol. 3, 101. The *Neue Preußische Zeitung* called John Brown the 'old Capitani Brown' and 'slave-freer'. 'Nord-Amerika. [Der Virginische Proceß]', *Neue Preußische Zeitung*, 12 November 1859; 'Nord-Amerika. [Die Vertheidigung des Sclavenbefreiers]', *Neue Preußische Zeitung*, 20 November 1859; 'Nord-Amerika. [Die Hinrichtung Brown's]', *Neue Preußische Zeitung*, 21 December 1859. For Great Britain and France, see Drescher, 'Servile Insurrection', 262–6.

19 See, for instance, the reports from New York under the heading 'Vereinigte Staaten von Nordamerika', *Allgemeine Zeitung*, 19 November 1859, 5285–6; 'Vereinigte Staaten von Nordamerika', *Allgemeine Zeitung*, 4 December 1859, 5528; 'Vereinigte Staaten von Nordamerika', *Allgemeine Zeitung*, 14 December 1859, 5704; 'Vereinigte Staaten von Nordamerika', *Allgemeine Zeitung*, 16 December 1859, 5740; Hermann Raster, 'Blicke auf die Politik der Verein. Staaten von Nordamerika. New-York, 13. Jan.', *Allgemeine Zeitung*, 2 February 1860, 533–4; Z 63 Köln [Julius Faucher?], 'Ein Putsch in den Vereinigten Staaten. Köln, 10. November', *Kölnische Zeitung*, 11 November 1859, 1; Roderich Arndt, 'America. Köln, 2. Dezember', *Kölnische Zeitung*, 3 December 1859, 1; 'America', *Kölnische Zeitung*, 8 December 1859, 3; *Kölnische Zeitung*, 11 December 1859, 3; *Kölnische Zeitung* 18 December 1859, 3; 'Nord-Amerika', *Neue Preußische Zeitung*, 2 December 1859; *Neue Preußische Zeitung*, 4 December 1859; and *Neue Preußische Zeitung*, 18 December 1859. On the United States being used as an argument for or against democracy, federalism, and so on in political debates from after the French Revolution to the 1830s as well as in the constitutional convention and in the parliament meeting in the Frankfurt Paulskirche during the revolutionary years of 1848 and 1849, see Depkat, *Amerikabilder in politischen Diskursen*; and Charlotte A. Lerg, *Amerika als Argument: Die deutsche Amerika-Forschung im Vormärz und ihre politische Deutung in der Revolution von 1848/49* (Bielefeld: Transcript, 2011). For Great Britain and France, see Drescher, 'Servile Insurrection', 266–9.

20 See, for example, the self-confident appraisals in 'États-Unis. (Correspondance particulière du Siècle.) New York, 1 novembre 1859', *Le Siècle*, 16 November 1859, 2.

of an imprudent remark uttered'.[21] The press reports stressed that the
fear of abolitionism and of slave revolts was destroying the important
achievements of American democracy, such as freedom of speech and
freedom of the press. The trend towards denunciation was said to be
growing to the point that a person in Virginia had more to fear when
expressing his opinion freely than in tsarist Russia. These kinds of exclusion and repression were explained by the instability of the slave system
and the awareness of that institution's unjustness. According to an article in the *Kölnische Zeitung*, for example, 'this fear is a direct admission
of guilt and indirect proof that the presence of the colossal powder keg
that has accumulated over the past forty years has made an insurrection
of this kind inevitable in the long run.' The unrest in Virginia and
Maryland was 'a revealing symptom of the volatility of a societal organization based on the repression of the weak by the strong, on slavery',
opined *Le Siècle*'s New York correspondent. The unrealistic attempt at
insurrection by a few individuals, he continued, had sufficed to threaten
the entire system.[22] According to European observers, the fact that such
a militarily insignificant action could trigger such strong reactions owed
to slavery's instability as an institution. The criticism by the European
press therefore did not apply to the entire United States but rather only
to the slave states in which the excesses were being reported.

European intellectuals further intensified this critique from the leading European newspapers. Whereas American intellectuals emphasized
that John Brown and his group were simply acting in accordance with
the founding ideas of the United States, their European colleagues saw
the death sentences given to the raiders of Harpers Ferry as a self-
renunciation of the United States as a nation. The Polish poet Cyprian
Kamil Norwid, for example, wrote an open letter to the United States
which included a poem 'To Citizen Brown'. In it he portrayed the execution of John Brown as a betrayal of George Washington and Tadeusz

---

21 Friedrich Joseph Karl Freiherr von Gerolt to the Prince Regent, 16 January 1860,
cited in Löffler, *Preußens und Sachsens Beziehungen zu den USA*, 40. On Gerolt, see
especially Enno Eimers, *Preußen und die USA 1850 bis 1867: Transatlantische
Wechselwirkungen* (Berlin: Duncker & Humblot, 2004), Chapter 2.1.

22 Z 63 Köln [Julius Faucher?], 'Ein Putsch in den Vereinigten Staaten', *Kölnische
Zeitung*, 11 November 1859, 1, 'Amérique. (Correspondance particulière du Siècle.)
New-York, le 19 novembre 1859', *Le Siècle*, 3 December 1859, 2. See also *Allgemeine
Zeitung*, 14 December 1859, 5704; and *Allgemeine Zeitung*, 2 February 1860, 534. On
Great Britain and France, see Drescher, 'Servile Insurrection', 266–9.

Kosciuśzko, the famous Polish freedom fighter of the American Revolution. As Norwid put it, Brown's death sentence proved that the stars on the American flag were nothing more than fireworks. By hanging Brown, America had hanged itself.[23]

On the day Brown was executed, Victor Hugo – himself an émigré from Napoleon's France – published a letter to the United States under the heading 'Un mot sur John Brown' (A Word on John Brown) in which he – like Thoreau and Emerson – compared John Brown to Christ: *Christus nos liberavit*, he wrote in Latin – Christ has set us free.[24] As Hugo explained to his European readers,

> Look, then, to what is taking place in that country of Washington at this present moment. In the Southern States of the Union there are slaves; and this circumstance is regarded with indignation, as the most monstrous of inconsistencies, by the pure and logical conscience of the Northern States. A white man, a free man, John Brown, sought to deliver these negro slaves from bondage . . . John Brown endeavored to commence the work of emancipation by the liberation of slaves in Virginia. Pious, austere, animated with the old Puritan spirit, inspired by the spirit of the Gospel, he sounded to these men, these oppressed brothers, the rallying cry of Freedom (*Christus nos liberavit*).[25]

Hugo disputed the impartiality and legality of the proceedings against Brown, challenged his death sentence, and called for vigilance in 'the civilized world', where such injustice could not be allowed to take place without comment: 'At this moment, America attracts the eyes of the

23 Jerzy Jedlicki, 'The Image of America in Poland, 1776–1945', *Reviews in American History* 14/4 (1986), 674–5.

24 Victor Hugo, 'Un mot sur John Brown. Hauteville-House, 2 décembre 1859', *Le Siècle*, 10 December 1859, 1–2, quotation at 1. Reprinted in Victor Hugo, 'Aux états-unis d'Amérique', in *Œuvres complètes de Victor Hugo: Actes et paroles*, ed. Paul Meurice and Gustave Simon (Paris: Albin Michel, 1938), vol. 2, 142–4. For a critical view of Hugo in exile, see David Baguley, *Napoleon III and His Régime: An Extravaganza* (Baton Rouge: Louisiana State University Press, 2000), Chapter 2.

25 'Victor Hugo on John Brown', *London News*, 10 Dec. 1859; also available under the title 'Victor Hugo's letter to the *London News* regarding John Brown', *London News* (n.d.), at en.wikisource.org. The article is a translation of Hugo, 'Un mot sur John Brown'; Hugo, 'Aux états-unis d'Amérique', 143.

whole of Europe.'[26] If John Brown really were to be hanged, responsibility would lie, Hugo argued, not only with the judge, or the governor, or the State of Virginia, but with the whole federation, which had done too little to prevent such a catastrophe. For 'viewed in a moral light, it seems to me that a portion of the enlightenment of humanity would be eclipsed, that even the ideas of justice and injustice would be obscured on the day which should witness the assassination of Emancipation by Liberty.'[27] The letter closed with a reference to George Washington as an ambiguous emblem of political freedom: 'Yes . . . there is something more terrible than Cain slaying Abel: It is Washington slaying Spartacus!'[28] Writing to the people of Crete a few years later in 1867, Victor Hugo ranked John Brown among the great freedom fighters of his time: 'Just as John Brown stood up for the negroes, and as Garibaldi stood up for Italy, so too is Zimbrakakis standing up for Crete.' Hugo sought to encourage the Cretans in their struggle against Turkish rule, and he called on them to follow John Brown's example: 'If he [Zimbrakakis] takes things to the very end, and he will, then he will be a great man, whether he succumbs like John Brown or prevails like Garibaldi.'[29] Thus John Brown was turned into an almost 'native' figure in European political struggles.

Beyond these shared responses in the European press, however, national political experience also influenced the reception of the raid on Harpers Ferry, in both scope and substance. In Great Britain the struggles of the British abolitionist movement and the successful legislative

---

26 'Victor Hugo's letter to the *London News*'; Hugo, 'Un mot sur John Brown', 1; Hugo, 'Aux états-unis d'Amérique', 143.

27 With this expression (*l'assassinat de la délivrance par la liberté*), Hugo refers to the execution of the idea of emancipation personified by the emancipator (of the slaves, that is John Brown) by the idea of liberty embodied by the nation of liberty (the United States). 'Victor Hugo's letter to the *London News*'; Hugo, 'Un mot sur John Brown', 1; Hugo, 'Aux états-unis d'Amérique', 144.

28 'Victor Hugo's letter to the *London News*'; Hugo, 'Un mot sur John Brown', 2; Hugo, 'Aux états-unis d'Amérique', 144. For a reprint of the English translation, see, for example, 'Victor Hugo on Old Brown', *Memphis Morning Enquirer*, 29 December 1859, p. 2. On the comparison between John Brown and Spartacus, see also Hartman, 'Transatlantic Spartacus', which analyses how the anarchist Joseph Déjacque reacted to Brown's act of violence.

29 'Réponse de Victor Hugo', in Elpis Melena, *Erlebnisse und Beobachtungen eines mehr als 20jährigen Aufenthaltes auf Kreta*, rev. new ed. (Zehdenick: Pandora, 2008), 173.

abolition of slavery in its own colonies mediated the perception and assessment of what John Brown had done. Granted, the British anti-slavery movement had declined since the Emancipation Act of 1833 and played only a marginal role in British politics by the late 1850s.[30] Nevertheless, decades of intense clashes over the issue of slavery and close contacts with the American Anti-Slavery Society had given rise to a keen sensitivity and interest in the subject and produced expert journalists and a well-informed readership.

The Times immediately judged the raid on Harpers Ferry to be an 'extraordinary incident' and devoted a great deal of coverage to it.[31] Other leading British newspapers did likewise. In the following weeks they regularly published brief notes or long articles about the raid's defeat, the trial, the reactions of the parties, attempts by the Democrats to instrumentalize it, the emergence of martyr worship in the North, the letters from Lawrence Thatcher, and reports on the riots in the South. Moreover, the Morning Chronicle and The Times, among others, printed key documents verbatim, such as Brown's Provisional Constitution and his address before the court. They also published dispatches and articles from the New York Herald, the New York Times and the Boston Journal, as well as letters from readers on the topic.[32]

As early as the beginning of November and based merely on the initial, meagre bulletins, journalists working for the Daily News and The Times began to write extensive and well-researched feature articles and background reports about the specific situation of the slaves and slavery in the border states of Virginia and Maryland, about the strategic position and salience of the town of Harpers Ferry, about slave rebellions and the political debates about slavery in the United States, and about the civil war in Kansas. They carefully interpreted the still fragmentary

---

30 See Drescher, 'Servile Insurrection', especially 256–7.

31 'The Last Mail from New York', The Times, 2 November 1859, 8.

32 See especially 'Extensive Negro Conspiracy in Virginia and Maryland', Morning Chronicle, 1 November 1859; 'The United States. (From Our Own Correspondent)' and 'America', The Times, 2 and 4 November 1859, 7, 10 respectively; as well as articles under the same titles on 7 November 1859, 9; 8 November 1859, 7; 12 November 1859, 9; 14, 15, and 17 November and 1 December 1859, all at 7; 9 December 1859, 9; and 13, 17 and 20 December 1859, all at 7. For an example of a reader's comment, see X., 'Hotel de Lille et d'Albion, Paris, Nov. 4, "The Insurrection at Harper's Ferry. To the Editor of the Times"', The Times, 8 November 1859, 9. For more on the Provisional Constitution and Brown's address, see Chapter p. 245, note 152 in this volume.

and contradictory information for their readers, explicitly drawing on context to make conclusions about the specific intentions of the actors and the meaning of their actions. By and large, they succeeded convincingly.[33]

The substance of the assessments, judgements and horizons of expectation communicated in the British papers was affected by the experience that the emancipation of slaves could be achieved by peaceful means with institutional political processes. Slavery was as solidly repudiated as the use of any form of violence to abolish it. At the same time, the British newspaper editors took the violence by John Brown and his group very seriously as a symptom and tactic and analysed it carefully, mindful of rebellions in the British colonies. For example, according to a feature article in *The Times* on 2 November 1859,

The insurgents, we can easily believe, thought that the seizure of a Government establishment, and the possession of rifles and cannon, would encourage the whole population [of slaves] to rise against their masters. Forty-eight hours might have been enough to make half the plantations in the State the scenes of the foulest crimes. The isolated and unprepared families in the country districts might have been set upon by their maddened slaves, and the whole system of slaveholding been so shaken as to necessitate some plan of abolition. This, at least, seems to have been the design of the leaders. That they could have expected to conquer the United States' Executive in a servile war, and to turn Virginia and Maryland into free States through victories gained by rebellious Negroes, seems out of the question. America is not like one of our own island colonies, where the Negroes outnumber the whites many fold.[34]

In this report, as in other analyses by the British press, the focus was on the instrumental, military dimension of John Brown's violent act.

As a rule, the German press generally continued to take reports of the raid on Harpers Ferry from British newspapers, especially from *The Times*, translating accounts, documents and letters from the readers or

---

33 See for example, 'London, Wednesday, Nov. 2', *Daily News*, 2 November 1859; 'The Last Mail from New York', *The Times*, 8 November 1859, 9.

34 'The Last Mail from New York', *The Times*, 2 November 1859, 8.

providing summaries of them. They also printed primary texts, such as the Baltimore telegrams with breaking news of the raid, Brown's address to the court, and the Provisional Constitution, after their publication in English papers. As the primary sources of news, the English papers were supplemented by a few telegrams from Wolff's Telegraphisches Bureau (WTB).[35] The articles based on the English press usually concentrated on factual descriptions but also provided some incisive assessments from editorials and correspondent reports.[36] All this meant that the German reporting fell short of that of the British press in precision and analytical power.[37]

There were exceptions to this rule, however. Some longer, well-informed feature articles in the *Kölnische Zeitung*, and especially the detailed correspondent reports from New York to Georg von Cotta's

35 On Wolff's Telegraphisches Bureau, which was established in Berlin in 1849 and also called the Continental-Telegraphen-Compagnie, see Rudolf Stöber, *Deutsche Pressegeschichte: Von den Anfängen bis zur Gegenwart*, 2nd ed. (Konstanz: Uni Taschenbücher, 2005), 131–3; and Dieter Basse, *Wolff's Telegraphisches Bureau 1849 bis 1933: Agenturpublizistik zwischen Politik und Wirtschaft* (Munich: De Gruyter Saur, 1991).

36 See, for example, 'America', *Kölnische Zeitung*, 2 November 1859, 5; and the articles with the same heading on 4 November 1859, 2; 6 November 1859, 3; 9 November 1859, 5; 15 November 1859, 2; 16 November 1859, 5; 19 November 1859, 5; 8 December 1859, 3; 11 December 1859, 3; 15 December 1859, 3; and 18 December 1859, 3; as well as the articles under the heading 'Vereinigte Staaten von Nordamerika', *Allgemeine Zeitung*, 4 November 1859, 5032; 8 November 1859, 5096; 11 November 1859, 5147; 16 November 1859, 5228; 18 November 1859, 5264; 21 November 1859, 5318; 4 December 1859, 5528; 16 December 1859, 5740; 19 December 1859, 5792; 20 December 1859, 5807–8; 24 December 1859, 5884; and 31 December 1859, 6000. See also the articles under the heading 'Nord-Amerika', *Neue Preußische Zeitung*, 1 November 1859; 8 November 1859; 12 November 1859; 15 November 1859; 20 November 1859; 27 November 1859; 2 December 1859. In addition to indicating the location and date, the reprints or renditions were marked in the *Allgemeine Zeitung* with the abbreviation 'E.Bl.' (*Englische Blätter*; that is, 'English papers'), or 'Times'. The *Kölnische Zeitung* usually mentions the source in the text.

37 The German novelist, journalist and poet Theodor Fontane, who composed 'spurious correspondent reports' of this kind for the *Neue Preußische Zeitung*, later asserted that the discrepancy between these reports and those written by correspondents who really were based abroad was not so very great, as long as the reporter knew the language, the country and its people: 'One draws his wisdom from the "The Times" or the "Standard", etc., and it means little whether the reproduction process takes place in Hampstead-Highgate or in Steglitz-Friedenau [a Berlin suburb].' Theodor Fontane, *Von Zwanzig bis Dreißig: Autobiographisches*, ed. Otto Drude (Frankfurt am Main and Leipzig: Insel-Verlag, 1997), 297. Fontane thereby aptly describes the work process, but caution is recommended when it comes to his assessment of the outcome.

Allgemeine Zeitung, offered their own reports, assessments and commentaries.[38] The feature articles in the *Kölnische Zeitung* were written by the editor Roderich Arndt in Cologne and probably by Julius Faucher in London and were based directly on reporting in American newspapers.[39] The reports to the *Allgemeine Zeitung* were written by Hermann Raster, who had fled to the United States after participating in the revolutions of 1848. There he became the coeditor of the *New Yorker Abendzeitung*, a moderately important German-language newspaper in the United States.[40] Raster intentionally interpreted the raid on Harpers Ferry from the perspective of the German émigré community, referred to German-language media in the United States and tried to make sense of the events in the context of the political and cultural experience (*Erfahrungsraum*) familiar to his readers in Germany.

The assessments and expectations (*Erwartungshorizont*) in these lead articles and correspondent reports written specifically for the German newspapers were influenced by the relatively recent revolutions of 1848–9. For example, Faucher wrote in the *Kölnische Zeitung* that he felt

38 See for example, Hermann Raster, 'Vereinigte Staaten von Nordamerika. New-York, 21. Oct.', *Allgemeine Zeitung*, 9 November 1859, 5115–6, and the articles under the same heading but with different dates on 19 November 1859, 5285–6; 29 November 1859, 5444; 14 December 1859, 5704; and 1 January 1860, 6–7. For the deciphering of correspondents' codes, see Bernhard Fischer (ed.), *Die Augsburger 'Allgemeine Zeitung' 1798–1866*, nach dem Redaktionsexemplar im Cotta-Archiv (Stiftung der 'Stuttgarter Zeitung'), 4 vols. (Munich: De Gruyter Saur, 2002–5). The articles by Raster used two different correspondent codes, but the editorial copy suggests that both are attributable to him. For information on the *Allgemeine Zeitung*, which Johan Friedrich Cotta (the publisher of Johann Wolfgang von Goethe, Friedrich Schiller and other writers of the German classical period) founded in 1798, see Günter Müchler, *'Wie ein treuer Spiegel': Die Geschichte der Cotta'schen Allgemeinen Zeitung* (Darmstadt: Wissenschaftliche Buchgesellschaft, 1998). The *Allgemeine Zeitung* remained the most important German newspaper until the mid-nineteenth century and maintained a network of correspondents unparalleled in Germany.

39 On the feature articles in the *Kölnische Zeitung* see Z 63 Köln [Julius Faucher?], 'Ein Putsch in den Vereinigten Staaten. Köln, 10. November', *Kölnische Zeitung*, 11 November 1859, 1; and Roderich Arndt, 'America. Köln, 2. Dezember', *Kölnische Zeitung*, 3 December 1859, 1. On the reporting about the United States in the *Kölnische Zeitung* until 1850 and the recruitment of Friedrich Kapp as its correspondent from the United States as of 1860, see Buchheim, *Die Geschichte der Kölnischen Zeitung*, vol. 2, Chapter 16; vol. 3, Chapter 11, and vol. 4, Chapter 2.3.

40 On Wilhelm Friedrich Hermann Raster, see A. E. Zucker, *The Forty-Eighters: Political Refugees of the German Revolution of 1848* (New York: Columbia University Press, 1950), 329.

'thrown back into a second improved and enlarged edition of the June Days uprising in Paris' when he read the first dispatches in the American papers. As he explained to his readers,

> It would hardly be worth bothering to waste even a single word to write about this essentially insignificant putsch, like the ones almost every little German country town had in 1848, if a few rather penetrating observations were not tied to it.[41]

Raster's report from New York on 21 October, which appeared on 9 November 1859, quoted the assessment by his New Yorker *Abendzeitung*:

> In this dry, sober America, where it has become almost an article of religious faith to say that the ballot is the sole remedy for all damages to state and society, you might think you're dreaming when you hear about an official pronunciamento in the style of Mexico or, if you prefer, Europe. Since the founding of the Union, this is the first time there has been this kind of upheaval with such momentous ultimate goals.[42]

The first act of violence produced by political ideology in the American republic since its founding! Raster felt that John Brown's raid on Harpers Ferry was so noteworthy because it seemed to be so un-American. He believed that this strike had set the United States on the road of European development in terms of violent political conflict. When considered against the likelihood that Brown's tactic was most probably inspired by Orsini, Raster's analysis showed remarkable political insight.

Nevertheless, this correspondent of the *Allgemeine Zeitung* did not want John Brown's raid to be seen as a revolutionary act. Raster concurred with the widely shared view in the North that Brown had primarily sought to take 'revenge on slave-owners', a motive that, given

---

41 Z 63 Köln [Julius Faucher?], 'Ein Putsch in den Vereinigten Staaten. Köln, 10. November', *Kölnische Zeitung*, 11 November 1859, 1.

42 'Vereinigte Staaten von Nordamerika. New-York, 21. Oct.', *Allgemeine Zeitung*, 9 November 1859, 5115. To a German audience in Raster's day, the word *pronunciamento* meant 'a public demonstration against the current government, signaling a call to insurrection'. *Allgemeine deutsche Real-Encyklopädie für die gebildeten Stände. Conversations-Lexikon. Elfte, umgearbeitete, verbesserte und vermehrte Auflage. In funfzehn Bänden*, Leipzig: F.A. Brockhaus 1864–1873, vol. 12, Prämissen bis Salier (1867), 126.

his experience in Kansas, had become 'a veritable idiosyncrasy'.[43] It was believed, Raster continues, that Brown had received money from 'the most fanatical abolitionists of the North', from 'a small band' who were to the Republicans something like 'the Communists in Europe were to the Constitutionalists', and was therefore thought to have decided to use this money 'to instigate a slave revolt'. But John Brown, it was said, completely miscalculated how the slaves would react. This did not surprise Raster, who regarded Brown as 'none too sharp a thinker and judge of real conditions but rather a plain American Bible-thumping Christian' who had concocted his opinions from the so-called Holy Scriptures, who was 'too ingenuously and simply organized' (that is, he lacked an organization like a workers' association), and who had naively failed to recognize the relationship between means and ends. Brown and his participants should therefore 'in no way be judged from the same points of view as European revolutionaries'. Raster maintained that they had distinguished themselves solely through personal courage and 'eager sacrifice', and he therefore considered the whole affair to be of interest more from a psychological than a political perspective and indeed saw John Brown as a genuine Michael Kohlhaas.[44]

This comment is a reference to the novella *Michael Kohlhaas*, published in 1810 by the German writer Heinrich von Kleist.[45] It is a fictionalized story of a pious, upstanding sixteenth-century horse breeder in rural Prussia who – after his patient and humiliating quest for legal redress of his violated rights fails – takes the law into his own hands and resorts to violence, becoming an 'avenging angel' and an 'angel of justice descended from heaven'. With this interpretation of John Brown as Michael Kohlhaas, Raster misconstrues Brown's attack on Harpers Ferry as an act of revenge. But if one perceives Kohlhaas's objective as the establishment of justice for its own sake, Brown's story can indeed be seen to express Kohlhaas's central ethical problem of the

---

43 'Vereinigte Staaten von Nordamerika. New-York, 21. Oct', *Allgemeine Zeitung*, 9 November 1859, 5115. For this interpretation, see above, p. 296.

44 'Vereinigte Staaten von Nordamerika. New-York, 21 Oct', *Allgemeine Zeitung*, 9 November 1859, 5115–16.

45 See Heinrich von Kleist, *Michael Kohlhaas (Aus einer alten Chronik)* (1808–10), in *Sämtliche Werke und Briefe*, 2 vols., ed. Helmut Sembdner, 8th ed. (Munich: Hanser, 1985), vol. 2, 9–103, or the English translation: Heinrich von Kleist, *Michael Kohlhaas: A Tale from an Old Chronicle*, in *Selected Prose of Heinrich von Kleist* (Brooklyn: Archipelago Books, 2010), 143–254.

legitimacy of individual violence in the face of the failure of the institutions of the state.[46]

The emphasis that Raster, the former revolutionary, placed on the psychological and literary dimension of John Brown's violent act coincided with the perception expressed by the Prussian ambassador to Washington, DC. Revealing an education in the ethics of German idealism, von Gerolt wrote in his report to Prince Regent Wilhelm that Brown was 'a man of unshakable courage and fanatical zeal', a man who 'has distinguished himself through opposition to the introduction of slavery and has thus become a martyr because of his moral act bound by duty'.[47]

Original reporting for German readers thus presented John Brown primarily as a courageous martyr. Whereas the reasons for his act of violence were sought at the level of individual psychology, the German evaluation of the raid on Harpers Ferry was carried out in military and instrumental terms, as it was in England as well. The fact that John Brown had perpetrated violence was not a problem either for the generation that had gone through the revolutions of 1848 nor for the liberal press in the German states. Journalists like Raster and Faucher, however, measured John Brown's violence against that of the revolutions in continental Europe. By comparison, Brown's appeared dilettantish, neither a shining example nor one worthy of imitation.

The French press, by comparison, was generally less normative and more analytical. Whereas the British papers condemned the raid on Harpers Ferry because John Brown had used force at all, and the German press criticized him because he had used individual violence, the French

---

46 For a discussion of the nature of Kohlhaas's violence (including its interpretation as terrorism), see especially Horst Sendler, *Michael Kohlhaas, Then and Now*, translated by Alan Cornell (Berlin and New York: de Gruyter, 1986); Andreas Gailus, *Passions of the Sign: Revolution and Language in Kant, Goethe, and Kleist* (Baltimore: The Johns Hopkins University Press, 2006), Chapter 3, e.g. 125–6; Thomas Pröll, 'Deutungsversuch eines Gewaltausbruchs: Die Kleistsche Figur Michael Kohlhaas als Symbol für die Ambivalenz des Gerechtigkeitsbegriffesre', in Gianluca Crepaldi, Andreas Kriwak and Thomas Pröll, *Kleist zur Gewalt: Transdisziplinäre Perspektiven* (Innsbruck: Innsbruck University Press, 2011), 31, 19; and Jeffrey Champlin, *The Making of a Terrorist: On Classic German Rogues*, preface by Avital Ronell (Evanston: Northwestern University Press, 2015), especially Chapter 4.

47 Friedrich Joseph Karl Freiherr von Gerolt to the Prince Regent, 5 November 1859, quoted in Löffler, *Preußens und Sachsens Beziehungen*, 39.

journalists focused particularly on trying to explain the discrepancy between the relative triviality of the violence and the immensity of the response.

Le Constitutionnel and *Le Siècle*, like *The Times* and the *Allgemeine Zeitung*, had their own correspondents in New York who wrote at regular intervals about political events and developments in the United States, and they were present in the courtroom during John Brown's trial.[48] 'Despite the noise from the supporters of slavery, the *black* insurrection at Harper's Ferry was not as meaningful as they would have it,' wrote the correspondent for *Le Siècle* in his article on October 22.

> It is purely and simply an affair in which some passionate men known for their unwavering devotion to the cause of emancipation ludicrously undertook to use violence to help achieve the principle of racial equality and human freedom. This attempt, made under conditions that rendered it utterly impossible, would have remained a ridiculous enterprise had it not shed the blood of some victims.

As this correspondent observed in the same report, the violence did have a considerable effect: 'This movement, as preposterous and absurd as it was, struck a raw nerve [*une douloureuse sensation*] in Virginia and Maryland.' The correspondents for *Le Siècle* and *Le Constitutionnel* primarily blamed this effect on the efforts of the Democrats to instrumentalize the violence for their own ends. According to the first to analyse this discrepancy, 'the democrats are unabashedly making hay out of the foolish would-be insurrection at Harper's Ferry.'[49] Other demagogues, too, who whipped up the debates

48 See, for example, 'Correspondance particulière du Constitutionnel. New-York, 26 octobre 1859', 9 November 1859, 2, 'Correspondance particulière du Constitutionnel. New-York, 12 novembre 1859', *Le Constitutionnel*, 28 November 1859, 2–3; and 'Gazette des Tribunaux: [Circuit-Cour de Charlestown (Virginie). Hon. Parker, juge. Jugement des insurgés de Harper's Ferry', *Le Siècle*, 16 November 1859, 3.

49 'Amérique. (Correspondance particulière du Siècle.) New York, 1er novembre 1959', *Le Siècle*, 16 November 1859, 2. A more detailed article on this topic appeared about two weeks later: 'Poorly inspired, the Democratic party endeavored to exploit the affair of Harper's Ferry for its own political advantage. It tried to draw into the affair some influential men from the black Republican party who in all likelihood had nothing to do with it.' 'Amérique. [Correspondance particulière du Siècle.] New-York, le 5 novembre 1859', *Le Siècle*, 21 November 1859, 2.

to gain advantage, as well as Virginia's authorities, seriously contributed to John Brown's popularity as a result of 'the violent and arbitrary
treatment of the prisoner' and the 'excessively severe persecution of an
enemy' who was already completely powerless. The press itself, which
'had significantly profited from it by switching its position for or
against in the interest of its own political stakes', was also held responsible for the media hype.[50] Irrespective of each newspaper's position on
abolition, the French press showed itself to be particularly sensitive to
the difference between the instrumental and the symbolic dimension
of John Brown's violence and to the dangers arising from the political
instrumentalization of that violence.

Overall, a positive assessment of John Brown prevailed in the
European press. This reception had an effect back in the United States,
where an awareness had emerged soon after the raid on Harpers Ferry
that the event would be noticed by the world public and where the
responses to it were even declared to be an indicator of the moral coor-
dinates of nations. For instance, in his speech entitled 'Lesson of the
Hour' from 1 November 1859, Wendell Phillips proclaimed, 'this blow,
like the first blow at Lexington, heard around the world, this blow at
Harper's Ferry reveals men.' And he continued confidently, 'Watch
those about you and you will see more of their temper and unheeded
purpose and real moral position of men than you would imagine. This
is the way nations are to be judged. Be not in a hurry; it will come soon
enough from this sentiment.'[51] The interest in foreign judgements of
the events was intense. Starting with articles from the *Examiner*
(London) and the *Freeman* (London), which the *Liberator* printed on
9 December, hosts of reports and commentaries from the European
press, especially British newspapers but also French and Russian ones,
found their way into the US media, as did speeches from leading
figures in the British anti-slavery movement. This reporting was

---

50 'Amérique. (Correspondance particulière du Siècle.) New York, 1er novembre
1959', *Le Siècle*, 16 November 1859, 2–3, 2; '(Correspondance particulière du
Constitutionnel.) New York, 12 novembre' and '(Correspondance particulière du
Constitutionnel.) New York, 15 novembre', *Le Constitutionnel*, 28 and 30 November
1859, both on p. 2.

51 'The Virginia Rebellion . . . Wendell Phillips on the Outbreak', *New York Times*,
2 November 1859, 1, reprinted with some changes in Wendell Phillips, *Speeches, Lectures,
and Letters* (Boston: Lee and Shepard, 1863), 263–88. For more information on this
speech, see above, p. 316.

systematically presented and appraised by the American anti-slavery movement.[52]

This appraisal was guided by an awareness that 'the judgments of a foreign country, in some sort, foreshadow those of future times,' as written in an introductory note to the chapter 'Opinions from Over Sea' in the American Anti-Slavery Society's booklet *The Anti-Slavery History of the John-Brown Year* on foreign reactions to John Brown.[53] In other words, people in the American anti-slavery movement believed that the attention John Brown and his action attracted from abroad portended the assessment by future generations. This notion galvanized the abolitionists because 'Pro-Slavery students . . . would find some profitable, if not pleasant, reading in the comments of the European press upon the Harper's Ferry inroad and its consequences,' as the editors of the American Anti-Slavery Society wrote.[54] The press reactions in Europe strengthened the advocates of the anti-slavery movements in their conviction that, in their fight against slavery and the slave owners, they were on the right side of history, the side of progress.

The political blockage in Russia

Although the news of the raid on Harpers Ferry drew attention throughout Europe, it landed on truly fertile ground in only one country, the one which might be the least expected: Russia. British, German and French journalists were basically sympathetic to the raid by John Brown

---

52 On European press comments received in the United States, see, for example, 'The Harper's Ferry Rising', *Examiner*, reprinted as 'The Harper's Ferry Rising', *Liberator*, 9 December 1859, 1; 'A London View of Old Brown. From the Times of Nov 5th', *Memphis Morning Enquirer*, 26 November 1859, 2; 'British Opinion on John Brown', *Harper's Weekly*, 14 January 1860, 23; 'The London Times on the Harper's Ferry Affair', *Ripley Bee*, 3 December 1859, col. D; 'The London Times upon Slave Insurrections', *Bangor Daily Whig and Courier*, 2 December 1859, col. B; and the section 'Opinions from Over Sea', in American Anti-Slavery Society, *The Anti-Slavery History of the John-Brown Year* (New York: American Anti-Slavery Society, 1861), 157–66, which also includes press commentaries from France and Russia. For a speech, see, for example, 'American Slavery. Mr. George Thompson in the City Hall. From the North British Daily Mail, Glasgow', *Liberator*, 30 March 1860, 1. Overall, see also Drescher, 'Servile Insurrection', 279–80.

53 American Anti-Slavery Society, *The Anti-Slavery History*, 157.

54 Ibid., 157.

but for various reasons also regarded it from a critical distance. Polish and French intellectuals added their powerful eloquence to the chorus of American voices glorifying John Brown and his act, but their commentaries failed to have any lasting influence. Ultimately, John Brown found a genuinely congenial translation and reception in the oppositional literary critic and writer Nikolai Gavrilovich Chernyshevsky in St Petersburg, as well as in Chernyshevsky's follower, Dmitry Vladimirovich Karakozov.

The keen interest that John Brown and his act of violence aroused in Russia stemmed from the similar political situation there. In both the United States and the tsarist empire, the political blockage lay in the question of emancipation, and Dmitry Vladimirovich Karakozov's terrorist act was a response to this blockage. Unlike the United States, Russia even made the first step towards liberating its unfree population – the legal abolition of serfdom – peacefully and through legislation. The second step – the implementation and regulation of the new freedom – was likewise achieved by law without initial violence even though emancipating the bonded population was a much greater challenge in Russia than in the rest of Europe and the United States. The Russian empire had to cope with freeing almost 22 million serfs belonging to the nobility and 25 million serfs belonging to the tsar's family and the state (compared to 800,000 slaves in the British colonies and 4 million slaves in the American South). Terence Emmons therefore rightly called emancipation in Russia 'probably the greatest single piece of state-directed social engineering in modern European history before the twentieth century'.[55] The problem with the policy adopted by the tsar and his administration was that it was not accepted by large sections of the population, and a political impasse emerged because there was no legal means for any further revisions to the legislation if the tsar rejected it.

Just as in Central and Western Europe, the debate about serfdom started in Russia around the mid-eighteenth century. For various reasons, however, this debate and the corresponding political measures

---

55 Terence Emmons, *The Russian Landed Gentry and the Peasant Emancipation of 1861* (Cambridge: Cambridge University Press, 1968), 414. Franco Venturi in his *Roots of Revolution* also emphasizes the political challenge of this reform. For the figures, see Petr Andreevich Zaionchkovskii, *Otmena krepostnogo prava v Rossii* (Moscow: Prosveshchenie, 1968), 15.

did not move beyond the initial steps until the mid-nineteenth century.[56] For example, Tsar Alexander I promised major reforms while mobilizing against Napoleon, but he did not implement them after the re-establishment of peace in Europe. This disappointed and embittered many of the officers who had served him in the campaign through Europe and who had returned to Russia with their own views on the implementation of freedom in Central Europe.

These officers reacted with collective violence. They began to plan the assassination of Alexander I or an insurrection to free the peasants in Russia and introduce a constitution on the American model. When Tsar Nicholas I ascended the throne on 14 December 1825, they attempted the 'first Russian revolution', but the revolt by these 'Decembrists' (*Dekabristy*) was suppressed on the same day.[57]

Partly in response to this revolt, ten secret commissions worked on a solution to the serfdom issue under Nicholas I. But the emancipation of the peasants was not recognized as a priority until Alexander II's ascension to the throne in 1855 and the shock of defeat in the Crimean War

56 On the emancipation of the peasants before Alexander II came to power, see Hugh Seton-Watson, *The Russian Empire 1801–1917* (Oxford: Oxford University Press, 1967), Parts 1–3; Sergei Germanovich Pushkarev, *The Emergence of Modern Russia, 1801–1917* (New York: Holt, Rinehart and Winston, 1963), Chapters 2.4–6, 3.5–8; Manfred Hildermeier, *Geschichte Russlands: Vom Mittelalter bis zur Oktoberrevolution*, 2nd ed. (Munich: C. H. Beck, 2013), 768–73; and in particular Bruce W. Lincoln, *The Great Reforms: Autocracy, Bureaucracy, and the Politics of Change in Imperial Russia* (Dekalb, IL: Northern Illinois University Press, 1990), Chapter 1; Aleksandr Iur'evich Polunov, *Russia in the Nineteenth Century: Autocracy, Reform, and Social Change, 1814–1914* (Armonk, NY: M. E. Sharpe, 2005), Introduction and Chapter 1; Zaionchkovskii, *Otmena krepostnogo prava v Rossii*, 51–62; and Jerome Blum, *Lord and Peasant in Russia: From the Ninth to the Nineteenth Century* (Princeton: Princeton University Press, 1961), Chapter 25. The significance of the enlightened administration is analysed in Bruce W. Lincoln, *In the Vanguard of the Reform: Russia's Enlightened Bureaucrats 1825–1861* (Dekalb, IL: Northern Illinois University Press, 1982); and also by David Moon in *The Abolition of Serfdom in Russia, 1762–1907* (New York: Routledge, 2001).

57 For an introduction see Venturi, *Roots of Revolution*, 1–9; Hildermeier, *Geschichte Russlands*, 751–63; and Avrahm Yarmolinsky, *Road to Revolution: A Century of Russian Radicalism* (London: Macmillan, 1957), Chapters 2–3; Adam B. Ulam, *Russia's Failed Revolutions: From the Decembrists to the Dissidents* (London: Basic Books, 1981), Chapter 1; Philip Pomper, *The Russian Revolutionary Intelligentsia* (Arlington Heights, IL: Harlan Davidson, 1970), 13–32; and especially Anatole Gregory Mazour, *The First Russian Revolution, 1825: The Decembrist Movement, Its Origins, Development, and Significance* (Stanford: Stanford University Press, 1964); and Hans Lemberg, *Die nationale Gedankenwelt der Dekabristen* (Cologne: Böhlau Verlag, 1963).

in 1856, which also persuaded conservatives of the urgency of reforms. As the new tsar informed the Muscovite nobility, 'It is better to begin abolishing serfdom from above than to wait for it to begin to abolish itself from below.'[58] The tsar believed that state initiatives for emancipation from bondage would serve as protection against revolutionary violence, and he thus formulated the guiding principle of revolution from above.

Implementing emancipation in Russia was an unprecedented, major political and administrative project, particularly because the first and second steps – the legal emancipation and its enactment – were conceived as taking place in one go, although it turned out to be more difficult than planned. The project began in April 1856, when the tsar entrusted his new minister of the interior with the task of emancipating the peasants. The matter did not start moving until a year later, when Alexander II authorized the nobility throughout the north-west of the empire to develop proposals for an 'improvement in the way of life for the peasants owned by the nobility' – as the emancipation from serfdom was euphemistically called. With this step, the topic of emancipation moved from the arcane domain of the court into the public sphere. Petitions subsequently flooded into St Petersburg from all the regions of the empire, and 44,000 serf-owning nobles elected about 1,400 representatives to forty-eight governorate committees to discuss the local situation of the serfs and feasible ways and means to emancipate them. Furthermore, Alexander II created a 'Main Committee on the Peasant Question' (*glavny komitet*, which had initially been called the *neglasny komitet* or 'secret committee') to assess and systematize the proposals from the governate committees. In February 1859 the tsar formed an editorial commission to formulate emancipation laws based on this material. By early 1860 the members of the editorial commission presented the result of their work to representatives of the governate

58 Alexander II, 'Speech to Representatives of the Moscow Nobility (March 30, 1856)', stetson.edu; Alexander II, 'Rech' Gosudaria Moskovskim Dvorianam, 30-go Marta 1856 g., po tekstu, privedennomu v zapiskakh senatora Solov'eva', *Russkaia Starina* 27 (1881), 228–9. This statement of Alexander II's motives for abolishing serfdom is incomplete, however. For a detailed study thereof, see Zaionchkovskii, *Otmena krepostnogo prava v Rossii*, 63–6; and, drawing on the previous, Daniel Field, *The End of Serfdom: Nobility and Bureaucracy in Russia, 1855–1861* (Cambridge, MA: Harvard University Press, 1976), Chapter 2. See also Hildermeier, *Geschichte Russlands*, 884–5.

committees, who had been invited to St Petersburg specifically for this purpose.[59] In September 1860 the editorial commission completed its work, and on 19 February 1861 Alexander II signed the Emancipation Manifesto,[60] as well as the 'Statutes on the Emancipation of the Serfs', the comprehensive legislation on the reform of the rural order in Russia.[61] With this signature, the almost 22 million serfs belonging to the nobility were emancipated.

In many ways the laws implementing emancipation and the way they came about corresponded to the pattern in the rest of Europe. In Russia, as in Prussia, the nobility and the reform-minded bureaucracy shaped the body of rules and regulations, while peasant unrest had no notable influence. Instead, the state budget came to play a particularly important role. The Russian government's decision to use private capital to finance the expansion of the railroads and steam shipping led to such a dire banking crisis that the progressive intellectuals in the editorial commission suddenly had to switch to a strict austerity policy and abandon all plans for public subsidization of the

---

59 See the classic account by Sergei Spiridonovich Tatishchev, *Imperator Aleksandr II: Ego zhizn' i tsarstvovanie* [1911] (Moscow: AST, 2006), Chapter 13; and Seton-Watson, *The Russian Empire, 1801–1917*, 332–48; Pushkarev, *The Emergence of Modern Russia, 1801–1917*, 132–4; Hildermeier, *Geschichte Russlands*, Chapter 33; Lincoln, *The Great Reforms*, 61–90; Polunov, *Russia in the Nineteenth Century*, Chapter 4; Blum, *Lord and Peasant in Russia*, Chapter 26; and especially Zaionchkovskii, *Otmena krepostnogo prava v Rossii*, Chapter 2; and, based on this, Field, *The End of Serfdom*, which examines the various groups that influenced this process; Emmons, *The Russian Landed Gentry*, on the role of the nobility; Larisa Georgievna Zakharova, *Samoderzhavie i otmena krepostnogo prava v Rossii 1856–1861* (Moscow: Izd-vo Moskovskogo universiteta, 1984), which analyses the work of the committees and other government institutions; and Lincoln, *In the Vanguard of Reform*, on the contributions of the civil service.

60 Manifest 19 fevralia 1861 goda, in *Polnoe sobranie zakonov Rossiiskoi imperii*, 2nd Collection (St Petersburg: Pechatano v Tip. II Otd. Sobstvennoi ego Imperatorskago Velichestva Kantseliarii, 1825–81), vol. 36, Part 1, no. 36650, 130–4; reprinted, for example, in Oleg Ivanovich Chistiakov (ed.), *Rossiiskoe zakonodatel'stvo X–XX vekov*, vol. 7: *Dokumenty krest'ianskoi reformy*, 26–31. An English translation is printed in Basil Dmytryshyn (ed.), *Imperial Russia: A Source Book, 1700–1917* (New York: Holt, Rinehart and Winston, 1967), 220–5.

61 *Vysochaishe utverzhdennoe Obshchee Polozhenie o krest'ianakh, vyshedshikh iz krepostnoi zavisimosti*, in *Polnoe sobranie zakonov Rossiiskoi imperii*, 2nd collection (1825–81), vol. 36, Part 1, no. 36657, 141–69. For a translation see 'Statutes on the Emancipation of the Serfs, February 19, 1861', in George Vernadsky (ed.), *A Source Book for Russian History from Early Times to 1917*, vol. 3: *Alexander II to the February Revolution* (New Haven and London: Yale University Press, 1972), 600–2.

compensation payments that the peasants would be required to make to the nobility.[62]

The emancipation that took effect with Alexander II's signature was therefore oriented primarily towards the interests of the nobility and the state. It freed all the serfs on the properties of the nobility, but established a transitional period during which the serfs had to continue paying levies and providing services, and they remained bound to the land. During this time, redemption contracts between the former serfs and their manorial lords were to be drawn up. The contracts had to be examined by government mediators (*mirovye posredniki*) to ensure that the size and type of the transferred land met the legal requirements. As soon as the redemption contracts were approved, the government advanced 80 per cent of the sum to the lord of the manor, and the former serf had to pay the remaining 20 per cent directly to his lord. If the serf could not pay the sum, he received a plot of land for free, but this was only a quarter of the usual size. The peasant community bore the responsibility for repaying the redemption sums that the government had advanced.[63]

With respect to the emergence of political violence, the emancipation of the peasants in Russia also resembled that of Western and Central Europe in significant ways: for instance, emancipation in all three regions was undertaken and successfully completed by strong central governments. Although often suggested otherwise in the literature, the distinguishing specifics of the procedure in Russia were not primarily the mode of land reallocation, the level of redemption payments, or the time frame of up to forty-nine years within which the payments had to

---

62 See Lincoln, *The Great Reforms*, 83–4.

63 See ibid., 87–9; Pushkarev, *The Emergence of Modern Russia, 1801–1917*, 132–41; Polunov, *Russia in the Nineteenth Century*, 105–9; Hildermeier, *Geschichte Russlands*, 891–5; and the detailed analyses in Zaionchkovskii, *Otmena krepostnogo prava v Rossii*, Chapters 3, 5–8; Petr Ivanovich Liashchenko, *History of the National Economy of Russia to the 1917 Revolution* (New York: Macmillan, 1949), 379–99; Michael T. Florinsky, *Russia: A History and an Interpretation* (New York: Macmillan, 1953), vol. 2, 921–8; and Carol Scott Leonard, *Agrarian Reform in Russia: The Road from Serfdom* (New York: Cambridge University Press, 2011), which examines the reform's effects on agricultural productivity. On the mediators 'in charge of implementing the [re]forms in situ', see Natalia F. Ust'iantseva, 'Accountable Only to God and the Senate', in Ben Eklof, John Bushnell and Larissa Zakharova (eds.) *Russia's Great Reforms, 1855–1881* (Bloomington: Indiana University Press, 1994), 161–80.

be made (by 1910, a shorter period than that in Bavaria, for example), even if the combination of these elements in Russia put the former serfs at a comparative disadvantage.[64]

Rather, the key differences relating to the emergence of political violence stemmed, first, from the fact that the traditional village community in Russia became even more important as a result of the new political functions it received. The former serfs remained a recognizable group, all the more so as Russia's late industrialization meant that cities contributed less to the dissolution of the peasants as a social class.[65] Second, while Western Europe had seen lengthy legislative processes in which diverse social groups and political institutions had participated through their influence, consultation, decision making, political violence and counterviolence,[66] in Russia the process of emancipation instead took the form of a solution negotiated all at once between the nobility and the bureaucracy – and for which ultimately the tsar himself was the only responsible authority.

It was precisely owing to the high expectations for the emancipation of the serfs in Russia that the final arrangement was met with great disappointment. This reaction did not escape the notice of Alexander II and his government. They thus took extensive precautions in dealing with peasant insurrections on the day the Emancipation Manifesto and its attendant laws were promulgated.[67] The expected unrest largely failed to materialize, but none of the social groups involved were satisfied with the tsar's policy. Otto von Bismarck, then

---

64 Russia retained the commons (as did France), so many peasants in Russia (unlike those in Prussia) had to accept plots that were smaller than those that they had farmed before the emancipation. Yet they had to make high redemption payments (which was not the case in France). The question about the effects of the agricultural reform in Russia and whether they could have been more positive for the peasants remains controversial to this day. The assessment here is based on Lincoln, *The Great Reforms*, 87–9; Polunov, *Russia in the Nineteenth Century*, Chapter 6, especially 125–32; Florinsky, *Russia*, 921–8; and Leonard, *Agrarian Reform in Russia*, Chapter 1.1. See also Hildermeier, *Geschichte Russlands*, 895–9.

65 Tsar Alexander III even reinforced the special status of former serfs yet again by partially retracting some of the freedom granted them under his father's emancipation laws. See Victor Leontovitsch, *The History of Liberalism in Russia* (Pittsburgh: University of Pittsburgh Press, 2012), Part 2, Chapter 4.

66 See section 1.3 in this book.

67 Hildermeier, *Geschichte Russlands*, 892.

402   The Invention of Terrorism

the Prussian ambassador to the St Petersburg court, recorded in his *Petersburger Journal* on 28 January 1861,

> It is impossible for the intended legislation to live up to all the hopes attached to it ... When one realizes that the whole of the peasant population on the lands of the crown and the nobility is dissatisfied with its lot and holds exaggerated expectations of the impending improvements; that the entire nobility openly displays its bitterness about the intended interventions in their already distressed financial circumstances; and that this country [Russia] has just as many people who are working systematically towards overthrowing the political structure as any other, then one cannot entirely deny the justification for the gloomy predictions about the immediate future of the country constituting society's current daily conversations.[68]

While a large proportion of the nobility continued to reject the emancipation per se and regarded it as an expropriation accepted only by necessity, the enlightened public considered its attendant laws an injustice to the peasants, and the serfs continued to wait for their true freedom.[69]

Tsar Alexander II, seeing no way to make comprehensive changes in his monumental legislation, was unwilling to intervene with amendments. All legal avenues for addressing this question through political institutions were thereby blocked. With his terrorist attack on the tsar, Dmitry Vladimirovich Karakozov was acting precisely on this issue.

---

68 Otto von Bismarck, 'Bericht betr. die Bauernbefreiung. Petersburg, den 28. Januar 1861', in Ludwig Raschdau (ed.), *Die politischen Berichte des Fürsten Bismarck aus Petersburg und Paris (1859–1862)*, vol. 2: *1861–1862* (2 vols., Berlin: Reimar Hobbing, 1920), 16.

69 On the reaction of former serfs, see Hildermeier, *Geschichte Russlands*, 892, 895; and specifically Daniel Field, 'The Year of Jubilee', in Eklof, Bushnell and Zakharova (eds.) *Russia's Great Reforms*, 40–57. On the disappointment of the intelligentsia, see, for example, the poet Nikolai Nekrasov's reaction, described by Chernyshevsky in his '[Zametki o Nekrasove] Zametki pri chtenii "Biograficheskikh svedenii" o Nekrasove, pomeshchennykh v I tome "Posmertnogo izdaniia" ego "Stikhotvorenii", SPB, 1879', in Nikolai Gavrilovich Chernyshevskii, *Polnoe sobranie sochinenii*, vol. 1 (Moskau: Goslitizdat, 1939–53), 747. For a general overview of the intelligentsia's critique and the resulting movements, see, for example, Lincoln, *The Great Reforms*, 163–8; Polunov, *Russia in the Nineteenth Century*, Chapter 7; and the following section of this chapter.

The radicalization of the Russian intelligentsia

Political communication and political action developed under different conditions in Russia than in the rest of Europe and the United States in the first half of the nineteenth century. These conditions contributed, among other things, to the fact that in Russia (just as in Central Europe) there was no social movement for the abolition of serfdom comparable to the abolitionist movements in Great Britain and the United States or with the national movement in Italy.

In Russia, the intelligentsia took the place of such social movements. Like the members of the abolitionist movement in the United States (and unlike the members of the revolutionary national movement in Italy for a long time), members of the intelligentsia initially placed their hopes for the abolition of serfdom on the existing political and institutional processes. And, just as in the United States, the dashing of these hopes led to a radicalization in their thought and action; that is, to an increasing acceptance of non-state violence as a means of achieving their political goals.

The institutions of the Russian state, however, responded more quickly, thoroughly and comprehensively to all expressions of oppositional political thought and action than did the organs of the United States government and even more so than those in Italy. The story in Russia is thus not about a series of attempts at insurrection and revolution (as in Italy) or a gradual process of radicalization over two decades (as in the United States), but rather about political generations that followed each other at short intervals, becoming ever more radical at an accelerating rate because of their successive experience of persecution. Chernyshevsky belonged to the fourth generation of the opposition. One of his readers, a member of the fifth generation, mounted the first terrorist attack in Russia.

The media and their public in the Russian Empire also differed somewhat from their nineteenth-century counterparts in Western and Central European countries and the United States.[70] Censorship and

---

70 On the concept of the public, the issues surrounding it, and the Russian term *obshchestvennost'*, see Guido Hausmann, 'Öffentlichkeit', in Thomas M. Bohn and Dietmar Neutatz (eds.), *Geschichte des Russischen Reiches und der Sowjetunion*, 2nd revised ed. (Cologne: UTB GmbH, 2009), 257–63; likewise Catriona Kelly and Vadim Volkov, 'Obshchestvennost'', Sobornost'': Collective Identities', in Catriona Kelly and David Shepherd (eds.), *Constructing Russian Culture in the Age of Revolution, 1881–1940* (Oxford: Oxford University Press, 1998), 26–7.

control of the press by the state were more the rule than the exception throughout continental Europe, but in Russia all the major newspapers were published by government agencies until Alexander II ascended the throne in 1855 (just four years before Brown's raid on Harpers Ferry). Peter the Great himself had founded the empire's first newspaper in 1703. It was replaced by *Sankt Peterburgskie vedomosti* (St Petersburg News) during the eighteenth century and supplemented by *Moskovskie vedomosti* (Moscow News), which were published by the Academy of Sciences and the Moscow University respectively. Other papers began appearing in the early nineteenth century, including *Severnaia pochta* (Northern Post), published by the Ministry of the Interior; *Russkii invalid* (Russian Disabled Veteran), published by the Ministry of War; and *Severniya pchela* (Northern Bee), which was an undercover organ of the Russian Empire's political police – the III. Otdelenie Sobstvennoi Ego Imperatorskogo Velichestva kantseliarii, or simply III. Otdelenie (aka the Third Section). The *Severnaia pchela* had 4,000 subscribers in the 1830s, making it the country's most read newspaper. Flanking these organs were the generally short-lived private press, satirical papers and local periodicals in provincial towns. Ever since Catherine II introduced censorship in Russia, all printed matter was subject to state approval. The censors checked texts to see that good morals were respected and that certain topics (such as Russia's military debacle in Crimea and the planned emancipation of the peasants) did not make their way into the Russian media.

Alexander II's reforms established the legal, economic and social conditions for the emergence of the commercial mass media. The tsar needed an enlightened public for his reforms, so he also relaxed censorship in the late 1850s. Furthermore, journalism became more important for many people because they had a keen interest in the progress of the reforms, which journalists were permitted to cover. As a consequence, thirty periodicals were established between 1851 and 1855, the last years of Tsar Nicholas I's reign, whereas five times that number were launched between 1856 and 1860, the first years under Tsar Alexander II.[71] However,

71 See Luise McReynolds, *The News under Russia's Old Regime: The Development of a Mass-Circulation Press* (Princeton: Princeton University Press, 2014), 18. On the press and censorship in Russia in the eighteenth century and the first half of the nineteenth, see McReynolds, *News*, Chapter 1; as well as the classic study by Boris Ivanovich Esin, *Russkaia dorevoiyutsionnaia gazeta 1702–1917 gg. Kratkii ocherk* (Moscow: Izd-vo

newspapers that explicitly positioned themselves as organs of a social movement with emancipatory objectives, such as William Lloyd Garrison's *Liberator* or *Fredrick Douglass' Paper* in the United States, remained inconceivable under Alexander II as well, and the censors continued to preselect publishable news.

Nonetheless, this close state control of the press meant neither that an enlightened public was absent in Russia nor that it lacked communications media and influence.[72] The advocates of emancipation and democratization turned instead to other forms of communication, media and genres of writing, and to foreign countries, using literary and musical gatherings, salons, chess clubs, universities and study circles (*kruzhki*). The array of media also included the belles lettres, encyclopedias and dictionaries, and the literary monthly journals (*tolstye zhurnaly*, or 'thick' journals), where book reviews and discussions of economic and social problems of other countries offered space for indirect reflections on Russia's own situation. In addition, there were the Russian émigré newspapers and books smuggled into the country from abroad. At gatherings in salons and clubs, people adhering to enlightened ideas read from banned texts and circulated them in handwritten copies. At universities and in study circles there were lectures on forbidden philosophical ideas or simply contemporary European history. Subtly, but unmistakably, writers addressed taboo topics through literature, as exemplified by Ivan Sergeevich Turgenev's *A Sportsman's Notebook*, a cycle of short stories describing the situation of the rural population in a realist tone, depicting peasant hardships and abuse by the aristocracy, clergy and

---

Mosk. un-ta, 1971), 8–27; Gary Marker, *Publishing, Printing, and the Origins of Intellectual Life in Russia, 1700–1800* (Princeton: Princeton University Press, 1985); Susan Joan Smith-Peter, *The Russian Provincial Newspaper and Its Public, 1788–1864* (Pittsburgh: University of Pittsburgh Press, 2008); and Hildermeier, *Geschichte Russlands*, Chapter 27, 2–3, Chapter 38, 2. On *Severnaia pchela*, see Nurit Schleifman, 'A Russian Daily Newspaper and Its New Readership: *Severnaia pchela 1825–1840*', *Cahiers du monde russe et soviétique* 28/2 (1987), 134. On censorship see the classic account by Mikhail Konstantinovich Lemke, *Nikolaevskie zhandarmy i literatura 1826–1855 gg.: Po podlinnym delam tret'iago otdeleniia sobstv. E. I. Velichestva kantseliarii* [1908] (The Hague: Europe Printing, 1965); Charles A. Ruud, *Fighting Words: Imperial Censorship and the Russian Press, 1804–1906* (Toronto: University of Toronto Press, 1982); and Marianna Tax Choldin, *A Fence around the Empire: Russian Censorship of Western Ideas under the Tsars* (Durham, NC: Duke University Press, 1985).

72 See also Hausmann, 'Öffentlichkeit'; Kelly and Volkov, 'Obshchestvennost', Sobornost': Collective Identities', 26–7.

police.[73] Editors of encyclopedias and dictionaries – following Diderot's example – explained the thinking that lay behind terms and concepts, and contributors to the literary monthlies discussed Russian questions tacitly through their examination of slavery in the United States and pauperism in England. In this way authors and their audiences developed Aesopean language, becoming experts in subtle discourse, encoded speaking and writing, and decoded listening and reading.[74]

Such public communication resulted in the tendency to engage in more or less coded conversations among insiders, because indirect discourse complicated communication and restricted the number of potential recipients. These circumstances made it impossible to build a broad social movement like that in Great Britain or the United States. But the intellectual elite crucial for the emergence of terrorism grew in this way just as well, or perhaps even more sustainably, because the official restrictions on what could be said lent special weight and heightened significance to statements that lay between the lines or beyond the permissible. For this reason, the intellectual elite in Russia was delineated earlier and more clearly than were its counterparts in the rest of Europe and the United States, and its members developed a consciousness of themselves as a specific group through the restrictions on their communication, the attendant punishments and the shared language that these restrictions engendered.[75]

---

73 Ivan Sergeevich Turgenev, *A Sportsman's Notebook* (New York and London: Everyman's Library, 1992), also known as *The Hunting Sketches* and *Sketches from a Hunter's Album*. On this book, see Reinhard Lauer, *Geschichte der russischen Literatur: Von 1700 bis zur Gegenwart* (Munich: C. H. Beck, 2003), 337–9; and Leonard Shapiro, *Turgenev: His Life and Times* (Cambridge, MA: Harvard University Press, 1982), 87, generally 86–8.

74 On the forms of communication and the media used by the enlightened public in Russia, see Hildermeier, *Geschichte Russlands*, Chapter 38.2; Pomper, *The Russian Revolutionary Intelligentsia*, 32–56; Robert L. Belknap, 'Survey of Russian Journals, 1840–1880', in Deborah A. Martinsen (ed.), *Literary Journals in Imperial Russia* (Cambridge: Cambridge University Press, 2010), 91–116; L. P. Gromova, 'Stanovlenie sistemy russkoi politicheskoi pressy XIX veka v emigratsii', in Zhirkova (ed.), *Zhurnalistika russkogo zarubezh'ia XIX–XX vekov: Uchebnoe posobie* (St Petersburg: Izd. S.-Peterb. un-ta, 2003), 29–94; and Lev Losev, *On the Beneficence of Censorship: Aesopian Language in Modern Russian Literature* (Munich: O. Sagner in Kommission, 1984). The phenomenon that censors permitted the discussion of controversial political questions as long as they seemed to concern the United States can also be observed for the German lands. See Depkat, *Amerikabilder in politischen Diskursen*, Chapter 4.

75 The principle of receiving increased attention and solidarity as a result of persecution was not unknown in countries with press freedom either. For example, when Garrison and Lovejoy spoke out in their papers against slavery or lynching, it

The necessity of inventing alternative and subversive media and indirect forms of communication in Russia thus contributed greatly to the particularly early emergence of intellectuals as a distinct social stratum with profound political significance. According to the French historian Christophe Charle, Russia can therefore 'claim the historical honour of being the first country in which intellectuals achieved social visibility and a collective political role'.[76] Indeed, the literary critic Vissarion Grigoryevich Belinsky described a new 'special class' as early as 1847: it received the name *intelligentsia* from its opponents only in the 1860s.[77] In the process of the emergence of terrorism, this social group of *intelligenty* assumed the function that social movements performed in other contexts and places, such as in the national movement in Italy or the abolitionist movement in the United States.

The intelligentsia has been defined variously ever since it arose in the nineteenth century. Most definitions agree that this social formation consists of an elite that is engaged socially and politically without having their own direct means of exercising power. 'The definition which we shall adopt . . . employs as its touchstone the sense of commitment to public welfare,' writes, for example, Richard Pipes:

> A member of the intelligentsia . . . is someone not wholly preoccupied
> with his personal well-being but at least as much and preferably much
> more concerned with that of society at large, and willing, to the best of
> his ability, to work on society's behalf . . . An intelligentsia thus defined
> emerges wherever there exists a significant discrepancy between those
> who control political and economic power, and those who represent (or
> believe themselves to represent) public opinion.[78]

---

also required courage, which lent their statements particular salience. The difference is merely that, in their case, transgressing the limits of what could be said was not punished by central government authority but rather by the violence of local representatives of the state in coordination with organized mobs.

76 Christophe Charle, *Les intellectuels en Europe au XIXe siècle: Essai d'histoire comparée* (Paris: Editions du Seuil, 1996), 246. See also Denis Sdvizhkov, *Das Zeitalter der Intelligenz: Zur vergleichenden Geschichte der Gebildeten in Europa bis zum Ersten Weltkrieg* (Göttingen: Vandenhoeck und Ruprecht, 2006), 154–6.

77 Quoted after Sdvizhkov, *Das Zeitalter der Intelligenz*, 154.

78 Richard Pipes, *Russia under the Old Regime* (New York: Penguin, 1992), 252–3. See also Kurt Röttgers, W. Goerdt, J. Rodriguez-Lores, W. Mackenthun and K. H. Wewetzer, 'Intelligenz, Intelligentsia, Intellektueller', in Joachim Ritter (ed.), *Historisches Wörterbuch*

Richard Pipes defines the intelligentsia as opposed to political and economic power. In the US case, it was individual abolitionists in the anti-slavery movement (such as Wendell Phillips or the Secret Six), who could be regarded as members of an intellectual elite thus defined because they felt responsible for the American republic without being able to achieve anything within available political institutions. In Russia, by contrast, the intelligentsia represented a discrete stratum of people who felt that same sense of responsibility for the future of their country but who were usually excluded from legal political channels of governance.[79] Given a corresponding process of radicalization, the intelligentsia offered fertile ground for the seeds of terrorism.

Such a process of radicalization can also be identified in Russia. It essentially corresponded to the processes of radicalization in Italy and the United States, with a major part of the intelligentsia believing that changes were essential but finding the political institutions either unwilling or unable to put them into effect, thus making violent action an attractive option for resolving the blockage. In the early 1860s, a few radical 'Westernizers' came to this assessment of the state's unwillingness or inability to reform the political system and to emancipate the peasants.

'Westernizers' (*zapadniki*) constituted a political current within the intelligentsia. In a debate in the 1830s about whether Russia should follow the historical development in Western Europe and the United States or whether the country should forge its own way, the Westernizers set themselves apart from the Slavophiles (*slavianofily*), who argued for taking a manifestly Russian approach to the issue.[80] Like the radical abolitionists in the United States, the radical Westernizers also initially rejected the use of violence to achieve their objectives. Only after a lengthy process of radicalization did they come to the conclusion that, in Russia, no change towards individual and political freedom could

der Philosophie, vol. 4: *I–K* (Basel: Schwabe, 1976), 445–61; Charle, *Les intellectuels en Europe*, 243–82; Sdvizhkov, *Das Zeitalter der Intelligenz*, 156; as well as Otto Wilhelm Müller's authoritative account, *Intelligencija: Untersuchungen zur Geschichte eines politischen Schlagwortes* (Frankfurt am Main: Athenäum Verlag, 1971); and the sociohistorical perspective from Hildermeier in *Geschichte Russlands*, Chapter 37.2.

79 See Sdvizhkov, *Das Zeitalter der Intelligenz*, 13.

80 For an introduction, see Klaus von Beyme, *Politische Theorien in Russland, 1789–1945* (Wiesbaden: Verlag für Sozialwissenschaften, 2001), Chapters 1.3, 2.1; as well as Hildermeier, *Geschichte Russlands*, Chapter 32.3.

be achieved without violence. Yet, unlike Italy or the United States, Russia did not have a steadily growing generational cohort (such as 'Young Italy' or those born around 1800 in the United States) whose members had experienced this radicalization process individually or together with friends and disciples. Instead, it was ever larger sections of new political generations. With few exceptions, the repressive measures of the Russian government managed to eliminate and silence the radical intellectuals of each political generation. However, those who had been executed, banned or exiled immediately became martyrs to the youth, who took their place in ever larger numbers as a new and more radical generation. In this way five more or less distinct generations emerged successively among the Westernizers in the intelligentsia.[81]

The revolutionary tradition in Russia began with the Decembrists. Most of the leading figures of this revolt were born in the 1790s and belonged to Russia's high aristocracy, whose families often owned thousands of serfs. Nevertheless, their highest ambition was to abolish serfdom. After their insurrection had failed, they were all executed or banished to Siberia. Silencing them also stifled the highly advanced and differentiated discussion of questions relating to emancipation and the drafting of a constitution for Russia. Their influence on the next generation therefore consisted less in their concrete political

---

81 The demarcation of five political–intellectual generations is new. Such a classification does not appear in the sources on the revolutionary movement in Russia, which typically differentiate between groups of intellectuals and characterize them as 'sons' and 'disciples'. The decision to view the people born around 1800 as the starting point for the question of radicalization and to adopt the resulting generational taxonomy and numerical reckoning stems from comparison with Italy and the United States and therefore represents an original synthesis of the literature on the emergence of the revolutionary movement in Russia. On this movement and the approaches that have generally structured it, see Venturi, *Roots of Revolution*; Pomper, *The Russian Revolutionary Intelligentsia*; Tomáš Garrigue Masaryk's *The Spirit of Russia: Studies in History, Literature and Philosophy* (London: Allen & Unwin, 1919), whose somewhat misleading title belies its main contribution as a history of political thought in Russia; Peter Scheibert, *Von Bakunin zu Lenin: Geschichte der russischen revolutionären Ideologien, 1840–1895*, vol. 1: *Die Formung des radikalen Denkens in der Auseinandersetzung mit deutschem Idealismus und französischem Bürgertum* (Leiden: Brill, 1956); Stuart Ramsay Tompkins, *The Russian Intelligentsia: Makers of the Revolutionary State* (Norman: University of Oklahoma Press, 1957); Beyme, *Politische Theorien in Russland*; Hildermeier, *Geschichte Russlands*, Chapter 32.3; and the literature cited below in this book.

ideas than in their example as heroic and altruistic fighters for free-dom. They established the idea in Russia of selfless sacrifice for the people.[82]

The second generation, the so-called intelligentsia of the 1830s and 1840s, had Turgenev, Michail Alexandrovich Bakunin, Vissarion Grigoryevich Belinsky, Alexander Ivanovich Herzen and Nikolai Platonovich Ogarëv as its leading lights. They were born in the 1810s and as schoolboys were deeply impressed by the Decembrist revolt. Their interest in political issues was awakened by the July revolution in Paris (1830) and the November revolt in Poland (1830–1). As university students Herzen and Ogarëv, for example, read texts by Charles Fourier and Henri de Saint-Simon, which were forbidden in Russia. In the late 1830s, after arrest and brief banishment that contributed to their radi-calization, Herzen, Bakunin and Belinsky were part of the Moscow (and later Berlin) circle (*kruzhok*) around the poet and intellectual Nikolai Vladimirovich Stankevich, where, together, they absorbed German idealism, which was likewise banned in Russia. In the early 1840s all the members of this circle actively pursued journalism. However, Belinsky died young, and both Bakunin and Herzen went abroad. In London Herzen founded the *Free Russian Press* and together with Ogarëv edited the almanac *Polyarnaya Zvezda* (Polar Star) (the title of a publication by the Decembrists) and the journal *Kolokol* (Bell), in which he wrote directly to Alexander II in a manner reminiscent of Mazzini. Through work on this journal, Herzen became the founder of *narodnichestvo* ('populism', from *narod* – 'people'), as the Russian liberation movement came to be called as of the 1870s.[83]

---

82 On the Decembrist revolt see also pp. 397–8 above. Lemberg, *Die nationale Gedankenwelt der Dekabristen*, Chapter 2, discusses the 'Decembrists as a generational community'.

83 There is abundant literature on the generation of the 1830s and 1840s, the emergence of Russian populism, and especially Bakunin and Herzen, but also Belinsky, Ogarëv and Stankevich and his circle. For an introduction, see Venturi, *Roots of Revolution*, Chapters 1–4; Scheibert, *Von Bakunin zu Lenin*, Chapters 5–15, 18–20; Pomper, *The Russian Revolutionary Intelligentsia*, 32–56; Ulam, *Prophets and Conspirators*, Chapter 2; and Hildermeier, *Geschichte Russlands*, 858–67. On the whole group (with the exception of Stankevich) see the classic work by Edward Hallet Carr, *The Romantic Exiles: A Nineteenth-Century Portrait Gallery* (London: V. Gollancz, 1933); on Bakunin see the likewise classic account by Ricarda Octavia Huch, *Michael Bakunin und die Anarchie* (Leipzig: Insel-Verlag, 1923); Edward Hallett Carr, *Michael Bakunin* (London: Macmillan, 1937); and especially Madeleine Grawitz, *Bakounine* (Paris: Plon,

The Petrashevsky circle constituted the third political–intellectual generation that emerged as a result of the Russian government's policy of repression. This group consisted of the students and younger colleagues of the 1840s generation, including Mikhail Yevgrafovich Saltykov-Shchedrin and Fyodor Mikhailovich Dostoyevsky, who later became a Slavophile. Almost all the members of this generation were born in the 1820s, and they congregated around Mikhail Vasilyevich Butashevich-Petrashevsky, who possessed a library of revolutionary literature. With few exceptions, they belonged to the lower nobility, were less wealthy than the members of the 1840s generation, and therefore needed paid employment in government service while lacking any personal experience in Western Europe. Lacking resources and therefore necessarily the largesse or worldliness which wealth can provide, the Petrashevskys were often ridiculed and remained almost unknown in the rest of Europe.

The Petrashevskys, however, were crucial to the emergence of the revolutionary movement. As Franco Venturi writes, their circle became 'the base for all Westernizers then in Russia who were not just liberals or moderates'. In his view, 'Petrashevsky's group was placed at the crossing of two roads. One was to lead the intelligentsia to play a political part; the other pointed to the creation of a more specifically revolutionary movement. The group itself harboured elements of both these trends.'[84] The issue of emancipating the peasants lay at the heart of what its members thought and did. In the course of the Russian government's reaction to the revolutions of 1848–9, the authorities arrested sixty members of this circle and sent twenty-three of them to a military

1990); and Valerii Nikitich Demin, *Bakunin* (Moscow: Molodaia gvardiia, 2006). On Belinsky, Herzen, Ogarëv and Stankevich, the best resources remain Herbert Eugene Bowman's *Vissarion Belinksi, 1811–1848: A Study in the Origins of Social Criticism in Russia* (Cambridge, MA: Harvard University Press, 1954); Irina Aleksandrovna Zhelvakova, *Gertsen* (Moscow: Molodaia gvardiia, 2010); Michel Mervaud, *Socialisme et liberté: La pensée et l'action de Nicolas Ogarev, 1813–1857* (Mont-Saint-Aigan: Université de Haute Normandie, 1984); and Edward J. Brown, *Stankevich and His Moscow Circle: 1830–1840* (Stanford: Stanford University Press, 1966). On the journals *Poliarnaia Zvezda* (by the Decembrists and Herzen) and *Kolokol*, see A. V. Zapadova (ed.), *Istoriia russkoi zhurnalistiki XVII–XIX vekov* (Moscow: Vysshaia shkola, 1963), 145–52, 303–28; and Boris Ivanovich Esin, *Istoriia russkoi zhurnalistiki XIX veka*, 2nd ed., revised and expanded (Moscow: Aspekt Press: Izd-vo Moskovskogo universiteta, 2003), 30–7, 101–13.

84 Venturi, *Roots of Revolution*, 80.

tribunal, where twenty-one of them were sentenced to death. Not until the moment they stood before the execution squad were their convictions converted to exile and hard labour in Siberia. Drawing on his own staged execution, Dostoevsky would go on to describe the cruelty of this form of pardon in his later writings.[85]

Nikolai Gavrilovich Chernyshevsky belonged to the fourth generation of the intelligentsia. Its members have gone down in history under various names: nihilists, *raznochintsy* (literally, people of miscellaneous ranks), or 1860ers (from the Russian designation of the sixth decade of nineteenth century that encompasses the reforms from 1855 to 1866). The leading representatives of this generation, besides Chernyshevsky himself, were Nikolai Alexandrovich Dobrolyubov, his younger colleague and friend, and Dmitri Ivanovich Pisarev.[86]

Chernyshevsky, the most important of the three, was born in 1828 in Saratov, south-east of Moscow on the Volga river. In 1846 he left his hometown to study at a seminary for orthodox priests in St Petersburg. He was politicized and radicalized during the revolutions of 1848–9, specifically by the speeches of Louis Blanc, which Chernyshevsky read

85 See Nikolai Bel'chikov, *Dostoevskii v protsesse Petrashevtsev* (Moscow: Nauka, 1971), 88. On Petrashevsky and the Petrashevskys, see Hildermeier, *Geschichte Russlands*, 867–8; Scheibert, *Von Bakunin zu Lenin*, Chapter 17; Venturi, *Roots of Revolution*, 79–89; Yarmolinsky, *Road to Revolution*, 75–90; Pomper, *The Russian Revolutionary Intelligentsia*, 50–6; as well as, specifically, John Evans, *The Petraševskij Circle* (The Hague: Mouton, 1974); Manfred Alexander, *Der Petraševskij-Prozess: Eine 'Verschwörung der Ideen' und ihre Verfolgung im Russland von Nikolaus I.* (Wiesbaden: Steiner, 1979); and B. F. Egorov, *Petrashevtsy* (Leningrad: Nauka, 1988).

86 On the term *raznochintsy* see Sdvizhkov, *Das Zeitalter der Intelligenz*, 15, 145; Hildermeier, *Geschichte Russlands*, 812–13; and specifically Christopher Becker, 'Raznochintsy: The Development of a Word and a Concept', *American Slavic and East European Review* 18/1 (1959), 70–4; and Elise Kimerling Wirtschafter, 'The Groups Between: *Raznochintsy*, Intelligentsia, Professionals', in Dominic Lieven (ed.), *The Cambridge History of Russia*, vol. 2: *Imperial Russia, 1689–1917* (Cambridge: Cambridge University Press, 2006), 245–63. On the 1860ers, or nihilists, see Pomper, *The Russian Revolutionary Intelligentsia*, Chapter 3; Ulam, *Prophets and Conspirators*, Chapter 6; O. V. Budnitskii, *Terrorizm v rossiiskom osvoboditel'nom dvizhenii: ideologiia, etika, psikhologiia (vtoraia polovina XIX – nachalo XX v.)* (Moscow: ROSSPEN, 2000), Chapter 1.1; and Hildermeier, *Geschichte Russlands*, 941–2. On Chernyshevsky, Dobrolyubov and Pisarev, see the introduction by Ralph E. Matlaw in Matlaw (ed.), *Belinsky, Chernyshevsky, and Dobrolyubov: Selected Criticism* (Bloomington: Indiana University Press, 1976); and Vladimir Rodionovich Shcherbina, *Revoliutsionno-demokraticheskaia kritika i sovremennost': Belinskii, Chernyshevskii, Dobroliubov* (Moscow: Nauka, 1980).

in the *Journal des débats*. In late 1848 he also encountered the writings of Fourier, Hegel and Feuerbach through various members of the Petrashevsky circle. After their arrest, Chernyshevsky joined the circle associated with Irinarkh Ivanovich Vvedensky, where discussions focused on literature, religion, socialist theory and the revolution and where he got to know and appreciate the banned writings of Belinsky and Herzen. The political implications of the dissertation that Chernyshevsky wrote meant that he could not pursue a university career, so he turned to journalism in 1853, becoming a full-time employee and, later, a coeditor of *Sovremennik* (The Contemporary), one of the most popular literary monthly journals with Western leanings. From 1856 to 1860 he succeeded in increasing the number of subscribers from 3,000 to 6,500.[87]

After Alexander II ascended the throne and it became known that the tsar intended to release Russian peasants from serfdom and to implement reforms, the intelligentsia briefly sided with the monarch. Chernyshevsky, too, pinned his hopes on the Russian government and a peaceful revolution from above. By 1858, though, he had come to suspect that the emancipation of the serfs by the tsar and the nobility would take place to the serfs' disadvantage. Disillusioned, he broke

---

87 For the best introduction to this, see Venturi, *Roots of Revolution*, Chapters 5–6; Yarmolinsky, *Road to Revolution*, 99–113; Ulam, *Prophets and Conspirators*, Chapter 3; Ulam, *Russia's Failed Revolutions*, 83–9; and Hildermeier, *Geschichte Russlands*, 942–3. See furthermore the classic work by Iurii Mikhailovich Steklov, *N. G. Chernyshevskii: ego zhizn' i deiatel'nost', 1828–1889* (Moscow: Gosizdat, 1928); Francis B. Randall, *N. G. Chernyshevskii* (New York: Twayne Publishers, 1967); William F. Woehrlin, *Chernyshevskii: The Man and the Journalist* (Cambridge, MA: Harvard University Press, 1971), Chapters 2, 4; Norman G. O. Pereira, *The Thought and Teachings of N. G. Černyševskij* (The Hague: Mouton, 1975); and Anatolii Petrovich Lanshchikov, *N. G. Chernyshevskii*, 2nd ed. (Moscow: Sovremennik, 1987), 48–78. Chernyshevsky does not have a good reputation in much of the literature on the Russian revolutionary movement. Isaiah Berlin, for example, writes that Chernyshevsky was 'not a man of original ideas' and criticizes 'his flat, dry, pedestrian style, his very dullness and lack of inspiration': Isaiah Berlin, *Russian Thinkers* (New York: Penguin Books, 1978), 224–5. Edward Hallet Carr is similarly negative in his introduction to Chernyshevsky's *What Is to Be Done?* (London: Virago, 1982), xiii–xxii. However, reading Chernyshevsky's work and the literature already cited about him contradicts such assessments of his work, as Cathy Porter also indicates in her new foreword to the edition of *What Is to Be Done?*. On the journal *Sovremennik*, see Zapadova, *Istoriia russkoi zhurnalistiki XVIII–XIX vekov*, 342–97; Belknap, 'Survey of Russian Journals', 106–14; and Esin, *Istoriia russkoi zhurnalistiki XIX veka*, 117–31.

completely with both the tsar and the intellectuals of the 1840s who – like Herzen in the *Kolokol* – still counted on the autocrat and rejected any use of violence. From that point until the emancipation, Chernyshevsky fostered a new, radical kind of journalism in *Sovremennik*, developing his own philosophy and a revolutionary lifestyle that became especially popular with the youth in schools, seminaries and universities and among young officers and public servants. He became the leading radical of his generation.[88]

The fifth generation of the intelligentsia was the radical student movement. It was born when the details of the emancipation laws were published on 19 February 1861, for among intellectuals they confirmed Chernyshevsky's views that the tsar was not a non-partisan father of the country but rather simply the grandest and most privileged noble of the land. A few days after the promulgation, demonstrations took place in Warsaw, which were bloodily suppressed by the Russian military. In the summer the government imposed new rules on Russian universities, tightening admission requirements and restricting the autonomy of student facilities, such as self-organized libraries and autonomous banks that helped support destitute students.

When these new regulations became known at the beginning of the winter semester, massive student protests erupted. For the first time the students connected their own demands with general social and political issues in their proclamations, manifestos and demonstrations. The first Russian underground newspaper, *Velikorus* (Great Russian), appeared from June to October 1861. The first calls to murder the tsar's family appeared in a proclamation titled 'Molodaya Rossiya' (Young Russia).[89]

---

88 For Herzen's efforts to support the tsar in reforms even after 1858; and on the break between him and Chernyshevsky, see the anonymous 'Pis'mo iz provintsii', reprinted as document no. 9 in E. L. Rudnitskaia (ed.), *Revoliutsionnii radikalizm v Rossii: vek deviatnadtsatyi* (Moscow: Arkheograficheskii tsentr, 1997), 80–5; Venturi, *Roots of Revolution*, 104–9, 158–61; Steklov, *N. G. Chernyshevskii*, vol. 2, Chapter 3; Randall, *N. G. Chernyshevskii*, Chapter 5.1–2; Woehrlin, *Chernyshevskii*, Chapter 8; Lanshchikov, *N. G. Chernyshevskii*, 212–22; as well as Nina Nikolaevna Novikova and Boris Michajlovich Kloss, *N. G. Chernyshevskii vo glave revoljutsionerov 1861 goda: Nekotorye itogi i perspektivy issledovaniia* (Moscow: Nauka, 1981), Chapter 1.

89 On the student movement, its public and secret facilities, and the conjecture that Chernyshevsky worked on *Velikorus* and a pamphlet to the peasants (which neither the police at the time nor historians later have been able to confirm because he was so careful), see Hildermeier, *Geschichte Russlands*, 943–4; Venturi, *Roots of Revolution*, 110, 170–8: Emiliia Samoilovna Vilenskaia, *Revoliutsionnoe podpol'e v Rossii, 60-e gody XIX*

The authorities responded by arresting more than 400 students. After a dramatic conflagration in St Petersburg in May 1862, whose cause was never identified but for which the revolutionary movement was held responsible, the government started taking action against the 1860ers as well as the student movement and its institutions. It temporarily banned *Sovremennik* and other literary monthly journals with Western leanings, and closed the chess clubs, the students' Sunday schools for workers and other places where revolutionaries were thought to gather. In addition, it arrested radical poets and writers such as Chernyshevsky and Pisarev. Despite lack of proof that they had engaged in subversive activities, they were sentenced to hard labour and exile in Siberia. The Russian authorities thereby managed to silence the 1860ers and suppress the revolutionary student movement as well.[90]

The authorities' success, however, was again short-lived. What remained of the student movement went underground in the summer of 1862, bringing forth the first Russian revolutionary underground movement, Zemlia i Volia (Land and Freedom). Chernyshevsky managed to publish his novel, *What Is to Be Done?*, while sitting in a prison cell, sending one last but powerful appeal to the young people of Russia. The novel and the underground movement it influenced became a model for Russian revolutionaries, all the way down to Lenin and Stalin.[91] Chernyshevsky attributed great significance to John

v. (Moscow: Nauka, 1965), Chapter 2; Ulam, *Prophets and Conspirators*, Chapters 4–5; Pomper, *The Russian Revolutionary Intelligentsia*, 75–83; Novikova and Kloss, *Chernyshevskii*, Chapter 2; Abbott Gleason, *Young Russia: The Genesis of Russian Radicalism in the 1860s* (New York: Viking Press, 1980), Chapters 4–6; and Guido Hausmann, *Universität und städtische Gesellschaft in Odessa, 1865–1917: Soziale und nationale Selbstorganisation in der Peripherie des Zarenreiches* (Stuttgart: Steiner, 1998), whose findings extend beyond the case in question. For the call to murder the tsar, see document no. 22, 'Molodaia Rossiia', reprinted in Rudnitskaia, *Revoliutsionnii radikalizm v Rossii*, 142–50.

90 On the temporary closure of *Sovremennik* and the journal *Russkoe slovo* and on their prohibition after the attempted assassination of Alexander II, see Ruud, *Fighting Words*, 130; and Esin, *Istoriia russkoi zhurnalistiki XIX veka*, 137–41. On banishment, see Steklov, *N. G. Chernyshevskii*, vol. 2, Parts 4–5; Randall, *N. G. Chernyshevskii*, Chapters 5.2, 7; Woehrlin, *Chernyshevskii*, Chapter 10; and Lanshchikov, *N. G. Chernyshevskii*, 244–96, 357–78.

91 See Venturi, *Roots of Revolution*, Chapter 10; Vilenskaia, *Revoliutsionnoe podpol'e v Rossii*, Chapter 3; Ulam, *Prophets and Conspirators*, Chapter 5; and Budnitskii,

Brown and his act of violence, both of which became a principal source of inspiration for his book and its revolutionary heroes.

The true Rakhmetov? John Brown as Chernyshevsky's model in *What Is to Be Done?*

Nikolai Gavrilovich Chernyshevsky had been keeping a critical, sympathetic eye on the democratic experiment in the United States for some time and was well informed about the economic, social, political and intellectual developments in North America, particularly the fierce debates about slavery in the United States.[92] As early as the November

---

Terrorizm v rossiiskom osvoboditel'nom dvizhenii, Chapter 1.2.

92 For example, Chernyshevsky created a chart with all the important American newspapers, in which he characterized their political orientation and their position on the matter of slavery. See David Hecht, *Russian Radicals Look to America, 1825–1894* (Cambridge, MA: Harvard University Press, 1947), 134. During the Cold War, American and Soviet scholars made Chernyshevsky and America into a subject of research, including his image of America, his sources of information, and what he wrote about the United States generally, with American scholars highlighting the positive aspects of his assessments, while Soviet scholarship focused on his critical remarks. For the latest publication on each side, see respectively Nikolai Nikolaevich Bolkhovitinov, 'Russian-American Cultural Relations: An Overview', in Norman E. Saul and Richard D. McKinzie (eds.), *Russian–American Dialogue on Cultural Relations, 1776–1914* (Columbia: University of Missouri Press, 1971), 1–25; and I. Popov, 'Iz amerikanskoi zhisni Dmitriia Sergeevicha Lopukhova', *Inostrannaia literatura* (1981), 251–6. Although American and Soviet scholarship repeatedly pointed out Chernyshevsky's special interest in John Brown, it did this only by simple reference to this fact or by summarizing Chernyshevksy's writings about John Brown without providing any deeper assessment of the significance for Chernyshevsky's work. See, for example, Bolkhovitinov, 'Russian–American Cultural Relations', 21; Hans Rogger, 'Russia and the Civil War', in Harold Melvin Hyman (ed.), *Heard Round the World: The Impact Abroad of the Civil War* (New York: Knopf, 1969), 197–8; and Iurii Serafimovich Melent'ev, 'Kritika N. G. Chernyshevskim burzhuaznoi demokratii SShA', *Uchenye zapiski Ural'skogo gosudarstvennogo universiteta imeni A. M. Gor'kogo* 24 (Sverdlovsk: Kafedra obshchestvennykh nauk, 1958), 208. Otherwise, they explained Chernyshevsky's sympathy for Brown by describing him as a role model for leading the masses in the United States into armed conflict. See, for example, I. I. Liagushenko, 'N. G. Chernyshevskii o grazhdanskoi voine v Soedinnennych Shtatakh Ameriki', Aftoreferat dissertatsii na soiskanie uchenoi stepeni dandidata istoricheskikh nauk, Leningradskii gosudarstvennyi ordena Lenina universitet imeni A. A. Zhdanova, Saransk 1952, 11; and I. Ia. Razumnikova, 'N. G. Chernyshevsky o grazhdanskoi voine v Soedinennych Shtatakh Ameriki, 1861–1865 gg.', in *Trudy Voronezhskogo*

1859 issue of *Sovremennik*, he devoted almost one-third of the 'Politics' section to John Brown. In this section, Chernyshevsky presented and commented on events he considered especially relevant to world politics. The importance he ascribed to John Brown and the raid on Harpers Ferry becomes evident from the title itself: 'European Issues. North American States and Brown'.[93] Drawing on reports 'in European newspapers' (only the London *Times* is cited, but the text also contains echoes of the reporting in *Le Siècle*),[94] Chernyshevsky briefly but accurately describes the course of events in the raid on Harpers Ferry, writing that a group of abolitionists had made a surprise attack on the arsenal, captured it and proclaimed the freedom of all the 'negroes' (*negry*).

---

gosudarstvennogo universiteta: Sbornik rabot istoriko-filologicheskogo fakul'teta 47 (1957), 36. Chernyshevsky's sympathy for Brown's attempt to free the slaves is analysed by others in terms of its implications for the emancipation of the serfs in Russia. See especially M. M. Malkin, 'Chernyshevskii i zaatlanticheskaia respublika (SShA)', in Vladislav Evgen'evich Evgen'ev-Maksimov, Aleksandr Alekseevich Voznesenskii and Sholom Israilevich Ganelin (eds.), *N. G. Chernyshevskii (1889–1939): Trudy nauchnoi sessii k piatidesiatiletiiu so dnia smerti* (Leningrad: Izdanie leningradskogo gosudarstvennogo universiteta, 1941), 323–5; Max M. Laserson, *The American Impact on Russia: Diplomatic and Ideological, 1784–1917* (New York: Macmillan, 1950), 246; and Popov, 'Iz amerikanskoi zhisny Dmitriia Sergeevicha Lopukhova', 251–2, 254, which provides the most detailed and thorough analysis of this matter. The question whether and how Brown's example might have influenced Chernyshevsky's thoughts and writing has been neither posed nor studied until now.

93 Nikolai Gavrilovich Chernyshevskii, 'No. 11-Noiabr' 1859 goda. Evropeiskie dela. – Severo-Amerikanskie Shtaty i Braun', in *Polnoe sobranie sochinenii N. G. Chernyshevskago*, vol. 5 (St Petersburg: Tipografiia tovarishchestva 'Obshchestvennaia Pol'za', 1906), on John Brown, see 440–2.

94 Ibid., 440. The reference to *The Times* is at 441. David Hecht, *Russian Radicals*, 86–7, comes to the following conclusion about Chernyshevsky's sources of information on the United States:

The main sources of information on America at Chernyshevsky's disposal and those whose context he himself indicates as having utilized may conveniently be summarized as follows: Western European and English magazines and newspapers, American newspapers, books by Europeans and Americans on America, and American literature ... The *Allgemeine Zeitung, Indépendance Belge, Revue des deux Mondes, Revue Brittanique, L'Annuaire de l'Économie Politique, Edinburgh Review, Athenaeum*, and the London *Times* were the important European and English periodicals which Chernyshevsky consulted in seeking news and information about the North American States. Although Chernyshevsky was familiar enough with the names and trends of the important American newspapers, the *New York Times* and *New York Herald* were apparently the only two that he managed to obtain even at irregular intervals.

When the militia from the nearby towns arrived, Brown and his men did not surrender, so they were surrounded and killed or arrested and sentenced to death. In Chernyshevsky's opinion, 'The incident is utterly trivial in terms of its size, but it is highly significant as the first of its kind.'[95] He thus made it clear from the outset that he considered the momentousness of the violent act committed by John Brown and his volunteers to lie not in the instrumental dimension of the violence but rather in the newness of the tactic.

What did Chernyshevsky see as being new about the raid on Harpers Ferry? In his opinion it was the first time the abolitionists had gone on the offensive, a position that had hitherto been the sole preserve of slavery's defenders. Chernyshevsky believed that socio-psychological reasons lay behind this step, that the perennial insults by the proponents of slavery had intensified the abolitionists' belief in their own power so much and had stoked their enthusiasm to such an extent that it had awakened their desire to take the initiative themselves. He recognized that their first attempt had failed, as almost all first attempts of this kind do. Nevertheless, Chernyshevsky was sure that this initial abortive endeavour would have substantial political consequences. He reasoned that at first the proponents of slavery would be strengthened following the raid on Harpers Ferry because they would receive support from timid people but that then the struggle between the abolitionists and slavery's defenders would gradually assume a new character. The abolitionists would eventually seek to avenge their first martyrs: Brown, the leader of the group that had fought so heroically at Harpers Ferry, as well as his fearless comrades. He believed that these struggles would cause the people in the northern and southern states to feel increasing shame because their political friends were being exposed to such attacks. Under pressure from the free citizens in North and South, the frontiers of slavery, which had kept expanding until that point, would shrink for the first time.[96] Chernyshevsky therefore believed that the particular import of John Brown's act lay in its symbolic, socio-psychological consequences.

Chernyshevsky was not only interested in the raid on Harpers Ferry as a new form of violence but also in the person of John Brown as 'the

---

95 Chernyshevskii, 'No. 11-Noiabr' 1859 goda', 441.
96 Ibid., 441.

leader of the first martyrs for the cause of the negroes [*negry*] in the United States'.[97] To introduce John Brown, he appended translated excerpts from the Provisional Constitution to his article, explaining that an 'indomitable energy and a deep, strong, moral feeling impart extraordinary originality to this constitution'.[98] Chernyshevsky also published his translation of most of a letter that a reader had written to the editor of *The Times* on John Brown and his character. Chernyshevsky wrote that this document would help acquaint his readers with the ideas of the radical abolitionists. The letter to the editor, which appeared anonymously in *The Times* on 8 November 1859, was also used by other newspapers in Europe to portray John Brown, but the almost complete translation of the letter in *Sovremennik* was an exception.[99]

Strictly speaking, almost none of the information in this letter is correct in the way the writer presents it. The writer, who had reportedly spoken several times with John Brown's friends and neighbours, recounted that Brown had been living peacefully in Kansas when 'a party of border ruffians' (which Chernyshevsky translated as *shaika golovorezov*, or 'band of cutthroats') attacked his farm one night, destroyed his home and fields and 'completely gratuitously' killed one of his children, and that Brown's wife died soon after from grief. In response to this attack, according to Chernyshevsky, Brown fell into a 'monomania which was cold, unusually shrewd, patient and desperately courageous'. He gathered a small group around him and went with these men to Missouri, where he rescued opponents of slavery from lynching, freed whole families from slavery, and destroyed the homes of men who were

---

97 Ibid., 441.

98 Chernyshevsky's translation of the Provisional Constitution is included in the 1906 collection of his works: Nikolai Gavrilovich Chernyshevskii, 'Vremennaia konstitutsiia i postanovleniia dlia naroda Soedinennich Shtatov', in *Polnoe sobranie sochinenii*, vol. 5, 444–6. This text is no longer included in the later Soviet editions of his works. For an annotated edition of excerpts of the text, see I. P. Dement'ev, 'N. G. Chernyshevskii i konstitutsiia Dzhona Brauna', *Voprosy istorii* 12 (1959), which argues convincingly that Chernyshevsky's translation was based on a reprint of the Provisional Constitution in the London *Times* on 4 November 1859. See Dement'ev, 'N. G. Chernyshevskii', 140.

99 The letter to the editor, which is identified here for the first time, is X., 'Hotel de Lille et d'Albion, Paris, Nov. 4. "The Insurrection at Harper's Ferry. To the Editor of the Times"', *The Times*, 8 November 1859, 9. On the partial or summarized presentations of the text in other European newspapers, see, for example, 'Une correspondance du *Times* donne les renseignements suivants sur Brown', *Journal des débats*, 11 November 1859, 2.

known for using terror to bring slavery to Kansas and sometimes also executed them. After the conflict had been resolved and peace restored, Brown is said to have reverted to being a farmer and peaceful citizen. But as soon as the Missourians invaded Kansas again, he left once more for retaliatory campaigns in Missouri, where the last rumour had him surrounded by attackers before charging right through them with all his comrades and vanishing without a trace into the night.[100]

What particularly impressed Chernyshevsky in this version of John Brown from the London *Times* becomes clear in an article published in *Sovremennik* in January 1861, which focused on the secession of South Carolina and the first other southern states from the Union.[101] Using a speech by William H. Seward, Chernyshevsky analysed the reactions in the North to secessionist aspirations and drew on the most recent literature to present the demographic, economic and social conditions in the North and South.[102] He then examined Abraham Lincoln's position on slavery and came to the same conclusion as John Brown – that the new president would leave slavery intact in the United States. He presented the long history of the conflict between the North and the South over the question of slavery. In this context, Chernyshevsky returned to the discussion of the civil war in Kansas and of John Brown. He indicated his conviction that the plantation owners definitely could have succeeded, through deception and violence, in forcing slavery upon the population of Kansas and the other territories that were yet to become states. He believed they might have even managed to conceal this 'if the

100 See X., 'To the Editors of the Times' and Chernyshevskii, 'No. 11-Noiabr' 1859 goda', 442.

101 Nikolai Gavrilovich Chernyshevskii, 'Ianvar' 1861. Rastorzhenie Severo-Amerikanskogo Sojuza. – Evropeiskie Dela', in V. Ia. Kirpotin, B. P. Koz'min, P. I. Lebedev-Polianskii, N. L. Meshcheriakov, I. D. Udal'tsov and N. M. Chernyshevskii (eds.), *Polnoe sobranie sochinenii v piatnadtsati tomakh* (Moscow: Gosudarstvennoe izdatel'stvo khudozhestvennoi literatury, 1939–1953), Vol. 8, A. P. Rybasov (ed.) (1950), 385–408.

102 The speech Chernyshevsky translated was delivered by William Henry Seward on 21 December 1860 (not on 23 December, the date given by Chernyshevsky), at the New England Dinner that was held by the New England Society of New York. It is published under the title 'Secession', in George E. Baker (ed.), *The Works of William H. Seward* (Boston: Houghton, Mifflin and Company, 1884), 644–50. Chernyshevsky cites John S. C. Abbott, *South and North; Or, Impressions Received During a Trip to Cuba and the South* (New York: Abbey & Abbot, 1860), as the source of the demographic, economic and social data he used.

settlers of the south-western territories had been apathetic or cowardly people'. But, according to Chernyshevsky, the settlers

> were very energetic and courageous people [*liudi ochen' energicheskie i khrabrie*]. They repulsed the bandits, forced their way into the lodgings that the plantation owners had set up for them, took revenge on their opponents for every insult [*za kazhduiu obidu otomshchaiut protivnikam*] and freed the slaves there as they left. What kind of settlers they were can be seen from the fact that John Brown – who had been convicted in Virginia about a year earlier of having tried to abolish slavery in the state by force – was a settler in Kansas.[103]

This version of the civil war in Kansas partially diverged from the actual local conditions but exactly matches the depiction in *The Times*'s anonymous letter to the editor.

It also reveals what counted for Chernyshevsky: the citizens of the free states who thought and acted morally were not about to put up with any nonsense, retaliating in kind whenever the proponents of slavery attacked. Nor did they shrink from taking the fight to their enemies. Instead of passively accepting what the immoral but powerful plantation owners wanted to impose on them against their will, these settlers took their fate, the fortunes of their state, and the future of the nation into their own hands. In this, Chernyshevsky truly grasped one of John Brown's central ideas: when faced with the peaceful surrender of the city of Lawrence and the attack on the defenceless Charles Sumner in the Senate, John Brown used arguments like 'an eye for an eye, a tooth for a tooth' (even if it included 'some killing') in order to 'fight fire with fire', 'to strike terror in the hearts of the advocates of slavery', and 'to show these barbarians that we, too, have rights', in order to justify the murders at Pottawatomie.[104]

The significance of John Brown and his act of violence for the political situation in the United States were not only subjects of analysis and keen interest for Chernyshevsky as a journalist. Even more than this, he came to see Brown as the embodiment and epitome of 'the new man'

---

103 Chernyshevskii, 'Ianvar' 1861', 398.
104 See above, p. 226.

who would appear in *What Is to Be Done? From Tales of New People.*[105] Chernyshevsky wrote this novel, whose title is a reference to Luke 3:10–14,[106] between December 1862 and April 1863 in the Alexeevsky Ravelin, the wing for political prisoners in the Peter and Paul Fortress in St Petersburg. Nevertheless *Sovremennik* was still able to publish it in a series of instalments in 1863. When the censors retroactively banned those issues of the journal, handwritten copies of the text continued circulating in Russia. In addition, in 1867 émigrés in Geneva published the first edition of the novel as a book in Russian, and translations followed in almost all European languages.[107]

---

105 Nikolai Gavrilovich Chernyshevskii, *Chto delat'? Iz rasskazov o novykh liudiakh*, ed. T. I. Ornatskaia and Ts. A. Reiser (Leningrad: Nauka, 1975). The following analysis is based on this authoritative, annotated, critical 1975 edition of the novel. For a review of the different versions and editions of the text, see the foreword in Andrew M. Drozd, *Chernyshevskii's What Is to Be Done? A Reevaluation* (Evanston: Northwestern University Press, 2001), ix–xi, especially ix–x. Translator's note: The quotations in the following passages are drawn from the 1989 edition of Chernyshevsky's *What Is to Be Done?*, translated by Michael R. Katz and annotated by William G. Wagner (Ithaca: Cornell University Press, 1989). It is based on the authoritative 1975 edition of the Russian text, for which Tamara I. Ornatskaia and Solomon A. Reiser corrected all obvious misprints and errors in the original 1863 publication in *Sovremennik*. While the two 1886 English translations of the novel provide a more authentic glimpse of how the original was read and understood in the English-speaking world, both have significant flaws. The American translation by Nathan Haskell Dole and S. S. Skidelsky follows the Russian quite literally, often too much so, and leaves out sexually suggestive references in a book which Chernyshevsky himself had already subjected to self-censorship and coded language, while the translation by Benjamin Tucker was itself a translation of the French translation and leaves out the entirety of Vera Pavlova's fourth dream, a crucial section of the novel.

106 '10 And the people asked him, saying, What shall we do then? 11 [John the Baptist] answereth and saith unto them, He that hath two coats, let him impart to him that hath none; and he that hath meat, let him do likewise. 12 Then came also publicans to be baptized, and said unto him, Master, what shall we do? 13 And he said unto them, Exact no more than that which is appointed you. 14 And the soldiers likewise demanded of him, saying, And what shall we do? And he said unto them, Do violence to no man, neither accuse any falsely; and be content with your wages.' In Russia the notion of 'the new man' or 'new people' harks back to the time of Peter the Great.

107 For the first publication of the novel, see *Sovremennik* 3–5 (1863). On the history of its writing and publication, see Solomon A. Reiser, 'Ot redaktora', in Chernyshevskii, *Chto delat'?*, 1975, 5–6; and Drozd, *Chernyshevskii's What Is to Be Done?*, 5–9. For the censors' discussion of the book, see Ruud, *Fighting Words*, 138, 153. A bibliography of the translations is provided by Boris L. Kandel', 'Bibliografia perevodov romana *Chto delat'?* na iazyki narodov SSSR i na inostrannye iazyki', in Chernyshevskii, *Chto delat'?*, 1975, 862–8.

The novel rapidly became the 'bible' for Russia's young revolutionaries, the object of intense philosophical and literary debate, and a
classic work of European revolutionary literature. Fyodor Mikhailovich
Dostoevsky responded to the novel remarkably quickly, publishing his
Notes from Underground in 1864 and, a few years later, *Demons* (also
known as *The Possessed* and *The Devils*).[108] Lev Nikolaevich Tolstoy
provided his own answer to Chernyshevsky's question by publishing
What Then Must We Do? (1886); Vladimir Ilyich Lenin, a devotee of
the novel like many Russian revolutionaries, wrote his own *What Is to
Be Done?*, subtitling it *Burning Questions of Our Movement* (1902).[109]
Anarchists like Pyotr Alexeyevich Kropotkin and Emma Goldman
were just as impressed and influenced by the work as were Rosa
Luxemburg and Georgi Valentinovich Plekhanov, the father of Russian
Marxism.[110] It seems no exaggeration to claim that Chernyshevsky had
'the greatest impact on Russian society' of any author in nineteenth-
century Russian literature and that 'no work in modern literature,
with the possible exception of *Uncle Tom's Cabin*, can compete with

---

108 Fyodor Dostoevsky, *Notes from the Underground*, translation by Richard
Pevear and Larissa Volokhonsky (New York: Vintage Classics, 1994); Fedor
Dostoevskii, *Polnoe sobranie sochinenii v tridtsati tomakh, tom desiatyi: Besy*
(Leningrad: Institut russkoi literatury, 1974), in English as *Demons*, translated by
Richard Pevear and Larissa Volokhonsky (New York: A. A. Knopf, 2000).

109 L. N. Tolstoi, *Tak chto zhe nam delat'? Ispoved'* (1886), Moskva: Need to add
publisher? 2011. For the English see Leo Tolstoy, *What Then Must We Do?* (Hartland:
Green, 1991); and V. I. Lenin, *Chto delat'? Nabolevshie voprosy nashego dvizheniia*
(Stuttgart: J.H.W. Dietz Nachf., 1902), English: Vladimir I. Lenin, *What Is to Be Done?*
(Oxford: Clarendon Press, 1963).

110 On the significance that Kropotkin attributed to the book, see Petr Kropotkin,
Ideals and Realities in Russian Literature (Westport, CT: Greenwood Press, 1970),
279–81. On its reception by Emma Goldman and Alexander Berkman, as well as in
the United States in general, see Steven Cassedy, 'Chernyshevskii Goes West: How
Jewish Immigration Helped Bring Russian Radicalism to America', *Russian History*
21/1 (1994), 1–21. On the history of how the novel was received overall, see the
introductory short overview by Reyser, 'Ot redaktora', 5; or Porter, 'New Preface', x–xii;
and Yarmolinsky, *Road to Revolution*, 120; Drozd, *Chernyshevskii's What Is to Be
Done?*, 9–19; Novikova and Kloss, *Chernyshevskij*, Chapter 3; E. I. Shcherbakova,
'Roman N. G. Chernyshevskogo "Chto delat'?" v vospriiatii radikal'noi molodezhi
serediny 60-kh godov XIX v.', *Vestnik Moskovskogo universiteta*, seriia 8: Istoriia/1
(1998), 59–68; Iu. D. Mishin, 'Sotsialisticheskaia kontseptsiia N. G. Chernynevskogo i
ee vliianie na revoliutsionnuiu mysl' Rossii 70-kh godov XIX v.', in Aleksei Pavlovich
Okladnikov (ed.), *N. G. Chernyshevskii i ego nasledie* (Novosibirsk: Nauka, 1980),
178–84; and A. N. Pekarik, 'V. I. Lenin i N. G. Chernyshevskii', in ibid., 25–31.

What Is to Be Done? in its effect on human lives and its power to make history.'[111]

In Chernyshevsky's novel, the 'new people' referred to in the Russian original's subtitle have the same features and attitudes as those he had ascribed to the settlers in Kansas, whereas Rakhmetov, the hero of the story, resembles John Brown. The 'new people' – those who are considered 'contemporary people' and are contrasted with the 'antediluvian types'[112] – are 'splendid' (*slavnye*) people:

> Each of them is a man of courage, unwavering and unyielding, capable of grappling with any task; upon doing so, he keeps a firm grasp on that task so that it doesn't slip away. This is one side of their character. On the other hand, each of them is a man of such irreproachable honesty that it never even occurs to us to ask, 'Can this man be relied upon unconditionally?'

They distinguish themselves by their 'cold-blooded practicality, measured and calculated activity, and active common sense.'[113] Chernyshevsky emphasizes with heavy symbolism that his character Lopukhov (one of his protagonists among the new people) 'had a rule never to yield to anyone except a woman', and he illustrates different situations of daily life in Russia to show that these 'contemporary' people do not let themselves be pushed around.[114] Such characterizations bear striking

---

111 Joseph N. Frank, 'N. G. Chernyshevsky: A Russian Utopia', *Southern Review* 3/1 (1967), 68. Frank credits Chernyshevsky with having greater influence than Marx because 'Chernyshevsky's novel, far more than Marx's *Capital*, supplied the emotional dynamic that eventually went to make the Russian Revolution.' Ibid. Irina Paperno comes to the same conclusion in *Chernyshevsky and the Age of Realism: A Study in the Semiotics of Behavior* (Stanford: Stanford University Press, 1988), 4. For Chernyshevsky's influence on the Russian women's movement specifically, see Richard Stites, *The Women's Liberation Movement in Russia: Feminism, Nihilism, and Bolshevism, 1860–1930* (Princeton: Princeton University Press, 1978), Chapter 4; and Bianka Pietrow-Ennker, *Rußlands 'Neue Menschen': Die Entwicklung der Frauenbewegung von den Anfängen bis zur Oktoberrevolution* (Frankfurt am Main: Campus, 1999).

112 For example Chernyshevskii, *Chto delat'?*, 271; Chernyshevsky, *What Is to Be Done?*, 353–4.

113 Chernyshevskii, *Chto delat'?*, 148–9; Chernyshevsky, *What Is to Be Done?*, 211–12.

114 Chernyshevskii, *Chto delat'?*, 147, 231; Chernyshevsky, *What Is to Be Done?*, 209, 354.

resemblance to the 'very energetic and courageous people' of Kansas, who exact revenge on their opponents for every insult, as well as to John Brown's 'cold, unusually shrewd, patient, and desperately courageous' monomania.[115]

It is the parallels between the hero of Chernyshevsky's novel, Rakhmetov, and John Brown that are decisive, however – that is, with the historical person of Brown and the figure of Chernyshevsky's imagination. Both belong to the 'new' and 'wonderful' people who distinguish themselves by their courageous, clever, determined and upstanding lifestyle. But they are also more: extraordinary (*osobennyi*), eminent people who live ascetically in spartan simplicity, abstaining from alcohol, luxury, women and amorous adventures; who watch their diets; and who attach importance to physical strength, seeking to develop and maintain it as much as possible. For all their 'wildness' they are also 'tactful', 'considerate and good'. They uphold the equal rights of men and women, cherish an ethics of duty and think in the categories of sin, guilt, repentance and punishment.[116] Chernyshevsky's key terms signal these parallels. Apart from conscious eating habits and physical exercise, Chernyshevsky could have borrowed these behaviours, character traits and convictions from the available sources already mentioned: the letter to the editor of *The Times* and John Brown's Provisional Constitution. Fredrick Douglass's description of his first longer meeting with Brown and his family documents the fact that these traits and beliefs indeed belonged to the historical person John Brown.[117]

Rakhmetov is the only character in the novel to receive the attribute of originality bestowed upon Brown in Chernyshevsky's political writings. In his November 1859 article, Chernyshevsky opined that an 'indomitable energy and a deep, strong, moral feeling impart extraordinary originality' to John Brown's constitution.[118] And in *What Is to Be Done?* he wrote that Rakhmetov, shortly before leaving the university,

---

115 Chernyshevskii, 'Ianvar' 1861', 398; Chernyshevskii, 'No. 11-Noiabr' 1859 goda', 442.

116 Chernyshevskii, *Chto delat'?*, 200, 209, 204–8, 210, 244, 226–8, 222, 220–3; Chernyshevsky, *What Is to Be Done?*, 271, 285, 278–85, 286, 324, 305–7, 300–1, 299–301. Translator's note: Rus. *dikost'*, lit. 'wildness', translated by Katz as 'rudeness', here amended in accordance with Chernyshevsky's descriptions, which suggest Rakhmetov's behaviour is not about rudeness or barbarity, but a deliberate disregard for bourgeois manners.

117 See, for example, Douglass, 'Life and Times', 715–19.

118 Chernyshevskii, 'Vremennaia konstitutsiia', 444–6.

had 'already adopted a set of original principles to govern his material, moral, and spiritual life', with originality being defined as including a 'connection between intellect and insanity'.[119] Extraordinary people, however, push the boundaries in more than just the intellectual sense: they push moral boundaries as well. Chernyshevsky has Rakhmetov explain that 'he himself isn't happy to be such a "gloomy monster" [*mrachnoe chudovishche*], but that circumstances are such that a person with his ardent love for the good can't help being a "gloomy monster." If it weren't for that, he might spend the whole day joking, laughing, singing, and dancing.' Elsewhere, the author describes his protagonist as 'a frightening man' (*strashnyi chelovek*).[120] This also presents a parallel to Heinrich von Kleist's novella *Michael Kohlhaas*, where the protagonist Kohlhaas is described as an 'extraordinary man' (*außerordentlicher Mann*) and as 'one of the most upright and at the same time terrible men of his time'.[121] This may very well have established a type.

However, Chernyshevsky also refers to both Rakhmetov and John Brown in Christian terms – ranging from 'the salt of the earth' to martyr (for John Brown); he even gives Rakhmetov a saint's halo.[122] Presumably, Chernyshevsky knew of Victor Hugo's comparison between John Brown and Christ. Through the press he may even have been familiar with the use of Christ and Crucifixion metaphors by Thoreau and Emerson. Like

119 Chernyshevskii, *Chto delat'?*, 206; Chernyshevsky, *What Is to Be Done?*, 280, 274. The question whether Chernyshevsky characterized any other people, documents or political phenomena in *Sovremennik* as 'original', and if so which ones, goes beyond the scope of the present book. The indirect description of originality as an amalgam of reason and madness appears in the novel in reference to Isaac Newton's late work, which Rakhmetov considers worth reading – because it was original – unlike the books by Macaulay, Guizot, Thiers, Ranke or Gervinus, for example. See Chernyshevskii, *Chto delat'?*, 201–2; Chernyshevsky, *What Is to Be Done?*, 273.

120 Chernyshevskii, *Chto delat'?*, 231, 309, also 222; Chernyshevsky, *What Is to Be Done?*, 310–11, 401, also 300–1.

121 Von Kleist, *Michael Kohlhaas (Aus einer alten Chronik)* (1808–10), 9; von Kleist, *Selected Prose of Heinrich von Kleist*, 163.

122 Chernyshevskii, *Chto delat'?*, 215; Chernyshevsky, *What Is to Be Done?*, 293 ('salt of the earth'). Chernyshevskii, 'No. 11-Noiabr' 1859 goda', 441 (*muchennik*/'martyr'); and Chernyshevskii, *Chto delat'?*, 212; Chernyshevsky, *What Is to Be Done?*, 289 (*siian'e* /'halo'). In this context, too, a separate study would be required to establish whether Chernyshevsky described other figures using Christian metaphors in his political writings, and if so, who. The phrase 'salt of the earth' comes from the Sermon on the Mount, in which Jesus tells his disciples, 'Ye are the salt of the earth . . . Ye are the light of the world' (Matthew 5:13–14).

Thoreau, Chernyshevsky notes that 'only honest and bold eyes' can perceive the extraordinary person as a higher type of the new man. The capacity to perceive therefore depends on the beholder.[123]

An additional indication that John Brown served as a role model for Rakhmetov is the prominent and in many respects special place that the United States, particularly the anti-slavery movement, has in *What Is to Be Done?*. For example, Chernyshevsky maintains that freedom and happiness are objectives both in personal life and in historical development.[124] He implicitly recommends reading Harriet Beecher Stowe, and as the editor of *Sovremennik* he sent a free copy of her novel *Uncle Tom's Cabin* to all the subscribers of the journal. He also has Lopukhov temporarily emigrate to the United States, where he assumes the name Charles Beaumont (literally 'beautiful hill' and phonetically close to *beau monde*; that is, 'beautiful world'), and where Lopukhov, alias Beaumont, becomes a 'rabid abolitionist'.[125] The conversations of the new people were often 'serious, about everything under the sun', but whereas the author identifies various scientific questions that his characters discuss, such as 'the chemical basis of agriculture according to Liebig's theory' or 'the laws of historical progress', the only truly political topic that Chernyshevsky addresses is 'the civil strife in Kansas which was the forerunner of the Great Civil War between the North and the South, which in turn was to be the forerunner of even greater events, not only in America'.[126]

Lastly, the country outside Russia that the extraordinary Rakhmetov absolutely must get to know with his own eyes is the United States. 'Indeed, the study of [the North American states] he considered more

---

123 Chernyshevskii, *Chto delat'?*, 214; Chernyshevsky, *What Is to Be Done?*, 292. For Thoreau's comments see above, p. 322. According to Hecht, *Russian Radicals*, 87, Chernyshevsky was at least familiar with Emerson's works.

124 Chernyshevskii, *Chto delat'?*, 60, 289–90; Chernyshevsky, *What Is to Be Done?*, 75, 270 ('there's no happiness without freedom'), 317–20. Malkin, 'Chernyshevsky i zaatlanticheskaya respublika [SŠA]', 320; and Popov, 'Iz amerikanskoy zhisny Dmitriya Sergeevicha Lopukhova', also note the prominence of abolitionism in *Chto delat'?*.

125 Chernyshevskii, *Chto delat'?*, 166, 330, 316–32, quotation at 318; Chernyshevsky, *What Is to Be Done?*, 230, 425, as well as 409–28, quotation at 412. On the distribution of *Uncle Tom's Cabin*, see Laserson, *The American Impact on Russia*, 249.

126 Chernyshevskii, *Chto delat'?*, 123; Chernyshevsky, *What Is to Be Done?*, 179 ('everything under the sun' and 'civil strife in Kansas'), 180 ('chemical basis' and 'laws of historical progress').

"necessary" for him than that of any other country,' he wrote to friends in Russia:

> He would remain there a long time, perhaps over a year, perhaps forever, if he found appropriate pursuits [*delo*]. But it was much more likely that in three years or so he'd return to Russia because it seemed that there – not now, but then, in three or four years – it would be 'necessary' for him to be in Russia [*no veroiatnee, chto goda cherez tri on vozvratitsia v Rossiiu, potomu chto, kazhetsia, v Rossii – ne teper', a togda, goda cherez tri-chetyre, – 'nuzhno' budet emu byt'*].[127]

Composed with the censor in mind, this passage implies that Rakhmetov wanted to learn from the abolitionists in North America and might even want to stay there if he could become active in the United States (in addition to meaning 'pursuit' or 'employment', *delo* also means 'action'), but that he could return to Russia if a revolution were to break out in three or four years. The somewhat circuitous, repetitive formulation in the Russian original directs attention to this expectation more effectively than its recapitulation can in English.

Until now, the source of inspiration for the figure of Rakhmetov has not been conclusively identified in the extensive secondary literature on Chernyshevsky's novel. The close examination that Irina Paperno, a scholar of Russian literature, undertook of Chernyshevsky's writings, notes, diaries and correspondence has revealed the influence that his personal experience and the history of ideas had on various concepts and modes of thinking in the novel. However, she remains quite unspecific about the 'ideal man' Rakhmetov: 'In the image of Rakhmetov, the symbolism of French Christian socialism is blended with that of the Russian Orthodox tradition.'[128] She refers to the work of a second specialist in her field, Joseph Frank, who sees this figure as the 'fateful fusion between the hagiographic pattern of Russian religious kenoticism and the coldly dispassionate calculations of English Utilitarianism.'[129]

---

127 Chernyshevskii, *Chto delat'?*, 214; Chernyshevsky, *What Is to Be Done?*, 291.

128 Paperno, *Chernyshevsky and the Age of Realism*, 187, 208.

129 Frank, 'N. G. Chernyshevsky', 83–4. Strictly speaking, in the passage Paperno cites, Frank refers to the whole novel. Kenoticism is defined as 'the doctrine of, or belief in, the kenosis of Christ', meaning 'the self-renunciation of the divine nature, at least in part, by Christ in the incarnation'. *The Oxford English Dictionary*, 1993, 'Kenosis'.

She also refers to the literary scholar Katerina Clark, who believed that Rakhmetov's life was modelled on that of a well-loved Russian saint, *The Life of Alexei, A Man of God*: 'In both texts an upper-class dandy undergoes a conversion, eschews worldly success and true love, dedicates himself to the faith, and uses incredible means of self-mortification to drive out temptations to waver in his resolve (Rakhmetov trains his will by lying on a bed of nails).'[130] Over the years, other authors have suggested several additional role models from literature and history – such as Nikolai Alexandrovich Dobrolyubov; the nobleman Pavel Alexandrovich Bakhmetev, with whom Chernyshevsky was acquainted; Mikhail Alexandrovich Bakunin; or Chernyshevsky himself. Yet other authors have argued that this character does not correspond to 'any specific model'; that it is rather 'a composite image based on the great men of history (Cromwell, Napoleon).'[131] Clearly, there is no scarcity of ideas as to the possible inspirations or models for Rakhmetov.

These suggestions from the literature indisputably apply to certain features of Chernyshevsky's most influential character, and it is difficult to weigh exactly how much of any particular model is dominant in him, including John Brown.[132] However, no theory thus far has taken account of the references to the United States and the anti-slavery movement. John Brown, when considered against his various presentations and interpretations (by himself and by others) and his national and international reception (both by Chernyshevsky and by others) at different times and in different publics, really is the figure best suited to embodying the contradictory facets of Rakhmetov the 'extraordinary man' in his own peculiar logic – the disciplined ascetic, the frightful moralist, the selfless helper, the representative man and the saint who is willing to make sacrifices for the cause of emancipation. To Chernyshevsky, John Brown embodied the freedom-loving and self-confident North American: the 'new man'.

Another aspect enters as well. The underlying reason why Nikolai Gavrilovich Chernyshevsky reacted in precisely this way to the news

130 Katerina Clark, *The Soviet Novel: History as Ritual*, 3rd ed. (Bloomington: Indiana University Press, 2000), 50. For the reference to this book, see Paperno, *Chernyshevsky and the Age of Realism*, 208.

131 See Drozd, *Chernyshevskii's What Is to Be Done?*, 126, note 105.

132 A further possibility to consider is Felice Orsini, another 'extraordinary man'. Arianna Arisi Rota and Roberto Balzani, 'Discovering Politics: Action and Recollection in the First Mazzinian Generation', in Patriarca and Riall, *The Risorgimento Revisited*, 89.

about John Brown lies in the parallels between his own political thinking and John Brown's. Further comparative research is needed on this
point as well. What is certain, however, is that Chernyshevsky, just like
John Brown, grew up with the Bible. As the son of an orthodox priest
and eventually as a seminarian, Chernyshevsky, too, was well versed in
the Old Testament. Without needing much additional information, he
understood the intentions and self-image of John Brown, the orthodox
Calvinist and puritanical holy warrior. Both Brown and Chernyshevsky
were well acquainted with the lives of the saints and the mechanisms of
martyrdom. Both men had direct or indirect roots in German idealism.
And for both of them, the demands for liberty and justice were something they lived out in their everyday practices, anchored in religion and
imbued with the active commitment to freedom and equality as its logical imperative. Chernyshevsky recognized John Brown and understood
his deed despite the distance and the linguistic and cultural translations
involved, for his thinking derived from a similar background.

Note one pivotal difference, however. Whereas Chernyshevsky's
influence flowed primarily from his writings – not least because he was
arrested as soon as he began to be active – John Brown (like Felice
Orsini) became a role model through the acts he perpetrated and their
impact. It was those acts that their imitators learned about directly, or
indirectly through Chernyshevsky's novel, and then tried to put into
practice in yet another set of cultural and political contexts.

6

Further development by imitators

The universalization of terrorist tactics

Wilhelm, Abraham, Alexander: three victims of terrorist attacks

On 14 July 1861, Oskar Wilhelm Becker, a student motivated by national-revolutionary aspirations, attacked the Prussian king (and later German emperor) Wilhelm I in the spa town of Baden-Baden. The resort was not Wilhelm I's favourite; he preferred the waters in Bad Ems and in the Habsburg spa of Bad Gastein. But his wife Augusta liked coming to the 'summer capital of Europe' in the northern Black Forest region and usually stayed for several weeks. She enjoyed being far from Berlin and close to her only daughter, Louise, who was married to Grand Duke Friedrich von Baden and often resided in the New Palace above the town during the summer.[1] As usual, Augusta had left Berlin in the early summer. Wilhelm followed later, arriving on 10 July at the Maison Messmer, which was located next to the spa building and directly on the park. The Prussian ruling couple had been returning to this hotel ever

---

1 On Wilhelm I see Jürgen Angelow, 'Wilhelm I. (1861–1888)', in Frank-Lothar Kroll (ed.), *Preußens Herrscher: Von den ersten Hohenzollern bis Wilhelm II* (Munich: C. H. Beck, 2000); Erich Marcks, *Kaiser Wilhelm I.* (Leipzig: Duncker, 1897); and Franz Herre, *Kaiser Wilhelm I. Der letzte Preuße* (Cologne: Kiepenheuer & Witsch, 1980). On Augusta see the classic by Marie von Bunsen, *Kaiserin Augusta* (Berlin: Karl Siegismund, 1940), Chapter 21.4; and Karin Feuerstein-Prasser, *Augusta: Kaiserin und Preußin* (Munich: Piper, 2011). The expression *la Capitale d'été de l'Europe* was coined by the French author Eugène Guinot. On this phenomenon, see Dagmar Kicherer, *Kleine Geschichte der Stadt Baden-Baden* (Karlsruhe: G. Braun, 2008), 85–126.

432 The Invention of Terrorism

since Wilhelm had first stayed there in 1849. The location was symboli-cally significant, because he had come to the city of Baden-Baden at the time while leading Prussian troops with a mandate from the Provisional Central Power in Frankfurt to put down the third attempted revolution in the Grand Duchy of Baden. After routing the revolutionary troops in the Rastatt fortress, he had pursued some of the fleeing revolutionaries to Baden-Baden as well. 'I came to you as an enemy; next time I will return as a friend,' he is reported to have told the republican-minded Messmers when he left. For more than forty years since then, Wilhelm and his wife had annually spent several weeks in the spa town and in this hotel.[2]

The attacker, Oskar Wilhelm Becker, was a twenty-two-year-old student of law and *Staatswissenschaften*, comparable to governance and public policy, in Leipzig. He had travelled by train to Baden-Baden, and it was his first time there. At the station, a boy offered to carry Becker's black leather suitcase into the town for six *Kreuzer*. Becker handed him the luggage and used the opportunity to inquire where the king of Prussia was staying, whether he went swimming or walking, and whether he was accompanied by constables or servants on these excur-sions. He learned that in the mornings the king usually rode or walked without escort along the promenade and Lichtentaler Allee.[3] Becker

2 See Wolfram Siemann, *The German Revolution of 1848–49* (Basingstoke: Macmillan, 1998), 209–11; Wolfgang von Hippel, *Revolution im deutschen Südwesten: Das Großherzogtum Baden 1848/49* (Stuttgart: Kohlhammer, 1998), 316–79; Kicherer, *Kleine Geschichte*, 107–14; Angelow, 'Wilhelm I', 251; and Herre, *Kaiser Wilhelm I*, 218–25. On the Messmer couple and their Maison Messmer, see the memoirs of the great-grandson, Reinhold Schneider, *Der Balkon: Aufzeichnungen eines Müßiggängers in Baden-Baden* (Wiesbaden: Insel-Verlag, 1957), 47–85, quotation at 59. The hotel was demolished in 1957 to make way for a parking lot. A new building now stands on the site, the Dorint Hotel Maison Messmer.

3 See GLA Karlsruhe, 250: Amtsgericht Baden-Baden-Verfahren 8 (General State Archive, Karlsruhe, 250: Baden-Baden Municipal Court Proceedings 8) (hereafter GLA Karlsruhe, 250/8): Zeugenaussage Johann Schäufler vor dem Amtsgericht Baden-Baden (testimony of Johann Schäufler before the Baden-Baden Municipal Court), 16 July 1861, Bl. (Blätter) 95–7, here Bl. 96; GLA Karlsruhe, 250/8: Becker's interrogation (*Verhör*), 14 July 1861, Bl. 47–8; and on Becker's luggage, GLA Karlsruhe, 250/8: Becker's interrogation (*Verhör*), Bl. 13–15: Bericht der Polizei an das Amtsgericht Baden-Baden über die Visitation Beckers (police report to the Baden-Baden Municipal Court on Becker's visitation). The fact that this was Becker's first time in Baden-Baden emerges from GLA Karlsruhe, 250/9, Bl. 313–25: interrogation of Oskar Wilhelm Becker before the Baden-Baden Municipal Court, 29 July 1861, afternoon, Bl. 314.

followed the recommendation of his porter and took a room in the Gasthaus zur Blume, then proceeded straight to the promenade to gather more information about the king of Prussia.[4] He learned from two journeymen masons at the spa building that Wilhelm I was staying at the Maison Messmer. Becker checked out the house several times, then went into town to eat and to ask where he could buy cigars. Afterwards, he sat in front of the Konversationshaus (today's spa building), drank a cup of coffee, and observed the Hotel Messmer. To recognize the king, Becker had bought a photograph of Wilhelm I before leaving Leipzig. When a man resembling the monarch on the photograph stepped out of the hotel, Becker asked a waiter whether the gentleman was the king of Prussia. The waiter confirmed that it was indeed the king. Thereupon Becker watched the gambling in the casino of the Konversationshaus a while longer and then went to bed early. Before going to sleep, he wrote a 'Note on the Motives for My Deed' ('Notiz über die Motive meiner That'). He tore up the first version due to an inkblot; he placed the second, pristine copy into his wallet.[5]

On 14 July 1861, a Sunday, Queen Augusta had set out early in the morning to Lichtental with her lady-in-waiting, Countess von Brühl.[6] The small town with its venerable Cistercian abbey is an easy half-hour walk away, along Lichtentaler Allee. The royal family liked to have their breakfast outside there, in the garden of the Zum Bären inn.[7] The road to Lichtental runs along the Oos river, whose meadows had been undergoing landscaping for a few years to resemble an English landscape park.[8] The king followed his wife somewhat later, taking the same path. He walked alone. Along the way a young man overtook him and

4 See GLA Karlsruhe, 250/8, Becker's interrogation, 14 July 1861, Bl. 47; and the receipt, in GLA Karlsruhe, 250/8, Becker's interrogation, 14 July 1861, Bl. 17.

5 See GLA Karlsruhe, 250/8, Becker's interrogation, 14 July 1861, Bl. 48–9.

6 There is no evidence in the sources that this date was consciously chosen as the anniversary of the storming of the Bastille. See also Reiner Haehling von Lanzenauer, *Das Baden-Badener Attentat* (Baden-Baden: Arbeitskreis für Stadtgeschichte, 1995), 34.

7 See GLA Karlsruhe, 250/8, testimony of Count von Flemming before the Baden-Baden Municipal Court, 16 July 1861, Bl. 98–105, 99. On the Prussian royal couple's fondness for breakfasting at the Wirtshaus zum Bären, see 'Das Attentat auf Seine Majestät den König', *Kölnische Rundschau*, 17 July 1861.

8 See Ulrich Coenen, *Von Aquae bis Baden-Baden: Die Baugeschichte der Stadt und ihr Beitrag zur Entwicklung der Kurarchitektur* (Aachen: Mainz, 2008), Chapter 6.1.2; Berndt Weigel, *Die Lichtentaler Allee: Denkmal der Gartenkunst in Baden-Baden* (Baden-Baden: Aquensis, 2005).

greeted him 'in a particularly friendly, almost warm way, doffing his hat and lowering it several times', as Wilhelm later recalled. 'Soon after, he shortened his steps, so I walked past him, whereupon he greeted me again.'[9] About halfway to Lichtental, at the Kettenbrücke ('chain bridge') where the Gunzen flows into the Oos, the footpath joined a country road lined with maple trees. At the bridge the king met the Prussian ambassador to the Baden Court, Friedrich Count von Flemming, who had also taken a morning walk to Lichtental and was already on his way back. Wilhelm invited his ambassador to accompany him, and they continued along the way together.[10]

Oskar Wilhelm Becker had also risen early that morning. He drank his morning coffee in his room, loaded both barrels of a small front-loading pistol (a *Doppelterzerole*) with powder and balls, and was on the promenade at six o'clock. There he sat on a bank, cocked the two hammers of his weapon, put it into his breast pocket, and waited. Shortly past seven he saw the king of Prussia, whom, as he later commented under questioning, he 'recognized from the photograph, the information collected yesterday, but definitely as such in particular after the general greetings'.[11] He sat in the gallery of the Konversationshaus, drank another cup of coffee there and hoped that Wilhelm I would walk past him. Around eight o'clock he saw a man in the distance, from behind, whom he thought was the king of Prussia. Becker followed him 'now with the intention of carrying out the attack'.[12] After both of them had advanced some way along Lichtentaler Allee, Becker passed Wilhelm I, who at that point 'was without any escort, greeted him in passing, walked a little further, and then crossed to the other side of the road, where I advanced slowly to allow the king to pass again'. Then he continued following the king of Prussia and saw another man join him.

Becker made his assassination attempt shortly thereafter. He quickly followed behind the king and his ambassador, and when he was five or six steps away did not take much time to aim but rather 'held the pistol

9 GLA Karlsruhe, 250/8, affidavit of Wilhelm I von Preußen, Baden, 14 July 1861, 11 a.m., Bl. 76–8, quotation at Bl. 76.

10 GLA Karlsruhe, 250/8, affidavit of Wilhelm I von Preußen, Bl. 76 and testimony of Flemming, Bl. 98–9.

11 See GLA Karlsruhe, 250/8, Becker's interrogation, 14 July 1861, Bl. 50, 52, quotation at Bl. 50.

12 Ibid., Bl. 50–1, quotations at Bl. 51.

approximately at chest level', thinking he would be most likely to hit him there, and fired both barrels. 'The King stood still for a moment, and I realized instantly that I had missed him,' Becker later told the examining magistrate. He threw away the pistol and his umbrella at once 'without really knowing why'.[13]

Figure 20. The attack. © Generallandesarchiv Karlsruhe, J-D B 6.

Flemming and Wilhelm I had walked about 150 paces when a shot was fired very close behind them. As Wilhelm wrote later, he 'immediately [felt] a pain in the left side of [his] neck', sensed 'a roaring in [his] whole head', and shouted 'My God, what was that!' Flemming saw the king 'raise his hands to his head as though to cover himself'. Both turned around, and Wilhelm caught sight of the young man who had just greeted him in such a friendly manner 'standing calmly three steps behind [them]'. As Flemming later told the court, he was at first 'so far from assuming the possibility of an attack on the king that [he] first

___

13 Ibid., Bl. 51–2, quotations at Bl. 52.

believed a reckless person must have lit a *pétard* [firecracker or firework]'.[14] But when he saw a young, pale-looking man motionless and unarmed, he 'went up to him straight away, asking "What was that? Who fired? Did you fire?" He replied, "I fired." And in response to [his] next question, "At what? At whom?" he clearly said, "At the King"'. Upon these words, Flemming grabbed the young man by the throat and called two people he saw nearby to help him arrest the attacker.[15]

Figure 21. Pistols. © Generallandesarchiv Karlsruhe, 250 Nr. 17.

The arrest of Oskar Wilhelm Becker was quick. Both people to whom Flemming had called for help reacted straight away. The lawyer Julius

---

14 GLA Karlsruhe, 250/8, affidavit of Wilhelm I von Preußen, Bl. 76; GLA Karlsruhe, 250/8, testimony of Flemming, Bl. 100–1, quotation at Bl. 100–1.

15 GLA Karlsruhe, 250/8, testimony of Flemming, Bl. 101. The minutes of the questioning and the written statement by the king diverge slightly from Flemming's statement. Becker described the verbal exchange as follows: 'Right after the shooting, the person escorting the king turned and said, "What is that?", whereupon I stood still and answered, "a shot". The escort asked: "Who shot?", to which I responded calmly: "I did". He then asked "at whom?", to which I responded "at the king"'. Becker also testified that Count Flemming grabbed his arm or the lapel of his jacket (GLA Karlsruhe, 250/8, Becker's interrogation, 14 July 1861, Bl. 52–3; and GLA Karlsruhe, 250/8, Becker's interrogation, 29 July, Bl. 318). Wilhelm I combined the questions and answers in his statement: 'Mr. Flemming asked him: "Who shot here? Did you shoot?" To which the man quite calmly answered: "I shot at the king"'. GLA Karlsruhe, 250/8, affidavit of Wilhelm I von Preußen, Bl. 76.

Süpfle and Carl Schill, a legal trainee, had been on their way from the Baden-Baden train station to Gernsbach, about fifty kilometres away.[16] They had seen the king of Prussia walking ahead of them on Lichtentaler Allee and had passed him because 'my companion really wanted to take a closer look at His Majesty,' as Süpfle testified in court. Suddenly they heard 'a loud noise', which Süpfle, like Flemming, initially took to be 'a firework shot at a distance'. When they turned around, they saw 'a thin cloud of powder ten to twelve feet behind His Majesty', and they heard an exchange of words between Flemming and a young man. 'Then we understood everything,' Schill told the court.[17] He rushed to help Flemming, knocked the attacker to the ground and held him there. 'While throwing him down, I shouted at him in my agitation, "You scoundrel" or "You dog of a dog, you shot at the king".'[18] Seeing this led the king and Count Flemming to intervene on behalf of the attacker. His majesty approached Süpfle with the words 'Don't do him any harm,' or 'Let him be,' and Flemming told Schill to stop mistreating the man. Thereupon, Süpfle doffed his hat and justified his behaviour: 'Your Majesty, consider this outburst as an expression of indignation from the people of Baden that an outrage like this has occurred on our soil.'[19] Meanwhile, Schill looked for the pistol. He found it a few steps away in a meadow, showed it to the king, and handed it over to Flemming.[20] By this point, the Paris merchant Damas Joseph Blanquet had also come upon the scene, having been on a walk alone twenty to twenty-five steps

16 See GLA Karlsruhe, 250/8, testimony of attorney Süpfle before the Baden-Baden Municipal Court, 14 July 1861, Bl. 24–9, Bl. 24; GLA Karlsruhe, 250/8, testimony of legal trainee Schill before the Baden-Baden Municipal Court, 14 July 1861, Bl. 29–33, Bl. 29–30.

17 GLA Karlsruhe, 250/8, testimony of Süpfle, Bl. 24–6; GLA Karlsruhe, 250/8, testimony of Schill, Bl. 31.

18 GLA Karlsruhe, 250/8, testimony of Süpfle, Bl. 26–7. The king's statement uses different words but conveys a similar message. According to the king, Süpfle called out, 'That is a shame and a disgrace for Baden; the people must avenge it.' GLA Karlsruhe, 250/8, affidavit of Wilhelm I von Preußen, Bl. 77.

19 GLA Karlsruhe, 250/8, testimony of Süpfle, Bl. 27.

20 GLA Karlsruhe, 250/8, testimony of Schill, Bl. 31. According to the minutes of the questioning, Becker commented on these events only: 'Then two men jumped in from the other side, one of them threw me to the ground and pinned me down. I could not observe the movements of the king during this time.' GLA Karlsruhe, 250/8, Becker's interrogation 14 July 1861, Bl. 53.

behind the king of Prussia on Lichtentaler Allee.[21] 'I ran up forthwith,' the French witness stated in the report, which was written in German.

> The king of Prussia said to me in French that he was not wounded, that he thought that the pistol was not loaded and the young man was crazy. I replied I did not believe that to be the case because I saw that the left shoulder of the king's topcoat had a tear, obviously caused by one of the bullets.[22]

The king then took off the coat, assured himself that the statement was correct, and told Mr Blanquet that he had 'a strange sensation in his ear', which the merchant interpreted as the consequence of a bullet that had probably flown past his majesty's ear.[23]

The men hailed a hackney that happened to be passing on the way from Lichtental to Baden-Baden and packed the attacker into it. He put up no resistance and made no attempt to flee. Instead, he identified himself as 'student Becker' and gave Flemming his wallet, saying, 'it contains everything that could provide explanation.'[24] Becker had just climbed into the coach with Süpfle and Schill when Carl Wilhelm Brandt, the former owner of the Hôtel du Nord in Berlin, arrived. Flemming told Brandt what had happened and Brandt went to the king to offer his help. According to Brandt's testimony, he asked where the shot had hit him and Wilhelm answered that 'it had not done him any harm.' Brandt then 'took hold of the king's cravat and assured myself that he was not wounded'. Meanwhile, Wilhelm I recounted to him 'that the perpetrator had encountered him that morning on Lichtentaler Allee and had greeted him in a friendly manner; he, the king, had thanked him amiably'.[25] Then he asked Brandt to see to the man who had shot at him. Brandt climbed into the coach, in which Schill and

---

21 See GLA Karlsruhe, 250/8, testimony of Damas Joseph Blanquet before the Baden-Baden Municipal Court, 14 July 1861, Bl. 9–12, Bl. 10; GLA Karlsruhe, 250/8, testimony of Damas Joseph Blanquet before the Baden-Baden Municipal Court, 15 July 1861, Bl. 65–8, Bl. 66.

22 GLA Karlsruhe, 250/8, testimony of Blanquet, Bl. 11.

23 GLA Karlsruhe, 250/8, affidavit of Wilhelm I von Preußen, Bl. 77; GLA Karlsruhe, 250/8, testimony of Blanquet, Bl. 11.

24 GLA Karlsruhe, 250/8, testimony of Flemming, Bl. 103.

25 See GLA Karlsruhe, 250/8, testimony of Carl Wilhelm Brandt before the Baden-Baden Municipal Court, 14 July 1861, Bl. 20–3, Bl. 20–1, quotation at Bl. 22.

Süpfle were already sitting with the attacker, with Flemming and Blanquet taking up positions next to the coachman.[26] Seeing the men off, the king advised them to 'treat Becker with forbearance'. Thereupon the coachman gave his signal, the horses started off, and the whole party drove into town to turn Becker over to the court.[27]

In the interim, Wilhelm I walked alone to Lichtental and returned home with his wife. He did not say a single word to her about the incident. Augusta did not learn about what had happened until others came by to congratulate her husband on his narrow escape.[28]

Almost four years later, on 14 April 1865, the actor John Wilkes Booth assassinated Abraham Lincoln in Washington, DC. The act was motivated by counterrevolutionary ideas: one of the intentions was at least to impede African Americans being granted citizenship rights throughout the United States even if Congress had already passed legislation emancipating the slaves.[29]

14 April 1865 was Good Friday. On this day, the end of the Civil War was symbolically celebrated in the port of Charleston in South Carolina. At Fort Sumter, General Robert Anderson again raised the very flag that

---

26 GLA Karlsruhe, 250/8, testimony of Brandt, Bl. 23.

27 Ibid., Bl. 103. Becker's statement under questioning about this process is utterly terse: 'In the meantime another Frenchman arrived, a hackney was hailed, and I had to drive to the municipal court with the king's companion, who called himself Count Flemming, and with the three other men.' GLA Karlsruhe, 250/8, Becker's interrogation, 14 July 1861, Bl. 53.

28 GLA Karlsruhe, 250/8, affidavit of Wilhelm I von Preußen, Bl. 77–6; Geheimes Staatsarchiv Preußischer Kulturbesitz, III. Hauptabteilung Ministerium der auswärtigen Angelegenheiten (hereafter GStA PK, III. HA MdA), I no. 8913: Attentat auf König Wilhelm I am 14. Juli 1861 (Attack on King Wilhelm I on 14 July 1861), 1861–1862 (hereafter, Attack), o.Z. (ohne Zählung), Flemming to Minister of Foreign Affairs von Schleinitz, 17 July 1861. See also Carola Dietze and Frithjof Benjamin Schenk, 'Traditionelle Herrscher in moderner Gefahr: Soldatisch-aristokratische Tugendhaftigkeit und das Konzept der Sicherheit im späten 19. Jahrhundert', Geschichte und Gesellschaft 35/3 (2009), 368–401.

29 From the vast body of literature on Lincoln and his presidency see especially the concise introduction by James M. McPherson, Abraham Lincoln (Oxford and New York: Oxford University Press, 2009); the classics by John G. Nicolay and John Hay, Abraham Lincoln: A History, 10 vols. (New York: The Century Co., 1890); and by David Herbert Donald, Lincoln (New York: Simon & Schuster, 1995); as well as Richard Carwardine, Lincoln: A Life of Purpose and Power (New York: Alfred A. Knopf, 2006); Michael Burlingame, Abraham Lincoln: A Life, 2 vols. (Baltimore: Johns Hopkins University Press, 2008); Ronald C. White, A. Lincoln: A Biography, 1st ed. (New York: Random House, 2009); and Jörg Nagler Abraham Lincoln: Amerikas großer Präsident. Eine Biographie (Munich: C. H. Beck, 2009).

he had taken down under Confederate bombardment four years earlier, marking the start of the Civil War.[30]

For Lincoln, this day began like many others. He rose at seven o'clock, read some verses in the Bible as usual, then went through his mail. After the family breakfast, his son Robert Todd Lincoln told him of the surrender in Appomattox, at which he had been present as an officer under Ulysses S. Grant. The rest of the day passed with receiving and hearing many petitioners and visitors, as well as holding a Cabinet meeting at which the main topic on the agenda was plans for the reconstruction of the southern states.[31] In the early afternoon, the president allowed himself for once to take a few hours away from his desk for a coach ride with his wife. They rode past the Capitol, whose cupola had just been completed, to the Navy Yard in south-east Washington, where they spontaneously visited the famous ironclad USS *Montauk*. Their conversation focused mainly on their personal future. Lincoln wanted to return to his law practice in Illinois after completing his second term as president, and he dreamed of travelling to Palestine and California. He also reminisced about old times in Springfield, and Mary Lincoln commented that she had not seen him look so happy in a long time. 'And well I may feel so, Mary,' her husband is reported to have said. 'I consider *this day*, the war, has come to a close.' Lincoln said that both of them should be more cheerful in the future; the war and the loss of their eleven-year-old son Willie had often made them very miserable. After returning to the White House, Lincoln received a few more visitors, quickly ate an early supper, and walked over to the War Department again.[32]

Then Lincoln and his wife set off to attend a performance of the comedy *Our American Cousin*.[33] Lincoln enjoyed the theatre and went

30 On what happened on 14 April, see especially Nicolay and Hay, *Abraham Lincoln*, vol. 10, Chapter 14, especially 277–86; and W. Emerson Reck, *A. Lincoln: His Last 24 Hours* (Jefferson: McFarland, 1987). On the celebrations in Charleston, see Nicolay and Hay, *Abraham Lincoln*, vol. 10, 277–80; Reck, *A. Lincoln*, 32; and Nagler *Abraham Lincoln*, 413.

31 On the Cabinet meetings during these days, see James Garfield Randall and Richard N. Current, *Lincoln, the President*, 4 vols. (New York: Dodd Mead & Co., 1945–55), vol. 4, 357–62; and Donald, *Lincoln*, 589–92.

32 See Reck, *A. Lincoln*, Chapters 5–6, quotation at 47.

33 Tom Taylor, *Our American Cousin: The Play that Changed History*, edited and with an introduction by Welford Dunaway Taylor (Washington, DC: Beacham Publishing, 1990).

often. There he could escape the war and the ceaseless flow of visitors to the White House for a few hours and turn his mind to other thoughts.[34] On this evening, however, neither of the Lincolns was really in a mood for the theatre. But Mary had planned this outing with the Grants, and the theatre had promoted the performance in the newspapers by announcing the presence of these heroes of the hour.[35] At the Cabinet meeting that morning, General Ulysses S. Grant had excused himself and his wife from the engagement at the theatre because they wanted to travel to New Jersey to see their children at last. Lincoln knew that many spectators would be coming to the performance especially to see Grant and him, and he did not want them to be doubly disappointed. He would certainly not find any peace at the White House, anyway. So off the Lincolns rode, stopping along the way to pick up Major Henry R. Rathbone and Clara Harris, a pair of young friends who were joining them instead of the Grants. They arrived at the theatre about half an hour into the play.[36]

Lincoln had correctly anticipated the audience's expectations. When he, his wife and their guests entered the theatre and tried to slip unnoticed into their box, he was greeted with 'deafening cheers' from the more than a thousand spectators, 'and the rising of all'. The actors interrupted the performance, and the orchestra played 'Hail to the Chief', the hymn that had been played for some years already on official occasions when the president appeared. Lincoln bowed in thanks for the warm welcome, and he, Mary and their two guests took the seats reserved for them to the right above the stage.[37] The actors resumed the performance. Because the play had been a hit in the United States for the past five

---

34 See Nicolay and Hay, *Abraham Lincoln*, 292; Donald, *Lincoln*, 568–70.

35 On Grant and the myth surrounding him at the end of the Civil War, see especially Jean Edward Smith, *Grant* (New York: Simon & Schuster, 2001), 409; Joan Waugh, *U.S. Grant: American Hero, American Myth* (Chapel Hill: University of North Carolina Press, NC, 2009), particularly 99–101.

36 On Grant's cancellation, which led to conspiracy theories against him, see Edward Steers, *Blood on the Moon: The Assassination of Abraham Lincoln* (Lexington: University Press of Kentucky, 2001), 96–8; and J. E. Smith, *Grant*, 409. On Lincoln's arrival at the theatre, see Reck, *A. Lincoln*, 38–40 and Chapter 6; and Timothy S. Good, 'The Lincoln Assassination: An Overview', in Timothy S. Good (ed.), *We Saw Lincoln Shot: One Hundred Eyewitness Accounts* (Jackson: University Press of Mississippi, 1995).

37 See Reck, *A. Lincoln*, Chapter 8; Good, 'Lincoln Assassination', 10. The quotations are from a letter that Jason S. Knox wrote to his father on 15 April 1865, reprinted in Good, *Lincoln Shot*, 40–1, quotation at 40.

years and the cast could assume that the audience would know the text well, they permitted themselves some wordplays in honour of the president. When the ailing heroine of the play needed to be protected from a draft, the protagonist did not respond with the words in the text, 'Well, you're not the only one that wants to escape the draft,' but extemporized instead: 'You are mistaken. The draft has already been stopped by order of the President!' The Lincolns responded to these and other punchlines with quiet chuckling or hearty laughs.[38]

The attack occurred at a different line, one at which the actors could be certain that everyone in the audience would be laughing. In the second scene of the third act, Harry Hawk, playing Asa Trenchard, called out to the mother of the girl he futilely adored, 'Don't know the manners of good society, eh? Wal, I guess I know enough to turn you inside out, old gal – you sockdologizing old mantrap.' He had the desired effect on this night, too. However, a shot rang out through the audience's laughter.[39] Shortly afterwards, a man dressed in black leapt from the president's box and landed somewhat clumsily on the stage. He deftly straightened himself up, and some members of the audience recognized him as the popular actor John Wilkes Booth. In his right hand he held a knife, which he waved in the air for all to see, and declaimed clearly with a tragic intonation Brutus' famous utterance: '*Sic semper tyrannis*', a phrase that had also been the rallying cry of the colonialists against King George III of England during the American Revolution and is still the heraldic motto of the state of Virginia. According to some witnesses, Booth also added, 'The South is avenged' or 'Virginia is avenged.' Then he ran across the stage and disappeared behind the set stage left. Some spectators heard him say to himself, 'I have done it.'[40]

---

38 Donald, *Lincoln*, 595; and Jason S. Knox, letter to his father, 15 April 1865, reprinted in Good, *Lincoln Shot*, 40. On the history of performances of *Our American Cousin*, see the introduction in Taylor, *Our American Cousin*.

39 See, for example, Good, 'Lincoln Assassination', 16–17; and for the quotation, Taylor, *American Cousin*, 82.

40 See Reck, *A. Lincoln*, Chapter 9. Will T. Kent referred to a 'tragical tone' in his affidavit on 15 April 1865; and Spencer Bronson wrote about a 'tragical attitude' in a letter to his sister on 16 April 1865, reprinted in Good, *Lincoln Shot*, 44, 57–8, quotation at 58. See also Terry Alford, *Fortune's Fool: The Life of John Wilkes Booth* (Oxford: Oxford University Press, 2015), 265–9, whose reconstruction diverges from the one here only with regard to the timing of Booth's words.

THE ASSASSINATION OF PRESIDENT LINCOLN.

Figure 22. The Assassination of President Lincoln, in Ford's
Theatre, Washington, DC, 14 April 1865. Library of Congress,
Prints and Photographs Division, LC-USZCz-1947.

It was daring to shoot Abraham Lincoln in public in a place full of Union soldiers. Most of the men in the audience were uniformed and armed. As an actor, however, John Wilkes Booth knew the theatre setting and the audience's reactions. He knew about the moment of surprise and about the fictional character who would control everything that was happening on the scene. His plan worked. Although the report of the pistol 'startled every one [*sic*] in the audience, it was evidently accepted by all as an introductory effect preceding some new situation in the play, several of which had been introduced in the earlier part of the performance', as Dr Charles Sabin Taft described the audience's first interpretation of the shot in his report to the US Department of War. Others initially assumed that a solider or a drunk in the audience had shot unintentionally, or that the man who leapt from the box was trying to save himself. Many were simply in denial, refusing to believe what they were experiencing. More than a thousand people sat momentarily paralyzed.[41] Their utter bewilderment explains why Booth

41 In a similar vein, see also Alford, *Fortune's Fool*, 267. The quotation is from Dr Charles Sabin Taft, official report, 16 April 1865, in Good, *Lincoln Shot*, 62–4, quotation at 63. Similar expressions can be found elsewhere in the sources. For the guesses that a soldier or a drunk had

almost reached the backdrop before Mary Lincoln's screams rang out from the president's box and Major Rathbone shouted, 'Stop that man,' echoed by Clara Harris, who called out, 'Stop that man! Won't somebody stop that man?' James P. Ferguson, who could see what was happening in the president's box from his seat on the other side of the theatre, was the first to cry out, 'My God – the President is shot!' Answering a question from the audience about what was going on, Clara Harris now also shouted, 'The President is shot!' Not until that moment did most of the audience realize that John Wilkes Booth had attacked Abraham Lincoln.[42]

In addition to the effect of surprise, John Wilkes Booth had the advantage of being on familiar territory, as he had often performed at Ford's Theatre and knew the place inside out. He slipped through the stage set and ran past various theatre crew members, threatening to knife anyone who stood in his way, and reached Baptist Alley through a back door. There, an unsuspecting theatre boy was holding Booth's horse by the reins, keeping it ready for him. Lieutenant John S. Knox and Major Joseph B. Steward, who were seated in the first and second parquet rows, were the first to react. They jumped up from their seats onto the stage and ran in pursuit. Knox got lost between the stage sets and the corridors behind the stage, and had to abandon the chase, whereas Stewart, who knew the house, at least succeeded in following the attacker to the rear exit. However, Booth slammed the door in his face, and the door jammed shut. In the short moment that Stewart needed to get the door open, Booth managed to swing himself onto his horse, bring the horse forward and ride off. He rode through Baptist Alley onto F Street and raced across the city to the Navy Yard Bridge (now Eleventh Street Bridges), which spanned the eastern branch of the Potomac (now Anacostia river).[43] He thereby reached

---

unintentionally fired a shot or that the man in black was trying to save his own life, see, for example, the letter from Charles A. Sanford to Goodrich, 16 April 1865; and the letter from Edwin Bates to his parents, 15 April 1865, in Good, *Lincoln Shot*, 47–9, quotation at 48, and 34–6, quotation at 34. Sanford goes on to write, 'We could not persuade ourselves that the President had been assassinated' and 'Everybody was confounded and paralyzed'. Good, *Lincoln Shot*, 48. 'Paralyzed' is the term used frequently to describe the first reaction of the audience.

42 Quoted in Reck, *A. Lincoln*, 113. See also Good, 'Lincoln Assassination', 22–3; Anthony S. Pitch, *'They Have Killed Papa Dead!' The Road to Ford's Theatre, Abraham Lincoln's Murder, and the Rage for Vengeance* (Hanover: Steerforth Press, 2008), 115; and Alford, *Fortune's Fool*, 267.

43 See Knox in Good, *Lincoln Shot*, 40; and Reck, *A. Lincoln*, 109–12; Kauffman, *American Brutus*, 8–9; Pitch, *'Papa Dead!'*, 116–17; and Alford, *Fortune's Fool*, 267–9.

southern Maryland, most of whose residents sympathized with the Confederates. Although the government in Washington launched a massive dragnet that very night, it was twelve days before Booth was found by a mounted Union army unit in a tobacco barn in northern Virginia. Against explicit orders, he was shot there by a Union soldier.[44]

When Booth disappeared between stage sets, most members of the audience at Ford's Theatre broke out of their stupor. A wild uproar immediately ensued. People jumped out of their seats, and according to an eye witness 'horror was stamped upon every face.' From all sides people were shouting 'Catch him, kill him,' 'hang him, shoot him,' 'kill him, lynch him!' While some of the spectators streamed to the exit, others stormed onto the stage to follow the attacker or to peer into the president's box. Panic broke out in places when some people in the crowd fell to the ground and others were pressed to the wall of the orchestra pit.[45] In all this chaos, calls rang out for a doctor, and a few doctors who had been sitting in the audience fought their way through to the president's box as quickly as possible. They gathered around Lincoln, who sat unconscious in his rocking chair, held by his wife so that he would not fall forward.[46]

All the doctors agreed that Lincoln would not be able to survive the injury he had sustained. The 0.44 calibre bullet from Booth's derringer pistol had entered the back of his head about two and a half inches behind the left ear and had penetrated nearly eight inches through his

---

44 The story of Booth's escape and the chase after him by the government is often recounted and is the subject of many books. Most of the descriptions have the same kind of limitations as the literature on the attack itself. Meticulous reconstructions of the twelve days are provided by Kauffman, *American Brutus*, Chapters 12–15; Pitch, '*Papa Dead!*'; and Alford, *Fortune's Fool*, Chapters 11–12. James L. Swanson, *Manhunt: The Twelve-Day Chase for Lincoln's Killer* (New York: William Morrow, 2006), is a dramatically told story but not always completely reliable.

45 In the order of the quotations: Albert Daggett, letter to friend Julie, 15 April 1865, in Good, *Lincoln Shot*, 45; and Bates, Bronson and Dr Taft, 'Letters or Other Texts from Bates, Bronson, and Dr. Taft', in Good, *Lincoln Shot*, 34, 58. Similar statements appear in many other eyewitness accounts. See also Michael W. Kauffman, *American Brutus: John Wilkes Booth and the Lincoln Conspiracies* (New York: Random House, 2004), 9–13; Thomas Goodrich and Debra Goodrich, *The Darkest Dawn: Lincoln, Booth, and the Great American Tragedy* (Bloomington: Indiana University Press, 2005), 99–102; Anthony S. Pitch, '*Papa Dead!*', 117.

46 See Dr Taft and Major Henry R. Rathbone, 'affidavit on 15 April 1865'; Clara Harris, letter, 29 April 1865; and Dr Charles Augustus Leale, letter to General Benjamin Butler, 20 July 1867, in Good, *Lincoln Shot*, 41–4, 69–71, 59–62; Charles Augustus Leale, *Lincoln's Last Hours* (n.p., 1909), 4–7; and Kauffman, *American Brutus*, 10–14, 226.

Figure 23. '$100,000 Reward! The murderer of our late beloved President, Abraham Lincoln, is still at large.' Library of Congress, Rare Book and Special Collections Division, LC-USZC4-5431.

brain before lodging behind one of his eye sockets.[47] When the diagnosis of the mortal injury spread in the theatre, the tumult turned to rage. Many men wept in their desperate helplessness and vented their anger on the theatre furnishings, swearing as they smashed the seats. Shame and self-reproach gnawed at the soldiers, who had done nothing to impede the attack on their commander-in-chief or to stop the assassin. The actors tried in vain to calm the audience.[48]

In the meantime, the doctors decided that Lincoln should not die in a theatre, as they thought there was something disreputable about the place. With the help of a few soldiers in the audience, they carried him out on a board through the crowd. By then the spectators were also willing to obey the request to leave the theatre and slowly made their way out to Tenth Street. Most of them remained standing there, waiting to see what would happen next. The doctors had the impression that Lincoln would not survive a trip back to the White House, so he was carried through the crowd to the home of William Petersen, a tailor who lived across from the theatre. The door was immediately opened to the small procession.[49] They laid the dying president on a guest bed, and the doctors examined him thoroughly once again. During the next few hours, they tried to stabilize his circulation and keep his limbs warm with brandy, hot water bottles, blankets and mustard plasters. Beyond that they were limited to keeping the wound open, as was the medical practice of the time, and to monitoring his pulse and breathing. As the new day dawned, Lincoln's breathing became ever more laboured and his pulse weaker. Without regaining consciousness, he died at 7:22 a.m.[50]

*   *   *

---

47 See the quotations from the autopsy reports in Reck, *A. Lincoln*, 167–9.

48 See for, example, the report by Bates and Knox in Good, *Lincoln Shot*, 35, 40; and especially Kauffman, *American Brutus*, 9–11; and Goodrich and Goodrich, *Darkest Dawn*, 99–102.

49 See Leale, *Lincoln's Last Hours*, 7–8; Reck, *A. Lincoln*, 118–26; Good, 'Lincoln Assassination', 23–6; Kauffman, *American Brutus*, 17–19; and Goodrich and Goodrich, *Darkest Dawn*, 102–3.

50 The best and most impressive description of these hours is in Gideon Welles's diary entry for 14 April 1865 in Howard K. Beale and Alan W. Brownsword (eds.), *Diary of Gideon Welles, Secretary of the Navy under Lincoln and Johnson*, 3 vols., Vol. 2: *April 1, 1864 – December 31, 1866* (New York: Norton, 1960), 280–90, especially 286–8; and Leale, *Lincoln's Last Hours*, 8–12. See also Reck, *A. Lincoln*, Chapter 11; Good, 'Lincoln Assassination', 26; and Pitch, *'Papa Dead!'*, Chapter 8.

Almost exactly one year after Lincoln's assassination, on 4 April 1866, the student Dmitry Vladimirovich Karakozov made an attempt on the life of the Russian emperor Alexander II. His motivations were social-revolutionary in nature, as he believed the tsar's emancipation laws for the Russian serfs did not go far enough.

It was widely known in Russia that Alexander II enjoyed going for daily walks. It was well known that the forty-seven-year-old tsar would even occasionally go on long walking tours, accompanied only by his daughter Maria, or one or several of his dogs. Since the tsar almost always wore his general's uniform, he was easily recognizable.[51] During the half-year of winter, the court usually resided in the Winter Palace. This imposing building complex is situated in the centre of St Petersburg on the bank of the river Neva. Thus, to get a little exercise and a breath of fresh air in the winter months, Alexander would, as a rule, go into the Summer Garden in the afternoon. The spacious city park designed under Peter the Great, with its old trees, white benches and artful marble statues, was just a few minutes up the river from the Winter Palace.[52]

While Alexander went for his walk in the Summer Garden, the park, which was enclosed in a high wrought iron fence, remained open to the public. Two policemen, however, were stationed at the entrance to the park. Their orders were to refuse entrance to anyone dressed poorly or

---

51 See here in particular Moss, *Russia in the Age of Alexander II*, 89–90; as well as Ulam, *Prophets and Conspirators*, 1–2; and N. P. Eroshkin, 'Vystrel u Letnego sada', *Voprosy istorii* 7 (1993), 170. See also Carola Dietze and Frithjof Benjamin Schenk, 'Traditionelle Herrscher in moderner Gefahr'.

52 On the Winter Palace, the Summer Garden and their history see, for example, Kulturstiftung Ruhr and Gemeinnütziger Verein Villa Hügel, *St. Petersburg um 1800. Ein goldenes Zeitalter des russischen Zarenreichs: Meisterwerke und authentische Zeugnisse der Zeit aus der Staatlichen Ermitage, Leningrad: Ausstellung Kulturstiftung Ruhr, Villa Hügel, Essen* (Recklinghausen: Verlag Aurel Bongers, 1990); Emmanuel Ducamp (ed.), *The Winter Palace, Saint Petersburg*, introduction and commentaries by Militsa Filipovna Korshunova with the collaboration of Tatiana Borisovna Bushmina and Tatiana Borisovna Semionova, preface by Mikhail Borisovich Piotrovsky (Paris and Saint Petersburg: Alain de Gourcuff and State Hermitage Museum, 1995); Susan P. McCaffray, *The Winter Palace and the People: Staging and Consuming Russia's Monarchy, 1754–1917* (Dekalb: Northern Illinois University Press, 2018); as well as Kira Mikhailovna Egorova, *Leningrad, House of Peter I: Summer Gardens and Palace of Peter I*, photos by M. Vakhromeyeva (Leningrad: Aurora Art Publishers, 1975); and Nina Vladimirovna Semennikova, *Letnii sad: Al'bom* (Leningrad: Iskusstvo, 1978).

acting conspicuously. Alexander was not afraid of interactions, and would always pause to converse with members of St Petersburg's good society who also enjoyed taking walks in the park. His two-horse equipage would stand at the northern gate of the garden in the direction of the Neva. It was common for people of all ages and social classes to gather around the carriage with its imperial coat of arms. The gate of the park opened then, as now, onto a bustling street that leads along the Neva to the bridges that connect St Peterburg's city centre with its residential districts. And so, if it was apparent to passers-by that the tsar had stopped in the park, many people would stay and wait a little while to catch a glimpse of the Emperor of All Russia when he came back to the carriage.[53]

Monday, 4 April, was cold and grey. The temperature was just barely above freezing and the rooftops of the city were enveloped in a grey cloudy haze. The snow had not yet completely melted, and the dirty clumps of its remains obstructed the sides of the streets and paths. On this day, twenty-five-year-old Dmitry Vladimirovich Karakozov, a former student of law at Moscow University, passed by the Winter Palace on his way to the Summer Garden, armed with a double-barrelled pistol, additional rounds and powder, two handwritten copies of his proclamation 'To My Worker Friends' ('Druz'iam-rabochim'), as well as morphine, strychnine and hydrogen cyanide, and waited there for the tsar so he could shoot him.[54]

His chance to act appeared very quickly. On the day of the attempt, Alexander II had come to the Summer Garden in the afternoon to go for a walk, accompanied as usual by his stately gordon setter Milord. In the park, he encountered his niece and nephew, Princess Maria Maximilianovna Badenskaia and Duke Nicolas Maximilianovich Leikhtenbergskii, and went on together with them as they talked.[55]

---

53 On this see Ulam, *Prophets and Conspirators*, 1–2; and Eroshkin, 'Vystrel u Letnego sada', 170.

54 See the indictment, printed in Mitrofan Mikhailovich Klevenskii and K. G. Kotel'nikov (eds.), *Pokushenie Karakozova: Stenograficheskii otchet po delu D. Karakozova, I. Khudiakova, N. Ishutina i dr.* (Moscow: Izdatel'stvo Tsentralkhiva R.S.F.S.R., 1928 and 1930), vol. 1, 6–7, as well as Alexei Alexeevich Shilov, 'Iz istorii revoliutsionnogo dvizheniia 1860-kh godov', *Golos minuvshego* 10/12 (1918), 162; Moss, *Russia in the Age of Alexander II*, 90; and Verhoeven, *The Odd Man Karakozov*, 66–7, 130–1, 142–3.

55 See Slesarchuk's testimony of 18 August 1866, printed in Klevenskii and Kotel'nikov, *Pokushenie Karakozova*, vol. 1, 13; as well as Tatishchev, *Imperator Aleksandr II*, 423; Ulam, *Prophets and Conspirators*, 2; Eroshkin, 'Vystrel u Letnego sada', 170 and Liashenko, *Aleksandr II*, 276.

Meanwhile, at the gate, the police officer and sergeant of the castle guard Stepan Zabolotin and the sergeant of the Gendarme squadron Luk'ian Slesarchuk were keeping guard. As the tsar returned to the carriage at four o'clock, the two of them hurried to hold out his overcoat, to unfold the lap quilt for him and to help him get in the vehicle. As this was going on, the tsar continued a conversation with a field officer. Neither of them was paying attention to the crowd that had formed all around the carriage. Nor did they notice that – just as the tsar was putting on his overcoat – a young man pulled a pistol out of the pocket of his peasant coat, aimed it at the tsar and fired a shot at close range.[56]

He missed. As the Russian historian Leonid Liashenko states, there are two versions as to how Alexander II was almost miraculously saved from danger. The first version states that 'the shooter was not overly well versed in the use of his weapon' and thus could only have hit the tsar by accident.[57] The second official version is, on the contrary, a 'pretty story', 'that a simple peasant saved the monarch from the shot of a member of the radical intelligentsia': the twenty-five-year-old hat maker of peasant origins named Osip Ivanovich Komissarov (also Komisarov) was supposedly near Karakozov during the assassination attempt, and in a moment of quick thinking bumped the shooter's elbow, thus diverting the shot.

This second version can be traced back to Eduard Ivanovich Totleben, a hero of the Crimean War during the defence of Sevastopol and adjutant general to the tsar. In contrast to the first version of the story, this one had the obvious advantage of reinforcing the idea that the simple

56 See the indictment and the testimony of Slesarchuk and Zabolotin from 18 August 1866, printed in Klevenskii and Kotel'nikov, *Pokushenie Karakozova*, vol. 1, 6, 13–14, as well as Tatishchev, *Imperator Aleksandr II*, 423; Ulam, *Prophets and Conspirators*, 2–3; Moss, *Russia in the Age of Alexander II*, 90; Eroshkin, 'Vystrel u Letnego sada', 170; Liashenko, *Aleksandr II*, 276; and Verhoeven, *The Odd Man Karakozov*, 178.

57 Liashenko, *Aleksandr II*, 347, note 7. Compare this version in Liashenko with that found in Klevenskii and Kotel'nikov, *Pokushenie Karakozova*, vol. 1, 292, note 4 to page 6, which also collects a number of important sources that confirm this version; and Boris Jakovlevich Bukhshtab, 'Posle vystrela Karakozova', in *Katorga i ssylka: Istoriko-revoliutsionnyi vestnik* 5/78 (1931), 54–5, 75–6, as well as Venturi, *Roots of Revolution*, 348; Moss, *Russia in the Age of Alexander II*, 90; and Verhoeven, *The Odd Man Karakozov*, 68–9.

Figure 24. *D. V. Karakozov's Attempt on the Life of the Tsar,
April 4, 1866.* Painting by Vasily Griner, watercolour on paper
and cardboard, St Petersburg, 1866. The Museum of Political
History of Russia, St Petersburg (KP-25550 F.IV-559).

people loved the tsar.[58] Karakozov himself explained his missed shot as a result of hastiness.[59]

Although Dmitry Karakozov still had another round loaded in his pistol, he immediately attempted to flee and ran along the Neva towards Prachechnyi Most (Laundry Bridge), which leads over the Fontanka river. But he did not make it far. While one can find mentions of all the bystanders standing 'frozen' in shock in some historical accounts, others state that the crowd overtook him and threatened to beat him. It is certain, however, that the two police officers ran after the assailant and got hold of him after fifteen *sazhen* (about 100 feet). Zabolotin and Slesarchuk, who were – as was customary in Russia at the time – armed only with sabres, detained Karakozov, and Zabolotin snatched away his pistol.[60]

Tsar Alexander II followed them and asked Karakozov if he was a Pole and why he had shot at him. There are several extant versions of this dialogue. The minister of the interior Count Pëtr Aleksandrovich Valuev noted in his diary entry for that same day, 'The Emperor asked him if he [Karakozov] was Russian and why he shot at him. (He probably asked if he [Karakozov] happened to be a Pole).'[61] According to Slesarchuk and Zabolotin's concurring testimonies four and a half months later, the tsar asked what Karakozov wanted (*Chto tebe nuzhno?*, 'what do you want?') and who he was (*Kto ty takoi?* 'Who are you

---

58 Liashenko, *Aleksandr II*, 347, note 7. The second version appears already on that same day in the diary of the minister of internal affairs, Count Pëtr Aleksandrovich Valuev, but with a qualifying *govoriat* ('they say'). See Petr Andreevich Zaionchkovskii (ed.), *Dnevnik P. A. Valueva ministra vnutrennikh del v dvukh tomakh*, vol. 2: *1865–1876* (Moscow: Izdatel'stvo akademii nauk SSSR, 1961), 114; and then, for example, in the indictment and in Komissarov's testimony of 18 August 1866, both printed in Klevenskii and Kotel'nikov, *Pokushenie Karakozova*, vol. 1, 6, 12–13; as well as in Tatishchev, *Imperator Aleksandr II*, 423; and, with disclaimers, in Ulam, *Prophets and Conspirators*, 3; and Eroshkin, 'Vystrel u Letnego sada', 170–1. On the origin of this version see Klevenskii and Kotel'nikov, *Pokushenie Karakozova*, vol. 1, 292, note 4 to page 6, as well as Buchshtab, 'Posle vystrela Karakozova', 54–5, 75–6; and Verhoeven, *The Odd Man Karakozov*, 66–70.

59 See Klevenskii and Kotel'nikov, *Pokushenie Karakozova*, vol. 1, 292, note 4 to page 6.

60 See the indictment and the testimonies of Slesarchuk and Zabolotin of 18 August 1866, printed in Klevenskii and Kotel'nikov, *Pokushenie Karakozova*, vol. 1, 6, 13–14; as well as Ulam, *Prophets and Conspirators*, 3, which provides both versions of the crowd's reactions; and the combination of variants in Eroshkin, 'Vystrel u Letnego sada', 170.

61 Zaionchkovskii, *Dnevnik P. A. Valueva*, 114.

anyway?').[62] The historian of imperial Russia Mikhail Dolbilov explains the difference between these versions as a kind of editing process. For this conclusion he draws on other 'examples of how Alexander's oral pronouncements mentioning "Poles" pejoratively were later "corrected" in the writing so as to have them sound nationally neutral, as it behoved an imperial ruler'. Dolbilov also points to the fact that this editing process is already discernible in Valuev's diary, and he remarks that the question whether Karakozov was a Pole suggests an agitation on Alexander's part, while Slesarchuk and Zabolotin's testimonies have the emperor word his questions calmly and in a business-like fashion.[63] Moreover, another archival source close to events that is at Dolbilov's disposal confirms the interpretation that Alexander asked Karakozov if he was a Pole.

When it comes to Karakozov's replies to the tsar, even more versions exist. According to his diary, Valuev had collected the following versions:

> The killer replied that he was Russian and that his majesty had supposedly deceived us for too long. Others say that he said his majesty had deprived the peasants of their share of land. Still others [say] that, turning to the crowd, he said: 'Boys, I fired for all of you' [*Rebiata, ia za vas strelial*]. This last version is confirmed from different sources.[64]

---

62 Testimonies of Slesarchuk and Zabolotin from 18 August 1866, printed in Klevenskii and Kotel'nikov, *Pokushenie Karakozova*, vol. 1, 13–14. For these and related versions and their rendering in the contemporary press and literature, see the comparison in Bukhshtab, 'Posle vystrela Karakozova', 69–75. The literature is divided as to which version it accepts as authentic. For instance, Venturi, *Roots of Revolution*, 347; and Eroshkin, 'Vystrel u Letnego sada', 170, write that the tsar asked Karakozov if he was a Pole, while Ulam, *Prophets and Conspirators*, 3; and Verhoeven, *The Odd Man Karakozov*, 176–8, 216, note 12, settle on the guards' version.

63 Mikhail Dolbilov, associate professor, Department of History, University of Maryland, College Park, Maryland, United States, email communication with the author from May to September 2020, especially emails on 12 May and 6 August 2020. On the specific meaning of the term 'Pole' in the political vocabulary of the Russian Empire as interpreted from a perspective of conceptual history, see Mikhail Dmitrievich Dolbilov, 'Poliak v imperskom politicheskom leksikone', in *'Poniatiia o Rossii': K istoricheskoi semantike imperskogo perioda*, ed. Aleksei Il'ich Miller, Denis Anatol'evich Sdvizhkov and Ingrid Shirle, Studia Europea (Moscow: Novoe literaturnoe obozrenie, 2012), 293–339.

64 Zaionchkovskii, *Dnevnik P. A. Valueva*, 114–15.

According to Slesarchuk and Zabolotin's concurring testimonies, the tsar received only the answer, 'A Russian' and 'Nothing' (*Nichego ne nuzhno*, literally, '(I) don't need anything/Nothing is needed').[65] Their version constitutes the most effective de-politicization of any answer Karakozov could have given and for this reason does not seem likely, but confirms Dolbilov's judgement that their replies had undergone an editing process.

Then the shooter suddenly reached into his coat pocket and pulled out a 'letter'. This letter, just like the pistol, was immediately snatched out of his hand by Slesarchuk. Zabolotin gave Alexander II the pistol, and the tsar briefly examined it. Then he asked Duke Leikhtenbergskii and Princess Badenskaia to convey the news of the attack to his brother and president of the Council of State, the Grand Duke Konstantin Nikolaevich Romanov, while the tsar himself set off on a direct path towards Kazan Cathedral on Nevsky Prospekt to thank God for saving him from danger (or so went the official account). He instructed Zabolotin and Slesarchuk to bring the assailant to Prince Dolgorukov; that is, to the headquarters of the Russian political police.[66] As police wagons did not yet exist, the two officers took the assailant away by holding him between them and leading him by foot towards the headquarters of the Third Section, which lay at the other end of the Summer Garden by Tsepnoi Most ('Chain Bridge', now Panteleimonovsky Most), where today's Ulitsa Pestelia (Pestel Street) crosses the Fontanka. A crowd of people followed them, and Karakozov continuously looked over his shoulder at them as they went. Thus the officers began to suspect that the assailant might have had accomplices in the crowd, and, once they reached Prachechny Most, put him in a droshky and rode the last part of the way with the prisoner. Karakozov would later be brought from the Third Section

65 Testimonies of Slesarchuk and Zabolotin from 18 August 1866, printed in Klevenskii and Kotel'nikov, *Pokushenie Karakozova*, vol. 1, 13–14. On these and related versions again see the comparison by Bukhshtab, 'Posle vystrela Karakozova', 69–75. Again, Ulam, *Prophets and Conspirators*, 3; and Verhoeven, *The Odd Man Karakozov*, 176–8, follow the guards' version, while Venturi, *Roots of Revolution*, 347; Eroshkin, 'Vystrel u Letnego sada', 170; and Liashenko, *Aleksandr II*, 276, hold the versions collected by Valuev to be true.

66 See the testimonies of Slesarchuk and Zabolotin from 18 August 1866, printed in Klevenskii and Kotel'nikov, *Pokushenie Karakozova*, vol. 1, 13–14, as well as Zaionchkovskii, *Dnevnik P. A. Valueva*, 115; Tatishchev, *Imperator Aleksandr II*, 423; Ulam, *Prophets and Conspirators*, 3; and Eroshkin, 'Vystrel u Letnego sada', 170.

states. He became involved (according to his own admission) as a spy
and as a 'blockade-runner' (smuggler) for the Confederates, in particular by buying the expensive medication quinine in the North and transporting it into the South. His dedication, however, did not go as far as
volunteering for service in the Confederate Army. 'I only have an arm to
give; my brains are worth twenty men, my money worth an hundred. I
have free pass everywhere, my profession, my name, is my passport,' as
he justified this decision to his sister. In the farewell letter to his mother,
the favourite son additionally declared that he had not joined the
Confederate troops for her sake.[103] In this sense, John Wilkes Booth
remained a spectator during these four years of a counterrevolutionary
movement's protracted collective struggle for nationhood.[104]

By April 1865, the Confederate States of America had failed
completely. The utopian republic of slaveowners had not been diplomatically recognized by the US government in Washington or any other
country in the world. Their efforts at internal nation building also failed
above all because the plantation aristocracy had not been able to win or
maintain the support of the small farmers. And, of course, last but not

---

103 See Booth, 'To Mary Ann Holmes Booth [Philadelphia, November] 1864', in
Rhodehamel and Taper, 'Right or Wrong, God Judge Me', 130; Clarke, The Unlocked Book,
113–15, quotation at 113–14, as well as Kauffman, American Brutus, 117, 130–1; and
Alford, Fortune's Fool, 115–16.

104 William A. Tidwell, James O. Hall and David Winfred Gaddy have argued in
Come Retribution: The Confederate Secret Service and the Assassination of Lincoln
(Jackson: University Press of Mississippi, 1988); and Tidwell, himself a high-ranking
secret service agent, argued again in April '65: Confederate Covert Action in the
American Civil War (Kent, OH: Kent State University Press, 1995), that John Wilkes
Booth was commissioned by Jefferson Davis and the Confederate government to
kidnap Lincoln, and that Booth worked closely with the Confederate Secret Service. If
this account is accurate, then Booth would not be a 'spectator' but – quite to the
contrary – a central figure within the movement. So far, however, these authors have
not been able to convince academic historical scholars – including the author of this
book – of the veracity of their arguments. This is due, first, to the lack of evidence for
the commission hypothesis and, second, to its contradicting too many established
facts (such as Booth's escape route). There is also another hypothesis connected to that
of the commission, according to which Booth belonged to the secret society known as
the Knights of the Golden Circle, which brought together sympathizers with the
southern states (on this see, in addition to the books named above, Lause, A Secret
Society History of the Civil War, 96). But this claim, too, is based on dubious sources
and is therefore equally unconvincing. Alford comes to the same conclusion regarding
both hypotheses in Fortune's Fool: on the first, see 92, 223, 233–4; and on the second,
207–8.

headquarters to Cell 6 of the Alexeevsky Ravelin, in the wing of the Peter and Paul Fortress designated for political prisoners – where, three years before, Nikolai Gavrilovich Chernyshevsky had been imprisoned and written his novel *What Is to Be Done?*[67]

In prior historical scholarship, these three terrorist acts have been treated as completely different, unconnected political murders. That is, when these acts have received any attention at all – whereby Booth's assassination has most certainly received the most attention, and Becker's attempt to shoot Wilhelm I the least – then they have been and are examined as three completely different acts in entirely different historical contexts that do not bear comparison with one another. This approach has precluded their joint treatment, let alone their systematic comparison, until today.

There are indeed significant differences between the three attacks. First, there is the terrorists' disparate aptitudes and planning: while Booth was able to kill Abraham Lincoln, Becker and Karakozov missed their mark. And while Booth was able to escape immediately, Karakozov was captured within 100 feet, and Becker made no attempt to flee. Second, Becker and Karakozov ultimately acted as individuals, while Booth – just like Orsini and Brown – operated with a group of conspirators. They planned to assassinate not only Abraham Lincoln, but also Vice President Andrew Johnson and Secretary of State William H. Seward, and thereby eliminate the entire senior leadership of the union. But in contrast to Booth, his co-conspirators were not successful in killing their intended victims.

As established at the beginning of this study, however, such differences between the acts of violence are irrelevant for determining the typology of the violence perpetrated. Likewise, the differences named above and a range of others are not relevant to the question of the comparability of their acts. For the hypothesis pursued here, the expansion of the groups of assailants and victims in Booth's case represents above all a serial extension of the same principle, and while the success

---

67 See the testimonies of Slesarchuk and Zabolotin from 18 August 1866, printed in Klevenskii and Kotel'nikov, *Pokushenie Karakozova*, vol. 1, 13–14, as well as ibid., 291, note 2 to page 5; Ulam, *Prophets and Conspirators*, 3; and Eroshkin, 'Vystrel u Letnego sada', 170, 172.

or the failure of the violence or their escape had significant effects on the public reaction and were indeed crucially relevant in the further development of this history, it is nevertheless irrelevant for the classification of the violence itself, as these differences do not affect the definition criteria central to classifying an act as political murder or terrorism. Not only is the instrumental and military success of a given attack immaterial in determining the nature of its violence; so also is the question whether the attack was successful in politico–symbolic terms, that is, whether they actually achieved the desired political and psychological effects. The only relevant question in determining the type of violence exercised is whether such an effect was intended.

Were the attackers in the position to transmit their political message and inspire not only fear and terror, but also sympathy and support? Measured by this criterion, the violent acts of the imitators – in contrast to the terrorist actions of Felice Orsini and John Brown – were not successful, at least not immediately. There are reasons for this failure, and the analysis of these reasons can function here as a kind of 'counter-sample', one that indicates the conditions for the success of terrorist violence. To put it another way: it is precisely the example of failed terrorist acts that allows us to verify the factors which, in the examinations of Orsini's and Brown's violent acts, were emphasized as decisive. These examples additionally illustrate three ways in which the politico–symbolic success of terrorist acts could be thwarted or contained in the nineteenth century.

The insufficient politico–symbolic success of the attacks by Becker, Booth and Karakozov has led to their being generally perceived not as intended terrorist actions that somehow failed, but instead as examples of the genre of 'classic' political murders. They have therefore been thus far either completely left out of the history of terrorism's origins or classified inadequately. With certain qualifications, this also applies to Dmitry Vladimirovich Karakozov's assassination attempt, as early Soviet studies had already clearly identified his attempt as the first example of terrorism in the Russian Empire (for example, Mitrofan Mikhailovich Klevenskii, who edited the 1928 publication of the court transcript of Karakozov's trial), and the Russian historian Oleg Budnitskii demonstrated in the year 2000 that this assassination attempt 'opened the epoch of terrorism in Russia', and also examined the influence that 'this in every respect unsuccessful attack had on Russian revolutionary thought and, in particular, on the development of the terrorist idea'.[68] With this, Budnitskii clearly identified Karakozov's attempt not as a terrorist act itself, but as the starting point for the history of terrorism in Russia. The American historian of Russia Claudia Verhoeven even defined Karakozov's attempt as the original instance of terrorism itself in her 2009 book: 'it may fairly be said that in all but name, terrorism was born of 1866.' Verhoeven further clarifies, however, that it was not the assassination attempt, but the Russian government's handling of Karakozov's attack which is responsible for the emergence of terrorism: 'Terrorism virtually emerged from the Russian autocracy's mishandling of April 4, 1866.'[69] Thus both Budnitskii and Verhoeven still characterize Karakozov's violent act itself as a traditional political assassination, even though the reception or reaction turned it into the starting point for the history of terrorism in Russia.

It will be argued here, in contrast, that the assassination attempts of Becker, Booth and Karakozov warrant being viewed as terrorist attacks,

---

68 Klevenskii, 'Predislovie', in Klevenskii and Kotel'nikov, *Pokushenie Karakozova*, vol. 1, iv–v and xii–xiii; as well as Budnitskii, *Terrorizm v rossiiskom osvoboditel'nom dvizhenii*, 34–5.

69 Verhoeven, *The Odd Man Karakozov*, 6, 10. Verhoeven implicitly contradicts this thesis, presented in the section of her book entitled 'Argument' (that is, that terrorism emerged from the government's reaction to Karakozov's assassination attempt), numerous times in both her book and in the article 'The Making of Russian Revolutionary Terrorism', e.g. 100, 102, without discussing these contradictions. Thus she contrasts Karakozov's assassination attempt as 'Russia's first modern tsaricide' (*The Odd Man Karakozov*, 12) with the 'tsaricides of the old type' who killed Paul I (ibid., 78). Furthermore, she accepts as fact the version of the tsar's two guards that Karakozov allegedly responded to the tsar's question regarding what he wanted with, 'Nothing, nothing'. The 'radical nature of Karakozov's act' expressed in this 'Nihil', Verhoeven writes, sets his act apart from John Wilkes Booth's assassination or the first attempt on the life of Bismarck by Ferdinand Cohen Blind, which were merely aimed against 'a *particular* abuse of power' and not against the exercise of power as such (ibid., 176 and 178). This argument – that is, that the nature of the violence perpetrated by Karakozov is new or different because it is especially radical, because of its nihilism – is not convincing. First, it ignores two sources. These are the more likely versions of Karakozov's replies to the tsar and his proclamation (which she certainly takes into account at other points, e.g. ibid., 143) in which he extensively and precisely lays out his grievances against the Russian tsars in general and Tsar Alexander II in particular (see for example pp. 395–402 of this volume). Second, Verhoeven leaves open the significance of the radicalism of this 'Nihil' for classifying violence as assassination or as terrorism (ibid., 176, 178). For this reason, her attribution of a special radicalism to Karakozov's act does not actually help to prove he was a terrorist.

for all three assassinations – as will be shown in the following – were violent acts that correspond not only to the definition of terrorism but to the logic of terrorist action as well, and are thus terrorist acts. It is therefore important to place these assassination attempts in the early history of terrorism. Indeed, these three violent acts not only represent early (if not the very first) copycat crimes following Orsini's and Brown's acts of violence, but also helped terrorism to develop further as a tactic and become politically and ideologically universalized: the three imitators invented the claim of responsibility, and their assassination attempts are examples of the three different political–ideological manifestations of terrorism – ethno-nationalist, radical right-wing and social-revolutionary – that have been evident since then. It is these three manifestations of terrorism, rather than religious terrorism, that became influential in the nineteenth and twentieth centuries. Thus the vast majority of violent acts – if not all – that are classified as terrorist in nature can be assigned to one or another of these three manifestations.

The three assailants and the violent acts they perpetrated will be the subject of a systematic comparative analysis below. In the narrative that follows, comprehensiveness is neither possible nor pursued, as was the case in the investigations of Felice Orsini and John Brown – that would require individual publications for each case. Thus in the following the focus will be, first, on examining the personalities of Becker, Booth and Karakozov and their respective political concerns, milieus and plans; second, on the reception of their models and related acts; third, on the invention of the claim of responsibility, which was a further development of terrorist tactics; and fourth, on the reception of their assassination attempts. Just as in the preceding chapters, these topics will be discussed with an eye to the main argument of the emergence of terrorism. The overarching goal of this is to show that the three perpetrators and their attacks correspond to the criteria for terrorist violence and the context in which it emerges – criteria that were defined here at the outset and already applied in the cases of Orsini's and Brown's acts of violence. The goal is also to establish that the three violent acts discussed are respectively ethno-nationalist, radical right-wing and social-revolutionary terrorist assassination attempts.

The attackers: novice, onlooker and theorist in matters of (counter)revolution

Oskar Wilhelm Becker, John Wilkes Booth, Dmitry Vladimirovich Karakozov and their acts of violence are all linked with significant social movements of their era. In comparison with the inventors and discoverers of terrorist tactics – Felice Orsini (in cooperation with Napoleon III) and John Brown – we can identify Becker, Booth and Karakozov as something closer to novices, onlookers and theorists in the (counter) revolutionary movements for which they intended to act. In the following the imitators, who were born over the course of the three years from 1838 to 1840, will be considered systematically in light of the origins of terrorism and the criterion of planning. In accordance with the factors worked out in the introduction and analogously to Felice Orsini and John Brown, the central questions will be, first, their education and familial socialization; second, the imitators' engagement in social movements and the political blockages as they saw them; third, their personal situations (to the extent that they seem relevant to their violent acts); and fourth, their secret preparations for their assassination attempts.

Familial socialization and education

The relatively marginal nature of the imitators' social and political standing, as well as the fact that they all lacked long-term practical experience in the (counter)revolutionary movements for which they intended to be active, becomes apparent immediately when we look at their familial socialization. Oskar Wilhelm Becker was born on 5 June 1839 in Odessa. His family was originally from Saxony, but his paternal grandfather had emigrated to Russia in 1805 to take a position as teacher in a gymnasium in Reval (now Tallinn, Estonia). Becker's father also joined the Russian civil service and taught at the Richelieu lyceum in Odessa. In 1861, Dr Paul Adam Becker was the headmaster of this school and bore the title of 'imperial active state councilor'.[70] Dmitry Vladimirovich

---

70 GLA Karlsruhe, 250/8, Bl. 38–56: Becker's interrogation, 14 July 1861, Bl. 38, 41–2; as well as Guido Hausmann, *Universität und städtische Gesellschaft in Odessa 1865–1917: Soziale und nationale Selbstorganisation an der Peripherie des Zarenreiches* (Stuttgart: Franz Steiner Verlag, 1998), 511.

Karakozov was born on 23 October 1840, the scion of an impoverished noble family in Zhmakino, a village located in the district of Serdobsk in the governorate of Saratov.[71] If Becker's or Karakozov's families defined themselves according to any of the revolutions of the previous years, or provided their sons with any expertise in the exercise of revolutionary violence, the information has so far failed to find its way into the histori-cal record.

Figure 25. Oskar Wilhelm Becker. ©
Generallandesarchiv Karlsruhe, 250 Nr. 10.

Only John Wilkes Booth came from a family with a revolutionary tradition. His grandfather Richard Booth was an English lawyer who, from London, had supported the uprising of the American colonies against the crown. It was not for nothing that he christened his two sons Junius Brutus and Algernon Sydney in honour of, respectively, the

---

71 Now Kolyshleyski District in Penza Oblast. The broad outlines of Karakozov's biography and information about his family are best represented in Klevenskii and Kotel'nikov, *Pokushenie Karakozova*, vol. 1, 291, note 2 to page 5. That volume also contains the more extensive notes on Karakozov himself dedicated to more specific questions.

anti-monarchical writer, Julius Caesar's assassin and the English politician who attempted to kill King Charles II. Born on 10 May 1838 in a whitewashed log cabin called 'the Farm' three miles from Belair (today Bel Air) in Maryland, John Wilkes Booth was named after his relative John Wilkes, a radical English Whig and erstwhile lord mayor of London who also stood up for the American rebels and passed the first parliamentary reforms in Great Britain. Booth's father, Junius Brutus Booth, was born in London and had already enjoyed a successful acting career in England and the Netherlands before he decided to emigrate to the United States. In the New World he became one of the most popular stage performers of his time.[72] In this sense, the revolutionary republican tradition that the family passed on to their son was more theoretical than practical in nature.

Figure 26. John Wilkes Booth. Library of Congress, Prints and Photographs Division, LC-DIG-ppmsca-19233. Photographer: Alexander Gardner.

72 On this see, alongside the memoirs of his sister Asia Booth Clarke, *The Unlocked Book: A Memoir of John Wilkes Booth* (New York: G. P. Putman's Sons, 1998), 31–7, 43, 88, note 1, in particular John Rhodehamel's and Louise Taper's (eds.) introduction to *'Right or Wrong, God Judge Me': The Writings of John Wilkes Booth* (Urbana: University of Illinois Press, 1997), 4; Kauffman, *American Brutus*, 81–5; and more recently Alford, *Fortune's Fool*, 11–12.

Just like Felice Orsini and in contrast to John Brown, all three attackers received an above-average education. Oskar Becker began attending a gymnasium in Kiev at fourteen years old and, at sixteen, the historic Kreuzschule in Dresden. After graduating from this famous secondary school, he studied law, governance and public policy at the University of Leipzig.[73] John Wilkes Booth spent his first school years in the private Belair Academy, then graduated from the Milton Academy (today the Milton Inn), a demanding boarding and preparatory school for boys in Cockneysville, north of Baltimore, run by a Quaker. Then he switched to the elite military academy of St Timothy's Hall in Catonsville, Maryland, which was attended by the sons of the most well-heeled slaveowning families of the Upper South.[74]

Dmitry Vladimirovich Karakozov finished secondary school in Penza, around sixty miles north-east of Zhmakino, in 1860, and began a course of study in law at Kazan University in 1861 (once again 300 miles to the north-east on the Volga river). He had, however, already been expelled from the university by the end of October 1861 for his involvement in student political activities. He was nevertheless allowed to return to his studies in Kazan two years later in the fall; he transferred to Moscow University one year later.[75] Owing to their education at prestigious public or private institutions, the three assassins can be counted among the intellectual elite of their day.

And yet, by the time of their assassination attempts, not one of the three attackers had finished their degrees. Becker was still enrolled in Leipzig in the summer semester of 1861. Karakozov was again expelled from university in the first half of the 1865–6 academic year, this time because he had not paid his school fees. In summer 1865, he travelled through the countryside – closely following the example of Chernyshevsky's hero Rakhmetov from *What Is to Be Done?*. When he returned to Moscow in the autumn, he was ill, could not pay the fees for

73 See the beginning of a curriculum vitae in GLA Karlsruhe, 250/10, Bl. 147 Box 66; and the summary of various documents in ibid., 250/12, compilation, Bl. 28.

74 See Clarke, *The Unlocked Book*, 51–61; Kauffman, *American Brutus*, 86–8, 90–1; Rhodehamel and Taper, 'Introduction', 4; as well as Alford, *Fortunes Fool*, 17–19, 25, 29–30.

75 For the most precise account see Klevenskii and Kotel'nikov, *Pokushenie Karakozova*, vol. 1, p. 291, note 2 to page 5; as well as Alexei Alexeevich Shilov, 'Pokushenie Karakozova 4 aprelia 1866 g', *Krasnyi arkhiv* 17/7 (1926), 130, note 1 to page 94.

Figure 27. Dmitry Vladimirovich Karakozov. State Archive of
the Russian Federation (GARF), f.1742, op.1, d.14778, 1.1.

the winter semester and so could not continue his studies.[76] Booth left
the military academy at fourteen after his father's early death in 1852, in
order to support his mother, and began his acting career a few years
later. By 1860, he had managed to become a 'star', known particularly for
his daring leaps and combat as well as his performances in Shakespeare's
plays, earning about $20,000 per year, which would be more than
$600,000 today.[77] This made the high-school dropout Booth the only
one of the three attackers who not only stood on his own two feet financially, but was even quite successful.

---

76 See Klevenskii and Kotel'nikov, *Pokushenie Karakozova*, vol. 1, 291, note 2 to
page 5; Shilov, 'Pokushenie Karakozova 4 aprelia 1866 g.', 130, note 1 to page 94; and
Verhoeven, *The Odd Man Karakozov*, 136–7.

77 See Clarke, *The Unlocked Book*, 61; Kauffman, *American Brutus*, 92 and Chapter
6–7; Rhodehamel and Taper, 'Introduction', 4–5, and 'Allow Me a Few Words!', 49–50; as
well as Alford, *Fortune's Fool*, 33–4 and Chapters 2–6, especially 159, 163. For the
conversion into today's currency Historical Currency Conversions, at futureboy.us, was
used.

Political blockages and engagement in social movements

Like Orsini and Brown, all three imitators were influenced early on in life by the political struggles of their time. For Oskar Wilhelm Becker it was the national question, as it had emerged in the revolutions of 1848–9, that became his most important political reference point. Becker was only ten years old when these revolutions took place, and he observed them from a distance in Odessa, but experienced them intensely nonetheless. He himself cited Prussia's role in the revolution and the interpretation which his social milieu gave to the events of the revolution as central to his decision to make an attempt on the life of Wilhelm I. As he said before the examining magistrate, 'At that time in Odessa, the view that Prussia didn't know how to make use of the relations of power was the prevalent, openly expressed belief among the large number of Germans living there.' This meant that in the eyes of the German diaspora in Odessa, Prussia had failed to use the opportunities afforded by the revolution to realize a German nation comprising all territorial states.[78]

Dmitry Karakozov had observed the living conditions of the peasant population from an early age. What was decisive for the formation of his political convictions, however, was the two years he spent in 'exile' at home in his village after his expulsion from Kazan University. During this time, he worked as a secretary to the peace arbitrator (*mirovoi posrednik*) for his local Serdobsk District to assist with the implementation of the emancipation laws. He quit this job after only two months, as he could not stand what he saw as the arrogance and lack of understanding of this important task on the part of his employer and other mediators.[79] Karakozov was in constant contact with the rural population and knew how hard life was becoming for many former serfs after their liberation, as they now often had to get by with less land and were burdened with large debts resulting from the fees they had to pay to buy their freedom. Karakozov had, furthermore, a connection to the older generation of the revolutionary intelligentsia (even if not a personal

78 GLA Karlsruhe, 250/9, Becker's interrogation, 27 July 1861, morning, Bl. 266–7.
79 Shilov, 'Iz istorii revolutsionnogo dvizheniia 1860-kh gg', 166; and especially Klevenskii and Kotel'nikov, *Pokushenie Karakozova*, 291, note 2 to page 5. The term 'exile' is used there in his cousin's testimony, who quotes Karakozov's words.

one) in the region where he grew up. Saratov is the home town of both Vissarion Belinsky and Nikolai Chernyshevsky, and Chernyshevsky taught there in the gymnasium from 1851 to 1854 after completing his studies, before he took up a position in St Petersburg.[80]

John Wilkes Booth likewise knew the institution of slavery from personal experience. Although his father had never bought slaves, he had borrowed several every year from his neighbours. In contrast to Karakozov, Booth's first-hand knowledge of slavery led him to the opposite conclusion: he began to advocate not *for* the betterment of (former) slaves, but against it. At thirteen years old, he had witnessed the so-called Christiana Riot as a student of the Milton Academy. The riot occurred because, after the adoption of the Fugitive Slave Act of 1850, a plantation owner from Maryland named Edward Gorsuch, along with one of his sons, a US Marshal and a posse, tried to capture and bring back four slaves who had escaped from his plantation to Christiana, Pennsylvania. When the pursuers reached Christiana, however, they found the slaves armed and supported by a group of abolitionists. The posse were surprised, not having expected the slaves to be prepared to defend their freedom with force. It is still unclear today who first resorted to violence, but, by the time the encounter was over, Gorsuch was dead, his son was seriously injured and the rest had fled. A judge later acquitted the slaves and their supporters. As Gorsuch's plantation was only a few miles from both the Milton Academy and the Booth's farm, and Gorsuch's youngest son was a schoolmate and friend of John Wilkes Booth, the latter probably felt a great deal of sympathy for the Gorsuchs and outrage at the 'bloody abolitionists'. At any rate, Booth referred to the incident in this spirit in 1860 in one of his few surviving political writings.[81] By the time he left the military academy he had already taken up the aristocratic bearing of the upper class of the slave states – the 'undemocratic feeling', as his sister Asia Booth Clarke called it – an attitude that stood in complete opposition to the beliefs and conduct of his rebellious,

---

80 See Ch. Vetrinskii (aka V. E. Cheshikhin), 'N. G. Chernyshevskii i karakozovtsy', in *Russkaia mysl'* 34/2 (1913), 103.

81 See John Wilkes Booth, '[Draft of a Speech] Philadelphia, Late December 1860', 64; and on that Kauffman, *American Brutus*, 88; Rhodehamel and Taper, 'Allow Me a Few Words!', 52–3; Alford, *Fortune's Fool*, 15, 26–7; and, specifically on the events in Christiana, Katz, *Resistance at Christiana*.

patriotic grandfather and father, who had both strived to live out republican ideas of equality.[82]

Moved early on by the great political questions of their time, politics occupied a high place in the lives of Oskar Wilhelm Becker, John Wilkes Booth and Dmitry Vladimirovich Karakozov – including in everyday life. All three attackers were intensely engaged in political developments. In the substance of their engagement they remained faithful to the political impressions of their childhoods, while the forms of their participation were strongly influenced by the opportunities available to them in their social milieu, their class positions and their individual roles. The political situation, as it appeared to them in light of their respective concerns, was decisive for them in their resolution to perpetrate an act of violence – just as it had been for Felice Orsini and John Brown. All three imitators believed that there was an obstacle standing in the way of their political goals. And just as in the case of their models, it was pivotal that they perceived political development through institutional channels as something that would not lead to the goal they sought. What varied, however, was the quality of their analyses of the political situation and therefore the political potential for their violent acts.

Of the three of them, Karakozov had the most experience in a social movement. He was involved in the Russian revolutionary student movement. As described earlier, this student movement – the fifth generation of the intelligentsia produced by the repressive policies of the tsarist government – had emerged in 1861, largely out of disappointment with Alexander II's long-awaited laws of emancipation. This disappointment, together with the outrage over the actions of Russian troops in Poland in 1863 and the opposition to a restrictive change in higher-education policy, led to a shift in awareness of the sociopolitical situation in the country among sections of the students. The astute critic of these government policies was Chernyshevsky. His journalism, his philosophy and the lifestyle he encouraged in his writings had a lasting influence on the student movement. Chernyshevsky and the members of the underground organization Zemlia i Volia believed in 1861 that a revolution would break out in Russia within the next five years.

---

82 Clarke, *The Unlocked Book*, 63–4, quotation at 63; and also Kauffman on this, *American Brutus*, 83–5; as well as Alford, *Fortune's Fool*, 30.

After Karakozov was expelled from Kazan University in 1861 for his participation in the student actions, and after he had gained experience with the emancipation laws, their implementation and their consequences as secretary to the mediator in Serdobsk, he continued his studies, as already noted, in Moscow. He lived there with his cousin Nikolai Andreevich Ishutin, who had grown up in Karakozov's family, and they considered themselves brothers. They formed the core of a politically active circle of friends, whose members included Petr Dmitrievich Ermolov, Maximilian Nikolaevich Zagibalov, Nikolai Pavlovich Stranden, Dmitrii Alexeevich Iurasov and Nikolai Pavlovich Peterson, among others. Apart from Ishutin, who came from a family of merchants, they were all of aristocratic background. Together the friends had attended the gymnasium or the aristocratic institute in Penza, then began studies in Moscow or Kazan and became active in the student-organized political demonstrations and actions of these years: struggles with university administrations over the autonomy of the student body, expressions of solidarity with the Polish (or January) Uprising of 1863, and initiatives inspired by early ideas of socialism. They had additionally also made contact with the underground organization Zemlia i Volia when it was already in decline.[83]

When some of the members of the circle of friends were expelled from the university for these activities, they began to engage more intensely in non-university contexts. Thus Ishutin and Iurasov, for example, assisted one of the leaders of the Polish Uprising of 1863

---

83 On specific figures and their biographies, the best resource is the systematic and detailed information in Klevenskii and Kotel'nikov, *Pokushenie Karakozova*, vol. 1, 304, note 39, 306, note 53, 308, note 66, 306, note 58, 307, note 59; as well as Venturi, *Roots of Revolution*, 331–2. On contact between the circle and Zemlia i Volia see Shilov, 'Pokushenie Karakozova 4 aprelia 1866 g.', 91. The word 'brother' for Ishutin appears, for example, in Karakozov's statements from 16 April 1866, printed in Klevenskii and Kotel'nikov, *Pokushenie Karakozova*, vol. 1, 94–5. The extent to which this circle was conspiratorial in nature is a matter of debate in scholarship. On this see in particular the differing assessments in Filippov, *Revoliutsionnaia narodnicheskaia organizatsiia*; Vilenskaia, *Revoliutsionnoe podpol'e v Rossii*, Chapter 4–5; as well as Verhoeven, *The Odd Man Karakozov*, 7–38, who sees the supposition of secret organizations as a construct created in retrospect. As the texts, especially the court transcripts, in fact do suggest caution as to the existence of such secret groups, the account here follows Verhoeven, even though the understanding of the group of friends as one of subversive thought and action does not exclude the possibility of individual clandestine actions, as will become clear in the following.

– Jarosław Żądło-Dąbrowski – in his escape from a Moscow prison: Ermolov hid him in his apartment temporarily, and Ishutin and Iurasov organized his escape abroad. There Dąbrowski engaged himself as one of the leaders of the 1871 Paris Commune. From 1863 the friends began forming various initiatives together with other students and a former guard officer: a bookbinding and tailoring cooperative, a self-managed cotton mill, an association for droshky drivers and a savings bank for students that provided funds for poor students to continue their studies. Ermolov, Stranden and Karakozov also opened people's schools in 1864 for poor children and taught there themselves. In all these activities it was Ishutin who stood at the forefront of the revolutionary group, and Karakozov, as his brother, cooperated. All these participants were inspired by the idea of disciplined, ascetic self-sacrifice.[84]

The friends diverged, however, in their concrete political goals. To be sure, they all shared Chernyshevsky's expectation of revolution by the mid-1860s, and as no revolution had yet occurred by that time, extended its arrival by five more years. Because of this expectation, the emancipation of the serfs appeared to them as a manoeuvre by the tsar to ward off his imminent overthrow. But they were divided – just as the Decembrists had been before them – as to what kind of revolution was needed in Russia. Some argued that Russia should take the Western path of political revolutions. They declared themselves in favour of political freedoms, a constitution, an elected government and its accountability to the people, as well as greater regional autonomy. Furthermore, they supported something more like a revolution from above than from below, and still placed hopes on the political understanding of the tsar.[85]

84 See Vetrinskii, 'N. G. Chernyshevskii i karakozovtsy', 104–5; as well as the introduction by Shilov, 'Pokushenie Karakozova 4 aprelia 1866 g.', 92; and Klevenskii, 'Predislovie', in Klevenskii and Kotel'nikov, Pokushenie Karakozova, vol. 1, iv, x, xiv. On specific activities of the group see Ishutin's court statement in particular, printed in Klevenskii and Kotel'nikov, Pokushenie Karakozova, vol. 1, 62–72, 67–8; Zagibalov's court statement, ibid., 86–90, 86–7, Venturi, Roots of Revolution, 332–5; and Stites, The Women's Liberation Movement in Russia, 118–21. Ishutin's description of a Petersburg model for these initiatives in his letter of 19 April 1866 also provides a good rendering of the cooperatives, printed in Shilov, 'Pokushenie Karakozova 4 aprelia 1866 g.', 96–9, especially 96–7.

85 See Klevenskii, 'Predislovie', in Klevenskii and Kotel'nikov, Pokushenie Karakozova, vol. 1, vii; and Venturi, Roots of Revolution, 334, 338, 342–3.

Others (including Ishutin and Karakozov) were of the view that what Russia required was not so much a political revolution as a social – or as Karakozov would declare later under interrogation – an 'economic' revolution. They wanted to pave the way for this revolution with the help of their initiatives and peaceful propaganda. The supporters of the social revolution not only criticized the liberation of the peasants, but also utterly disapproved of the tsar's other liberal reforms. It was said of Ishutin, for example, that – upon hearing from a St Petersburg group that wanted a political revolution – he told a friend that if the group were successful in bringing about a purely political coup, 'the people in Russia will have it one hundred times worse than now, as they'll think up some kind of constitution and will stuff Russian life into a framework of western life.' The middle and upper social strata would support this constitution, as it would guarantee personal freedom and stimulate industry and trade, but would not protect against the development of pauperism and a proletariat: it would, to the contrary, only deepen poverty.[86] These political changes and their accompanying social shifts were seen on the horizon. Thus, for Karakozov, and similarly to John Brown's case, it was a matter of racing against the clock, of pre-empting an important political change. This was a factor that should not be underestimated in his decision to undertake an act of terrorism.[87]

John Wilkes Booth had been involved in two social movements, although he stood only on the sidelines in each of them. He was a fierce defender of the American political and social status quo as he knew it. He therefore fought against all further changes to American society. After he left the military academy, he began regularly attending the meetings of what was known as the Know-Nothing movement. This nativist and militantly xenophobic movement, which competed electorally as the American Party and was especially successful in Maryland,

---

86 See Shilov's introduction to 'Pokushenie Karakozova 4 aprelia 1866 g.', 92–3. The quote from Ishutin can be found there as well (the term 'economic' is in Karakozov's testimony from 16 April 1866, ibid., 95), and in Klevenskii, 'Predislovie', in Klevenskii and Kotel'nikov, *Pokushenie Karakozova*, vol. 1, x–xiii, for Ishutin's quote, x. On this see also Venturi, *Roots of Revolution*, 334–5.

87 On this see Claudia Verhoeven, 'Time of Terror, Terror of Time: On the Impatience of Russian Revolutionary Terrorism (Early 1860s–Early 1880s)', *Jahrbücher für Geschichte Osteuropas* 58/2 (2010), 254–73, which examines the case of Karakozov and other Russian revolutionaries.

emerged at the beginning of the 1850s in reaction to mass immigration from Ireland and Germany. Its stated goal was to defend 'democracy' and the 'Protestant character' of the United States from the new immigrants, drawing its ideological driving force from anti-Catholicism.[88] It is unknown whether Booth participated in the violent riots against immigrants in which the movement was involved. His sister writes only about the secret meetings of 'a so-called "debating society"', and about a mass rally for Henry Winter Davis, the American Party representative from Baltimore, where Booth served as marshal. It is also through her that we know that her brother, generally speaking, would use any opportunity to get into political arguments and disputes, whether appropriately timed or not.[89]

A 'star engagement' in Montgomery, Alabama, in October and November 1860 had a radicalizing effect on Booth. During these weeks of the presidential campaign and election, he witnessed the shock caused by the election of Republican Abraham Lincoln in the Deep South. He heard speeches from two well-known 'Fire-Eaters' who spoke on the subject, Robert Toombs and William L. Yancey. Booth was a friend of the latter's son, Ben, and took every chance to discuss political questions with Yancey senior.[90]

The Fire-Eaters had emerged in the early 1850s in reaction to the anti-slavery movement in the north, and agitated for the political independence of the slave states.[91] The problem of emancipation and the problem of nationhood in the US were thus strangely linked: the Fire-Eaters were convinced that maintaining slavery was essential for the republican form of government and that their vision of an ideal society

---

88 On this see Heideking and Mauch, *Geschichte der USA*, 134; as well as Hochgeschwender, *Amerikanische Religion*, 109–11.

89 Clarke, *The Unlocked Book*, 72, 75, 91, 104–5. Booth's early political engagement has only been considered cursorily in scholarship. Kauffman, for example, only covers it in one and a half paragraphs in *American Brutus* (see 93–4 and the reference at 111), and Terry Alford, *Fortune's Fool*, 35–56, also dedicates a mere paragraph to this activism, narrowly defined.

90 On this and the echoes of Yancey in Booth's writings, see Rhodehamel and Taper, 'Allow Me a Few Words!', 47–54, especially 49, 65, note 11; and, on the basis of new sources, see Alford, *Fortune's Fool*, 96–7. On Booth's sympathies for the slave states more generally, see Kauffman, *American Brutus*, 92–4 and Chapter 6. Kauffman discusses Booth's stay in Montgomery at 111, but assigns no special significance to it.

91 On the Fire-Eaters and their reaction to John Brown's raid on Harpers Ferry, also see above, pp. 351–2.

could only be realized in an independent republic of slave states. Their utopian expectation was that all the mistakes and inadequacies of the American political system that existed in their time would disappear in a nation of slaveowners, and they saw secession as the precondition for this ideal republic.[92] Against this they feared the growing power of the federal government in Washington and the accompanying loss of rights on the level of individual states. In taking up these views, the Fire-Eaters saw themselves as direct heirs to the old republicanism of the founding fathers. As Eric Walther writes,

> For them, localism, the creation of government as a check on power instead of a grant of power, and the slaveholders' preoccupation with the liberty and equality of all white men reveal secessionist thinking as locked into the eighteenth-century world of their revolutionary parents and grandparents as opposed to the mid-nineteenth-century America transformed by Jacksonian democracy.[93]

The Fire-Eaters therefore typically described themselves as by no means radicals but rather as conservative politicians who had merely stepped up to defend the founding principles of the United States, 'liberty, independence and honor'.[94]

The Fire-Eaters' moment came in the winter of 1860–1. In the 1850s the movement had essentially consisted of a mere dozen men. Their advocacy of 'a romantic, millenarian renewal' was in line with important trends in American society at the time: the reform societies of the Second Awakening and the messianic Protestantism from which the anti-slavery movement had emerged.[95] And, just like other social movements, the Fire-Eaters used the media and public sphere to achieve their goals. But they were still considered too extreme to garner a larger base of support, and therefore remained a 'small but vocal group of

---

92 See especially Ulrich Bonnell Phillips, *The Course of the South to Secession: An Interpretation* (New York: Appleton-Century Company, Inc, 1939), Chapter 6, quotation at 128; as well as the introductory and concluding chapters in Eric H. Walther, *The Fire-Eaters* (Baton Rouge: Louisiana State University Press, 1992).

93 Walther, *The Fire-Eaters*, 298.

94 Ibid., 300.

95 Ibid., 301.

472 The Invention of Terrorism

southerners' that was influential at every level of the government.[96] It was only the shock of the raid on Harpers Ferry and the even greater shock of Lincoln's presidential victory that led to the Fire-Eaters' growth from a small counterrevolutionary avant-garde to a broad secession movement in a short space of time. For now, they 'suddenly seemed prophetic, conservative, and wise instead of irresponsible, radical, and rash'. This secession movement took control in winter 1860–1 with the founding of the Confederate States of America.[97]

With the start of the secession crisis, Booth initially advocated for the unconditional preservation of both the Union and slavery, in accordance with his foundational beliefs and disposition. His line of reasoning borrowed both from the Fire-Eaters and from the great Union Meetings in the north. 'You know it [slavery] is not a sin. And if it was. The Constitution forbids you to interfere with it' – so he declared to an imaginary public in an imagined speech written in December 1860, shortly before South Carolina seceded from the Union.[98] He harshly criticized the abolitionist movement and held its intellectual leaders responsible for the crisis. He believed that the people of the northern states (among which he counted himself a member in this case) were culpable in two ways: first because they had agitated against slavery and thus illegitimately interfered in the affairs of the South, and second because

96 Thus argues Eric Walther in *The Fire-Eaters* – see especially 301, quotation at 1. Walther thereby argues convincingly against Ronald G. Walters, who excludes Freemasons, 'proslavery, mobs and nativism' from 'true reform movements' in his book *American Reformers, 1815–1860* (New York: Farrar, Straus and Giroux, 1978): 'Proslavery writers often criticized Northern and Southern ways of life and presented alternative visions of society (and in that sense they were reformers), but they did not have a distinctive organizational structure to spread their ideas and to channel the energies of the faithful. Instead of building a movement, they used publications and existing political bodies to carry the word.' Since this form of organization was born of necessity due to minimal resonance, this criterion does not actually contradict the categorization of the secessionists as a modern reform movement. On the presence of the Fire-Eaters in the press, see Ratner and Teeter, *Fanatics and Fire-Eaters*.

97 Walther, *The Fire-Eaters*, 298–9. Also see Dwight Lowell Dumond, *The Secession Movement, 1860–1861* (New York: The Macmillan Company, 1931).

98 John Wilkes Booth, '[Draft of a Speech] Philadelphia, Late December 1860', in Rhodehamel and Taper, *'Right or Wrong, God Judge Me'*, 62–3. The orthography and punctuation here and below belong to the original. On Booth's intellectual debts see the editors' corresponding commentary to the text. Further commentary on the draft of this speech and its context can be found in Kauffman, *American Brutus*, 111–13; as well as Alford, *Fortune's Fool*, 100–3. The latter also situates Booth's political positions at 97–100.

instead of supporting the rights of the southern states, they were consciously subverting them. 'What has been the cause of all this [the secession crisis] why nothing but the constant agitation of the slavery question,' wrote Booth, continuing elsewhere, 'The Laws have not been enforced that would protect southern rights [in reference to the Fugitive Slave Act of 1850], others have been passed to enfringe those [*sic*] rights [that is, the personal-liberty laws of some northern states].'[99] Booth wrote that the slave states had demanded justice, but that had proven futile. They had only received empty promises from the north: 'She [the South] has cryed called for justice in vain; we of the North have promised & promised but that has been all.'[100] Thus he saw it as justified for the South to reject any further attempts to be palmed off with promises, to draw the necessary conclusions, take action and leave the Union: 'deny that justice and anything Ay even cession [*sic*] is warrantable.' Using violence to impede that secession, in contrast, would amount to tyranny: 'She [the South] is fighting in a just cause . . . We must not use force against her. If we do then are we greater tyrants! Than George the 3d: ever was towards our fathers!'[101] Thus to save the Union, Booth argued in December 1860, it would be necessary to comply with the demands of the slave states in every way.

After secession and the beginning of the civil war, Booth sided with the Confederate States of America. He identified himself with the southern states in a farewell letter to his mother from November 1864 using his typically theatrical style, idiosyncratic orthography and punctuation: He called the Confederacy 'my Country', its inhabitants 'my brave countrymen' and their cause the 'cause of liberty & justice' as well as '*the cause I love*'.[102]

Like so many Marylanders – a state that did not join the Confederacy and stayed in the Union – Booth dedicated himself to the southern

99 Booth, '[Draft of a Speech] Philadelphia, Late December 1860', in Rhodehamel and Taper, '*Right or Wrong, God Judge Me*', 62, 57. On the Fugitive Slave Act and its political consequences see also above, pp. 217–18.

100 Booth, '[Draft of a Speech] Philadelphia, Late December 1860', in Rhodehamel and Taper, '*Right or Wrong, God Judge Me*', 59.

101 Ibid., 62.

102 Booth, 'To Mary Ann Holmes Booth [Philadelphia, November] 1864', in Rhodehamel and Taper, '*Right or Wrong, God Judge Me*', quotation at 130–1. On Booth's conduct in the first years of the war see Kauffman, *American Brutus*, 116–29; and Alford, *Fortune's Fool*, 103–16, as well as Chapter 5.

least, the Confederate rebels lost the war they had begun four years earlier: on 9 April 1865, Robert E. Lee capitulated as commander-in-chief of the Army of Northern Virginia. As the most significant army within the Confederacy, its elimination practically meant the end of the American Civil War.[105]

With this, all collective forms of violence and all legal means of political influence for the supporters of slavery were exhausted and closed off for the foreseeable future. They were blocked from political involvement. Booth correctly recognized this threatening blockage, but was neither able nor willing to accept it. After the Confederate capital of Richmond fell and the news of Lee's surrender arrived in Washington, he let out his frustration at a shooting range and declared to a friend in a heated tone that things were by no means 'gone up' for the southern states, as general Joe Johnston was still in the field.[106] The time to act, he implied, had not yet passed.

In Booth's eyes, moreover, the defeat of the Confederacy would be accompanied by the political loss of the Union. For like many of Lincoln's opponents in the North, Booth suspected that Lincoln would now establish himself as the king of the United States of America and do away with democracy – just like Napoleon I and Napoleon III in France. He had the Bonapartes in mind and the danger of Lincoln becoming a dictator when he sang a song to his sister one evening, ending with the refrain, 'In 1865 when Lincoln shall be king,' and he went on to explain to her,

> That Sectional Candidate [that is, only elected with northern votes] should never have been President ... This man's appearance, his pedigree, his coarse low jokes and anecdotes, his vulgar similes, and his policy, are a disgrace to the seat he holds ... *He* is Bonaparte in one great move, that is, by overturning this blind Republic and making himself a king. This man's re-election which will follow his success, I tell you, will be a reign! The subjects, bastard subjects, of

---

105 On this see above, around p. 439; McPherson, *Battle Cry of Freedom*, Chapter 12.IV and 18.I, as well as 848–50; Paul D. Escott, *After Secession: Jefferson Davis and the Failure of Confederate Nationalism* (Baton Rouge: Louisiana State University Press, 1978); and William Marvel, *Lee's Last Retreat: The Flight to Appomattox* (Chapel Hill: University of North Carolina Press, 2002).

106 See Kauffman, *American Brutus*, 207; as well as Alford, *Fortune's Fool*, 252–3.

other countries, apostates, are eager to overturn this government. You'll see, you'll see that *re-election* means *succession*.[107]

Booth saw Lincoln as a tyrant, 'a greater tyrant than they ever knew', as he wrote in his journal after the assassination.[108]

Lincoln, in Booth's eyes, was an illegitimate president in every way. And this president, he feared, would not follow the Constitution and stick to political decorum by stopping at two terms in office. He would, with the help of immigrants from Europe, turn the US into a monarchy and crown himself king, similar to what had transpired in France. Booth's aristocratic, elitist ideology and the formative influence of the Know-Nothing movement on his thinking are readily apparent here in his appraisal of the post-war situation. To assassinate the illegitimate president and thereby prevent him from realizing these supposed goals was, for Booth, a just and legitimate act – and time was short.

For Oskar Wilhelm Becker, the national unification of Germany was a deeply personal and emotional cause. As he told the examining magistrate, he had essentially always held on to the interpretation that his social milieu in Odessa had given the revolutionary events in 1848–9. In order to prove this, he referred to his 'Prophecies for the year 1860 and those that follow' ('Prophezeiungen für das Jahr 1860 und die folgenden'), written in 1859. In this unpublished text, he articulated his vision of 'the aforementioned state of the world as I imagine it in the near future'. There he states, for example, 'It is hard to know what to make of Prussia. On the one hand it is impossible to say that it has a weak policy and yet it is unable to achieve any success at all in general European affairs, nor in the specifically German one.'[109] Nor was the German Confederation capable, in Becker's eyes, of bringing about a solution to the German question. 'After a lot of useless talk, the

---

107 Asia Booth Clarke, *John Wilkes Booth: A Sister's Memoir*, edited and with an introduction by Terry Alford (Jackson: University Press of Mississippi 1999), 88.

108 Booth, 'Diary. Zekiah Swamp and Nanjemoy Creek, Charles County, Maryland, 17 and 22 April 1865', 154. Also see Booth, '[Draft of a Speech] Philadelphia, Late December 1860', 56; and the commentary on this in Kauffman, *American Brutus*, 120–1, 141–3; as well as Alford, *Fortune's Fool*, 198, 244–6.

109 GLA Karlsruhe, 250/10, Bl. 83, Box 52: Oskar Becker's letter to the bookseller Lehmann of 29 November 1859; GLA Karlsruhe, 250/10, Bl. 85–101, Box 53: Prophezeiungen, Bl. 86–7.

Bundestag will eventually be transformed,' he predicted for the years 1861–2. But in Becker's opinion this would not lead to any improvement on the status of the 'German question'. For the years 1866–7 he prophesied, 'The Germans are disgruntled over the sad state of their political circumstances.'[110] It was this discontentment that he wanted to remedy.

Becker had formed this picture of the political atmosphere in the German-speaking lands by reading newspapers in Leipzig during the late 1850s and the 1860s. The image he thus pieced together confirmed his earlier Odessan perspective on the German question. 'From the very beginning of my university studies [subsequent insertion: 'and even before that'], I busied myself with reading newspapers in my leisure time,' began Becker's explanation at the very first interrogation in his case.

> In this I found the view expressed everywhere that the Germans were in need of a unification, and that it could not be easily achieved other than through Prussia. I was also convinced that the king of Prussia himself was working toward this goal, but believed that, based on the policies of the current Prussian government, the king of Prussia was not up to this task. Thus I came to the thought that an attempt on his life would be useful to the unification of Germany.[111]

This is how Becker justified his attack on King Wilhelm I by conscious analogy with Orsini's attack on Napoleon III.[112]

In 1861, the blockage to the formation of a German state could have indeed appeared total. The collective violence of the revolutions of 1848–9 and the institutions that had emerged from them had not produced any solution to the German question, and the repression dealt out by the princes and governments in response to the revolutions had only subdued and thereby deferred the question. At the end of the 1850s, hopes for a 'new era' had again begun to proliferate. Repression had abated, and in Prussia Crown Prince Wilhelm became regent. His wife Augusta leaned towards liberal views, and both stood in opposition to

---

110 GLA Karlsruhe, 250/10, Prophezeiungen, Bl. 88–9, 95.
111 GLA Karlsruhe, 250/8, Becker's interrogation, 14 July 1861, Bl. 43.
112 For more evidence on this see later in this chapter, for example p. 504.

the ultraconservatives associated with the so-called 'Kreuzzeitung' (the *Neue Preußische Zeitung*, generally referred to as the 'Cross Newspaper', because of the Prussian iron cross in the title), who had defined politics under Friedrich Wilhelm IV. Initially the prince regent had even appointed what was considered to be a liberal Cabinet.[113]

With the Italian War of 1859, however, it eventually became clear that, as far as the national question was concerned, no unified state would emerge under Wilhelm either. 'The revolutionary elements (now dubbed nationalities)' remained suspect to the Hohenzollern prince regent,[114] and he was not (yet) prepared to take up policies that ruthlessly pursued Prussian advantages above all else. When Otto von Bismarck noted, in reference to the conflict in Italy, that 'the present situation again has a great destiny for Prussia in the cards', Wilhelm responded to this with annoyance. To stab Austria in the back in its hour of need, in the opinion of the prince regent, would be wrong.[115]

The fact that there was no movement on the German situation weighed all the more heavily as the comparison to Italy forced itself on everyone: The successes of the national movement from 1859 onwards showed that national territorial fragmentation did not have to be accepted as irrevocable. In Italy, the princes had quickly fled from their lands and the territories then held referendums on annexations to Sardinia–Piedmont. This now appeared to many to be the model for the process of unification in Germany. Wilhelm, however, stuck with the German confederation of princes. But then even the limited efforts at reform that he tried to accomplish within this framework had come to nothing by 1861. With this, not only the revolutionary attempts of 1848–9, but also all attempts the princes had undertaken since then to work towards a stronger German unity, seemed to have collapsed. The political blockage was complete.

113 On this see Blasius, *Geschichte der politischen Kriminalität in Deutschland*, 47–55; Nipperdey, *Deutsche Geschichte*, vol. 1, Chapter VI.4, as well as Lenger, *Gebhardt* 15: *Industrielle Revolution und Nationalstaatsgründung*, section §11a.

114 Quoted from Herre, *Kaiser Wilhelm I*, 268.

115 On the Italian War see above, pp. 169–73. On Prussia's and especially on Wilhelm's attitude towards the Italian war and the demands directed at Prussia, see Nipperdey, *Deutsche Geschichte* 1, 693–95; and Lenger, *Gebhardt* 15: *Industrielle Revolution und Nationalstaatsgründung*, 266–7. Also see the detailed account in Marcks, *Kaiser Wilhelm I.*, 130–5; as well as Herre, *Kaiser Wilhelm I*, 268–71 (the quotations can also be found here, 269–70).

Oskar Wilhelm Becker was not involved in the German national movement, for example within the recently founded German National Association
(Deutscher Nationalverein) that called for a national parliament and a
central government under Prussian leadership.[116] Since many at the time
nevertheless presumed that Becker had been instigated to act by the national
movement, the student associations or fraternities (*Burschenschaften*) were
under suspicion after his assassination attempt. After all, they had begun
agitating to unify and democratize Germany immediately after the wars of
liberation against Napoleon, and the Carlsbad Decrees following Karl
Ludwig Sand's attack and the repressions of the *Vormärz* period (the
so-called *Demagogenverfolgung* or 'persecution of the demagogues') were
aimed chiefly against members of the universities and particularly against
the student associations. And as a result of this, the authorities still held a
deep-seated distrust of these students at the beginning of the 1860s.[117]

Only a few days after Becker's assassination attempt, the Ministry of
Justice received confidential reports from the police which claimed that
a 'conspiracy' had formed in a fraternity called Germania, 'a secret close-
knit society with republican tendencies'. It was further suspected that
the most recent attack had been propagandized by Karl d'Ester, who
supposedly had already been planning the assassination of the king and
prince of Prussia in 1849. The liberal ministry reacted cautiously to this
information and, when it shared the information with the court, stated
explicitly that 'more exact details on the supposed conspiracy' were not
available as yet.[118] Becker himself stated immediately at his first interrogation that he had 'never been in any fraternity' and that he had 'no
friends or close associates' among the students. The police investigations
largely confirmed his assertions.[119]

---

116 Lenger, *Gebhardt* 15: *Industrielle Revolution und Nationalstaatsgründung*, 288–9.

117 On this see for example Hahn and Berding, *Gebhardt*, vol. 14: *Reformen,
Restauration und Revolution*, section §6c; Jensen, *The Battle against Anarchist Terrorism*,
64; and especially Williamson, 'Thought Is in Itself a Dangerous Operation', and in this
book below, pp. 609–612.

118 GLA Karlsruhe, 250/9, Ministry of Justice to the Baden District Court, 22 July
1861, Bl. 70.

119 GLA Karlsruhe, 250/8, Becker's interrogation, Bl. 39. For confirmation of his
claims see ibid., telegram of the Leipzig public prosecutor's office to the Baden-Baden
District Court, 14 July 1861, Bl. 63; telegram of the Saxon foreign minister Baron von
Beust to the Baden minister of state and foreign affairs Baron von Roggenbach, 15 July
1861 (copy), Bl. 92–4 (also in GStA PK, III. HA MdA, I No. 8913: Attack); GLA

Nor did Oskar Wilhelm Becker have any direct connection with international revolutionary movements. Another seemingly hot lead also quickly turned out to be a dead end: Becker's contact with Alexander Herzen in London. 'Oscar Becker 21 [*sic*] year-old stud[iosus] Jur[is] b[orn] in Odessa, 1859 in Leipzig, son of a gymnasium teacher in Odessa, eccentric, connected to Herzen' read a telegram from the Prussian Interior Ministry, which transmitted the first results of the investigation in Berlin to Baden-Baden on the afternoon of 15 July. This was followed immediately by an update clearing him of the Herzen connection: 'According to another report of the agent sent to Leipzig, Becker's connection to Herzen is limited to apparently sending unsolicited essays for the Kolokol,' was the message that came on the very next day.[120] Becker actually had only tried – as confirmed by his own testimony and the documents themselves – to send Herzen an essay on 'Duke Biron of Churland's overthrow and exile to Siberia'. But the text never arrived in London.[121] The magistrate's assessment in his final

---

Karlsruhe, report of the Prussian police officer Rockenstein, 15 July 1861, Bl. 209–11; ibid., 250/9, police director in Halle an der Saale to Illaire, 16 July 1861, Bl. 293–4, together with the report of Leipzig police commissioner Dr Urban, 15 July 1861 (ibid., Bl. 295–6); as well as GStA PK, III. HA MdA, I No. 8913: Attack, Prussian envoy in Dresden Karl Friedrich von Savigny to the Prussian minister of state and foreign affairs Alexander von Schleinitz, 18 July 1861, along with appendices.

120 GLA Karlsruhe, 250/8, telegram of the Prussian Ministry of the Interior to Illaire, 15 July 1861, transmitted to the Baden District Court on the same day (copy), Bl. 79; and ibid., telegram from the Prussian Ministry of the Interior to Illaire, 16 July 1861 (copy), Bl. 157. The second telegram contained the report of police officer Rockenstein, who was employed by the Prussian Ministry of the Interior in Leipzig. It reads, 'According to the writings he left behind, he [Becker] was engaged in literary works for the "Bell" [*Kolokol*], especially in translations from Russian into German. Thus there were also two letters from Herzen in London, but they were only about literary works'. GLA Karlsruhe, 250/8, report of the Prussian police officer Rockenstein, 15 July 1861, Bl. 209–11.

121 This is a reference to Ernst Johann von Biron, favourite of Tsarina Anna Ivanovna, who became Duke of Kurland in 1737, but who was sentenced to death soon after her death. His sentence was later reduced to exile for life. On Becker's contact with Herzen see GLA Karlsruhe, 250/9, Becker's interrogation, 26 July 1861, afternoon, Bl. 253–4; the mail notice for a parcel with a manuscript by Oskar Becker to Alexander Herzen, 24 January 1860, in German and English with a very tentative address (GLA Karlsruhe, 250/10, Bl. 107–8, Boxes 58–9), as well as a letter by Alexander Herzen to Oskar Becker, 27 January 1860 (GLA Karlsruhe, 250/10, Bl. 109, Box 60). In addition, Oskar Becker must have tried to transmit a comedy by Alexander Herzen to one Ferdinand Schneider in Berlin, who did not want to make use of it. See GLA Karlsruhe, 250/10, o.Z. [103], Box 55.

report, correspondingly, described Becker's relationship with Alexander Herzen 'as an apparently trivial one'. He wrote in conclusion, 'Becker was not a member of a fraternity, he has never belonged to a political association, and [there] is not the slightest hint that he ever entered into close alliance with anyone on political matters.'[122] His conclusion still seems persuasive today.

It was really only through newspapers that Oskar Wilhelm Becker participated, on a purely theoretical level, in political life. The *Leipziger Journal* reported that while at university he would periodically be noticed

> for his chronic reading of newspapers and journals at the Lese-Museum ['Reading Museum', a reading society that subscribed to the most important newspapers and journals and provided them for reading], where he would be seen absorbed in organs of the most varied tendencies with an expression of restless, ravenous appetite, with both his elbows on the table, and with his feet, thrust out widely, as if nailed in place.

At dinner in Seidels Speisekeller on the market square, he would also read the *Deutsche Allgemeine Zeitung* every day.[123] In addition, he would go regularly to Café Döderlein or Café von Gehricke and there read the remaining relevant German newspapers of various political stripes: besides the *Deutsche Allgemeine Zeitung*, he read the Augsburg *Allgemeine Zeitung*, the *Leipziger Zeitung*, the *Kölnische Zeitung*, the *National-Zeitung* and the Berlin *Kladderadatsch*.[124] As already mentioned, he also knew Herzen and Ogarëv's newspaper *Kolokol*.

---

122 GLA Karlsruhe, 250/12, Collection, Bl. 32. The previous quotation can be found in ibid., Bl. 45.

123 GLA Karlsruhe 250/10, Bl. 372–9: testimony of the university police officer (*Pedell*) Emil Seyfart to the University Court of Leipzig, 15 July 1861 (copy), Bl. 374. Becker was not very considerate in getting his newspaper, as Seyfart testifies: several times, Becker sat down 'in Seidel's pub very close to me, took the newspaper away from me with the words: "Are you reading?", ignored me completely for a while, but later apologized as if he had only just recognized me'. Ibid., Bl. 376. On the concept and the function of reading societies in Germany, see Siemann, *The German Revolution of 1848–49*, 121.

124 GLA Karlsruhe, 250/9, Becker's interrogation, 26 July 1861, afternoon, Bl. 254–5.

Thus, as a reader, Becker consumed newspapers both intensely and extensively.

But it did not end with the purely passive reading of newspapers. Becker produced sheets 'with excerpts from different newspapers and with his own notations of ideas on German conditions', which he wanted to use as material for articles in Russian papers – a project which he gave up on after some time.[125] In order to earn some extra money he did translate a number of articles and wrote his own articles and essays which he offered to newspapers.[126] Newspapers and the world of public opinion were in consequence an integral part of Oskar Wilhelm Becker's life in many ways. He was entirely lacking, however, in any practical experience of political involvement.

Becker, Booth and Karakozov all saw themselves connected to political goals that were also the goals of significant social movements in their own time. These movements used various means in their struggles, ranging from institutionalized politics to collective military violence. Becker, Booth and Karakozov were engaged in these struggles to varying degrees. While Dmitry Vladimirovich Karakozov participated in the activities of the radical Russian student movement both intellectually and practically, John Wilkes Booth's contribution remained at best marginal both within the Know-Nothing movement and in terms of Confederate political and military activities, and Oskar Wilhelm Becker's political work was purely theoretical.

None of the three attackers could fall back on a store of experience or networks at the time of their acts of violence, in contrast to Felice Orsini and John Brown. None of the three imitators had active movement experience in dealing with media and publicity, as for example in writing books or articles in support of their cause, through connections with journalists or through public lectures. The press and the public might have showered John Wilkes Booth with the attention of a star, but this publicity was the result of his personality and his work as an actor, and

---

125 Ibid., 254.

126 In addition to the essay on the Duke of Kurland Ernst Johann von Biron, which he had tried in vain to submit to the *Kolokol*, there is also a treatise on a Russian painter which he translated from Russian into German, and which actually appeared in an illustrated newspaper. It remains unclear which illustrated newspaper is referred to here. Possible candidates would be the *Berliner Illustrierte Montags-Zeitung* or *Über Land und Meer: Allgemeine illustrierte Zeitung* from Stuttgart.

was not connected to his political commitments. Finally, none of the three imitators had any experience with political violence, whether through previous attempts at rebellion, ostentatiously brutal assassinations or military conflict.[127]

Personal crises

As shown above, while social movements and the political situation were of decisive importance for the three imitators and their acts of violence, they had relatively little experience in these movements. What did play a greater role than in the cases of Felice Orsini and John Brown were the personal crises faced by Becker, Booth and Karakozov.

Becker anguished over his inability to fully integrate into German life. Having been raised by German immigrants in Odessa, his life between two worlds became a fundamental problem of identity for him. Although he was born in Russia, he had 'been imprinted with such a love for Germany' that he always gravitated towards it, as he reported under interrogation. While he had a 'completely German disposition', he was nevertheless 'always seen somehow as a foreigner'.[128] Even his Saxon relatives believed that he 'didn't really fit into German society'. Maybe, Becker thought, he had come to Germany too late to be able to fully adapt to German social conditions.[129] As things were, Becker was indeed considered a bit strange and had few social contacts outside his family circle.

On top of the identity crisis came his existential crisis. Becker began to suspect that, because he was seen as a foreigner, he had almost no professional path open to him: 'As a result I found few indications that I would later be able to make a career in Germany,' he stated in his interrogation.[130] At the same time, he was totally animated by the idea of doing something for Germany. While still a pupil in secondary school he had attempted to join the Prussian military, and had registered with the

---

127 These statements would have to be revised should it be proved that Booth also participated in the militant assaults of the Know-Nothing movement, as he would then have had concrete experience in effecting political violence.

128 GLA Karlsruhe, 250/9, Becker's interrogation, 27 July 1861, afternoon, Bl. 283–4.

129 GLA Karlsruhe, 250/9, Becker's interrogation, 29 July 1861, afternoon, Bl. 323.

130 GLA Karlsruhe, 250/9, Becker's interrogation, 27 July 1861, afternoon, Bl. 284.

Habsburg forces after the outbreak of the Austrian–Italian War. But the war was already over by the time he could even be enlisted.[131] This is why Becker then continued with his studies in Leipzig, aiming to become an interpreter at an embassy in the Orient. He concentrated on the culture and history of the Near and Middle East and took Persian, Arabic and Turkish as secondary subjects. But the nearer Becker came to his goal, 'the more I came to regret ever having taken up these plans for diplomatic assignment in the Orient, because the necessary consequence of completing this plan would be my separation from Germany'. He also doubted that he would be able to do enough for Germany by going down this path. Assassinating the king of Prussia looked like a way out of this situation: 'I came to the opinion that I could nevertheless do something beneficial for Germany by carrying out the assassination of the king of Prussia and thereby act in a way conducive to German unification.'[132] He believed this was a worthy goal since he, if his act 'brought about a beneficial effect, would be able to achieve more than by dedicatedly working towards this goal over the course of a long life'.[133] Becker considered an assassination to be a chance to do something for Germany as a foreigner in Germany. The fact that the death penalty awaited him might have also seemed to be a way out of his crises of identity and purpose.

The imminent defeat of the Confederate States of America also brought John Wilkes Booth to a crisis in his identity and purpose. He felt responsible, because he had only made an insufficient effort towards fulfilling his duty to fight for the Confederacy: 'But dearest Mother, though, I owe you all, *there* is another duty,' he explained to her in his farewell letter of November 1864:

A noble duty for the sake of liberty and humanity due to my Country – For, four years I have lived (I may say) A *slave* in the north (A favored slave its true, but no less hateful to me on that account.) Not daring to express my thoughts or sentiments ... I have cursed my wilful idleness, And begun to deem myself a coward and to despise my own existence.

---

131 Ibid.
132 Ibid., Bl. 285–6.
133 Ibid., Bl. 279.

Thus the moment had come when fate was leading him away from her, 'to do what work I can for a poor oppressed downtrodden people'.[134] John Wilkes Booth felt duty-bound to act for the cause of the Confederacy in order not to lose all respect for himself in the face of its defeat.

With Lee's capitulation and the end of the Confederate States fast approaching, Booth also came to the realization that he had lost the nation which he wanted to be a part of, the object of his patriotism. He wrote on this in his farewell letter 'To Whom It May Concern': 'How I have loved the *old flag* [of the United States, that is, of the Union] can never, now, be known.' A few years before this, no flag in the 'entire world' had been so 'pure and spotless'.

> But I have of late been seeing and hearing of the *bloody deeds* of which She has *been made, the emblem* [probably an allusion to the Atlanta campaign, which was over by the beginning of September 1864]. And would shudder to think how changed she had grown . . . till now (in my eyes) her once bright red stripes look like *bloody gashes* on the face of Heaven.[135]

After the brutal acts of war perpetrated by Union generals in the southern states, Booth was neither able nor willing to identify with the North any more. 'Great God! I have no longer a country!' he exclaimed on 14 April on Pennsylvania Avenue, as a column of 440 prisoners of war from General Ewell's army marched by him. The army included some of his comrades from the days of the Richmond Grays.[136]

In Dmitry Vladimirovich Karakozov's case, too, a personal crisis can partially explain why he was prepared to risk his life and to make the leap from idea to action. While ill after travelling back to Moscow from the provinces in 1865, he was admitted at the medical clinic of Moscow University in November. The doctors admitted him and took him under

134 Booth, 'To Mary Ann Holmes Booth [Philadelphia, November] 1864', 130. Also see Alford on this, *Fortune's Fool*, 169, 175, 199–200.

135 Booth, 'To Whom It May Concern [Philadelphia, November] 1864', 126.

136 Testimony of John Mathews, 'Impeachment of the President', *House Report Seven* (serial set 1314), 40th Cong., 1st sess. (1867), 782–5, as quoted in the commentary of Rhodehamel and Taper to Booth, 'To the Editors of the *National Intelligencer*. Washington, D.C., 14 April 1865', in footnote, 151. On this see Alford, *Fortune's Fool*, 260–1. On Booth's temporary enlistment in the Richmond Grays, see below, pp. 500–1.

their care for two months.[137] In the middle of December 1865, one month after his admission, his condition worsened dramatically. He told his friends that he wanted to poison himself since he would die soon in any case. When they asked him what the matter was, he told them that the director at the university clinic had explained to his students that he – Karakozov – had *febris cerebralis* (a type of 'brain inflammation') and that this illness was life-threatening. The friends then consulted with the advanced medical student responsible for Karakozov. He tried to ease their concerns but confirmed nonetheless that, according to the latest research by a German professor of medicine named Felix Niemeyer, the majority of cases which showed the symptoms diagnosed in Karakozov ended in mental aberration and suicide.[138] From a contemporary medical and psychological perspective, the question of what kind of illness the director and his student might have been talking about is difficult to answer with any precision.

As Karakozov's physical state stabilized at the beginning of the new year, he was released from the clinic in mid-January 1866. But he now felt, at least psychologically, worse than before. He bought himself a pistol and would stay the whole day alone in his room without speaking a word to anyone, or wander around Moscow brooding over suicide. 'In the middle of the great fasting period' – that is, on or around 23 February – he went to St Petersburg for consultations with various doctors and medical institutions. There, too, no one was able to help him, at least in his opinion.[139]

---

137 See Klevenskii and Kotel'nikov, *Pokushenie Karakozova*, vol. 1, 298, note 10 to page 10; and Verhoeven, *The Odd Man Karakozov*, 137.

138 See Zagibalov's testimony in Klevenskii and Kotel'nikov, *Pokushenie Karakozova*, vol. 1, 89, as well as 289, note 10 to page 10; and Verhoeven, *The Odd Man Karakozov*, 138.

139 See Ishutin's testimony in Klevenskii and Kotel'nikov, *Pokushenie Karakozova*, vol. 1, 28–30, especially 29–30; Kobylin's testimony in ibid., 227–36; and, on it, Verhoeven, *The Odd Man Karakozov*, 139–41, whose dating of Karakozov's trip to St Petersburg at the beginning of February is ultimately unconvincing. Karakozov was still in Moscow at the beginning of Russian Orthodox carnival (*maslenitsa*), which lasted from 31 January to 6 February in 1866, and he himself indicated in his court testimony that he travelled to Petersburg at the end of February. A statement by Iurasov confirms this, and the indictment, where the quotation here in the text above is taken from, settles on this information. See Karakozov's court testimony on 24 August 1866, printed in Klevenskii and Kotel'nikov, *Pokushenie Karakozova*, vol. 1, 238; Iurasov's testimony on 22 August 1866, 131–4, 133; and the indictment, ibid., 6–10, 8.

In this situation of incurable illness (whether imagined or not), tsaricide, which had previously been a merely theoretical discussion, became a real possibility for Karakozov. He began to reproach his friends, saying that all their activities could only 'achieve philanthropic goals', 'but that a more or less severe, decisive fact' was necessary (*rezkii . . . reshitel'nyi fakt*). What he meant by this was 'some kind of decisive step' (*kakoi-nibud' reshitel'nyi shag*), as Ishutin would explain later to the judge from the Supreme Criminal Court, Prince Ol'denburgskii, who was not yet familiar with Johann Gottlieb Fichte's philosophy of the act and Charles (aka Karl) Follen's calls to action (that is, assassinations of princes), namely 'tsaricide'.[140] Under interrogation Karakozov later explicitly described how the decisive impulse for his assassination attempt came out of his illness: 'Initially it led me to the thought of suicide, but later, as the goal emerged of not dying for nothing, and rather of using it for the people, I was filled with the energy to carry out my plans.'[141] Just like Oskar Wilhelm Becker and John Wilkes Booth, Dmitry Vladimirovich Karakozov attempted to give meaning to his life through his act of violence.

Plans and their secret preparation

All three imitators planned their violent acts and prepared for them in secret. The level of planning, however, was not up to the level of their models; that is, their preparations took up less time and were less thorough than the plans and preparations undertaken by Felice Orsini and John Brown.

---

140 Ishutin's testimony in Klevenskii and Kotel'nikov, *Pokushenie Karakozova*, vol. 1, 69. Also see Verhoeven, *The Odd Man Karakozov*, Chapter 4, which cites parts of this quote as an epigraph (85), and pp. 492–3 in this volume. On the emergence of the philosophy of the act in German idealism and the reception of these ideas in Karl Follen's circle (to which Karl Ludwig Sand also belonged), see in particular Ries, 'Making Terrorism Thinkable'; as well as George S. Williamson, '"Thought Is in Itself a Dangerous Operation": The Campaign against "Revolutionary Machinations" in Germany, 1819–1828', *German Studies Review* 38/2 (2015), 285–306, 296.

141 Karakozov's statements to the investigatory commission of 16 April 1866, in Shilov, 'Pokushenie Karakozova 4 aprelia 1866 g.', 94. Also see the repetition of these statements (ibid., 95); as well as his testimony before the court on 18 August 1866, printed in Klevenskii and Kotel'nikov, *Pokushenie Karakozova*, vol. 1, 11. Claudia Verhoeven thematizes this connection in *The Odd Man Karakozov*, Chapter 6.

Oskar Wilhelm Becker's plans required the least time. During his interrogation, however, he put a strong emphasis on the intellectual development and preparation for his act, since in his eyes they refuted the supposition that he was of unsound mind. As he explained to the examining magistrate, he had already been convinced for a long time that the king of Prussia needed to be killed; for a few weeks he had then toyed with the idea: 'I myself wanted to sacrifice myself to this purpose.' He had made the 'firm decision' only in the week before, he said, and then began at once with the necessary preparations.[142]

These preparations ranged from purchasing a photo of the king, a pair of glasses ('in order to see better in the performance of my act'), a new black frock with trousers, and a new black hat ('to be better dressed'); to buying two double-barrelled pistols with powder horn, powder, bullets, primers and wadding and doing shooting practice at the Leipzig shooting range; and, finally, to intellectual preparations as well: looking up the entries on 'Charlotte Corday', 'François Ravaillac', and 'Karl Sand' (the assassins of Jean-Paul Marat, Henri IV of France and August von Kotzebue respectively), as well as 'Baden[-Baden]' in the *Konversationslexikon* (encyclopedia of conversational lexicon) at the Brockhaus bookstore in Leipzig.[143] In all likelihood, Felice Orsini and John Brown had not yet made it into the encyclopedias, but Becker had read about them in the newspapers.

Becker learned from the Thursday newspapers that the king of Prussia had left for Baden-Baden and that he had also already arrived there. The very next day, Friday, 12 July, around noon – as he stated to the examining magistrate – he took a train from Leipzig to Frankfurt, arriving early on Saturday. From there he travelled at 10 a.m. to Baden-Baden on the next departing express train and arrived there on Saturday afternoon

---

142 See GLA Karlsruhe, 250/8, Oskar Wilhelm Becker's interrogation before the Baden-Baden District Court, 14 July 1861, Bl. 38–46, quotes at Bl. 44; GLA Karlsruhe, 250/9, Becker's interrogation, 5 August 1861, morning, Bl. 445–6.

143 See GLA Karlsruhe, 250/8, Becker's interrogation, 14 July 1861, Bl. 45–6; GLA Karlsruhe, 250/8, Becker's interrogation, 20 July 1861, morning, Bl. 248–50; GLA Karlsruhe, 250/9, Becker's interrogation, 22 July 1861, afternoon, Bl. 10; GLA Karlsruhe, 250/9, Becker's interrogation, 27 July 1861, afternoon, Bl. 289–90; and GLA Karlsruhe, 250/9, Becker's interrogation, 29 July 1861, afternoon, Bl. 323. The quote regarding his glasses is in GLA Karlsruhe, 250/8, Becker's interrogation, 20 July 1861, afternoon, Bl. 270.

shortly after 3:30 p.m.[144] Thus Becker had been considering the idea of committing the assassination 'for a few weeks' and spent one week on practical preparations.

With between eight and nine months of preparation for his act, John Wilkes Booth invested the most time. In this he oriented his plans – similarly to John Brown – around the political and practical situation. Beginning in August 1864, Booth planned to abduct Lincoln and bring him to the South. This was an idea that was common among supporters of the Confederacy at that time, and Booth was not the only one to pursue it. After being carried off to the South, the Union president was to be exchanged for Confederate soldiers being held as prisoners of war in the North who were desperately needed if the war was to be contin-ued.[145] For this plan to work, it would have to be assumed that Lincoln would be kept alive.

But even this plan transitioned naturally into an assassination plot. As John Rhodehamel and Louise Taper have argued convincingly, anyone who planned to abduct Lincoln had to take into account the risk that he might die in the process. Due to Abraham Lincoln's legendary height and strength, any kidnapper would have to assume that the presi-dent would defend himself effectively and vigorously against any attempt at capture.[146] Furthermore, the thought of assassinating Lincoln had become an *idée fixe* for John Wilkes Booth since the beginning of 1863 – when Lincoln signed the Emancipation Proclamation – and from autumn 1864 might have already been an alternative he seriously consid-ered: at the end of October, Booth travelled to Montreal for a meeting with Confederate agents, where he spoke at length with George Nicholas

---

144 GLA Karlsruhe, 250/8, Becker's interrogation, 14 July 1861, Bl. 46–7. According to this information, Becker must have left Leipzig on Friday on a train scheduled for 11:08 a.m. and travelled without changing trains via Corbetha (now Korbetha), Kassel and Giessen to Frankfurt am Main, where his train arrived at 9:40 a.m. on Saturday. There he could have taken an express train to Mannheim at 10:30 a.m. In Heidelberg he had a connection at 1 p.m. for an express train towards Basel, with which he could arrive in what is today the Oos district of Baden-Baden at 3:08 p.m. At 3:10 p.m., there was a connection between Oos and Baden-Baden, with a given duration of eight to ten minutes. See the timetables no. 48 and no. 57–8 in the *Eisenbahn- Post- und Dampfschiff-Cours-Buch 1861*.

145 See Rhodehamel and Taper, 'A Star of the First Magnitude', 71; Kauffman, *American Brutus*, 132–5; and Alford, *Fortune's Fool*, Chapter 7 and 199–213.

146 John H. Rhodehamel and Louise Taper, 'Might Makes Right', in Rhodehamel and Taper, '*Right or Wrong, God Judge Me*', 118.

Sanders, a former diplomat in the Pierce administration, who had been involved in a conspiracy against Napoleon III in 1853 and had personally met Felice Orsini in London.[147]

In the following winter months, it became clear to Booth that implementing the hostage plan was more difficult than he had anticipated for a number of reasons. An abduction attempt after Lincoln's inauguration in March 1865, for example, failed when the president changed his schedule at short notice. Time was slipping away from Booth and his co-conspirators: the war was coming to an end and it was becoming increasingly clear that the southern states would no longer be in the position to turn things around. On 3 April, Confederate troops evacuated their capital of Richmond and fled further to the South and the West. It was too late to take Lincoln hostage and exchange him for Confederate soldiers; Booth had invested his time and money in the plan for nothing.[148]

Thus it only required a small impetus for Booth to go from planning a kidnapping to planning a terrorist assassination. This came on 11 April 1865. Union victory brought forth the question of Reconstruction: the question of how the southern states would be rebuilt and reintegrated into the Union. One of the primary issues of Reconstruction was how to carry out emancipation in the former slave states. Emancipation was a two-step process, legal emancipation followed by the social and economic implementation of emancipation so that it became a reality. The major question for the process of Reconstruction therefore was how to implement freedom.[149] By the end of the war, President Abraham Lincoln still had no clear ideas on how to do this. After the news of Lee's capitulation reached the inhabitants of Washington on the morning of 10 April, the White House was surrounded by people who continuously called out for the president over the course of the day. Lincoln finally came out to address a few words to the crowd but put off a longer

---

147 Ibid., 119; Kauffman, *American Brutus*, 140–1, 342–3; as well as Alford, *Fortune's Fool*, 166, 187. On Sanders and his acquaintance with Orsini, also see Lause, *A Secret Society History of the Civil War*, especially 1, 17, 92–3, 103, 123.

148 On this see Rhodehamel and Tapper, 'Might Makes Right', 119–22; Kauffman, *American Brutus*, Chapters 8–10; as well as Alford, *Fortune's Fool*, 213–17, 231–43, 255.

149 See Heideking and Mauch, *Geschichte der USA*, Chapter 4.3; Finzsch, Horton and Horton, *Von Benin nach Baltimore*, 315–26; and especially Eric Foner, *Reconstruction: America's Unfinished Revolution, 1863–1877* (New York: History Book Club, 2005).

communication until his speech on the next day that would be part of the official victory festivities.[150]

This speech on 11 April, in which Lincoln wanted to present his first reflections on plans for Reconstruction, was important to the president, and he prepared it with care. There was the burning and controversial question of what place African Americans were to have in the future of American society. Since regiments of African American volunteers had fought on the side of the Union, black civil rights activists and radical Republicans were demanding that African American men should now be given citizenship and the right to vote. Lincoln did not want to go quite that far. He declared to the crowd in front of the White House, 'I would myself prefer that it [the ballot] were now conferred on the very intelligent, and on those who serve our cause as soldiers.' This nevertheless made him the first American president to ever publicly support voting rights for African Americans and to reflect on what the emancipation of the slaves could mean for their political rights.[151]

Booth was standing in the crowd on 11 April and listened to the speech which Lincoln delivered from the White House. For him this speech became the spark to act. 'That means nigger citizenship,' he is supposed to have said to his companion and co-conspirator. 'Now, by God! I'll put him through.' At this he turned around and pushed his way through the crowd.[152] In contrast to Becker, Booth did not need to buy a weapon or practise firing, as he had been dealing with weapons at least since his education at the military academy, and was, moreover, a good shot. Three days later, on 14 April 1865, he shot Abraham Lincoln in Ford's Theatre.

For Dmitry Vladimirovich Karakozov, we have evidence of two phases in which he made secret plans: the weeks after his release from the clinic in mid-January and the period starting from the second

---

150 See Abraham Lincoln, 'Response to Serenade, April 10, 1865', in *The Collected Works of Abraham Lincoln*, vol. 8, 393–4. On Lincoln's first efforts for Reconstruction, see Randall and Current, *Lincoln the President*, vol. 4: *Last Full Measure*, 344–8; and Donald, *Lincoln*, 571–81.

151 Lincoln, 'Last Public Address, April 11, 1865', 403. On the significance of the speech for Lincoln, see Donald, *Lincoln*, 580–5.

152 Lincoln, 'Last Public Address, April 11, 1865', 403. John Wilkes Booth is quoted from Kauffman, *American Brutus*, 210. Also in Alford, *Fortune's Fool*, 256–7, quote at 257.

week of March 1866. Together his plans amounted to no more than two and a half months, with his preparations intensifying in the last three weeks before his attack on the tsar. The question of how to trigger the outbreak of a revolution had long been the subject of Karakozov's discussions in his circle of friends. Among other ideas, tsaricide had come up as a theoretical possibility in July 1865, on the principle of 'the end justifies the means.' The formulation of this principle, which has ancient roots, was taken up again with some effect by Charles Follen and other representatives of the radical fraternities in Giessen, Jena and Heidelberg in their justifications for the political murder of German princes. But it was only when Karakozov began to believe he was incurably ill that the option of assassinating the tsar became thinkable as a practical possibility. When he took off for St Petersburg at the end of February, Ishutin was already concerned that his brother wanted to try to kill the tsar. He based this concern on a number of compelling hints which he presented to the court: Karakozov's poor health after his release from the hospital in mid-January, his reproach of philanthropy in combination with his call for a 'decisive act' (that is, tsaricide), his purchase of a pistol, and his trip to St Petersburg at the end of February.[153] According to this reconstruction of events, Karakozov would then have come up with the idea of an attack on the tsar by mid-January, or about one and a half to two and a half months before the assassination attempt.

But it was only when Karakozov believed he had confirmed that he was incurably sick that he actually decided to carry out the attack. He appears to have received this confirmation in the second week of March. Karakozov initially sought out various medical institutions in St

---

153 See in particular Ishutin's testimony from 20 August 1866 and Klevenskii, 'Predislovie', in Klevenskii and Kotel'nikov, *Pokushenie Karakozova*, vol. 1, 70–2 and v, as well as Shilov, 'Pokushenie Karakozova 4 aprelia 1866 g.', 91–2; and Venturi, *Roots of Revolution*, 335. On Follen see, most recently, Williamson, 'Thought Is in Itself a Dangerous Operation', 296; as well as Ries, 'Making Terrorism Thinkable'. The chronology of his discharge from the hospital, his purchase of a pistol and trip to St Petersburg follows Verhoeven, *The Odd Man Karakozov*, 136–43. She, however, does not pose the question raised here as to when it was precisely that Karakozov's idea of committing an assassination attempt on the tsar became concrete for him, as Verhoeven is above all interested in Karakozov's psycho-physical condition. On the period in which Karakozov formulated his reproach of philanthropy, see Ishutin's testimony Klevenskii and Kotel'nikov, *Pokushenie Karakozova*, vol. 1, 68–70.

Petersburg, including the Therapeutic Clinic of the Medical–Surgical Academy. As he stated in court, Karakozov came to this clinic 'to be cured'. There he met the doctor Alexander Alexandrovich Kobylin, one year his junior, who had just finished his studies and took over his treatment.[154] Kobylin prescribed some medicine to his patient, but he came back a few days later and complained that it wasn't helping. Another doctor took over his treatment, diagnosed him with hypochondria and refused to change the medication. When Karakozov appeared again, Kobylin tried to treat him with electric shocks. On 11 March he prescribed him morphine.[155] When Karakozov ran out of money, he was allowed to move into Kobylin's apartment and sleep and eat there 'in the sixth week' of Orthodox fasting – which in 1866 fell on the third week of March, or from 13 to 19 March 1866.[156]

Over the course of the treatment, a bond of trust formed between Karakozov and his young doctor. They began to get into discussions, especially about Karakozov's health and politics.[157] One day Karakozov

154 Karakozov's testimony, 24 August 1866, reprinted in Klevenskii and Kotel'nikov, *Pokushenie Karakozova*, vol. 1, 236–45, quotation at 236. The information on Kobylin follows Shilov, 'Pokushenie Karakozova 4 aprelia 1866 g.', 130, note 2 to page 95. To the question of when he came to the clinic, Karakozov testified that he had already met Kobylin 'shortly after his arrival from Moscow', and, upon further inquiry, mentioned the fourth or fifth week of Lent, that is, the period from Sunday, 27 February to Saturday, 12 March 1866 (ibid., 238). Kobylin in his testimony gave Monday of the fifth week of fasting, that is, 7 March 1866 (see Kobylin's testimony, 24 August 1866, reprinted in Klevenskii and Kotel'nikov, *Pokushenie Karakozova*, vol. 1, 227–36, 229). Verhoeven, *The Odd Man Karakozov*, 140, dates the meeting to the 'end of the first week of March', that is, 4 or 5 March 1866, but does not provide a citation. In view of Kobylin's strategy during testimony, as he generally tried to minimize his points of contact with Karakozov and to present them as motivated purely by professional and humanitarian reasons, and in view of concurring testimony on what else happened in this time, the earlier point indicated by Karakozov appears to be more probable, that is, the period after Sunday, 27 February 1866.

155 See Kobylin's and Karakozov's testimony, 24 August 1866, reprinted in Klevenskii and Kotel'nikov, *Pokushenie Karakozova*, vol. 1, 229–30, 237; as well as Verhoeven, *The Odd Man Karakozov*, 141.

156 This dating follows Karakozov's testimony (24 August 1866, reprinted in Klevenskii and Kotel'nikov, *Pokushenie Karakozova*, vol. 1, 237). Kobylin named the Monday of the seventh week of fasting, that is, 21 March 1866, as the date of Karakozov's move-in (testimony, 24 August 1866, in Klevenskii and Kotel'nikov, *Pokushenie Karakozova*, vol. 1, 231). Also in Verhoeven, *The Odd Man Karakozov*, 141–2.

157 On this see Kobylin's and Karakozov's testimony on 24 August 1866, reprinted in Klevenskii and Kotel'nikov, *Pokushenie Karakozova*, vol. 1, 230–2, 237–40.

went so far as to venture the opinion – as he would later testify in court – 'that propaganda by words [*slovesnaia propaganda*] was not enough . . . and thereby hinted that propaganda by deed [*fakticheskaia propaganda*] is necessary, that crimes are necessary, that assassinations are necessary, but I did not state this directly'.[158] He seemed to feel he had reached an understanding with Kobylin when he made this statement, as the doctor in his turn told Karakozov more or less openly that there was a group in St Petersburg connected to the younger brother of the tsar (and in the case of tsaricide that meant a potential heir to the throne), Grand Duke Konstantin Nikolayevich Romanov, and that this group desired 'the welfare of the working people'.[159] This information was pivotal for Karakozov's decision – outside any ideology – to go ahead with the assassination. He later stated before the Investigative Commission (Sledstvennaia Komissiia), 'This thought emerged for me at the time when I heard about the existence of a party that wanted to bring about a coup to benefit Grand Duke Konstantin Nikolayevich.' In addition to this he also named his illness as important.[160] Besides this, Karakozov spoke with Kobylin about the state of his health and – as Karakozov said in court – also, finally, about his intention

to commit the crime if, indeed, the state of my health worsens, and I asked him, among other things, what course my illness might take, to which he did not give a satisfactory reply, and that's why, following our discussions, when I saw that I didn't have long to live and over-whelmed by my difficult condition, I told him my intention of committing the crime to his face.[161]

158 Karakozov's court testimony on 24 August 1866, reprinted in Klevenskii and Kotel'nikov, *Pokushenie Karakozova*, vol. 1, 240. On Karakozov's idea of *fakticheskaia propaganda* see the discussion above at p. 487, and further at 529–30.

159 Karakozov's testimony, 16 April 1866, printed in Shilov, 'Pokushenie Karakozova 4 aprelia 1866 g', 94. On this also see Verhoeven, *The Odd Man Karakozov*, 145–6.

160 Information provided by Karakozov to the Investigative Commission, 16 April 1866, printed in Shilov, 'Pokushenie Karakozova 4 aprelia 1866 g', 94–5, quotation at 94. There were also strategical defence reasons that led Karakozov to emphasize this motive more and more over time. See Verhoeven, *The Odd Man Karakozov*, 144–5.

161 Karakozov's court testimony, 24 August 1866, in Klevenskii and Kotel'nikov, *Pokushenie Karakozova*, vol. 1, 237; also quoted in Verhoeven, *The Odd Man Karakozov*, 146.

Karakozov went to Moscow again for Holy Week (20 to 27 March 1866), where he met with his circle of friends on Monday, 21 March; by Wednesday, 23 March, he was already back in St Petersburg.[162]

It is not easy to reconstruct *when exactly* the decisive conversation between Karakozov and Kobylin took place, and therefore also when Karakozov made his final decision to carry out the attack.[163] There is evidence, however, that around seven in the evening on Sunday, 13 March 1866, Karakozov walked up and down between the University of St Petersburg and the second Cadet building and passed out the hand-written copies of his proclamation 'To My Worker Friends' ('Druz'iam rabochim') to students. On the following Sunday, 20 March, the same proclamation was found at the St Petersburg Putilin factory and was given to the authorities after the assassination attempt.[164] Later in this chapter there will be a more detailed consideration of the proclamation and how Karakozov produced and spread it. Here, the only relevant fact is that Karakozov wrote political proclamations to prepare the way for his assassination and disseminated them, and that he had already announced a date of no later than 5 April 1866 for the assassination, writing this on the envelope of the proclamation found in the Putilin factory, albeit in convoluted form.[165]

When one takes all the evidence together, the following picture emerges: after his trip from Moscow to St Petersburg, Karakozov

162 See the indictment, reprinted in Klevenskii and Kotel'nikov, *Pokushenie Karakozova*, vol. 1, 9; and the many references to this journey in Karakozov's testimony on 24 August 1866, in Klevenskii and Kotel'nikov, *Pokushenie Karakozova*, vol. 1, 237. Venturi, *Roots of Revolution*, 347, gives 25 March for the date of the meeting in Moscow and 29 March for his return; Verhoeven, *The Odd Man Karakozov*, 141–2, indicates 24 March for Karakozov's departure and 30 March for his return, without citing a source.

163 Claudia Verhoeven's account gives the impression that Karakozov's decision to carry out the assassination was made only shortly before the act of violence itself: in a conversation with Kobylin on 30 March or even only on 4 April 1866 in a depressive delirium (*The Odd Man Karakozov*, 142–3, 145–6). Her account assumes – contradicting the explicit indications in the sources – that there was only a single 'fateful conversation' between Kobylin and Karakozov. Her interpretation is based on a different reconstruction of the data and ignores the sources that indicate Karakozov's active preparations for the assassination.

164 See the indictment, reprinted in Klevenskii and Kotel'nikov, *Pokushenie Karakozova*, vol. 1, 9; as well as Shilov, 'Iz istorii revoliutsionnogo dvizheniia 1860-kh gg.', 164.

165 On this see below, pp. 514, 518–20.

initially sought a cure for his illness and held out the possibility of continuing other forms of political activity should recovery turn out to be possible. In St Petersburg he met Kobylin and they began their discussions. On Friday, 11 March, Kobylin prescribed him morphine. During Holy Week, the sixth week of fasting, which began on Sunday, 13 March, Karakozov moved into Kobylin's apartment. After this date Karakozov seems not to have made any further attempts to find medical treatment. At some point in the course of the second week of March – or between 7 March and 13 March 1866 – he gave up all hope of being cured. Furthermore, the idea of assassinating the tsar became more plausible to him with the information about Konstantin's faction, so that he now devoted himself entirely to this political goal. By Sunday, 13 March 1866, he was already passing out his proclamation at the university; in the proclamation from Sunday, 20 March 1866, he announced his intention to assassinate the tsar by 5 April. Karakozov thus dedicated at least three weeks to the direct planning and preparation of his act of violence.

At this intermediary point, it can be noted that both the imitators themselves (Becker, Booth and Karakozov) and the acts of violence they carried out meet the criteria for the definition and the causes of terrorist violence laid out in the first part of this book. As the two previous chapters have shown, their assassination attempts meet the definition of 'political violence against a political order from below which is well planned, meant to be shocking and supposed to spread feelings of insecurity and fear, but which also generates sympathy and support' and is directed 'bottom-up' against an opponent who – in principle – is much more powerful. Whether these assassination attempts were also *supposed* to 'spread feelings of insecurity and fear' and at the same time 'generate sympathy and support' (even if it did not turn out as intended) is the subject of the following analysis.[166]

The supporting criteria that we introduced in the first chapter were likewise fulfilled by the perpetrators: all three belonged to the intellectual elite in their respective societies, were intensely engaged with

---

166 Waldmann, *Terrorismus*, 12; as translated in Carola Dietze and Claudia Verhoeven, 'Introduction', paper presented at the conference on Terrorism and Modernity: Global Perspectives on Nineteenth Century Political Violence, Tulane University, New Orleans, Louisiana, 23–6 October 2008, 6. Also see the corresponding remarks in Chapter 1, pp. 47–9.

Further development by imitators   497

political questions and were affected early on by the central political struggles of their time regarding the establishment of the nation and freedom. They were, furthermore, active in the context of social movements that were formed in relation to these struggles: Becker in connection to the German national movement, Booth to the radical right-wing and counterrevolutionary Know-Nothings and the Fire-Eaters, and Karakozov to the social-revolutionary student movement. All three imitators understood the political situation as blocked and saw the legal possibilities of political action as too limited and ineffective as a result of this blockage; all three sought a form of sense-making and accepted a great degree of risk.

When compared with Felice Orsini and John Brown, Becker, Booth and Karakozov do nevertheless fulfil some of these criteria less adequately or completely. In their respective social movements, the imitators were not to the manor born – unlike Orsini and Brown – and they also accumulated less experience in these movements, especially with respect to dealing with the public, the media and violence. They had had no share in the collective violence that preceded their acts; in their cases that violence had been carried out by others. The imitators prepared for their acts of violence less thoroughly and carefully, and their political analyses were less incisive. By contrast, their personal crises took on greater significance.

What emerges from this is that the imitators seem generally less politically and socially savvy than Orsini or Brown, as the forms of their political involvement were more of a passive, receptive and theoretical–discursive nature at the time of their assassination attempts. The essays, speeches and proclamations which all three imitators wrote are emblems for this political life that remained unfulfilled: Becker's essays were not published, Booth's speeches never had a real audience and Becker, Booth and Karakozov's justifications for their acts were only able to achieve uncertain success in reaching their intended audience. These testimonies of their desperate and urgent involvement with politics remained, right up to their assassination attempts, in the fantasy realm of the personal and private, and, after their attacks, drifted into the archives to reach the public only decades later after being exhumed by historians.

Another point is decisive here: without models, none of the three imitators would have carried out their assassination attempts. It was only after learning about Felice Orsini's and John Brown's acts of violence – even if mediated through the figure of Rakhmetov – that they came to see the idea of a violent act as attractive. The violence of Orsini and Brown therefore represented central reference points for Becker, Booth and Karakozov in their thought and action. The decisive significance of the models also means, conversely, that Becker, Booth and Karakozov have to be integrated into the history of the emergence of terrorism on these grounds – and this aspect remains independent of their invention of the claim of responsibility or how individually successful they were in imitatively adopting, implementing or advancing the tactics employed by those who had discovered or invented them.

Orsini and Brown: interpersonal, medial and transmedial models

In contrast to Brown's reception of Orsini and similar to Chernyshevsky's reception of Brown, all three imitators left behind explicit references to their models. Among them, however, the orientation of the references varies: Becker, Booth and Karakozov aligned themselves primarily either with Felice Orsini or with John Brown. And, in their content, these references reflect the connections to their respective political concerns. Becker, who felt strongly about the national unification of Germany, saw Orsini as a model because the latter had triggered the process of forming an Italian nation state, precisely by means of his assassination attempt, just as Becker hoped to do for Germany. For Dmitry Vladimirovich Karakozov, it was the figure of John Brown, as mediated through Chernyshevsky's reception and interpretation, that provided him with a decisive example. To him, the crucial issue was that of emancipating and improving the lives of an unfree population, no less a problem in Russia than in the United States. In this sense, the greatest level of abstraction reveals itself in John Wilkes Booth's reception of his models – most of all John Brown but also, to a lesser extent, Felice Orsini – as he recognized that Brown's violent tactics in support of emancipation could be separated from their ends and that these means could be used equally well in opposition to Brown's goals. Here the former governor of Virginia, Henry A. Wise, had already preceded him in providing an example of this political repurposing.[167]

Just as varied were the ways in which the imitators learned about their predecessors. This process was dependent on the respective spatial proximity and distance between the imitator and his model, as well as on the media they used, and therefore also dependent on the general conditions of politics and media in their countries.

Karakozov's path of engagement with his model was especially rich in mediation. John Brown was a figure he learned about through other media, specifically through reading Chernyshevsky's novel *What Is to Be Done?*. As discussed in Chapter 5, the interpretation embedded in the novel is based primarily on representations from Western European newspapers, and these were themselves based on reports from American newspapers or journalists, as well as letters from readers.

Karakozov and his revolutionary student friends worshiped Chernyshevsky, and they tried to apply the political ideas developed in his novel to their own lives. Ishutin later stated, 'Only three significant people ever lived on Earth: Jesus Christ, the apostle Paul and Chernyshevsky.'[168] And Leonid Egorovich Obolenskii, who was close to the circle of friends, wrote in his memoirs that the group had 'imitated Rakhmetov', Chenyshevsky's hero, 'and not much was missing, and they had even slept on nails'.[169] Another close associate of the group, Petr Fedorovich Nikolaev, dismisses this as nonsense in his memoirs. And yet he also describes how Ishutin and Karakozov actually did resemble Rakhmetov in a number of different qualities, and that 'Karakozov was very similar to Nikitushka Lomov,' referring to one of Rakhmetov's nicknames.[170] So it should come as no surprise that Stranden and Iurasov planned to free Chernyshevsky from his exile in Siberia in a forced-labour

---

167 See above, p. 338–45.

168 Cited in Klevenskii, 'Predislovie', in Klevenskii and Kotel'nikov, *Pokushenie Karakozova*, vol. 1, viii; as well as in Shilov, 'Pokushenie Karakozova 4 aprelia 1866 g.', 93; and also in Venturi, *Roots of Revolution*, 331.

169 As quoted in Nikolaev, printed in Ch. Vetrinskii (= V. E. Cheshikhin), 'N. G. Chernyshevskii i karakozovcy', 104.

170 Ibid.; also quoted in Verhoeven, *The Odd Man Karakozov*, 40. Generally, for the comparison, also see Stites, *The Women's Liberation Movement in Russia*, 118.

camp – a project that failed with their own arrest following Karakozov's assassination attempt.[171]

It has been the conclusion both of contemporaries and of recent scholarship that Karakozov and his group of friends sought to embody Chernyshevsky's novel and, in particular, its hero Rakhmetov. This is further corroborated by the fact that after Karakozov's assassination attempt on Tsar Alexander II several contemporaries instantly recognized and confirmed the similarity to Rakhmetov: 'He was, probably, a madman, who wanted to take on the role of Rakhmetov from the novel *What Is to Be Done?*', noted Pavel Petrovich Maevsky, another acquaintance of the group, immediately after the attack; Obolenskii stated in court, 'I compared him to Rakhmetov from Chernyshevsky's novel.'[172] It was obvious to his contemporaries that Karakozov had emulated Rakhmetov. The preceding analysis has shown, furthermore, that there are good reasons to conclude that the character was based on the example of John Brown.

It was John Wilkes Booth who had the least-mediated interpersonal path of reception. Booth was employed as an actor for the company of the Old Marshall Theatre in Richmond when John Brown made his raid on Harpers Ferry. Booth was thereby able to experience the reactions in Virginia's state capital at first hand. On 19 November he was just on his way with a couple of colleagues from his hotel to the theatre when the bells in front of the capitol began ringing the alarm. Governor Wise had received information that northern abolitionists were planning to liberate Brown, and again mobilized the Richmond militia in response. The train that was to bring the Richmond Grays to Harpers Ferry waited directly across from the Old Marshall Theatre in the Broad Street Depot. Seeing that, nothing could keep Booth in the city any more. He dropped everything, went over to the train, and convinced two militia members he knew to sell him a uniform and take him with them. When they

171 Nikolaev, printed in Ch. Vetrinskii (= V. E. Cheshikhin), 'N. G. Chernyshevskii i karakozovcy', 106; and also, generally, Shilov, 'Pokushenie Karakozova 4 aprelia 1866 g.', 93; Klevenskii, 'Predislovie', in Klevenskii and Kotel'nikov, *Pokushenie Karakozova*, vol. 1, viii–x; Venturi, *Roots of Revolution*, 331–5, 344; Paperno, *Chernyshevsky and the Age of Realism*, 29–30; as well as Verhoeven, *The Odd Man Karakozov*, 40.

172 Quote from Maevsky from Shcherbakova, 'Roman N. G. Chernyshevskogo "Chto delat'?" v vospriiatii radikal'noi molodezhi serediny 60-kh godov XIX v.', 68; Obolenskii quoted in Ch. Vetrinskii (= V. E. Cheshikhin), 'N. G. Chernyshevskii i karakozovtsy', 104; and in Verhoeven, *The Odd Man Karakozov*, 40, 199, footnote 7.

arrived in Charles Town, the warnings of the attempt to free Brown turned out to be unfounded, and instead of beating back abolitionists the Richmond Grays – with Booth among them – found themselves guarding the prison or, as cavalrymen, the road to Martinsburg. Booth additionally occupied himself as a scout and as a sergeant in the quarter-master's department.[173]

On 1 December, the day before Brown's execution, Booth managed to visit John Brown and his fellow prisoners in their cells. The Richmond Grays were, moreover, appointed to stand guard at the execution. Booth stood close to the gallows, not far from Thomas J. Jackson (later 'Stonewall' Jackson) and the cadets of the Virginia Military Institute.[174] When the trapdoor opened, John Brown fell into the hole, and the hemp rope slowly strangled him to death, Booth is said to have gone quite pale. 'I called attention to it,' later reported Philip Whitlock, who was standing next to him, in his autobiography, 'and he said he felt very faint – and would then give anything for a good drink of whiskey.'[175] Booth was still able to talk to John Brown himself and witnessed his execution first-hand. Thus he had formed a personal impression of him that would serve him as a model in the use of violence, even if Booth was not yet conscious of this.

We know from Booth's sister's memoirs that Brown had made a strong impression on him by the time he left Charles Town. He brought her one of Brown's pikes as well as a piece of wood from the box in which Brown's casket was transported. He wore this piece of wood like a relic and said repeatedly, 'He was a brave old man . . . John Brown was a man inspired, the grandest character of the century!'[176]

What had so impressed Booth about Brown was his readiness to act. For Booth, Brown was a model of decisive action; he had followed his

---

173 On this see Clarke's (not, however, entirely correct) memoirs, *The Unlocked Book*, 111–12; Kauffman, *American Brutus*, 103–7; and above all the precise investigations by Angela Smythe, 'Has He Been Hiding in Plain Sight? John Wilkes Booth and the Richmond Grays', in 'Antebellum Richmond, John Wilkes Booth and the Richmond Grays', 10 May 2010, antebellumrichmond.com; as well as Alford, *Fortune's Fool*, 68–76.

174 Alford, *Fortune's Fool*, 77–81.

175 'The Life of Philip Whitlock, by Himself', unpublished manuscript, Virginia Historical Society, quoted from Kauffman, *American Brutus*, 106. For biographical information on Whitlock, see Smythe, 'Has He Been Hiding in Plain Sight?'.

176 Clark, *The Unlocked Book*, 112, 122; as well as Alford, *Fortune's Fool*, 81.

words with honourable deeds, as Booth explained in his imaginary speech from December 1860:

> For John Brown was executed (yes, and justly) by his country's laws for attempting in another way, mearly [sic] what these abolitionists are doing now[177] . . . I may say I helped to hang John Brown and while I live, I shall think with joy upon the day when I saw the sun go down upon one trator [sic] *less* within our land. His treason was no more than theirs, *for open force is holier than hidden craft. The Lion is more noble than the fox.*[178]

According to Booth, all abolitionists were traitors to the US Constitution. But, while John Brown had used open violence in a knightly manner that could be countered with manly retaliation, Booth saw the Republicans' use of political and institutional processes (which were not actually a threat, although they were quite feared in the South) for the emancipation of the slaves as sly and devious.

One year after the raid on Harpers Ferry and shortly after Lincoln's election, Booth accordingly called the men of the North to action so that they might counter the empty promises of the past with something worthy of trust: 'But I could wish you would prove to the south, with deeds, instead of words, that she shall have those rights which she demands, those rights which are her due,' he called out to his imaginary audience. At another point (two and a half years before the appearance of Chernyshevsky's novel *What Is to Be Done?*) he writes, 'What is to be done? If argument has no more resources, it is time for all good citizens . . . in, this, her hour of need to come to action.'[179] According to Booth, it was deeds, not words, which were needed, as in his view words could no longer be trusted and had lost the power to convince.

And yet Booth identifies violence here as the last resource available. According to him, free men had to resort to this last means only if circumstances required it: 'For God be my witness that I love peace,' he emphasized to his imaginary listeners, 'but Gentlemen there is a time when peace becomes a burden. There is a time when men should act for

---

177 Lincoln was familiar with this argument, as the quote on p. 368 indicates.
178 Booth, '[Draft of a Speech] Philadelphia, late December 1860', 60.
179 Ibid., 59.

themselves and not under the guidance of a few political leaders who use ^them^ only for their own ends.'[180] By deciding to use force in this way, Booth writes, it must be with a readiness to give up one's life for one's ideals and country. Violence was for Booth the last means of action, when all political and institutional paths had been exhausted or when they were used once and for all against one's very own interests. At a time like this, he believed, all free men were called upon to sacrifice themselves for what was truly important to them – and John Brown had provided an example of this.

While John Wilkes Booth was able to both speak to and see his model in the flesh, Oskar Wilhelm Becker was limited to following Felice Orsini's assassination attempt and its consequences in the press. The *Deutsche Allgemeine Zeitung*, which he read every day at dinner, reported on the attempt in many long articles.[181] His 'Prophecies for the Year 1860 and Those That Follow' from 1859 show how these reports made an impression on him. There he writes, for example, as a prediction for the years 1865 to 1867:

> Very secret societies. Napoleon III is no longer safe on his throne . . .
> An attempt is made on his life . . . the terrifying infernal machine has nearly had its effect. It is only thanks to a strange incident that Napoleon did not lose his life. His son, however, who was at his side, lies dead. One of Napoleon's adjutants is maimed in a terrible way . . .
> The episode makes a great sensation all over Europe . . . The only thing on which Napoleon is still counting is a national war with England. The precarious position in which England finds itself gives Napoleon III hope. They are building up arms against each other in England and France. Germany is also arming itself, as to all appearances it will join in the war against France.[182]

---

180 Ibid., 58. Words marked with carets (^) were inserted in the original between the lines or in the margins. See John H. Rhodehamel and Louise Taper, 'Editorial Method', in Rhodehamel and Taper, *'Right or Wrong, God Judge Me'*, 23.

181 On coverage in German-speaking countries see above, pp. 141–5, 158–61, 165; and also, especially, the thorough article 'Das Attentat auf den Kaiser Napoleon', *Deutsche Allgemeine Zeitung*, 19 January 1858, 115–16 (= 1–2), as well as the reporting on the following pages through 119.

182 GLA Karlsruhe 250/10, 'Prophezeiungen', Bl. 99b and 100. The dating of the 'Prophezeiungen für die Jahre 1865 bis 1867' is not explicitly noted in the file in this case, and is derived from the year names before and after it.

At the trial, furthermore, both the defendant himself and his defence lawyer identified Felice Orsini as the actual and most important model for Becker's attempt to shoot the king of Prussia. Becker 'wanted to promote German unification' with his assassination attempt, 'just as Orsini's assassination attempt on Emperor Napoleon had acted as a stimulus for the unification of Italy,' as his lawyer put it in his summary of his client's statements.[183] Oskar Becker had attempted to emulate Felice Orsini.

Beyond this, Becker also revealed a number of additional sources of inspiration to the examining magistrate. According to this testimony, he had read Machiavelli's *The Prince* intensely as a pupil in secondary school in Dresden: he studied the book itself as well as commentaries on it – for example Karl Bollmann's *Vertheidigung des Machiavellismus* (A Defence of Machiavellianism) – and also read Adolf Trendelenburg's speech in honour of Frederick the Great, 'Machiavell u. Antimachiavell' (Machiavelli and Anti-Machiavelli) and made notes of his own to all these texts.[184] Around Easter 1859 he wrote his own tract, giving it the pretentious title of 'Das Buch des Fürsten von Oskar Becker, Studiosus Lipsiensis jur[is] et cam[eralium]' (The Book of the Prince by Oskar Becker, Student of Law and Governance and Public Policy at Leipzig University) and the motto 'Wickedness is a science as well as an art' (*Schlechtigkeit ist eine Wissenschaft sowohl als eine Kunst*). In his treatise, Becker concluded that a democratic form of government is the best and monarchy, conversely, the worst, and argued, in at times ungrammatical and clumsy German, for harsh realpolitik by emulating Machiavellianism:

---

183 'Oskar Becker's Proceß. (Von unseren eigenen Berichterstattern.) . . . Bruchsal, 24 September', *Kölnische Zeitung*, 26 September 1861, second edition, 1.

184 Niccolò Machiavelli, *Il principe. Discorsi sopra la prima deca di Tito Liovio*, Milano 1968 (Opere di Niccolò Machiavelli 1); Friedrich II, 'Anti-Machiavel ou Essai de critique sur Le Prince de Machivel', ed. François M.A. Voltaire, Den Haag 1740 in: *Friedrich II. König von Preußen, Antimachiavell und Testamente*, Berlin 1912 (Die Werke Friedrichs des Großen in deutscher Übersetzung 7); Karl Bollmann, *Vertheidigung des Macchiavellismus*, Quedlinburg 1858; Friedrich Adolf Trendelenburg, *Machiavell u. Antimachiavell. Vortrag zum Gedächtnis Friederichs des Grossen gehalten am 25. Jan. 1855 in der königlichen Akademie der Wissenschaften*, Berlin 1855. On Becker's preoccupation with Machiavelli see GLA Karlsruhe 250/9, Becker's interrogation, 26 July 1861, afternoon, Bl. 249–50; and GLA Karlsruhe 250/12, compilation, Bl. 41–3.

One can reach the throne in one of two ways: either one belongs to the ruling family and receives the throne by inheritance, or one obtains it through personal competence, either by doing away with the legitimate heir to the throne or, if there is a democratic or aristocratic constitution, by removing the current rulers and taking their place.

At another point he notes that someone who 'has made the grand plan of becoming the ruler of a nation' should not shy away from 'spilling a little blood', and recommended that a would-be usurper, among other things, extirpate the ruling family 'or at least their most important members', as, he writes, 'The people will thus have no one to turn to and you will be able to rule absolutely securely.'[185] Becker accordingly considered murder for political goals advisable as long as they promoted one's own interests or the interests of state, and he considered terrorist assassination to be a modern form of this political thought. In court in the city of Bruchsal, he lectured the jury on this point: 'The Machiavellianism of the 19th century works by other, by intellectual means, such as treason, bribery and so on, and Orsini's assassination attempt should be identified as the highest achievement of this Machiavellianism.'[186] He thereby provided an updated reading for the historical tract, transferring it from the Italian situation to the German one.

In making these statements, Becker also took up the thought attributed to Charles Follen on the relations of ends to means. In the interrogations, the examining magistrate in Baden-Baden devoted considerable attention to this question. Again and again the district judge pointed out the criminal nature of the assassination and the disparity between means and ends: 'You couldn't possibly have believed that you had even the vaguest pretext for such a misdeed?' he replied to Becker after the latter had stated his motive.[187] Becker openly confessed to the evil of his methods, but he remained nevertheless steadfast in the belief that the ends justified the use of the means: 'I recognize that my deed, in itself, is reprehensible, but the motives for it were at least well

---

185 GLA Karlsruhe, 250/10, Bl. 114–28: Das Buch des Fürsten von Oskar Becker, Studiosus Lipsiensis jur[is] et cam[eralium], Bl. 114, 118, 123–4.

186 'Oskar Beckers Prozeß. (Von unseren eigenen Berichterstattern.) . . . Bruchsal, 23. September', *Kölnische Zeitung*, 26 September 1861, first edition, 3.

187 GLA Karlsruhe, 250/9, Becker's interrogation, 27 July 1861, afternoon, Bl. 287–8.

intended, and likewise the goal was good that I thought to achieve through this.' And he stated repeatedly that in order 'to achieve this goal, I didn't even recoil from this evil measure; or to put it better, I deemed this means, in itself reprehensible, to be permitted in achieving this great end'.[188] In his opinion, the end justified the means, however criminal they may have been.

Becker also found illustrative material and models for his view in many places besides Orsini's assassination: in the history of the Roman Empire;[189] in the assassinations of Henry IV of France, Jean-Paul Marat and August von Kotzebue; and especially in recent Russian history. Becker had read the memoirs of Princess Ekaterina Romanovna Vorontsova-Dashkova, who, at eighteen years old, was involved in the *coup d'état* against Peter III which brought his widow Catherine the Great to power. In her memoirs, Dashkova indirectly describes the assassination of the tsar.[190] 'The memoirs of Fonvizin, a witness of the troubled period under Emperors Paul I, Alexander I and Nicolas I', which were published in Russian by the Leipzig publisher Gerhard, were given to Becker for corrections.[191] These memoirs had inspired Becker to write an essay on the assassination of Paul I himself.

A comparison of this essay with Becker's interpretation of his assassination attempt in the interrogations suggests that the assassination of Paul I also served as a foil for his own act and influenced his expectations about the public reaction.

---

188 Ibid., Bl. 282, 272. Also see ibid., 29 July 1861, afternoon, Bl. 321: 'I have no regrets! But this does not originate in moral depravity, I have only used evil means to pursue a goal that I consider good.'

189 On Becker's preoccupation with Roman history, see GLA Karlsruhe, 250/10, Das Buch des Fürsten.

190 Ibid., 250/9, Becker's interrogation, 26 July 1861, afternoon, Bl. 251. Dashkova's memoirs first appeared in 1840 in English, in 1857 in German, and in 1859 in French. Becker probably had access to the German translation. E. R. Dashkova, *Memoirs of the Princess Daschkaw, Lady of Honour to Catherine II. Empress of All the Russias: Written by Herself: Comprising Letters of the Empress and Other Correspondence*, edited from the originals by Mrs. W. Bradford, in two volumes (London: Henry Colburn, Publisher, 1840); on her involvement in the *coup d'état*, see ibid., 1–118.

191 Mikhail Alexandrovich Fon-Vizin, *Zapiski Fon-Vizina, ochevidtsa smutnykh vremen tsarstvovanii Pavla I, Alexandra I, Nikolaia I/Memoiren des Herrn von Wisin, eines Augenzeugen der erregten Zeiten unter Paul I., Alexander I. und Nicolaus I.* (Leipzig: Wolfgang Gerhard, 1859).

When an action becomes necessary, men will be found who feel themselves called to it. Paul's government was eam [Latin 'for her', that is, for Catherine] too onerous and at the same time harmful to Russia than could be any further tolerated . . . Owing to Paul's unpopularity . . . it was natural that it would become clear to many that it was necessary to secure liberation from Paul's tyranny somehow or other. Therefore whoever could show how this could be done would boldly be able to expect the support of many others.[192]

A monarch who is unpopular and harmful to the state he rules, a person who draws the conclusions from this situation and boldly finds a way to 'remove' the monarch, broad support for this act from all sides: this was also essentially Becker's evaluation of the situation in Germany, and why he saw the country's liberation from the 'tyranny' of Wilhelm I as a glorious deed.[193]

Accordingly, an array of political assassinations from the ancient and contemporary history of Western Europe and Russia served as models for Becker, while Orsini's attack on Napoleon III had an especially deep impact on his thinking and action due to its spectacular success and proximity in time and substance.

What holds true for Becker also holds for the two other copycats. The existence of explicit references to one precedent does not exclude other sources of influence. It has been documented, for example, that John Wilkes Booth followed the US media coverage of the 'Orsini attempt' and its author. He bragged that, if he had tried to do it, he would not have failed; he later spoke to George Nicholas Sanders about Orsini.[194] Furthermore it is extremely likely that Oskar Wilhelm Becker also devoured the articles on John Brown in all the major German newspapers. Likewise, Dmitry Vladimirovich Karakozov and his circle certainly knew of Orsini's and Booth's acts of violence directly through the Russian press. In Moscow people were familiar with Booth's words '*Sic semper tyrannis*,' and Ishutin has been shown to have inquired about

---

192 GLA Karlsruhe, 250/10, Bl. 129–36: 'On the assassination of Pavel I', Bl. 129, 136.
193 Ibid., Bl. 129, 136–7.
194 On Booth's admiration for Corday and Orsini and on his bragging, see Alford, *Fortune's Fool*, 248–9; and on the conversation with Sanders see above, pp. 489–90. Regarding the model provided by Orsini and other Italian nationalists for assassination and violent insurrection inside and outside of Italy, see Jensen, *The Battle against Anarchist Terrorism*, 20–1 and 73, footnote 46.

how to build 'Orsini-bombs'.[195] The fact that they began to discuss the possibility of tsaricide in the summer of 1865, of all times, suggests that they may have been inspired by reports of Booth's assassination of Lincoln. The nature of these possible connections, however, has yet to be examined more closely.

Here, it is important to take the character of the reporting into account and how its expression in each country influenced Orsini's and Brown's potential attractiveness for their respective imitators. While Becker could hardly have identified himself with an American religious fundamentalist like Brown, Booth – who was described by contemporaries (both men and women) as the embodiment of an ideal, athletic masculinity and as one of the most attractive men of his time – was probably able to imagine himself quite easily in the role of the handsome and heroic revolutionary Orsini in court.

They also had other models and sources of inspiration. In both Becker's and Karakozov's cases, there are references to the writing and activities of the radical German fraternities (*Burschenschaften*) and, in Booth's case, to Charlotte Corday, who carried out the assassination of the French revolutionary Jean-Paul Marat, as well as to plays, for example James Fenimore Cooper's *Wept of Wish-ton Wish*, Friedrich Schiller's *William Tell* and, above all, Shakespeare's *Julius Caesar*.[196] But whatever other models there may have been and whatever influence may be attributed to them, the fact remains that Felice Orsini and John Brown had a remarkably groundbreaking and style-forming effect – whether directly or mediated through the figure of Rakhmetov. An additional indication of this was Booth and Becker's black clothing, which could have been an attempt to re-create Orsini's appearance in court.[197]

Beyond this there could have been another link in the transnational reception chain between the United States and Europe: Mikhail Alexandrovich Bakunin. Bakunin escaped from Siberian exile in the

---

195 See on this Venturi, *Roots of Revolution*, 337, 344.

196 See on this Alford, *Fortune's Fool*, 246–8.

197 On Karakozov, whose peasant coat (*armiak*) came to shape the style of the revolutionary movement in Russia, see Verhoeven, *The Odd Man Karakozov*, Chapter 5; and, subsequently, also Lynn Patyk, 'Dressed to Kill and Die: Russian Revolutionary Terrorism, Gender, and Dress', *Jahrbücher für Geschichte Osteuropas* 58/2 (2010), 192–209. This phenomenon still needs to be examined in connection to the revolutionary movements and violent actors outside Russia.

summer of 1861, fled via Japan to the United States and travelled across North America to Western Europe. During this journey, he also stayed in Boston. In the following years, while in Europe, he was in contact with members of Zemlia i Volia as well as with members of the Polish national movement. Thus, potentially, there were still many other possibilities for transfers of ideas and of experiences in the application of political violence that will have to be examined in detail elsewhere.[198]

Deed, propaganda, self-sacrifice: inventing the claim of responsibility

What exactly did Becker, Booth and Karakozov learn from their respective role models? And what did the three copycats think – rightly or wrongly – of the effect their violence would have on each of the political situations as they – rightly or wrongly – interpreted them? The reckoning of the three attackers differed in the details and according to the respective circumstances in which they found themselves. There are nevertheless three elements that were significant to all of them and that impart an essentially terrorist nature to their violent acts: the combination of sensational deed, propaganda and a readiness to sacrifice themselves. The significance of these three elements and their combined effect was something they had learned to assess from the example of their models John Brown and Felice Orsini.

The emergence of a new genre of text, that is, the terrorist claim of responsibility, a claim created by each of the three imitators, has to be seen in this context. The question has hardly been considered in earlier scholarship – and not at all from a comparative perspective. Neither Felice Orsini nor John Brown had made use of any written claim of responsibility for their violent deeds. The documents left by Brown at the Kennedy farm represent at best a starting point in this direction. It was only after the fact that Orsini and Brown had the chance to claim personal and political responsibility and to explain their acts of violence: through the letters to Napoleon III and the interview with Wise and other prominent people. These personal and political confessions subsequently became the basis for the

---

198 On Bakunin and the scholarship on him also see above, pp. 409–10.

psychological effect of their actions as well as their elevation to the status of martyr. This set a precedent. It was precisely this cohesion of sensational act, legitimizing confession, personal readiness for self-sacrifice and political success, emerging out of the combined effect of these elements, that the imitators observed and understood and that led them to invent the claim of responsibility. Possibly, they did this on their own in each case, but they may also have learned from one another in the process.

They hardly ever commented on how they perceived Orsini´s and Brown´s violent tactics. Here, too, we encounter the fact that, alongside the models of Orsini and Brown, there are other sources of influence and models whose weight should be gauged individually. However, the fact that each of the three imitators wrote a claim of responsibility is itself already an indication of the important role played by Felice Orsini and John Brown in this process.

What is a terrorist claim of responsibility? What are the characteristics of this form of confession? And how, generally speaking, is the genre understood today? The philosopher Hermann Lübbe, one of the few academics from the humanities and social sciences to have worked on the claim of responsibility as a genre (and not only for specific groups like the Red Army Faction or Al-Qaida), characterizes this variety of text as a 'part of terrorist activities' that fulfils the functions constitutive of the 'political purpose' of terrorism.[199] These functions, according to Lübbe, consist in the first order of 'attracting publicity' (*Publizitätsverschaffung*) generally: 'An acting subject, an organization, steps out of its anonymity and transforms the turmoil caused by a spectacular act into its own intense publicity.' Attracting publicity, for Lübbe, implies the identification of the actors with their act. Second, Lübbe writes, the claim of responsibility fulfils the function of a 'denial of triviality [*Trivialitätsdementi*] vis-à-vis the act for which the confessors claim responsibility', that is, the claim of responsibility should identify

---

199 Lübbe, 'Bekennerschreiben und freundlichere Konsensdementis', 128. This does not mean that there does not also exist terrorism which lacks claims of responsibility, or whose responsibility claims are misleading. On this see Hoffman, 'Aaron M. Hoffman, 'Voice and Silence: Why Groups Take Credit for Acts of Terror', *Journal of Peace Research* 47/5 (2010), 615–26'; and Erin M. Kearns, Brendan Conlon and Joseph K. Young, 'Lying about Terrorism', *Studies in Conflict & Terrorism* 37/5 (2014), 422–39.

the act confessed as a political act and thereby free it from trivial criminality. Third, taking credit brings attention to the 'need for legitimation' (*Legitimationsbedarf*) that terrorist acts evoke. Fourth, claims of responsibility provide this legitimation. And, fifth, they provoke fear and – as one must add – sympathy.[200]

Lübbe does not focus on either the act or martyrdom or the political consequences. Nonetheless his characterization confirms the significance of the claim of responsibility for terrorist tactics as well as the pivotal function that the claim fulfils between the act on the one hand and martyrdom and potential political success on the other. His description shows how the interrelation of sensational act, propaganda (in the sense of attracting publicity), denials of triviality, legitimation and the attempt to generate specific psychological effects are constitutive of the genre. Typically, identification of one's self also enters as a condition for self-sacrifice and martyrdom.

The written confessions of all three imitators meet this definition, although the process of their writing took different forms. In this, their respective personal situations played no less a role than the intended function of their texts in the intended function of their violent actions. Shortly before his assassination attempt, Oskar Wilhelm Becker wrote his confession in only one copy and kept it with him. As already stated, he declared in the interrogation that he had written the document on the evening before the attack in the Gasthaus zur Blume. While writing it, it had been very important to him that it be flawless.[201]

John Wilkes Booth also wrote his claim of responsibility only shortly before his act of violence, more precisely on 14 April in the National Hotel. According to an article in the *New York Daily Tribune*, Booth appeared at the reception desk at approximately 4 p.m. and asked somewhat nervously for writing paper and an envelope. He was about to start writing when the thought occurred to him that one of the people standing nearby could read what he was writing. He is then reported to have gone to the hotel office and asked whether he could sit there to write.

---

200 Lübbe, 'Bekennerschreiben und freundlichere Konsensdementis', 128–30.

201 GLA Karlsruhe, 250/8, Becker's interrogation, 14 July 1861, Bl. 48–9, as well as in this volume, p. 432.

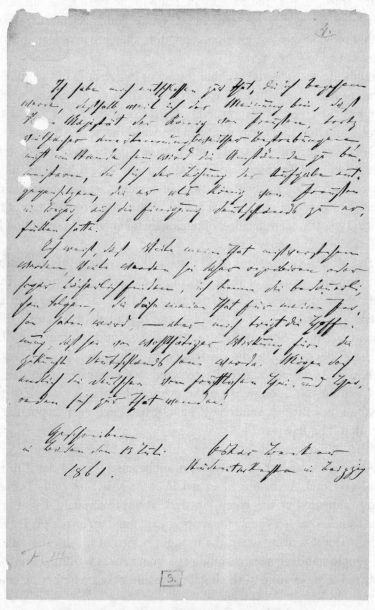

Figure 28. Oskar Wilhelm Becker, letter of confession.
Generallandesarchiv Karlsruhe, 250 Nr. 10.

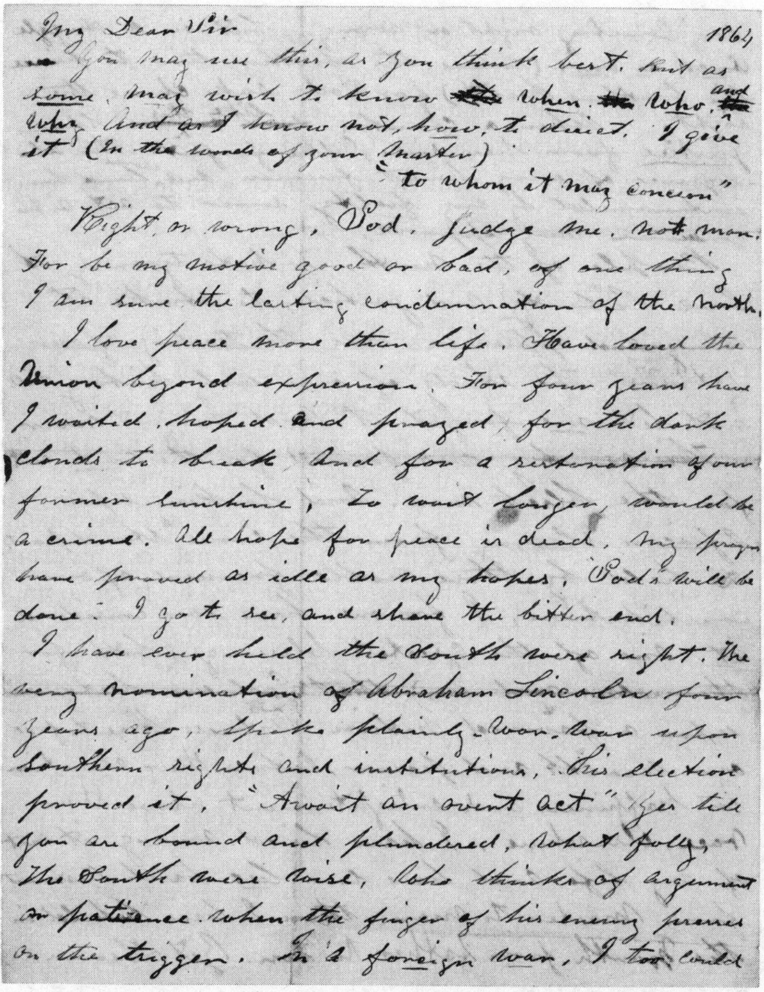

My Dear Sir   1864

You may use this, as you think best. But as some, may wish to know when, who, and why And as I know not, how to direct. I give it (In the words of your Master)
                    "to whom it may concern"

Right or wrong, God, judge me, not man. For be my motive good or bad, of one thing I am sure the lasting condemnation of the North.

I love peace more than life. Have loved the Union beyond expression. For four years have I waited, hoped and prayed, for the dark clouds to break And for a restoration of our former sunshine. To wait longer, would be a crime. All hope for peace is dead. My prayers have proved as idle as my hopes. God's will be done. I go to see, and share the bitter end.

I have ever held the South were right. The very nomination of Abraham Lincoln four years ago, spoke plainly. War. War upon Southern rights and institutions. His election proved it. "Await an overt act" Yes till you are bound and plundered. What folly. The South were wise. Who thinks of argument or patience when the finger of his enemy presses on the trigger. In 's foreign war, I too could

Figure 29. 'To Whom It May Concern', 1864. Papers Relating to John Wilkes Booth, National Archives Identifier 6783029, General Records of the Department of Justice, 1790-2002, RG 60, National Archives at College Park, College Park, MD.

Once in the office, he is said to have begun writing immediately, but after a few words he paused again and asked in an earnest tone of voice,

> 'Merrick, is this the year 1864 or '65.' 'You are surely joking, John,' replied Mr. M., 'you certainly know what year it is.' 'Sincerely, I do not,' he rejoined, and on being told, resumed writing. It was then that Mr. M. noticed something troubled and agitated in Booth's appearance, which was entirely at variance with his usual quiet deportment.

After Booth had finished writing the letter, he is reported to have sealed the envelope, put it in his pocket and left the hotel.[202]

Dmitry Vladimirovich Karakozov composed his proclamation at least three weeks before his assassination attempt and made approximately eighty copies of it, later claiming in court that he made these copies on his own and without any assistance from others.[203]

The use of the texts as well as the risks it occasioned were likewise various. Oskar Wilhelm Becker made no effort to publicize his claim of responsibility, and this even though he considered his letter so important. We know this from his behaviour immediately after his arrest: in the carriage from Lichtentaler Allee to Baden-Baden the former Berliner and hotel owner Brandt asked the would-be assassin, 'what motive he had for his deed'. Becker only replied, 'You will find that in my wallet.' Beyond these words he remained silent throughout the entire ride.[204] He thereby completely delegated the political statement of his act to this piece of writing, which he kept in his wallet.

Once they had arrived in the city, Count von Flemming exited the carriage in order to immediately inform various people and institutions about the assassination attempt. He entrusted Becker's pistol and wallet to Brandt, who handed them to the city director, Kuntz, commenting that the motive for the crime lay in the wallet in written

---

202 'The Great Calamity! . . . Special Dispatch to the N.Y. Tribune. Washington, Saturday, April – 4.50 p.m., *New York Daily Tribune*, 17 April 1865, 1; excerpted in Booth, 'To the Editors of the National Intelligencer', 150, note 1.

203 See Shilov, 'Iz istorii revoliutsionnogo dvizheniia 1860-kh gg', 163. The archive copy is written by hand (see ibid., 162).

204 GLA Karlsruhe, 250/8, testimony of Brandt, Bl. 23.

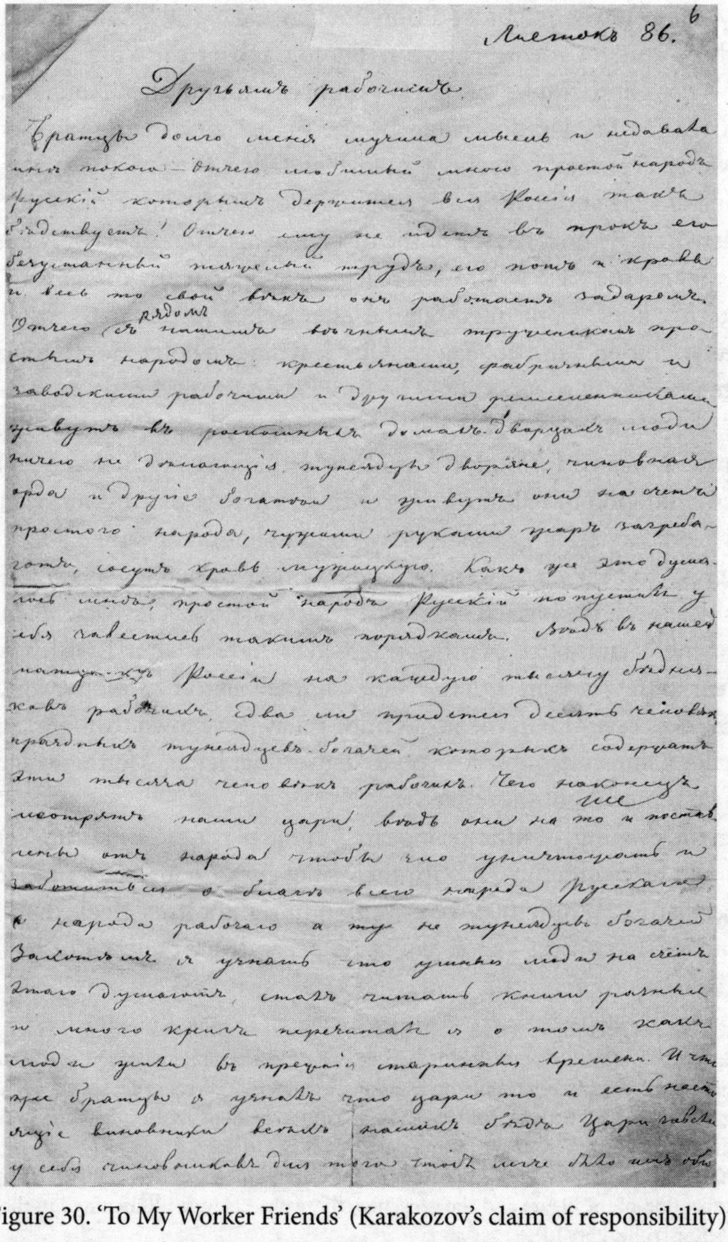
Листокъ 86. 6

Друзьямъ рабочимъ.

Братцы долго меня мучила мысль и недавала
мнѣ покоя — отчего любимый мною простой народъ
русскій которымъ держится вся Россія такъ
бѣдствуетъ! Отчего ему не идетъ въ прокъ его
безпрестанный тяжелый трудъ, его потъ и кровь
и весь то свой вѣкъ онъ работаетъ задаромъ.
Отчего рядомъ съ нашимъ вѣчнымъ тружеником про-
стымъ народомъ: крестьянами, фабричными и
заводскими рабочими и другими ремесленниками
живутъ въ роскошныхъ домахъ-дворцахъ люди
ничего не дѣлающіе, тунеядцы дворяне, чиновная
орда и другіе богатеи и живутъ они на счетъ
простого народа, чужими руками жаръ загреба-
ютъ, сосутъ кровь мужицкую. Какъ же это допус-
каетъ міръ, простой народъ русскій попустилъ у
себя завестись такимъ порядкамъ. Вѣдь въ нашей
матушкѣ-Руси Россіи на каждую тысячу бѣдняковъ
рабочихъ, едва ли придется десять человѣкъ
праздныхъ тунеядцевъ-богачей, которыхъ содержатъ
эти тысяча человѣкъ рабочихъ. Чего наконецъ
смотрятъ наши цари, вѣдь они на то и постав-
лены отъ народа чтобы его уничтожать и
заботиться о благѣ всего народа русскаго,
и народа рабочаго а ужъ не тунеядцевъ богачей.
Захотѣлъ я узнать что умные люди на счетъ
этого думаютъ, сталъ читать книги разные
и много кое-чего перечиталъ я о томъ какъ
люди жили въ прежнія старинныя времена. И что
же братцы я узналъ что цари то и есть насто-
ящіе виновники всѣхъ нашихъ бѣдъ. Цари завели
у себя чиновниковъ для того чтобъ легче было имъ обо

Figure 30. 'To My Worker Friends' (Karakozov's claim of responsibility). State Archive of the Russian Federation (GARF), f. 272, op.1, d.10, l.6.

form.[205] Kuntz himself then turned both items over to the court. The junior lawyer on duty at the district court examined the wallet on the very same day and, in addition to two cigars, a Saxon groschen, Becker's student identification, a photograph of the king of Prussia and two photographs of Becker himself, found the 'Note on the Motives for My Deed' written by the perpetrator in the inn on the previous evening.[206] Becker's note had fallen immediately into the hands of state authorities: a Prussian diplomat, the director of the city Baden-Baden and a lawyer of the district court, thus effectively ensuring that his message would not reach the public in any direct way.

John Wilkes Booth entrusted the letter he had written in the National Hotel to a friend and colleague. After leaving the hotel, Booth took his rented horse out of its stall. As he rode down Pennsylvania Avenue, he met the actor John Matthews (also Mathews) near Willard's Hotel. Matthews was performing at Ford's Theatre, and Booth had known him since childhood in Baltimore. According to Matthews's testimony given two years later to an investigatory commission, they spoke about the column of officer war prisoners from Ewell's army making its way up the avenue. Booth then asked, 'Johnny, I wish to ask you a favor; will you do it for me?' And, once Matthews agreed, 'I have a letter I wish you to deliver to the publishers of the National Intelligencer to-morrow morning, unless I see you in the mean time. I may leave town to-night, and it will not be much trouble for you to deliver that letter.' Matthews agreed to help him and put the letter away.[207]

In the evening, Matthews appeared in the play *Our American Cousin* and was held under arrest with the rest of the ensemble after Lincoln's assassination. While they were waiting in the theatre's cloakroom and shouts of 'hang' and 'lynch' could be heard from the theatre hall, he

205 GLA Karlsruhe, 250/12, compilation of accusing and exonerating evidence in the investigation of Oskar Wilhelm Becker from Odessa, student of law and cameral sciences in Leipzig, in relation to an assassination attempt directed against His Majesty King Wilhelm I of Prussia, and thereby an attack of high treason intended and/or undertaken against the German Confederation, Bl. 1–70, 12.

206 GLA Karlsruhe, 250/8, findings of Dr Gerstner, 14 July 1861, Bl. 18–19. With the exception of the cigars and the groschen, these objects were all included in the files (GLA Karlsruhe, 250/10).

207 Testimony of John Matthews, in 'Impeachment of the President', *House Report Seven*, as quoted in Booth, 'To the Editors of the National Intelligencer. Washington, D.C., April 14, 1865', 150–3, footnote 5, quotation at 151–2.

remembered – as he testified later – Booth's letter: 'I opened it, and glanced hastily over the letter. I saw it was a statement of what he was going to do. I read it very hurriedly.' In this way, he read the letter a few times and then burned it – out of fear that he would be found with the letter and therefore tied to the assassination.[208]

In witness questioning, Matthews still made several efforts over the following years to describe the content of the letter; in 1881 he even tried to 'reconstruct' the text at the instigation of a journalist. The result of this reconstruction was a text that for the most part corresponds to Booth's 'To Whom It May Concern' from November 1864. He had given this letter to his sister probably in February 1865 to keep in her safe, and it was generally known to the public by 1881.[209] It is therefore quite possible that Matthews used this letter in his reconstruction, as both Edward Steers and John Rhodehamel consider likely.[210]

In 1867, however, Matthews himself had already written explicitly, 'The first two pages were written in the spirit and style of the Philadelphia letter' ('To Whom It May Concern') 'and it was only at the concluding paragraph that anything was said bearing upon what had transpired.'[211] If one then considers the situation in which Booth wrote the letter, it seems all the more likely that he actually did repeat large sections of 'To Whom It May Concern' on 14 April in the National Hotel. According to the research of the journalist at the New York Tribune, the entire scene from Booth's request for paper to his departure cannot have taken more than twenty minutes. Booth is supposed to have arrived at the hotel around 4 p.m. By half past the hour he had already been seen on horseback on Pennsylvania Avenue, talking to John Matthews.[212] Moreover, Booth is said to have written without pause – with the exception of the date.

---

208 Testimony of John Matthews, in 40th Congress, 1st session, *Impeachment of the President*, as quoted in Booth, 'To the Editors of the National Intelligencer. Washington, D.C., April 14, 1865', 150, footnote 5, quotation at 152.

209 Clark, *The Unlocked Book*, 123–4; Booth, 'To Whom It May Concern [Philadelphia, November] 1864', 127, footnote 1; and Booth, 'To the Editors of the National Intelligencer. Washington, D.C., April 14, 1865', footnote 5, 151.

210 See Steers, *Blood on the Moon*, 111; and Booth, 'To the Editors of the National Intelligencer. Washington, D.C., April 14, 1865', note 5, 151.

211 John Matthews in a letter to the *National Intelligencer* from 18 July 1867, cited in Booth, 'To the Editors of the National Intelligencer. Washington, D.C., April 14, 1865', note 5, 153.

212 'The Great Calamity! ... Special Dispatch to the N. Y. Tribune. Washington, Saturday, April – 4.50 p.m.', *New York Daily Tribune*, 17 April 1865, 1.

Writing a text of around 1,500 words of such exceptional importance in such a short period of time would be unusual even for people already used to expressing themselves in writing. Booth, however, was an actor. It was not the writing but the memorization of lengthy texts that was his profession. In this respect it seems highly probable – considering Booth's situation – that his letter to the *National Intelligencer* was broadly identical to the one in his sister's safe. Ultimately, both texts served almost the very same purpose.[213]

Dmitry Vladimirovich Karakozov distributed copies of his 'proclamation' (*proklamatsiia*, as he himself called his confession) before his assassination attempt. According to the Russian historian and archivist Alexei Alexeevich Shilov, who published Karakozov's text for the first time in 1918, the proclamations, which were seized by agents of the Third Section during Karakozov's body search, had been placed in an envelope marked 'Leave henceforth until needed until 5 April; if such a need does not arise over the course of this period, burn immediately.'[214] For 'burn', Karakozov had used the Old Testament word *vsesozhzhenie* (instead of the standard *sozhzhenie*), the Russian translation of the Greek ὁλοκαύτωσις (*holokautōsis*), which in the Bible denotes an animal sacrifice that is completely consumed by fire.

As Karakozov later testified, he had spread his proclamation by 'strewing' envelopes in three places (he used the term *razbrasyvanie*), 'where it could fall into the hands of workers as quickly as possible, predominantly near the works and factories located on the Vyborgskaia and Peterburgskaia sides'. He had similarly tried to spread his proclamations among the students of St Petersburg University, namely 'with the goal of inciting workers and the youth to participate in the coup he was

---

213 This observation has not yet figured in Booth scholarship. Kauffman, *American Brutus*, 223; and Alford, *Fortune's Fool*, 254, describe the scene in question, but mostly in order to provide a sense of Booth's own state of mind, where it does not seem to be clear to Kauffman that Booth wrote his letter for the *National Intelligencer*, as he mistakenly claims that Booth deposited his finished letter in a mailbox. Swanson, *Manhunt*, 16, cites a part of the article from the *New York Tribune* without any additional commentary. Pitch, *'Papa Dead!'*, 89, also only recounts the scene and draws no conclusions from it about the content of the letter.

214 Shilov, 'Iz istorii revoliutsionnogo dvizheniia 1860-kh gg', 162, 163–4 for the following quotation.

preparing'.[215] In court he was unable to say precisely how many copies of his proclamation had been circulated, as he testified he had always distributed the copies immediately after making them.

Distributing a claim of responsibility before a terrorist attack carries the risk that the text will fall into the hands of security organs before the attack, and this is exactly what happened in Karakozov's case. On 14 March 1866, an anonymous letter went out through the city post marked 'Very important. Deliver without delay' to the governor general of St Petersburg, Alexander Arkadyevich Suvorov.[216] The letter contained one copy of the proclamation in the original envelope, on which Karakozov had written, 'To the students of the University. Open in one week.' In an accompanying letter the anonymous sender described how Karakozov had distributed his appeals to students:

> Your Grace,
>
> Having received the letter included here yesterday evening on the street from an unknown person, with the request to read it and share it with students within a week, I, upon arriving home, decided to open this letter immediately and, having read the disturbing appeal against my Sovereign contained therein, I decided to present it to your Grace, in the hope that you will take measures to cease the further dissemination of these appeals.
>
> The man who handed me this letter will in all likelihood even today be walking around the buildings of the university and second cadet building, in expectation of passing students.
>
> A Student.

The sender then added that the governor general, should he wish to speak with him, could arrange this by printing the codeword 'N°N°N° is requested' in the *Vedomosti S.-Peterburgskoi gorodskoi politsii* (News of the St Petersburg Police). He had carefully noted on the proclamation

---

215 As cited in Shilov, 'Iz istorii revoliutsionnogo dvizheniia 1860-kh gg.', 163. On this also see the indictment printed in Klevenskii and Kotel'nikov, *Pokushenie Karakozova*, vol. 1, 8–9; as well as Venturi, *Roots of Revolution*, 345.

216 As cited in Klevenskii and Kotel'nikov, *Pokushenie Karakozova*, vol. 1, 9, 297–8 note 8, quotation at 297. Also see Ulam, *Prophets and Conspirators*, 2.

envelope, 'Received on 13 March at 7 o'clock in the evening.'[217] This meant that Karakozov's proclamation had been in the possession of the state authorities for almost three weeks before he had made the assassination attempt.

The authorities took both the letter and the proclamation seriously. Two days later, in issue no. 57 of the *Vedomosti S.-Peterburgskoi gorodskoi politsii* from 16 March 1866, the friendly invitation to NºNºNº actually did appear for an audience on the following day, 17 March, at the chancellery of the governor general. Instead of the student, however, only another letter came on that day in which NºNºNº gave his extremely courteous and wordy thanks for the invitation in *Vedomosti*. He apologized that, 'owing to illness,' he could not appear on 17 March, and promised to make up for this 'promptly.' According to Klevenskii, who also described and reprinted the student's letter in his publication of the court records, the file ends there. The 'student' did not appear, and apparently no one attempted to investigate the activities of the person distributing rebellious proclamations in front of the university and the cadet building without his help either.[218] As a result, Karakozov remained free to continue with his preparations for the assassination.

There are significant differences between the three responsibility texts in terms of length and style. Oskar Wilhelm Becker appropriately titled his text 'Note on the Motives of My Deed'. The document comprises 120 words, is written in Becker's typically cumbersome style and reads as follows:

> I have decided on the deed which I will commit because I believe that His Majesty the King of Prussia, in spite of many efforts worthy of recognition, will not be able to cope with the circumstances that oppose the resolution of the task with regard to the unification of Germany which he, as King of Prussia, would have to fulfil. I know that many will not understand my deed; many will therefore rebuke it or even find it ridiculous; I know the unfortunate consequences that my deed will have for my person – but I am carried by the hope that it will have a beneficial effect upon Germany's future. May the Germans finally turn away from fruitless equivocating and to action!

---

217 Description and quotes from Klevenskii and Kotel'nikov, *Pokushenie Karakozova*, vol. 1, note 8, 297.

218 See ibid., vol. 1, note 8, 297–8; and also Ulam, *Prophets and Conspirators*, 2.

Written in Baden, the 13th of July, 1861 / Oskar Becker, Student of law
in Leipzig.[219]

Becker presents the political background and the intentions behind his
act quickly and succinctly, even with his wordy presentation, and
provides all the important information needed for the public to classify
his act of violence.

Dmitry Vladimirovich Karakozov's proclamation, at 887 words, is
more than seven times longer than Becker's note and in many sections
resembles something more like a political-historical essay in style. He
gave his appeal the title 'To My Worker Friends' ('Druz'iam rabochim')
and began as follows:

> Brothers, I have long been tormented by the thought and had no peace
> – why does the simple Russian people, whom I love and which holds all
> of Russia together, suffer from such misery! Why does his untiring hard
> labour, his sweat and blood, not bring him any benefit, and he works his
> whole lifetime for nothing? Why, alongside our eternal toiler the simple
> people: peasants, the workers of the factories and mills and other crafts-
> men, do people live in luxurious palatial homes who do nothing, para-
> site nobility, the bureaucratic horde and other rich men, and they live at
> the expense of the simple people . . . How can it be, I thought, that the
> simple Russian people would allow itself to be placed in such a system.[220]

---

219 GLA Karlsruhe, 250/10, Bl. 4: 'Ich habe mich entschlossen zur That, die ich begehen
werde, deshalb weil ich der Meinung bin, daß Seine Majestät der König von Preußen trotz
vielfacher anerkennungswerther Bestrebungen, nicht im Stande sein wird die Umstände zu
bemeistern, die sich der Lösung der Aufgabe entgegensetzen, die er als König von Preußen
in Bezug auf die Einigung Deutschlands zu erfüllen hätte. Ich weiß, daß Viele meine That
nicht verstehen werden, Viele werden sie daher reprobiren oder sogar lächerlich finden, ich
kenne die bedauerlichen Folgen, die diese meine That für meine Person haben wird – aber
mich trägt die Hoffnung, daß sie von wohlthätiger Wirkung für die Zukunft Deutschlands
sein werde. Mögen doch endlich die Deutschen vom fruchtlosen Hin- und Herreden sich
zur That wenden! Geschrieben in Baden, den 13. Juli 1861 / Oskar Becker, Student der
Rechte in Leipzig.' Also see the facsimile of the document at p. 512.
220 Shilov, 'Iz istorii revoliutsionnogo dvizheniia 1860-kh gg.', 160–2, quotation at
160. For a reprint with changed punctuation, see Klevenskii and Kotel'nikov, *Pokushenie
Karakozova*, vol. 1, 7, note 5, 292–4. Also see the facsimile at 548; as well as Venturi,
Roots of Revolution, 345–6. Claudia Verhoeven devotes scant attention to Karakozov's
proclamation. She cites it several times (see *The Odd Man Karakozov*, 130, 143, 179), but
does not analyse or evaluate it.

For every thousand working poor there were ten rich parasites 'in our mother Russia', making their living off a thousand working people. Karakozov continues, writing that he had wanted to know what intelligent people thought about these questions and that he had read many books about how people lived in earlier times.

Thus he had discovered that it was the tsars who were 'the real culprits for all our misfortune'. They created civil servants (*chinovniki*) to make it easier to loot the people through all kinds of taxes, and a standing army to break any resistance against it. The tsars had paid for these services by awarding land which had hitherto been farmed by the peasantry, who had in turn been pressed into 'slavery' by the civil servants and nobility. This was how serfdom had been introduced in Russia, and tsars, civil servants and landowners had begun to live at the expense of peasant labour. From this it was apparent that the tsar was merely the most important landowner in the country, who would never lend a hand to the peasants because he was the greatest enemy of the simple people.[221]

The tsar's 'freedom' (*volia*, by which he means the Emancipation Edict) is just a continuation of this relationship. Thus 'the very smallest piece of land was cut out from the squire's property, and then the peasant was made to pay large amounts of money for this, but where was this already ruined peasant to get the money to buy himself the land that he had worked for centuries?'[222] The peasants, writes Karakozov, could not believe at first that the tsar was capable of such a betrayal; they thought it was the landowners who had robbed them of 'real freedom' (*nastoiashchaia volia*) and had neither obeyed them nor the civil arbitrators. But then the tsar sent his generals and troops to the disobedient peasants, who were then hanged or shot. And so the peasants were left with no other choice than to accept this 'freedom – slavery' (*priniali etu voliu nevoliu*) and their lives became even worse than before.[223] Karakozov claims to have observed this himself in different places in Russia. If the money (*otkup*) for their freedom was not paid or if there was a remaining balance owed to the tax authorities, the peasant would be

221 Shilov, 'Iz istorii revoliutsionnogo dvizheniia 1860-kh gg.', 160–1, quotation at 160; Klevenskii and Kotel'nikov, *Pokushenie Karakozova*, vol. 1, 293.

222 Shilov, 'Iz istorii revoliutsionnogo dvizheniia 1860-kh gg.', 161; Klevenskii and Kotel'nikov, *Pokushenie Karakozova*, vol. 1, 293.

223 Ibid.

robbed of his last horse, his last cow, the livestock would be sold at auction just so the money could fill the tsar's pockets.

It made him sad that his 'beloved people' was 'perishing' and he had decided 'to destroy the criminal tsar' (*unichtozhit' tsaria-zlodeia*) and die for his beloved people.[224] The appeal ends with references to his act as well as some recommendations for handling the text in the reader's hands. Karakozov did not sign the proclamation in his own name, and it contained no other indication of his identity.

The longest claim of responsibility is that of John Wilkes Booth. The letter 'To Whom It May Concern' from November 1864, as well as John Matthews's reconstruction of the later text, span about 1,500 words and are thereby each almost twice as long as Karakozov's confession.

The November letter begins somewhat cryptically and in Booth's characteristic style:

My Dear Sir[225]
You may use this, as you think best, but as some, may wish to know ~~the when, the who~~ and ~~the why~~, and as I know not, *how*, to direct, I give it. (In the words of your Master)
'To whom it may concern'

It was with these words that President Abraham Lincoln had recently addressed a text to the Confederate representatives in negotiations for peace. 'Master' is therefore a reference to Lincoln. Booth continues:

Right, or wrong, God, judge me, not man. For be my motive good or bad, of one thing I am sure, the lasting condemnation of the north.
I love peace more than life. Have loved the Union beyond expression. For four years I have waited, hoped and prayed, for the dark clouds to break, And [*sic*] for a restoration of our former sunshine, to wait longer would be a crime. All hope for peace is dead, my prayers

---

224 Ibid.
225 Booth, 'To Whom It May Concern [Philadelphia, November] 1864', 124. According to the commentary by the editors, the letter is apparently addressed to Booth's brother-in-law John Sleeper Clarke, who supported the Union and with whom Booth had recently had a violent argument over the Civil War. See Booth, 'To Whom It May Concern [Philadelphia, November] 1864', footnote 2, 128.

have proved idle as my hopes. God's will be done. I go to see, and share the bitter end.[226]

John Matthews later reconstructed the beginning of the text written at the National Hotel as follows:

To My Countrymen: For years I have devoted my time, my energies, and every dollar I possessed to the furtherance of an object. I have been baffled and disappointed. The hour has come when I must change my plan. Many, I know – the vulgar herd – will blame me for what I am about to do, but posterity, I am sure, will justify me.

Then it continues as in the first letter: 'Right or wrong, God judge me, not man.' And so on.[227]

Booth signed the surviving letter with 'A *Confederate*, At present doing duty *upon his own responsibility*. J Wilkes Booth';[228] while in Matthews's reconstruction it ends with a reference to Shakespeare's *Julius Caesar*: 'I answer with Brutus: He who loves his country better than gold or life. John W. Booth.'[229]

If one applies Lübbe's criteria here, the texts of Becker, Booth and Karakozov display all the elements and functions that are typical of the claim of responsibility as a genre (with one significant exception). Becker's text contains an identification ('Oskar Becker, student of law in Leipzig'), one political denial of triviality ('but I am carried by the hope that it will have a beneficial effect upon Germany's future') and an indication of its purpose in attracting publicity and legitimation ('Note on the Motives for My Deed'). He provides a legitimation of the assassination attempt in his motive: Becker wanted to promote German

226 Booth, 'To Whom It May Concern [Philadelphia, November] 1864', 124. The explanation uses the additional information provided by the editors, note 3, 128–9.

227 Booth, 'To the Editors of the *National Intelligencer*. Washington, D.C., April 14, 1865', 147.

228 Booth, 'To Whom It May Concern [Philadelphia, November] 1864', 127.

229 Booth, 'To the Editors of the *National Intelligencer*. Washington, D.C., April 14, 1865', 150; and – almost identical – another version of the letter printed in note 5, 153. The content of the letter 'To Whom It May Concern' and its reconstructions have also received little attention in earlier scholarship, probably because no document with the exact wording of Booth's claim of responsibility has survived. Kauffman does not discuss it in *American Brutus*, and Alford only devotes one paragraph to it in *Fortune's Fool*, 260.

unification by killing Wilhelm I. This unification, in his view, could only take place through Prussia. The Prussian king, however, seemed unsuited to this task. He therefore had to be killed. To him this killing appeared to be the only way to open the path to German unification. His attempt to ensure its psychological effect is laid out in the call to action ('May the Germans finally . . .'). This means that Oskar Wilhelm Becker's written confession is perhaps the first claim of responsibility in history to be consciously composed as such.

John Wilkes Booth's letters likewise display all the elements and functions of a claim of responsibility. In both versions – from November 1864 and from 14 April 1865 – Booth signed with his full name (identification). He anticipates the public interest motivating his own attempt to attract publicity with the phrase 'but as some, may wish to know ~~the when, the who~~ and ~~the why~~ [sic]'. Pompous phrases like 'Right, or wrong, God, judge me, not man' function as political denials of triviality. This formulation also marks the need for legitimation.

Booth dedicates significant space to the attempt to justify his use of violence. He describes violence essentially as the last resort: 'God grant, it [the preservation of the Union] may be done in a peaceful way. If not, it must be done with blood. Ay with blood & Justice,' was his declaration to his imaginary public already in December 1860, by which he meant the preservation of the Union on the conditions of the slave states.[230] Since then, however, collective violence had been applied on a massive scale in the Civil War. But its application had not led to the desired and – in Booth's eyes – only correct and legitimate result: 'I love peace more than life,' it reads in this connection in the November letter, and then also in the reconstructed letter: 'All hope for peace is dead, my prayers have proved as idle as my hopes.'[231] It was Booth's conviction that, in this situation, conscience must lead one to act, especially if the nation itself had left the path of justice, inverted right and wrong and thereby forfeited its legitimacy: 'When a country ~~such as ours~~ ^like this^ spurns *justice* from her side, She forfeits the allegiance of every honest freeman, and ^should^ leave him untrammeled [sic] by any fealty soever, to act,

---

230 Booth, '[Draft of Speech] Philadelphia, late December 1860', 60.

231 Booth, 'To Whom It May Concern [Philadelphia, November] 1864', 124; Booth, 'To the Editors of the National Intelligencer. Washington, D.C., April 14, 1865', 147.

as his conscience may approve.'[232] He logically signed this as 'A *Confederate*, ~~At present~~ doing duty *upon his own responsibility*.'[233] In Booth's verbose explanation, the legitimacy of his own violence was therefore based in the illegitimacy of state action.

In contrast to this, the substantive reasons Booth uses in his letters to justify his violence remain vague. This also has consequences for the psychological effect of his text. It is clear that the concept of 'justice' for the slave states was crucial to Booth and that it denotes the right of the slave states to preserve their social order, and therefore slavery, and that it also includes the right of secession. Booth, after all, was convinced that in the United States supremacy belonged to the whites: 'This country was formed for the *white* not for the black man,' he writes again and again. 'And looking upon *African slavery* from the same stand-point, ~~as~~ held by those noble framers of our Constitution. I for one, have ever considered *it* [slavery], one of the greatest blessings (both for themselves [the slaves] and us), that God even [*sic*] bestowed upon a favored nation.'[234] Lincoln's policy, he claims, is only preparing the way 'for their total annihilation' – probably an allusion to race war. Booth adds to the 1864 November letter that the Union was forcing the southern states to choose between 'extermination' and 'slavery for *themselves* (worse than death).'[235]

In terms of psychological effects, Booth's text is not particularly geared towards its public. He accuses the population of the North of forgetting 'the teaching of our fathers', being as they were 'to hate tyranny to love liberty and justice, to strike at wrong and oppression'. But more than anything else what he presents here is a testimonial of his love for the southern states. In both letters it is clear that Booth hopes his act of violence will once more stave off the defeat of the Confederate States. He does not, however, dedicate a single word in either text to his belief that Lincoln was an illegitimate president who wanted to eliminate democracy in the United States and install himself as dictator.

232 Booth, 'To Whom It May Concern [Philadelphia, November] 1864', 124; Booth, 'To the Editors of the National Intelligencer. Washington, D.C., April 14, 1865', 147.

233 Booth, 'To Whom It May Concern [Philadelphia, November] 1864', 127. On the question of legitimacy in a broader theoretical and historical context see Dietze, 'Legitimacy and Security from a Historical Perspective'.

234 Ibid., 125; Booth, 'To the Editors of the National Intelligencer. Washington, D.C., April 14, 1865', 147.

235 Booth, 'To Whom It May Concern [Philadelphia, November] 1864', 125; Booth, 'To the Editors of the National Intelligencer. Washington, D.C., April 14, 1865', 147–8.

Dmitry Vladimirovich Karakozov's proclamation displays quite the opposite set of priorities. His proclamation contains no explicit examination of the legitimacy of the violence he planned to carry out; the need to legitimize his assassination attempt is signalled only by the fact that he wrote the proclamation at all.

In contrast, Karakozov does provide extensive legitimation in terms of the substance of his grievances. This legitimation begins with the socio-political situation in Russia and subsequently attempts to demonstrate both the tsars' historical guilt and their renewed guilt in the form of the Emancipation Edict, which, he argues, came at the expense of the emancipated serfs. A brief denial of triviality follows – specifically that he had decided to 'destroy the criminal tsar' because his 'beloved people is perishing in this way'.[236] Karakozov follows with additional remarks on its substantive legitimation, in which he outlines his future utopia of a Russia without the tsar and all his good-for-nothings: the land will be distributed to the people who actually use it, capital will no longer be drained into the coffers of the tsar and his aides but will remain in the hands of the working population who can reuse it profitably, the Russian people will find the ways and means to rule themselves. In short, without the tsar and his apparatus, everyone would have enough and be happy. This would be 'true freedom' (*nastoiashchaia volia*).

Finally, Karakozov makes some concrete remarks on the psychological effect of his crime. He apparently thought that it would influence the general population in the following way: 'May the Russian people recognize their most important, most powerful enemy, be it Alexander II or Alexander III and so on, that doesn't matter.' He closes with an equally concrete instruction for creating publicity: 'Let each one of you who receives this sheet in your hands copy it out and give it to acquaintances to read, and let them pass it on into other hands.' What this proclamation lacks is an identification. His distribution of it before his act, however, explains this.[237]

---

236 Shilov, 'Iz istorii revoliutsionnogo dvizheniia 1860-kh gg.', 161; Klevenskii and Kotel'nikov, *Pokushenie Karakozova*, vol. 1, 293–4, quotation at 294.

237 As Karakozov later explained in court, he even kept his real name secret from doctor Kobylin, with whom he lived and discussed his plans for the assassination, so that no one could keep him from spreading his propaganda (and presumably from preparing for the assassination as well). See Karakozov's court testimony on 24 August 1866 in Klevenskii and Kotel'nikov, *Pokushenie Karakozova*, vol. 1, for instance at 238.

The arguments of the three claims of responsibility are not entirely original. To the contrary: Booth's references to Shakespeare's plays are rather obvious; John Rhodehamel and Louise Taper have also identified the quote from Lincoln. Other passages employ *topoi* that had long become discursive fixtures for supporters of slavery, as for example the warning of a race war, or the assertion that the United States had been created for 'the *white* not for the black man', or that slavery was the 'greatest blessing' for the institution's own victims.

Alexei Alexeevich Shilov has already established that the text of Karakozov's proclamation stands in a tradition of revolutionary proclamations, displaying this in both content and style, for example, 'To the Young Generation' (*K molodomu pokoleniu*, 1861), 'Young Russia' (*Molodaia Rossiia*, 1862), Chernyshevsky's 'To the Lords' Peasants' (*Barskim krest'ianam...*, 1864) as well as the proclamation to the peasants entitled 'They Have Oppressed You a Long Time, Brothers' ('Dolgo davili vas, bratsy').[238] Furthermore, Shilov referred to echoes of characterizations of Nicholas I's bureaucracy through the writings of the 'natural school', who, with Belinsky, Herzen, Turgenev, Dostoevsky and Saltykov-Shchedrin, comprised some of the most prominent representatives of the second and third generation of political intellectuals. He also found echoes of the so-called 'Russian Truth' document ('Russkaia Pravda') from the pen of the Decembrist Pavel Ivanovich Pestel. The text proposed the creation of a Russian republic with Jacobinist characteristics.[239] On the other hand, Mitrofan Mikhailovich Klevenskii worked out and illuminated the precise differences between the political ideas in Chernyshevsky and Karakozov's proclamations.[240] These

---

238 See Shilov, 'Iz istorii revoliutsionnogo dvizheniia 1860-kh gg', 164; as well as Venturi, *Roots of Revolution*, 345. For the proclamations 'To the Young Generation', 'Young Russia', 'To the Lords' Peasants' and 'They Have Oppressed You a Long Time, Brothers', see Rudnitskaia, *Revoliutsionnyi radicalism v Rossii*, documents 12, 22, 10, 25.

239 Shilov, 'Iz istorii revoliutsionnogo dvizheniia 1860-kh gg', 164; and 'Pokushenie Karakozova 4 aprelia 1866 g', 93. On the Decembrists, see above, pp. 397–8, 410; on the 'natural school', see Adolf Stender-Peterson, *Geschichte der russischen Literatur*, 5th ed. (Munich: C. H. Beck, 1993), Part 2, Chapter II.3; and Richard Peace, 'The Nineteenth Century: The Natural School and Its Aftermath, 1840–55', in Charles A. Moser (ed.), *The Cambridge History of Russian Literature* (Cambridge: Cambridge University Press, 1992), 189–247.

240 Klevenskii, 'Predislovie', in Klevenskii and Kotel'nikov, *Pokushenie Karakozova*, vol. 1, XI.

affinities and differences would need to be examined separately at another point.

It is decisive here, however, that the texts of Becker, Booth and Karakozov display other similarities more strongly linked to their time, which derive from the modelling function fulfilled by Felice Orsini and John Brown. This concerns, first of all, the idea of the 'deed' that is significant in all three texts. Becker uses the term 'deed' four times in his 'Note' of 120 words, in which the *deed* – just as with Orsini and Brown – is contrasted with the *word*: 'May the Germans finally turn away from fruitless equivocating and to action!'[241] Booth also made a call 'to act', 'untrammeled by any fealty soever', only following one's own conscience, and in another place in the same letter he writes, 'But there is no time for words,' which he contrasts to his own action, specifically to taking 'such a step' as his.[242] Karakozov had already explained to his friends the distinction between what he considered to be a necessary 'violent', 'decisive fact' (*rezkii, reshitel'nyi fakt*), a 'decisive step' (*reshitel'nyi shag*), and the kinds of 'facts' and 'steps' of his friends in their philanthropic activities.[243] Moreover, he had also explicitly distinguished between verbal propaganda (*slovesnaia propaganda*) and propaganda of the deed (*fakticheskaia propaganda*) in conversation with Kobylin.[244]

---

241 GLA Karlsruhe, 250/10, Bl. 4.

242 Booth, 'To Whom It May Concern [Philadelphia, November] 1864', 124, 126; Booth, 'To the Editors of the National Intelligencer. Washington, D.C., April 14, 1865', 147–8.

243 Ishutin's testimony in Klevenskii and Kotel'nikov, *Pokushenie Karakozova*, vol. 1, 69. Also see pp. 486–7 in this volume.

244 See Karakozov's court testimony on 24 August 1866, printed in Klevenskii and Kotel'nikov, *Pokushenie Karakozova*, vol. 1, 240; as well as earlier in this volume, pp. 486–7, 494. Claudia Verhoeven, *The Odd Man Karakozov*, 147–9, attributes the invention of 'propaganda of the deed' to Karakozov: ' "Factual Propaganda" Is Karakozov's Concept'. She then, however, reports (ibid., 213, note 106), that the concept was initially advanced by the Italian revolutionaries Carlo Pisacane, Errico Malatesta and Carlo Cafiero and that the expression's coinage is usually attributed to the French anarchist Paul Brousse in a text from 1877. But, according to Verhoeven, what all of these figures had meant by this was 'collective action', while Karakozov had already used the term in 1866 for what it tended to mean later, specifically assassinations. The history of the term must therefore be revised, 'for it was in fact Karakozov who coined the phrase in 1866: *fakticheskaia propaganda*. And he meant by it precisely singular, serial assassinations' (ibid.). This is not correct, because assassinations were only one of the possible activities which Karakozov subsumed under the term *fakticheskaia propaganda*, and Paul

These terms do not appear in Karakozov's proclamation; he likewise avoided other equivalents of the idea of deed (for example the term *delo* – in the sense of act, deed – which Chernyshevsky employed). Instead he speaks concretely of 'destroy[ing] the criminal tsar' (*unichtozhit' tsaria-zlodeia*), likely because Karakozov sought to align himself linguistically with his target audience, which also and specifically included the working population with limited education. This segment of the population would have been able to make even less of terms like 'decisive facts' or 'steps' than the presiding judge of the criminal court, Prince Oldenburgskii.

The philosophy of the deed nonetheless did find its way into Karakozov's proclamation, specifically in the idea of the 'new man'. According to Chernyshevsky these 'new people' are distinguished by an 'untiring, tactical vigor'. Thus Karakozov, following Chernyshevsky's reception of Brown, gave his readers a call to action in the last sentence of his proclamation: 'May the workers recognize that . . . they must take care of themselves and not place their hopes on anyone else besides themselves, that they seize happiness for themselves and liberate Russia from its robbers and wrongdoers.' The model of John Brown, as Chernyshevsky portrayed him vigorously driving the Missourians out of Kansas, is clearly present in Karakozov's formulation.

A further similarity among the three claims of responsibility is the way the authors broach the issue of their readiness for self-sacrifice. Oskar Wilhelm Becker states this succinctly and unpretentiously: 'I know the unfortunate consequences that my deed will have for my person.'[245] He explained this more in court:

> I know well that my whole future is ruined, and I have always expected the death penalty, even if I should miss the king completely or not fatally. I did not only prepare for this deed in the knowledge that I would have to suffer the death penalty, but also with the outlook that I would not be considered in my right mind.[246]

Brousse's term, strongly influenced by Orsini's assassination attempt, referred to both individuals and small bands of conspirators. On this see Miller, 'The Intellectual Origins of Modern Terrorism in Europe', 42; and Jensen, *The Battle against Anarchist Terrorism*, 16. Karakozov's use of the term points more towards his reception of Western European ideas than to his own creativity.

245 GLA Karlsruhe, 250/10, Bl.4.
246 GLA Karlsruhe, 250/9, Becker's questioning on the morning of 27 July 1861, Bl. 274–5.

Becker had already anticipated the death penalty regardless of whether he killed the king or not. Hence the constant play of 'sacrifice' motifs (*Opfer* and *Aufopfern*) when he is questioned: Oskar Becker wanted to become a martyr for Germany. But he was also prepared to be seen as mad or mentally ill – even today a widespread reaction to terrorists.

In his letter of November 1864, Booth repeatedly mentions his own readiness to make sacrifices, including financial sacrifices. At the beginning he writes, 'I go to see, and share the bitter end', which implies that he will sacrifice himself; this is then followed by the sacrifice of happiness and money: 'I know how foolish I shall be deemed, for undertaking such a step, as this, Where on the one side, I have many friends, and everything to make me happy. Where my profession *alone* has gained me an income of *more than* Twenty thousand dollars a year', and again: 'If success attends me, I go penniless to her side [that is, of the South]'.[247] In Matthews's reconstruction, it reads right at the beginning: 'For years I have devoted my time, my energies, and every dollar I possessed to the furtherance of an object'.[248] According to his letters, Booth made a strong effort to get recognition in the South for his contribution.

For Karakozov, too, self-sacrifice plays a central role in his proclamation. He writes, for example, that he is saddened that his 'beloved people' are perishing and that he has therefore decided to 'destroy the criminal tsar' and to die for his beloved people himself.[249] And yet beyond this self-sacrifice, Karakozov had also thought through the psychological effect that his readiness to sacrifice would have on his sympathizers:

> If I succeed in my plan, I will die with the thought that my death would bring a benefit for my good friend, the Russian peasant. And if it doesn't succeed, I believe that there will be people who will follow my path. Where I did not succeed – they will succeed. My death will be a model for them and inspire them.[250]

---

247 Booth, 'To Whom It May Concern [Philadelphia, November] 1864', 124, 126.

248 Booth, 'To the Editors of the National Intelligencer. Washington, D.C., April 14, 1865', 147.

249 Shilov, 'Iz istorii revoliutsionnogo dvizheniia 1860-kh gg.', 161; Klevenskii and Kotel'nikov, *Pokushenie Karakozova*, vol. 1, 293–4, quotation at 294.

250 Shilov, 'Iz istorii revoliutsionnogo dvizheniia 1860-kh gg.', 161; Klevenskii and Kotel'nikov, *Pokushenie Karakozova*, vol. 1, 294. On the idea of 'serial assassinations', see also Verhoeven, *The Odd Man Karakozov*, 147–9, whose argument that Karakozov had responded to Kobylin's criticism and that of another friend with this idea is not, however, convincing, as she assumes that the idea is a new one.

Karakozov assumed that no matter what, his sacrifice would advance the cause of the revolutionary movement in Russia – directly or indirectly. Karakozov had no doubt that his 'enterprise' would 'pay' politically, as John Brown had thought in his case.

While both Becker and Booth anticipated incomprehension and criticism, Karakozov did not consider this an issue. He drew clear lines between friend and foe, in which his enemies' disapproval could not challenge him and his friends' sympathy was presupposed as a given. Becker, on the other hand, wrote regarding public reaction, 'I know that many will not understand my deed; many will therefore rebuke it or even find it ridiculous.' It was precisely in anticipation of such reactions that he sought to explain his motives. And Booth wrote analogously in his letter from November 1864: 'Right, or wrong, God, judge me, not man. For be my motive good or bad, of one thing I am sure, the lasting condemnation of the north.' In Matthews's reconstruction it then says, 'Many, I know – the vulgar herd – will blame me for what I am about to do, but posterity, I am sure, will justify me.' The addressing of criticism and lack of understanding in these confessions can be read as an indication of the novelty and immaturity of the genre (and possibly also of its authors).

But, at least in Booth's case, his anticipation of being rejected also suggests that he understood the violence he perpetrated – an understanding he had gained explicitly from the example set by John Brown. Booth thus wrote in his November 1864 letter with smug exaggeration,

> When I aided in the capture and ~~the g~~ execution of John Brown, (Who was a murderer on our Western Border, and who was fairly *tried* and *convicted*, – . . . of treason, – And who by the way has since been made a God – I was proud of my little share in the transaction, for I deemed it my duty And that I was helping our common country to perform an act of justice. But what was a crime in poor John Brown is now considered (by themselves) ^as^ the greatest and only virtue, of the whole Republican party. Strange transmigration, *vice* to become a *virtue*. Simply because *more* indulge in it. I thought then, *as now*, that the abolitionists, *were the only traitors* in the land . . .[251]

---

251 Booth, 'To Whom It May Concern [Philadelphia, November] 1864', 125.

The same action that in John Brown's case – according to Booth – was still rightly and clearly regarded and condemned as treason and therefore also as an injustice was now, by virtue of its origin in the federal government, regarded as just. In his eyes this was an absurd reversal of morality.

For Booth, John Brown appears here as a moral landmark of a world in which good and evil were still fixed and took their usual and proper place, a landmark that undoubtedly marked the site of the crime. At the same time, he describes John Brown as 'poor' because he had merely acted too early. Four years later, when – in Booth's telling – the entire Republican Party, including the president, were doing as John Brown had done, the old abolitionist would no longer have landed on the scaffold as a result of his act.[252] Brown's apotheosis, which Booth clearly had in mind, could be seen as a clear indication of this transformation of the moral dimensions and beliefs of his society. Through the example of John Brown, Booth comes to the conclusion of a relativity in political and moral judgements; that is, his claim of responsibility reaches the very same conclusion that Brown himself had formulated in his letters before execution: that it is not the act itself but the political circumstances that determine punishment and judgement.

The extent to which Booth was under the impression of the attack on Harpers Ferry and the interpretations of this event becomes clear when one takes these statements about John Brown together with his anticipation of criticism from the North and his designation of the US Constitution (as well as the rights of the South enshrined therein) as 'sacred'.[253] He saw himself, analogous to Brown but with reversed political positions, as a defender of the 'higher law' of the American Constitution and the God-given social order of the southern states, which for him represented the state of legitimacy – a legitimacy that was existentially threatened by what was in his view the illegitimate military power of the Union, led by an illegitimate commander-in-chief, and by the Union's illegitimate legislation. (Booth was not concerned about

---

252 Booth's sister supplies an appropriate comparison between Lincoln and John Brown: 'He [Lincoln] is walking in the footprints of John Brown, but no more fit to stand with that rugged old hero – Great God! No . . . a man springing from the ashes of old Assanothime Brown [sic – Booth means Osawatomie Brown].' Clarke, *The Unlocked Book*, 122.

253 Booth, 'To Whom It May Concern [Philadelphia, November] 1864', 125; and 'To Mary Ann Holmes Booth [Philadelphia, November] 1864', 131.

political details, such as the fact that the Confederacy had started the war.) It is precisely this assumption of a conflict between legitimacy and legality – a mode of thinking he had come to know through John Brown and his act of violence – as well as his self-image of defending legitimacy against legality, that makes Booth's act of violence a terrorist act.

The significance of the deed–propaganda–sacrifice triad is legible in the confessions of each of the three imitators. But how did they imagine the interaction of these three aspects in relation to the public? That is, what did they think about the psychological and symbolic effects of their actions? Were these attacks *intended* to 'spread uncertainty and horror' as well as 'generate sympathy and willingness to support'?[254]

Different kinds of sources relating to Becker, Booth and Karakozov provide varying information in answer to these questions. While the claim of responsibility in Karakozov's case already gives a number of valuable leads, Becker's 'note' on this question says comparatively little. In his case, court files can be used to fill in the gaps, as there he provided to the examining magistrate detailed information on his models, the political background and the intention and logic of his actions, information he even presented with a certain pride. John Wilkes Booth, on the other hand, who was shot on the run, could only reflect on his actions in his diary. That is why his diary entries are used here as the best source for these questions.

Becker explained to the Baden-Baden magistrate that he had hoped the indirect effect of the assassination would be 'an amendment of the Federal Constitution in a unified sense' (Becker's awkward term for unification). He stressed that he had carried out his deed 'by no means with regard to the king's mode of governing *in Prussia itself*' but only with regard to his policy on Germany, and clarified, 'I demand from the king of Prussia that he bring about the unification of Germany, and that he should do so at all costs.'[255] He cited as role models King Frederick the Great and King Vittorio Emanuele II, who had been confirmed only four months earlier as king of a united Italy. Compared to these two monarchs, Becker considered the Prussian king Wilhelm I to be too limited and harmless:

---

254 Waldmann, *Terrorismus*, 12; also see p. 46 in this volume.

255 GLA Karlsruhe, 250/9, Becker's interrogation, 27 July 1861, morning, Bl. 276, 275 and Bl. 271 (emphasis in the original).

If the present king of Prussia had a greater spirit, suited to his task, he would find in himself the means to achieve his goal . . . I acknowledge the great righteousness of the present king of Prussia; but I do not believe that this is the quality which can bring about the unification of Germany.[256]

The Prussian king Wilhelm I was, according to Becker, simply the wrong man for the important political position he occupied.

Decisive for the classification of his act of violence is the fact that Becker was not at all sure whether Wilhelm's son Frederick, who according to the dynastic principle would have taken over the government after a successful assassination, was much more suitable than his father. During the interrogation he explained that he 'had not heard anything from the current Crown prince that would make him particularly capable of achieving the unification of Germany'. But he was convinced that the assassination attempt would further the cause of German unification quite independently of the Crown prince's particular aptitudes, since 'the moral impression that my deed will exert on the German nation and the Crown prince of Prussia will be conducive to the development of Germany in a unified sense.'[257] Becker thus believed it was the psychological effect of his act on the royal family and the German public which would be significant, and not whether or not the assassination was successful.

The decisive factors in Becker's calculation were thus the public and the psychological effects of his deed, and he regarded both factors as crucial for the success of his plan. He saw himself as a role model, in the same way that he had recognized Orsini's assassination attempt as exemplary: he hoped that his deed could be 'imitated' by those who, like himself, 'could be enthusiastic about a similar sacrifice at the sight of another sacrificing himself for a purpose'. As he explained to the examining magistrate, this did not always have to be an assassination; if 'some will at least make small sacrifices, e.g. in pecuniary terms', much had already been achieved in his view.[258] More important,

256 GLA Karlsruhe, 250/9, Bl. 265–80: Becker's interrogation, 27 July 1861, morning, Bl. 269–70.

257 Ibid., Bl. 272.

258 Ibid., Bl. 273 and Bl. 279. He did not state how and for what he wanted to use the money collected.

however, were the attacks to follow, as Becker was clearly aware: 'If my deed remains quite isolated, its effect naturally fades away.' Therefore his plan was as follows:

> But if one thinks that among the forty million Germans some would be willing to make the same sacrifice as I, then the princes of Germany would be terrorized [*terrorisiert werden*], or given an external incentive to meet the needs of the idea of unity, while in the present circumstances they can ignore public opinion without fear.[259]

Becker thus reckoned that a sufficiently large number of people would follow him and also carry out assassination attempts on German heads of state so that no prince would feel safe in his small state any longer. Only when the crowned heads of state felt the direct pressure of public opinion would they be prepared to give up their sovereignty and unite Germany.

Becker thus addressed the psychological message of his assassination attempt to two groups simultaneously: he sought sympathy, support and enthusiastic followers among the German population;[260] at the same time, he wanted to spread insecurity and terror among the ruling princes of Germany, thus forcing them to change their policies. For this strategy of threat and intimidation he used the term 'terrorize' (*terrorisieren*) as a transitive verb.

The importance that Becker attached to the psychological effect and the public reaction was so great that the question whether or not the king of Prussia was dead became irrelevant to him. The minutes of the interrogations repeatedly record statements like the following:

> I would also like to point out that I was of the opinion that even if I did not succeed in carrying out the assassination, it would have the same effect on the transformation of Germany in a unified sense as if

---

259 Ibid., Bl. 273.

260 As Becker testified, he had first thought of securing followers by addressing other students. But he abandoned this idea without clarifying the reasons for this: 'I do not have accomplices, only once in the beginning did I think of associating with a student for this so that he would repeat an assassination attempt if I failed. But I did not speak to any students or third parties about this.' GLA Karlsruhe, 250/9, Becker's interrogation, 5 August 1861, morning, Bl. 441.

it were successful. Specifically I was thinking of its moral effect on the German people and on the king himself.[261]

Whether successful or not, the psychological effect of the assassination on the public and the princes would be, in Becker's view, equally powerful – exactly as it had been in Orsini's case.

Consequently, he also considered it possible that his act, even in the event of its failure, would lead to the intended goal, 'since perhaps the king of Prussia – although it is again quite unlikely – would pursue a different a[nd] more correct policy in regard to German unification'.[262] Napoleon III had provided an example. For Becker, the victim of his violence and the target of the attack were therefore not identical, and the attack was for him a highly symbolic act. In this respect, the goal of influencing the public and the princes in the desired way could be achieved even if the act of violence failed while its message still reached its audience. It was not the death of Wilhelm I that was decisive for Becker; rather, it was a question of successful communication.

From Becker's perspective, whether his message of violence would be successfully communicated to the German public or not depended on whether he could convey the motives of his assassination attempt to the public and the princes. As he had already attempted in his 'note', Becker repeatedly expressed his worry during his interrogations that his act would be 'rebuked [reprobirt] by many, and completely misunderstood, especially if the motive would not become adequately known to the public, that I have acted in the belief that I was doing something conducive to the unification of Germany'.[263] Becker was convinced that his attempted murder would be rejected if the public did not understand his reasons for undertaking it. Furthermore, he explained what a 'colossal effect' he had hoped for from his assassination attempt, precisely because 'such an act has not yet been recorded in the annals of German history'.[264]

---

261 GLA Karlsruhe, 250/9, Bl. 438–54, Becker's interrogation, 5 August 1861, morning, Bl. 441. Also see, for example: 'Even if my attempt did not succeed, I still hoped for it to have a beneficial effect on Germany.' GLA Karlsruhe, 250/9, Becker's interrogation, 27 July 1861, morning, Bl. 276; as well as ibid., Bl. 278.

262 GLA Karlsruhe, 250/9, Becker's interrogation, 27 July 1861, morning, Bl. 278.

263 Ibid., Bl. 275.

264 'Oskar Becker's Proceß. (Von unseren eigenen Berichtstattern.) ... Bruchsal, 23. September' and 'Oskar Becker's Proceß. (Von unseren eigenen Berichtstattern.) ... Bruchsal, 24. September', Kölnische Zeitung, 26 September 1861, first edition, 3, and second edition, 1.

The success or failure of his enterprise for him thus depended on his reaching the public. He was aware, moreover, that as an initial spark this required a spectacular act, and regarded the extraordinary nature of the act as a possible prerequisite for this spectacle.

John Wilkes Booth's diary also clearly shows the importance he attached to the public reception of his motives. He read newspapers while on the run and learned that his letter had not been printed in the press, and that not only the general public disapproved of his act, but his friends and colleagues as well.[265]

His first entry, which he dated both 'April 13th' and '14 Friday the Ides' and which was probably composed on 17 April 1865, was written in Zekiah Swamp, a marshy area in southern Maryland north-east of the Potomac, where he hid for six days before he managed to cross over the Potomac to Virginia. Here he writes: 'This night (before the deed), I wrote a long article and left it for one of the Editors of the National Inteligencer [sic], in which I fully set forth our reasons for our proceedings. He or the Govmt'. At this point the entry breaks off.[266] Booth probably had intended to write that John Matthews or the government had withheld the article – he came back to the subject in his next entry. Titled 'Friday 21', although probably written on 22 April 1865, it reads,

After being hunted like a dog through swamps, woods, and last night being chased by gun boats till I was forced to return wet cold and starving, with every mans [sic] hand against me, I am here in despair. And why; For doing what Brutus was honored for, what made Tell a Hero. And yet I for striking down a greater tyrant than they ever knew am looked upon as a common cutthroat . . . The little, the very little I left behind to clear my name, the Govmt will not allow to be printed. So ends all. For my country I have given up all that makes life sweet and Holy, brought misery on my family, and am sure there is no pardon in Heaven for me since man condemns me so . . . To night I will once more try the river with the intent to cross, though I have a

265 The best overview of public reactions can be found in Alford, *Fortune's Fool*, 280–2.

266 Booth, 'Diary. Zekiah Swamp and Nanjemoy Creek, Charles County, Maryland, 17 and 22 April 1865', 154. On this see the editor's notes, especially footnote 2 at 155–6 and note 7 at 156; as well as Alford, *Fortune's Fool*, 278–80.

greater desire to return to Washington and in a measure clear my name which I feel I can do. I do not repent the blow I struck. I may before God but not to man. I think I have done well, though I am abandoned, with the curse of Cain upon me. When if the world knew my heart, *that one* blow would have made me great, though I did desire no greatness.

The diary ends with the sentence 'I do not wish to shed a drop of blood, but "I must fight the course" Tis all thats [sic] left me.'[267] These are Booth's last surviving political statements.

The diary entries quoted document, first, the significance which Booth attributed to the public reaction. His expectations of the public's reception of his act of violence become clear. According to his diary, Booth had assumed that those who sympathized with the confederation, whom he had also regarded as his own potential sympathizers, would respond in the press by explaining, supporting and legitimizing his actions, that he would be received with open arms, and that he would be celebrated as a hero – indeed as a god. He measured his expectations explicitly against the dramatic heroes of Brutus from Shakespeare's *Julius Caesar* and Schiller's *William Tell*, but presumably also against John Brown's reception in the northern states, where Brown – as Booth himself had noted – had been declared a god.

But his expectations were bitterly disappointed. Booth, fleeing through southern Maryland and northern Virginia, would learn that most doors remained closed to him and that even the people who had stood predominantly on the side of the Confederates during the war despised him as a common 'cutthroat' and extended 'the cold hand' to him. Thus he learned that he had no sympathizers or that those he had did not dare to show sympathy.[268] The paramount importance that Booth ascribed to this lack of public and interpersonal sympathy is the most apparent where he wrote that there could be 'no pardon in Heaven' for him, 'since man condemns me so'. With this he granted sovereignty

267 Booth, 'Diary. Zekiah Swamp and Nanjemoy Creek, Charles County, Maryland, 17 and 22 April 1865', 154–5. Also see the editor's commentary in notes 8, 10, at 157; as well as Alford, *Fortune's Fool*, 284–7.

268 Booth, 'Diary. Zekiah Swamp and Nanjemoy Creek, Charles County, Maryland, 17 and 22 April 1865', 154.

to public reaction in interpreting his actions and himself began to question the legitimacy of his action.[269]

The diary entries furthermore show the importance Booth attached to his claim of responsibility. He blamed the hostile reactions with which he was met at every turn entirely on the fact that his letter to the *National Intelligencer* had not been published and his noble motives had been entirely withheld from the public. Indeed, the non-appearance of his confession letter meant that the functions characterized by Hermann Lübbe as 'attracting publicity' and 'denying triviality', which were to set the act apart from common murder, could not be performed, nor could the 'need for legitimation' be either declared or met. The communicative act had failed – Booth's message had not reached its audience. The murder of President Abraham Lincoln remained unexplained and unjustified. The stigma – the curse of Cain, as Booth called it – stuck to him, and no transformation from stigma to charisma took place.

For Dmitry Vladimirovich Karakozov, too, the reactions were central in calculating the effect of his violent act. This can already be seen in his proclamation and how he dealt with it: first, there is the fact that he tried to write as many copies as possible in his own hand and to circulate them among potential sympathizers. Second, he explicitly invited his readers to join him in disseminating the proclamation, suggesting towards the end of the text (as already quoted), 'Let each one of you who receives this sheet in your hands copy it out and give it to acquaintances to read, and let them pass it on into other hands.'[270] Karakozov tried to initiate a subversive snowball effect to reach his potential sympathizers. Third, he expressly considered and described his act as propaganda by deed (*fakticheskaia propaganda*), and provided many concrete reflections in his proclamation on the effect of this propaganda, that is, on the psychological effect of his violence.[271]

In calculating the intended psychological effects of the assassination, Karakozov differentiated precisely between friend and foe. Then, within

269 On this, also see Alford, *Fortune's Fool*, 287.
270 Shilov, 'Iz istorii revoliutsionnogo dvizheniia 1860-kh gg.', 162; Klevenskii and Kotel'nikov, *Pokushenie Karakozova*, vol. 1, 294.
271 Karakozov's court testimony on 24 August 1866, printed in Klevenskii and Kotel'nikov, *Pokushenie Karakozova*, vol. 1, 240. On this, see Venturi, *Roots of Revolution*, 345; and Verhoeven, *The Odd Man Karakozov*, 147–9.

the group of potential sympathizers, he further distinguished between radical activists and the uneducated Russian population, whose sympathy he counted on. To the radical activists his act of violence – regardless of its success or failure – was to be a model worth imitating. For the general Russian population, however, he wanted to create a didactic spectacle: 'May the Russian people recognize their most important, most powerful enemy, be it Alexander II or Alexander III and so on, that doesn't matter,' he says in his proclamation.[272]

As far as the psychological effect on the enemy was concerned, Karakozov's calculation was quite similar to that of Becker. At least according to the statements of other court witnesses, his aim was to frighten the tsar, his government and his aids so deeply through his violent act that they would be compelled to carry out social reforms: 'You can force the government to carry out social reforms by intimidating them,' Ermolov is said to have explained with regard to Karakozov's intentions.[273] Just like Becker, Karakozov was also aware that there would be no such intimidation if it remained only a matter of his lone act; he therefore needed successors.

Beyond this, Karakozov hoped that shooting the tsar would act as a trigger that could set the entire Russian political field in motion. In a written interrogation he remarked on the necessity of this crime to produce the political revolution (*perevorot*) that would lead to the improvement of the material well-being of 'the simple people', and Klevensky concludes from this in his foreword that the murder of the tsar was intended to 'stir up the whole of society and immediately provoke a social revolution'.[274] This led Venturi to conclude, 'However strange it may appear at first sight, if we follow the strand of revolutionary movements from *Zemlya i Volya* onwards, we are inevitably led to conclude that the pistol shot becomes an exact substitute' for appeals to the tsar.[275]

---

272 Shilov, 'Iz istorii revoliutsionnogo dvizheniia 1860-kh gg', 161; Klevenskii and Kotel'nikov, *Pokushenie Karakozova*, vol. 1, 294.

273 As cited in Klevenskii, 'Predislovie', in Klevenskii and Kotel'nikov, *Pokushenie Karakozova*, vol. 1, xii.

274 Karakozov's testimony from 16 April 1866 in Shilov, 'Pokushenie Karakozova 4 aprelia 1866 g', 95; and Klevenskii, 'Predislovie', in Klevenskii and Kotel'nikov, *Pokushenie Karakozova*, vol. 1, xii.

275 Venturi, *Roots of Revolution*, 335.

542   The Invention of Terrorism

Thus both the development of social movements towards political violence and the expectations of the political consequences of the terrorist attack show strong parallels with the violent acts of Felice Orsini and Oskar Wilhelm Becker, only that in Russia the social question was in the foreground and Karakozov no longer felt compelled to formulate the goals of social change through revolution as a continuation of the revolutions in the West – instead, he did so precisely by drawing it in distinction to them.

The assassination attempts of Becker, Booth and Karakozov show all the important elements of terrorism, including the combination of sensational act and propaganda. In Peter Waldmann's definition, these acts were shocking violent attacks against political orders 'from below', *intended* by their perpetrators to 'spread feelings of insecurity and fear' but also 'generate sympathy and support'.[276] As expressed in the political intentions and goals of the three terrorists, the political dimensions of Becker's, Karakozov's and Booth's acts of violence were, respectively: German unification at any price, sparking a social revolution for the betterment of the emancipated serfs, and averting the collapse of the Confederate States of America and the practical implementation of measures to ensure freedom for the former slaves.

Peter Waldmann additionally emphasizes the importance of communication: 'Terrorism, it must be remembered, is primarily a communication strategy.'[277] Becker and Karakozov were acting precisely in accordance with this logic by claiming they could achieve their goals – forcing the German princes to unite Germany or rousing the Russian people to action and showing them their true enemy – regardless of whether they killed Wilhelm I or Alexander II, as long as the public understood the reasons for their actions. With this they wanted to transmit two different messages at the same time (entirely corresponding to the definition of terrorism): on the one hand, intimidating the princes and, on the other, appealing for sympathy and successors among the general population. Booth, who unlike Becker and Karakozov actually succeeded in killing his victim, reflected more deeply on public reaction and thus showed he understood its significance for his action.

---

276 Waldmann, *Terrorismus*, 12.
277 Ibid., 15.

In all three cases, the shock effect necessary (by definition) for the terrorist act to work was tied to the prominence of the victim. It was just as shocking to attack the ruler appointed by God and the God-given social order of the monarchy as it was to attack the president elected by the people. All three imitators ambushed the head of state and prepared their plans secretly, and thus represented attacks against the political order organized 'from below'.

Once again, all of Peter Waldmann's definitional criteria are fulfilled in the attacks by Becker, Booth and Karakozov. And what is more, the three imitators did not just bring these elements together by chance, but rather combined them after thinking through their internal connections. They had analysed the acts carried out by their role models in one way or another; established the connection between deed, propaganda and sacrifice; and understood the functional mechanisms of terrorist tactics that resulted from Orsini's cooperation with Napoleon III and Brown's attack on Harpers Ferry.

But how did their claims of responsibility and the news of the attacks on Wilhelm I, Abraham Lincoln and Alexander II actually spread, and what reactions did they provoke? Just as with Orsini and Brown, the media were of central importance here for the reception and transmission of their writings and the news of their acts. The assumption, however, that the mass media or the manual dissemination of written claims of responsibility would inform a wider section of the population about the assassinations and the assassins' motives was initially nothing more than a bet on the future. The question of how these messages would be spread and received was as open in the moment of their acts as the question of what reactions these messages would provoke. Indeed, so was the question of whether they could – as the assassins had calculated – actually provoke fear and terror as well as sympathy and support.

Politico–symbolic failure

As previously with the violent acts of Felice Orsini and John Brown, the success of the terrorist attacks committed by Oskar Wilhelm Becker, John Wilkes Booth and Dmitry Vladimirovich Karakozov depended on public and political reactions. All three acts of violence initially failed on precisely this point; that is, they were unable to provoke the desired reactions – sympathy and support as well as fear and terror – from their governments or from the general population.

Why were these three attacks politically unsuccessful? The answers to this question refer once again to the decisive conditions for the success of Orsini's and Brown's acts of violence and thus to the conditions for the success of terrorist violence in general. Their successes depended first of all on the fact that the acts were spectacular, perceived as sensational and reported as events in the national and international press. The second prerequisite was that the violence was perceived as symbolic (and not primarily as instrumental), and that its symbolic content, message and call to action could be conveyed and would be understood. Third, it was crucial that governments or other powerful groups tried to instrumentalize the acts of terrorist violence politically and it was only really through this instrumentalization of the acts that they won political significance. Whether these conditions for success were met or not depended in turn on the existing political and social conditions already in place.

In the following analysis, the imitators' attacks will be examined with regard to these three conditions of success: first, the spectacular nature of the respective events as well as the popular and media reactions; second, their success or failure in transmitting their respective messages; and third, the reactions of the state.

Spectacularity and (media) event

The hypothesis to explain the failure of the terrorist attacks that comes first and most obviously to mind might be that the violent actions carried out by Becker, Booth and Karakozov were not spectacular enough. Neither Becker, nor Booth, nor Karakozov produced the scandal of a bomb attack like Orsini, nor did they attack a small town like Brown. They used ordinary revolvers for their violent attacks and only directed them against one person, their respective head of state.

But that does not get at the heart of it: each of the imitators' attacks actually *was* spectacular, and became the starting point for national and international media events. And even if they did not all achieve the same intensity of reaction as Orsini's and Brown's acts of violence, they each contained the potential for successful terrorist acts – they were acts that, in relation to their respective messages, were essentially capable of generating sympathy and support, fear and terror.

Even if this may seem unlikely from today's perspective, Oskar Wilhelm Becker's assassination attempt immediately became a national and international sensation and was covered as headline news. Once Count Flemming had left the carriage in which he and his aides had brought Becker back to Baden-Baden, he reported the assassination shortly after 11 a.m. to the Prussian minister of state and foreign affairs Baron von Schleinitz by telegram. For the time being, a ban was placed on the use of the telegraph by private individuals.

Flemming's telegram arrived in Berlin about an hour later. The text read,

This morning at 9 o'clock in Lichtenthaler Allee a double-barreled pistol [*Doppelterzerol*] was fired on His Majesty the King at point blank range by the Leipzig student Oskar Becker from Odessa. God's protection saved the king's life. A bullet went through the collar of the coat and caused a contusion on the left side of the neck not dangerous in character. His Majesty returned to His apartment on foot. I was in the king's company and arrested the student Becker who was handed over to the Grand Ducal Court. Count Flemming.[278]

The head of the Foreign Office had this message forwarded by telegram immediately and literally to all Prussian missions, to the royal consulates general in Warsaw and Bucharest, to members of the royal house and to the ministers of state.[279] All Prussian provinces were also informed.

Before these telegrams were received by the various embassies and addressees, however, many of them had already received corresponding telegraphic messages from the prince of Hohenzollern, whom Flemming had informed in passing in Lichtentaler Allee.[280] The authorities in

---

278 GStA PK, III. HA MdA, I No. 8913: Attack, o.Z., telegram no. 678 from Graf Flemming to the Minister [of Foreign Affairs] Baron von Schleinitz in Berlin on 14 July 1861 from Baden, time of transmission: 11 o'clock 4 min. a.m., time of arrival in Berlin: 12 o'clock 17 min. p.m. See, furthermore, the report, 'Berlin, 15. Juli', in *Kölnische Zeitung*, 17 July 1861.

279 GStA PK, III. HA MdA, I No. 8913: Attack, o.Z., memorandum I 13578 of 14 July 1861. Also see *Neue Preußische Zeitung*, 16 July 1861, 1; as well as the report, 'Berlin, 15. Juli', *Kölnische Zeitung*, 17 July 1861.

280 GStA PK, III. HA MdA, I No. 8913: Attack, o.Z., political report of the envoy to Stuttgart von der Schulenburg-Priemern to the Minister of Foreign Affairs von Schleinitz, 15 July 1861; GStA PK, III. HA MdA, I No. 8913: Attack, o.Z., telegram of the

Baden-Baden and other spa guests had also immediately taken the initi-ative and passed on the message by telegram as soon as they learned of the assassination attempt.[281]

In Baden-Baden itself, 'the message spread rapidly from group to group and caused disbelief everywhere,' as *L'illustration de Bade* wrote.[282] On the same day one could read the following note about the assassina-tion attempt in the *Badeblatt für die Großherzogliche Stadt Baden*:

> Baden, 14 July. Our city is in unusual frightful excitement owing to the news that this morning around 9 o'clock an assassination attempt took place on His Majesty the King of Prussia by means of a double pistol shot. Fortunately, the perpetrator missed his target both times and the one bullet only passed through the coat near the neck.[283]

At the last moment before the newspaper went to print, this informa-tion had been inserted between advertisements and stock market prices.

On the very same evening the people of Baden-Baden were given the opportunity to express their feelings of solidarity with the king 'in an appropriate way', with a torchlight procession in which 'the entire citi-zenship along with civil servants' participated with 500 to 600 torches and several thousand people. When they arrived at the king of Prussia's hotel, they assembled in the surrounding streets and listened to the performances of the choral society and the spa orchestra, who honoured

envoy to Vienna von Solms to the Minister of Foreign Affairs von Schleinitz, 14 July 1861, time of transmission: 7:55 p.m., time of arrival in Berlin: 9:40 p.m.; GStA PK, III. HA MdA, I No. 8913: Attack, o.Z. von Heydebrandt und der Lasa, Prussian envoy to the court of Weimar, to the Minister of Foreign Affairs von Schleinitz from 15 July 1861.

281 GLA Karlsruhe, 250/8, Bl. 4: telegraphic dispatch to the grand ducal Ministry of Justice; GLA Karlsruhe, 250/8, Bl. 6–8: telegram to the state prosecutor to the Royal Court of Appeals in Leipzig (draft); GLA Karlsruhe, dept. 236, Baden Ministry of the Interior, no. 8653, o.Z.: Report of the city director Kuntz in Baden to the President of the Baden Ministry of the Interior Lamey; GStA PK, III. HA MdA, I No. 8913: Attack, o.Z., memorandum I 13450, 14 July 1861: telegram of the Baden-Baden chancellery secretary Schaffner to the Minister of Foreign Affairs von Schleinitz, 14 July 1861, time of transmission 11:25 a.m.

282 *L'illustration de Bade: Journal littéraire et artistique de la vallée du Rhin et de la Forêt-Noire*, 18 July 1861, 60.

283 *Badeblatt für die Großherzogliche Stadt Baden: Amtliche Fremdenliste. Liste officielle des étrangers*, Sunday, 14 July 1861, 458.

Wilhelm I with, among other pieces, 'God Save the Queen'. Again and again they let out cheers for the king, who from time to time appeared on the balcony with his wife. *L'illustration de Bade* extoled this 'enormous demonstration' as a demonstration of European solidarity with Wilhelm of Prussia.

In the German states, news of the assassination was first spread by word of mouth among personnel and passengers on railway trains much like the news of John Brown's exploits. In addition, there was a telegram from Wolff's telegraph agency.[284] The two forms of media – telegraph and word of mouth – also worked in combination. 'Amazement', 'bewilderment' and 'deep disgust', 'pain', 'deepest indignation', 'tremendous agitation', 'deepest sympathy' in response to the 'cursed deed' and 'great joy' over the 'happy deliverance' make up the constantly recurring vocabulary with which the immediate reactions to the attempted assassination were described.[285] Whether in family circles or coffee houses, on public squares or walking paths, wherever the news reached, 'it hit everyone like a bolt of lightning'.[286] In public spaces, orchestras spontaneously played the Prussian anthem 'Heil Dir im Siegerkranz' (Hail Thee, Laurel Wreathed), and the audience joined them 'with enthusiastic cheers to His Majesty'.[287] Many houses in Berlin were 'illuminated' with lights and candles and draped with Prussian flags.[288]

Government offices all over Germany and Europe also received the news of Becker's assassination attempt that same evening. The Prussian envoys hurried to pass on the news to the respective princes. The princes, for their part, reacted with declarations of loyalty and telegrams with their congratulations.[289] Soon after, Wilhelm I's family

284 *Neue Preußische Zeitung*, 16 July 1861, 1.

285 See for example the reports from Berlin from 14 and 15 July 1861 in the *Wochenblatt*, 18 July 1861, 499; and in the *Badeblatt*, 17 July 1861, 477; *Neue Preußische Zeitung*, 16 July 1861, 1; *Staats- und gelehrte Zeitung des Hamburgischen unpartheyischen Correspondenten*, 16 July 1861, 1.

286 *Neue Preußische Zeitung*, 16 July 1861, 1.

287 Reports from Berlin from 14 and 15 July 1861 in the *Wochenblatt*, 18 July 1861, 499; and in the *Badeblatt*, 17 July 1861, 477.

288 'Berlin, 15. Juli', *Kölnische Zeitung*, 17 July 1861; *Neue Preußische Zeitung*, 16 July 1861, 1.

289 See, for example, GStA PK, III. HA MdA, I No. 8913: Attack, o.Z., telegram from Prince Gustav zu Ysenburg und Büdingen to von Schleinitz, 14 July 1861, 8 p.m.; GStA PK, III. HA MdA, I No. 8913: Attack, o.Z., Ysenburg to Minister of Foreign Affairs von Schleinitz, 15 July 1861; and GStA PK, III. HA MdA, I No. 8913: Attack, o.Z.,

members arrived, as did court emissaries with handwritten letters from their princes.

> Envoys arrived from all over Europe to convey congratulations to the king; a great number of princes from German and English families, ambassadors, high officials, delegations from cities and universities, diplomatic and military representatives have come to express their active sympathy and friendship on behalf of their sovereigns or on their own behalf,

read the description in *L'illustration de Bade*, and in this case the European dimension of the event was not exaggerated.[290]

To inform the general population, on the very evening of its receipt, 14 July 1861, the Prussian government published Flemming's telegram in a special edition of the Prussian *Staatsanzeiger* (Official State Gazette) and of the *Allgemeine Preußische Zeitung*.[291] In addition, some private newspapers reprinted the telegram word for word in special editions which they sent to their subscribers.[292] Over the course of Monday morning, new reports from Baden-Baden were received by government authorities in Berlin,[293] reports which found their way not only to officials and to members of Wilhelm I's family, but also to Wolff's telegraph office.[294] Thus one could read in the newspaper on 17 July 1861 that His Majesty the King had 'had quite a good night' and that 'sufficient sleep' had had a 'favorable effect on his energy', and then on 18 July that His

---

Prussian embassy at the Electoral Hessian Court, von Sydow, political report no. LXL Cassel, 15 July 1861.

290 *L'illustration de Bade*, 25 July 1861, 67.

291 See GStA PK, III. HA MdA, I No. 8913: Attack, o.Z., M[inisterium] d[er] a[uswärtigen] A[ngelegenheiten] (Foreign Ministry) to the Königl. Hofmarschall-Amt (Office of the Royal Major-Domo) from Berlin on 15 July 1861, as well as the report, 'Berlin, 15. Juli', *Kölnische Zeitung*, 17 July 1861.

292 *Volks-Zeitung*, 14 July 1861. *Neue Preußische Zeitung*, 16 July 1861, 1, mentions a special edition; they also printed the telegram on 16 July in the next regular printing, on the very first page. For reprints, also see, for example, *Die Presse*, 15 July 1861, 1; *Staats- und gelehrte Zeitung*, 16 July 1861, 1; *Volks-Zeitung*, 16 July 1861, 1.

293 GStA PK, III. HA MdA, I No. 8913: Attack, o.Z., Count Flemming's telegram from 15 July 1861, time of transmission 8:45 a.m., time of arrival in Berlin 9:35 a.m.

294 Memorandum in GStA PK, III. HA MdA, I No. 8913: Attack, o.Z., on the telegram of Count Flemming from 15 July 1861, time of transmission 8:45 a.m., time of arrival in Berlin 9:35 a.m.

Majesty the King had 'slept very well in the foregoing night', and felt thereby 'refreshed', and that no 'substantial change ... had otherwise occurred since yesterday'.[295] These bulletins from the king's personal physician now appeared on a daily basis, most often on the first page of German newspapers; the public loyal to the king probably regarded them as reassuring information.[296]

Becker's assassination attempt also received attention internationally. Just as in Germany, the first reports appeared in the newspapers of the European capitals outside the German states – for example in London, Paris and St Petersburg – on 15 or 16 July; that is, on the Monday or Tuesday following the attempt.[297] But the news even found its way into the provincial newspapers, which often appeared only two or three times per week, appearing in the very next issue following the attack.[298]

The news reached the United States with the ship *City of Baltimore*, which left port in Liverpool on 17 July 1861. On 18 July, the ship made a stopover in Queenstown (now Cobh in the south of the Republic of

295 GStA PK, III. HA MdA, I No. 8913: Attack, o.Z., telegram of Count Flemming, special envoy and authorized representative minister in Carlsruhe to the Minister of Foreign Affairs von Schleinitz in Berlin from Baden on 17 July 1861, 9:35 a.m., arrival 10:44 a.m.; GStA PK, III. HA MdA, I No. 8913: Attack, o.Z., telegram of Count Flemming, special envoy and authorized representative minister in Carlsruhe to the Minister of Foreign Affairs von Schleinitz in Berlin from Baden on 18 July 1861, 10:11 a.m., arrival 11:16 a.m.

296 See for example the *Kölnische Zeitung*, 17 July 1861; *National-Zeitung* (evening edition), 18 July 1861, 1, 4; *National-Zeitung* (evening edition), 20 July 1861, 1; *Berliner Börsen-Zeitung* (evening edition), 18 July 1861, 1; *Berliner Börsen-Zeitung* (evening edition), 19 July 1861, 1; *Berliner Börsen-Zeitung* (evening edition), 20 July 1861, 1457; *Staats- und gelehrte Zeitung*, 17 July 1861, 1 and 18 July 1861, 2; *Königlich Preußischer Staats-Anzeiger*, 17 July 1861, 1381; 18 July 1861, 1385; 19 July 1861, 1393; 20 July 1861, 1401; and 21 July 1861, 1409; *Volks-Zeitung*, 17 July 1861, 1; and 18 July 1861, 1.

297 For Great Britain, see *The Times*, 15 July 1861; *Manchester Examiner and Times*, 15 July 1861; *Morning Star*, 15 July 1861, 2; for France, see *La gazette de France*, 16 July 1861, 1; *Journal des débats*, Paris, 16 July 1861, 1; *Le Temps*, 16 July 1861, 1; for Russia, see *Sankt Peterburgskie vedomosti*, 4 July 1861, 840; and *Severnaia pchela*, 4 July 1861, 599.

298 For the Netherlands, for example, see the *Zierikzeesche Courant*, which appeared Wednesday and Saturday, the edition of Wednesday, 17 July 1861, 2: 'Jongste Tijdingen' (Latest News); in the *Goessche Courant*, which appeared Monday and Thursday, the edition on Thursday, 18 July 1861, 2: 'Buitenlandsche Berigten' (International Reports) and in the *Zierikzeesche Nieuwsbode*, which appeared Wednesday and Saturday, the edition of Saturday, 20 July 1861, 1: 'Duitschland' (Germany), with extensive reports from Berlin and Baden-Baden.

Ireland) and then passed Cape Race on 25 July at 10 p.m. There, as usual, the canister of European newspapers was thrown overboard and fished out of the water by the yacht of the Associated Press, which would then telegraph the reports from St John's to New York while the ship continued on its journey there.[299] On 25 July, however, the fog was so thick at Cape Race that a newspaper package was lost and the Associated Press staff in St John's only received the newspapers that had subsequently been brought onboard in Queenstown.[300]

The editors of the *New York Times* shared what they found there with their readers:

> The proceedings of Parliament had been unimportant, and political news generally was uninteresting. The most notable item is an attempt on the life of the King of Prussia, made at Baden on the 14th inst., by a young student from Liepsic, who fired a pistol at him, the ball from which grazed his neck.[301]

When the other news canister was finally found, a 'second dispatch' from St John's essentially repeated this information.[302]

In the days following the assassination attempt, both the German and the international media reported extensively on the exact course and setting of the attack, as well as on the Prussian royal couple and their own reactions to it.[303] This included a letter of thanks from

---

299 On the *City of Baltimore*, a ship of the Inman Line, and its function in communication between Europe and the United States, see the article 'European News by Mail: Arrival of the Steamship City of Baltimore', *New York Times*, 5 Jan. 1870, 5, as well as 'The Ships List, Ship Descriptions', and 'Inman Line', theshipslist.com.

300 'Four Days Later from Europe: The City of Baltimore off Cape Race. St. Johns, N.F., Friday, July 26', *New York Times*, 27 July 1861, 5.

301 'News of the Day', *New York Times*, 27 July 1861, 4.

302 'The King of Prussia was fired at at Baden, on the 14th, by a young student from Leipsic, named Becker, who was arrested. The ball slightly grazed the king's neck', 'Second Dispatch. St. Johns, Friday, July 26', *New York Times*, 27 July 1861, 5.

303 See, for example, *Journal des débats*, 16 July 1861, 1; *Morning Star*, London, 17 July 1861, 2; *La gazette de France*, 18 July 1861, 1; *Goessche Courant*, 18 July 1861, 2; *Journal des débats*, 18 July 1861, 1–2; *Le Temps*, 18 July 1861, 1; *La gazette de France*, 19 July 1861, 2; *Le Temps*, 19 July 1861, 1; *The Times*, London, 19 July 1861, 12; *La gazette de France*, 20 July 1861, 1; *Manchester Examiner and Times*, 20 July 1861; *Sankt Peterburgskie vedomosti*, 8 July 1861, 861; *Severnaia pchela*, 8 July 1861, 614; *The Times*, 20 July 1861, 9; *Zierikzeesche Nieuwsbode*, 20 July 1861, 1; *Severnaia pchela*, 10 July 1861,

Wilhelm I to the city of Baden-Baden and the announcement of plans to establish a King Wilhelm Foundation in his honour,[304] as well as reports on the king's injuries and translations of his health bulletins.[305] There were additionally reports on reactions in Baden-Baden and throughout Germany.[306] These included reports on Becker, his conduct following the assassination attempt and in court, and reports on the progress of the investigations and what the sentence might be.[307] There were even reports on thanksgiving services held for the king,[308] and on the arrival of envoys from all over Europe who congratulated him on surviving the attack.[309] There were also occasional reports about earlier attempts on the life of Wilhelm I and about the Prussian government's press and public relations work. Finally, space was also given to the economic and political consequences of the assassination attempt, such as the decline of stock market prices, the attacks on German

---

618; *Sankt Peterburgskie vedomosti*, 11 July 1861, 874; *Sankt Peterburgskie vedomosti*, 12 July 1861, 878.

304 See, for example, *La gazette de France*, 18 July 1861, 1; *Journal des débats*, 18 July 1861, 2; *The Times*, 20 July 1861, 9; *Zierikzeesche Nieuwsbode*, 20 July 1861, 1; and *Sankt Peterburgskie vedomosti*, 11 July 1861, 874. On the letters of thanks, see, for example, *La gazette de France*, 18 July 1861, 1; *Journal des débats*, 18 July 1861, 2; *The Times*, 20 July 1861, 9; *Le Temps*, 23 July 1861.

305 See, for example, *Journal des débats*, 16 July 1861, 1; *Morning Star*, 17 July 1861, 2; *La gazette de France*, 18 July 1861, 1, 2; *Journal des débats*, 18 July 1861, 2; *Severnaia pchela*, 8 July 1861, 614; *Zierikzeesche Nieuwsbode*, 20 July 1861, 1; *Severnaia pchela*, 10 July 1861, 618; *La gazette de France*, 23 July 1861, 2; *Journal des débats*, 25 July 1861, 1; *Sankt Peterburgskie vedomosti*, 11 July 1861, 874.

306 See, for example, *Morning Star*, 17 July 1861, 2; *La gazette de France*, 18 July 1861, 2; *Journal des débats*, 18 July 1861, 1; *Le Temps*, 18 July 1861, 1; *La gazette de France*, 20 July 1861, 1; *Zierikzeesche Nieuwsbode*, 20 July 1861, 1; *Sankt Peterburgskie vedomosti*, 9 July 1861, 869.

307 See, for example, *Morning Star*, 17 July1861, 2; *La gazette de France*, 18 July 1861, 2; *Journal des débats*, 18 July 1861, 1–2; *Le Temps*, 18 July 1861, 1; *La Gazette de France*, 19 July 1861, 2; *Le Temps*, 19 July 1861, 1; *La Gazette de France*, 20 July 1861, 1; *Manchester Examiner and Times*, 20 July 1861, *The Times*, 20 July 1861, 9; *Journal des débats*, 22 July 1861, 1; *Morning Star*, 22 July 1861; *Severnaia pchela*, 10 July 1861, 618; *Sankt Peterburgskie vedomosti*, 11 July 1861, 874; *Le Temps*, 23 July 1861; *Journal des débats*, 25 July 1861, 1.

308 See, for example, *La gazette de France*, 23 July 1861, 2; *Zierikzeesche Nieuwsbode*, 20 July 1861, 1; *Sankt Peterburgskie vedomosti*, 9 July 1861, 869.

309 See, for example, *La gazette de France*, 18 July 1861, 2; *Le Temps*, 18 July 1861, 1; *La gazette de France*, 19 July 1861, 1; *La gazette de France*, 20 July 1861, 1; *Manchester Examiner and Times*, 20 July 1861; *The Times*, 20 July 1861, 9; *Zierikzeesche Nieuwsbode*, 20 July 1861, 1; *Sankt Peterburgskie vedomosti*, 9 July 1861, 869.

liberals, the possibility of renewed persecutions like the *Demagogenverfolgung* in Germany or the possibility that Wilhelm I might renounce the throne.[310]

US newspapers reported less extensively, but they nevertheless also published articles with more details, summarizing reports from European newspapers such as the *Journal des débats*, providing information on Becker and reprinting Wilhelm I's letter of thanks in translation. Their significance for the American public is probably described quite precisely by the fact that these reports were classified in the *Chicago Tribune* as 'Foreign Gossip' and printed next to curiosities such as a report on the largest gorilla in the British Museum.[311]

As in the cases of Orsini and Brown, we can also recognize peculiarities of national reporting in Oskar Wilhelm Becker's case. In France, for example, the press focused more strongly on Baden-Baden as a place and on legal questions, while Russian newspapers dealt extensively with the perpetrator's background. German newspapers were used as a source for telegrams and articles for reprinting in all newspapers, although materials were taken from other European newspapers as well. British and Russian newspapers distinguished their coverage by selecting and combining articles more carefully, thereby imposing fewer repetitions and contradictions on their readers. French newspapers and the *Sankt Peterburgskie Vedomosti* also stood out for their independently researched and well-written original articles from journalists who contributed their own views, interpretations and judgements, and, in France, also took responsibility for the text by signing their own names.[312] In addition, the French press published (possibly

310 See, for example, reports on earlier attacks: *La gazette de France*, 23 July 1861, 2; on press and public relations work: *La gazette de France*, 20 July 1861, 1; *Sankt Peterburgskie vedomosti*, 9 July 1861, 869. For reflections on political and economic consequences, see *The Times*, 16 July 1861, 9; *Le Temps*, 18 July 1861, 1; *Sankt Peterburgskie vedomosti*, 9 July 1861, 869; *Goessche Courant*, 22 August 1861, 2; *Le Temps*, 23 July 1861; *Sankt Peterburgskie vedomosti*, 12 July 1861, 878; *Zierikzeesche Nieuwsbode*, 24 August 1861, 1.

311 See, for example, 'The Attempt on the Life of the King of Prussia', *New York Times*, 30 July 1861, 5; 'European News', *New York Times*, 2 August 1861, 1; 'The Attempted Assassination of the King of Prussia', *Chicago Tribune*, 5 August 1861, 3; 'Foreign Gossip', *Chicago Tribune*, 19 August 1861, 3.

312 For France, see especially *Journal des débats*, 18 July 1861, 1; *Le Temps*, 18 July 1861, 1; *Le Temps*, 23 July 1861; and for Russia especially *Sankt Peterburgskie vedomosti*, 9 July 1861, 869, and 11 July 1861, 874.

fictitious) letters to the editor,[313] and extensive and conflicting political commentary in which the significance of the assassination attempt was discussed.[314]

As in Germany, there was also a fierce media debate about Becker's attack in France, and in individual cases French and German media engaged and argued over differing interpretations, such that one can speak of an international media discussion and international media event.[315] Oskar Wilhelm Becker's act, therefore, was a media sensation.

The same applies to John Wilkes Booth's assassination of Lincoln. What followed this assassination, in terms of both popular reactions and media event, has already been examined and described on various occasions in the academic literature, making only a brief sketch here sufficient.[316]

In the evening immediately after the assassination, and during the night from Friday, 14 April to Saturday, 15 April 1865, the news of the murder of the president and of the attacks on other members of the government had already spread in Washington, DC with great speed. Soon, Lincoln's close friends, family and Cabinet members had gathered in the stuffy little room in Petersen's house around the bed where Lincoln lay. Among the Cabinet members was Secretary of War Edwin M. Stanton, who took over as a capable organizer during the state of emergency.

Meanwhile, many people – the majority of them African Americans – were waiting anxiously outside the military roadblocks through the night and the rain for news of their president. Quite a few of them feared that the emancipation of the slaves depended on Lincoln and that with his death the liberation would be challenged again. Wild rumours were circulating throughout the District of Columbia. They intensified the

313 See La gazette de France, 19 July 1861, 2.

314 See especially Le Temps, 17 July 1861; and La gazette de France, 17, 18, 19 and 20 July 1861, all on page 1.

315 See, for example, 'On lit dans le Journal de Francfort', Le Temps, 20 July 1861.

316 See Reck, A. Lincoln, Chapter 11; and especially Turner, Beware the People Weeping; Carolyn L. Harrell, When the Bells Tolled for Lincoln: Southern Reaction to the Assassination (Macon, GA: Mercer University Press, 1997); as well as Hodes, Mourning Lincoln; and, on the long-term reception, Gabor S. Boritt, The Lincoln Enigma: The Changing Faces of an American Icon (New York: Oxford University Press, 2001).

feelings of frustration, fear and terror that most people felt in the face of the brutal series of systematic and violent attacks on the Union government. Many people, men and women alike, broke into tears in response to the unbelievable events.[317]

Reports of the event were sent out nationally and internationally on the same night. The *New York Tribune* was the fastest to respond: shortly after the assassination, an acquaintance of the journalists who worked in the Washington office of the *Tribune* ran breathlessly to his friends and informed them that Lincoln had been shot. The office staff quickly wrote a few lines about the news and handed them to the office messenger boy. He then sped off to the telegraph office with the note and had it sent to the editorial office in New York. Twelve more messages followed by midnight, with the last message of the day having already identified John Wilkes Booth as the perpetrator.[318]

In addition to that, two telegraphers from the War Department who had been in the audience at Ford's Theatre had run directly to their department and the military telegraph office after the assassination to inform their superiors. The latter, in their turn, immediately put the call out to all available telegraphers in the city to occupy every telegraph machine at their disposal. This team immediately sent messages and orders to Union troops throughout the country as soon as they received them from Secretary of War Stanton, who remained at the bedside of the dying president.

Stanton wrote the first official message for the press at 1:30 a.m. on Saturday morning. Three-quarters of an hour later, at 2:15 a.m., this message was sent by telegraph to the commanding general in New York City; the *New York Times* and the *New York Herald* integrated it into the first column of their leading articles for the Saturday editions, dating the message at 2:30 a.m. Further reports, in which Booth was first described as the perpetrator, followed in the early hours of the morning.[319] Thus people in the northern states were already relatively well informed on the following day – Saturday, 15 April 1865. Booth's act of violence was also perceived as spectacular, arousing intense emotions and triggering

---

317 See Reck, *A. Lincoln*, 135–49; Turner, *Beware the People Weeping*, 26, 55–60; as well as Hodes, *Mourning Lincoln*, Chapter 2 and 68–9.

318 See Reck, *A. Lincoln*, 145; and Turner, *Beware the People Weeping*, 53.

319 Reck, *A. Lincoln*, 140–1; and Turner, *Beware the People Weeping*, 53.

a profound psychological effect in its immediate aftermath and far beyond it.

This applies also to Karakozov's would-be 'decisive fact'. After this assassination attempt there was an immense media storm, which, however, revolved primarily around the supposed saviour of the tsar, Osip Ivanovich Komissarov: a 'substitution strategy', according to Claudia Verhoeven, that served to 'preserve the myth of timeless unity between tsar and people, and with this myth to suppress the history that Karakozov was trying to make'.[320] According to her, it was 'impossible' to write about Karakozov, 'due to both the severity of the reaction and a sheer lack of information', because an official investigative report on the attack was not published until 3 August 1866.[321] On the other hand, the Russian émigré press did discuss the event in depth.[322]

Instead of Karakozov, it was Komissarov who was raised to the status of 'Russia's first modern mass media star'.[323] He was fêted at the Mariinsky Theatre and at various banquets in his honour, as well as in letters, telegrams, poems, songs and compositions all over the country; courted by high society; elevated to the nobility; and immortalized in photographs, on coins and in a bust. Within a week of the assassination attempt, Komissarov's portrait was available everywhere as a photograph, lithograph or etching, individually or in illustrated newspapers, and was bought in the thousands; soon there were also cakes, sweets, chocolate, beer, cigarettes and jewellery with his likeness, as well as a whole series of publications with titles like 'The Fourth of April and Its Patriotic Importance for Russia', 'God Saved the Tsar' or 'Thanks to the Almighty for the Salvation of the Tsar'.[324]

---

320 Verhoeven, *The Odd Man Karakozov*, 69; contrary to Verhoeven's claims (ibid., 68), a detailed version of this argument can already be found in Bukhshtab, 'Posle vystrela Karakozova', 74–6. See, furthermore, for example, Venturi, *Roots of Revolution*, 348.

321 Verhoeven, *The Odd Man Karakozov*, 69, and, on the publication of the official report see Chapter 1, for example, 11.

322 On this see Budnitskii, *Terrorizm v rossiiskom osvoboditel'nom dvizhenii*, 35–7, who includes references to additional sources.

323 Verhoeven, *The Odd Man Karakozov*, 70.

324 See Bukhshtab, 'Posle vystrela Karakozova', Parts 2, 4; Eroshkin, 'Vystrel u Letnego sada', 171; as well as Verhoeven, *The Odd Man Karakozov*, 67–73, 77.

Figure 31. Osip Ivanovich Komissarov-Kostromskoi (portrait
photograph, 1866). State Museum of the Political History of
Russia, St Petersburg. KP-52182/388 F.III-15348/2.

But it was not only expressions of sympathy for the tsar's saviour
that were omnipresent. Patriotic rallies for the tsar himself were ubiq-
uitous as well. As Bukhshtab discovered through reports from employees of the Third Section from all over the Russian Empire, these
patriotic celebrations followed a programme that took more or less the
same form throughout the country and strongly resembled the celebrations in the German states. Cities all over the Russian Empire were
similarly illuminated, and the population came out to the central
squares for the festivities. These celebrations were often tied to public
meals, while high society gathered together afterwards for a shared
feast. There were also theatre performances throughout Russia, similar
to those in Germany, in which the patriotic song 'God Save the Tsar!'
('Bozhe, Tsaria khrani!') could not be missed. Funds were gathered
everywhere in the country to erect churches, bell towers or altars in

honour of Alexander II and his saviour Komissarov, to establish chari-
table foundations and to arrange gifts for Komissarov. And, finally,
there were also deputations, telegrams, thanksgiving addresses and
poems sent from all over the empire to the capital, lauding the tsar's
escape from harm.[325] Taken together, all these activities probably had
the effect of drowning the memory of the threat posed by Karakozov's
attempted assassination.

Stalled communications

While all three imitators succeeded in drawing the attention of the
national and international media to their attacks, it turned out to be
difficult for Becker, Booth and Karakozov to communicate the concerns
and motives behind their violence. Unlike Napoleon III and Governor
Wise, Lincoln's members of Cabinet, as well as Wilhelm I, Alexander II
and their governments, refused to cooperate in any way with the assassins or to give them a space to represent themselves. Because of this, the
successors were unable to achieve any effect either through conversations or letters from prison, nor were they able to spread their claims of
responsibility unhindered or use the court as a site to create propaganda
for themselves.

Following their acts of violence, none of the three attackers was given
the opportunity to contact the public outside the courtroom: as prisoners, Oskar Wilhelm Becker and Dmitry Vladimirovich Karakozov were
completely isolated from the public. John Wilkes Booth, on the other
hand, was detained by soldiers of the 16th Regiment of the New York
Volunteer Cavalry in a courtyard near Bowling Green, Virginia, on the
night of 25–6 April 1865. Since Booth did not want to surrender, the
Union soldiers set fire to the tobacco barn in which he was hiding. One
of the soldiers, Sergeant Boston Corbett, observed Booth's reactions to
the fire through the cracks between the wooden planks. He fired at the
moment Booth aimed his weapon to 'fight his way out', as it appeared to
Corbett. He later testified that he wanted to prevent Booth from attacking his comrades.

---

325 See Bukhshtab, 'Posle vystrela Karakozova', 52–4.

Figure 32. Sergeant Thomas H. 'Boston'
Corbett, *16th New York Volunteer Cavalry, who shot John Wilkes Booth, April
26, 1865* from a page in the album, *The Lincoln Conspiracy*, 1865, albumen
silver print, 3 3/8 x 2 1/16 in. (8.6 x 5.3 cm), George Eastman Museum.

Booth's entire body was paralyzed as a result of the gunshot and he died shortly thereafter on the veranda of the farmhouse. The last words he is said to have spoken, in a whisper, were: 'Useless, useless'.[326] Therefore none of the three successors to Orsini and Brown was able to present his concerns in any depth or detail.

John Wilkes Booth and Dmitry Vladimirovich Karakozov also largely failed to spread their claims of responsibility. As already stated, immediately after the assassination John Matthews burned Booth's letter to the *National Intelligencer* in the dressing room of Ford's Theatre because he was afraid of being associated with Lincoln's murder through the letter. The letter 'To Whom It May Concern' was handed over by Booth's brother-in-law to US Marshall William Milward as a representative of the federal authorities on 18 April 1865. Milward even allowed this letter to be printed in the *Philadelphia Inquirer* on 19 April. But following that, both this letter and Booth's farewell letter to his mother were considered lost for 110 years. It was not until 1977 that the two letters were rediscovered at the National Archives in Justice Department files by James Otis Hall, an amateur historian and expert on the Lincoln assassination.[327]

It was similar in Karakozov's case: although his proclamation 'To My Worker Friends' remained intact – when Karakozov took out a 'letter' from the pocket of his peasant coat after being arrested by the two policemen, this was in all likelihood one of the two copies of the proclamation which he was carrying.[328] But the policeman Slesarchuk immediately snatched the document from him, stopping Karakozov from sharing his proclamation with the people. What happened to the

326 See Swanson, *Manhunt*, Chapter 9 and 311–43 in particular, and especially Scott Martelle, *The Madman and the Assassin: The Strange Life of Boston Corbett, the Man Who Killed John Wilkes Booth* (Chicago: Chicago Review Press Incorporated, 2015), xi–xii.

327 Booth, 'To Whom It May Concern [Philadelphia, November] 1864', first note at 127–8.

328 Alongside the two copies of the proclamation found during the search conducted after the arrest in the headquarters of the Third Section (which had each been placed in separate envelopes, so that they could be mistaken for letters), they also found a letter to a certain Nikolai Andreevich (who would later turn out to be Ishutin), which Karakozov was still carrying by mistake (see Klevenskii and Kotel'nikov, *Pokushenie Karakozova*, vol. 1, 7). It is hardly plausible that he would take this letter to Ishutin out of his coat immediately after being arrested.

approximately eighty copies which he had distributed in advance is unknown (with the exception of those mailed to the governor general of St Petersburg). The two copies which Karakozov carried with him were immediately put under lock and key in the headquarters of the Third Section. Apart from an indirect reproduction in the court records, they remained locked away until Alexei Alexeevich Shilov published them in a historical journal after the October Revolution, or about fifty years after the assassination attempt.[329]

If the state's attempt to maintain secrecy is counted as an additional criterion in identifying claims-of-responsibility letters as such, then this criterion would be fulfilled in both cases – regardless of all the many differences between the two systems of tsarist autocracy and American democracy. It was only private and professional commitment and a change in the political system that ensured that the claims of responsibility would finally make their way to the public after all – but as historical documents.

Thus Becker succeeded best in bringing his motives into the public eye, even though the Prussian government also tried to withhold relevant reports. On the morning after the assassination attempt, the heads of the ministries met at eleven o'clock in the Foreign Office and formulated an official announcement based on the reports received from Baden-Baden, subsequently published in the *Staatsanzeiger* and on posters on Berlin's street corners. This official announcement was intended to counteract the disturbing rumours circulating in the city about the state of the king's health.[330] It began with the evocation of divine protection and at the very end mentioned Becker's explanation, which only read: 'The motive for the act of violence is political fanaticism, the nature of which is not in doubt, but which cannot currently be discussed in more detail with regard to the judicial inquiry.'[331] This announcement was soon after published in most of the large German newspapers, adopting the language regulation of the Prussian government in their own reprinting.[332] The announcement was also translated

329 Shilov, 'Iz istorii revoliutsionnogo dvizheniia 1860-kh gg.'.
330 *Neue Preußische Zeitung*, 16 July 1861, 1; and *Volks-Zeitung*, 16 July 1861, 1.
331 *Vossische Zeitung*, 16 July 1861, 2; *Neue Preußische Zeitung*, 17 July 1861, 1.
332 See, for example, the *Staats- und gelehrte Zeitung*, 17 July 1861, 1; *Kölnische Zeitung*, 17 July 1861, 1. Even the Baden-Baden *Wochenblatt*, 18 July 1861, 499, which as a local publication should have been better informed, stuck to the official formulation.

frequently and disseminated internationally.[333] There was no room in this for possible feelings of sympathy with the assassin, for support or for enthusiastic imitation.

Nonetheless, this attempt to curate the information at the state and editorial level had already failed the moment the announcement had been conceived. Newspaper readers had already been able to learn from a special edition of the *Vossische Zeitung* on 14 July 1861 'that the student Becker had stated as the reason for his assassination attempt that he had not considered the king of Prussia, whom he held in high esteem due to his personal qualities, up to the German task' (that is, German unification). This is what a letter said that he had kept on him.[334] Since the Baden-Baden telegraph office had been shut down for private messages, a courier had brought this message to Frankfurt by express train, and then it was further distributed from there.

In addition, the *Neue Preußische Zeitung* (also called the *Kreuzzeitung*), which had been ousted from the centre of power by Wilhelm I, published a report by the Berlin hotel owner and witness Brandt on 16 July. Brandt had attended Becker's first interrogation and tried – for the *Kreuzzeitung*, among other papers – to quote Becker's statement on his deed 'quite literally', as the paper claimed:

> Baden, 13 July 1861. The motive owing to which I will shoot His Majesty the King of Prussia is that he cannot bring about German unity or overcome the circumstances in order that unity take place; thus he must die, in order that another accomplish it. They will ridicule me for the deed, or consider me to be hysterical, but I must carry out the deed to make the German fatherland happy. Oscar Becker, Stud[iosus] Jur[is] from Leipzig.[335]

Since the original wording remained for the time being under lock and key, this now became the version of Becker's statement used for further

---

333 See, for example, the full or excerpted printing in *La gazette de France*, 18 July 1861, 1–2; *Journal des débats*, 18 July 1861, 2; *Manchester Examiner and Times*, 19 July 1861; *Severnaia pchela*, 8 July 1861, 614.

334 Extra to *Vossische Zeitung* 162 (14 July 1861). This report also appeared, among other places, in *Staats- und gelehrte Zeitung*, 16 July 1861, 2; *Neue Preußische Zeitung*, 16 July 1861, 1; *Volks-Zeitung*, 16 July 1861, 1; *Die Presse* (evening edition), 15 July 1861, 1.

335 *Neue Preußische Zeitung*, 16 July 1861, 1.

political interpretations of the act on both the national and international level.

Speculations over Becker's remarkably bad writing style and 'education level', as a graduate of the *Kreuzschule* and a student at university, contributed significantly to the sensation his case provoked in the German states. During the court proceedings in mid-September 1861, however, the original version of his confession was read out and his own style became officially known.[336]

Finally, the three imitators were unable to convert their court proceedings into propaganda for themselves and their cause. John Wilkes Booth was shot on the run. But it is questionable whether – if he had survived his capture – he would have been able to compensate for the lack of publicity for his letter with his own effective public speeches and appearances in court. The trial of his co-conspirators took place under strict security before a military tribunal at the initiative of the secretary of war, Edwin Stanton. Like many of his contemporaries in the North, Stanton was convinced that the assassination of the Union's highest commander was a violation of martial law by the Confederate leadership: 'Killing the nation's commander-in-chief was viewed as a military crime and an offense against the law of war.' A military tribunal therefore seemed fitting, the more so as it left the possibility open to the government to influence the case and ensure that the

---

336 The term 'education level' (*Bildungsstufe*) is taken from the *Kölnische Zeitung*, 21 July 1861. Also see, for example, *Kölnische Zeitung*, 17 July 1861; *Staats- und gelehrte Zeitung*, 17 July 1861, 1; the reports on Becker's motives in *Journal des débats*, 16 July 1861, 1; *Manchester Examiner and Times*, 16 July 1861; *The Times*, 16 July 1861, 9; *Morning Star*, 17 July 1861, 2; *Sankt Peterburgskie vedomosti*, 5 July 1861, 846; *Severnaia pchela*, 5 July 1861, 603; *Le Temps*, 18 July 1861, 1; *La gazette de France*, 19 July 1861, 2; *Zierikzeesche Nieuwsbode*, 20 July 1861, 1; as well as the reprinting of the reconstructed letter in *La gazette de France*, 19 July 1861, 2; *Le Temps*, 19 July 1861, 1; *Manchester Examiner and Times*, 20 July 1861; *Sankt Peterburgskie vedomosti*, 8 July 1861, 861; *Severnaia pchela*, 8 July 1861, 614; *The Times*, 20 July 1861, 9; 'The Attempt on the Life of the King of Prussia', *New York Times*, 30 July 1861, 5; 'European News', *New York Times*, 2 August 1861, 1; 'The Attempted Assassination of the King of Prussia', *Chicago Tribune*, 5 August 1861, 3; 'Foreign Gossip', *Chicago Tribune*, 19 August 1861, 3. For a reproduction of the original letter of confession from the court proceedings, see, for example, 'Oskar Becker's Proceß. (Von unseren eigenen Berichterstattern.) Bruchsal, 23. September', *Kölnische Zeitung*, 25 September 1861, 2.

conspirators received the punishment which most of their contemporaries saw as their just deserts.[337]

The procedural rules for the tribunal nevertheless stipulated keeping verbatim stenographic transcripts. Stenography was a new documentation technique that was used probably for only the second time in this form in a court case in the United States.[338] The contract to prepare the transcripts was received – just as in the first proceedings to be documented in this way by the government – by Benjamin (also Benn) Pitman. His brother had invented a widely used version of stenography in 1837 and they had developed and popularized it together. He had received the right to publish the finished transcripts for public sale, as long as the publications were consistent with strict standards of accuracy and the government did not incur any costs; his employees had to swear 'to record the evidence faithfully and truly' over the course of the proceedings. As a result of these arrangements, all the records were published word for word in the *National Intelligencer* and the *Philadelphia Daily Inquirer*, as well as in various multi-volume book editions after the tribunal's conclusion. An unabridged hardback edition comprises three volumes of 1,584 pages, while the paperback edition appeared in sixteen volumes.[339] Such an accurate reproduction of questions, answers and patient discussions of detail would have left Booth little room for flaming rhetoric and dramatic gestures.

Two institutions were responsible for investigating Karakozov's assassination attempt, both working out of the public eye. After he had been taken to the headquarters of the Third Section, the matter was transferred to a permanent 'Investigative Commission' (Sledstvennaia Komissiia), founded by Alexander II in 1862 in response to criticism of the emancipation legislation, which stood above all ministries and the Third Section. The Investigative Commission began work the day after the assassination attempt.[340] It still hadn't completed its work when

---

337 See Steers, 'Introduction', quotation at xii.

338 The probable first instance was also a military tribunal headed by the Union. See Benn Pitman, *The Trials for Treason at Indianapolis, Disclosing the Plans for Establishing a North-Western Confederacy: Being the Official Record of the Trials before the Military Commission . . . Containing the Testimony, Arguments, Finding and Sentence* (Cincinnati: Moore, Wilsatch & Baldwin, 1865).

339 See Steers, 'Introduction', xiii–xiv, quotation at xiii.

340 See Klevenskii, 'Predislovie', in Klevenskii and Kotel'nikov, *Pokushenie Karakozova*, vol. 1, xiii; on the Investigative Commission in general see Jonathan W. Daly, *Autocracy under Siege: Security Police and Opposition in Russia, 1866–1905*

Alexander II gave the order at the end of June to form a 'Supreme Criminal Court' (Verkhovnyi Ugolovnyi Sud) – at that time no firmly institutionalized court of this kind yet existed in the Russian Empire. This haste was necessary as the tsar wanted the proceedings against Karakozov to conclude before the wedding celebrations of his son, and these were to begin in mid-September.[341]

By order of the tsar, the court met – just like the Supreme Criminal Courts which had tried the Decembrists in 1826 and the Petrashevsky Circle in 1849 – in the apartment of the commander of the Peter and Paul Fortress, which also held political prisoners.[342] To the chagrin of the chairman, Prince Pavel Pavlovich Gagarin, the court had to meet once again behind closed doors – contrary to the court regulations which the tsar had reformed shortly before, providing for public hearings. Tellingly, the reason given for this reversal was Karakozov's claim of responsibility, which was not to be made public, as will be explained later.[343]

In the trial against Karakozov and his circle of friends, stenographers were used for the first time in a court case in the Russian Empire, transcribing the entire trial verbatim. In doing so, the government in St Petersburg may have followed the example of the US government at the military tribunal in Washington against Booth's co-conspirators. Unlike what was practised in the United States, however, these transcripts were not published daily in the press; indeed they would not appear in print at all for more than sixty years, until Klevenskii and Kotel'nikov published them as a book.[344]

(DeKalb: Northern Illinois University Press, 1998), 16; and on the commission and the trial see Eroshkin, 'Vystrel u Letnego sada', 171–2; and Verhoeven, *Odd Man Karakozov*, Chapter 1, 17.

341 On this see, for example, Avrahm Yarmolinsky, *Road to Revolution: A Century of Russian Radicalism* (London: Princeton University Press, 1957), 141; and Eroshkin, 'Vystrel u Letnego sada', 172.

342 See Klevenskii, 'Predislovie', in Klevenskii and Kotel'nikov, *Pokushenie Karakozova*, vol. 1, xvi–xvii; Venturi, *Roots of Revolution*, 349; and Verhoeven, *The Odd Man Karakozov*, 25–6.

343 See the statements of the chairman, Prince Gagarin, printed in Klevenskii and Kotel'nikov, *Pokushenie Karakozova*, vol. 1, 5; as well as Klevenskii, 'Predislovie', ibid., xvii; and Eroshkin, 'Vystrel u Letnego sada', 172. On the court reforms and Prince Gagarin's dissatisfaction, see Verhoeven, *The Odd Man Karakozov*, 13–14, 26.

344 Klevenskii and Kotel'nikov, *Pokushenie Karakozova*, vol. 1. On the use of a stenographer and the history of the transcripts, see Klevenskii, 'Predislovie', in ibid., vol. 1, xvii; as well as Klevenskii and Kotel'nikov, 'Ot Redaktsii', in ibid., xix–xx; Eroshkin, 'Vystrel u Letnego sada', 172; as well as Verhoeven, *The Odd Man Karakozov*, 26.

Since Karakozov's investigation and trial took place behind closed doors, the interested public only received official information about the assassination attempt four months after it took place. The first release was a censored version of the official report of the Investigative Commission, published on 3 August in the newspaper *Severnaia pochta*; the second was the verdict of the Supreme Criminal Court from 31 August 1866, in which the court sentenced Karakozov to death.[345] The tsar rejected his request for a pardon, and Karakozov was hanged on 3 September 1866, on Smolensk Field – an uncultivated strip of land next to a cemetery of the same name on Vasilyevsky Island in St Petersburg. This execution was public and no small event.[346]

Only Oskar Wilhelm Becker received a normal, public trial before the presiding jury court of the Baden Middle Rhine District. He was charged with the 'offense of carrying out an attempted murder according to § 205, 106, 107 and 114 of the Baden Criminal Code'. The trial was public, and Becker could not have complained about a lack of attention in the national and international press: 'Correspondents from about 42 German and French newspapers' were present, 'as well as about 70 persons of distinction' and various 'legal notables also from France and Switzerland', as well as 'a number of Russians', reported the *Kölnische Zeitung*. The defendant had prepared himself for his trial and appeared elegantly dressed 'in black clothes of the most modern cut, a black Parisian hat [held] in a hand clothed in a grey kid glove'.[347] Here, too, the accused had probably followed the lead of his role model, Felice Orsini.

Nevertheless, Becker failed to convey his message convincingly or to impress his audience in the court in the necessary way. This was first due to the fact that in court he attempted to reinterpret his attack on Wilhelm I as a 'mock assassination' (*Schein-Attentat*) with explicit reference to Felice Orsini. Thus he explained in the courtroom:

---

345 See Verhoeven, *The Odd Man Karakozov*, 11, 19.

346 See Klevenskii and Kotel'nikov, *Pokushenie Karakozova*, vol. 1, 291, note 2 to page 5; Shilov, 'Pokushenie Karakozova 4 aprelia 1866 g', 130, note 1 to page 94; as well as Venturi, *Roots of Revolution*, 349; Eroshkin, 'Vystrel u Letnego sada', 172–3; and Verhoeven, *The Odd Man Karakozov*, Chapter 7.

347 'Oskar Becker's Proceß. (Von unseren eigenen Berichterstattern.) Bruchsal, 23. September', *Kölnische Zeitung*, 25 September 1861, first edition, 2–3.

It must astonish everyone and cause a sensation everywhere *that I did not carry out any assassination attempt on the king at all*; I will now explain the *real* facts of the case: I first came up with the idea of an assassination attempt with regard to the situation in Italy, when I had to tell myself that Orsini's assassination attempt contributed to Italian unification. I said to myself that an attempt on the life of the king of Prussia would have to have a similar effect for Germany; an assassination attempt in Germany is so unheard-of, and it was never part of my plan to really kill the king, knowing full well that the Crown prince would be himself no more able to comprehend and fulfil his task; it is therefore also very understandable that I proceeded to a mere appearance of an assassination attempt [*Schein-Attentat*].[348]

Since it had been unnecessary for Orsini to kill Napoleon III in order to achieve his goal of Italian unification, and because he had been aware that the Crown prince was no better prepared to carry out his task than the king, Becker, too, had not really wanted to kill the Prussian king, or so he said. He had, nevertheless, wanted to attain German unification through the attack: it was thus a fake terrorist act. This argument, which seems to be the result of his talks with the examining magistrate, was not very credible following his earlier remarks. Furthermore, it destroyed the impact of his terrorist assassination attempt by depriving the act of any potential to spread fear and terror.

More than this, Becker also gambled away all the support and sympathy he might have had behind him until that moment. He was not able to embody the role of the handsome and heroic revolutionary shaped so exemplarily by Orsini: Becker often got entangled in depictions of peculiar trivialities and broke into tears again and again. The correspondents from the *Kölnische Zeitung* and other newspapers conveyed directly to their readers his inability to fulfil and persevere in the role of his choosing: 'Since I only came up with the idea of an assassination attempt through Orsini', as they quoted Becker,

who, without achieving the effect he intended, brought about the unification of Italy, I also hoped to be able to produce a similar effect through a *mock assassination* . . . But now that I do not at all believe

---

348 *Kölnische Zeitung*, 25 September 1861, second edition, 1.

that the personage of the king is one that is to be removed from Germany, but instead believe that in Germany . . . (At these words the accused broke into tears accompanied by convulsive spasms.)[349]

Becker was aware that he could not explain the idea behind his deed to the court and his audience in the hall, nor did he any longer understand it himself.

So Becker continuously collapsed in front of the assembled audience in the courtroom. He had abandoned his 'original idea of dying a martyr's death', he explained, 'after he had found out about the misfortune in his family', by which he meant his family's dismay on hearing about the assassination attempt. And he again burst into tears during these remarks, as the *Kölnische Zeitung* reported.[350] Thus Becker succeeded neither in turning stigma into charisma, nor in addressing a message and a call to action to the German population. Nor was he successful in spreading fear and terror among Germany's princes. Perhaps he received sympathy in the sense of compassion. Compared to the ideal of a national-revolutionary hero, his behaviour was simply too human.

Becker, Booth and Karakozov had planned, and expected, to reach the public with their own explanations of their actions, but they succeeded only belatedly, or not at all. Unlike Felice Orsini or John Brown, none of their prison letters were published, and none of them were able to give interviews to high government officials or press representatives after their assassination attempts. The three of them were likewise unable to muster letters of support that could have stimulated a grand conspiracy of important persons. Additionally, they also lacked friends and comrades-in-arms who might have published sympathetic explanatory letters about the acts and the perpetrators, or delivered sermons and speeches in support of the assassinations after the attack. Famous intellectuals and philosophers did not speak out for the violent acts, but spoke, if at all, only against them.

There were no converts to their violence, and Becker, Booth and Karakozov were not immediately transformed into German, American or Russian icons. Although their assassinations were recognized as symbolic

---

349 Ibid.
350 Ibid.

acts of violence that reached beyond themselves, none of the assassins succeeded in filling this symbolic dimension with the messages they wanted to convey and which, in their view, would have allowed the general population to identify with them and their messages and thus re-enact their radicalization. They could not occupy the place of reference in the symbolic structure of violence, and so their acts – even in the case of success – remained meaningless in the eyes of the vast majority of the population, or were subject to differing and independent interpretations.

Political reactions

The decisive cause of the political failure of Becker, Booth and Karakozov's terrorist attacks lies in public reactions. In contrast to the reactions following Orsini's and Brown's attacks, there were no powerful social figures and groups who would, for their own purposes, productively instrumentalize the aims of the three imitators, their violence or their person and thereby lend them political significance, such as Napoleon III, Charles Demorny, Governor Henry A. Wise and Clement L. Vallandigham had done for Orsini and Brown.

Instead, the Prussian, American and Russian governments and public confronted the violence and its perpetrators with strategies that were capable of breaking the political success of their terrorist attacks for the time being or even preventing it in the long term. These strategies were able to largely contain, suppress or channel the development and political effectiveness of sympathy and support, fear and terror, and thereby prevent or manage the transformation of the protagonists into heroes and martyrs, or into barbarians and demons, respectively. This also allowed them to contain the radicalization and polarization of society at least to a certain degree, or to focus these processes on likely social breaking points, that is, already existing social conflicts.

The different strategies in the three societies are modes of response that are still pursued today: marginalization, militarization, repression and externalization.[351] Of these strategies, marginalization and militarization acted to depoliticize the response to the terrorist provocation – at

---

351 Verhoeven, 'The Making of Russian Revolutionary Terrorism', 103–16, has already described the strategy of externalization in the Russian government's handling of Karakozov's assassination attempt – not in name, however, but in substance.

least if one takes as a basis a narrow conception of politics.[352] Repression and externalization, on the other hand, resulted in increased politicization. They represent forms of second-order political instrumentalization. Repression and externalization do not work directly with the political messages and goals of the perpetrators of terrorist violence, but react to the act of violence itself. These strategies for dealing with terrorist violence cannot be strictly separated from one another. They can also be combined, as in the following examples and as the later history of counterterrorism shows. The differences between the strategies, however, remain significant enough that it is worth distinguishing them analytically.

The reactions to Oskar Wilhelm Becker's assassination attempt present one example of depoliticization through marginalization. It was, first of all, the expressions of universal approval of Wilhelm I and the general grief among the population that served to isolate the perpetrator and thus depoliticize his act. Franz Dunker's liberal-democratic Berlin *Volks-Zeitung*, for example, says,

> The recent assassination attempt is directed against a king whose conscientiousness, respect for the rule of law, rectitude of heart and simplicity of character distinguish him from many at the heads of empires . . . He is not simply loved and revered by his people out of loyal custom or political-theoretical opinion, but out of serious and justified conviction.[353]

Wilhelm I, newly ascended to the throne – this was the tenor in many newspapers in the German-speaking world – was justifiably esteemed by the entire population. Becker had chosen the wrong victim to assassinate.

---

352 The term and concept behind the term 'militarization' used here differs somewhat from the term as it is used by other authors, such as Richard Bach Jensen. This difference is mainly one of context: the process of militarization described here takes place and must be comprehended in the context of a war situation, while militarization as analysed by Richard Bach Jensen is set in civil societies in peacetime, that is, martial law. Because of these different political contexts, the political effects are different. Militarization in peacetime is more likely to backfire and provoke new terrorist responses, if it is ruthlessly implemented. For a comparison of different approaches, including militarization in peacetime, see also Jensen, *The Battle against Anarchist Terrorism*, especially Chapter 4.

353 *Volks-Zeitung*, 18 July 1861, 1.

Evocations of unity and impartiality continued the perpetrator's isolation. The venerable *Staats- und gelehrte Zeitung des Hamburgischen unpartheyischen Correspondenten*, for example, wrote,

> A fanatic dares to promote 'German unity' by attempting to murder the first German sovereign. The whole of Germany is terrified by this misdeed. There is only a single voice of indignation over this in the [city of the] royal residence as everywhere [in Germany]. Only deep sadness can issue from the fact that such a visible danger to life can suddenly descend and entire states can abruptly be put in fear by political fanaticism.[354]

As this admonition from Hamburg reads, deep sadness – and not instrumentalizing reactions – is the only appropriate response to such a crime.

In addition to these attempts to isolate the perpetrator politically, there were also efforts to externalize him. As his own daily read, the *Deutsche Allgemeine Zeitung*, wrote, Becker was 'neither a Prussian nor a German by birth but a Russian, and only his family's resettlement in Germany brought him closer to our national interests'.[355] This view well suited all those who wished to externalize him. The fact that Becker had been born in Odessa made it possible to define him as a Russian and thus as a foreigner. In this way, the question of group belonging took the place of the political question that had been the main motivation for Becker's act of violence.

These attempts at depoliticization by isolating and externalizing Becker had the express purpose of averting reactionary political measures. In view of the universal love for Wilhelm I, as Berlin's *Volks-Zeitung* wrote, an assassination attempt that was 'so unrelated to the mood of the times, to the excitement of the times, to personal conditions and in such contradiction with the whole undivided feeling of the people' could only be 'the fruit of the most individual lunacy'. And as the paper added, an individual act so out of sync with its time 'had to remain unrelated to time and history in its consequences as well!'[356] Behind these statements was the fear that – just as after Karl Sand's assassination of August von

---

354 *Staats- und gelehrte Zeitung*, 18 July 1861, 2.
355 *Deutsche Allgemeine Zeitung*, as quoted in the *National-Zeitung*, 18 July 1861, 1.
356 *Volks-Zeitung*, 18 July 1861, 1.

Kotzebue – the government's response could be 'a new Carlsbad' and the 'establishment of a standing federal police commission of ominous memory', as well as surveillance measures and restrictions of freedom of expression and the press that had affected the universities, the national movement, and liberals in particular. The liberal-democratic *Volks-Zeitung*'s interpretation of Becker's act of violence as 'out of sync' therefore served to prevent the implementation of similar measures once again.

For the same reason, the Viennese *Die Presse* displayed calculated optimism. It hoped that 'by now' times had 'changed in Germany as well' 'and the supporters of the policy of revenge' had become a vanishingly small, although still not powerless, group, so that 'Becker's crime' would not be strong enough 'to reform the Bundestag backwards, and to conjure the horrors of federal police violence as it was practised in the 1820s'.[357] The newspaper also cited the unanimous condemnation of the assassination by the population as grounds for hope, together with the many expressions of solidarity with the king, which in general the news reports so strongly emphasized.

The majority of the liberal papers were more sceptical, however, and prophesied that the assassination attempt would be instrumentalized for political ends: 'Unfortunately, various parties will interpret the heinous assassination attempt in their own interests,' feared the *Hamburgische unpartheyische Correspondent*. And the newspaper's assessment would turn out to be correct.[358]

In fact, the semi-official *Neue Hannoversche Zeitung* made an immediate attempt at such an instrumentalization. In accordance with the logic of the political situation, it contradicted the liberal newspapers' efforts to isolate Becker and instead linked him to various political groups. Thus, according to the Hanover newspaper, it was certain 'that only the democratic tendencies of the [German] National Association [Deutscher Nationalverein], raised to fanatical exaltation, were at the root of the crime'. The newspaper also made detailed references to Becker's connections with Herzen and his 'correspondence articles for various revolutionary newspapers'.[359] According to the article, this was

---

357 *Die Presse*, 17 July 1861, 1.
358 *Staats- und gelehrte Zeitung*, 18 July 1861, 2.
359 *Neue Hannoversche Zeitung*, cited in the *Berliner Börsen-Zeitung*, 19 July 1861,

no case of 'the most individual lunacy' outside time and history, as the Berlin *Volks-Zeitung* had claimed, but something quite the opposite: the act of a member of a dangerous 'fanatical revolutionary party'.[360] The aim here was not to depoliticize the assassination attempt through isolation and externalization, but rather to politicize it by drawing connections. Broadly speaking, the connection made between the assassination attempt on the one hand and the national movement and idea on the other was indeed correct.

The *Neue Preußische Zeitung* (aka the *Kreuzzeitung*) agreed. The ultraconservative paper (which had lost its influential position with Wilhelm's accession to power and his liberal government) also undertook to associate the assassination with the liberals' efforts towards unification generally and with the activities of the German National Association in particular.

> Just as Sand's deed was nothing but the fanatical and criminal extreme of the demagogy of its time, so the student Becker's assassination attempt can only be understood by trying to see it in its connection with certain aspirations towards German unity. One cannot denounce the German princes as the main obstacle to German unity for ten full years; one cannot preach for ten full years, loudly and quietly, about the necessity of eliminating the German princes without igniting the thought of the shortest and most thorough way to their elimination in an energetic and fanatical head.[361]

Just like the liberal press, this newspaper also took Sand's assassination as a yardstick and point of reference, while trying, at the same time, to equate the attacks of Becker and Sand as much as possible. In addition to political generalization, historical generalization also played a role in the paper's ultraconservative interpretation.

And yet the *Kreuzzeitung's* analysis was quite accurate with regard to Oskar Wilhelm Becker's tactical considerations. The newspaper's political instrumentalization of the event began at the point where it indirectly insinuated that the liberals shared responsibility for the

---

1446.
  360 Ibid.
  361 *Neue Preußische Zeitung*, 17 July 1861, 1.

assassination attempt and directly accused them of cynically exploiting the violence for their own purposes.

> The effect of the successful assassination: There will be no doubt in Prussia as to what we would have lost in our dear king, and even if the temporal concurrence of the act with certain, almost tangible actions toward German unity may only be a coincidence: We know of a party that would have understood how to best exploit the success [of the assassination]. But the failure might also have been taken into account, and if – as they say – the assassination attempt of Orsini did not remain without influence even on Emperor Napoleon then one may have succumbed to the assumption of expecting a similar result in the present case as well.[362]

The reference made by the *Neue Preußische Zeitung* to Orsini's assassination attempt was correct, but the idea that Becker's beliefs were shared by the majority of German liberals and were in their interest was an assumption meant to discredit the liberal movement as a whole.[363] The *Kreuzzeitung* went even further in the same issue and attacked the liberal Prussian government by implying that it had deliberately withheld police protection from the king. This bordered on a highly treasonous conspiracy theory.

But the *Kreuzzeitung* remained largely alone in its attempts at political instrumentalization of this kind. Most of the other major newspapers in the German-speaking world immediately rejected its efforts actively, deploying sound arguments while doing so. The *National-Zeitung* demanded positive evidence for the political insinuations, as 'one must not blame any party in the state for a positive crime without providing one's reasons, in order to assist the authorities in the

---

362 Ibid.

363 The official reaction after the attacks of Max Hödel and Karl Nobiling on 11 May 1861 was quite similar, except that the general insinuation in this case was directed at social democracy. See Carola Dietze, 'Terrorismus im 19. Jahrhundert: Politische Attentate, rechtliche Reaktionen, Polizeistrategien und öffentlicher Diskurs in Europa und den Vereinigten Staaten 1878–1901', in Karl Härter, Beatrice de Graaf, Gerhard Sälter and Eva Wiebel (eds.), *Vom Majestätsverbrechen zum Terrorismus: Politische Kriminalität, Recht, Justiz und Polizei zwischen Früher Neuzeit und 20. Jahrhundert* (Frankfurt am Main: Klostermann, 2012), 184–9. On the attempts, see Dietze, 'Von Kornblumen, Heringen und Drohbriefen'.

prosecution.'[364] Additionally, the liberal *National-Zeitung*, by republishing commentary from the *Karlsruhe Zeitung*, warned urgently against the longer-term consequences of instrumentalizing political violence:

> Sand's nonsensical murder once offered cause and pretext for a reaction that was hardly any less nonsensical. But from that whirlwind sown the following generations then reaped the harvest of the revolutions of 1830 and 1848, and we ourselves recently saw the last edifices of Metternich's statesmanship collapse disgracefully before our very eyes. Our day will not turn the disastrous deed into a source of new disaster. There is no sufficient means of protection against a, God willing, non-recurring individual repetition of an individual act of nonsense; but courage and trust in God will protect the knightly king from the knaves. The general fight against political assassination, however, will not be waged in our time with an intensified reaction, but with the intelligent management of our public affairs, as it [our time] has learned there is a stronger defense against common crimes in education and benevolence than in pillory and the torture chamber.[365]

As these papers argued, there could be no complete protection against individual perpetrators. One can only ensure that such violence does not become a source of new violence, and try to prevent new outbreaks of political violence through good government. In this way, the attacks on the liberals and the national movement were successfully rejected.

Just like the liberal press, the Prussian government, as the object of the *Kreuzzeitung*'s accusatory interpretation, had no reason to take up its argument on the attacks and use them as a guide in its political action – nor did the king, for that matter, who had appointed that government. Attempts to identify Becker with the liberals generally and thereby charge the assassination attempt with significance were therefore unable to pick up any political momentum.[366] Neither the apotheosis nor the

---

364 *National-Zeitung*, 19 July 1861.

365 *Karlsruher Zeitung*, as quoted in the *National-Zeitung* (evening edition), 18 July 1861, 1.

366 This is the decisive difference between this moment and the political situation in 1878, when the Anti-socialist Laws (*Sozialistengesetze*) followed the assassination attempts of Max Hödel and Karl Nobiling. On this see Dietze, 'Terrorismus im 19.

demonization of the assassin took place, nor did any process of polarizing or further radicalizing society occur.

In the northern states of the United States, John Wilkes Booth's assassination was interpreted as part of the Civil War.[367] War Secretary Edwin M. Stanton suspected that the Confederate government was behind the assassination and that this was a last desperate attempt to turn the tide for the South. According to this interpretation, the assassination was a military act that took place within the scope of the Civil War; Lincoln had been murdered as president and supreme military commander. As the example of the military tribunal earlier has already shown, this interpretation played a decisive role in the reactions of the entire American government.[368] An official interpretation of this kind, within the framework of military action, largely ruled out a demonization of the assassin himself, not least because it placed responsibility for the act mostly with the Confederate government and reduced Booth to its instrument. By contrast, the more routine comparisons of the assassin with devils and demons in church sermons in the North were too stereotypical and were therefore unable to attain sufficient power of persuasion for the broader population.[369]

Stanton's interpretation of the assassination as an act of war, on the other hand, was spontaneously shared by a large part of the population in the Northern states and shaped the immediate reactions on the street as well. By the night of the assassination – when only rumours of Lincoln's murder were circulating and media reports had yet to make their influence felt – civilians and soldiers showed no compromise in dealing with supporters of the assassination: 'I recall a soldier shooting to death a man who said he was glad Booth had shot Lincoln,' reported a cavalryman from Ohio. In Baltimore, someone who had approved of Booth's crime was branded a traitor – his hair was sheared and he was

---

Jahrhundert', 184–9, which also includes an analysis of relevant scholarship, as well as Dietze, 'Von Kornblumen, Heringen und Drohbriefen'; and Jensen, *The Battle against Anarchist Terrorism*, 23–4. With regard to terrorist violence at the end of the nineteenth century, Jensen similarly emphasizes that the political authorities and the media could help curb anarchist terrorism as well as promote it (ibid., 57).

367 On this, albeit with a somewhat different focus and more extensive reference to relevant scholarship, see again Dietze, 'Terrorismus im 19. Jahrhundert', 192–4.

368 See above, p. 562.

369 On this see Turner, *Beware the People Weeping*, 80.

punished by flogging. These were not isolated cases.[370] Such reactions to expressions of sympathy and support did not prevent hard-boiled opponents of Lincoln from feeling the corresponding emotions, but they could suppress their public appearance and thus their chance of manifestation and of having a political impact at least for the time being.[371]

In former Confederate territory, even the news of Lincoln's assassination was withheld. Only Union army commanders serving as occupying forces in the South received telegrams informing them about the assassination of the president. As a rule, they only published the news under strict military precautions, out of the fear of both insurrections by the population in the South and retaliatory measures against the civilian population by Union soldiers in the occupied territories.[372] In consequence, by means of direct military repression Union troops in the southern states prevented expressions of sympathy and support, and at least temporarily deprived sympathizers of the chance to be politically effective.

Militarization shaped the interpretation of the assassination and the reactions to the murder in at least two ways. Interpreting the assassin and the assassination in wartime resulted in the depoliticization of both, as the murder was generally attributed to the logic of war and also, more specifically, to the enemy's methods of waging war, and the concrete political reasons that had inspired Booth to his act – the conviction that Lincoln had ruled as a tyrant and the fear that he would now grant the freed slaves substantial rights – were subsumed into the general war aims of the enemy. The militaristic way of dealing with the reactions led in turn to the depoliticization of the public, as one side of the spectrum was suppressed in its ability to express and effect itself politically and – at least temporarily – silenced.

In addition, many potential sympathizers in the southern states considered the assassination to be a mistake – at least at a moment when the Confederacy had been defeated militarily and the states belonging to it were dependent on the benevolence of the Union. Thus the president of the Confederacy, Jefferson Davis, later noted in his written

---

370 See Reck, *A. Lincoln*, quotation at 135; Harrell, *When the Bells Tolled for Lincoln*, 97; Hodes, *Mourning Lincoln*, 81, 84–90; and especially Turner, *Beware the People Weeping*, 26–52.

371 On this, see Hodes, *Mourning Lincoln*, 74–9, 83–4.

372 See Reck, *A. Lincoln*, 141; and on the reactions in individual cities and regions, Harrell, *When the Bells Tolled for Lincoln*.

reaction to the assassination that, while one could not expect him to earnestly mourn the death of such an unyielding opponent, he could only regard Lincoln's assassination 'in view of its political consequences' as 'a great misfortune to the South'. Lincoln 'had power over the Northern people, and was without personal malignity toward the people of the South. His successor [Andrew Johnson of Tennesee] was without power in the North, and the embodiment of malignity toward the Southern people.' Similar analyses were also recorded by many other southerners – high-ranking politicians and military personnel as well as men and women among the general population.[373]

What actually became the decisive moment for Booth's failure was therefore not Matthews's destruction of his letter to the *National Intelligencer*, but Booth's lack of political analysis. The reactions to the assassination in the North and South prove that most people understood his motives – or at least the broad outlines thereof – even without his being able to spread his letter. But neither could politicians from the southern states be expected to express sympathy with Booth's act of violence, nor could they have found it opportune – at the time it would only have worsened the negotiating position of the South. And anyone who publicly expressed sympathy, evinced a willingness to support Booth and his co-conspirators or provided concrete help had to reckon with harsh consequences for himself and his family. In this sense, the strategy of militarization in wartime was successful in completely and totally depoliticizing the terrorist attack, at least as far as the assassin's potential sympathizers were concerned.

Contrary to what one might assume at first glance, Lincoln's supporters were also depoliticized, even though – or perhaps precisely because – they were free to express their emotions and political views. Through the assassination of the (in his view) 'sectional candidate' who 'should never have become president' and represented a 'desecration' of the office he held, Booth had paved the way for an immediate apotheosis. Like John Brown, Lincoln was now seen as Moses, liberator of the slaves, but the American president had also led his people through 'the blood-red sea of rebellion', for which he (just like Moses) was allowed to see the Promised Land, but not to enter it. The fact that Lincoln had just been murdered on Good Friday offered further grounds for manifold

---

373 See Harrell, *When the Bells Tolled for Lincoln*, 42.

comparisons to Christ: just like Moses and Jesus of Nazareth, God had taken Lincoln, 'the Savior of his land', to himself after he had fulfilled his task. Lincoln immediately entered the pantheon of the American nation as a radiant icon, comparable only to George Washington and even standing above him. He was once and for all withdrawn from day-to-day political debates.[374]

Alexander II, his government and the Russian public reacted to the assassination attempt by Karakozov with repression and externalization; that is, they developed the very same 'politics of revenge' that the liberal press in the German states had feared and presented as outdated in reference to the Carlsbad Decrees.[375]

The government's policy of repression was largely based on the cooperation of a reactionary and a former revolutionary. Three days after the assassination attempt, Tsar Alexander II replaced the chairman of his permanent Investigative Commission. Its new leader was Count Mikhail Nikolaevich Murav'ev (also Murav'ev-Vilensky). As governor general, he had put down the January Uprising in Congress Poland in 1863 and acquired the nickname 'the hangman'.[376] On the night of 19 April, a man named Ignaty Ignatevich Korevo appeared at the office of Moscow's chief of police and reported that he had a need to be personally introduced to the chairman of the Investigative Commission in St Petersburg; he had a secret which he could only confide to Murav'ev. He added that he knew important Karakozov collaborators. There were no obstacles to the fulfilment of his wishes in the office of the senior police official. By 22 April, and again on 24 April, Korevo had testified to the Investigative Commission.[377]

---

374 See Turner, *Beware the People Weeping*, 82–3; Hodes, *Mourning Lincoln*, Chapter 4; Carwardine, *Lincoln*, Chapter 7, quotation at 320; Nagler, *Abraham Lincoln*, 418–19; and particularly Philip B. Kunhardt III, Peter W. Kunhardt and Peter W. Kunhardt Jr, *Looking for Lincoln: The Making of an American Icon* (New York: Alfred A. Knopf, 2008).

375 Also see Dietze, 'Terrorismus im 19. Jahrhundert', 189–92, which considers the question in a comparative perspective, and Jensen, *The Battle against Anarchist Terrorism*, for example 22, 57, 61.

376 See Klevenskii, 'Predislovie', in Klevenskii and Kotel'nikov, *Pokushenie Karakozova*, vol. 1, xiii; Venturi, *Roots of Revolution*, 347; Ulam, *Prophets and Conspirators*, 8–9; Eroshkin, 'Vystrel u Letnego sada', 171; Verhoeven, *The Odd Man Karakozov*, 17–18; and Verhoeven, 'The Making of Russian Revolutionary Terrorism', 104.

377 On this see Shilov, 'Pokushenie Karakozova 4 aprelia 1866 g.', 131, note 7 to page 99; and Verhoeven, *The Odd Man Karakozov*, 33, which by and large follows Shilov.

Ignaty Ignatevich Korevo was about a year younger than Karakozov (born 1841). Before the Investigative Commission, he stated that his father had died when he was three or four years old. He had attended the lyceum in Odessa and, due to his good performance, had received a state scholarship to attend Moscow University, which had been withdrawn from him 'in the most outrageous way', however. This is why he had approached Karakozov's circle of friends, only 'to use them to get money' and complete his studies. The friends, however, had fully integrated him into the group, even though there had been conflicts between Korevo and some other group members.[378]

In his testimony before the Investigative Commission, Korevo went straight to the point and painted a picture of a great conspiracy *à la* Carboneria and the Decembrists. As his written testimony for the commission shows, Korevo was indeed able to provide considerable insider information; he tacked on so many imaginative additions to them, however, and interpreted them within such a distorted framework that everything took on the wrong light. Korevo stated before the commission that there was a 'revolutionary society by the name of Organizatsiia' ('the Organization') in Moscow that was connected 'to other societies' (he named the Konstantinian party, a 'Val'paraiso' society and a society of revolutionary officers) 'and to Poland', receiving from them poison and arms. A secret society existed within Organizatsiia that called itself 'Ad' ('Hell' in Russian). This circle, according to Korevo, was made up of Karakozov's closest circle of friends: Ishutin, Ermolov, Jurasov, Zagibalov and Stranden, as well as two more people. Members of this secret group identified themselves as *mortusy* ('dead men') and their 'noblest duty' was to murder the tsar. In this connection Korevo imaginatively depicted, for example, how the group decided on the next tsaricide by drawing lots.[379]

---

378 Korevo's testimony from 22 April 1866, printed in Shilov, 'Pokushenie Karakozova 4 aprelia 1866 g', 99–107, 105, quotation at 106. Verhoeven also partially discusses this in *The Odd Man Karakozov*, 33.

379 Korevo's testimony from 22 April 1866, printed in Shilov, 'Pokushenie Karakozova 4 aprelia 1866 g.', 99–103; and discussed, for example, in Eroshkin, 'Vystrel u Letnego sada', 172; and Verhoeven, *The Odd Man Karakozov*, 19–23, 33; as well as Verhoeven, 'The Making of Russian Revolutionary Terrorism', 108–13. As Jensen points out for the end of the nineteenth century: '"Chosen by lot" became, quite erroneously, the standard explanation for how anarchist assassins were selected; in fact no evidence has been produced that this method was ever used.' See Jensen, *The Battle against Anarchist Terrorism*, 37.

Korevo's narrative made reference to Poland, using it as a suggested means of externalization. This allegation conveniently tied in with the suspicion already entertained by Murav'ev and not far from the minds of large parts of the Russian public – after all, the empire had only recently dealt with Polish uprisings. So rumours immediately began to spread that the assassin must have been a Pole, and various newspapers reported the tsar's question to Karakozov as 'Are you a Pole?' while Mikhail Nikiforovich Katkov – a conservative Slavophile writer and editor of the *Moskovskie Vedomosti* – claimed on 8 April that the assassin was a Pole named Olszewski: supposedly, Karakozov's facial features and Polish language skills indicated this. But other nationalities were also taken into account. For example, various newspapers reported that the Karakozov family had never really been officially registered as Russian nobility and that the name sounded Tatar. Still others brought – even if ironically – German and Jewish roots into play.[380] Karakozov was allowed to be anything – except the Russian that he was.

Even more than that, Korevo's narrative contained all the essential elements of the great 'revolutionary conspiracy' that conservatives had been warning against since 1815.[381] Thus the story of this 'denunciator' (Klevenskii) mixed the motif of the secret society as part of an open society (which had existed among the Decembrists) with the motif of revolutionary officers and Poles (references to the Decembrists and the January Uprising of 1863), garnished with references to the Russian version of Filippo Buonarroti's secret organization, the Apofasimeni ('those sentenced to death'). Also in play were widely shared ideas about the inner life of secret societies, such as the Carboneria.[382]

---

380 For the tsar's question and the different versions thereof, see above, p. 454. For analysis of it and its repetition in newspapers at the time, see Bukhshtab, 'Posle vystrela Karakozova', 69–71; as well as Verhoeven, 'The Making of Russian Revolutionary Terrorism', 103–5. For Murav'ev's definition of Karakozov as a Pole see especially Dolbilov, 'Poliak v imperskom politicheskom leksikone', 321, note 59.

381 This has previously been observed by George Williamson, 'Thought Is in Itself a Dangerous Operation', 305, note 50 to page 298. Conspiracy theories also developed later around John Wilkes Booth's assassination of Lincoln. For these theories, see, for example, James McKinley, *Assassination in America* (New York: Harper & Row, 1977), Chapter 1; and especially Lloyd Lewis, *The Assassination of Lincoln: History and Myth* (Lincoln: University of Nebraska Press, 1994).

382 On this see above, pp. 102–3, 106, 112–13, 123. Claudia Verhoeven, *The Odd Man Karakozov*, 59, names the Jacobins and the Carboneria as archetypes.

A narrative such as this one could hardly have been created without prior knowledge, and so Korevo could not have been completely ignorant of the history of insurgent movements and their tactics. After all, the Moscow friends' group had assumed that they were close enough in shared convictions to trust him. It is likely that he knew Oskar Wilhelm Becker's case (and maybe even Becker himself), because Korevo had attended the lyceum that Becker's father had directed – perhaps even in the year when Becker had carried out his assassination attempt on Wilhelm I. He must have also heard of the Greek conspiratorial group modelled on the Carboneria (the Filiki Etaireia, 'Society of Friends') while in Odessa. In 1821, an officer in the Russian service had begun the Greek Revolution there. Furthermore, pronounced parallels existed with the demagogue conspiracy theory that followed Sand's assassination of August von Kotzebue.[383]

But however this bouquet of disparate strands from the history of European uprisings since the age of Napoleon was assembled, the result hit the mark for the chairman of the Investigative Commission. Following Korevo's statement, Murav'ev suggested to the tsar that he pay the informant one thousand silver roubles. What happened to him after this is unknown.[384]

Korevo's tale of conspiracy theories provided a good basis for the persecution of real or fictitious revolutionary conspiracies and conspirators; it went directly into the indictment and shaped the interrogations of those arrested. The Investigative Commission subsequently unleashed a 'white terror' (as Herzen wrote in *Kolokol*) under Murav'ev's leadership. The 'thick journals' of the Western-oriented intelligentsia (*Russkoe slovo* and *Sovremennik*, which Chernyshevsky had edited before his exile) were banned, and in St Petersburg and Moscow, but also in many places in the provinces, the commission had hundreds of people arrested and interrogated and their homes searched. As Klevenskii writes, not only members of Karakozov's circle were affected, 'but also their friends, the friends of these friends, etc.' Murav'ev and his friends did not shy away from 'robust' interrogation methods: Karakozov was tortured and

---

383 See above, pp. 570–1; and on the parallels see Williamson, 'Thought Is in Itself a Dangerous Operation', 305, note 50 to page 298.

384 See Shilov, 'Pokushenie Karakozova 4 aprelia 1866 g.', 131, note 7 to page 99; and Verhoeven, *The Odd Man Karakozov*, 33.

others were threatened with torture. The dungeons of the Peter and Paul Fortress were packed and overcrowded.[385]

The excessive number of arrests and interrogations probably served at least as much to intimidate as they did to procure information. The official report of the Investigative Commission, as well as the censored version published on 3 August 1866, were based more on Korevo's conspiracy narrative than on the extensive material that the commission had compiled on the Karakozov case (the archived part alone comprised almost 6,000 pages).[386] One has to grant Murav'ev that, even with a large staff, it would have been impossible not only to collect so much material in a mere four months, but also to sift through it and evaluate it systematically. This is one of the reasons why Korevo's ready-made interpretation might have appeared to be a very handy resource to the head of the Investigative Commission.

As far as the reception of Karakozov's assassination attempt is concerned, two effects developed as a result of the conspiracy narrative and these repressive measures. On the one hand, the theory of the large-scale conspiracy successfully obscured Karakozov's actual political intentions and had a lasting influence on the interpretation of the origin and background of the assassination attempt.[387] On the other hand, in view of the frightening repressions, nobody would have thought to voice support for Karakozov publicly. Only a few cases of denunciations were recorded in the police investigation files: a toast to Karakozov, the Revolution and the Guillotine and a Pole's dismay that the tsar still had not kicked the bucket. Furthermore, in May 1866, the investigators discovered that photographs of Karakozov were being circulated. Finally, unknown persons – rumour had it that they were students – had located his anonymous grave on Golodai Island (today Dekabristov Island,

---

385 See the indictment, as well as Klevenskii, 'Predislovie', in Klevenskii and Kotel'nikov, *Pokushenie Karakozova*, vol. 1, 8 and xiv–xv, quotation at xiv; Bukhshtab, 'Posle vystrela Karakozova', 70; Venturi, *Roots of Revolution*, 347–8; Ulam, *Prophets and Conspirators*, 9–10; Eroshkin, 'Vystrel u Letnego sada', 171; Verhoeven, *The Odd Man Karakozov*, 16–18; and Verhoeven, 'The Making of Russian Revolutionary Terrorism', 108–11.

386 On the scale of the material, see Shilov, 'Pokushenie Karakozova 4 aprelia 1866 g', 91; and Klevenskii, 'Predislovie', in Klevenskii and Kotel'nikov, *Pokushenie Karakozova*, vol. 1, xv.

387 On this, see Verhoeven, *The Odd Man Karakozov*, 32–3. On the varying interpretations of *Organizatsiia* and *Ad* in scholarship, see Verhoeven's introduction for a general overview, and, as an example, Venturi, *Roots of Revolution*, 336–8.

which means 'Island of the Decembrists') and repeatedly left fresh flowers there.[388] These, however, were exceptions.

In the overall picture, the assassination attempt had underscored the loyalty and close connection of the vast majority of the population to the tsar and his autocratic government. This was not least due to the fact that most people in the countryside saw Karakozov's assassination attempt as an attack by an aristocrat on 'Alexander the Liberator' – that is, as an attack by an aristocrat who wanted to prevent the further implementation of the peasant liberation by assassinating its executor.[389] How could the peasants' experience have led them to believe anything different?

Tsar Alexander II and his government reacted to the attack by changing personnel and enacting far-reaching political measures. Similar to Napoleon III's actions following Orsini's attack in France, before the month was over the tsar replaced several highly stationed members of his government who were considered liberal (including the governor general of St Petersburg, Suvorov, who had failed to follow up on the tip from the anonymous student) and replaced them with conservative hardliners. The new appointees immediately established various new police and security organs. Legislative measures then followed – also analogous to measures taken in France. Thus governors were empowered to ban all public assemblies and to close all societies or cooperatives that they regarded as a threat to state security – the first step towards a reversal of the Great Reforms that Alexander II had carried out in the years since he took power. More laws of this nature followed.[390] In short, Alexander slowed down the process of reforms in reaction to Karakozov's assassination attempt. Instead of the revolution the would-be assassin had hoped for, his act of violence marked the end of a particularly active period of political, social and societal reforms in Russia.[391]

---

388 On this and other incidents see Bukhshtab, 'Posle vystrela Karakozova', 67–9; and Verhoeven, *The Odd Man Karakozov*, 79, 84, 150.

389 On this see Bukhshtab, 'Posle vystrela Karakozova', especially 76–9; as well as Venturi, *Roots of Revolution*, 348; and Ulam, *Prophets and Conspirators*, 5.

390 On this, see Yarmolinsky, *Road to Revolution*, 142–3; Ulam, *Prophets and Conspirators*, 7, 11; Eroshkin, 'Vystrel u Letnego sada', 171; as well as Daly, *Autocracy under Siege*, 18–20.

391 See Venturi, *Roots of Revolution*, 347; Ulam, *Prophets and Conspirators*, 11–13; and Hildermeier, *Geschichte Russlands*, 944.

In the medium and long term, the various strategies of reaction through marginalization, militarization, repression and externalization led in consequence to different political processes. To certain and varying extents, these processes followed the logic of action inherent in the strategies described. That, to varying degrees, the processes followed the logic of action inherent in these strategies is due to the fact that the processes which developed out of the reaction strategies and their results cannot be attributed solely to the ways in which authorities reacted to the terrorist provocations. They were also conditioned, and ever more so the longer they continued, by many other people, constellations, decisions, developments and factors that were independent of the strategies of reaction to the acts of violence themselves. This means that even if the logic of action inherent in the reactions described has the potential to shape further social and political developments more or less intensely, they have no inherent determinism, and this in turn means that, within these political processes and developments, a change of course – away from the logic of action inherent in the strategies of reaction described and towards other more reconciliatory processes, for instance – is possible if the levers decisive to making that shift are used.

The limits of the strategy of repression and externalization used in Russia were probably most firmly rooted in the logic of the strategy itself. Thus the combination of repression and externalization made it possible to suppress potential sympathy and support for Karakozov and redirect it towards Komissarov, and in this way largely direct the emergence of heroes and demons, focusing social polarization on predetermined breaking points, such as the relationship with Poland.

But the Russian government's reactions were so massive that they were perceived as an overreaction even by observers who were in favour of the tsar and autocracy. One year after the assassination, for example, the writer and censor A. V. Nikitenko noted in his diary, 'Our most dangerous internal enemies are not the Poles and not the nihilists, but those statesmen who create nihilists by provoking indignation and aversion to the regime, those who close the *zemstvos* [local self-governing organs created in the course of the reforms] and undermine the courts.'[392] As the censor observed, the reactions intended to protect the state

---

[392] As quoted in Daly, *Autocracy under Siege*, 20, accompanied by similar statements from other monarchists.

undermined the legitimacy of the political order more than internal political enemies ever could have.

To quote Rainer Paris, this overreaction following Karakozov's assassination attempt had the effect of 'unmasking' the government itself – just like the overreaction in the southern states following John Brown's raid on Harpers Ferry. If the stigmatization of the other via terrorist provocation is to succeed, so goes the idea taken up from Paris at the beginning of this study, 'the other must betray himself. Through his reaction, he must expose himself as the one whom the provocateur wanted to expose. The provocation has ripped the mask off his face and revealed him as the actual culprit.'[393] According to Paris, the ultimate purpose of demonstratively breaking the norm is to prove that the norm itself is illegitimate. In evaluating the success or failure of an act of violence, however, it is decisive that – as Paris emphasizes – the exposure is 'a function of the reaction, not of the initial situation': 'Only insofar as the provocation stimulates the desired action is it the cause and trigger of this process.'[394] This means that the reaction has to be taken seriously as an independent element and its consequences can no longer be automatically attributed to the provocation.

In his proclamation, Karakozov attempted to prove the norm illegitimate. He had argued in his text, appealing to history, that the tsar was actually the one to blame for widespread poverty and that he was the greatest enemy of the common people. But he had hardly been able to penetrate the public consciousness with his proclamation at all.[395] Thus it was only the overreaction of the tsar and his government after the assassination attempt that led implicitly to the unmasking which Karakozov had tried to carry out explicitly but vainly.

In this way, the state reactions to Karakozov's assassination became a further step towards radicalization. This path would lead to the establishment of the executive committee of Narodnaia Volia at the end of the 1870s. Members of the social-radical groups and political generations to follow made reference to Karakozov's example; he became a cult figure alongside Chernyshevsky. In this respect, they also belatedly confirmed

---

393 Paris, 'Der kurze Atem der Provokation', 63. On this also see above, pp. 63–4 and especially 70–1.

394 Paris, 'Der kurze Atem der Provokation', 64.

395 See above, pp. 514–16, 559.

Karakozov's assertion that his act of violence – whether it would succeed or not – was a model worth imitating.[396] The members of the executive committee of Narodnaia Volia organized a whole series of terrorist attacks, to one of which Alexander II finally fell victim in 1881.[397]

In the United States, the limits of militarization as a strategy for dealing with terrorist violence were revealed in at least two respects. On the one hand, these limits became noticeable as soon as the official military interpretation lost plausibility. Significantly, new interpretations of the assassination and its background led to the assassin's demonization after all, and their effects are still felt today.[398] On the other hand, the further development of American right-wing terrorism since the 1860s illustrates the limits of the militarization strategy. Contrary to what many had hoped, American society missed perhaps its best chance of resolving the fundamental social and political conflicts surrounding emancipation and its implementation in the years after the Civil War. Due to financial and political considerations, the Union's military occupation of the former Confederate states could not be effectively sustained permanently. Given that these sociopolitical conflicts continued to exist, the limits of the military response to Booth's terrorist attack corresponded precisely to the limits of the will and ability to exercise military control. The end of this control resulted in an intensification of terrorist violence.

The later development of right-wing terrorism in the United States is closely linked to the political conflicts in implementing emancipation under Reconstruction. After Lincoln's assassination, Reconstruction passed into the hands of President Andrew Johnson, himself a former slaveholder from Tennessee. Johnson was convinced that African

---

396 On Karakozov's assertion above, see pp. 531–40; and on his cult status for succeeding groups, Venturi, *Roots of Revolution*, 351; and Budnitskii, *Terrorizm v rossiiskom osvoboditel'nom dvizhenii*, 37–8.

397 On this see Venturi, *Roots of Revolution*, 350–3 and Chapters 15–22; Yarmolinsky, *Road to Revolution*, 144–8 and Chapters 8–14; Budnitskii, *Terrorizm v rossiiskom osvoboditel'nom dvizhenii*, 38–77; as well as Hildermeier, *Geschichte Russlands*, 944–51.

398 It is precisely this demonization which Terry Alford references to explain the incredible fact that he produced the first scholarly biography of John Wilkes Booth in 2015 – 150 years after the assassination of Lincoln, on which there is otherwise no lack of literature. See Alford, *Fortune's Fool*, 1–3, as well as the myths about John Wilkes Booth discussed in the epilogue.

Americans had no place in the US political community. In contrast to the southern states' initial expectations, he pursued a highly conciliatory policy towards the former Confederacy, for example by leaving all concrete legislation regarding those emancipated up to the states themselves.[399]

Thus the presidential Reconstruction in the southern states resulted in the attempt to return as far as possible to the *status quo ante*. At the end of 1865, the legislative bodies in these states issued special Black Codes whose main intention was to force the newly freed African Americans to work on the plantations by other means: the coercive power that slaveowners had previously exercised over their slaves in private ownership was delegated to the state and its institutions – the courts, police and militia. These institutions were only open to white Americans of European descent, many of whom were recruited from among veterans of the Confederate armies. Large numbers of them soon began to terrorize the African American population, for example by mistreating those who did not want to sign an employment contract with a plantation. This violence and the Black Codes clearly refuted the validity of Andrew Johnson's view that the former states of the Confederacy could and should be given a free hand in reintegrating into the Union.[400] Such a policy was a recipe for virtual re-enslavement.

On these grounds, the legislative branch then took over southern reintegration with the congressional Reconstruction. The 39th Congress – in which the Republicans had clear majorities in both houses – reacted initially by passing the Fourteenth Amendment to the Constitution. This amendment declared all people born in the United States to be American citizens whose rights could not be curtailed or restricted. This overruled the Supreme Court's decision in the *Dred Scott* case.[401] In the Reconstruction Act, which temporarily placed the southern states under

---

399 On this see Heideking and Mauch, *Geschichte der USA*, 149–50; Finzsch, Horton and Horton, *Von Benin nach Baltimore*, 315, 319–20; and Foner, *Reconstruction*, 176–96; as well as more specifically Bergeron, *Andrew Johnson's Civil War and Reconstruction*.

400 See Heideking and Mauch, *Geschichte der USA*, 150; and Foner, *Reconstruction*, 119–23, 196–216.

401 The House Joint Resolution proposing the Fourteenth Amendment to the Constitution, June 16, 1866, Enrolled Acts and Resolutions of Congress, 1789–1999, General Records of the United States Government, RG 11, NAB, NARA, ourdocuments.gov. On the origins and creation of the Fourteenth Amendment see Foner, *Reconstruction*, 251–61.

military rule, Congress gave African Americans the right to vote for the first time and officially rejected the view that European Americans and African Americans were too different to be able to work together in a single political system. Finally, in the Fifteenth Amendment to the Constitution, Congress made it illegal to prevent American citizens from voting on the basis of race.[402] At the same time, Congress initiated a process in which the populations of the individual states in the South (including African American men and excluding former Confederates) elected representatives to constitutional conventions as well as governors, state governments and congresses in which African Americans were represented for the first time. The impact of this second American revolution was significant.[403]

Nevertheless, the emancipation policies supported by Congress had their limits, and these limits also point to the limits of the military handling of John Wilkes Booth's terrorist attack: Congress required the military power of the individual states and the president as commander-in-chief to enforce emancipation. This was especially important since, in the years from 1868 to 1871, the Ku Klux Klan and related organizations flooded the US South with a wave of right-wing terrorist violence.

Members of these terrorist organizations – mostly local notables in cooperation with middle- and lower-class whites – attempted as far as possible to reverse the changes enacted in the southern states by congressional Reconstruction.[404] To achieve this goal they threatened, abused, raped, shot and lynched African Americans who had participated in the constitutional conventions or who had distinguished themselves otherwise: in political or other public office, or in schools, churches and businesses. White Americans who had stood on the side of the Union during the Civil War, who were active in the Republican Party or who simply

---

402 The House Joint Resolution proposing the Fifteenth Amendment to the Constitution, December 7, 1868, Enrolled Acts and Resolutions of Congress, 1789–1999, General Records of the United States Government, RG 11, NAB, NARA, ourdocuments.gov. On the origins and creation of the Fifteenth Amendment, see Foner, *Reconstruction*, 446–9.

403 On congressional Reconstruction, see Heideking and Mauch, *Geschichte der USA*, 151–4; Finzsch, Horton and Horton, *Von Benin nach Baltimore*, 320–4; and Foner, *Reconstruction*, Chapter 6. The term 'Second American Revolution' is found in *Reconstruction*, 449.

404 Heideking and Mauch, *Geschichte der USA*, 154; and Foner, *Reconstruction*, 426.

treated African Americans as equals were also targeted by right-wing terrorists.[405]

Importantly, with this violence, the Ku Klux Klan and similar groups denied legitimacy to the Republican Reconstruction states by demonstrating that these states were unable to protect their own supporters. Since the violence was met with considerable sympathy and approval among the white population in the South, many southern governors were unwilling or unable to fight it effectively. Only after Congress had set up its own investigating committee, enacted a series of Enforcement Acts as well as the Ku Klux Klan Act and confirmed a dedicated attorney general who took up the matter seriously, was the violence (temporarily) contained.[406]

It will have to be left to additional research to determine whether, and to what extent, John Wilkes Booth served as a model and positive point of reference for these right-wing terrorists. What *is* certain is that members of the Ku Klux Klan and related organizations pursued the same basic goals as Booth. Moreover, they used the same methods, although the right-wing terrorists after the Civil War added other institutions and forms of violence directly related to slavery, such as patrols and lynching. Finally, a cursory glance at the blogs of today's Confederate supporters indicates that Lincoln's assassin is still present and has taken on the status of a hero. This is why John Wilkes Booth can be seen not only as the object of a belated demonization but also – at least within this section of a particular public sphere – as the object of a belated heroization, making him into an icon, a status shift that went hand in hand with a successful transformation of stigma into charisma.[407]

In the German states, the handling of the Oskar Wilhelm Becker case continued to be characterized by supreme unflappability. Unlike Orsini, Brown and Karakozov, Becker was not sentenced to death. The jury for the Baden Middle Rhine District Court sentenced him to twenty years in the 'correction house' or prison. But when his father and other family

---

405 On violence from right-wing terrorist organizations in these years see Finzsch, Horton and Horton, *Von Benin nach Baltimore*, 327–31; Foner, *Reconstruction*, 425–44; and especially Stephen Budiansky, *The Bloody Shirt: Terror after the Civil War* (New York: Penguin Books, 2009).

406 Foner, *Reconstruction*, 443–4, 454–9.

407 Also see the additional examples in Alford, *Fortune's Fool*, especially 332–3.

members appealed to Wilhelm I with a request for pardon in the autumn of 1866, the Prussian king interceded with his son-in-law, the Grand Duke of Baden, on their behalf. The latter consequently pardoned Becker on the condition that he would have to go abroad immediately and would not be allowed on German soil again. Becker first travelled to Brussels and, from there, to Egypt, where he died a few years later.[408] The fact that, outside Baden, he has been largely forgotten today, speaks to the effectiveness of the strategy of marginalization following his terrorist attack. However, the Prussian king's appointment of Otto von Bismarck as prime minister on 22 September 1862 might have also contributed to Becker's oblivion. Bismarck displayed precisely the qualities that Oskar Wilhelm Becker had found wanting in Wilhelm I, and broke through the political blockage to forming a nation state – modelled entirely on Italy – in the course of the subsequent decade, not least by using state-sanctioned collective violence.

408 On the sentence see 'Oskar Becker's Proceß. (Von unseren eigenen Berichterstattern.) Bruchsal, 24. September', *Kölnische Zeitung*, 26. 9. 1861, second edition, 1. On the request for pardon see Dr Ph. Eduard Weber, 9 October 1866, from the parsonage in Hosterwitz near Pillnitz by Dresden to Wilhelm I, as well as Dr Paul Becker, 15 November 1866 from Dresden to Wilhelm I, GStA PK, I. HA, Rep. 89 Secret Civil Cabinet, Recent Period No. 15257: Acts of the Royal Secret Cabinet. Subj.: Attempts carried out on the life of His Majesty the King Bl. 18–19 und Bl. 21. On the further course of the pardon, see ibid., 22–9.

Conclusion

The invention of terrorism

This book's point of departure was the abiding topicality and political relevance of terrorism and its history. From that perspective, it was hoped that comprehending the beginnings of terrorism as part of Western modernity and the first globalization that burgeoned in the nineteenth century could also help explain phenomena of terrorist violence arising a century and a half later in the context of this modernity's second globalization.

The central question of this volume is therefore how the terrorism so prevalent today developed historically. The story of its origins is described as a process of invention. Within a few years, a small group of actors in Europe, the United States and Russia went one by one through a collective transnational learning process and brought forth a new kind of political violence known today as terrorism. Felice Orsini, with his attempt on the life of the French emperor in 1858, must be considered the inventor of this new type of violence, although, paradoxically, it took cooperation with his intended victim, Napoleon III, to transform the abortive attack into a successful terrorist act. The second major inventor of terrorism was John Brown. All the evidence indicates that he followed the American media coverage of Orsini's assassination attempt and of his cooperation with the French emperor and that Brown subsequently sought to use the tactic of terrorism himself when he raided the arsenal and the weapons factories of the US military in Harpers Ferry. Terrorism's inventors include the first copycats as well: Oskar Wilhelm Becker, the would-be assassin of Prussian king Wilhelm I in 1861; John Wilkes Booth, who murdered US president Abraham Lincoln in 1865; and Dmitry Vladimirovich Karakozov, whose attack on Tsar Alexander II failed in 1866. These three men learned of Orsini's and Brown's methods through a variety of different channels, imitated them, and simultaneously developed terrorism as a tactic. All three attackers contributed an important innovation that long remained characteristic of terrorist attacks: the written claim of responsibility. Terrorism, just like the railway and artificial fertilizer, must therefore be regarded as an invention of the nineteenth century, except that it is not a scientific or technological invention but rather an invention of a logic of action in the realms of policy, society and the media.

The basic methodological question is how to identify the first consequential terrorist attacks as such. This is especially important insofar as nineteenth-century actors did not use the term as it is used today. In order to select certain acts of violence out of the historical abundance of similar phenomena and to demonstrate how those acts became historical and media events and thus sites of the invention of terrorist logic, it was necessary first to define terrorism; second, to name the central elements of the logic of violent terrorist action; and third, to inquire into the causes and dynamics of such violence. In order to do this, this book took the requisite components from social science research and assembled them into a theory of terrorism. These theoretical components facilitated this study of the five selected cases for the verifiability or the absence of the necessary attributes, elements, conditions, interdependencies, contexts and factors and thus whether a given violent act can be classified as terrorism.

These five cases are among the first acts of violence that exhibit all the essential attributes of the theory, in terms both of characterizing the perpetrators as terrorists and of labelling their violent deeds as acts of terrorism. In this respect, historical analysis can not only empirically validate the theoretical components derived from the social sciences (at least for the period examined), but can also point out and illustrate the ways in which these elements function and interact. In addition, theoretical elements mentioned in the literature of the social sciences and included here, but generally still underestimated in research on terrorism, have been strengthened. As the following compilation of findings indicates, historical analysis therefore opens an array of new perspectives, including ones relevant to research on violence in the social sciences.

With regard to the definition of terrorism, this study – contrary to the usual statements in the literature – establishes that, despite the existence of many different explanations of terrorism, well-conceived scholarly definitions agree in all the main points. This book takes up the work of Peter Waldmann, who defines terrorism as 'violence against a political order from below which is planned and prepared [*planmäßig vorbereitet*] and meant to be shocking. Such acts of violence are supposed to spread feelings of insecurity and intense fear, but they are also meant to generate sympathy and support'.[1] Waldmann emphasizes the political dimension of terrorist violence manifested in the political objectives of the terrorists, although he also includes the social and economic dimension. To address the logic of action, this study draws on the sociology of power as explored by Rainer Paris, who conceives of terrorism as a special form of provocation. He defines a provocation 'as a deliberate, surprising norm violation intended to draw the other into an open conflict and prompt a reaction that morally discredits and exposes that party in the eyes of third parties'.[2] In conjunction with Waldmann's definition, Paris's analysis of terrorism as provocation adds the concept of exposure, according to which attackers seek to challenge and discredit the legitimacy of a powerful opponent.

The acts of violence perpetrated by Felice Orsini, John Brown, Oskar Wilhelm Becker, John Wilkes Booth and Dmitry Vladimirovich Karakozov meet all of Waldmann's criteria for the definition of terrorism. What each of them did was premeditated and intended to shock. Their deeds were calculated to spread fear and horror among political opponents and to garner support among potential sympathizers. The acts were aimed at the political order in different ways depending on where the perpetrators lived. As the historical analysis in this book has

---

1 Peter Waldmann, *Terrorismus: Provokation der Macht* (Munich: Gerling-Akademischer-Verlag, 1998), 12.

2 Rainer Paris, 'Der kurze Atem der Provokation', in Rainer Paris, *Stachel und Speer* (Frankfurt am Main: Suhrkamp, 1998), 58.

also shown, provocation is a pivotal element in the learning process involved in the invention of terrorism as a tactic and to various extents is demonstrable for each of these protagonists. While Orsini did not entirely grasp this aspect of his violent act, John Brown, in particular, reckoned with it successfully.

The bearing that political ends have on the identification of terrorism is controversial in social science scholarship. Whereas some authors stress that terrorism as a tactic is open to all political ends and subject matters, Waldmann has found that three political directions can be identified, at least for the nineteenth and twentieth centuries: social-revolutionary, ethno-nationalist and radical right-wing terrorism.[3] Waldmann describes these three basic ideas with twentieth-century terrorist organizations in mind, focusing on the Red Army Faction in Germany and Action Directe in France as prime examples of social-revolutionary terrorism. In this context, it is understandable that Waldmann identifies revolutionary terrorism with Marxist ideas. The first volume of Marx's *Capital*, however, did not appear until 1867 – a year after Karakozov's attempt to assassinate the tsar. It is therefore crucial to broaden our understanding of the guiding ideas that provided (and in many cases still provide) motivations for terrorists. This will allow us to include, within Waldmann's typology of political motives, the first violent acts whose social logic classifies them as terrorism and which demonstrably had an important impact on terrorism's subsequent history.

If the context of the history of ideas behind the violent attacks examined in this book is taken seriously, then social-revolutionary terrorism is definable by the guiding idea of personal and social freedom and equality. By the same token, ethno-nationalist terrorism can be defined by the ideas of political participation and national self-determination. By contrast, it is an act of radical right-wing terrorism when the perpetrators want their violence to prevent, undermine or annul personal, social and political freedom and equality.

By raising the degree of abstraction in this way, the cases studied in this volume encompass the spectrum that Waldmann outlines. While Orsini was pursuing national objectives and Brown aimed at social-revolutionary ones, Becker was acting out of national and Booth from

---

3 Waldmann, *Terrorismus*, 19 and Chapter 6.

counterrevolutionary motives. For this reason, it is argued here that one may consider the attacks by Becker, Booth and Karakozov as the conclusion of the process of inventing terrorism's rationale and political parameters of terrorism not only as a tactic but also in terms of its three political directions – at least as far as the nineteenth and twentieth centuries go.

Perspectives on the theory of terrorism

In this book, the causes of terrorism have been sought at various levels. As became apparent in the theoretical components, it is, to begin with, significant on a wide social scale that in social science research political and economic processes of modernization and a number of its effects are considered necessary conditions and facilitating factors of insurrectionist violence generally and terrorist violence specifically. Authors such as Samuel Huntington and Ted Robert Gurr assert that these modernization processes lead to an increase in violent conflicts in many cases, and the social scientist Charles Tilly points out in his historically oriented scholarship that modernization processes as well as their concomitant revolutions in Europe ushered in a great deal of politicization and association along with new conflicts of interest and collective forms of action. Among the necessary conditions and facilitating factors, the primary ones that come to mind are the development of mass media and rapid transnational communications and forms of transport that afford those who would commit violent acts increased accessibility to targets, co-conspirators and the public and make news readily available to the overall population.

The 'transformation of the world' in the nineteenth century was driven by profound processes of modernization and international and regional communication and connections in Europe, Russia and the United States.[4] Those processes formed essential prerequisites for terrorism, as the historical contextualization of the five acts of terrorism treated here shows. By the middle of the century, the speed and regularity of travelling transatlantic steamships, the emergence of national and transnational rail and telegraph networks, press agencies and – thanks

---

4 Osterhammel, *The Transformation of the World*.

not least to the penny press – the intensified consumption of media by much of the population, had created the necessary conditions and facilitating factors in Europe, Russia and the United States alike. This historical study has shown that effective terrorist tactics were invented for the first time precisely when the necessary preconditions existed for the functioning of terrorism as a tactic, preconditions that later social scientists identified as necessary for terrorism to work.

Yet mass media and rapid communications and transport not only proved to be necessary factors in facilitating the potential success of terrorist attacks; they also established the conditions for the invention and development of terrorist tactics in the aforementioned serial, collective, transnational learning process. This latter finding, too, is new. Together, these results support a hypothesis that has circulated for some time in scholarship but has not yet been thoroughly studied and documented, namely that the invention of terrorism is a product of modernity – specifically, the modernity of the nineteenth century.

Social movements are one of the phenomena that have accompanied the political, economic and social transformations since the second half of the eighteenth century. As explained in the discussion of this study's theoretical components, particularly in relation to research by Charles Tilly and Dieter Rucht, social movements arose as a new kind of political association resulting from the politicization of broad segments of the population that were using heretofore unknown approaches to actively change their society. Donatella Della Porta finds that social movements were crucial to the emergence of terrorism in the twentieth century because it was in them that terrorists received the world view, experienced the political socialization, and underwent the radicalization that justified the use of violence in their own eyes and in those of their sympathizers. Della Porta thus corroborates the research of Lawrence Freedman and Martha Crenshaw, who contend that terrorism is neither a psychopathological act nor a tactic of first choice but rather the result of learning processes based on the fact that other attempts to exert political influence have not achieved their objective.

The five perpetrators from the nineteenth century studied in this volume largely confirm the picture drawn by scholarship in the social sciences as regards the twentieth and twenty-first centuries. First, the national democrats and abolitionists constituted the kind of proactive movements that organized themselves at the national, transnational and transatlantic levels. Second, there are demonstrable processes of political socialization and radicalization in and around these movements, especially for the two primary inventors of terrorism, Felice Orsini and John Brown: Orsini belonged to the national democratic movement in the Italian states and tried repeatedly to pursue the quest for an Italian republic through collective violence and institutional political channels. Only when he saw that all collective, military and political avenues were blocked did he seek other courses of action and decide to use individual violence: a spectacular assassination of Napoleon III. John Brown belonged to the abolitionist movement and fought to end slavery in the United States. At first, he intended to lead fugitive slaves in a kind of guerrilla war in the Appalachians. He modified this plan, however, moving in the direction of terrorist tactics just as the first detailed reports of Orsini's attack on Napoleon III appeared in the United States. To that extent, the second result of this historical analysis is that terrorism emerged from the first great social movements in history, a result which confirms the considerations of Wolfgang Mommsen and Eric Hobsbawm.

The imitators Becker, Booth and Karakozov were likewise associated with social movements, but far less closely or enduringly than Orsini and Brown. One may conclude that engagement in social movements is less significant as a prerequisite for the adoption and further development of terrorism than for the invention of this tactic. At the same time, the relative lack of previous involvement correlates with a lack of both networking and experience in political or publicizing activity at the time of the violent act and consequently facilitated the political failure of the terrorist attacks.

This study's theoretical components, insofar as the wider social conditions for terrorism are concerned, include the element of political blockage, building on the work of Martha Crenshaw and Luigi Bonanate. According to their view, the use of terrorist tactics is likely if a dissatisfied elite identifies social grievances that it deems changeable in principle but finds that it cannot change because it is denied a political voice and because mobilizing relatively large groups within the population is unpromising or even impossible.

Such political blockages were identified in all the cases studied in this book. In different ways all five perpetrators belonged to an elite; all five were highly dissatisfied with, indeed even troubled by, the political developments in the societies to which they belonged and, as a result, all five denied the legitimacy of both the political order in which they lived and its representatives. Orsini saw the restoration of the monarchies in Italy's territorial states after the revolution of 1848–9 as illegitimate. For Brown, it was the perpetuation and consolidation of slavery in the United States. Becker criticized the unwillingness and inability of the German sovereigns to unify the German territories into a nation state. Booth found it intolerable that the Confederate States had been defeated, that slavery had been abolished, and that rights of citizenship might be granted to emancipated slaves after the Civil War. Moreover, he feared that Abraham Lincoln, like Napoleon I and Napoleon III in France, would end democracy and establish himself as the monarch of the United States. Karakozov felt that the tsar had forfeited his right to rule Russia because the emancipation laws had disadvantaged the peasants it had freed from serfdom.

All five perpetrators, however, lacked effective legal channels for political participation, and some of them had already seen in practice that the population could not be stirred to take collective action in order to change the political situation. Orsini had failed again and again in his efforts to ignite revolutionary insurrections in Italy and lived in exile after the revolutions of 1848–9. Brown was aware that abolishing slavery through collective violence was inconceivable in the United States because radical abolitionist parties had not even managed to win majorities in elections. During the raid on Harpers Ferry, Brown also found that fewer slaves rallied around him than would have been necessary for a guerrilla war. Nonetheless, some of the five protagonists, such as Orsini and Karakozov, hoped – in vain – to spark a revolution through their terrorist violence. The historical analysis in this study has thus shown that terrorism as a tactic of political violence originated as a continuation and culmination of the great revolutions in North America and France, at a moment when the existing political orders were regarded as illegitimate but when the social conditions for revolution did not exist. Terrorism emerged as a means for bringing the revolutions to completion in a non-revolutionary situation.

By contrast, the cross-check to identify societies with no political blockages in the American–European–Russian space of communication during the relevant period found that terrorist violence, too, was absent there. On the question of abolishing serfdom and slavery, a comparison shows that the political system of absolute monarchy in which a sovereign, as long as he was powerful enough, was able to carry through a decision even against the interests of the influential nobility (while still counting on its loyalty) in most cases outperformed American democracy. After all, the founding fathers had deliberately prevented the creation of a strong central authority, granting the planter aristocracy the possibility of exerting disproportionate legislative, executive and judicial influence thanks precisely to its slaveownership. They had thereby enabled the planter aristocracy to defeat any initiative jeopardizing the foundations of its wealth and power. Changes in this imbalance were not possible until the demographic relationship between the North and the South shifted.

Causal analysis shows that overall social factors are supplemented by others at the individual and organizational levels. Key factors for the individual are political ideologies, ideas and experiences that foster the use of violence and legitimate it in the eyes of the perpetrator. In addition, there is the willingness to make sacrifices and the desire to find meaning, gain recognition and, indeed, attain immortality – in other words, the yearning for transcendence.

The historical analysis has shown that two ideas – personal freedom (liberty) and political freedom (nationhood) – accounted for much of the aforementioned political, economic and social processes of modernization and promoted the invention and further development of terrorism, too. Reform movements inspired by Christianity, national religious notions, Christian doctrines and the precedents set by Christian martyrs were sources of the willingness to make sacrifices and of the longing for transcendence, proving decisive in the emergence of terrorism. As for organizational factors, there is evidence in Orsini's case that competition with other groups also played a part in the choice to use terrorist violence. In many instances, the force of time figured in as well; that is, the feeling of having to pre-empt decisive developments.

Last but not least, the theoretical analysis revealed that public and political reactions determine the success or failure of terrorist attacks. As stressed especially by Rainer Paris, not every kind of reaction serves the intentions of terrorist perpetrators of violence, however; rather, the purpose of terrorist provocation is met only if the powerful other responds in such a way as to reveal itself to be what the terrorist set out to expose. This self-exposure, according to Paris, occurs primarily through overreaction.

All the terrorist acts studied here were nationally and internationally popular and media events. They bore out Rainer Paris's observation that the intentions behind a terrorist attack are not fulfilled until the public reacts to it. Whereas interpreting the terrorist attacks as instrumental violence took away their political barb, interpreting their symbolic dimension and the response to such political symbolism brought about processes by which the perpetrators were turned into icons among their sympathizers and demonized among their political opponents. The two processes reinforced each other, granting the terrorists and their acts of violence social influence they did not really have until then and enabling them to polarize and radicalize the public. Precisely in the cases of Orsini and Brown, it became apparent that attempts at instrumentalization by powerful political actors proved significant and effective for enhancing their magnitude, an essential process for the political success of terrorist attacks.

In summary, terrorism originated in the nineteenth century as a product of European and American modernity in terms both of its characteristic form in media and technology, and of its political and ideational substance, as well as in religious thought patterns and models. By about the mid-1800s, Europe, Russia and the United States already constituted a shared communication space thanks to the transnational revolution in technology, communications and the media. As a result, Orsini is not only part of European but also of American history, just as John Brown is part of both American and Russian history. From a political and ideological perspective, the emergence of terrorism represented a shift in the form of political violence, one facilitated and triggered by the dramatic processes of change taking place at the turn from the eighteenth to the nineteenth century: the processes of emancipation and nation building, political and social revolutions first in America and France and then in other European countries, the emergence of mass media and the mass public, and the formation of the first social movements shaped by Christian values. Terrorism was invented as a continuation of revolutionary violence sustained by the politicization and political participation of much of the population and legitimated by the appeal to political participation and national self-determination or human dignity, natural law and higher divine law – in a political order considered illegitimate but sanctioned by positive law. In other words, terrorism is a post-revolutionary form of violence invented in a non-revolutionary situation in Europe, the United States and Russia.

New perspectives on the history of terrorism

What bearing do the outcomes in this book have on the depictions and narratives dominating research on terrorism thus far? To what extent do they change the picture of terrorism's emergence and history? To address these questions, the present section first delves into the relation between terrorist assassinations and 'classical' political murders as documented from time immemorial. Following that, the results of this book are compared to the established narratives of terrorism's history, first to the periodization of the history of terrorism and to the connection between religion and modernity, second to the emergence of terrorism and the significance of the French Revolution in that process, third to the chronology and geography of terrorism's history and the role of Russia and the United States, fourth to ideas and other factors that drove or otherwise facilitated the invention of terrorism, and fifth to Rapoport's four-wave theory.

Terrorist assassination as a democratization of political murder

The differences between traditional political murder as recounted in history since antiquity and terrorist assassination, the origins of which are the focus of this book, are exemplified well by Oskar Wilhelm Becker's attack on Wilhelm I, king of Prussia. At first glance Becker's terrorist assassination attempt closely resembles conventional political murder, yet Becker's statements before the examining magistrate bring the dissimilarities of the two kinds of violence to light with exceptional clarity.

Becker's attempt on the life of Wilhelm I diverges from earlier political murders because of the relation between instrumental and symbolic violence.[5] Whereas conventional assassinations accomplish their

---

5 Waldmann, *Terrorismus*, 15.

immediate political objective with the death of the victim, the link between Becker's political objective – the unification of Germany – and his attack was indirect. He did explain that he had wanted to murder the king of Prussia because he believed the king to be incapable of unifying Germany, but this murder would have led directly to the goal (and would thereby be classifiable as 'political murder') only if it had been Becker's primary concern either to kill Wilhelm I or to bring the Crown prince to power. He intended neither, however. By murdering the king, Becker hoped to achieve a psychological effect that would advance the project of German unification. As Becker later (accurately) tried to explain by analogy with Orsini's attack on Napoleon III, Wilhelm I did not actually have to die in order to achieve this effect. In other words, Becker's attack on Wilhelm I was an attempt to indirectly push the public to achieve Becker's goal for him.

Another difference lies in the assassin's person. Whereas traditional political assassinations were usually carried out by members of powerful political elites in the victim's milieu (such as senators, high nobility and ranking military officers) or with imperial or ecclesiastical legitimation, Oskar Wilhelm Becker was a student from the educated middle class and as such belonged to the social elite but had no political power whatsoever.[6] Becker decided independently to try to murder the king without any justification derived from membership in a particular estate, from some position of power that he or his family held, or from official authority. The twenty-two-year-old student was keenly aware that people might well find his act ridiculous and absurd because of his low status. He had, however, correctly recognized that, despite being part of a social elite unaffiliated with the court and despite his lack of higher legitimation, he, too, could trigger the desired shock in a public informed through mass media and that this shock effect was what mattered most.

It is against this background that the invention of the claim of responsibility is to be understood, since the subordinate social rank of the assassin determined the possibilities of gaining access to relevant information and to the political public. Orsini, Becker, Booth and Karakozov

---

6 The significance of the difference between the hitherto usual palace coups and assassination by a 'civilian' such as Karakozov has already been emphasized by Verhoeven, 'The Making of Russian Revolutionary Terrorism', 102.

did *not* belong to the state's powerful political elite. Their political views did *not* derive from an intimate knowledge of the head of state and his milieu but rather from the media. They operated *without* consulting with or receiving consent from a part of the political elite, who might have been able to use their influence to guarantee the desired reception of their acts. Instead, the assassins committed their attacks as professional revolutionaries, students or actors having no government connections, hoping that the population would understand their motives, which were only indirectly tied to their attempted murders. These protagonists therefore had to take the classical political murder a step further. Orsini did so by receiving the political and journalistic backing of the most powerful man in France – his victim, Napoleon III – the three imitators did this by inventing the claim of responsibility to explain what they did.[7] Only in this way did they stand a chance of gaining the public's ear, which was the necessary precondition for their political success.

In many respects the media played an important role in this process of transformation and further development because the various elements of change were interdependent. For Orsini, Becker, Booth and Karakozov, as citizens, subjects or even exiles operating far from the centres of power, the existence of a political public, the use of media and their own active interest in politics were essential to their ability to shape their political opinion, to see themselves in a position to assess public opinion, or, as with Becker, to localize their victims. The very existence of mass media and the fact that broad swathes of the public were participating in the political system justified the hope of the assassins that the motives behind their violence would become public without their having the necessary sociopolitical communication networks at their disposal. In this respect, too, the mass media were a prerequisite, perhaps even the decisive one, for the transformation of classical political murder into a terrorist assassination, a prerequisite particularly for the use of assassination as a political resource by new social strata and thus for democratizing the perpetration of a specific kind of political violence. The democratization of the potential victims followed immediately, as with Émile Henry's bombing of the Café Terminus in Paris – an early

---

7 In principle the same is true of John Brown, who is excluded in this context because he did not carry out an assassination.

example of an assault on the general population, which in the bomber's eyes stood for the bourgeoisie.[8]

This does not mean that there has been nothing but terrorist assassinations since their invention and that political murders have been completely supplanted as a type of political violence. There were and still are murders and attempted murders instrumentally conceived to eliminate political actors and committed by powerful individuals surrounding them, but increasingly also by persons far from and without power. One example is Claus Schenk Graf von Stauffenberg's attack on Adolf Hitler on 20 July 1944, an act classifiable as an effort to commit traditional political murder. This is because killing Hitler was the central and the necessary condition for the success of von Stauffenberg's plan and not public reaction to the bomb attack he had undertaken. A second example is Georg Elser, a carpenter who sought to kill Adolf Hitler and other top National Socialist leaders in a wholly instrumental sense, which is why his attack in the Munich Beer Hall (Bürgerbräukeller) on 8 November 1939 also constitutes attempted political murder, not a terrorist attack. Two things follow from this line of reasoning. First, political murder has not remained a prerogative of the nobility in the subsequent course of history; that act, too, has undergone democratization. Second, older forms of political violence like political murder persist, even though new ones, such as the terrorist attack, arise and take their place alongside the earlier kinds.

From the standard narrative to a new history of terrorism

What implications do this book's results have for a global history of terrorism; that is, for a narrative that encompasses the history of the whole world since antiquity? This aspiration is evident in both Rapoport's developmental theory of terrorism and the standard narrative developed by Laqueur, including the later changes and additions by him and other authors as discussed in the introduction to this book. Compared to these two still dominant versions of terrorism's history, the present study reveals many elements in common but also significant amendments and innovations.

---

8 See especially John Merriman, *The Dynamite Club: How a Bombing in Fin-de-Siècle Paris Ignited the Age of Modern Terror* (Boston: Houghton Mifflin Harcourt, 2009).

The history of terrorism to date is framed in terms of a sequence extending from a premodern, religious type to a modern political–secular variety and then to a new religious form of the phenomenon. Rapoport and Laqueur (and many authors after them) have suggested that examples of premodern, religiously inspired terrorism are the Jewish Sicarii in ancient Jerusalem, the Assassins in medieval Persia and Syria, and India's Thugs. For Rapoport and Laqueur, the shift to modern political–secular terrorism came with the French Revolution and the emergence of modern transport and communication technologies, and both authors contend that the Russian group Narodnaia Volia and the European anarchists who committed assassinations and other acts of violence from the late 1870s were the first active terrorists of the political–secular type. According to Rapoport's four-wave theory, modern terrorism from that point onward encompasses four international ideological waves: anarchist, anti-colonial, new-left and religious. Laqueur pays special attention to the events that relate to these waves, but he also treats cases of ethno-nationalist and radical right-wing terrorism. The two authors agree that terrorism in the actual sense originated in Europe and that radical immigrants from the old continent brought it with them to the United States. Finally, Rapoport and Laqueur both note a return to religious terrorism since the 1970s. Implicit in these versions of terrorism's history is the narrative of a religiously shaped premodernity, a secular modernity shaped by politics and ideology, and a neoreligious postmodernity.

The findings of this book show that the differentiation between a premodern religious terrorism and a modern political–secular one is untenable as formulated up to now. Other research supports this result for the premodern kind of terrorism. For instance, studies by David Teegarden on the ancient world, by Warren C. Brown on the Middle Ages, by David Cook on the Ismaili (the Assassins), by Johannes Dillinger on the early modern era, and by Kim A. Wagner on the Thugs show that premodern, religious terrorism of the kind described above did not exist in these cases.[9] A possible exception to this may have been

9 See David A. Teegarden, 'Acting like Harmodius and Aristogeiton: Tyrannicide in Ancient Greek Political Culture', in Carola Dietze and Claudia Verhoeven (eds.), *The Oxford Handbook of the History of Terrorism*; and, in the same volume, Warren C. Brown, 'Instrumental Terror in Medieval Europe'; David Cook, 'Ismaili Assassins as Early Terrorists?'; Johannes Dillinger, 'Early Modern Forerunners of Terrorism in

the Sicarii in their struggle against the Roman Empire, as Kai Trampedach illustrates. Thus current research on the three examples of religiously motivated terrorism to which Rapoport and Laqueur refer for the period from the beginning of history to the 1870s discounts all but perhaps one of them: the Sicarii. Their conflict with the Romans, however, does not demonstrate religiously inspired violence in the strict sense but rather resistance to the Roman Empire's direct imperial rule in Judaea – a struggle chiefly about political objectives.[10] Consequently, the Sicarii embodied an amalgam of political and religious motives similar to the national-democratic movement Young Italy for which Orsini tried to foment rebellions before he fell out with Giuseppe Mazzini, and the Calvinist abolitionist John Brown, who studied the history of the Sicarii as a model. Booth and the declared atheist Karakozov also entertained religious notions, but their precise form and their significance for the violence the two men perpetrated has yet to be studied in detail.[11] These findings suggest it is misleading to state that there is a difference between premodern religious terrorism, modern secular terrorism and post-modern religious terrorism.[12] The question is rather about the different forms and constellations that the amalgamation of religion, politics and violence has taken on over the centuries.

As for the emergence of what Rapoport and Laqueur describe as 'modern' terrorism, the results of this book yield new historical interlink-ages along with a new timeline and geography. In addition to this, new actors come into view. First, the new timeline assigns the French Revolution a different role. This revolution, which in narratives of moder-nity and modernization typically functions as a hinge connecting premodernity and modernity, can no longer serve in the conventional manner as the shift to modern political–secular terrorism. As Ronen

---

Europe and Nineteenth-Century Historians'; and Kim A. Wagner, '"Thugs and Assassins": "New Terrorism" and the Resurrection of Colonial Knowledge'. Accordingly, the violence of the Ismaili is regarded as political murder. The question of the target groups, the intended public effect and the reception call for closer examination.

10 See Kai Trampedach, 'Terrorism and Theocracy: On the Radical Resistance Movement against Roman Rule in Judea', in Dietze and Verhoeven, *The Oxford Handbook of the History of Terrorism*.

11 On Karakozov, see Verhoeven, *The Odd Man Karakozov*, Chapter 7. On Booth see the cited political tracts.

12 Martin Schulze Wessel argues similarly in 'Terrorismusstudien: Bemerkungen zur Entwicklung eines Forschungsfelds', in *Geschichte und Gesellschaft* 35/3 (2009), 363.

Steinberg shows, terror as a form of the state's perpetration of violence has nothing directly to do with the invention of terrorism. It merely provided the name for this kind of political violence.[13] Nevertheless, the French Revolution looms large in the invention of terrorism in this book as well, albeit in a way other than that assumed in the foremost versions of terrorism's history. Thus the significance of the French Revolution for the emergence of terrorism lay less in the paradigmatic aspect of Jacobin terror than in the Revolution's political ideals – the demands for personal, political and national freedom and equality – for whose realization and dissemination the Revolutionaries strove. This is true not only for the French Revolution but also for the American Revolution and the ideas of democracy and human rights quite generally.

This book places the process of terrorism's emergence in Western rather than Eastern Europe, and casts the United States as an integrative, even pivotal, part of this history. This geographic recontextualization also moves the invention of terrorism back by about twenty years, placing it around the middle of the nineteenth century – 1858 (Orsini's attack on Napoleon III) and 1859 (John Brown's raid on Harpers Ferry) – rather than 1876 (when 'propaganda of the deed' was first proposed as a strategy at the Anarchist International), 1879 (when Narodnaia Volia made its first attempt on the life of the tsar) and 1881 (the year of the first bombings by Irish nationalists). In addition, Felice Orsini, John Brown, Oskar Wilhelm Becker, John Wilkes Booth and Dmitry Vladimirovich Karakozov are cast as inventors (Orsini and Booth) and as imitators (Becker, Booth and Karakozov) who develop terrorist tactics further. They replace Narodnaia Volia and the attacks by European anarchists, who until then had figured as the first genuine terrorists (that is, the first modern terrorists or the first active terrorists of the political–secular type). These shifts and recontextualizations, none of which may seem especially sweeping on their own at first glance, render a different history of terrorism when taken together and in light of the new settings within which they must be placed and when seen with the new perspectives that they open.

---

13 On this point see the terminological historical studies in Verhoeven, *Odd Man Karakozov*, 175; and especially the article by Ronen Steinberg, 'Situating the Reign of Terror in the History of Modern Terrorism: The Meaning and Practice of Political Violence in Revolutionary France', in Dietze and Verhoeven, *The Oxford Handbook of the History of Terrorism*.

As this book's findings show, Enlightenment philosophy and the rise of nationalism and democracy as revolutionary principles drove the emergence of terrorism just as much as did the call for personal freedom – in other words for the elimination of slavery and serfdom – as articulated in American abolitionism and the Russian revolutionary movement. At the very moment these revolutionary appeals became policy, with the Emancipation Proclamation in the United States and the end of serfdom in Europe, counterrevolutionary ideologies such as white supremacy became another force behind terrorism. Anarchism, with its 'propaganda of the deed', did not follow until the phenomenon had already taken shape in other political contexts. What Martha Crenshaw has written about the emergence of terrorist groups in the twentieth century thus also applies to the emergence of terrorism in general. In a situation without revolutionary conditions, elites in national or social movements discovered terrorist violence as a means of continuing and consummating the great revolutions. As it soon turned out, that very resource also lent itself to use by elites of counterrevolutionary movements to thwart change and to defend or restore structures of segregated feudal society. This development confirms the observations by such researchers as Ford and O'Sullivan mentioned in the introduction to this book: ideas play a key role in the emergence of terrorism. In the early history of terrorism, however, the ideas are much less abstract and ideological than those two authors and other writers assume.

This book shows that these shifts and recontextualizations coincide with the factors that various authors have repeatedly linked to the emergence of terrorism in modern times. Indeed, the way these factors function is better integrated and explained in the new history of terrorism laid out in the preceding chapters than in the dominant narratives so far. The historical analysis conducted here has confirmed the hypothesis offered by Rapoport and other authors that changes in the technology of transport and communication were necessary precursors to terrorism's emergence. But it has also shown how especially pronounced they were in Western Europe and the United States, leading to the logical conclusion that terrorism was invented there, and not in Russia or Ireland.

Similarly, there are several other factors that in the past have only been suggested but that now have been verified by the empirical study in this book. The unsuccessful revolutions of 1848–9 did in fact have a great bearing on the emergence of terrorism, as concretely proven in

Orsini's case. In turn, it is also obvious that this significance was much more direct and profound where these revolutions actually took place: France, Italy and Central Europe. The same is true for the experience of, and experimentation with, types of insurgent violence, the emergence of the political subject (that is, the cultivation of civic awareness and initiative), the emergence of the professional revolutionary as a type, and the establishment of a new legal culture with public judicial proceedings or challenges to the legitimacy of the political order. All these concrete and practical facets related to everyday life figured earlier and more intensely in France and the United States than, say, in Russia, where, partly for that reason (the lack of experience in and experimentation with types of insurgent violence and so on), factors relating to the history of ideas (the influences of literature, the philosophy of history and social theories) play a greater role.

By contrast, the criteria by which the hitherto dominant narratives have ascribed to the United States a purely receptive role in the history of terrorism do not hold up under empirical examination. Proponents of such narratives have attributed terrorism primarily to individuals seeking to ignite revolution and overthrow systems or even to socialists and anarchists alone (who in the United States were supposed to have been especially dominant among European immigrants). It is important to note, in general, that terrorist tactics have also been practised by persons of counterrevolutionary persuasion since their inception. More concretely, it can be shown in specific examples that John Brown and the radical abolitionist movement thought of themselves in precisely that way, as revolutionaries. Their stated aim was to precipitate the second American Revolution, and John Wilkes Booth tried nothing less than to bring down the Lincoln administration, which had begun to implement some of these revolutionary ideas. When Rapoport goes on to demand that terrorists have a theory of action in order to classify an act of violence as terrorism (a theory that he asserts European terrorist movements had in contrast to American terrorist movements), such a criterion seems ill-suited to terrorism. What criteria should that theory meet? At most, one can insist upon deliberate and premeditated action, as stated in Peter Waldmann's definition. Terrorism in the United States was thus only an import in the sense that, by all accounts, John Brown got the basic idea of terrorist tactics from Orsini. But because Brown subsequently put this idea into practice himself, further developing it and then (to continue with the metaphor) exporting it to Russia, and because he also became the paragon of the tactic's autochthonous further development in the United States, the United States occupies a key place in the process by which terrorism was invented. 'Bringing the United States back in' must therefore be the guiding principle of a new history of terrorism.

That leaves Rapoport's four-wave theory, which states that modern terrorism since its emergence is divisible into four international ideological waves: anarchic, anticolonial, new-left and religious. According to the findings of this book, a historical explanation for the wave-like emergence of terrorist activities posited by this developmental theory of international terrorism, for the 'energy' driving them, and for their duration of a generation per wave lies in each era's specific manifestations of the ideas of personal and political freedom, in the social movements that sought to advance or prevent the realization of these ideas, and in the political blockages those movements encountered in their attempts to do so. However, if the results of this book can be related to Rapoport's theory in this way, then the four-wave theory would have to become a five- or even six-wave theory. The fifth wave would be necessary in order to accommodate at least the abolitionist wave before the anarchic–nihilistic one, and the sixth because this abolitionist wave parallels a national-democratic wave that eventually sustained innumerable ethno-nationalist ones.

Perspectives for further research

But was terrorism not actually invented in Germany forty years earlier – in 1819 – by Karl Ludwig Sand with his assassination of August von Kotzebue? In German research, the invention of terrorism has time and again been seen in connection with this act of political violence.[14]

Sand and his assassination of Kotzebue do in fact have all the important elements in the theory of terrorism as developed in this book. In

14 See Hermann Lübbe, for example, 'Tugendterror: Höhere Moral als Quelle politischer Gewalt', *Totalitarismus und Demokratie* 1/2 (2004), 203–17; and Sylvia Schraut, '"Wie der Hass gegen den Staatsrath von Kotzebue, und der Gedanke, ihn zu ermorden, in Sand entstand": Ein politischer Mord und seine Nachwirkungen', in Christine Hikel and Sylvia Schraut (eds.), *Terrorismus und Geschlecht* (Frankfurt am Main: Campus, 2012), 145–66.

Sand's case as well (to cite Peter Waldmann's definition once again), the act was a premeditated, shocking, underground attack on a political order; was intended 'to spread feelings of insecurity and fear but ... also ... sympathy and support', and had a political dimension, namely the perpetrator's German nationalist objectives. The attack also had a religious aspect. Sand, a Lutheran, considered himself to be a warrior of God. As a student of theology at the University of Jena, he was a member of the educated elite; as the treasurer of a student patriotic fraternity, he was, like John Wilkes Booth, a rather peripheral member of the national movement, which had sprung from the wars of liberation against Napoleon I. The decisions taken at the Congress of Vienna were a major political setback to the aspirations of this movement, with the path to a German nation state seemingly blocked. Sand's victim, the playwright August von Kotzebue, was a politically insignificant, but vocal and eloquent, critic of the national movement and the student fraternities. By murdering Kotzebue, Sand was pursuing a primarily symbolic end. After all, to justify the murder he committed, Sand composed a placard entitled 'Death Knell for August von Kotzebue' ('Todesstoß dem August von Kotzebue'), which he intended to attach to a church door with a dagger dramatizing the way Luther was said to have nailed his ninety-five theses to the door of a church. Although this act did not happen, the placard served as a written claim of responsibility.[15] The reception of Sand's violent act also fits the definition of terrorism used in this book, for vast swathes of the population, including the nationally minded intellectuals, sympathized with Sand and celebrated him as a martyr. By contrast, the assassination instilled fear among the members of the princely governments, with Metternich tentatively coining the verb 'to sandize' (*sandisieren*) in reference to this new kind of terrorist attack.[16]

---

15 See Dirk Blasius, *Geschichte der politischen Kriminalität in Deutschland (1800–1980): Eine Studie zu Justiz und Staatsverbrechen* (Frankfurt am Main: Suhrkamp, 1983), 28–9; Hagen Schulze, 'Sand, Kotzebue und das Blut des Verräters (1819)', in Alexander Demandt (ed.), *Das Attentat in der Geschichte* (Cologne: Böhlau, 1996), with mention of the written claim of responsibility appearing at 223; Wolfram Siemann, *Metternich: Staatsmann zwischen Restauration und Moderne* (Munich: C. H. Beck, 2010), Chapter 9 (the term *Gotteskrieger*, or warrior of God, appears at 64); and especially George S. Williamson, 'What Killed August von Kotzebue? The Temptations of Virtue and the Political Theology of German Nationalism, 1789–1819', *Journal of Modern History* 72/4 (2000), 890–943.

16 See the contemporary description of the reactions as recorded in Karl August Varnhagen von Ense, *Denkwürdigkeiten des eignen Lebens, vol. 3 (1815–1834)*, in Karl

Hence, there are many sound arguments for having the history of terrorism begin in 1819 in the German-speaking realm and for considering Karl Ludwig Sand as the inventor of the tactic.

This reasoning has not been taken up in this book, however. Indeed, it is possible that Karl Ludwig Sand was the first terrorist in history, but the history of terrorism did not begin with him. As far as one can tell from the historical record and research currently available, Sand's murder of Kotzebue was not followed up by anything other than isolated copycat acts in the German lands directly after his act (for instance, the attempted assassination of Nassau's president of government, Carl von Ibell, in July 1819). Of the five perpetrators at the centre of this book, only Oskar Wilhelm Becker is known to have ever heard of Sand.

The results of this book provide three explanations for the finding that Sand does not stand at the beginning of the history of terrorism and that – from a global point of view – he was not a central figure in the invention of terrorism. First, although the conditions and facilitating factors within the German-speaking realm were established enough for the assassination to incite the desired reactions in the German lands, transnational communications and transport were too underdeveloped to provide Sand with the international audience and acclaim later garnered by the five cases studied in this book.[17] And even if a sufficiently extensive and dense dissemination and reception by the media had existed, reports of Sand's violent act would most probably have fallen on deaf ears everywhere.

After all – to name the second reason why the history of terrorism did not begin with Sand – around 1820 the basic political conditions in the countries which would develop into a European and American space of communication were not yet ripe for Sand's demonstrated tactic. That is, his violence could not yet have been met with understanding and interest: from Spain, Italy and Greece to Russia, national democrats at that time were still counting on the collective violence of

---

August Varnhagen von Ense, *Werke in fünf Bänden*, ed. Konrad Feilchenfeldt, 1st completely annotated ed. (Frankfurt am Main: Deutsche Klassiker-Verlag, 1987–94), 422–3. The word quoted from Metternich is found in Siemann, *Metternich*, 66. See also Blasius, *Geschichte*, 30–3.

17 On the range of the reception, see Siemann, *Metternich*, 64–5; Schraut, 'Hass', 147.

insurrection, while in the United States it seemed that the political authorities had managed to solve the issue of slavery with the Missouri compromise.

Lastly, Sand's assassination of Kotzebue held little attraction for imitators, at least in the medium term, because it quickly proved to be politically futile. Instead of bringing the German-speaking territories closer to national unity, the assassination became a primary catalyst for the Carlsbad Decrees, which led to a pervasive regime of surveillance and harsh repression targeting the national movement. But success was essential to encourage imitation, as shown by the five cases treated in this book. As a result of its political failure, Karl Ludwig Sand's terrorist attack did not recommend itself for imitation, and it remained on the whole an isolated act. By contrast, Felice Orsini's attack on Napoleon III was the seminal moment in a reception history that led to type-spawning terrorist groups and organizations in Europe and the United States by way of John Brown and the three imitators, especially John Wilkes Booth and Dmitry Vladimirovich Karakozov.

Nevertheless, the example of Karl Ludwig Sand indicates that the invention of terrorism, as shown in the cases of Orsini, Brown, Becker, Booth and Karakozov, has antecedents. That prehistory has yet to be studied – in two dimensions. First, it could be that the attack by Karl Ludwig Sand is only one among other such acts of violence that remained relatively isolated but that must now be classified as terrorism. Sylvia Schraut, for instance, has suggested that Charlotte Corday's assassination of Jacobin Jean-Paul Marat on 13 July 1793 is the point at which the history of terrorism began.[18] Francisco A. Ortega has proposed the attempted assassination of Simón Bolívar in 1828 in Bogotá, Colombia, as an example of such an act of violence.[19] In addition, David Rapoport has pointed out the operations of the Sons of the American Revolution, who, for example, were responsible for the Boston Tea Party. Rapoport, in deciding it would not be useful to include the Sons of the American Revolution in the history of terrorism, provides the explanation that

---

18 Sylvia Schraut, 'Terrorismus – Geschlecht – Erinnerung: Eine Einführung', in Christine Hikel and Sylvia Schraut (eds.), *Terrorismus und Geschlecht: Politische Gewalt in Europa seit dem 19. Jahrhundert* (Frankfurt am Main: Campus; 2012), 7.

19 Francisco A. Ortega, Universidad Nacional de Colombia, personal communication, 13 June 2012.

their operations remained at a national level, and thus lacked a crucial scope in their reception.[20] This line of thought coincides with the reasoning also adopted in this book with regard to the attack by Karl Ludwig Sand. However, such cases would be illuminating to study with a focus on the criteria of terrorism and the range and intensity of these cases' reception.

Second, the five cases analysed in this book were preceded by an increase in political attacks, at least in Europe during the Napoleonic Wars and the following decades. Just a few of the spectacular incidents were the various attempts on the life of Napoleon I; the assassination of Charles Ferdinand de Bourbon, Duke de Berry, in February 1820; the Cato Street Conspiracy against the British Cabinet, discovered in February 1820; and the attack on the French king Louis-Philippe I ('the Citizen King'), with an 'infernal machine' (a self-built volley gun) in July 1835.

However, a good deal of evidence indicates that all these attacks still fall within the genre of political murder, for their underlying logic was instrumental. The perpetrators were intent on, respectively, removing a usurper who was altogether invincible militarily; killing the potential heir to the throne of France, wiping out the royal family and ending the restoration; exacting revenge for the Peterloo massacre and the repression of the Six Acts and carrying out a revolutionary *coup d'état*; and murdering the king of the French – the would-be perpetrator himself was an abiding follower of Napoleon and his family.[21] Accordingly, these acts of violence would not qualify as terrorism yet.

All the same, the number, rapid succession, scale and interaction of these and other attacks conveyed a threatening scenario that presumably exceeded the impact of the individual acts themselves, especially because they were accompanied by multiple insurrections and revolutions. These acts of violence, their reception and their dynamics still need to be researched, as Wolfram Siemann also notes:

As remarkable as it seems, scholarship has not yet even begun to address the politically motivated terrorism that swept Europe at

---

20 See p. 16, note 34.

21 These examples are also cited in Siemann, *Metternich*, 67–9. On the assassination of the Duke de Berry, see Natalie Scholz, '"Quel Spectacle": Der Tod des Herzogs von Berry und seine melodramatische Bewältigung', *Zeitenblicke. Online-Journal für die Geschichtswissenschaften* 3/1 (2004), zeitenblicke.de.

that time and to take it seriously as a coherent phenomenon. There is no history of the attacks in Europe and the perception of the specifically targeted dynasties . . . It is still completely unexplained how vast the menacing scenario building since 1815 was to the ruling dynasties, how intensely the revolutionary perpetrators communicated or how keenly aware they were of each other, which ideological patterns they followed, and how acutely the targeted monarchs experienced them . . . How much reality was packed in the writer Nicolas Chamfort's slogan 'Peace to the shacks! War on the palaces!' which Georg Büchner adopted from the French Revolution?[22]

Further basic historical research on this topic is needed. However, such work should not stop at examining the attempts on the lives of individuals who were attacked as representatives of revolution or counterrevolution. It should also extend to pogroms such as the Hep Hep riots, which were directed against the emancipation of the Jews in various German and other European countries and which must be seen in relation to the history of counterrevolutionary right-wing terrorism.[23]

But it is not only the prehistory leading to the invention of terrorism by the five violent actors studied in this book that has important gaps which need to be filled by future historical research. Despite the many works of specialized literature dedicated to selected topic areas, the history of the reception of the violence committed by Felice Orsini and John Brown is also incomplete, as is the later course of terrorism in the nineteenth century. The question thus arises whether there were

---

22 Siemann, *Metternich*, 68.

23 On these pogroms and their place in history, see especially Jacob Katz, *Die Hep-Hep-Verfolgungen des Jahres 1819*, with an afterword by Stefan Rohrbacher (Berlin: Metropol, 1994); Christhard Hoffmann, Werner Bergmann and Helmut Walser Smith, introduction to Christhard Hoffmann, Werner Bergmann and Helmut Walser Smith (eds.), *Exclusionary Violence: Antisemitic Riots in Modern German History: Social History, Popular Culture, and Politics in Germany* (Ann Arbor, MI: University of Michigan Press, 2002); and Stefan Rohrbacher, 'The "Hep Hep" Riots of 1819: Anti-Jewish Ideology, Agitation, and Violence', in ibid., 23–42. On media-related aspects see Stephanie Schlesier, 'Die Hep-Hep Verfolgungen von 1819: Antijüdische Berichterstattung der Zeitungen?', in Michael Nagel and Mosche Zimmermann (eds.), *Judenfeindschaft und Antisemitismus in der deutschen Presse über fünf Jahrhunderte: Erscheinungsformen, Rezeption, Debatte und Gegenwehr* (Bremen: Ed. Lumière, 2013), 123–46.

616   Conclusion

still other early imitators. As Hans-Jürgen Bömelburg has commented, the 1863 insurrection in Warsaw, Poland, was preceded by several incidents: Ludwik Jaroszyński's attempt on 3 July 1862 to assassinate Grand Duke Konstantin, who was the viceroy of Poland and brother of Tsar Alexander II, and two unsuccessful attempts – one by Ludwik Ryll on 7 August 1862, the other by Jan Rzońca just eight days later – on the life of Count Alexander Wielopolski, the Polish statesman who headed the civil administration.[24] The point of each of these deeds was to trigger an insurrection and repressive responses by the establishment. One research question is whether these cases were copycat acts modelled directly on the acts by Orsini and Brown. The Polish national revolutionaries maintained close links with both the Italian national movement and the Russian underground movement Zemlia i Volia and had contact with Bakunin, from whom they could have gathered additional information about John Brown beyond press reports and literature. It seems quite plausible that the violent acts by Jaroszyński, Ryll and Rzońca should be ranked with those by Becker, Booth and Karakozov.

A further matter to clarify is whether the theory developed in this book also holds for the future history of terrorism. The theoretical components have withstood examination in the cases studied in the preceding chapters, but can they also explain terrorists and their violent acts in the subsequent course of history in the nineteenth, twentieth and twenty-first centuries? One could object that the political situation around the mid-1800s was in some respects so unique that other explanatory approaches must be sought in history since the mid-nineteenth century. A definitive answer as to the explanatory power of the theoretical components explained in this book necessitates further empirical studies of actors, groups, movements and networks, as well as of the ideas and ideologies driving them. It also requires further research on the relevant sociopolitical structures and dynamics; the national and transnational processes of reception; and the development of weapons, transport and media technology. That work goes beyond the scope of the present volume. However, everything suggests that the theoretically grounded explanatory patterns developed in this volume are also

---

24 Hans-Jürgen Bömelburg, Gutachten zur Habilitationsschrift von Frau Carola Dietze 'Taten statt Worte: Acht Jahre in der Erfindung des Terrorismus', 2013, 7–8.

applicable to later acts and their perpetrators, ranging from anarchist or nihilist attacks and left- and right-wing terrorism to Al-Qaida, the Islamic State (IS) and their diverse offshoots.

To name some broad strokes: the three central ideas that have emerged in this book – the vision of personal freedom and equality; the notion of political participation and national self-determination; and the aim of preventing, undermining or rescinding freedom and equality – continued to spark the violence carried out by terrorist actors.

However, the specific concerns to which each of these ideas referred changed with the circumstances of space and time. After the legal emancipation of slaves and serfs, the idea of personal freedom and equality was, on the one hand, extended to new groups, first to women and Jews in the nineteenth century and then, today, for example, to homosexuals and transgender people. The underlying idea that the legal implementation of personal freedom is not enough and that people who have been given their freedom are entitled to justice and the economic wherewithal to lead a dignified life has been discussed in a number of social philosophies since the Enlightenment. It was the overriding motive behind Karakozov's attempt on the tsar's life. Over the course of the nineteenth century, this idea was developed further in a wide spectrum of social-revolutionary literature by socialist and anarchist theorists of different leanings and was tailored to the relevant issues of their time and place, such as those of rural workers in Spain and of the proletariat in Germany. These ideas inspired corresponding movements from which in turn occasional individual perpetrators of violence emerged. Parallel processes took place within the ethno-nationalist and counter-revolutionary camp. In the history of terrorism specifically and of violence in general, however, the scholarly focus on the violence committed in the name of these three ideas in the nineteenth and twentieth centuries has varied considerably from one country to the next.

The history of terrorism in the nineteenth century is fundamentally a repeat or continuation of the developments treated in this volume. The terrorist tactic of the kind used by Orsini and Becker was immediately embraced by the national movements of Poland and Ireland. For instance, another assassination attempt against Alexander II took place at the 1867 World Exhibition in Paris, this time by a Pole. Irish subjects who had fought in the American Civil War returned to Ireland with terrorist tactics, including an attempt wholly in the style of John Brown to seize the weapons from a military garrison in England in February 1867 and thereby spark an insurrection, and Italian nationalist revolutionaries influenced the Fenians.[25]

Among social revolutionaries in the line of Brown and Karakozov, there were initially no further imitators who tried to use terrorist tactics in Europe after the attempts by Becker, Booth and Karakozov had failed as measured against their political objectives and their ambitions in terms of public agitation. Instead, there were again many efforts to push through social-revolutionary goals by means of collective violence, including the Paris Commune of 1871 and the insurrections in Spain and Italy from 1873 to 1877. Some of these attempts fed on anarchist ideas, with figures such as Mikhail Alexandrovich Bakunin and Errico Malatesta playing an active role. However, like the revolutions of 1848–9 and later attempts such as Orsini's to fan insurrections, all endeavours to achieve sustainable social-revolutionary changes through collective violence failed in the 1870s. As a result, individual violence began to reappear as an option once again. As Richard Bach Jensen comments in his study on the emergence of anarchic terrorism, 'It was in the context of the apparent failure of Bakunin's collectivism together with the increasing repressiveness of the police and the authorities that the theory of "propaganda by deed" developed and became widely known.'[26]

These ethno-nationalist and anarchist or nihilist movements, the acts of violence to which they gave rise, and the way society and the state reacted to them have been researched relatively well.[27] That literature,

---

25 Lindsay Clutterbuck, 'The Progenitors of Terrorism: Russian Revolutionaries or Extreme Irish Republicans?', *Terrorism and Political Violence* 16/1 (2004), 154–81; Burleigh, *Blood & Rage*, Chapter 1; Jensen, *The Battle against Anarchist Terrorism*, 73; and Nial Whelehan, 'Modern Rebels? Irish Republicans in the Late Nineteenth Century', in Dietze and Verhoeven, *The Oxford Handbook of the History of Terrorism*.

26 Jensen, *The Battle against Anarchist Terrorism*, 16. Similarly, see Requate, 'Die Faszination anarchistischer Attentate im Frankreich des ausgehenden 19. Jahrhunderts', 103–5.

27 For Germany see, for example, Andrew R. Carlson, 'Anarchism and Individual Terror in the German Empire, 1870–1890', in Wolfgang J. Mommsen and Gerhard Hirschfeld (eds.), *Social Protest, Violence, and Terror in Nineteenth- and Twentieth-Century Europe* (New York: St Martin's Press, 1982), 207–36; Elun T. Gabriel, *Assassins and Conspirators: Anarchism, Socialism, and Political Culture in Imperial Germany* (DeKalb: NIU Press, 2014); and Ulrich Sieg, *Geist und Gewalt: Deutsche Philosophen zwischen Kaiserreich und Nationalsozialismus* (Munich: Carl Hanser Verlag, 2013). Sieg

however, is largely of only national scope. Considering the manifold transnational connections and reception processes in the late nineteenth century, this national frame limits its ability to explain.[28] To develop a history of terrorism in the *longue durée* – that is, a comprehensive, long-term view of the history of terrorism – there is a need for research that systematically links into an overarching theoretical framework, and in this way facilitates analysis of the interaction between social circumstances, ideas, political dynamics, actors, networks, rationales and acts of violence, as well as reactions to them, and that reveals important national and transnational models and reception processes. After all, the rudiments of the elements and preconditions for terrorist action defined in this book as central to terrorist action are also apparent in the last third of

---

starts from the assassination attempts by Max Hödel and Karl Nobiling on Wilhelm I in 1878 and the moral and ethical crisis German society identified because of these attacks, and then analyses the way German philosophy tried to contribute to overcoming this crisis (ibid., 19–57). For France, see Merriman, *Dynamite Club*; and Vivien Bouhey, 'Anarchist Terrorism in Fin-de-Siècle France and its Borderlands', in Dietze and Verhoeven, *The Oxford Handbook of the History of Terrorism*. For Russia see Manfred Hildermeier, *The Russian Socialist Revolutionary Party before the First World War* (New York: St Martin's Press, 2000); Norman M. Naimark, *Terrorists and Social Democrats: The Russian Revolutionary Movement under Alexander III* (Cambridge, MA: Harvard University Press, 1983); and Oleg Vitalevich Budnitskii, *Terrorizm v rossiiskom osvoboditel'nom dvizhenii* (Moscow: n.p., 2000). For Switzerland, see Nino Kühnis, *Anarchisten! Von Vorläufern und Erleuchteten, von Ungeziefer und Läusen: Zur kollektiven Identität einer radikalen Gemeinschaft in der Schweiz, 1885–1914* (Bielefeld: Transcript, 2015).

28 See also Robert Gerwarth and Heinz-Gerhard Haupt, 'Internationalising Historical Research on Terrorist Movements in Twentieth-Century Europe', *European Review of History – Revue européenne d'histoire* 14/3 (2007), 275–81. The most important exception is Jensen, *The Battle against Anarchist Terrorism*. See also Richard Bach Jensen, 'Daggers, Rifles and Dynamite', *Terrorism and Political Violence* 16/1 (2010), 116–53; and Richard Bach Jensen, 'The First Global Wave of Terrorism and International Counter-terrorism, 1905–1914', in Jussi Hanhimäki and Bernhard Blumenau (eds.), *An International History of Terrorism: Western and Non-Western Experience* (London and New York: Routledge, 2013), 16–33; as well as Alexander Sedlmaier, 'The Consuming Visions of Late Nineteenth- and Early Twentieth-Century Anarchists: Actualising Political Violence Transnationally', *European Review of History – Revue européenne d'histoire* 14/3 (2007), 283–300; Fabian Lemmes, 'Der anarchistische Terrorismus des 19. Jahrhunderts und sein soziales Umfeld', in Stefan Malthaner and Peter Waldmann (eds.), *Radikale Milieus: Das soziale Umfeld terroristischer Gruppen* (Frankfurt am Main: Campus Verlag, 2012), 73–117; and a book of popular history by Alex Butterworth, *The World that Never Was: A True Story of Dreamers, Schemers, Anarchists and Secret Agents* (London: Bodley Head, 2010).

the nineteenth century for national and social-revolutionary terrorism: national and anarchist or nihilistic movements, political blockages arising, for example, from the predominantly repressive policies towards these movements and their goals in most countries, the failure of collective violence, national and transnational processes of reception, and the resulting copycat acts.

Contrary to the impression generated by the emphasis on the social and/or national revolutionary origins of terrorism in the dominant narrative of terrorism's history and in historical research to date, the medium- and long-term impact of this tactic's *counter*revolutionary use has been just as great, if not even greater, since John Wilkes Booth. This is especially true of the United States of the nineteenth and early twentieth centuries, where terrorism motivated by a desire for emancipation and equality was relatively rare, occurring as part of the anarchist movement, for instance. In most cases, terrorist violence was used to fight against emancipation. The Ku Klux Klan and other right-wing terrorist groups and organizations assassinated politicians standing up for freedmen and murdered emancipated slaves because they dared to exercise their legal rights granted them as citizens during the Reconstruction era or simply behaved as human beings of equal value with equal rights. Moreover, right-wing organizations attacked people who accepted such behaviour by the emancipated slaves because it acknowledged and encouraged them.[29]

Such counterrevolutionary uses of terrorist tactics occurred in Europe and Russia as well. The freeing of the serfs was accompanied by another process of emancipation that in most European countries was much more protracted than the freeing of the bonded population: the emancipation of the Jews. In the German states, it dragged on until 1869, when emancipation was granted in the North German Confederation, and 1871, when equal rights became the law of the German Empire; in Russia, this process was not even completed until the Revolution in 1917. Ever since then Europe has had to contend (and is still contending) with right-wing extremist movements that resort to terrorism to deny equality and integration to the Jewish population and

---

29 In addition to the literature on the Ku Klux Klan, see especially Foner, *Reconstruction*; Finzsch, Horton and Horton, *Von Benin nach Baltimore*, 327–31; and Budiansky, *The Bloody Shirt*.

other groups. This history of right-wing terrorism in Europe runs parallel to that in the United States, where, after the legal emancipation of the former slaves, broad movements developed that time and again up to the present day have violently resisted the enforcement and elaboration of this emancipation.

This part of terrorism's history – right up to today's right-wing terrorism directed by the National Socialist Underground against immigrants in the Federal Republic of Germany and violence against African Americans and people of colour in the United States – requires research that would build on the results presented in this book, systematically integrate this aspect into the history of terrorism and connect it with the history of terror. Important questions in this context might be, for example, what significance did models of forms of violence have? And how important were mutual processes of reception and transfer between counterrevolutionary movements in Europe, Russia and the United States in the latter half of the nineteenth century and the early twentieth century? The evident significance of such processes of reception and transfer in the late twentieth and early twenty-first centuries makes this question especially relevant.[30]

These political manifestations of social-revolutionary, ethno-nationalist and radical right-wing terrorism are by no means obsolete today. Broadly speaking, as in this book, they encompass a span ranging from emancipatory terrorism, whose intent is to assert enlightened, revolutionary demands; to anti-emancipatory terrorism, the aim of which is to prevent the realization of those demands; and to ethno-nationalist terrorism. With the use of such relatively general distinctions, it also

---

30 On the history of right-wing terrorism in Europe and especially in Germany and Austria, see Hoffman, *Right-Wing Terrorism in Europe*, a RAND note (Santa Monica: Rand, 1984); Armin Pfahl-Traughber, *Rechtsextremismus in der Bundesrepublik* (Munich: C. H. Beck, 1999); Gideon Botsch, *Die extreme Rechte in der Bundesrepublik Deutschland, 1949 bis heute* (Darmstadt: Wissenschaftliche Buchgesellschaft, 2012); Robert Gerwarth, "'Krieg im Frieden': Der "Weiße Terror" in den Nachfolgestaaten des Habsburgerreiches', in Weinhauer and Requate, *Gewalt ohne Ausweg?*, 123–36; and Christoph Kopke, Rechtsterrorismus und rechte Gewalt in der Geschichte der Bundesrepublik Deutschland, in: Heidi Beutin, Wolfgang Beutin und Ulrich Praefke (eds.), Rassismus. Ursprung – Funktion – Bekämpfung, Frankfurt am Main u.a.: Peter Lang 2014, 43–60. On processes of reception and transfer, see especially Michael Sturm and Daniel Schmidt, "'Action over Words": The Anatomy of Right-Wing Terrorism in 20th Century Europe', in Dietze and Verhoeven, *The Oxford Handbook of the History of Terrorism*.

seems possible to classify groups engaged in 'religious terrorism' according to the political demands that they advance.[31]

However, that classification occasionally produces new combinations
that are unusual from a European, American and Russian perspective.
The ideologies underlying the attacks by Al-Qaida on 11 September 2001,
for instance, have been alternately described as fascist, nihilist and anarchist. Linked too closely to specific movements in the history of European,
American and Russian thinking, none of these descriptions is really
convincing. By contrast, this book's political classification scheme could
subsume Al-Qaida as a movement seeking to impede the establishment
of at least some enlightened revolutionary objectives and to dismantle
nation states in the Islamic world while delegitimizing the global
political order and national authority structures and building religiously
sanctioned governance. This approach might help to facilitate a political–
ideological positioning that makes sense in light of European, Russian
and US political experience yet avoids European, Russian and American
historical terminology that is too specific for transfer to the political issues
of the Near and Middle East, and which acknowledges that the political
issues and the ideas responding to them are also reactions to European,
Russian and American history and policies.[32]

Since the nineteenth century, other factors that have proven decisive
in the cases studied in this volume have promoted the repetition and
continuation of the developments that have been examined. In the 1800s
they had already widened the social spectrum of the groups of perpetrators, escalated the technological level of terrorist tactics, and extended
the geographic range of their use. The mobilization of women, for example, was one factor that contributed to the expansion of the perpetrators'
social base, not least because the demand for the personal freedom and
equality of serfs and slaves also reached women of all social strata during
the first women's movement. They heard and called for that kind of
recognition for themselves as well as other groups. They, too, began to

---

31 The political objectives of religious terrorists are also stressed by Klaus Weinhauer,
'Religiös motivierter Terrorismus in der europäischen Diaspora: Transnationale
Netzwerke, lokale Kleingruppen, Medienkommunikation', in Weinhauer and Requate,
Gewalt ohne Ausweg?, 301–16.

32 See Ayman al-Zawāhirī and Osama Ibn-Lādin, *The Al Qaeda Reader*, ed. and
trans. Raymond Ibrahim, with an introduction by Victor Davis Hanson (New York:
Doubleday, 2007).

exert political force. For instance, the Russian revolutionaries Vera Ivanova Zasulich and Sophia Lvovna Perovskaia gained international fame as terrorists, with Perovskaia, a member of Narodnaia Volia, participating in various attacks on Tsar Alexander II.[33]

The intensification of terrorist attacks was primarily a result of new scientific and technical inventions. In 1866, the year of Karakozov's abortive attempt on the life of Tsar Alexander II, Alfred Nobel invented dynamite, whose detonation could unleash a blast of hitherto unprecedented power without the perpetrators having to risk their own lives. The knowledge necessary for its use circulated quickly through a subversive category of literature on do-it-yourself bomb making.[34] This genre has gone through interesting cycles ever since, creating its own imitators.

In the second half of the nineteenth and the beginning of the twentieth century, the intensification of transport and communication in and beyond the European–Russian–American space brought about an increasing globalization of the exchange of news and the possibilities of action even within strata of the general population, an expansion that fostered the still further geographic dissemination of terrorism. Whereas assassins, say, from the Italian diaspora in the United States crossed the Atlantic expressly to stage an attack on the Italian king, the terrorist attacks in Russia (especially those by Zasulich and Perovskaia) were no longer known about and imitated only in Europe and the United States

---

33 On women terrorists in Russia, see especially the classics by Vera Broido, *Apostles into Terrorists: Women and the Revolutionary Movement in the Russia of Alexander II* (London: Smith, 1977); Richard Stites, *The Women's Liberation Movement in Russia: Feminism, Nihilism, and Bolshevism, 1860–1930* (Princeton, NJ: Princeton University Press, 1978), Chapter 5; and Barbara Alpern Engel and Clifford N. Rosenthal, *Five Sisters: Women against the Tsar: The Memoirs of Five Young Anarchist Women of the 1870's* (Boston: Allen & Unwin, 1987); as well as the sources in Oleg Vital'evich Budnitskii (ed.), *Zhenshchiny-terroristki v Rossii* (Rostov on Don: Feniks, 1996). See moreover Ana Siljak, *Angel of Vengeance: The 'Girl Assassin', the Governor of St. Petersburg, and Russia's Revolutionary World* (New York: St Martin's Press, 2008); and Ana Siljak, '"The Beauteous Terrorist": Russian Women and Terrorism in Literature at the Turn of the Century', in Dietze and Verhoeven, *The Oxford Handbook of the History of Terrorism*. For the second half of the twentieth century and the early twenty-first century in an interntional perspective, see in the same volume Julie Rajan, 'Women Terrorists in Postcolonial Conflicts Globally'.

34 See Simon Werrett, 'The Science of Destruction: Terrorism and Technology in the Nineteenth Century', in Dietze and Verhoeven, *The Oxford Handbook of the History of Terrorism*; and, in the same volume, Ann Larabee, 'Propaganda of the Deed: The Emergence of the Radical Weapons Manual in the Late Nineteenth Century'.

but also in China, India, Japan, the Philippines and elsewhere.[35] In colonies, terrorist tactics were often used against the colonial rulers to pursue national democratic and/or ethno-nationalist objectives, right up to the struggles over decolonization and nation-building in the 1960s.[36]

Such medial and technical scientific developments continued in the twentieth and early twenty-first centuries. The invention of the telephone and the spread of the radio further accelerated the exchange of news in the late nineteenth and early twentieth centuries. The invention and proliferation of new media such as television and satellite technology ushered in a qualitatively and quantitatively new dissemination of news about attacks. A steadily growing public was informed ever more quickly. By the 1972 Olympic Games in Munich, a global audience was able to follow the terrorist attack by the Palestinian Black September group on the Israeli Olympic team in real time. The Internet has made it possible to transmit and receive images and messages independently of government or private agencies, thus enabling terrorist groups to prepare and broadcast shocking acts of violence – including executions – through media on their own. In the area of scientific and technical developments, the invention of the aeroplane and the expansion of air

---

35 For these specific interactions, see Richard Bach Jensen, 'Global Terrorism and Transnational Counterterrorism: Policing Anarchist Migration across the Atlantic: Italy and Argentina, 1890–1914', in Dietze and Verhoeven, *The Oxford Handbook of the History of Terrorism*; and, in the same volume, Müller, 'China and the "Anarchist Wave of Assassinations": Politics, Violence, and Modernity in East Asia around the Turn of the Twentieth Century'; Durba Ghosh, 'An Archive of "Political Trouble in India": History-Writing, Anticolonial Violence, and Colonial Counterinsurgency, 1905–1937'; and Mark Driscoll, 'Terrorism against Modernity: The Amakasu Incident and Japan's "Age of Terror", 1920s–1930s'. See also Benedict Anderson, *Under Three Flags: Anarchism and the Anti-colonial Imagination* (London: Verso, 2005); and Neeti Nair, 'Bhagat Singh as "Satyagrahi": The Limits to Non-violence in Late Colonial India', *Modern Asian Studies* 43/3 (2009), 649–81; and generally Jensen, 'The First Global Wave of Terrorism and International Counter-terrorism, 1905–1914'.

36 See Ryan Gingeras, 'The Internal Macedonian Revolutionary Organization: "Oriental" Terrorism, Counterinsurgency, and the End of the Ottoman Empire', in Dietze and Verhoeven, *The Oxford Handbook of the History of Terrorism*; and, in the same volume, Mate Nikola Tokić, 'Twentieth Century West Balkan Terrorism, from Sarajevo to the End of State Socialism'; Timothy H. Parsons, 'Manifestations of Imperial Terror in Colonial Kenya, 1890s–1960s'; Ami Pedahzur and Arie Perliger, 'The Evolution of Jewish Terrorism'; and Sedgwick, 'Anti-colonial Terrorism: Egypt and the Muslim Brotherhood to 1954'. See also Bruce Hoffman, *Anonymous Soldiers: The Struggle for Israel, 1917–1947* (New York: Alfred A. Knopf, 2015); and p. 1 in this volume.

traffic gave rise to hijacking, too. For several decades it primarily involved spectacular acts of hostage taking, a tactic that led to hijacked planes themselves being used as bombs during global prime time in front of running cameras on 11 September 2001.[37]

Additional social, economic, political and legal changes influenced the specific organization and financing of individual attacks and affected the perpetrators as well as the structures of their organizations, including emerging forms of rationalization and industrialization. All these new media, transport and weapons technologies have prompted further globalization and intensification in the use of terrorist tactics and have increased the destructive potential of individual terrorist attacks, attacks which inherently tend to escalate and constantly generate new shock effects.

Essentially, however, the elements of terrorist tactics and their logic of action have not changed. Just like the five violent perpetrators studied in this book, terrorists still generally pursue their political ends by conducting 'violence against a political order from below which is planned and prepared and meant to be shocking. Such acts of violence are supposed to spread feelings of insecurity and intense fear, but they are also meant to generate sympathy and support.'[38] Their intent is to show up a powerful opponent, disavow the legitimacy of that other's power, and prompt a reaction 'that morally discredits and exposes that party in the eyes of third parties'.[39] This also means that the reactions can be a powerful resource in the struggle against terrorism.[40]

Terrorist attacks, as demonstrated by the nineteenth-century inventors of this tactic, are not infrequently provocations to incite an overreaction to repression and violence, even to war. Whether these provocations succeed – that is, whether the response consists mostly of violence or rather of an approach that complements indispensable police work with at least some convincing arguments and ideas, strong

---

37 See Annette Vowinckel, *Flugzeugentführungen: Eine Kulturgeschichte* (Göttingen: Wallstein Verlag, 2011).

38 Waldmann, *Terrorismus*, 12.

39 Paris, 'Der kurze Atem der Provokation', 58. On the question of legitimacy in a broader theoretical and historical context see Dietze, 'Legitimacy and Security from a Historical Perspective'.

40 Richardson, *What Terrorists Want*, for instance at xxii, also stresses the potential of this insight for counterterrorism.

symbols and policies that help establish or restore the legitimacy of the social and political order – depends now as it did then on public, intellectual and political reactions. In those responses, as in everything else described in the preceding chapters, we are perhaps still far more directly the heirs of the nineteenth and twentieth centuries than we would often like to believe.

Acknowledgements from the German edition

The present book is a shortened and revised version of a manuscript accepted by the Department of Historical and Cultural Studies of the Justus-Liebig-University of Giessen as a habilitation thesis in summer 2013. It is a great pleasure for me to take this opportunity to thank all those who have supported and accompanied my work in one way or another over the years.

A project outline on terrorism as media event, written as an application proposal in June 2005, was the beginning of the research project from which this book emerged. The first conversations with Ulrich Sieg and my doctoral supervisor Hartmut Lehmann on the subject and outline pointed the way forward in many respects. This book could not have been written if I had not been accepted on the Research Training Group's programme 'Transnational Media Events from Early Modern Times to the Present', based at the Justus-Liebig-University of Giessen and supported by the German Research Foundation. Doing research and working in this group was a great privilege for me, and at the same time it was a task I accepted with joy. My special thanks go to Friedrich Lenger, then spokesperson of the Research Training Group, who, after my move from Göttingen to Giessen, offered me a new academic home at his chair, first as a post-doctoral fellow and later as assistant professor (*Akademische Rätin*). From the first ideas and colloquium lectures to habilitation, he has accompanied this research project and all associated endeavours with suggestions and valuable advice, was a good and important teacher to me in many respects, and gave me his constant support. Moreover, I owe an additional debt of gratitude to a number of colleagues and staff of the Research Training Group and the university for disciplinary and interdisciplinary discussions and to many doctoral students of the first funding period – especially Martin Steinseifer and Marion Tendam – for proactively integrating me into ongoing theoretical debates.

This path led on from the Giessen Research Training Group to the German Historical Institute (GHI) in Washington, DC, which offered an ideal starting point for research on terrorism and its history. I am grateful to the members of the advisory board of the institute for many stimulating discussions on the margins of meetings, but above all for giving me the opportunity to work as a research fellow at the GHI for some years, living and working in Washington. I would also like to thank Christof Mauch, then director, as well as acting directors Gisela Mettele and Anke Ortlepp, for their support of my project, for example by providing the opportunity to organize conferences and workshops on my research topic. Particularly important for this book was the 'Terrorism and Modernity: Global Perspectives on Nineteenth-Century Political Violence' conference, which took place in New Orleans in 2008. The initiative for this event, which Claudia Verhoeven participated in as co-convener, came from Christof Mauch. It could not have succeeded without the warm and thoughtful commitment of Samuel C. Ramer and Margaret M. Keenan, respectively of the Department of History and the Murphy Institute of Political Economy at Tulane University in New Orleans. Equally indispensable was the always competent support from the experienced staff at GHI: Christa Brown and Bärbel Thomas. My thanks also go to the generous support of the conference by the executive director of the Max Weber Foundation, Harald Rosenbach, and the support and active participation of Mareike König and GHI Paris, Benedikt Stuchtey and GHI London, as well as the German Historical Institutes in Moscow and Warsaw. I would like to thank all the conference participants for the stimulating discussions. The work on the *Oxford Handbook of the History of Terrorism*, which included many of the conference contributions, offered a framework to continue these discussions and to expand it with a view to other epochs and regions. I am grateful to Claudia Verhoeven, historian of ancient history Kai Trampedach, medievalist Warren C. Brown and early modern historian

Johannes Dillinger for their comments, hints and interesting discussions in their reading of my habilitation manuscript. This feedback has flowed into this book in various ways.

I would furthermore like to thank deputy director Dirk Schuhmann at the German Historical Institute in Washington, as well as other staff members and interns, especially my office colleagues Bernd Schäfer and Patricia Casey Sutcliffe and their families. During the Medieval History Seminar at GHI, I participated in interesting talks about violence and modernity with Patrick J. Geary, Dame Janet Nelson and Barbara H. Rosenwein. Outside the German Historical Institute, Jerry Z. Muller and Bruce Hoffman showed an abiding interest in my work, Michael David-Fox initiated an association with the University of Maryland and invited me to the Russian History Workshop and the Stammtisch at Tunnicliff's, and the discussions with Andrew Zimmerman and Johanna Bockman as part of our reading group proved to be stimulating. To all of the above as well as Michael C. Kimmage, Nathan Stoltzfus, Axel Frohn, Irit Dekel, Michael Weinman, Charles Wenner, William McTighe (†) and his family, and many of my neighbours on Independence Avenue and 5th Street SE, I am also grateful for integrating me into their lives at various opportunities so that I at once felt welcome and soon very much at home in the United States.

The Library of Congress (LOC), my focal point while working on this book in Washington, was a historian's paradise. I always found it to be an extraordinary privilege to live in close proximity to this wonderful library and to be able to work every spare minute with its excellent resources and holdings. The LOC staff – particularly those of the European Reading Room, the Main Reading Room and the Newspaper Reading Room – provided me with a great deal of advice and support. This also applies to the staff of the National Archives and Records Administration and the Moorland-Spingarn Research Center at Howard University in Washington; the Circuit Clerks Office in Charles Town, the West Virginia Archives and the History Department in Charleston, West Virginia; the Boston Public Library and the Massachusetts Historical Society in Boston as well as the American Antiquarian Society in Worcester, Massachusetts; the Abraham Lincoln Presidential Library in Springfield, Illinois; the Hudson Library & Historical Society in Hudson and the Ohio Historical Society in Columbus, Ohio; the Kansas Historical Society in Topeka, Kansas; the St Louis Mercantile Library in

St Louis, Missouri; and, especially, the Library of Virginia in Richmond, Virginia.

In my research in Russia, the German Historical Institute in Moscow and its staff assisted me in myriad ways, from obtaining visas to finding information and additional newspaper research right through to procuring a room directly in the archive's dormitory, where I enjoyed many interesting discussions with historians from all over Russia. Outside the GHI, I would especially like to thank Oleg Vital'evich Budnitskii and his wife for advice and discussions, first in Moscow and later also in Washington, as well as Nina Mikhailovna Kolosova for her friendly welcome and hospitality during my research in St Petersburg. Furthermore, I would like to thank the staff of the State Archive of the Russian Federation in Moscow and the Russian National Library in St Petersburg for their friendly support, advice and suggestions.

Upon my return to Giessen, a new group of colleagues gave me a kind welcome. This was very valuable during my reacculturation to the quiet of quaint middle Hesse, and I would like to give warm thanks to this group. David Kuchenbuch was the first to comment on my ideas for the overall concept of this work during a lunch in the cafeteria. An invitation to the Institute for Advanced Study Konstanz supported by the German Research Foundation, part of the of the Excellence Cluster 'Cultural Foundations of Integration' at the University of Constance, and to the Netherlands Institute for Advanced Studies in Wassenaar enabled me to concentrate on the writing phase and offered me an ideal environment to discuss my research project with fellows and colleagues. My thanks go to the management, advisory boards and staff of both institutions; to the professors who supported my applications with their evaluations; to the University of Giessen and the Department of Historical and Cultural Studies that enabled me to take up these fellowships; to Christopher Möllmann, who initiated the invitation to Constance; to Beatrice de Graaf, who put me in contact with NIAS; to the student research assistants in Constance; and to Isabell Franziska Frank, who supported me with their work, and a special thanks to Nina Fischer and Guido Golüke. Before I submitted the habilitation thesis, Joost Jonkers, Thomas Kailer and Henning Trüper read and commented on individual chapters, while Gábor Demszki, Sabine Dworog and Friedrich Lenger read and commented on the full text. I am grateful to them for numerous suggestions and improvements. Sabine Dworog was immensely important to the creation of this book in the writing phase, reading all parts of the text as works in progress as part of a 'writing exchange'. This book benefited greatly from her persistent critical questions and constructive comments.

In Germany, the staff of the library of the Giessen Historical Institute and the university libraries of Frankfurt, Giessen and Constance supported my work on this book in many ways. I would also like to thank the staff of the German Literature Archive in Marbach, the German National Library in Frankfurt am Main, the Secret State Archive of Prussian Cultural Heritage in Berlin (Dahlem), the General State Archive in Karlsruhe, the Museum for Communication in Frankfurt am Main, the City Archive in Baden-Baden, the City Archive in Leipzig and the State Library in Berlin – especially the director and staff of the news-paper department in Berlin's Westhafen. In France, I thank the staff of the Archives nationales in Pierrefitte-sur-Seine, and in the Netherlands the staff of the NIAS library, Dindy van Maanen and Erwin Nolet, as well as the staff of the International Institute for Social History in Amsterdam, the Royal Library in The Hague and the Leiden University Library.

A Heisenberg scholarship from the German Research Foundation allowed me to partially revise the habilitation thesis for printing. The evaluations of the reviewers of the habilitation committee (Friedrich Lenger, Hans Jürgen Bömelburg and Jürgen Osterhammel), as well as the evaluations of the anonymous reviewers of the German Research Foundation, proved very helpful. Moreover, the comments by Hartmut Lehmann and Martin H. Geyer on the complete manuscript were extremely valuable. Sabine Dworog, Iwan Iwanov, Lukas Keller and Laura Meneghello proofread individual chapters; Iwan Iwanov and Lukas Keller further helped me with various research questions and assistance with reproduction rights for illustrations. I would like to thank all of the above and also Ute Daniel, Diethelm Klippel, Anna, my neighbour, and other friends and acquaintances for their support. Last, but not least, my thanks go to the Hamburg Institute for Social Research and its publishing house for including the book in the Hamburger Edition catalog, to the publishing team and especially to the publishing director Birgit Otte for her sympathetic dedication and her persistent commitment in the preparation of the publication.

As always, the interest, understanding and manifold support of my immediate and extended family provided the basis for everything that resulted in this book. My thanks go first and foremost to my husband. This book is dedicated to my host parents during the 1992–3 academic year in St Petersburg, Nina Mikhailovna Kolosova and Sergei Maksimovich Vonskii (†), as well as CB. They opened the horizons and perspectives that are reflected in this book.

Giessen and Constance, June 2016

Acknowledgements for the English edition

This book is a slightly revised and expanded translation of my work published by Hamburger Edition in 2016. In the English translation, only the bibliography has been abridged. It is with great pleasure that I acknowledge the manifold support I have received over the course of this project.

The financial support of the Deutsche Forschungsgemeinschaft / German Research Foundation (DFG) made this translation possible – and this in a number of ways. A Heisenberg-Fellowship of the DFG enabled me to prepare an application for this translation as well as the translation itself, while two institutions funded by the DFG jointly financed the high costs of translating this voluminous book. These comprise the 'Cultural Foundations of Social Integration' Centre of Excellence at the University of Konstanz and the Collaborative Research Centre / Transregio 138 'Dynamics of Security. Types of Securitization from a Historical Perspective,' established at the Justus-Liebig-Universität Giessen and the Philipps-Universität Marburg. I am much indebted to both initiatives. In the Konstanz Centre of Excellence, my special thanks go to Christopher Möllmann, who first suggested an English translation of my book in 2014, and who invited me to apply for a grant. I also wish to thank Rudolf Schlögl and the members of the Centre's Plenary Assembly, who kindly supported my application, submitted in 2016, once the original German version was in print, and who permitted me to work at the Seeburg Castle in Kreuzlingen in the summer semester of 2017. The discussions over lunch in Seeburg's kitchen with Ulrich Bröckling, Michael Neumann, Albert Schirrmeister, and Martial Staub were unforgettable. In the Collaborative Research Centre, I wish to thank Angela Marciniak and the Executive Board, especially Christoph Kampmann, former Chairperson of the Research Centre, and Horst Carl, formerly Deputy Chairperson, for their generous support of my application. I also thank the Centre of Excellence, the Collaborative Research Centre and their staff for accompanying this translation project with help and advice.

This translation would also not have been possible without the support of the staff of Hamburger Edition and Verso Books. My special thanks go to the former publishing director of Hamburger Edition, Birgit Otte, for her generous support and to the foreign rights representative Paula Bradish, not least for valuable help and advice based on her own experience as a translator. In his report on the German manuscript, Geoff Eley not only recommended my book for publication by Verso, but also urged them to publish it unabridged. It is a great honor for me that he wrote an early review of the German book, and I want to express my deep gratitude for this and for his kind recommendation. I am also indebted to Sebastian Budgen for his understanding and patience when the translation was due but not yet finished, and for his support in bringing the project to completion and turning it into a book. It is also a pleasure to acknowledge the expert assistance of John Gaunt in copyediting the manuscript and the support of Duncan Ranslem, Jacob Stevens and Rowan Wilson at Verso Books.

I am very grateful to all the translators, who worked hard with me to turn this translation into a precise rendering of the German original and at the same time a readable English text geared towards an English-speaking public. In the case of this book, this work not only comprised the usual re-arrangement of word order and division of long German sentences, but it also involved additional research on the part of the translators as well as myself. Finding the appropriate historical vocabulary, hunting for original English citations and available translations of primary and secondary sources, and providing the original Italian, French, and Russian sources for direct translation all took time and work. Besides, the translators discussed individual sections of their text with me, and raised valuable queries that resulted in a number of additions to, and a few revisions of, the German text. I wish to thank the translators for all the time they have invested and for all the commitment and dedication they have shown in the four years it took to complete this translation project. The book is better for their input.

I also want to thank colleagues and staff from the universities of Giessen, Konstanz and Jena and other institutions, who provided me with information, advice, and support in different ways. In particular, this pertains to the former heads of the Historical Institute at Jena University, Gisela Mettele and Achim Hack, as well as to the librarians and staff at the Kommunikations-, Informations-, Medienzentrum Konstanz and the Thüringer Universitäts- und Landesbibliothek Jena. In February 2018, Joachim Whaley invited me to Cambridge, where I was able to hunt for English sources and translations in the University Library. In September 2018, the President of Jena University, Walter Rosenthal, in a different context supported a trip to New York and an opportunity to conduct research in the New York Public Library. While at the Collaborative Research Centre in Giessen, Iwan Iwanov reliably checked transliterations from Cyrillic, and Lukas Keller worked as my research assistant and helped the translation project immeasurably. So, too, did Lisa Gersdorf, Sebastian Hansen, and Lukas Lücking at the University of Jena as well as Anke Munzert from the staff of the chair of Modern History. Franziska Schedewie kindly put me in contact with Mikhail Dolbilov, who generously discussed details of Dmitry Vladimirovich Karakozov's attempt on Alexander I with me. Christine Hartig and Maike Rotzoll helped me with their expertise on questions concerning the history of medicine. Meike G. Werner put me in contact with Alexandra Campana, who read the first proofs with unparalleled accuracy. I am much indebted to all of them.

Last, but definitely not least, I want to express my profound gratitude to Richard Bach Jensen, who kindly volunteered to be the first expert reader of the entire translation and who suggested and discussed with me valuable additions in content and improvements in style. This was a very special token of friendship, and the book owes him much. But, of course, any errors of fact or interpretation are mine alone.

My entire family has shown unfailing support and understanding for my preoccupation on various occasions with multiple versions of this translation. To my parents, Eva-Maria and Jürgen Dietze, my mother-in-law, Traude A. Stiefenhofer (†), and my sister in-law, Christine S. Marklewitz, especially: Thank you! My greatest thanks and my greatest debt are due to my husband, Marc T. Stiefenhofer. This book is dedicated to him and to my English family, especially Julia Holden-White and Harriet Holden-White, who – among many other things – taught me the Queen's English and falconry in Cornish barns and on horseback on the moors. Even more importantly, they accepted me as their German daughter and sister. This relationship has always been very special for me.

June 2021

Index